Garfield
FAT CAT 3-PACK
VOLUME 10

BY
JIM DAVIS

BALLANTINE BOOKS · NEW YORK

2016 Ballantine Books Trade Paperback Edition

Based on the Garfield® characters created by Jim Davis

Published in the United States by Ballantine Books, an imprint of Random House,
a division of Penguin Random House LLC, New York.

Originally published as three separate volumes, in both black and white and colorized editions, by Ballantine Books, an imprint of Random House, a division of Penguin Random House LLC, as *Life In the Fat Lane* in 1995 (black and white) and 2014 (colorized), *Garfield Tons of Fun* in 1996 (black and white) and 2015 (colorized), and *Garfield Bigger and Better* in 1996 (black and white) and 2015 (colorized). This compilation was originally published in black and white in 1999.

ISBN 978-0-425-28558-9

Printed in China on acid-free paper

randomhousebooks.com

First Colorized Edition

9 8 7 6 5 4

Garfield
life in the fat lane

BY JIM DAVIS

Ballantine Books • **New York**

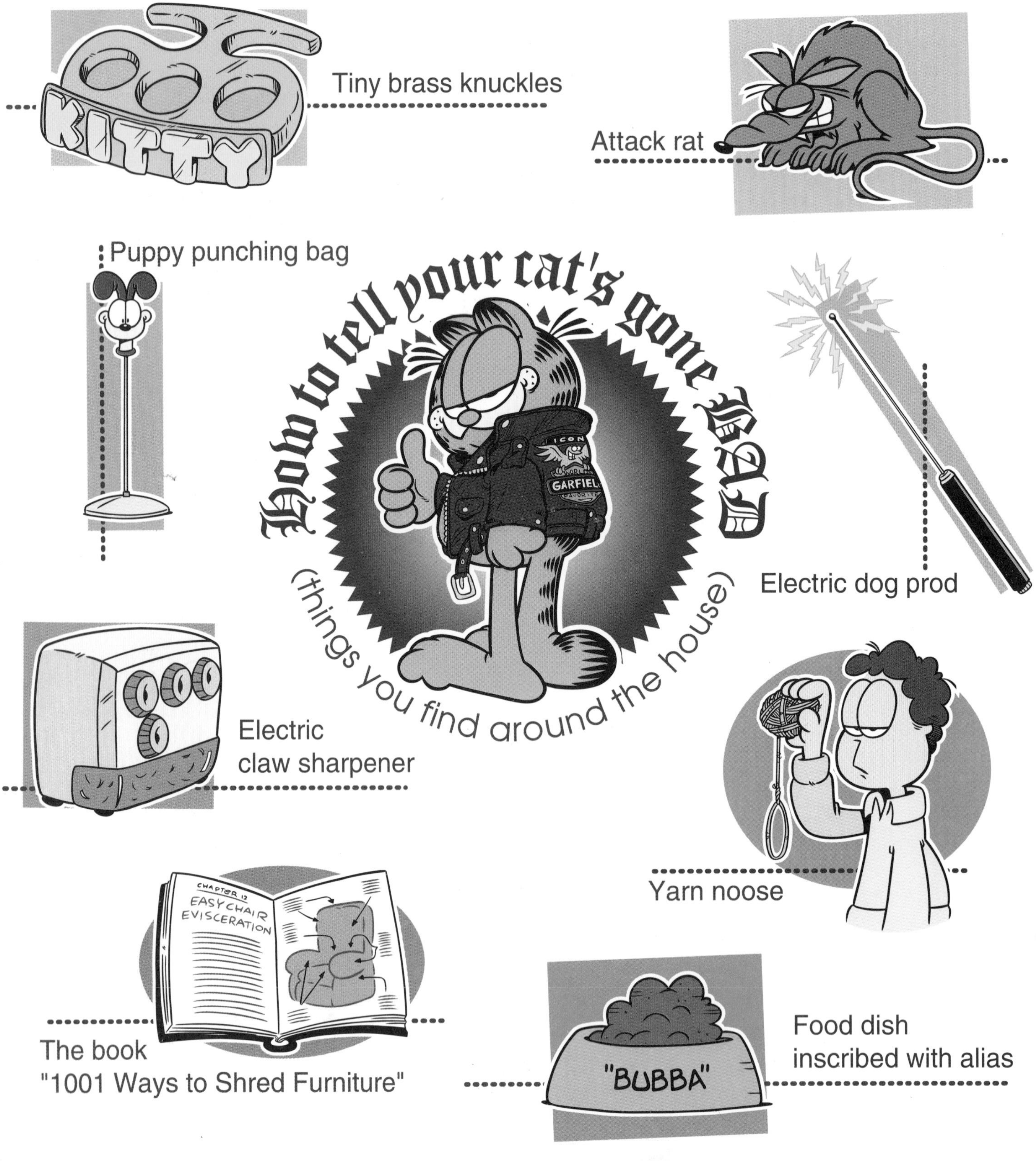
How to tell your cat's gone BAD
(things you find around the house)
KITTY
Tiny brass knuckles
Attack rat
Puppy punching bag
Electric dog prod
GARFIELD
Electric
claw sharpener
Yarn noose
CHAPTER 12
EASY CHAIR
EVISCERATION
The book
"1001 Ways to Shred Furniture"
"BUBBA"
Food dish
inscribed with alias

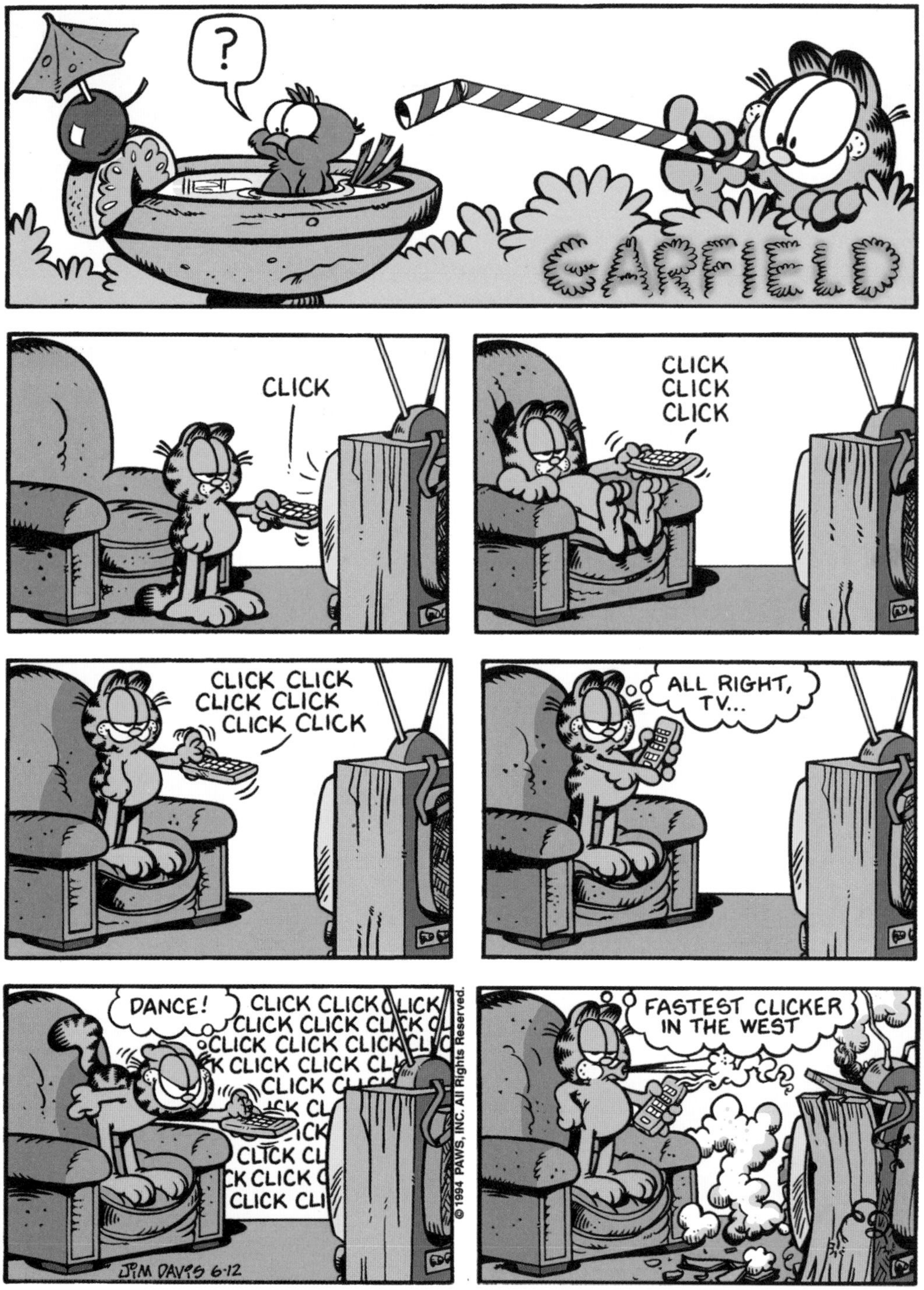
?
GARFIELD
CLICK
CLICK
CLICK
CLICK
CLICK CLICK
CLICK CLICK
CLICK CLICK
ALL RIGHT, TV...
DANCE!
CLICK CLICK
JIM DAVIS 6-12
© 1994 PAWS, INC. All Rights Reserved.
FASTEST CLICKER IN THE WEST

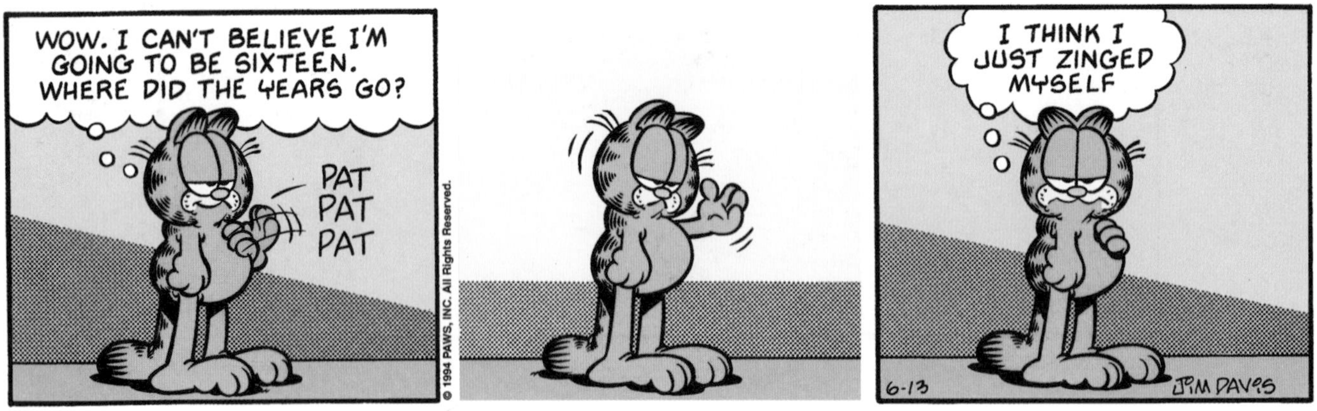
WOW. I CAN'T BELIEVE I'M GOING TO BE SIXTEEN. WHERE DID THE YEARS GO?
PAT PAT PAT
© 1994 PAWS, INC. All Rights Reserved.
I THINK I JUST ZINGED MYSELF
6-13
JIM DAVIS

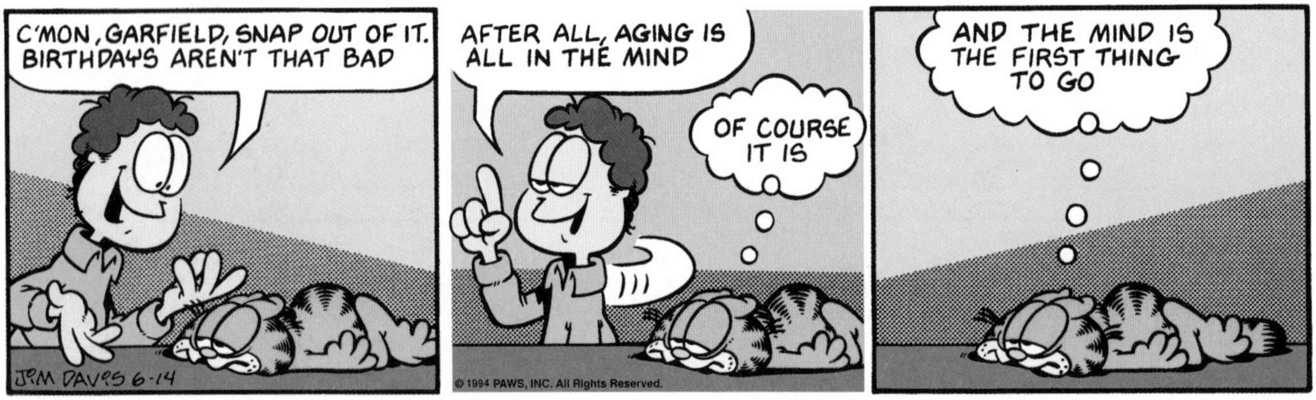
C'MON, GARFIELD, SNAP OUT OF IT. BIRTHDAYS AREN'T THAT BAD
JIM DAVIS 6-14
AFTER ALL, AGING IS ALL IN THE MIND
OF COURSE IT IS
© 1994 PAWS, INC. All Rights Reserved.
AND THE MIND IS THE FIRST THING TO GO

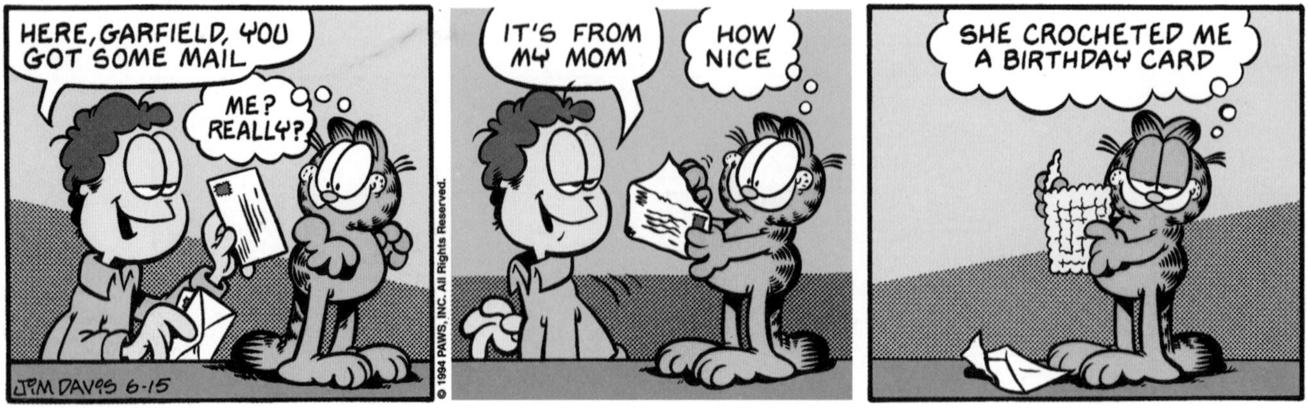
HERE, GARFIELD, YOU GOT SOME MAIL
ME? REALLY?
JIM DAVIS 6-15
© 1994 PAWS, INC. All Rights Reserved.
IT'S FROM MY MOM
HOW NICE
SHE CROCHETED ME A BIRTHDAY CARD

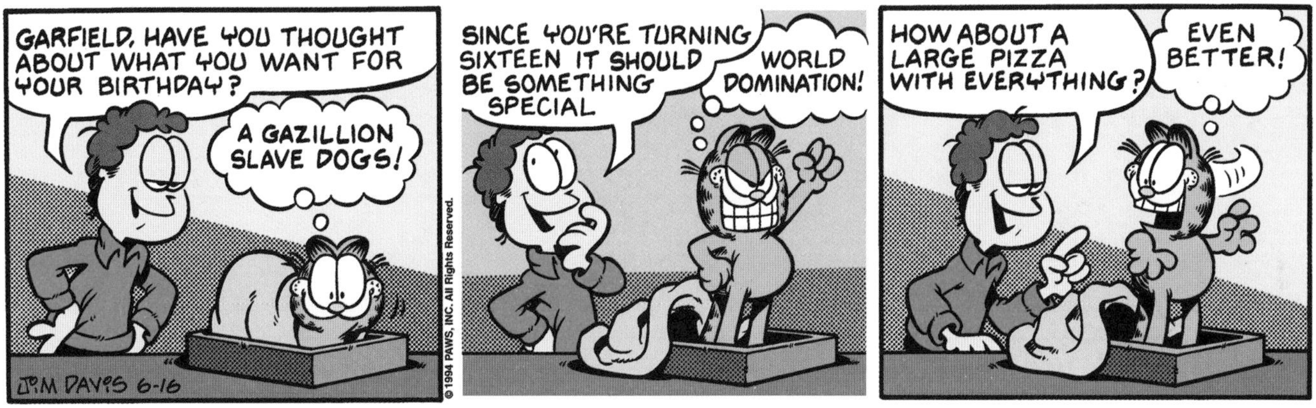
GARFIELD, HAVE YOU THOUGHT ABOUT WHAT YOU WANT FOR YOUR BIRTHDAY?
A GAZILLION SLAVE DOGS!
JIM DAVIS 6-16
© 1994 PAWS, INC. All Rights Reserved.
SINCE YOU'RE TURNING SIXTEEN IT SHOULD BE SOMETHING SPECIAL
WORLD DOMINATION!
HOW ABOUT A LARGE PIZZA WITH EVERYTHING?
EVEN BETTER!

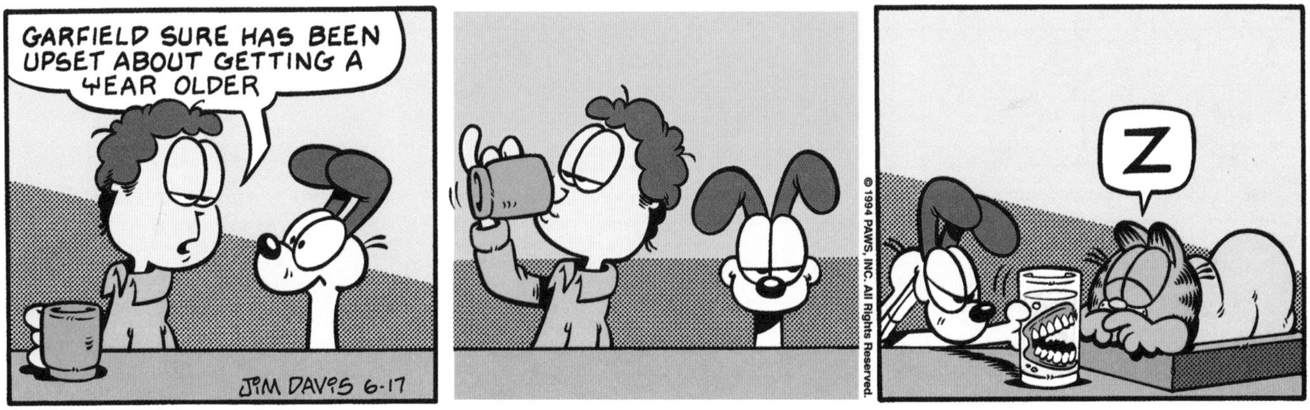
GARFIELD SURE HAS BEEN UPSET ABOUT GETTING A YEAR OLDER
JIM DAVIS 6-17
© 1994 PAWS, INC. All Rights Reserved.
Z

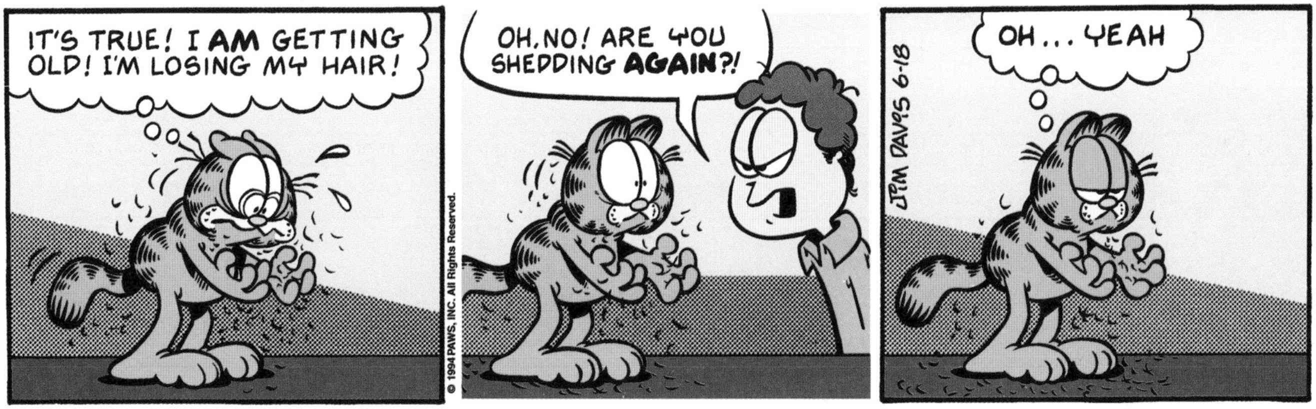
IT'S TRUE! I **AM** GETTING OLD! I'M LOSING MY HAIR!
© 1994 PAWS, INC. All Rights Reserved.
OH, NO! ARE YOU SHEDDING **AGAIN**?!
JIM DAVIS 6-18
OH... YEAH

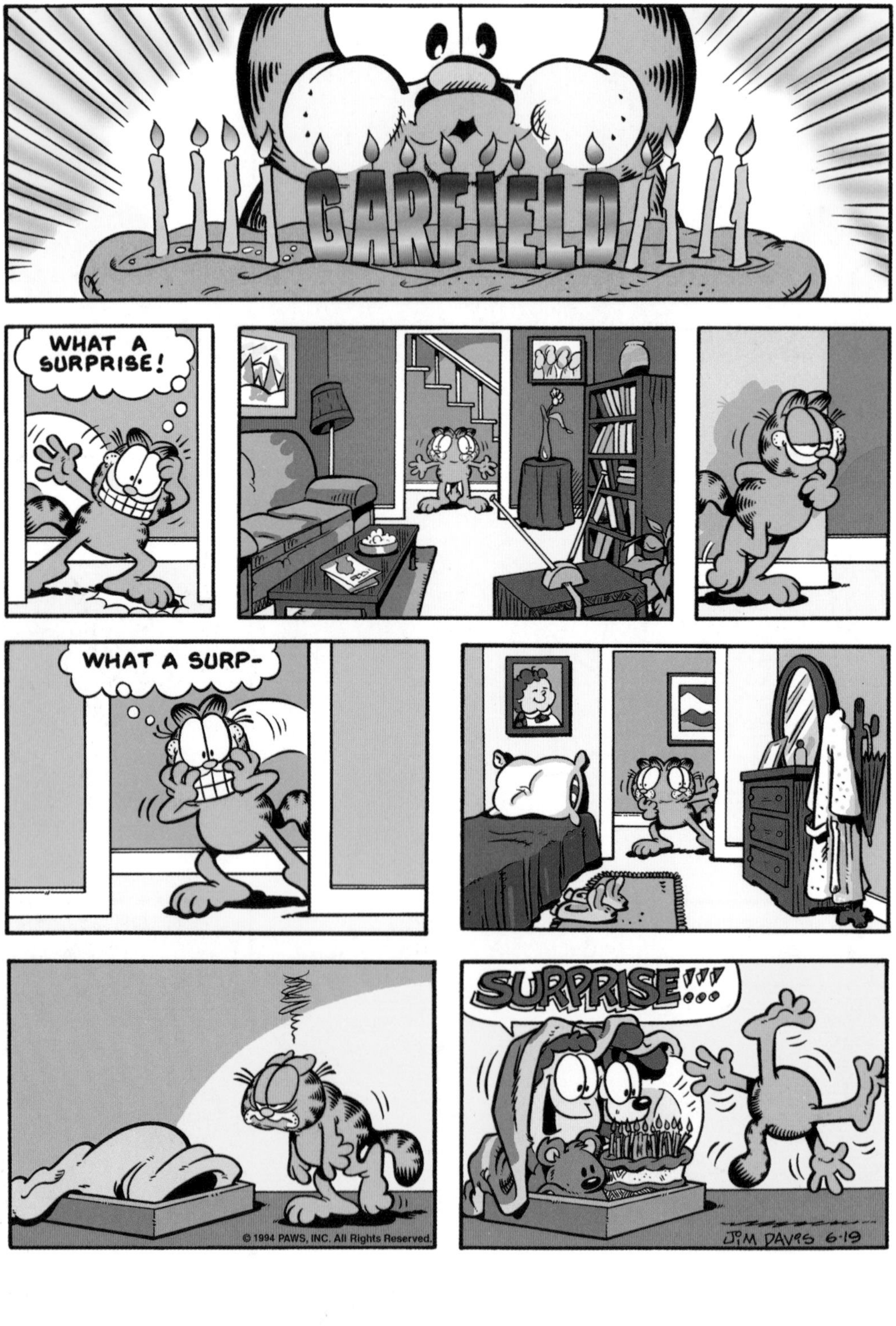
GARFIELD
WHAT A SURPRISE!
WHAT A SURP-
SURPRISE!!!
© 1994 PAWS, INC. All Rights Reserved.
JIM DAVIS 6-19

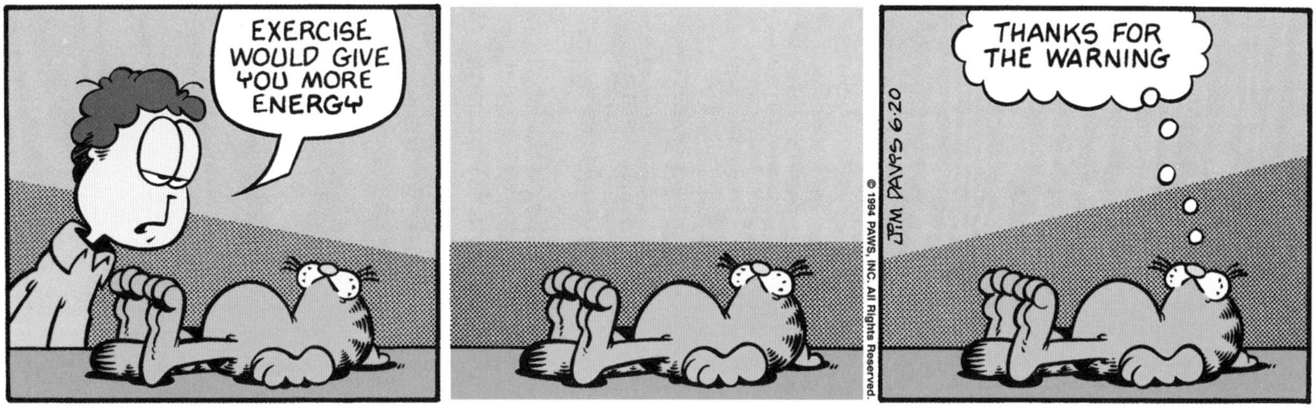
EXERCISE WOULD GIVE YOU MORE ENERGY
© 1994 PAWS, INC. All Rights Reserved.
JIM DAVIS 6-20
THANKS FOR THE WARNING

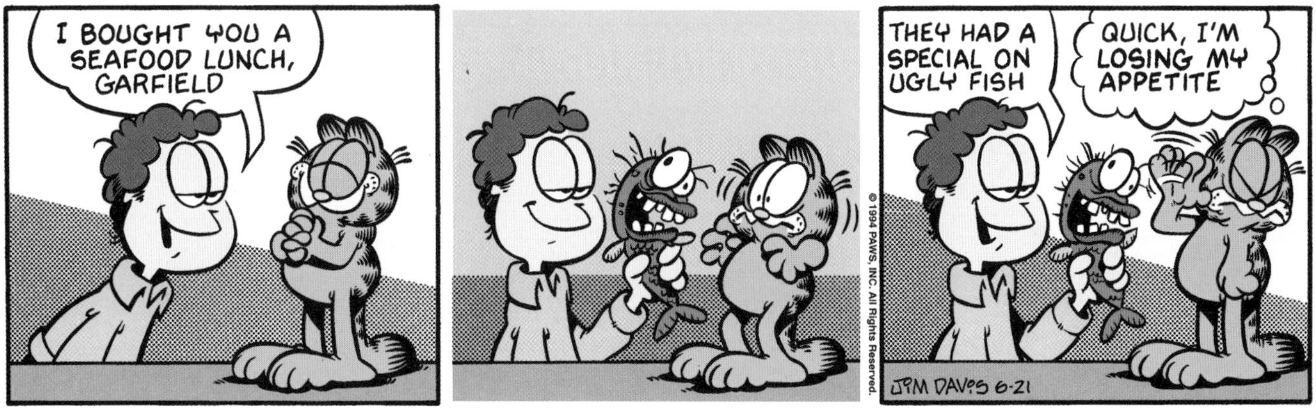
I BOUGHT YOU A SEAFOOD LUNCH, GARFIELD
© 1994 PAWS, INC. All Rights Reserved.
THEY HAD A SPECIAL ON UGLY FISH
QUICK, I'M LOSING MY APPETITE
JIM DAVIS 6-21

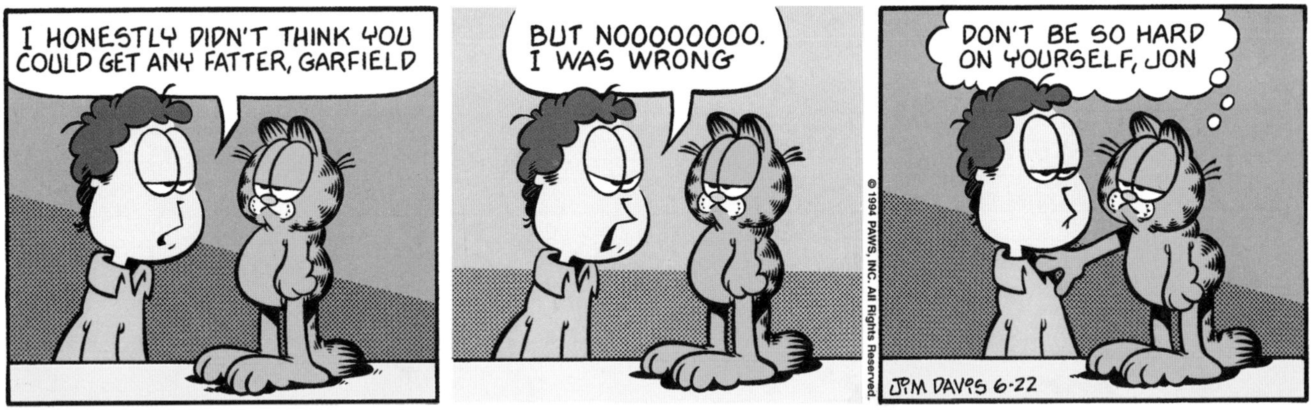
I HONESTLY DIDN'T THINK YOU COULD GET ANY FATTER, GARFIELD
BUT NOOOOOOOO. I WAS WRONG
© 1994 PAWS, INC. All Rights Reserved.
DON'T BE SO HARD ON YOURSELF, JON
JIM DAVIS 6-22

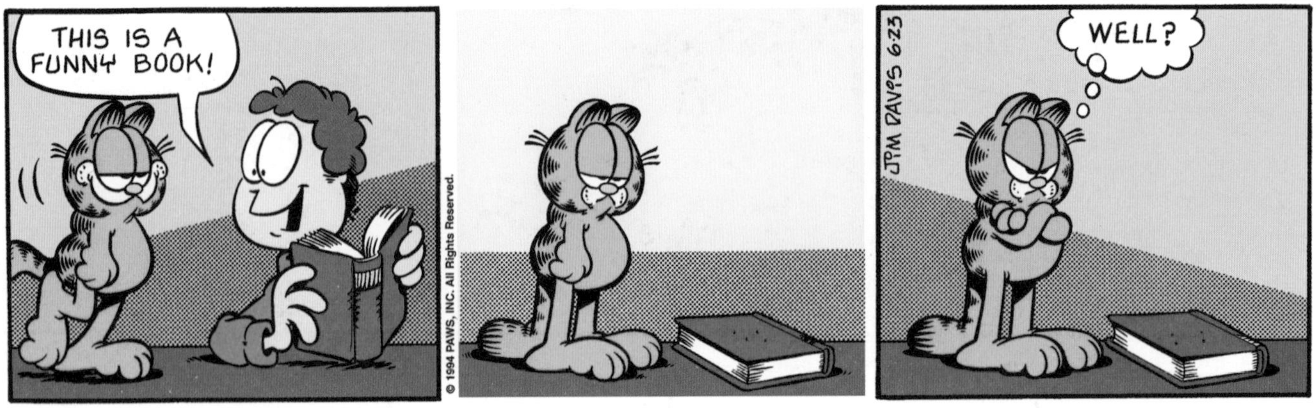
THIS IS A FUNNY BOOK!
WELL?
JIM DAVIS 6-23
© 1994 PAWS, INC. All Rights Reserved.

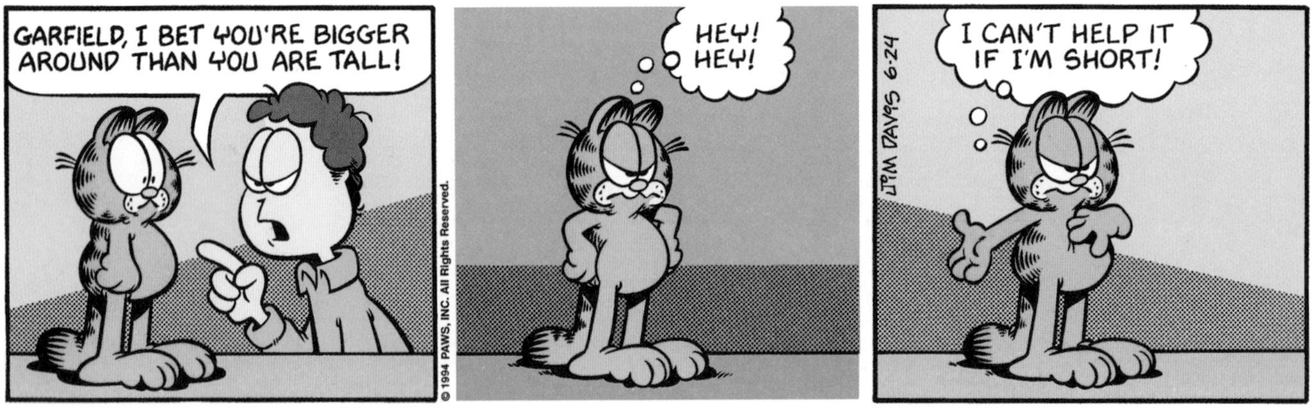
GARFIELD, I BET YOU'RE BIGGER AROUND THAN YOU ARE TALL!
HEY! HEY!
I CAN'T HELP IT IF I'M SHORT!
JIM DAVIS 6-24
© 1994 PAWS, INC. All Rights Reserved.

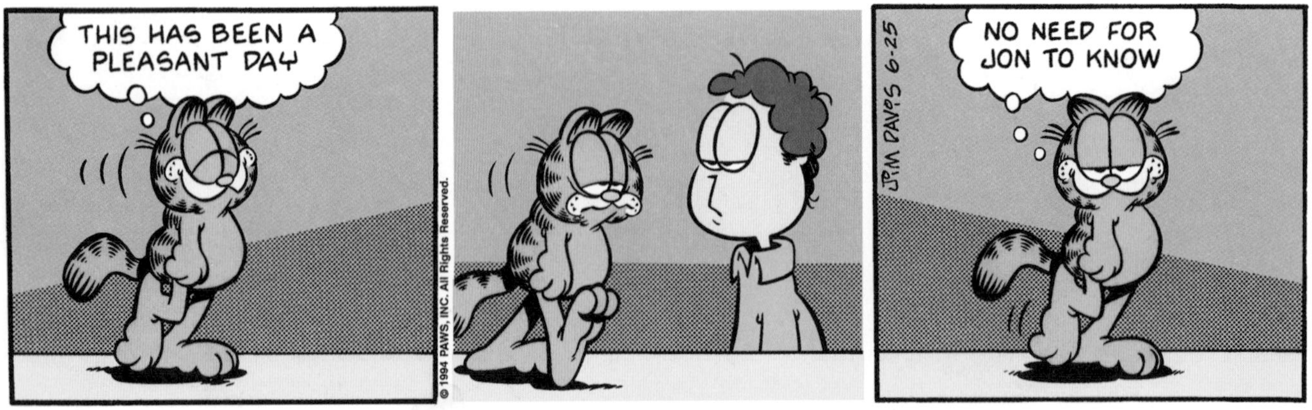
THIS HAS BEEN A PLEASANT DAY
NO NEED FOR JON TO KNOW
JIM DAVIS 6-25
© 1994 PAWS, INC. All Rights Reserved.

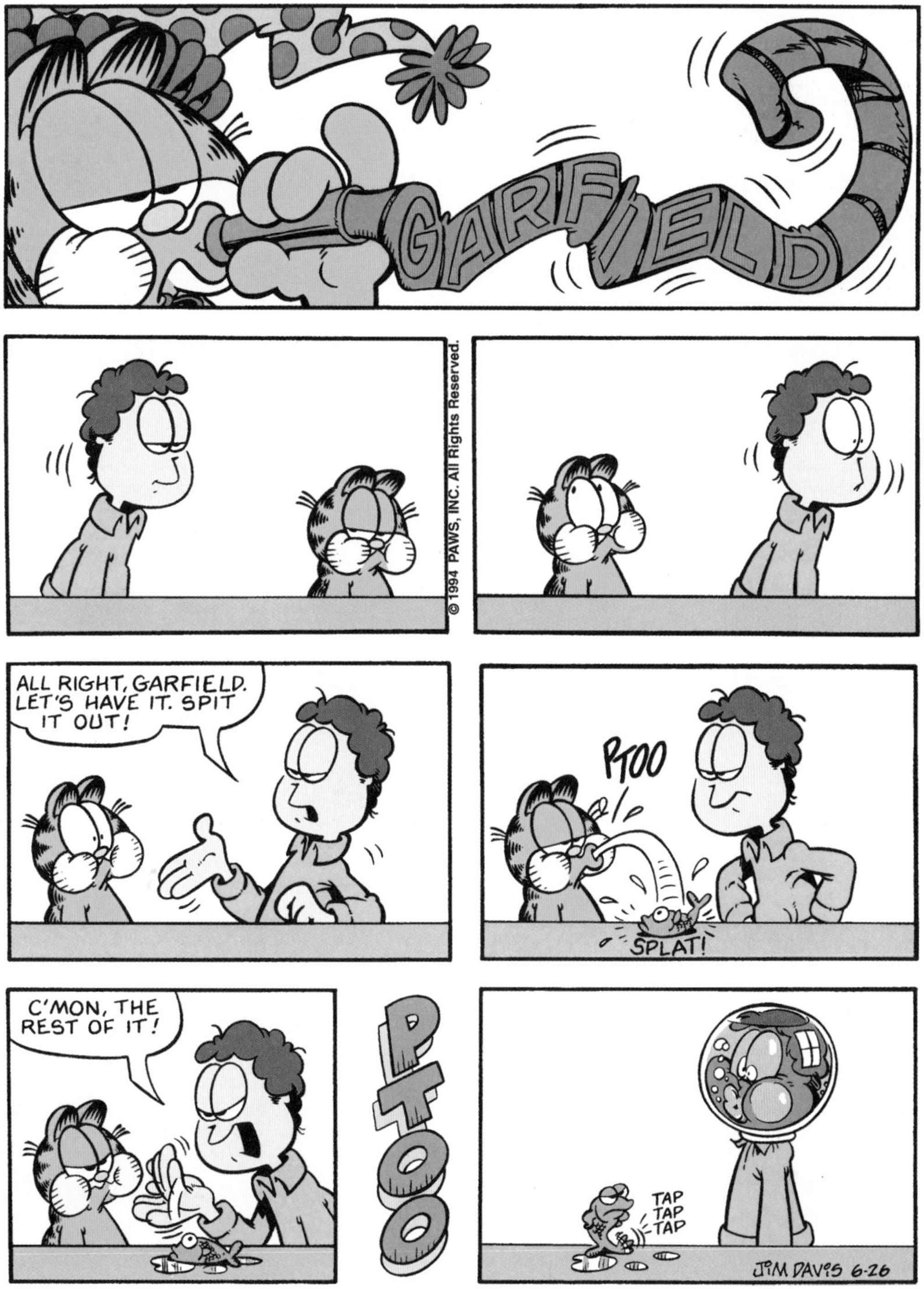
GARFIELD
© 1994 PAWS, INC. All Rights Reserved.
ALL RIGHT, GARFIELD. LET'S HAVE IT. SPIT IT OUT!
PTOO
SPLAT!
C'MON, THE REST OF IT!
PTOO
TAP TAP TAP
JIM DAVIS 6-26

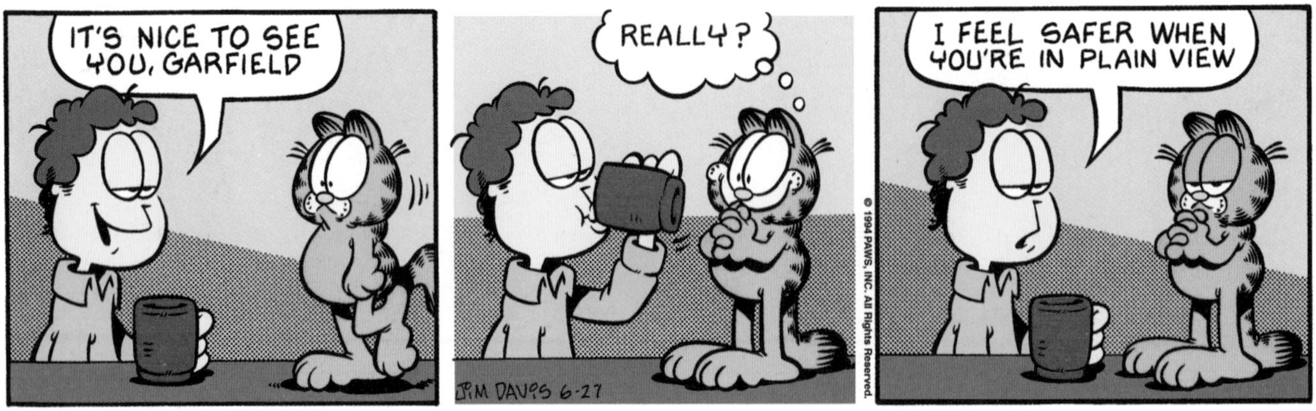
IT'S NICE TO SEE YOU, GARFIELD
REALLY?
I FEEL SAFER WHEN YOU'RE IN PLAIN VIEW
JIM DAVIS 6-27
© 1994 PAWS, INC. All Rights Reserved.

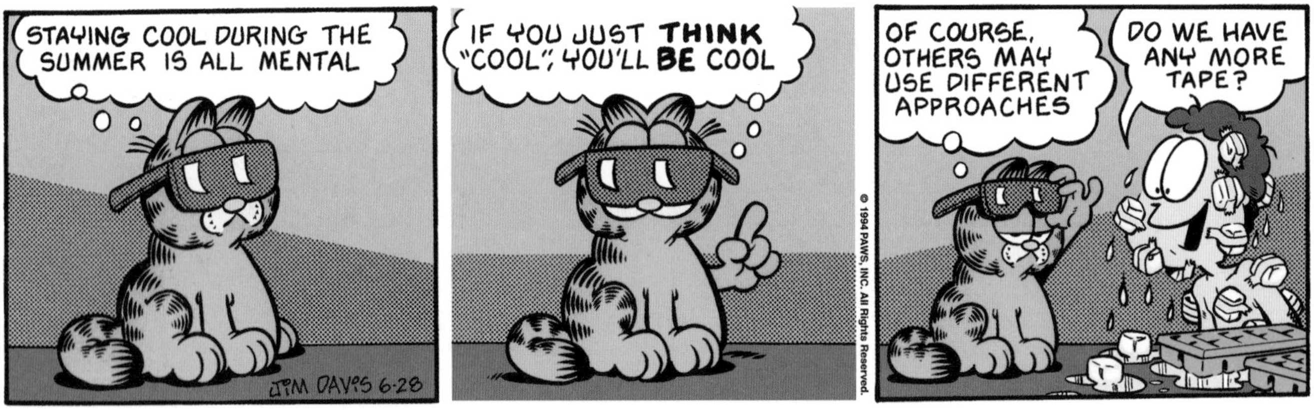
STAYING COOL DURING THE SUMMER IS ALL MENTAL
IF YOU JUST **THINK** "COOL", YOU'LL **BE** COOL
OF COURSE, OTHERS MAY USE DIFFERENT APPROACHES
DO WE HAVE ANY MORE TAPE?
JIM DAVIS 6-28
© 1994 PAWS, INC. All Rights Reserved.

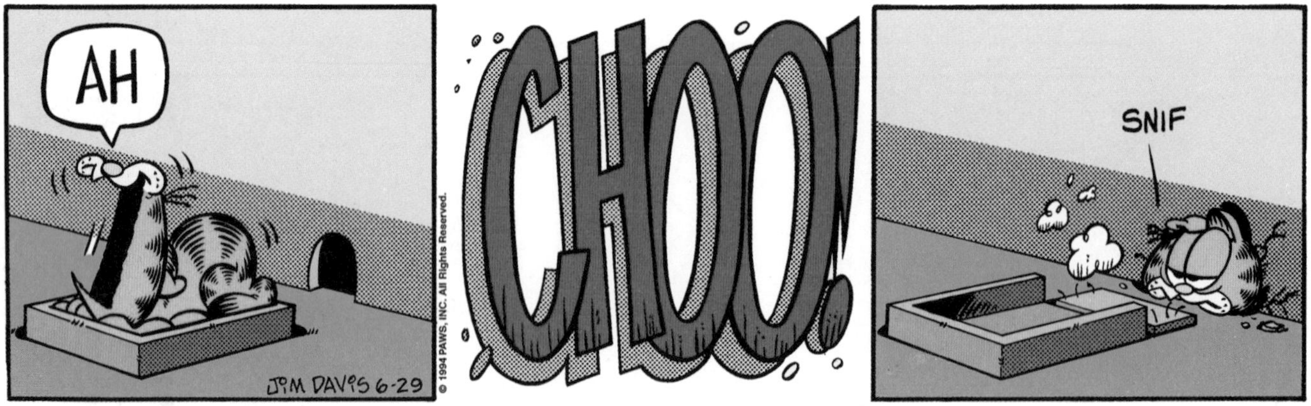
AH
CHOO!
SNIF
JIM DAVIS 6-29
© 1994 PAWS, INC. All Rights Reserved.

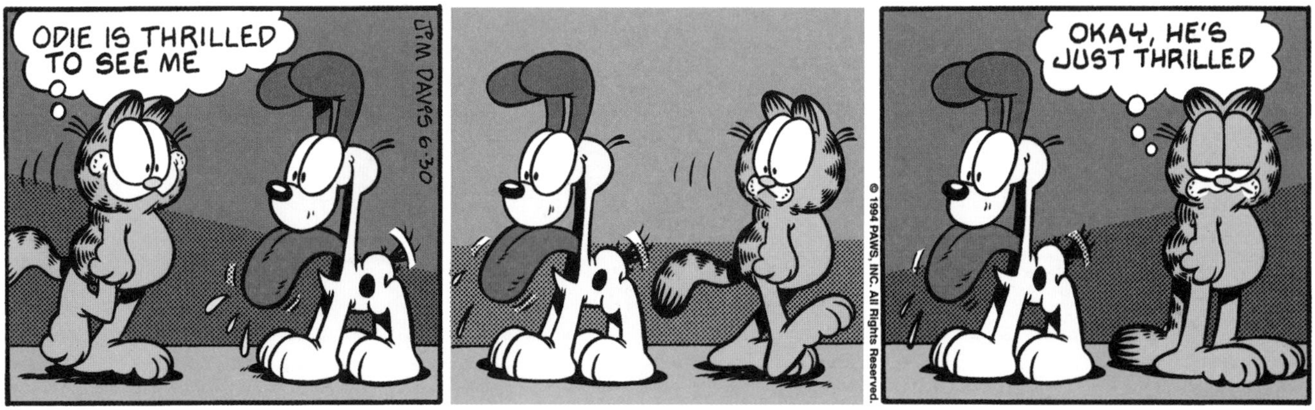
ODIE IS THRILLED TO SEE ME
JIM DAVIS 6-30
© 1994 PAWS, INC. All Rights Reserved.
OKAY, HE'S JUST THRILLED

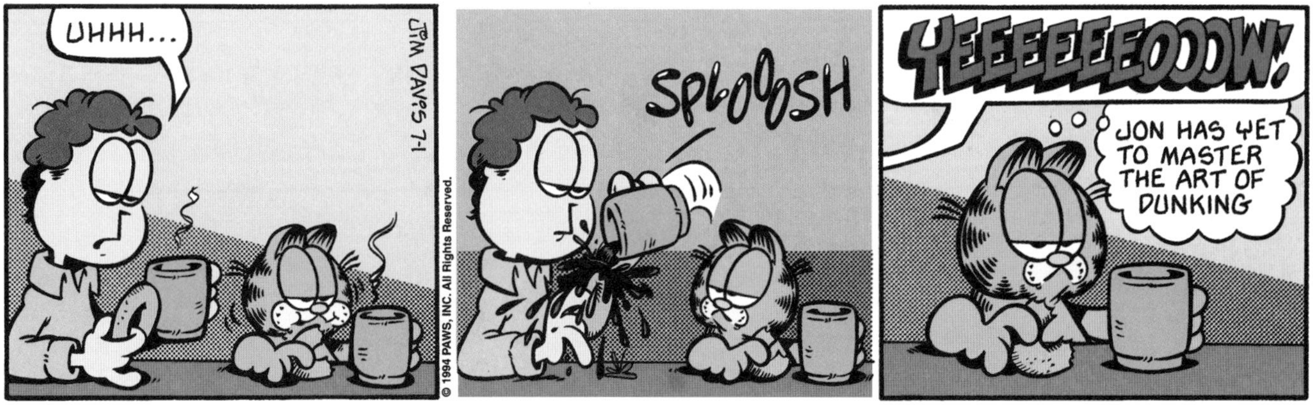
UHHH...
JIM DAVIS 7-1
© 1994 PAWS, INC. All Rights Reserved.
SPLOOOSH
YEEEEEEOOOW!
JON HAS YET TO MASTER THE ART OF DUNKING

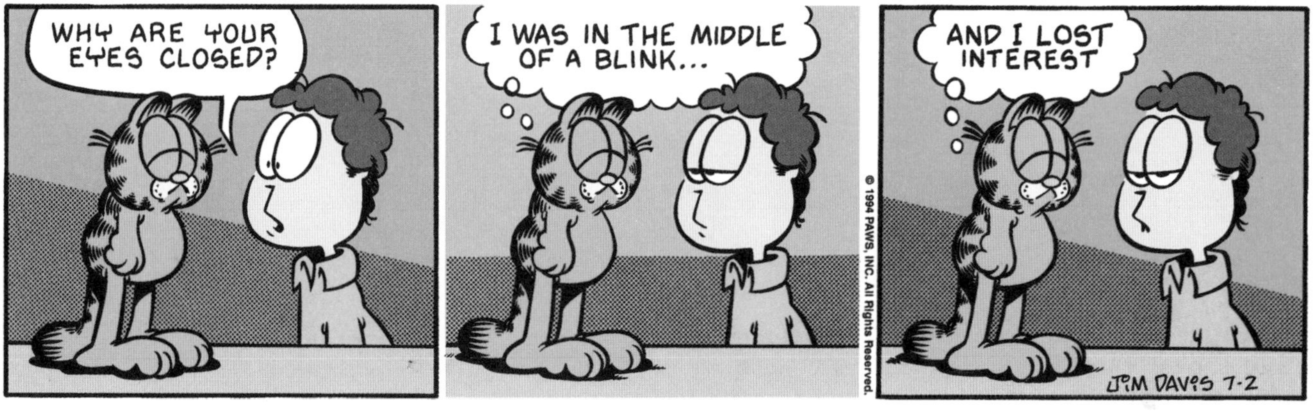
WHY ARE YOUR EYES CLOSED?
I WAS IN THE MIDDLE OF A BLINK...
© 1994 PAWS, INC. All Rights Reserved.
AND I LOST INTEREST
JIM DAVIS 7-2

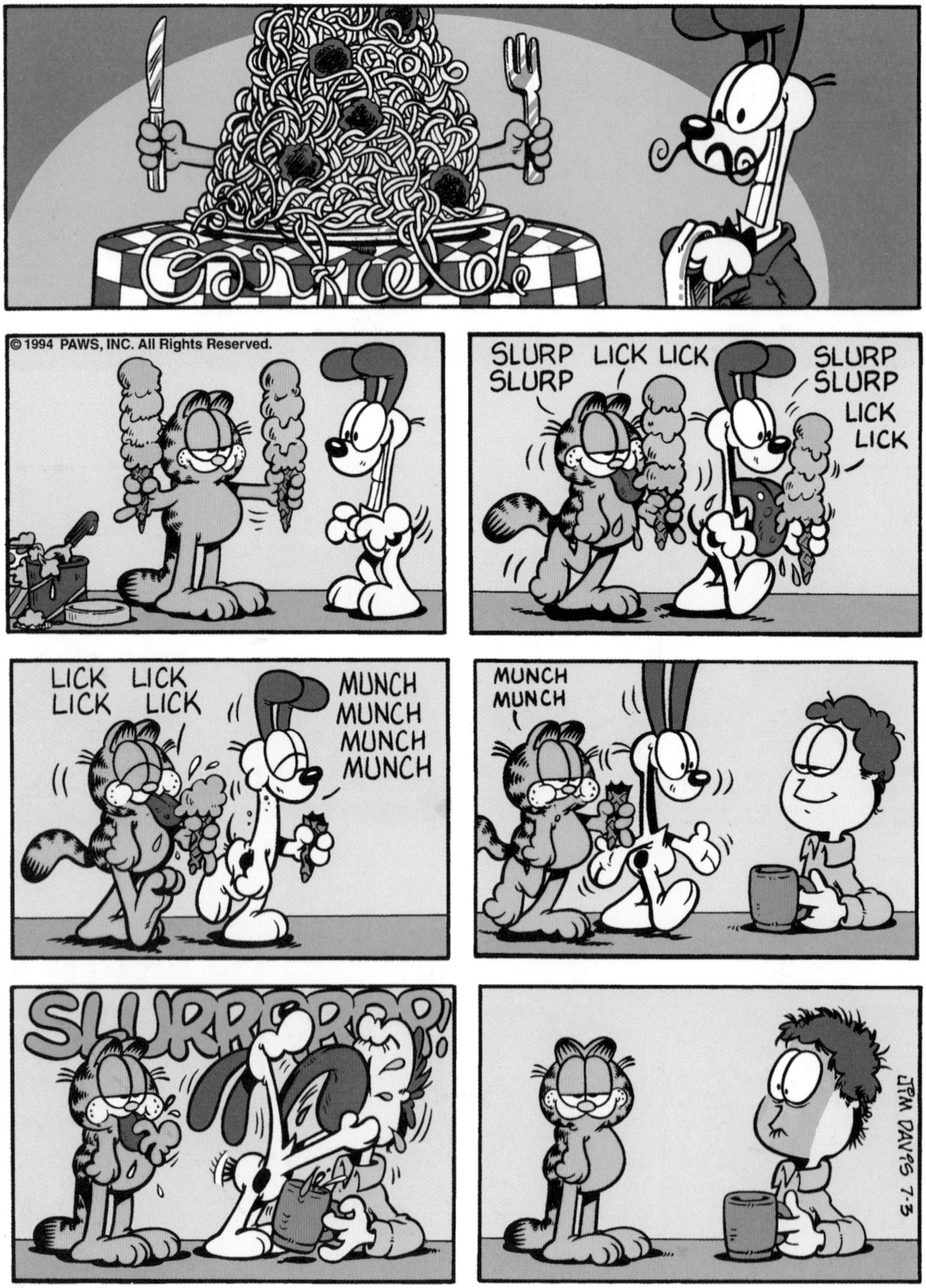
© 1994 PAWS, INC. All Rights Reserved.
SLURP SLURP
LICK LICK
SLURP SLURP
LICK LICK
LICK LICK
LICK LICK
MUNCH MUNCH MUNCH MUNCH
MUNCH MUNCH
SLURRRRRP!
JIM DAVIS 7-3

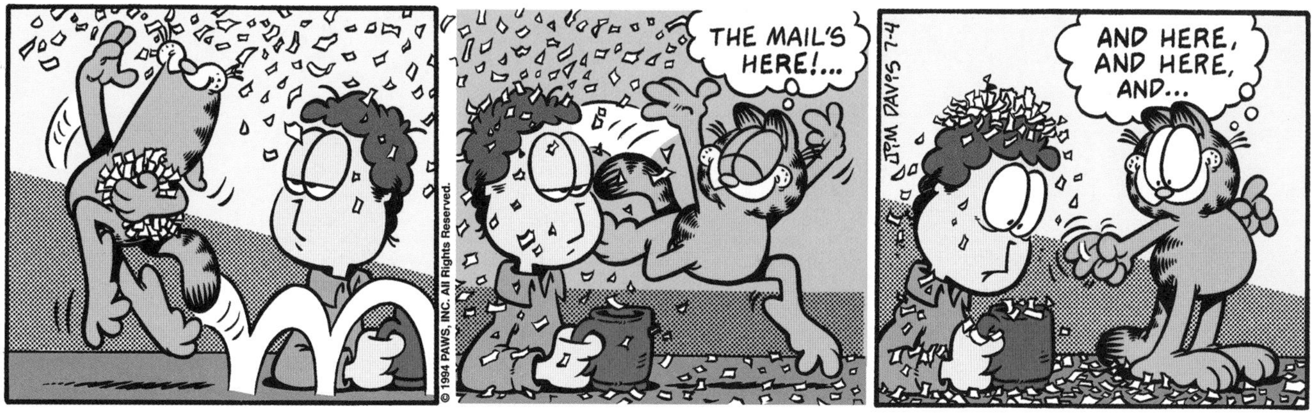
© 1994 PAWS, INC. All Rights Reserved.
THE MAIL'S HERE!...
JIM DAVIS 7-4
AND HERE, AND HERE, AND...

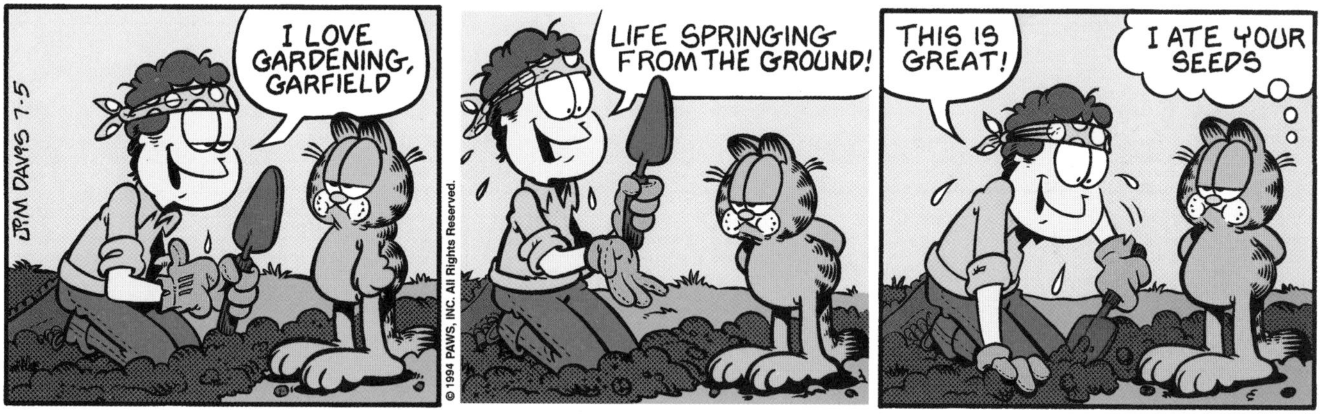
JIM DAVIS 7-5
I LOVE GARDENING, GARFIELD
© 1994 PAWS, INC. All Rights Reserved.
LIFE SPRINGING FROM THE GROUND!
THIS IS GREAT!
I ATE YOUR SEEDS

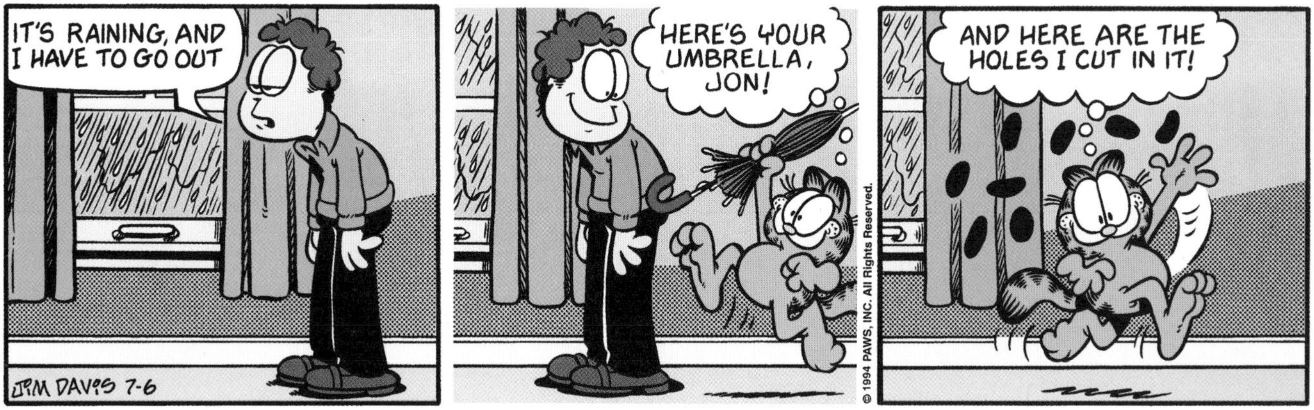
IT'S RAINING, AND I HAVE TO GO OUT
JIM DAVIS 7-6
HERE'S YOUR UMBRELLA, JON!
© 1994 PAWS, INC. All Rights Reserved.
AND HERE ARE THE HOLES I CUT IN IT!

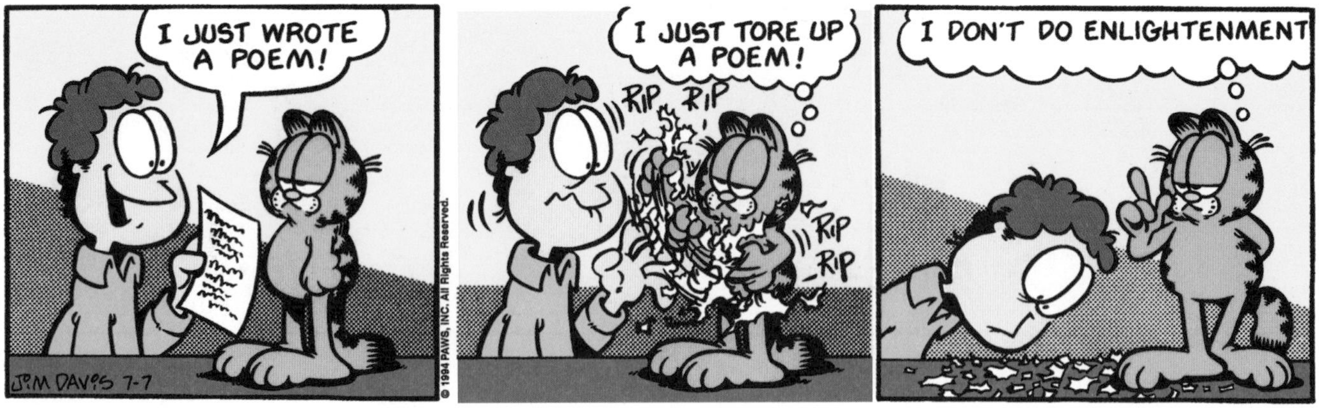
I JUST WROTE A POEM!
JIM DAVIS 7-7
© 1994 PAWS, INC. All Rights Reserved.
I JUST TORE UP A POEM!
RIP RIP
RIP
RIP
I DON'T DO ENLIGHTENMENT

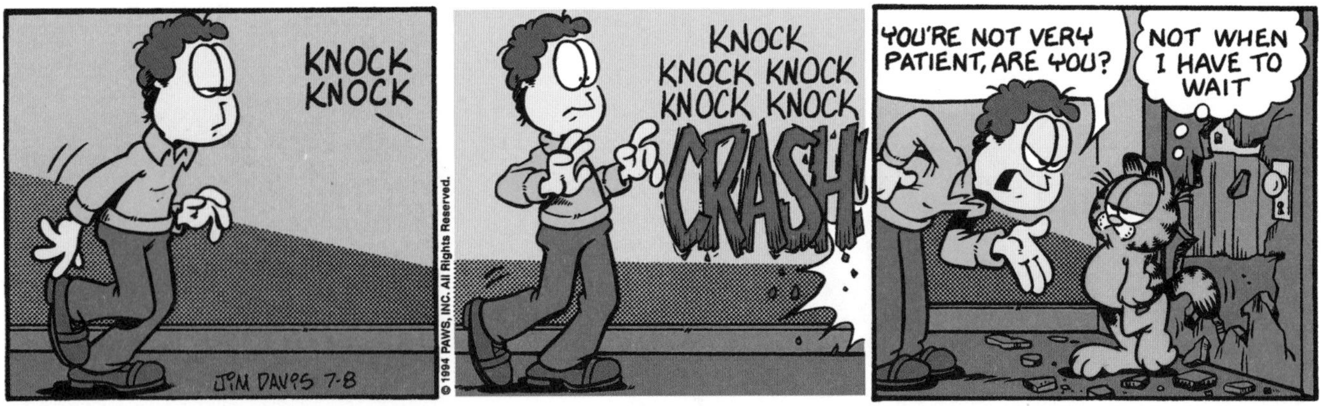
KNOCK KNOCK
JIM DAVIS 7-8
© 1994 PAWS, INC. All Rights Reserved.
KNOCK KNOCK KNOCK KNOCK KNOCK
CRASH!
YOU'RE NOT VERY PATIENT, ARE YOU?
NOT WHEN I HAVE TO WAIT

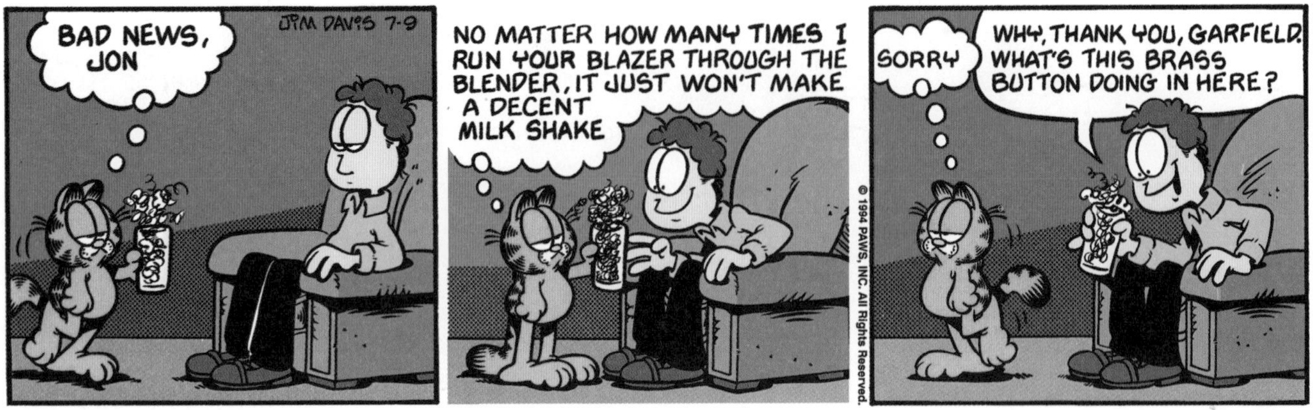
BAD NEWS, JON
JIM DAVIS 7-9
NO MATTER HOW MANY TIMES I RUN YOUR BLAZER THROUGH THE BLENDER, IT JUST WON'T MAKE A DECENT MILK SHAKE
© 1994 PAWS, INC. All Rights Reserved.
SORRY
WHY, THANK YOU, GARFIELD. WHAT'S THIS BRASS BUTTON DOING IN HERE?

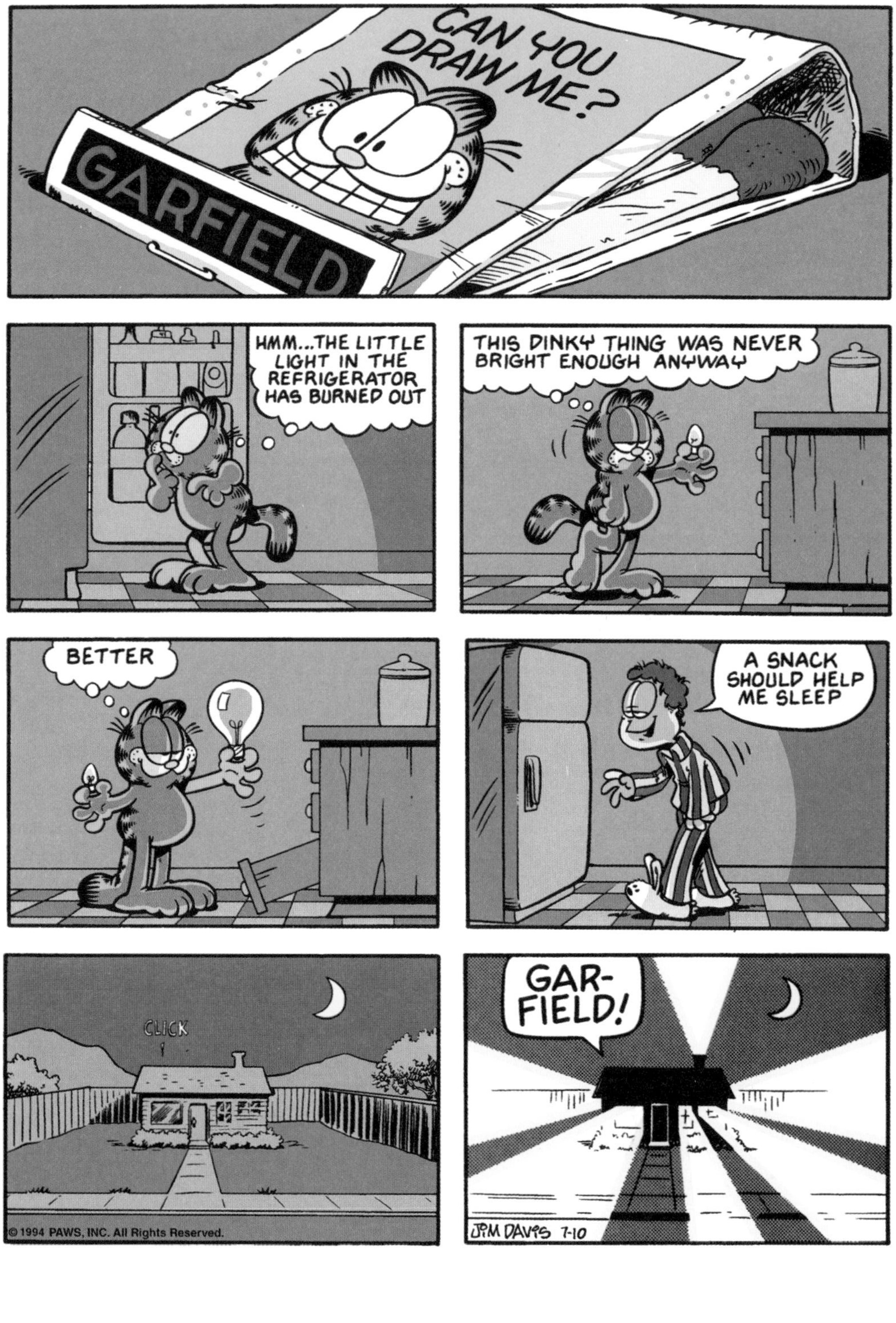
CAN YOU DRAW ME?
GARFIELD
HMM...THE LITTLE LIGHT IN THE REFRIGERATOR HAS BURNED OUT
THIS DINKY THING WAS NEVER BRIGHT ENOUGH ANYWAY
BETTER
A SNACK SHOULD HELP ME SLEEP
CLICK
GAR-FIELD!
© 1994 PAWS, INC. All Rights Reserved.
JIM DAVIS 7-10

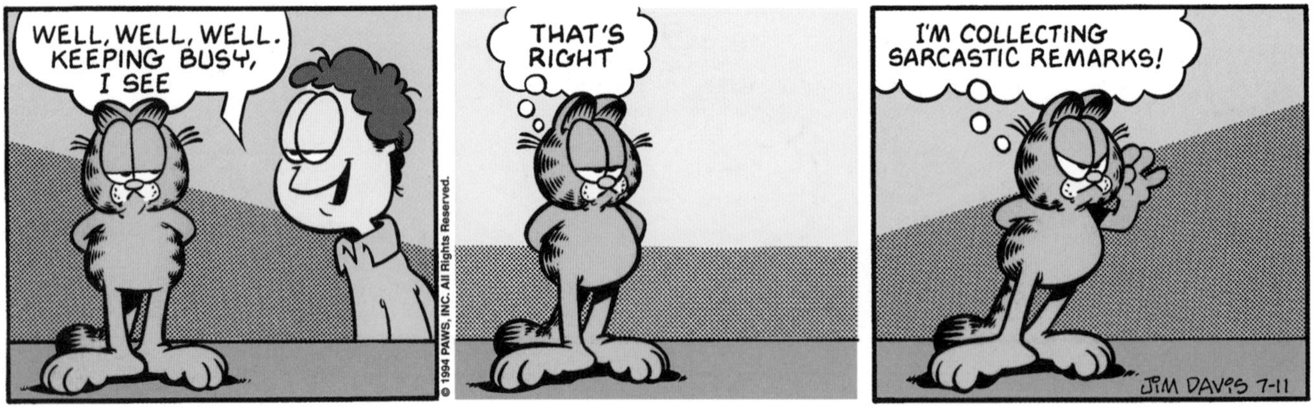
WELL, WELL, WELL. KEEPING BUSY, I SEE
THAT'S RIGHT
I'M COLLECTING SARCASTIC REMARKS!
© 1994 PAWS, INC. All Rights Reserved.
JIM DAVIS 7-11

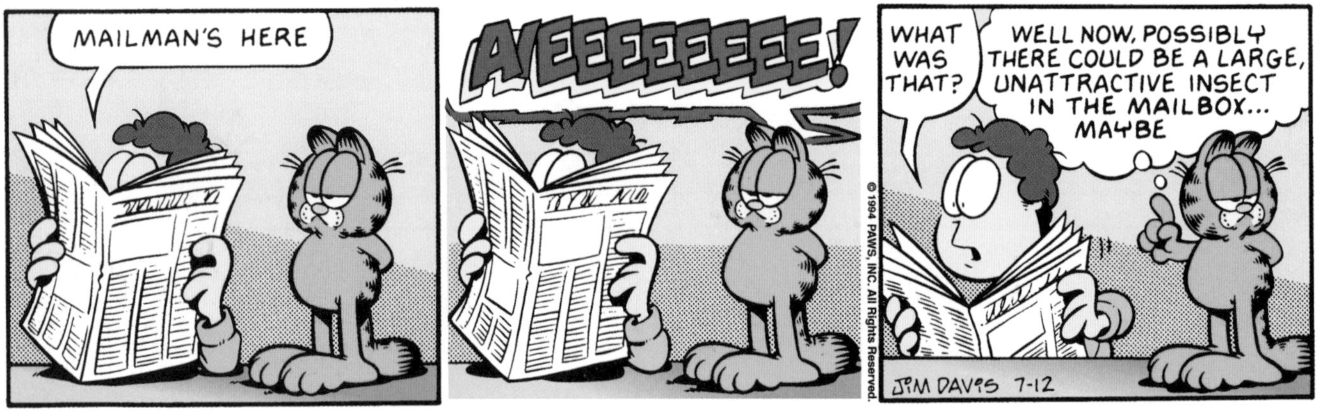
MAILMAN'S HERE
AIEEEEEEEEE!
WHAT WAS THAT?
WELL NOW, POSSIBLY THERE COULD BE A LARGE, UNATTRACTIVE INSECT IN THE MAILBOX... MAYBE
© 1994 PAWS, INC. All Rights Reserved.
JIM DAVIS 7-12

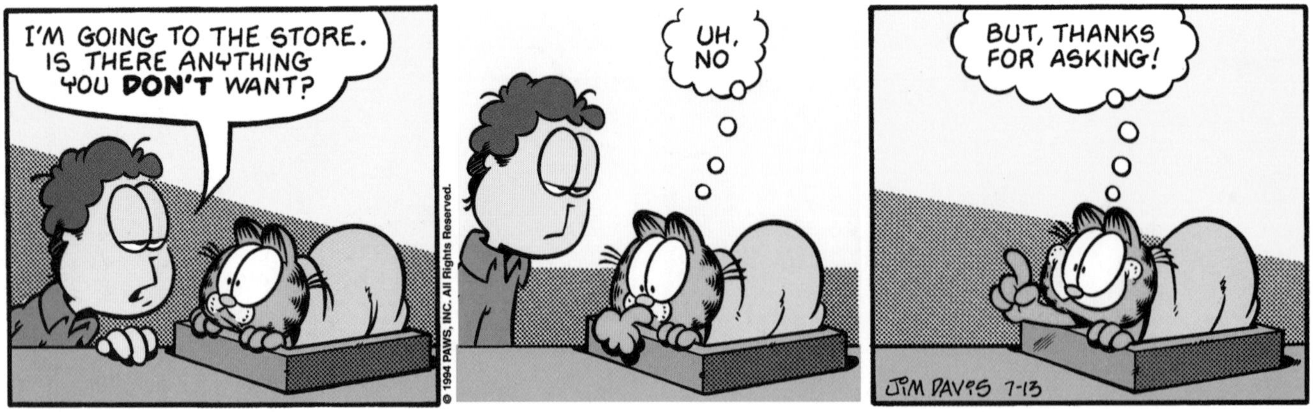
I'M GOING TO THE STORE. IS THERE ANYTHING YOU **DON'T** WANT?
UH, NO
BUT, THANKS FOR ASKING!
© 1994 PAWS, INC. All Rights Reserved.
JIM DAVIS 7-13

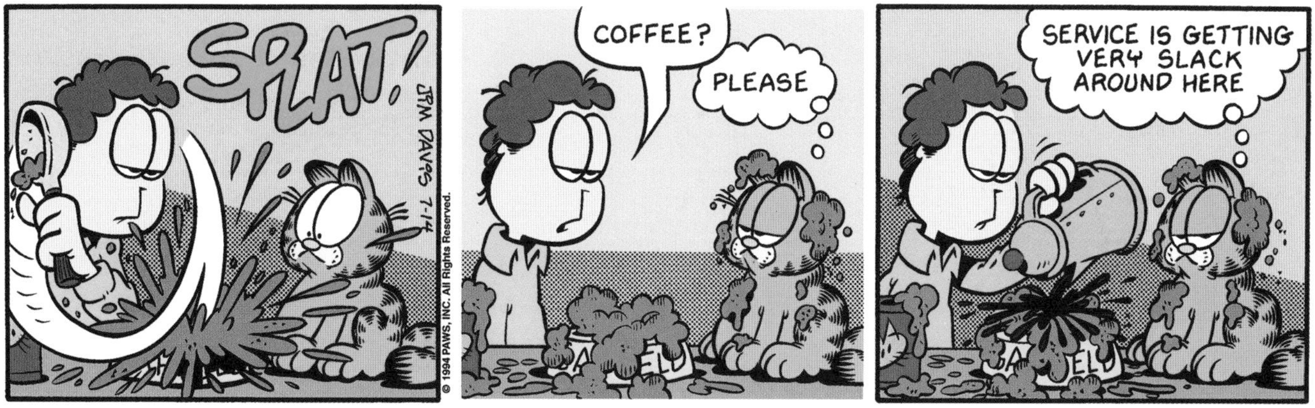
SPLAT!
JIM DAVIS 7-14
© 1994 PAWS, INC. All Rights Reserved.
COFFEE?
PLEASE
SERVICE IS GETTING VERY SLACK AROUND HERE

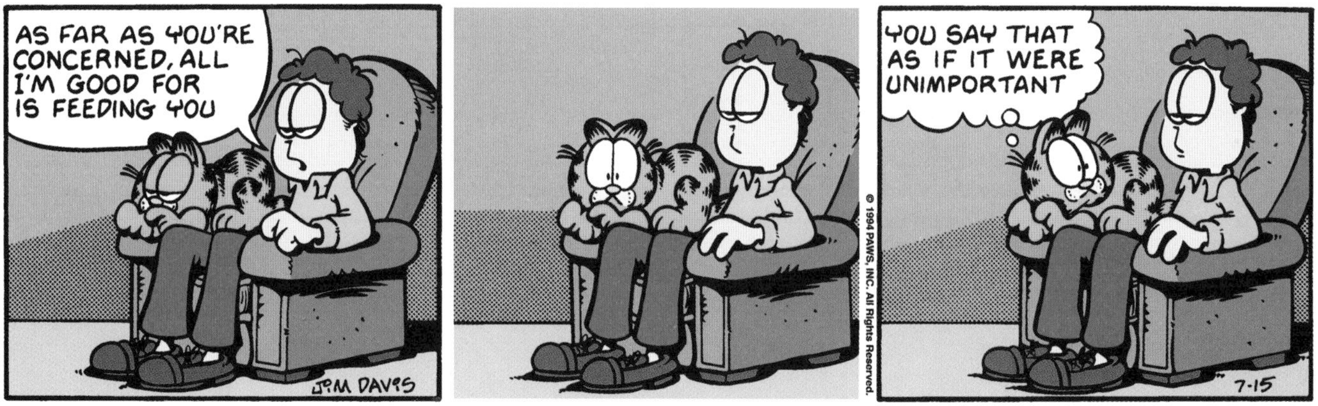
AS FAR AS YOU'RE CONCERNED, ALL I'M GOOD FOR IS FEEDING YOU
JIM DAVIS
© 1994 PAWS, INC. All Rights Reserved.
YOU SAY THAT AS IF IT WERE UNIMPORTANT
7-15

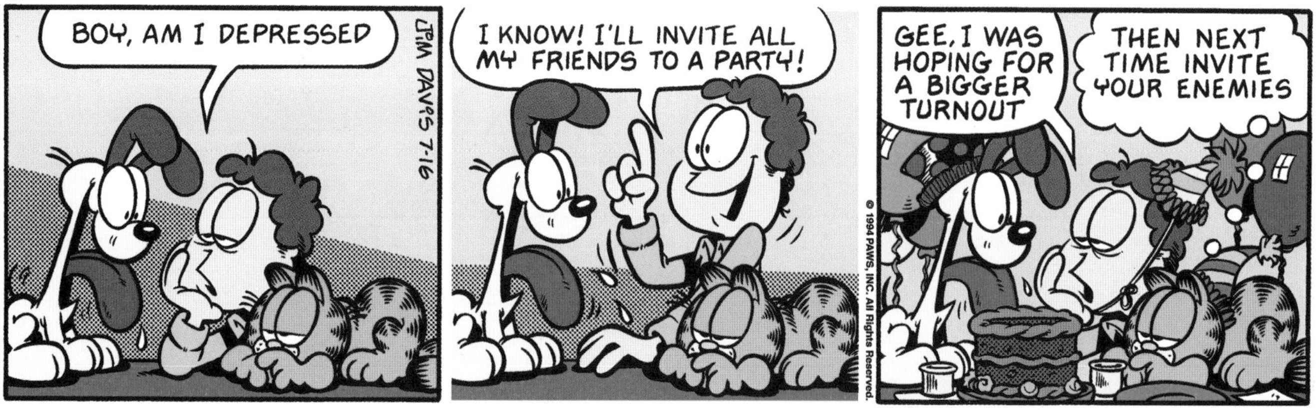
BOY, AM I DEPRESSED
JIM DAVIS 7-16
I KNOW! I'LL INVITE ALL MY FRIENDS TO A PARTY!
© 1994 PAWS, INC. All Rights Reserved.
GEE, I WAS HOPING FOR A BIGGER TURNOUT
THEN NEXT TIME INVITE YOUR ENEMIES

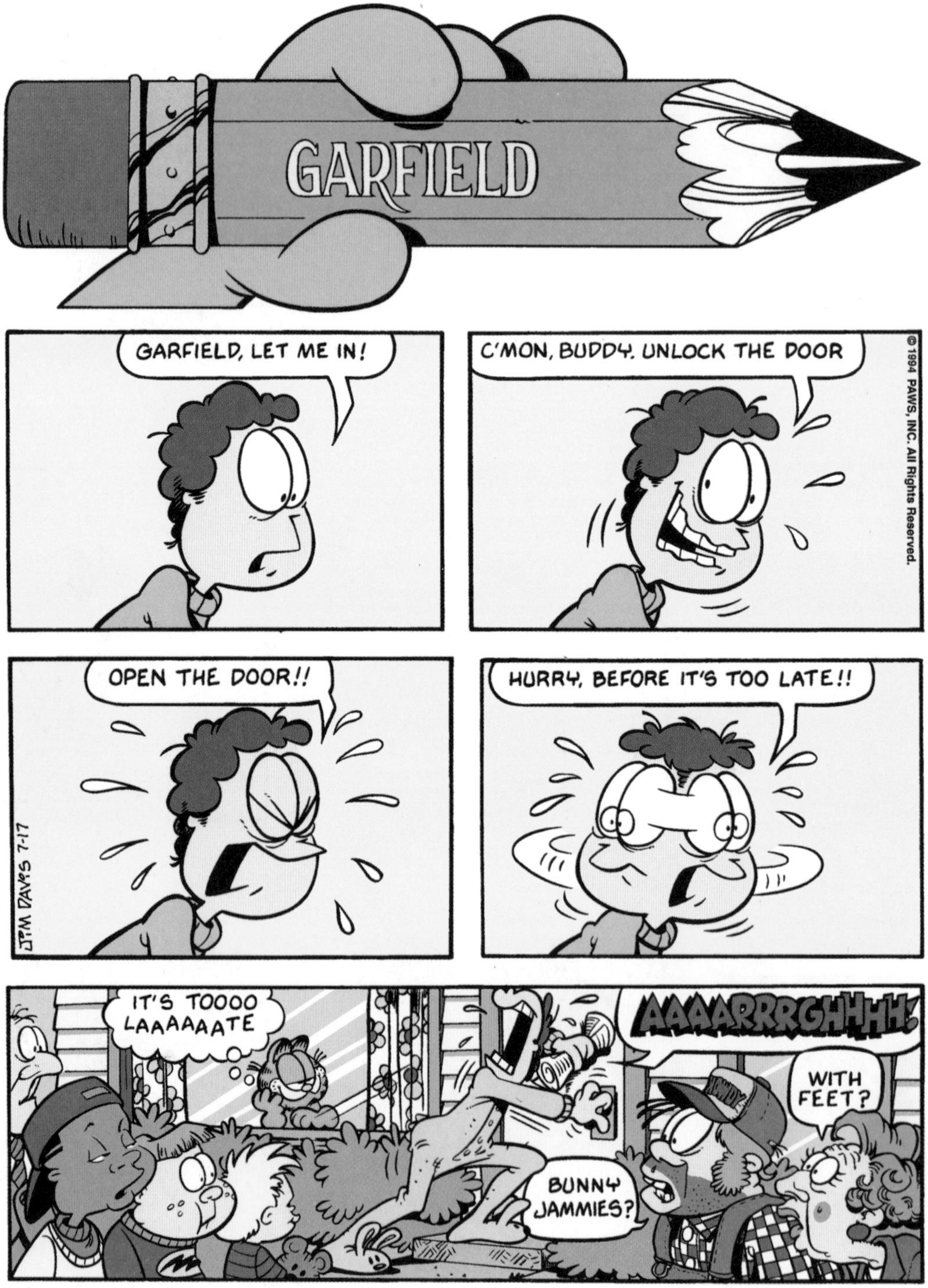
GARFIELD
GARFIELD, LET ME IN!
C'MON, BUDDY. UNLOCK THE DOOR
© 1994 PAWS, INC. All Rights Reserved.
OPEN THE DOOR!!
JIM DAVIS 7-17
HURRY, BEFORE IT'S TOO LATE!!
IT'S TOOOO LAAAAAATE
AAAARRRGHHHH!
WITH FEET?
BUNNY JAMMIES?

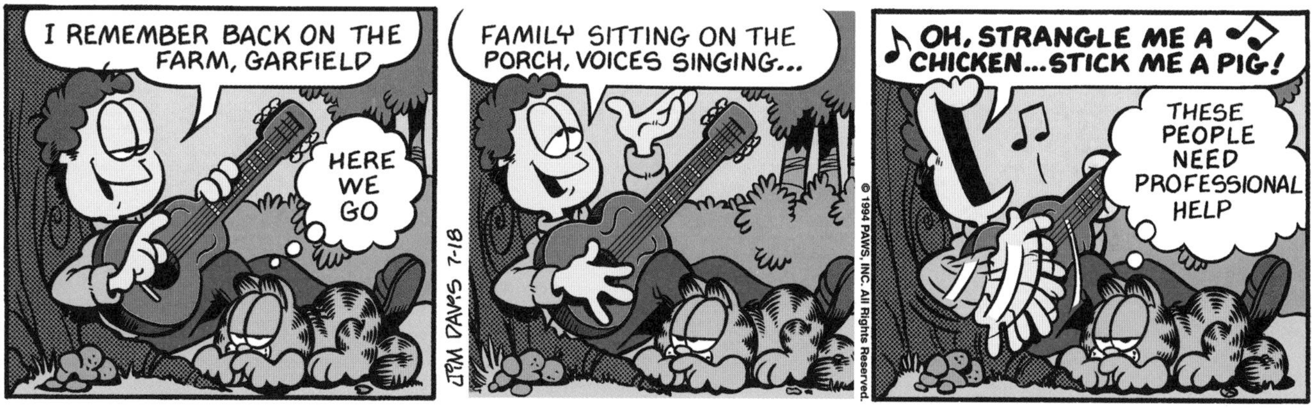
I REMEMBER BACK ON THE FARM, GARFIELD
HERE WE GO
JIM DAVIS 7-18
FAMILY SITTING ON THE PORCH, VOICES SINGING...
© 1994 PAWS, INC. All Rights Reserved.
OH, STRANGLE ME A CHICKEN...STICK ME A PIG!
THESE PEOPLE NEED PROFESSIONAL HELP

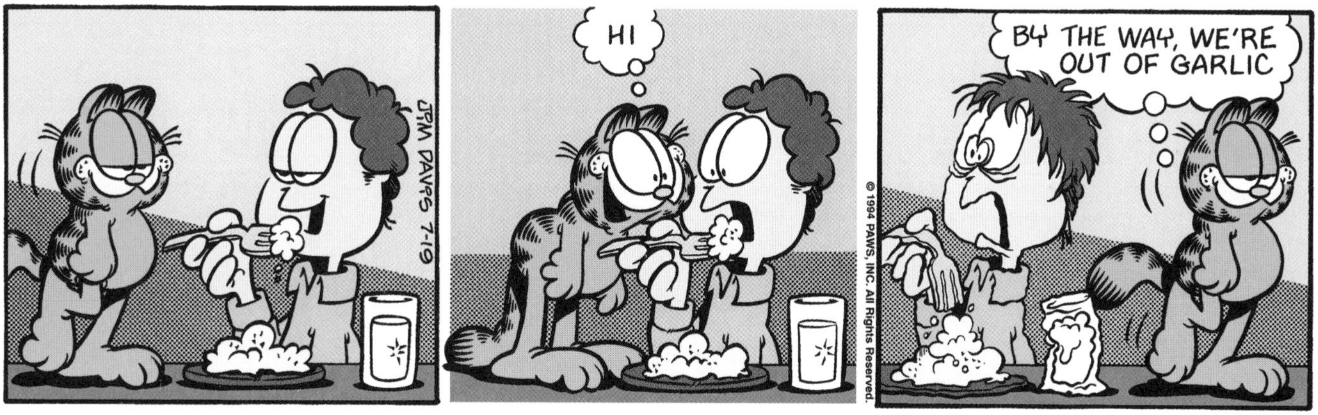
JIM DAVIS 7-19
HI
© 1994 PAWS, INC. All Rights Reserved.
BY THE WAY, WE'RE OUT OF GARLIC

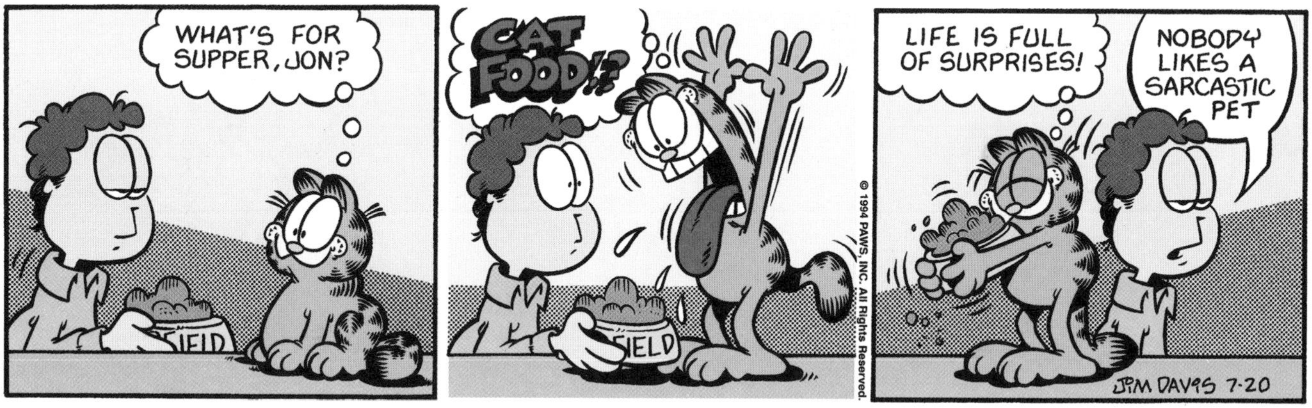
WHAT'S FOR SUPPER, JON?
CAT FOOD!?
© 1994 PAWS, INC. All Rights Reserved.
LIFE IS FULL OF SURPRISES!
NOBODY LIKES A SARCASTIC PET
JIM DAVIS 7-20

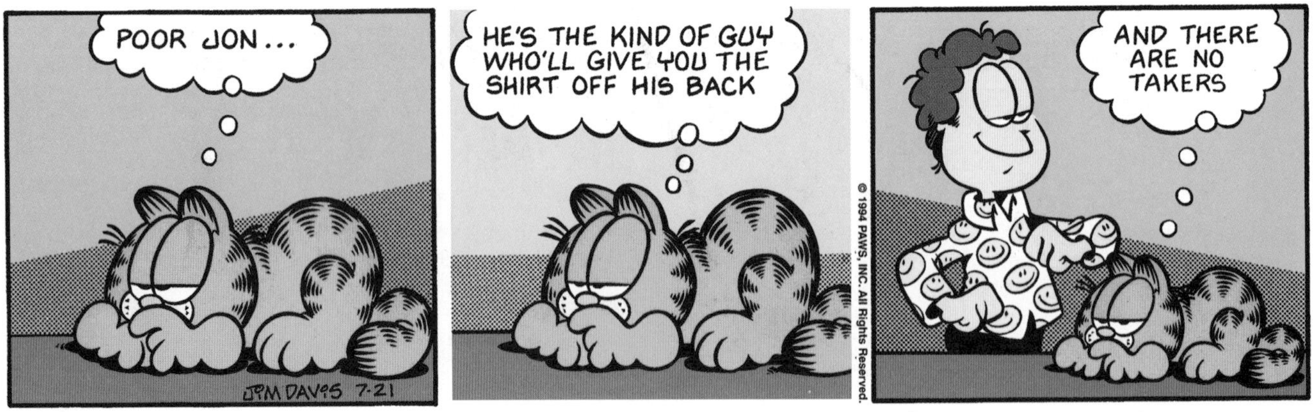
POOR JON...
HE'S THE KIND OF GUY WHO'LL GIVE YOU THE SHIRT OFF HIS BACK
AND THERE ARE NO TAKERS
JIM DAVIS 7-21

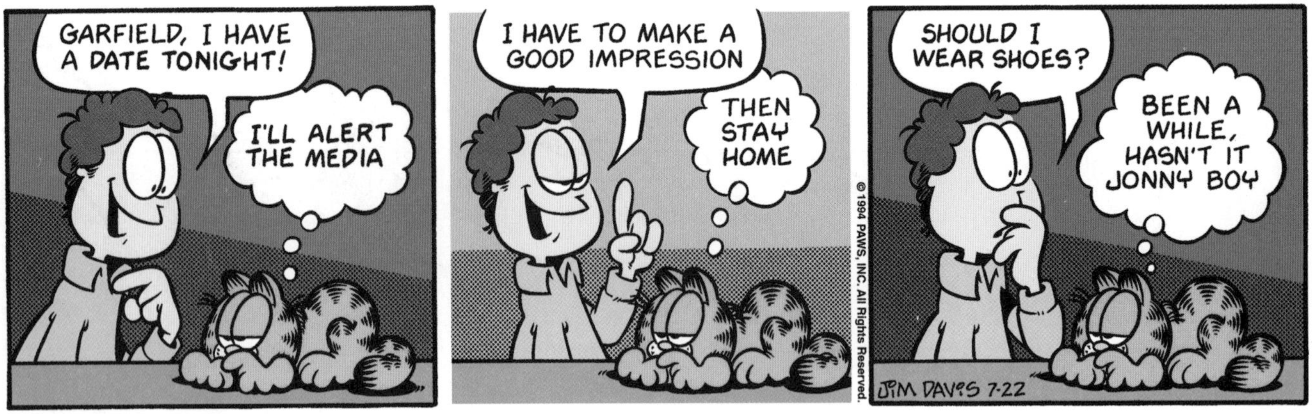
GARFIELD, I HAVE A DATE TONIGHT!
I'LL ALERT THE MEDIA
I HAVE TO MAKE A GOOD IMPRESSION
THEN STAY HOME
SHOULD I WEAR SHOES?
BEEN A WHILE, HASN'T IT JONNY BOY
JIM DAVIS 7-22

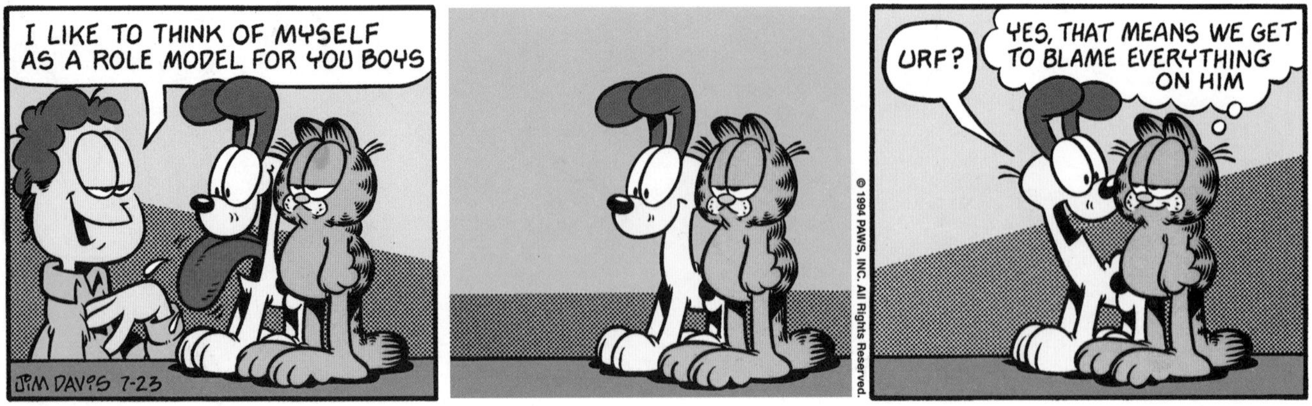
I LIKE TO THINK OF MYSELF AS A ROLE MODEL FOR YOU BOYS
JIM DAVIS 7-23
URF?
YES, THAT MEANS WE GET TO BLAME EVERYTHING ON HIM

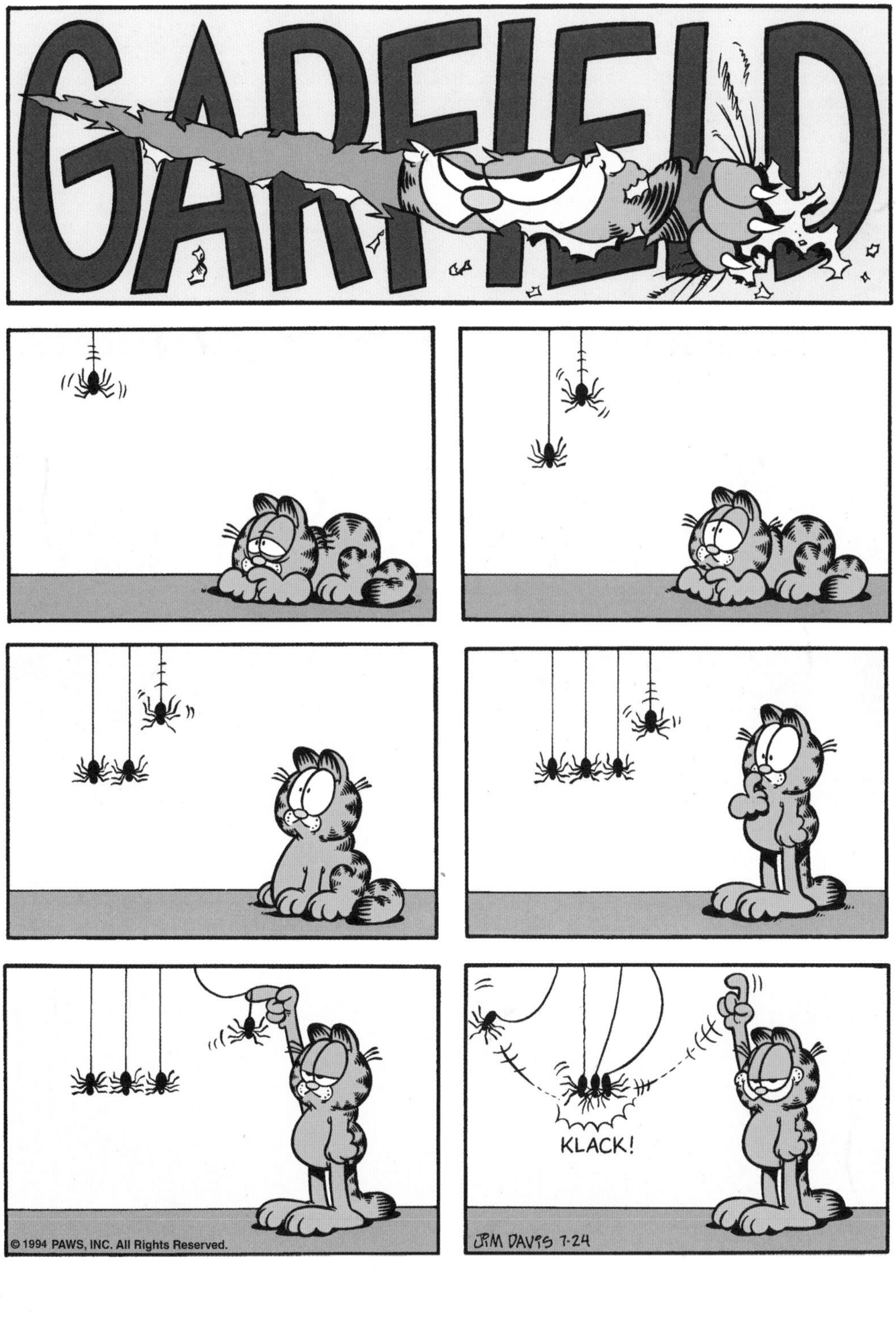
GARFIELD
KLACK!
© 1994 PAWS, INC. All Rights Reserved.
JIM DAVIS 7-24

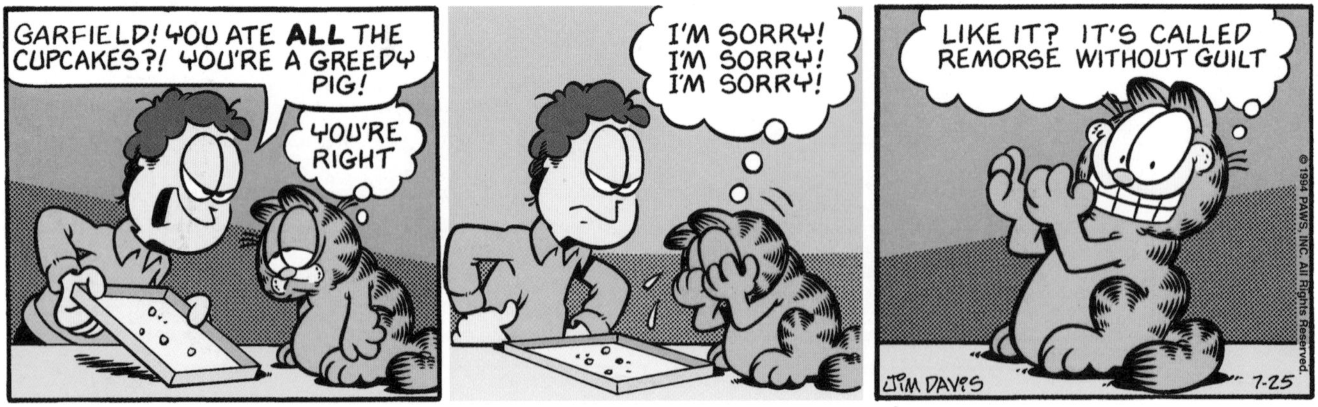
GARFIELD! YOU ATE ALL THE CUPCAKES?! YOU'RE A GREEDY PIG!
YOU'RE RIGHT
I'M SORRY! I'M SORRY! I'M SORRY!
LIKE IT? IT'S CALLED REMORSE WITHOUT GUILT
© 1994 PAWS, INC. All Rights Reserved.
JIM DAVIS 7-25

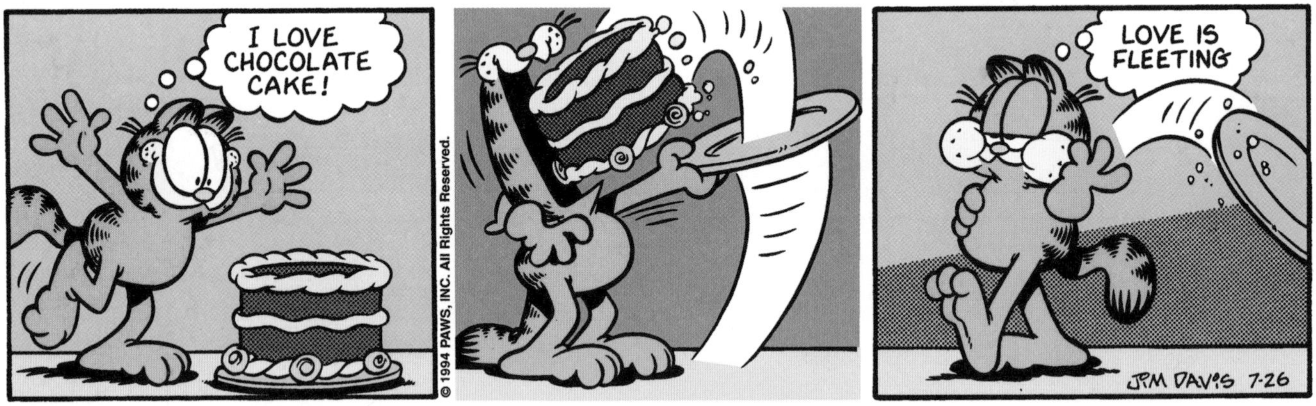
I LOVE CHOCOLATE CAKE!
© 1994 PAWS, INC. All Rights Reserved.
LOVE IS FLEETING
JIM DAVIS 7-26

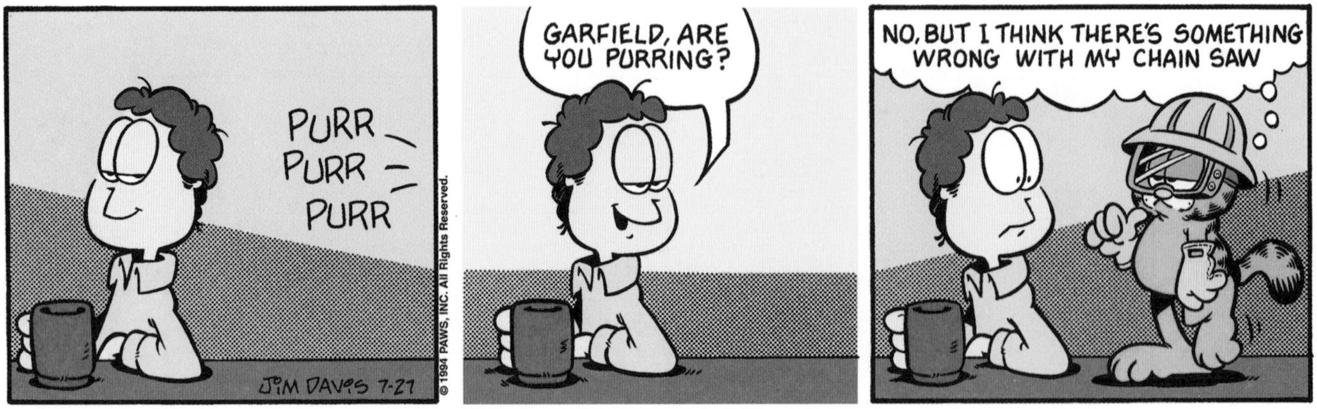
PURR PURR PURR
JIM DAVIS 7-27
© 1994 PAWS, INC. All Rights Reserved.
GARFIELD, ARE YOU PURRING?
NO, BUT I THINK THERE'S SOMETHING WRONG WITH MY CHAIN SAW

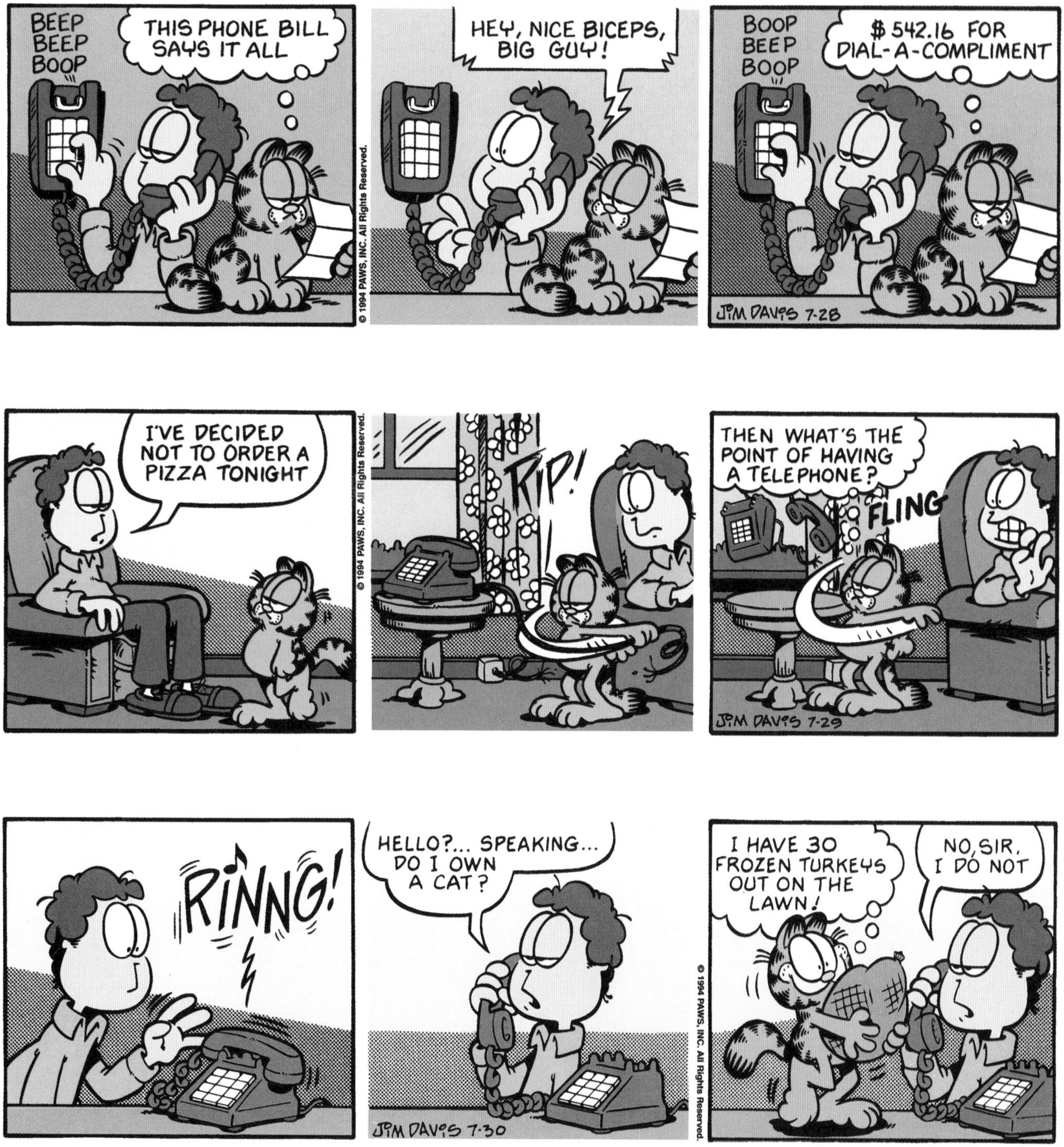
BEEP BEEP BOOP
THIS PHONE BILL SAYS IT ALL
© 1994 PAWS, INC. All Rights Reserved.
HEY, NICE BICEPS, BIG GUY!
BOOP BEEP BOOP
$ 542.16 FOR DIAL-A-COMPLIMENT
JIM DAVIS 7-28
I'VE DECIDED NOT TO ORDER A PIZZA TONIGHT
© 1994 PAWS, INC. All Rights Reserved.
RIP!
THEN WHAT'S THE POINT OF HAVING A TELEPHONE?
FLING
JIM DAVIS 7-29
RINNG!
HELLO?... SPEAKING... DO I OWN A CAT?
JIM DAVIS 7-30
© 1994 PAWS, INC. All Rights Reserved.
I HAVE 30 FROZEN TURKEYS OUT ON THE LAWN!
NO, SIR, I DO NOT

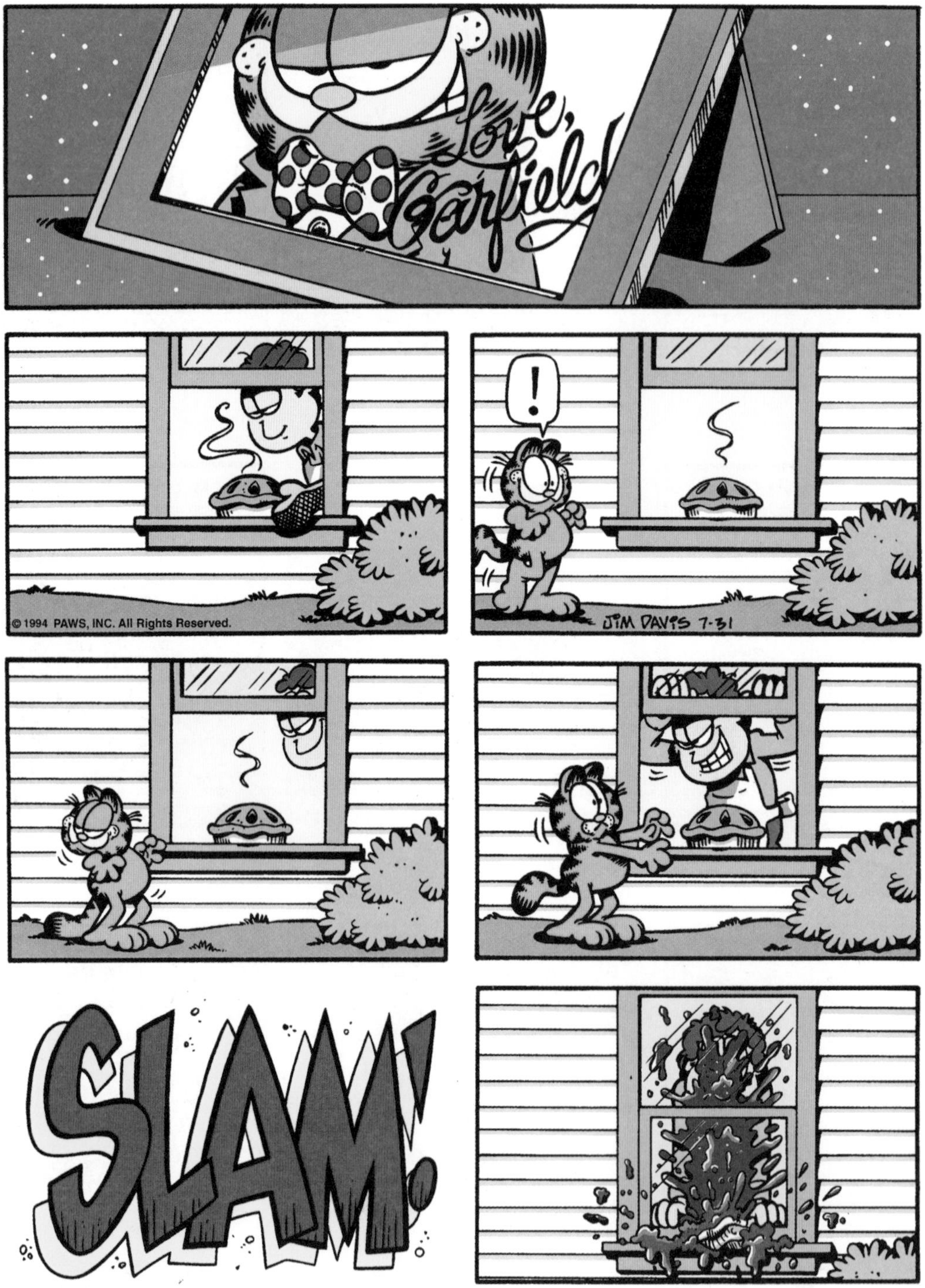

Love, Garfield
© 1994 PAWS, INC. All Rights Reserved.
!
JIM DAVIS 7-31
SLAM!

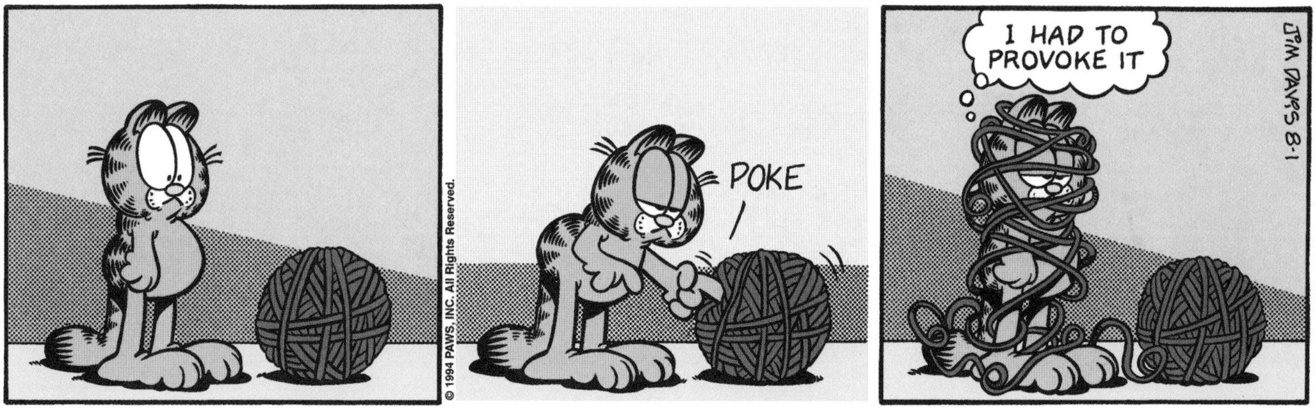
© 1994 PAWS, INC. All Rights Reserved.
POKE
I HAD TO PROVOKE IT
JIM DAVIS 8-1

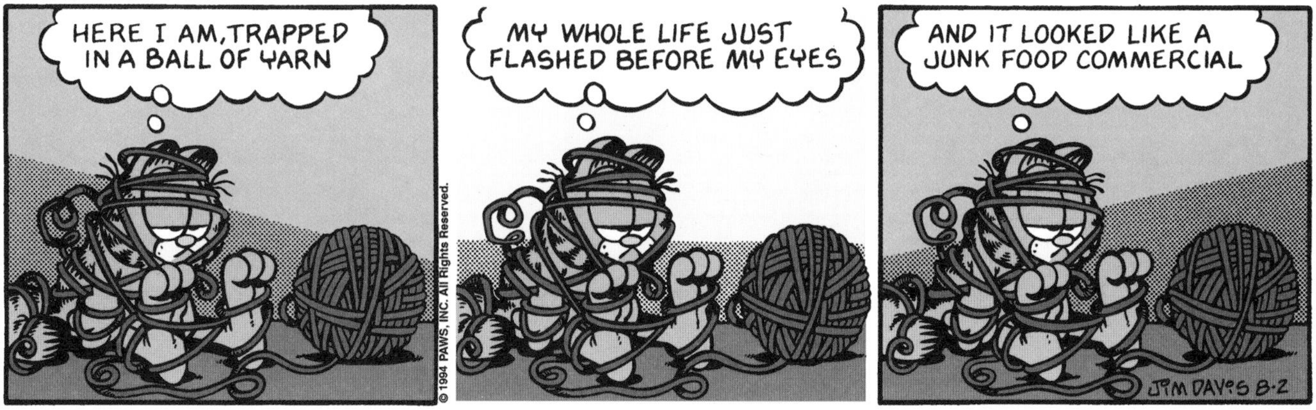
HERE I AM, TRAPPED IN A BALL OF YARN
© 1994 PAWS, INC. All Rights Reserved.
MY WHOLE LIFE JUST FLASHED BEFORE MY EYES
AND IT LOOKED LIKE A JUNK FOOD COMMERCIAL
JIM DAVIS 8-2

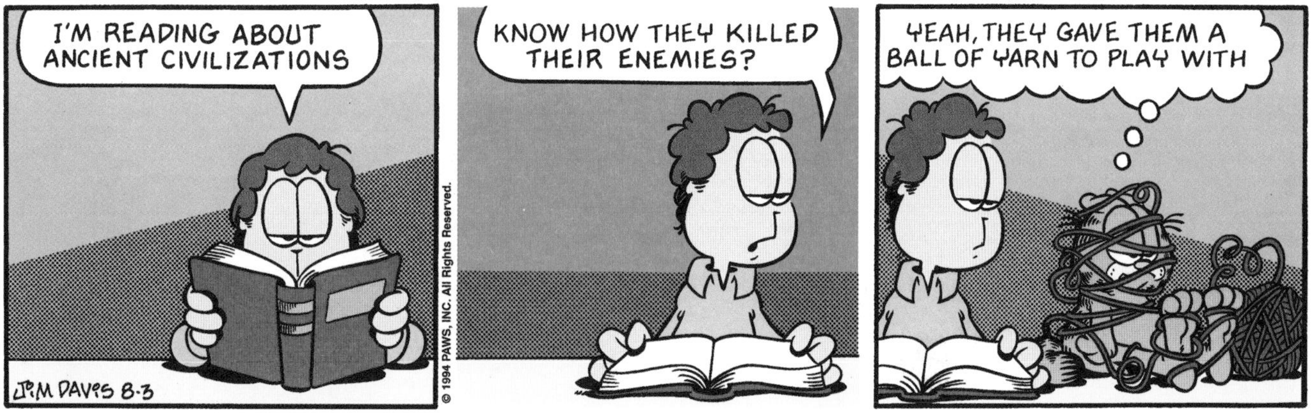
I'M READING ABOUT ANCIENT CIVILIZATIONS
JIM DAVIS 8-3
© 1994 PAWS, INC. All Rights Reserved.
KNOW HOW THEY KILLED THEIR ENEMIES?
YEAH, THEY GAVE THEM A BALL OF YARN TO PLAY WITH

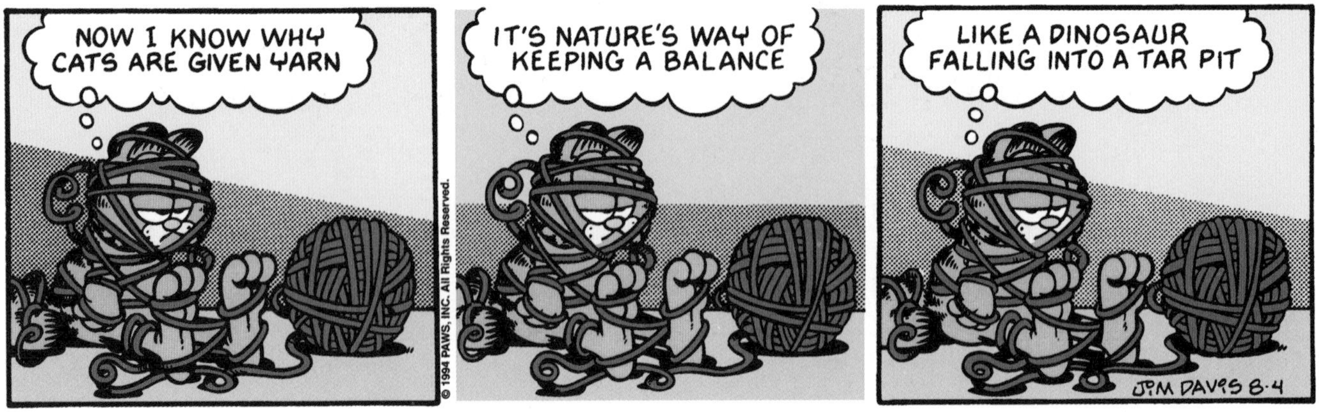
NOW I KNOW WHY CATS ARE GIVEN YARN
IT'S NATURE'S WAY OF KEEPING A BALANCE
LIKE A DINOSAUR FALLING INTO A TAR PIT
© 1994 PAWS, INC. All Rights Reserved.
JIM DAVIS 8-4

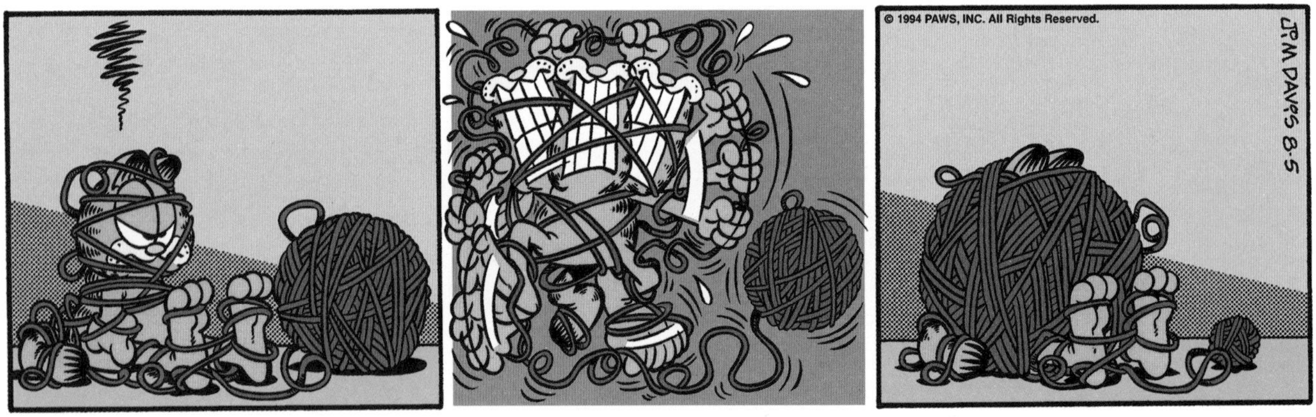
© 1994 PAWS, INC. All Rights Reserved.
JIM DAVIS 8-5

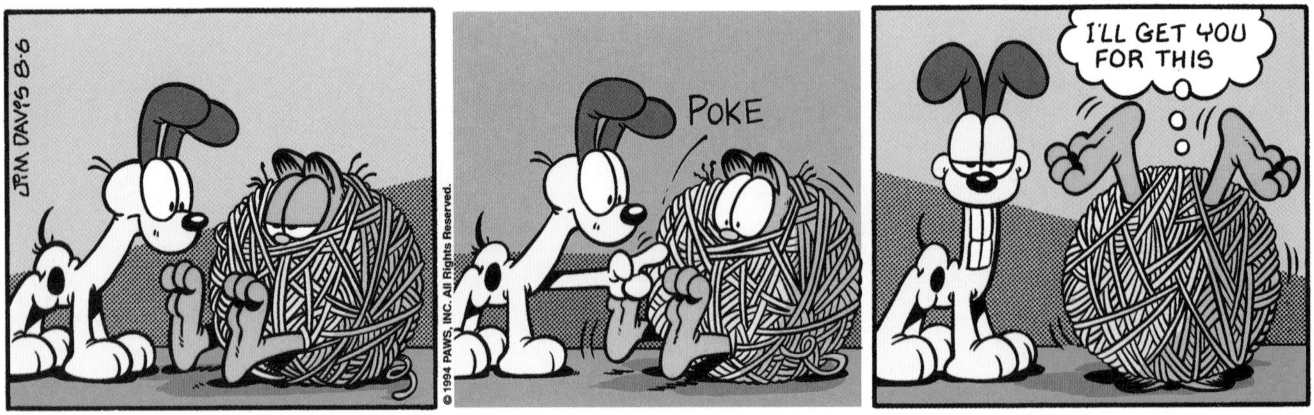
JIM DAVIS 8-6
POKE
I'LL GET YOU FOR THIS
© 1994 PAWS, INC. All Rights Reserved.

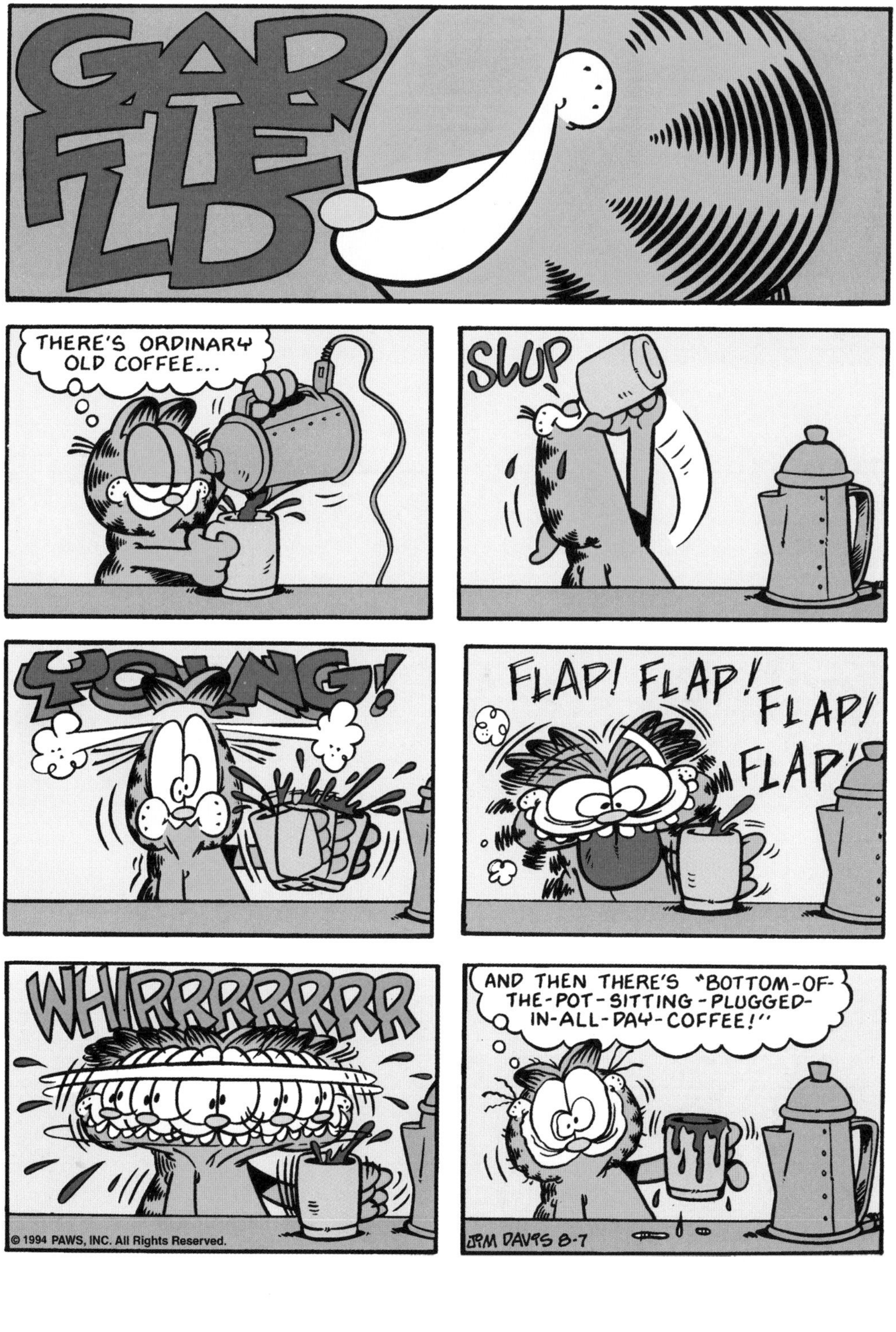
GARFIELD
THERE'S ORDINARY OLD COFFEE...
SLUP
YOWNG!
FLAP! FLAP! FLAP! FLAP!
WHIRRRRRRRR
AND THEN THERE'S "BOTTOM-OF-THE-POT-SITTING-PLUGGED-IN-ALL-DAY-COFFEE!"
© 1994 PAWS, INC. All Rights Reserved.
JIM DAVIS 8-7

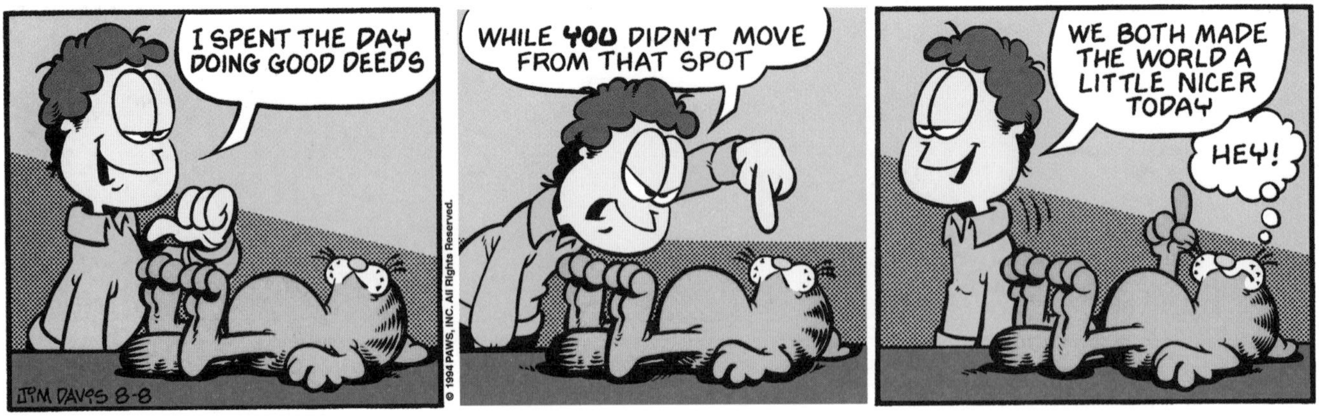
I SPENT THE DAY DOING GOOD DEEDS
WHILE YOU DIDN'T MOVE FROM THAT SPOT
WE BOTH MADE THE WORLD A LITTLE NICER TODAY
HEY!
JIM DAVIS 8-8
© 1994 PAWS, INC. All Rights Reserved.

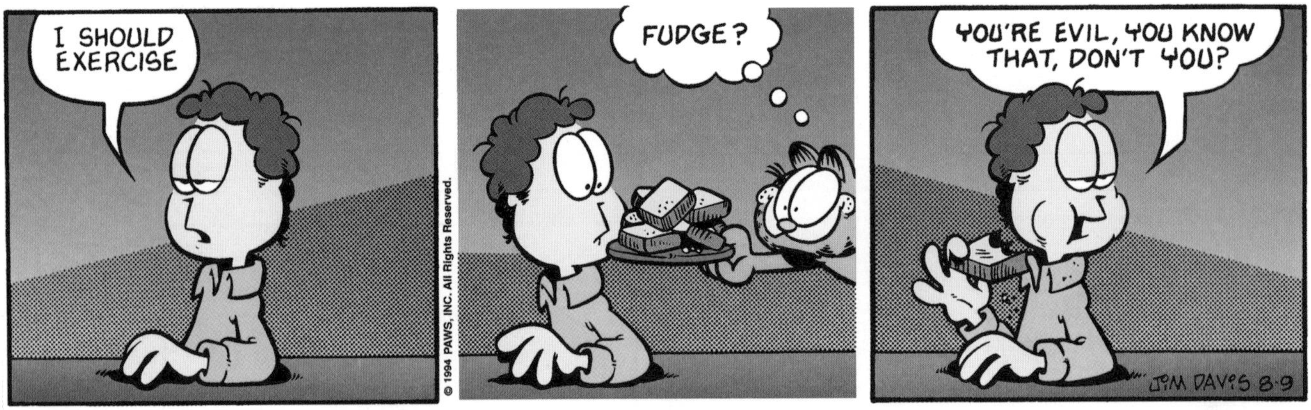
I SHOULD EXERCISE
FUDGE?
YOU'RE EVIL, YOU KNOW THAT, DON'T YOU?
JIM DAVIS 8-9
© 1994 PAWS, INC. All Rights Reserved.

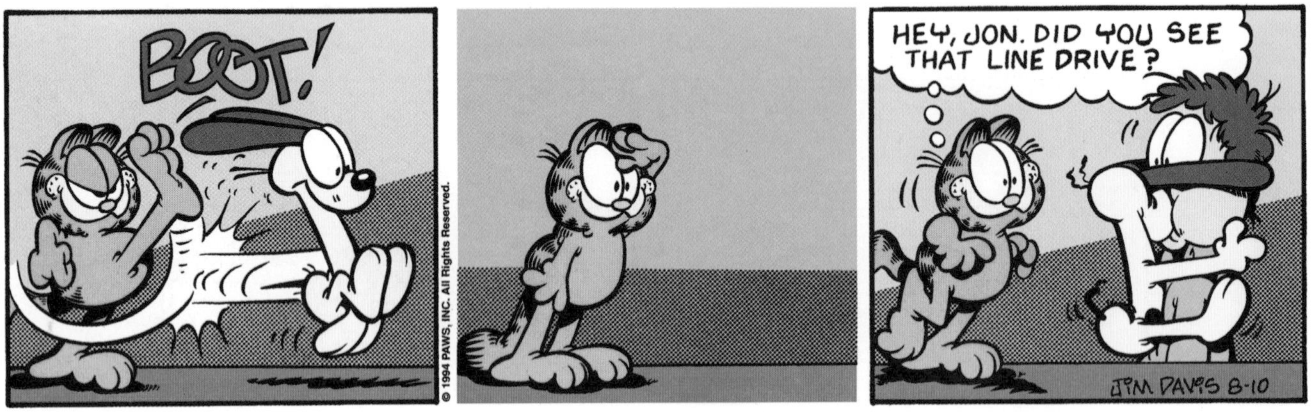
BOOT!
HEY, JON. DID YOU SEE THAT LINE DRIVE?
JIM DAVIS 8-10
© 1994 PAWS, INC. All Rights Reserved.

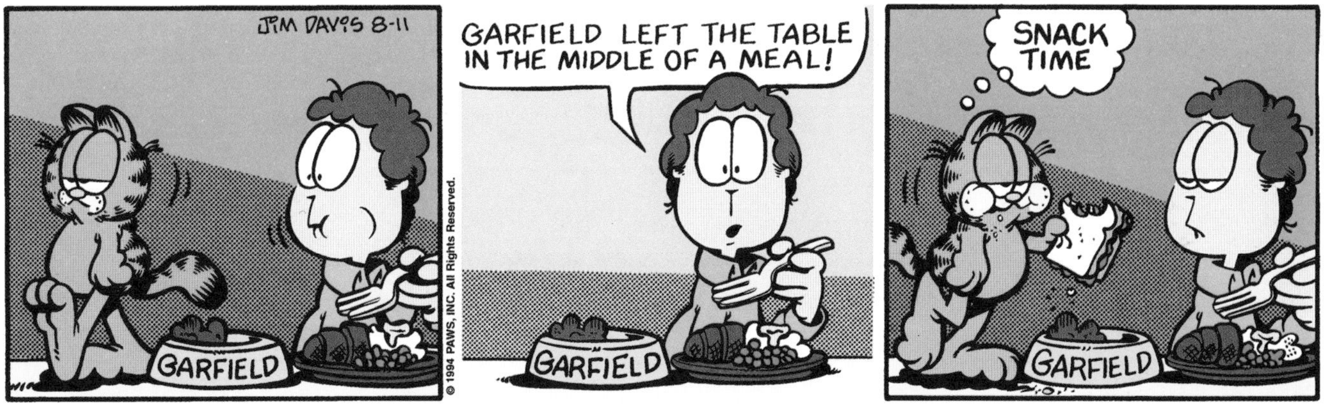
JIM DAVIS 8-11
GARFIELD
GARFIELD LEFT THE TABLE IN THE MIDDLE OF A MEAL!
GARFIELD
SNACK TIME
GARFIELD

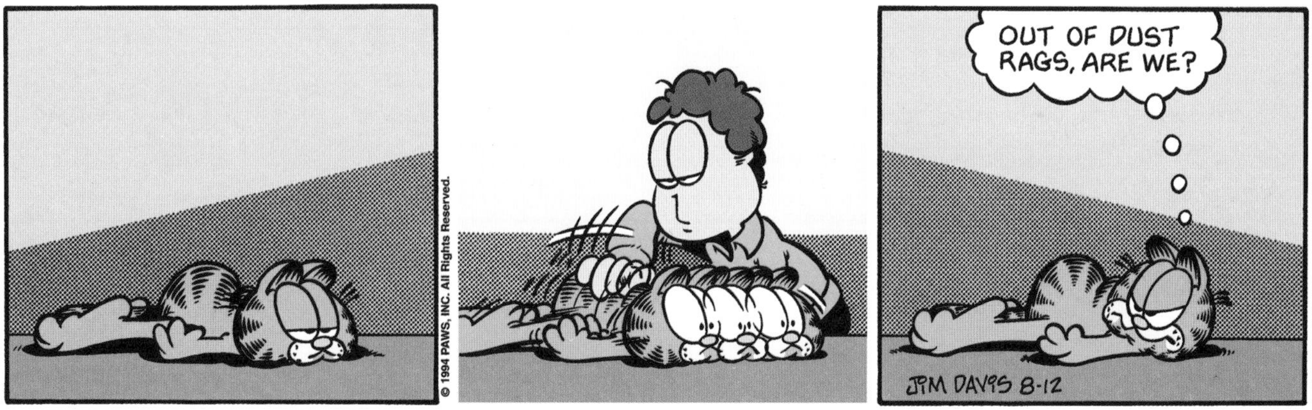
OUT OF DUST RAGS, ARE WE?
JIM DAVIS 8-12

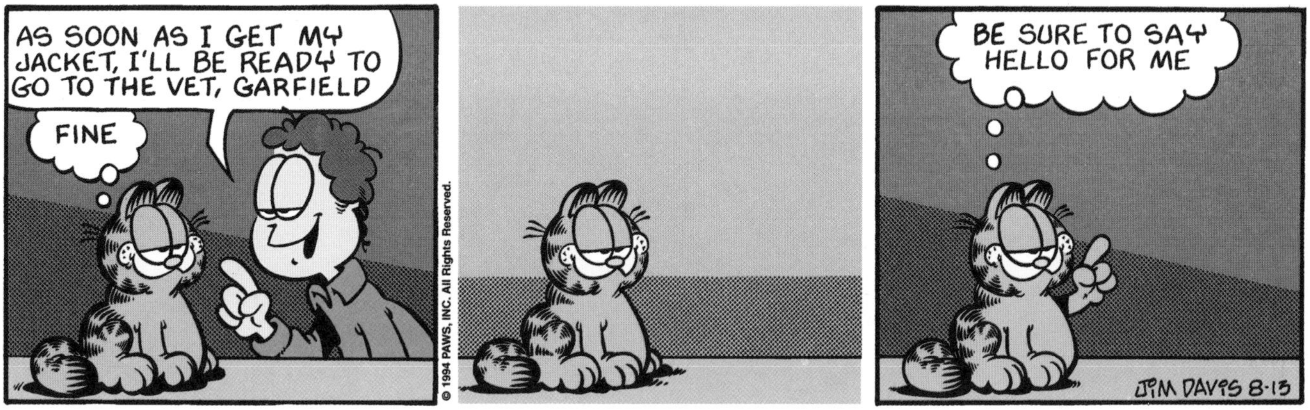
AS SOON AS I GET MY JACKET, I'LL BE READY TO GO TO THE VET, GARFIELD
FINE
BE SURE TO SAY HELLO FOR ME
JIM DAVIS 8-13

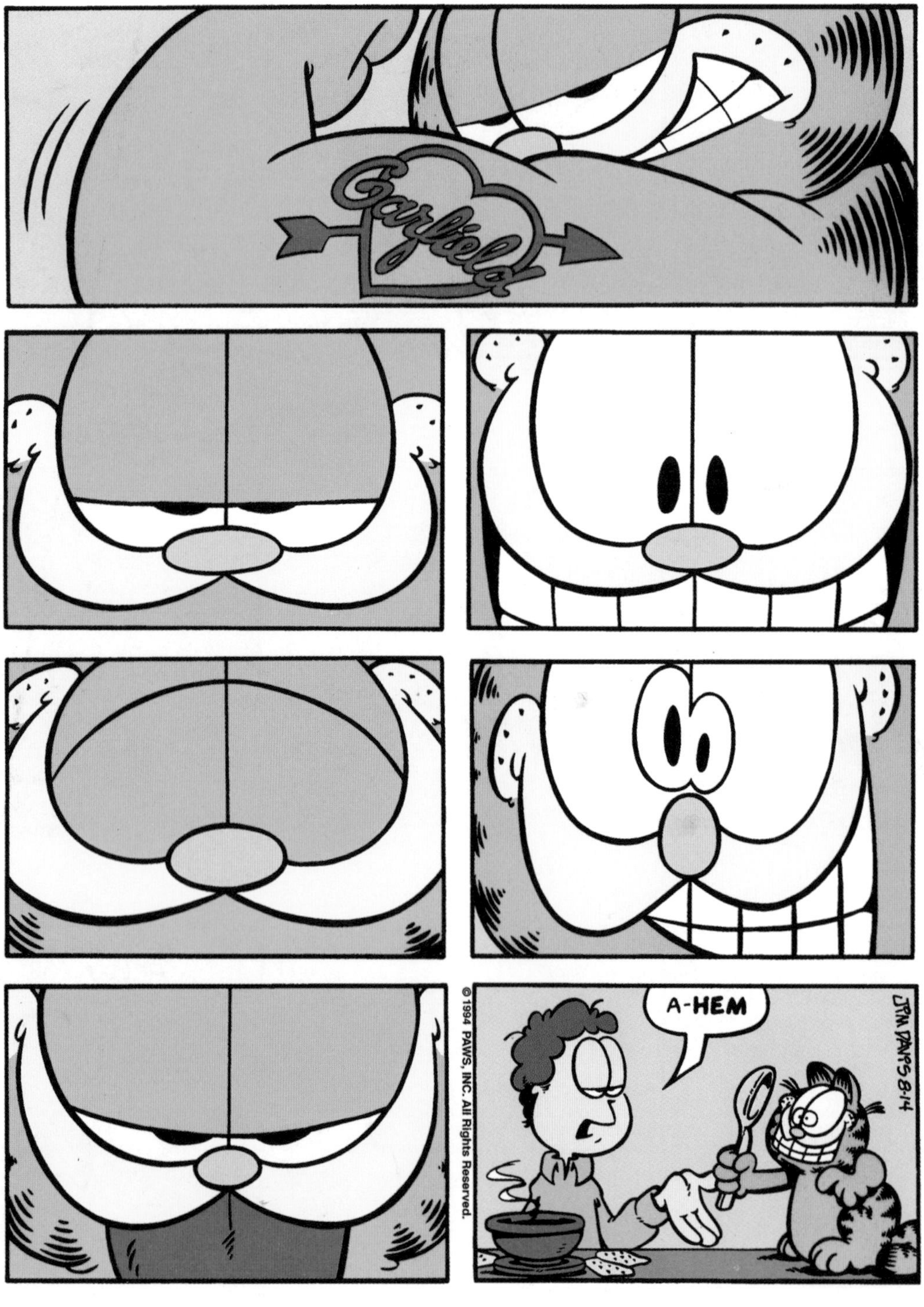
A-HEM

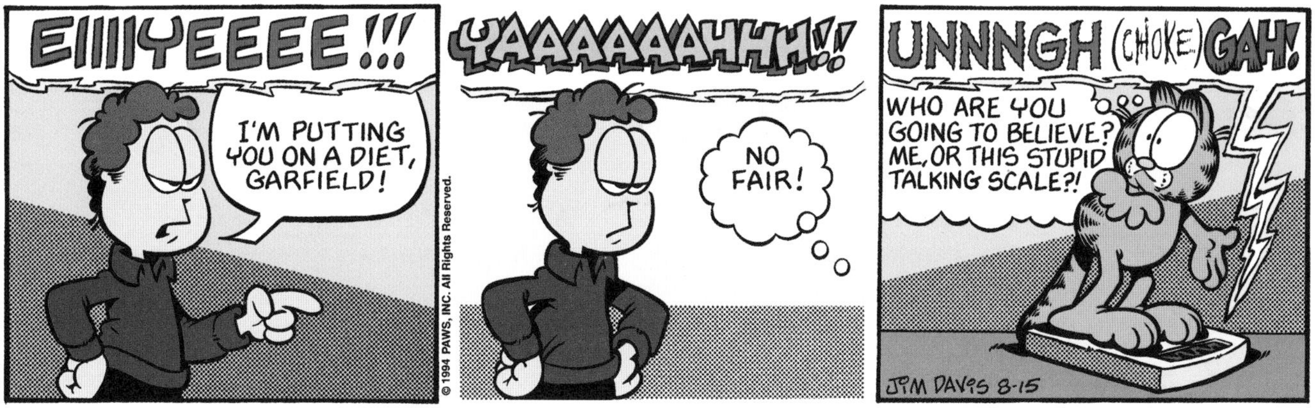
EIIIIYEEEE!!!
I'M PUTTING YOU ON A DIET, GARFIELD!
© 1994 PAWS, INC. All Rights Reserved.
YAAAAAAHHH!!
NO FAIR!
UNNNGH (CHOKE) GAH!
WHO ARE YOU GOING TO BELIEVE? ME, OR THIS STUPID TALKING SCALE?!
JIM DAVIS 8-15

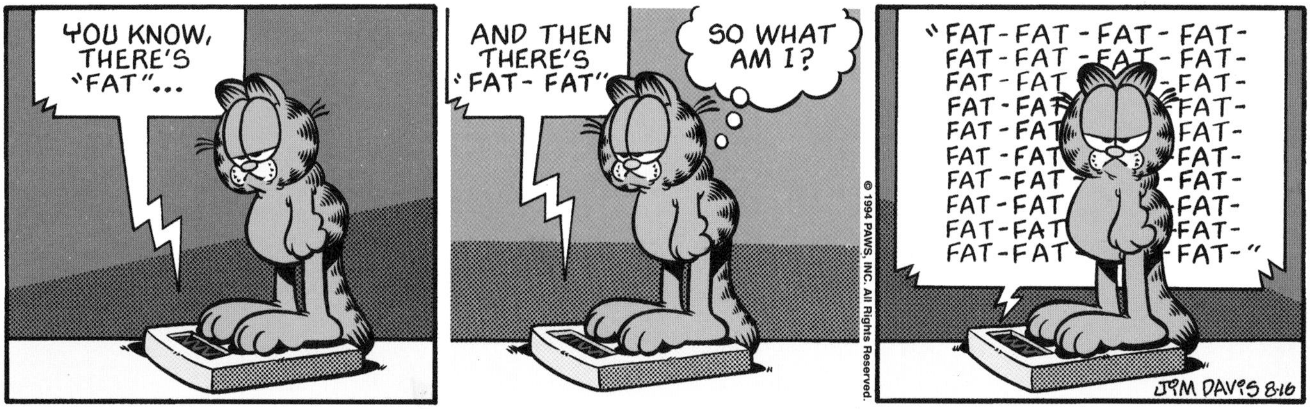
YOU KNOW, THERE'S "FAT"...
AND THEN THERE'S "FAT- FAT"
SO WHAT AM I?
© 1994 PAWS, INC. All Rights Reserved.
"FAT-FAT-FAT-FAT- FAT-FAT-FAT-FAT- FAT-FAT-FAT- FAT-FAT-FAT- FAT-FAT-FAT- FAT-FAT-FAT- FAT-FAT-FAT- FAT-FAT-FAT- FAT-FAT-FAT- FAT-FAT-FAT-"
JIM DAVIS 8-16

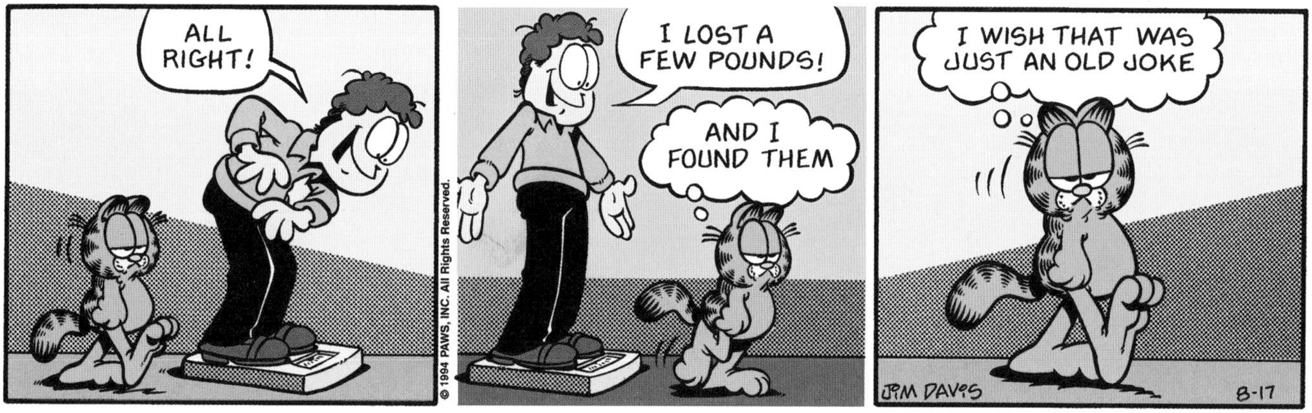
ALL RIGHT!
© 1994 PAWS, INC. All Rights Reserved.
I LOST A FEW POUNDS!
AND I FOUND THEM
I WISH THAT WAS JUST AN OLD JOKE
JIM DAVIS 8-17

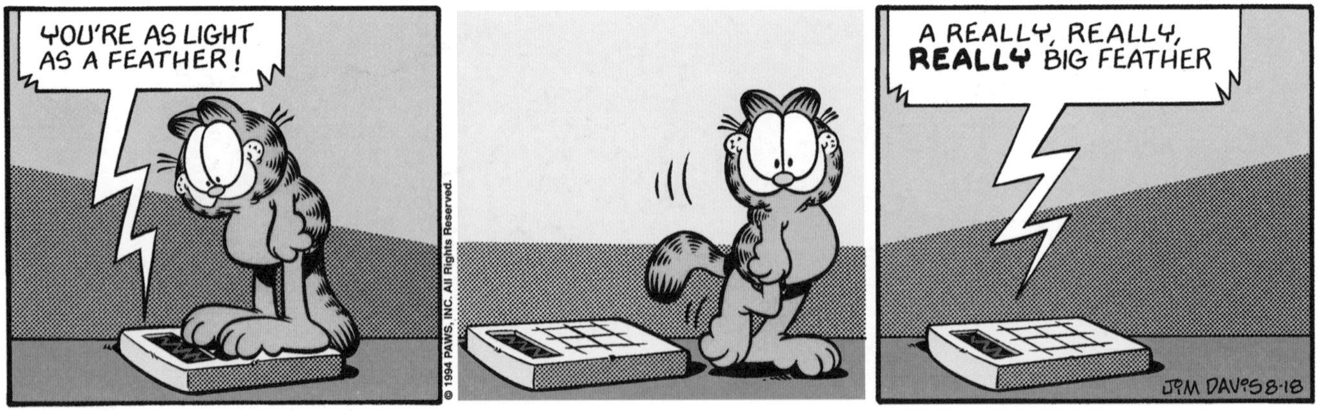
YOU'RE AS LIGHT AS A FEATHER!
© 1994 PAWS, INC. All Rights Reserved.
A REALLY, REALLY, **REALLY** BIG FEATHER
JIM DAVIS 8-18

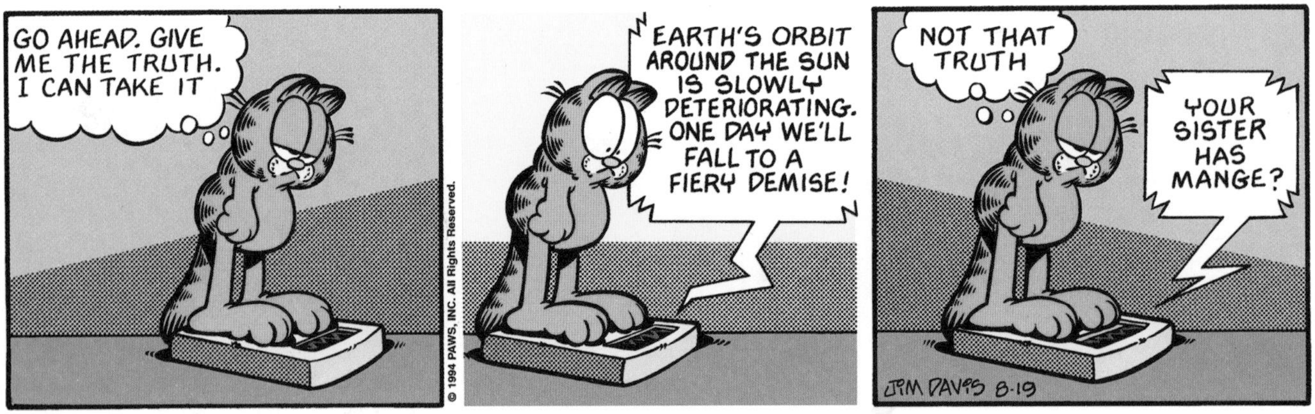
GO AHEAD. GIVE ME THE TRUTH. I CAN TAKE IT
© 1994 PAWS, INC. All Rights Reserved.
EARTH'S ORBIT AROUND THE SUN IS SLOWLY DETERIORATING. ONE DAY WE'LL FALL TO A FIERY DEMISE!
NOT THAT TRUTH
YOUR SISTER HAS MANGE?
JIM DAVIS 8-19

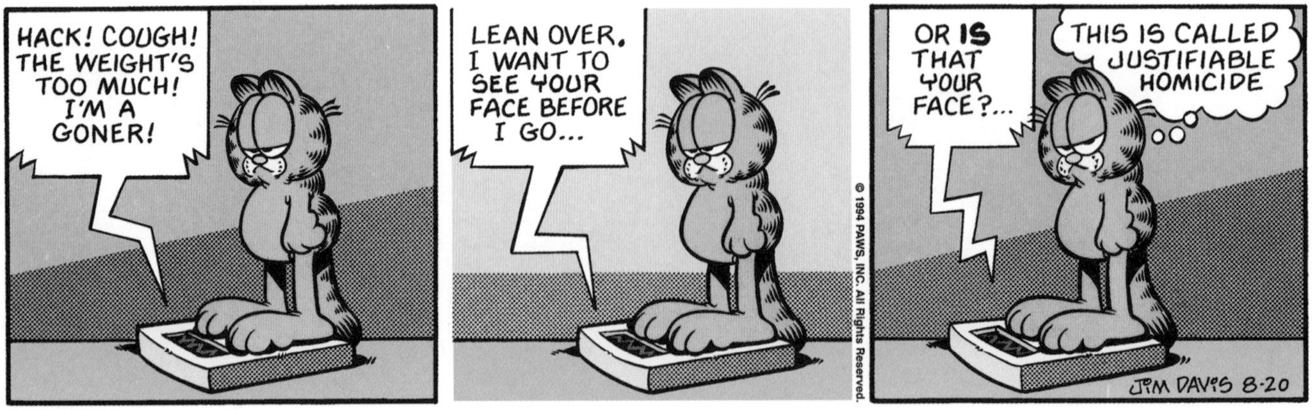
HACK! COUGH! THE WEIGHT'S TOO MUCH! I'M A GONER!
LEAN OVER. I WANT TO SEE YOUR FACE BEFORE I GO...
© 1994 PAWS, INC. All Rights Reserved.
OR **IS** THAT YOUR FACE?...
THIS IS CALLED JUSTIFIABLE HOMICIDE
JIM DAVIS 8-20

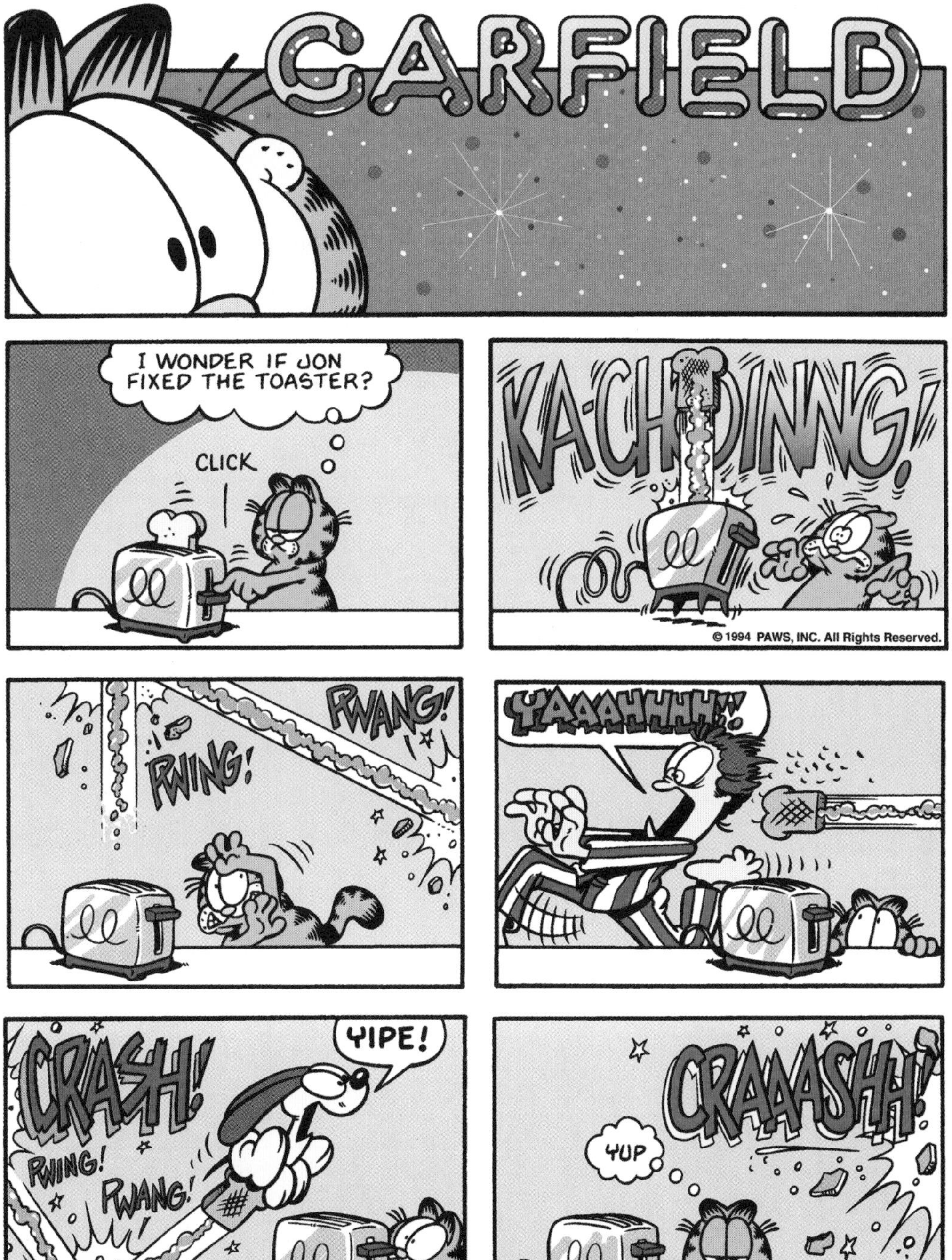
GARFIELD
I WONDER IF JON FIXED THE TOASTER?
CLICK
KA-CHOINNG!
© 1994 PAWS, INC. All Rights Reserved.
PWANG!
PWING!
YAAAHHHH!
CRASH!
YIPE!
PWING!
PWANG!
YUP
CRAAASHH!
JIM DAVIS 8-21

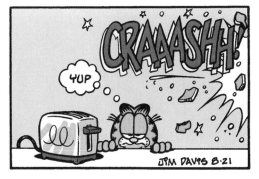

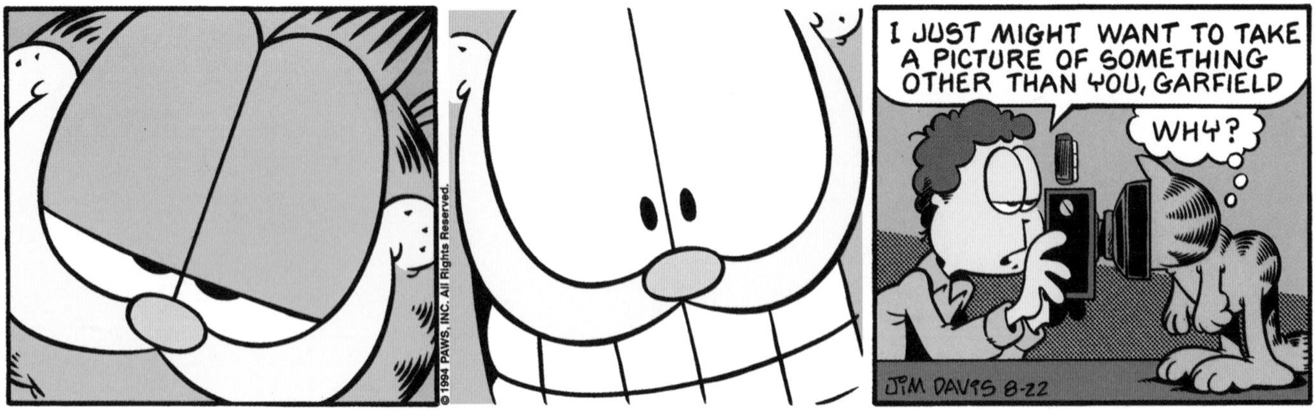
© 1994 PAWS, INC. All Rights Reserved.
I JUST MIGHT WANT TO TAKE A PICTURE OF SOMETHING OTHER THAN YOU, GARFIELD
WHY?
JIM DAVIS 8-22

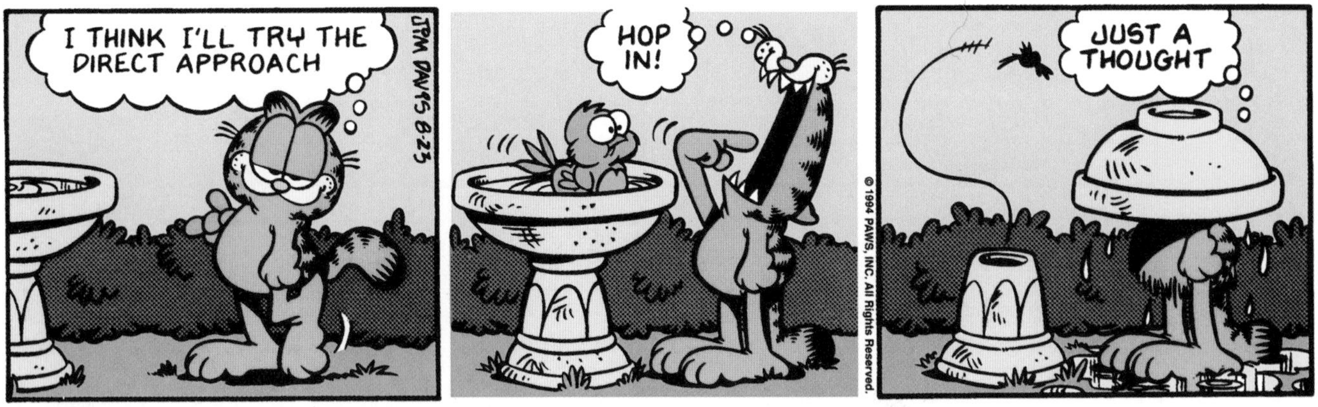
I THINK I'LL TRY THE DIRECT APPROACH
JIM DAVIS 8-23
HOP IN!
© 1994 PAWS, INC. All Rights Reserved.
JUST A THOUGHT

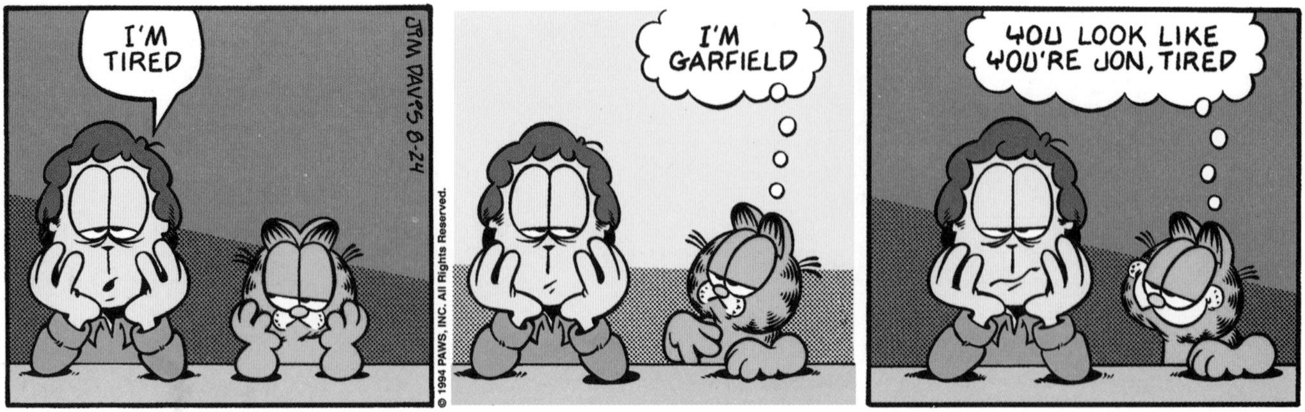
I'M TIRED
JIM DAVIS 8-24
© 1994 PAWS, INC. All Rights Reserved.
I'M GARFIELD
YOU LOOK LIKE YOU'RE JON, TIRED

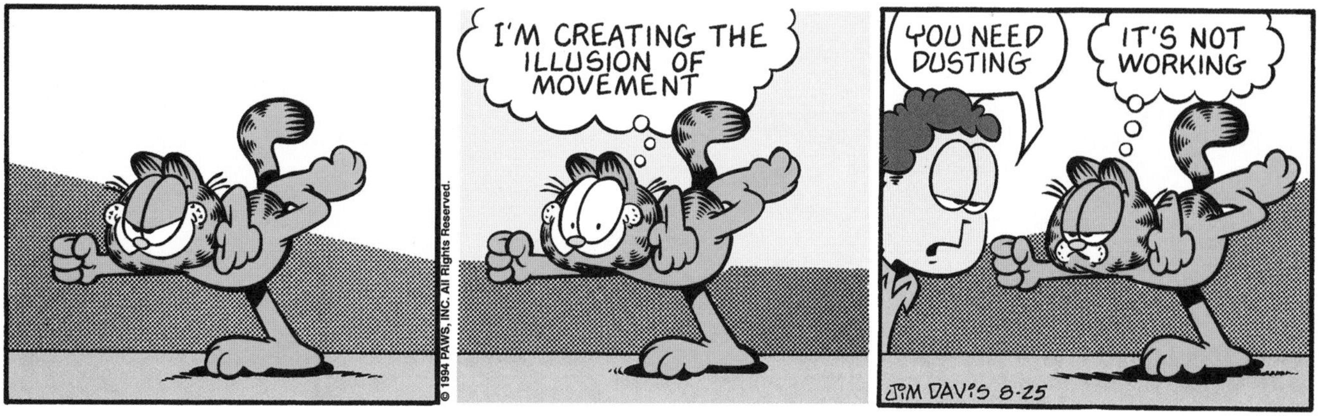
© 1994 PAWS, INC. All Rights Reserved.
I'M CREATING THE ILLUSION OF MOVEMENT
YOU NEED DUSTING
IT'S NOT WORKING
JIM DAVIS 8-25

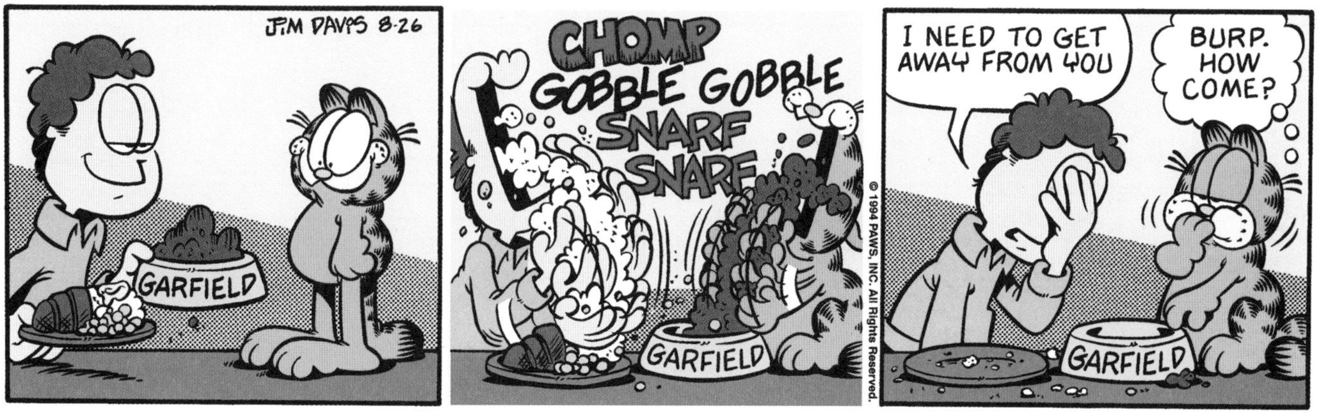
JIM DAVIS 8-26
GARFIELD
CHOMP
GOBBLE GOBBLE
SNARF SNARF
GARFIELD
© 1994 PAWS, INC. All Rights Reserved.
I NEED TO GET AWAY FROM YOU
BURP. HOW COME?
GARFIELD

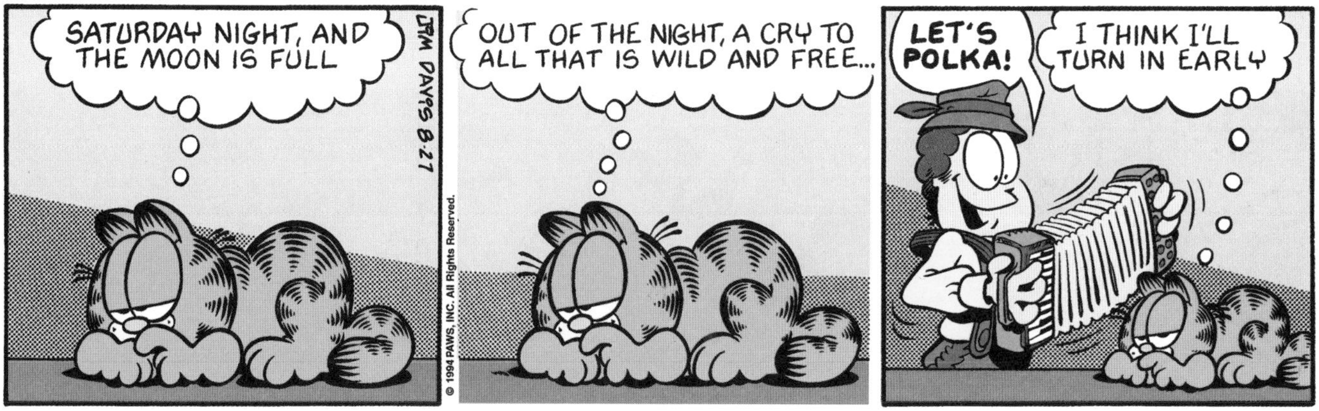
SATURDAY NIGHT, AND THE MOON IS FULL
JIM DAVIS 8-27
© 1994 PAWS, INC. All Rights Reserved.
OUT OF THE NIGHT, A CRY TO ALL THAT IS WILD AND FREE...
LET'S POLKA!
I THINK I'LL TURN IN EARLY

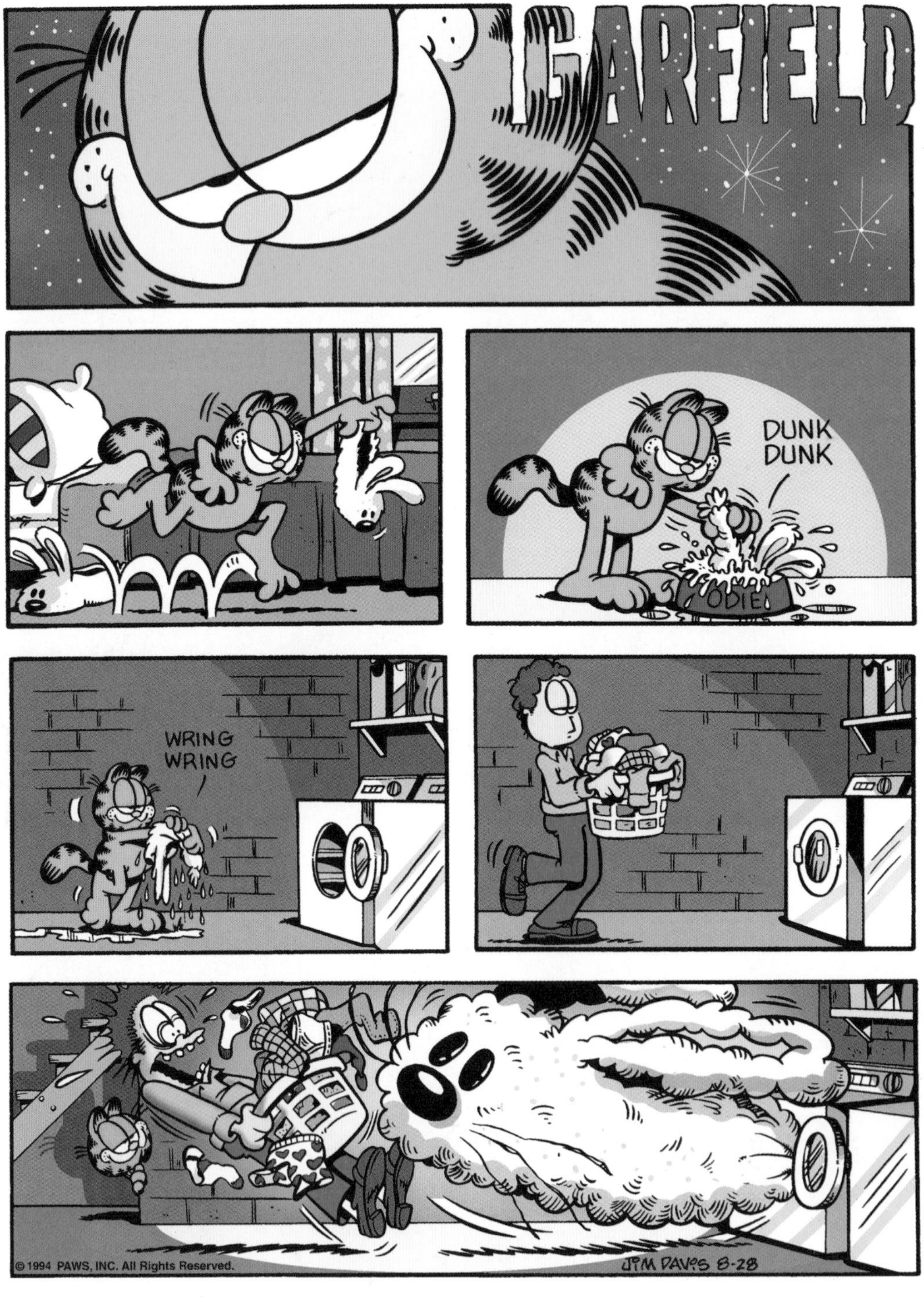
GARFIELD
DUNK DUNK
ODIE
WRING WRING
© 1994 PAWS, INC. All Rights Reserved.
JIM DAVIS 8-28

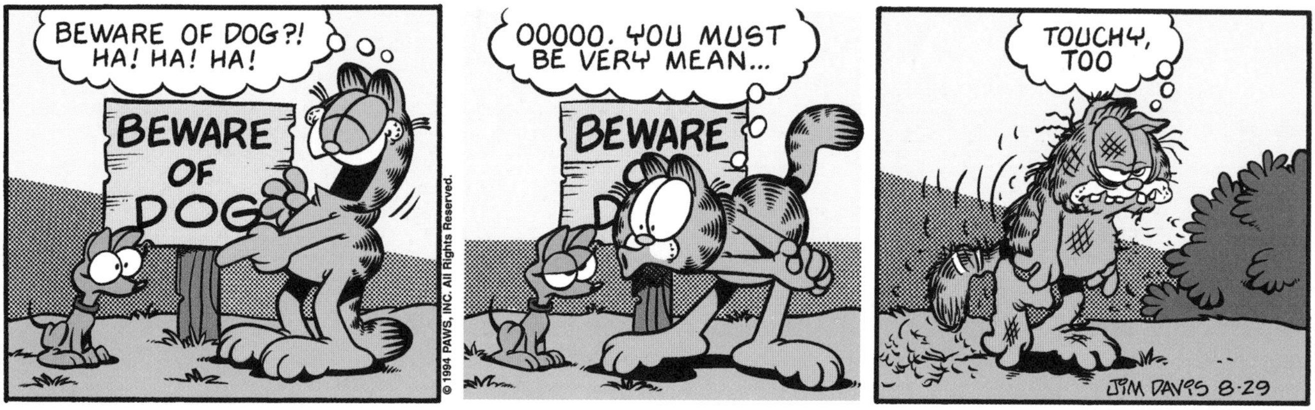
BEWARE OF DOG?! HA! HA! HA!
BEWARE OF DOG
© 1994 PAWS, INC. All Rights Reserved.
OOOOO. YOU MUST BE VERY MEAN...
BEWARE
TOUCHY, TOO
JIM DAVIS 8-29

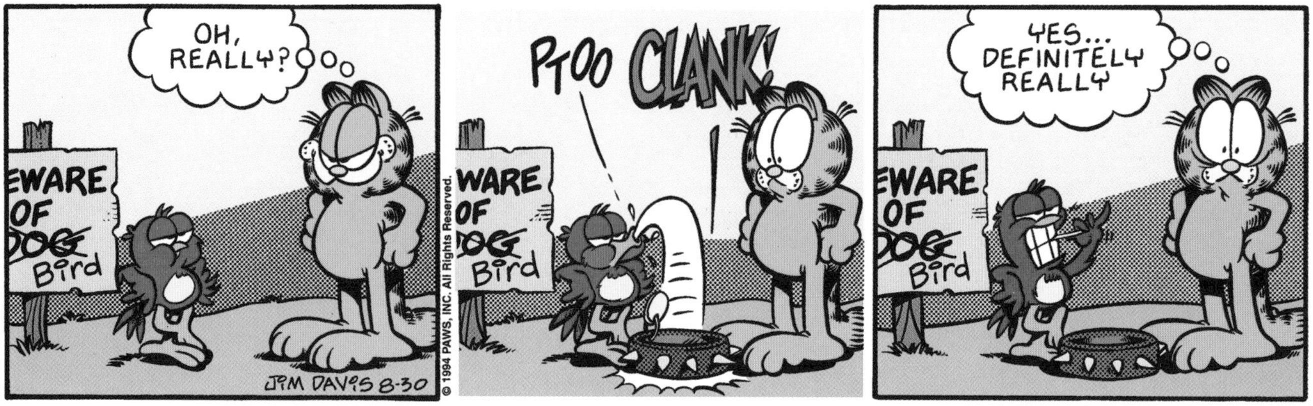
OH, REALLY?
EWARE OF DOG Bird
JIM DAVIS 8-30
© 1994 PAWS, INC. All Rights Reserved.
PTOO
CLANK!
WARE OF DOG Bird
YES... DEFINITELY REALLY
EWARE OF DOG Bird

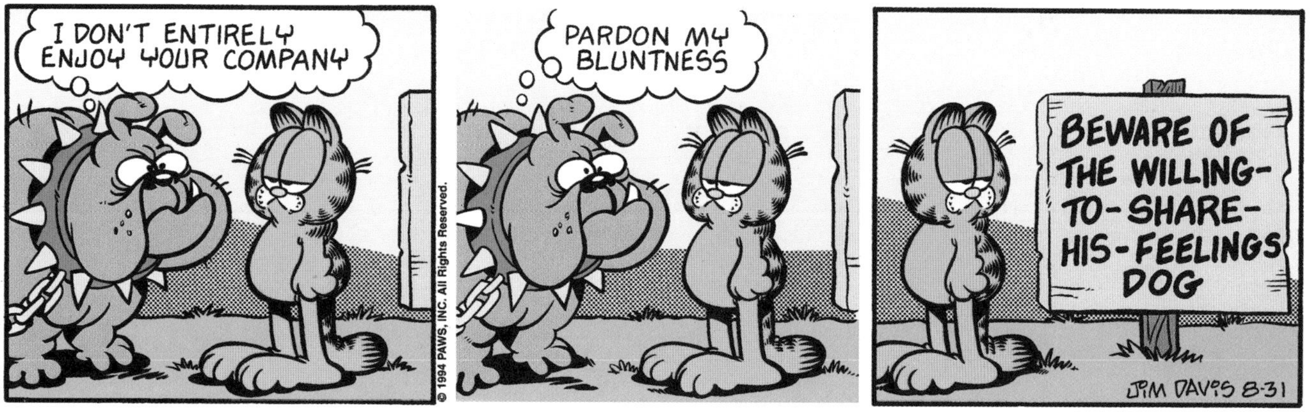
I DON'T ENTIRELY ENJOY YOUR COMPANY
© 1994 PAWS, INC. All Rights Reserved.
PARDON MY BLUNTNESS
BEWARE OF THE WILLING-TO-SHARE-HIS-FEELINGS DOG
JIM DAVIS 8-31

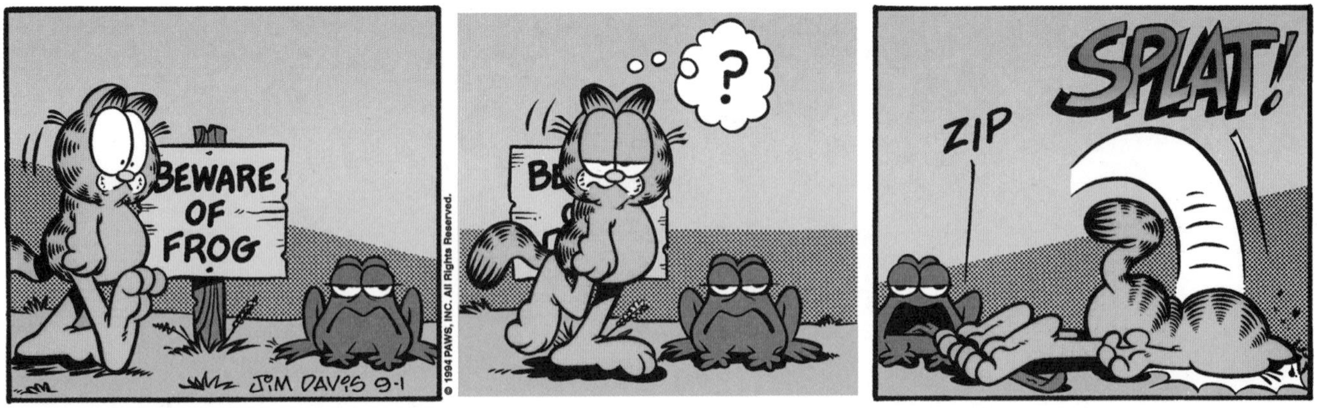
BEWARE OF FROG
JIM DAVIS 9-1
© 1994 PAWS, INC. All Rights Reserved.
?
ZIP
SPLAT!

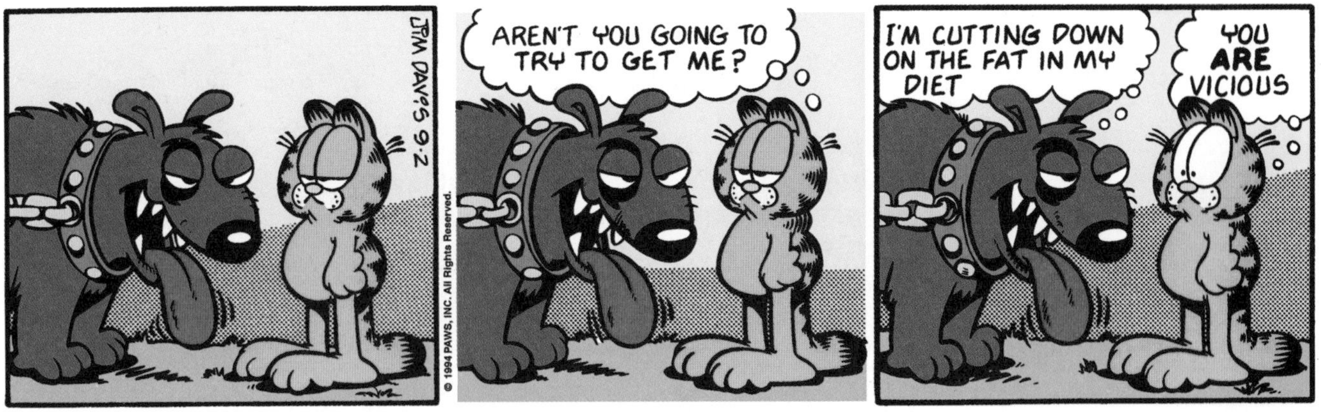
JIM DAVIS 9-2
© 1994 PAWS, INC. All Rights Reserved.
AREN'T YOU GOING TO TRY TO GET ME?
I'M CUTTING DOWN ON THE FAT IN MY DIET
YOU **ARE** VICIOUS

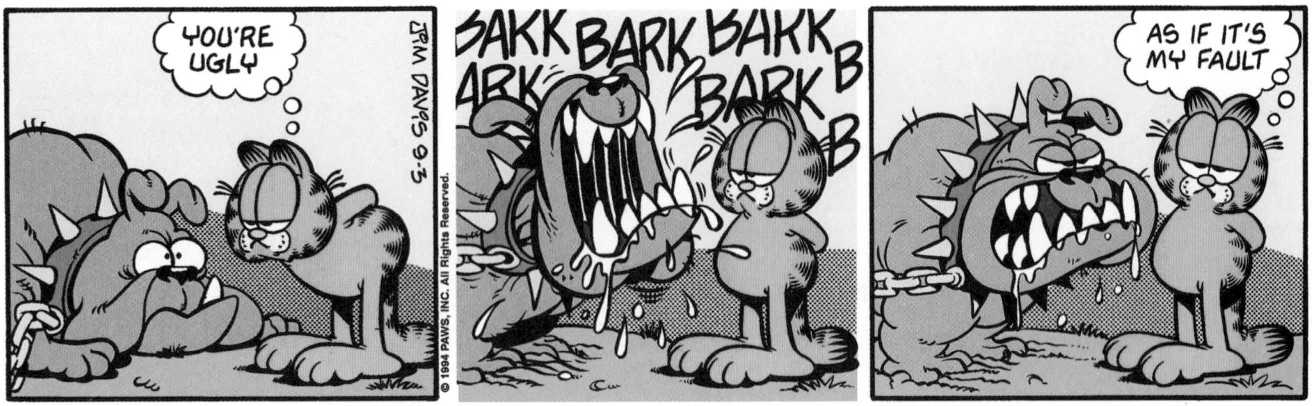
YOU'RE UGLY
JIM DAVIS 9-3
© 1994 PAWS, INC. All Rights Reserved.
BARK BARK BARK
BARK
AS IF IT'S MY FAULT

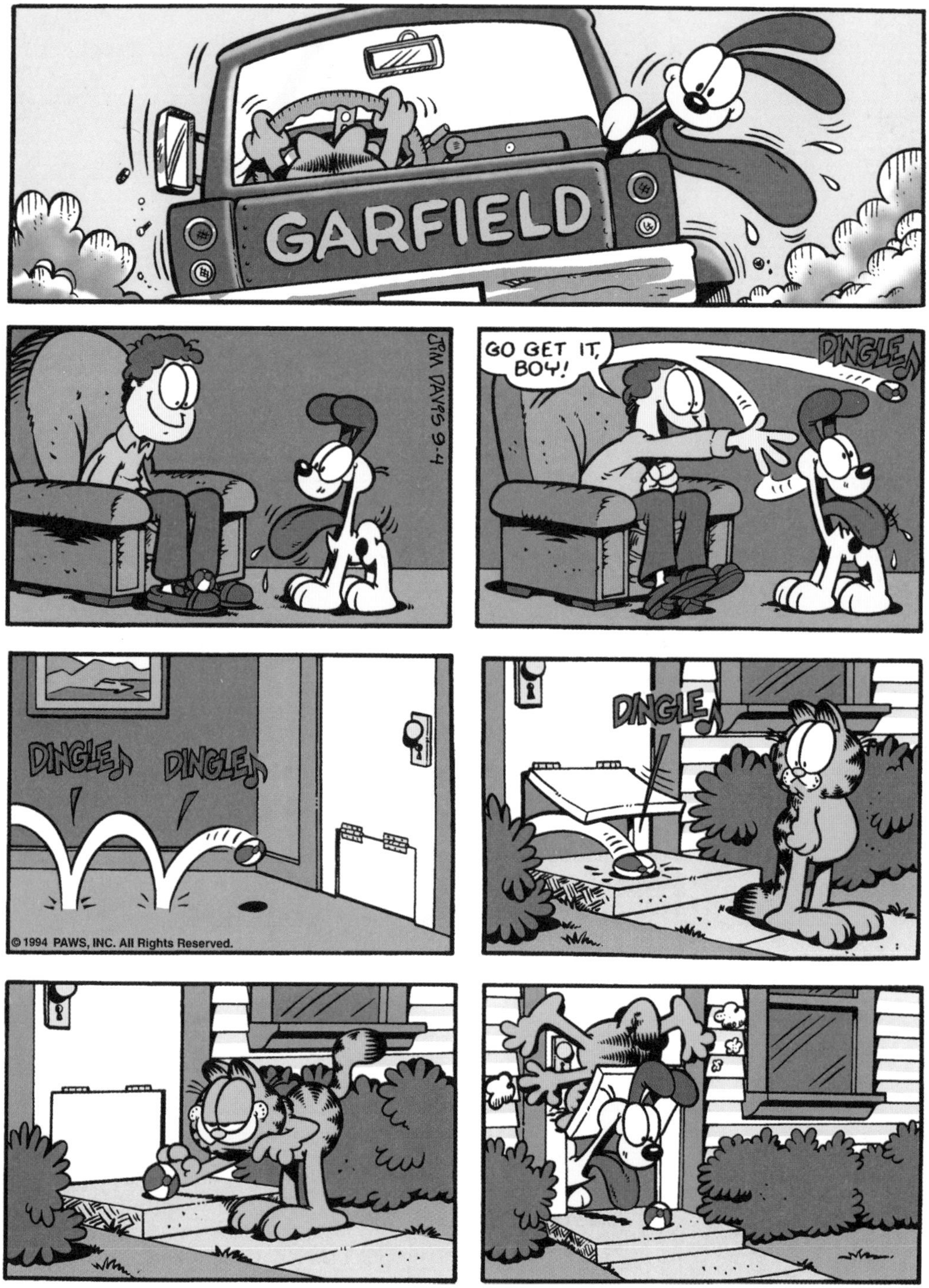
GARFIELD
JIM DAVIS 9-4
GO GET IT, BOY!
DINGLE
DINGLE
DINGLE
DINGLE

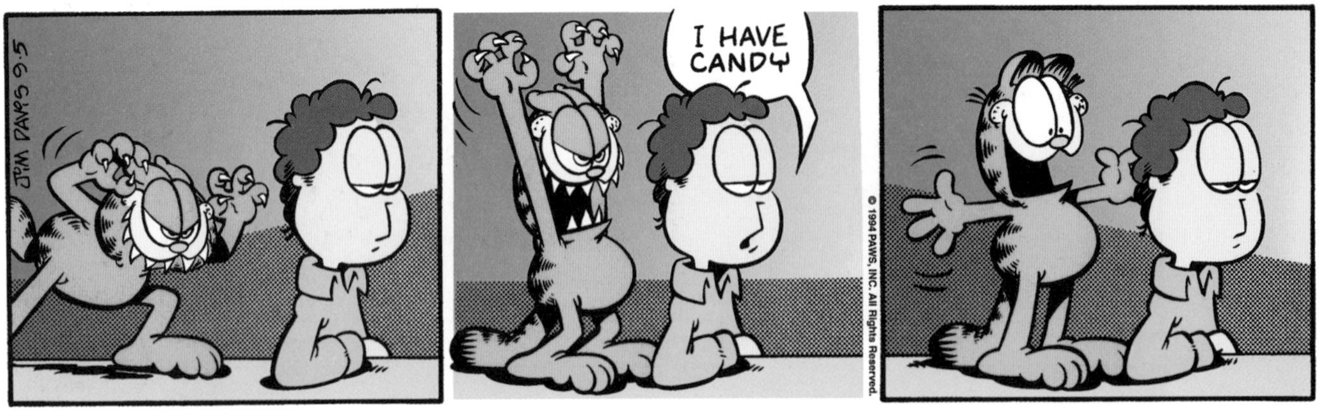
JIM DAVIS 9-5
I HAVE CANDY
© 1994 PAWS, INC. All Rights Reserved.

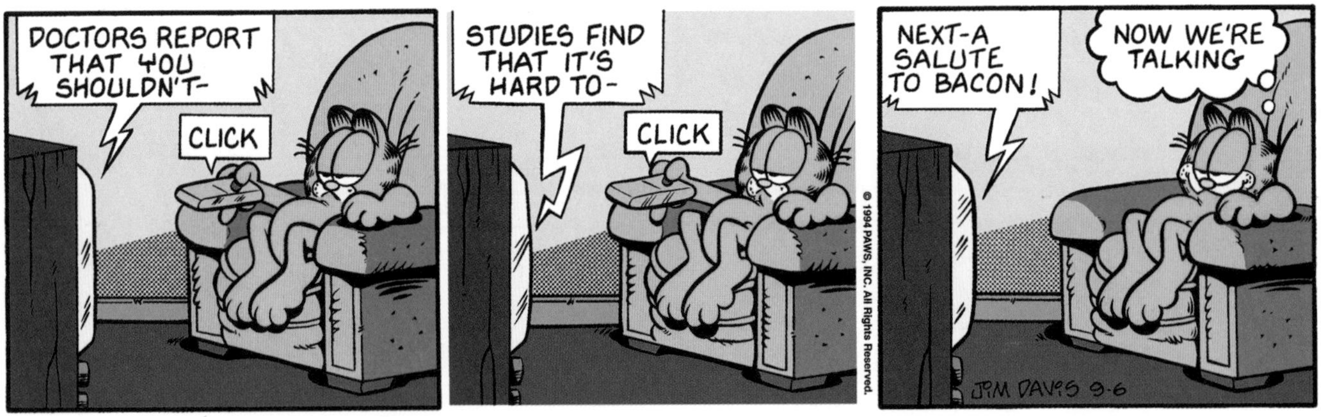
DOCTORS REPORT THAT YOU SHOULDN'T-
CLICK
STUDIES FIND THAT IT'S HARD TO-
CLICK
© 1994 PAWS, INC. All Rights Reserved.
NEXT-A SALUTE TO BACON!
NOW WE'RE TALKING
JIM DAVIS 9-6

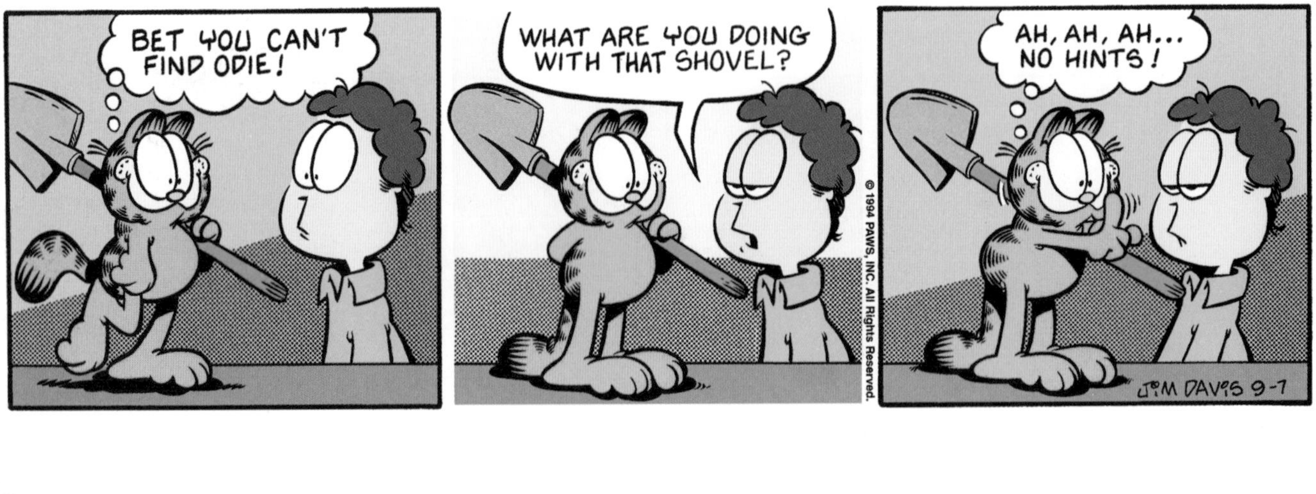
BET YOU CAN'T FIND ODIE!
WHAT ARE YOU DOING WITH THAT SHOVEL?
© 1994 PAWS, INC. All Rights Reserved.
AH, AH, AH... NO HINTS!
JIM DAVIS 9-7

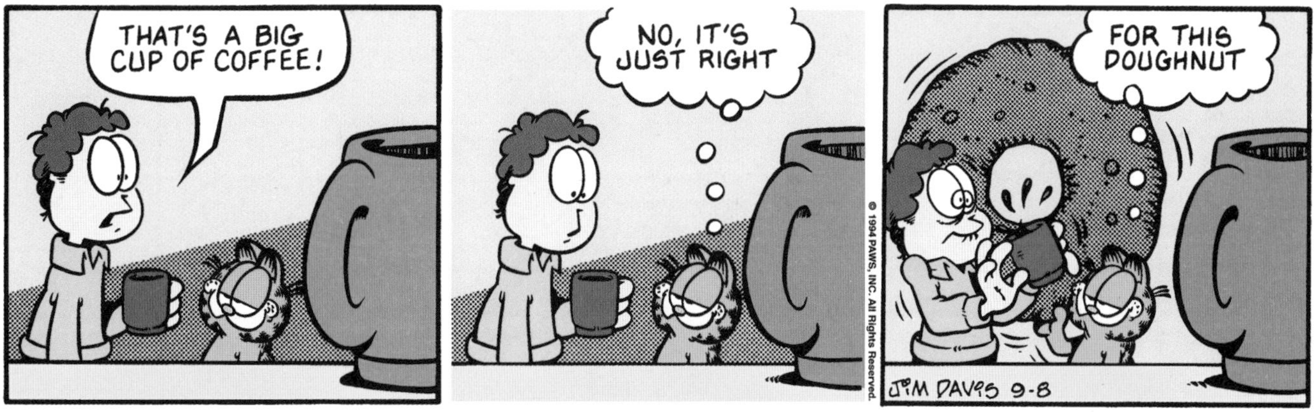
THAT'S A BIG CUP OF COFFEE!
NO, IT'S JUST RIGHT
FOR THIS DOUGHNUT
© 1994 PAWS, INC. All Rights Reserved.
JIM DAVIS 9-8

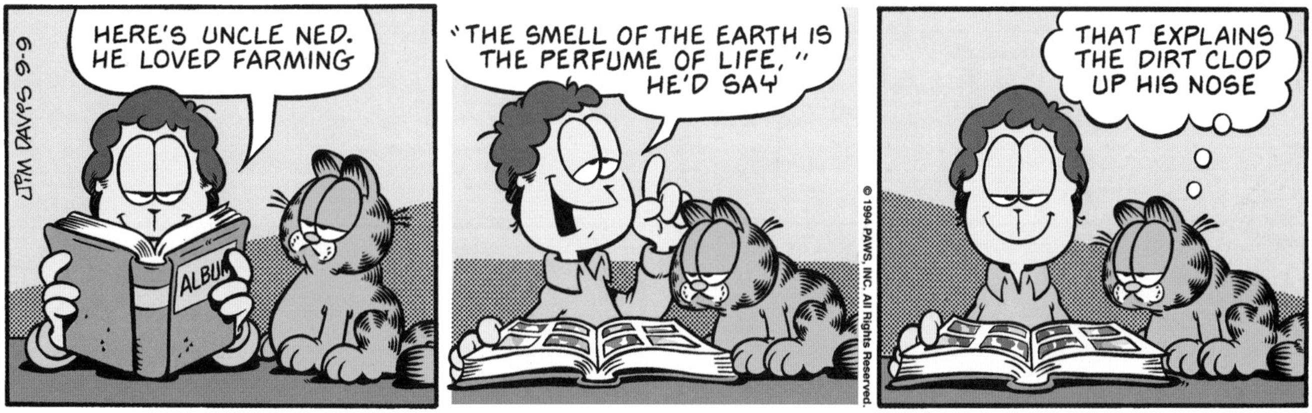
JIM DAVIS 9-9
HERE'S UNCLE NED. HE LOVED FARMING
ALBUM
"THE SMELL OF THE EARTH IS THE PERFUME OF LIFE," HE'D SAY
© 1994 PAWS, INC. All Rights Reserved.
THAT EXPLAINS THE DIRT CLOD UP HIS NOSE

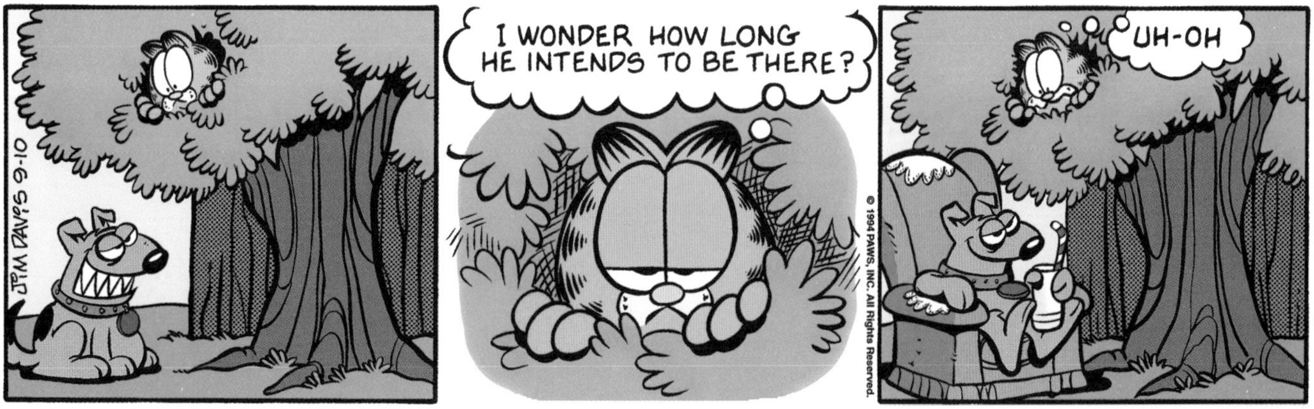
JIM DAVIS 9-10
I WONDER HOW LONG HE INTENDS TO BE THERE?
© 1994 PAWS, INC. All Rights Reserved.
UH-OH

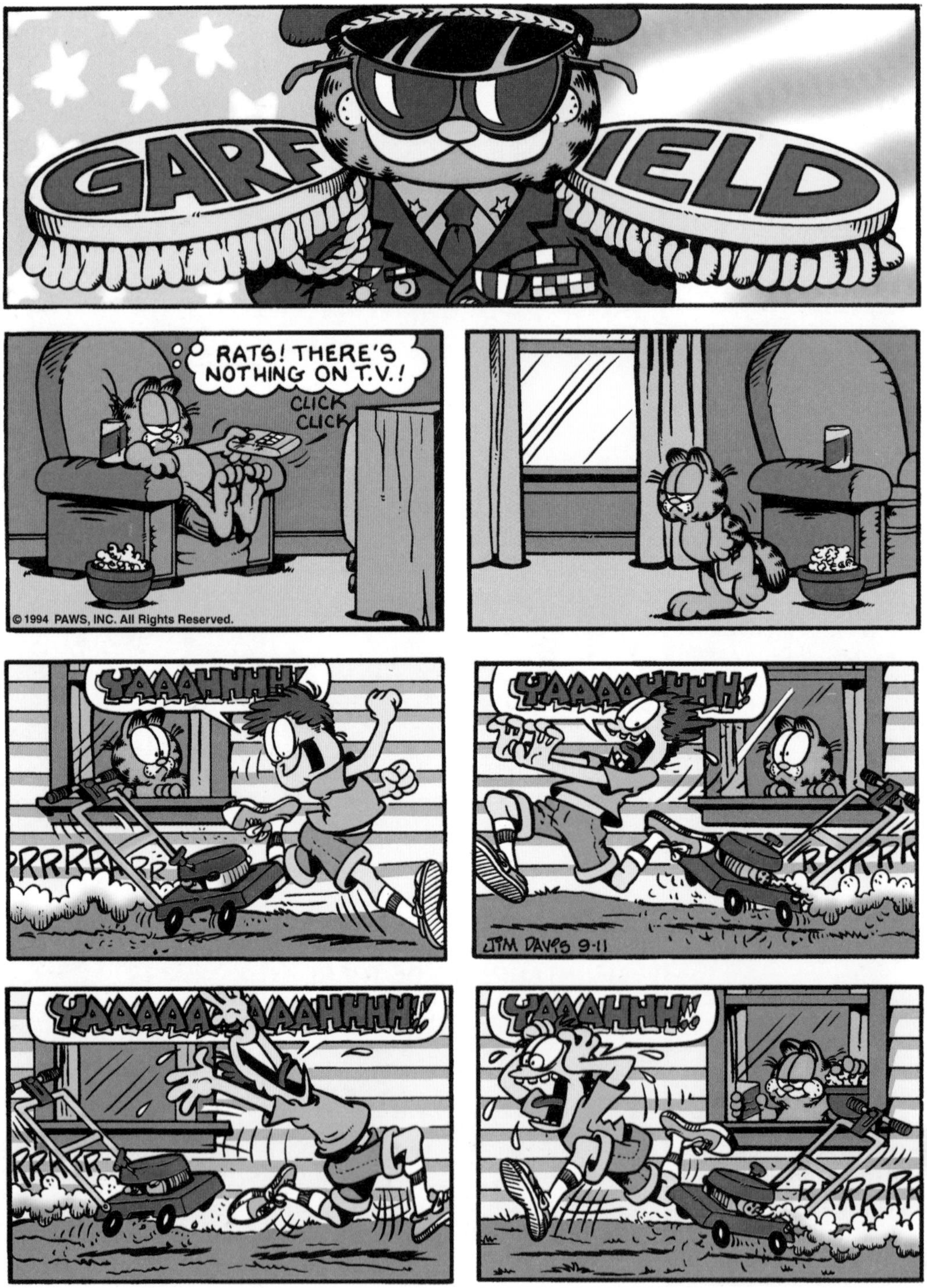

GARFIELD
RATS! THERE'S NOTHING ON T.V.!
CLICK CLICK
© 1994 PAWS, INC. All Rights Reserved.
YAAAHHHH!
YAAAAHHHH!
JIM DAVIS 9-11
YAAAAAAAAHHHH!!
YAAAHHH!!!

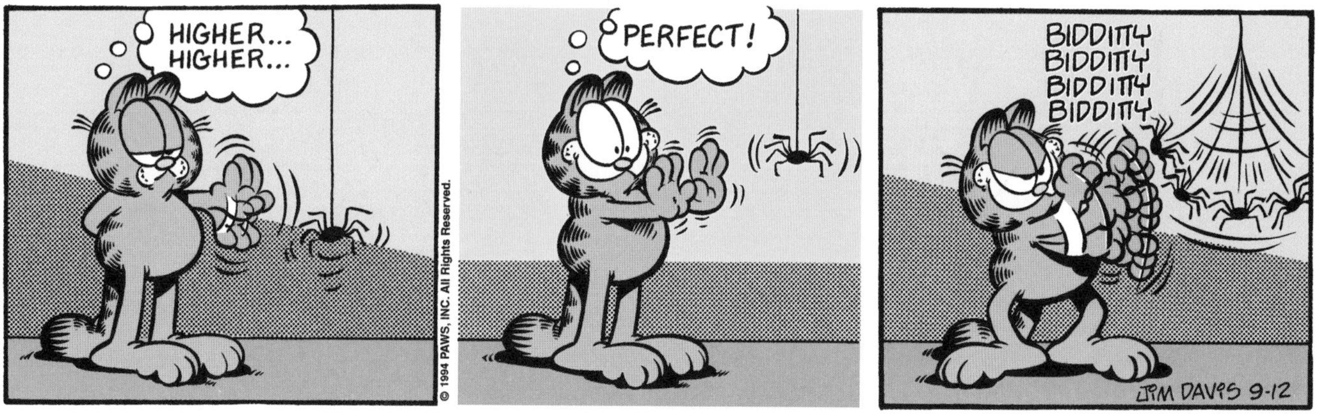
HIGHER...
HIGHER...
© 1994 PAWS, INC. All Rights Reserved.
PERFECT!
BIDDITTY
BIDDITTY
BIDDITTY
BIDDITTY
JIM DAVIS 9-12

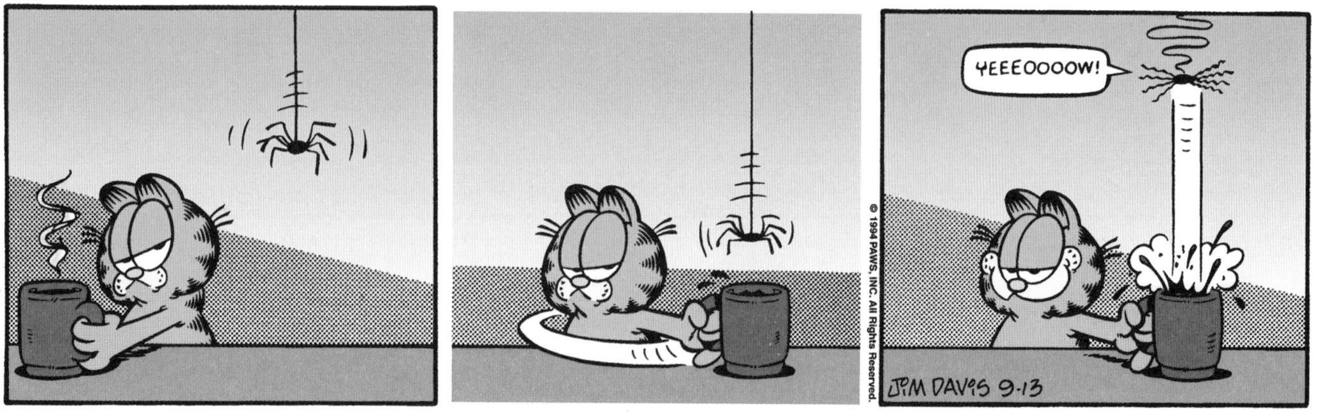
© 1994 PAWS, INC. All Rights Reserved.
YEEEOOOOW!
JIM DAVIS 9-13

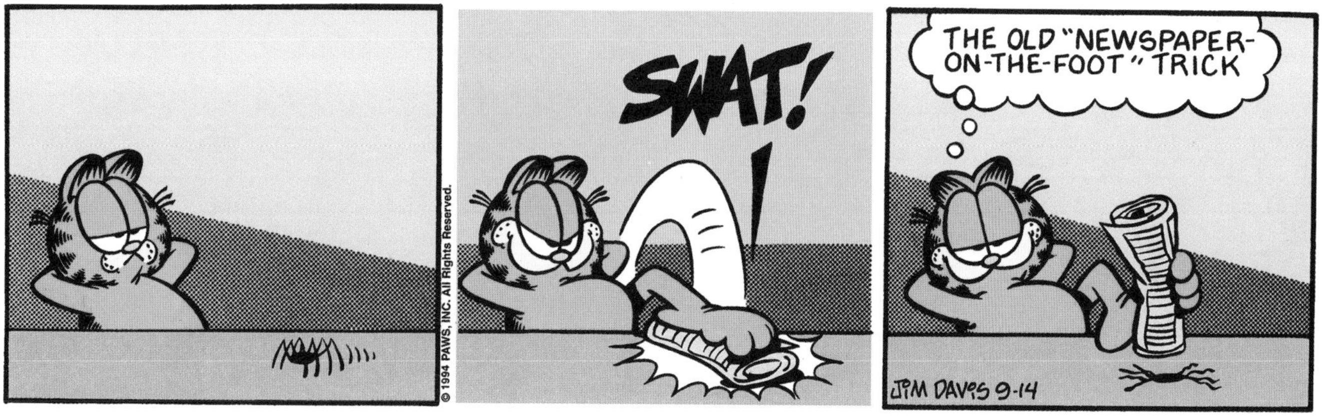
© 1994 PAWS, INC. All Rights Reserved.
SWAT!
THE OLD "NEWSPAPER-ON-THE-FOOT" TRICK
JIM DAVIS 9-14

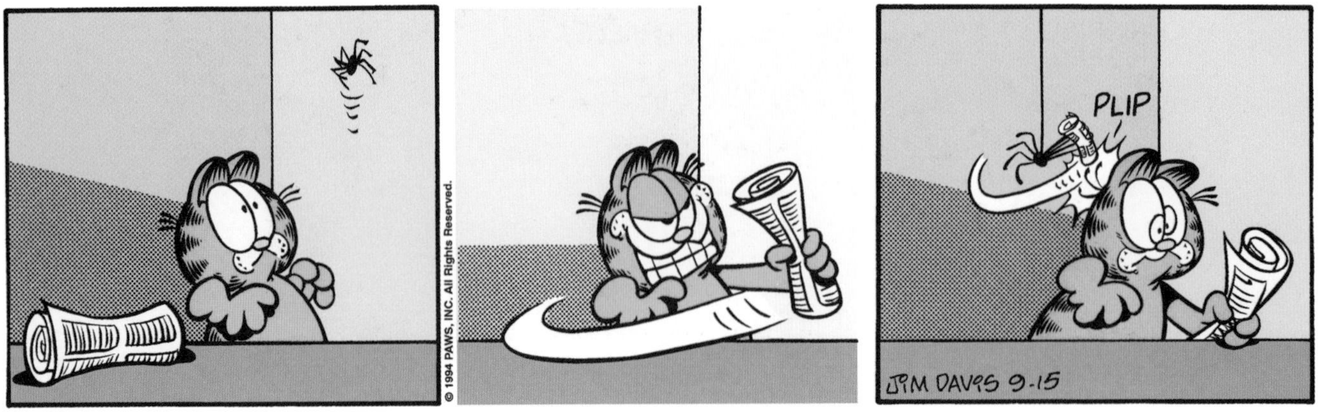
© 1994 PAWS, INC. All Rights Reserved.
PLIP
JIM DAVIS 9-15

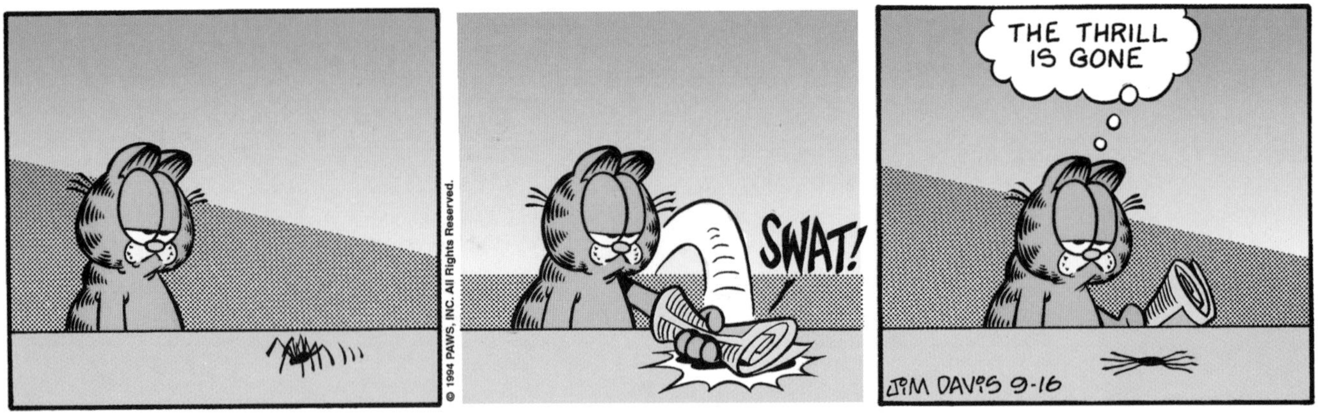
© 1994 PAWS, INC. All Rights Reserved.
SWAT!
THE THRILL IS GONE
JIM DAVIS 9-16

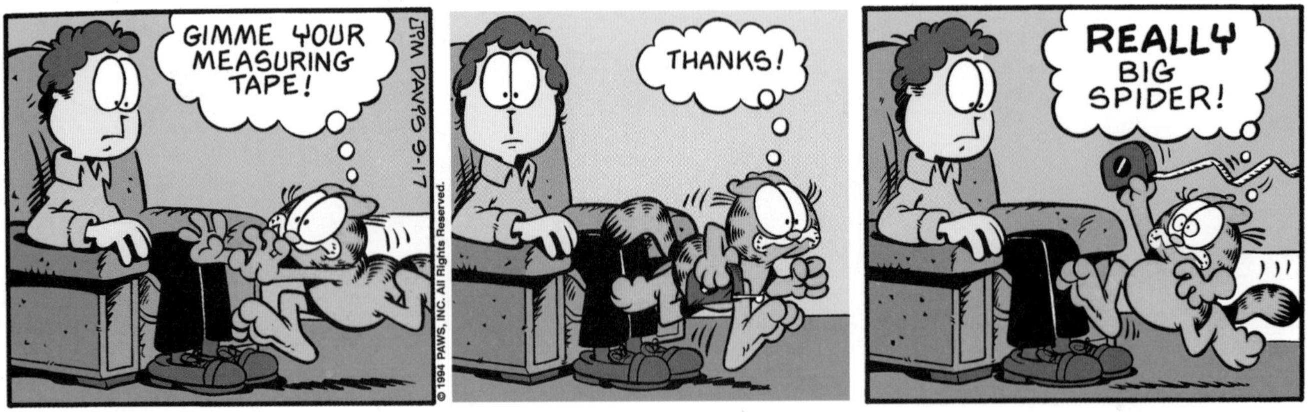
GIMME YOUR MEASURING TAPE!
JIM DAVIS 9-17
© 1994 PAWS, INC. All Rights Reserved.
THANKS!
REALLY BIG SPIDER!

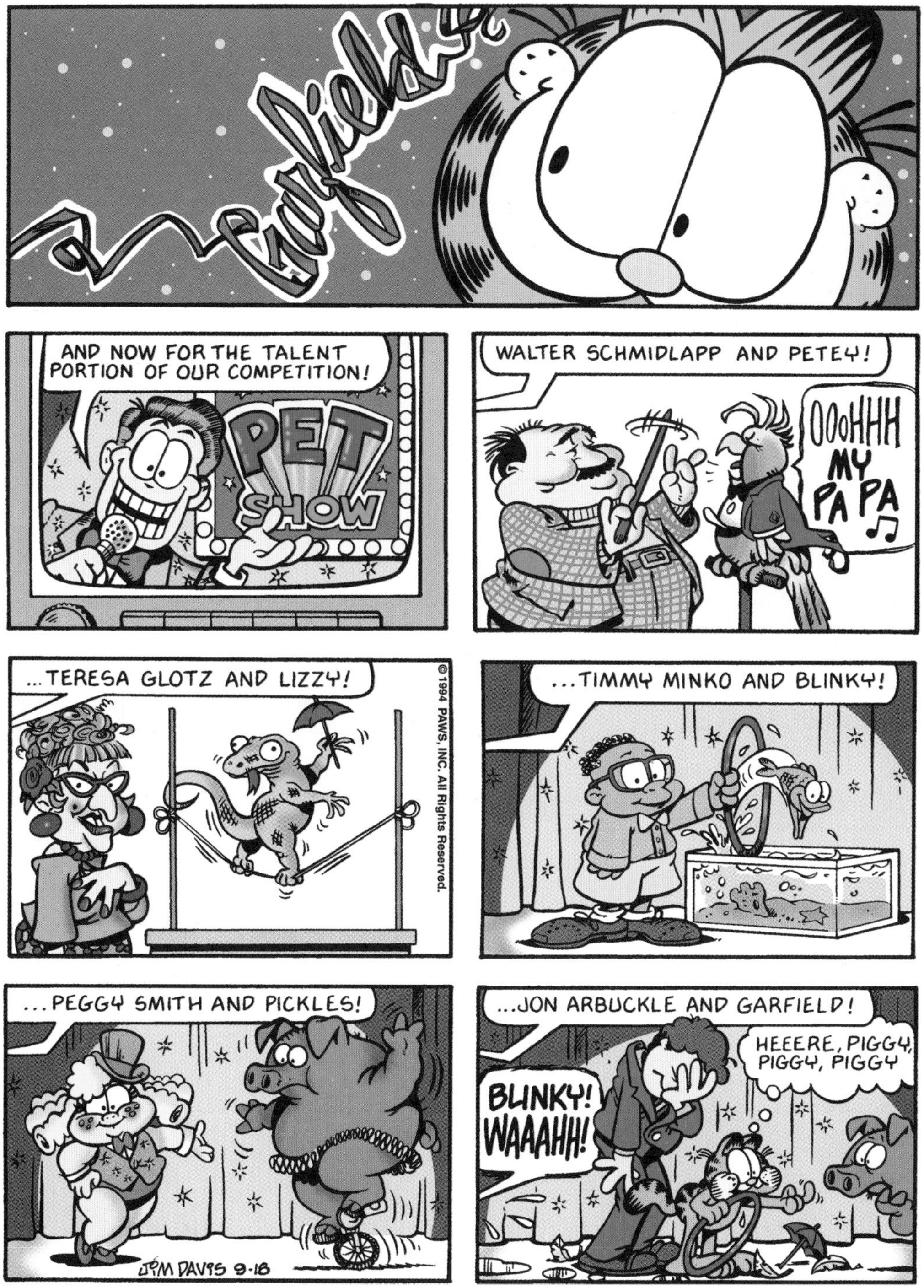
Garfield
AND NOW FOR THE TALENT PORTION OF OUR COMPETITION!
PET SHOW
WALTER SCHMIDLAPP AND PETEY!
OOoHHH MY PA PA
...TERESA GLOTZ AND LIZZY!
© 1994 PAWS, INC. All Rights Reserved.
...TIMMY MINKO AND BLINKY!
...PEGGY SMITH AND PICKLES!
JIM DAVIS 9-18
...JON ARBUCKLE AND GARFIELD!
HEEERE, PIGGY, PIGGY, PIGGY
BLINKY! WAAAHH!

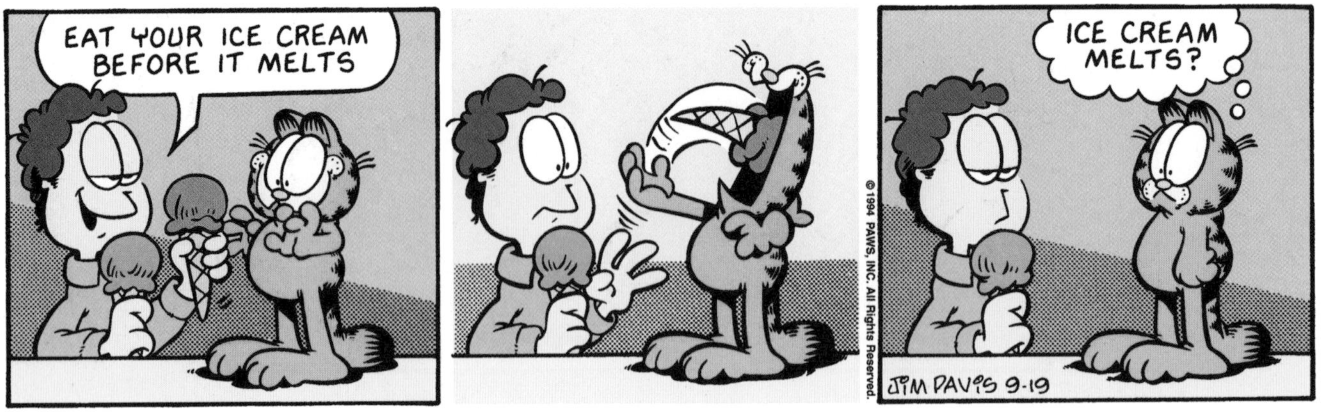
EAT YOUR ICE CREAM BEFORE IT MELTS
ICE CREAM MELTS?
© 1994 PAWS, INC. All Rights Reserved.
JIM DAVIS 9-19

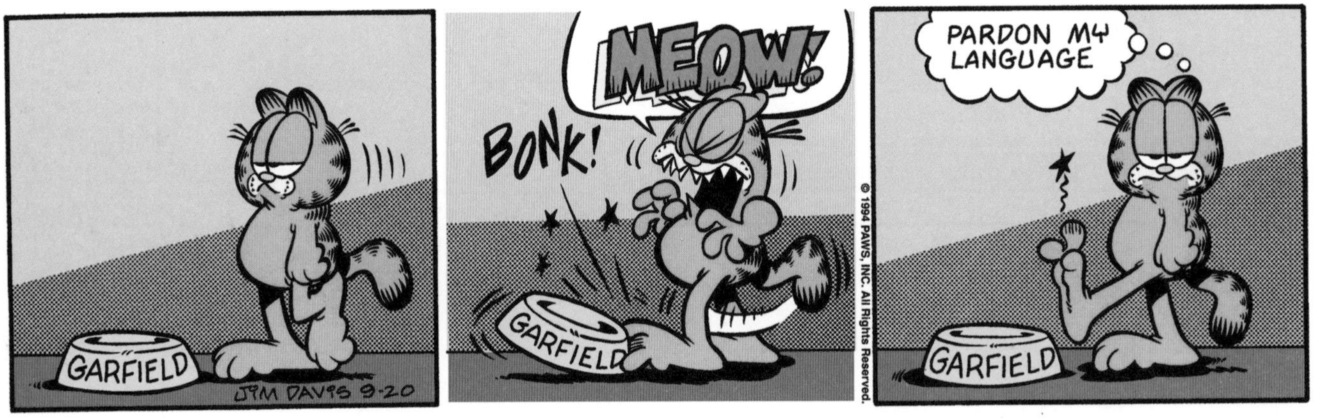
GARFIELD
JIM DAVIS 9-20
MEOW!
BONK!
GARFIELD
PARDON MY LANGUAGE
GARFIELD
© 1994 PAWS, INC. All Rights Reserved.

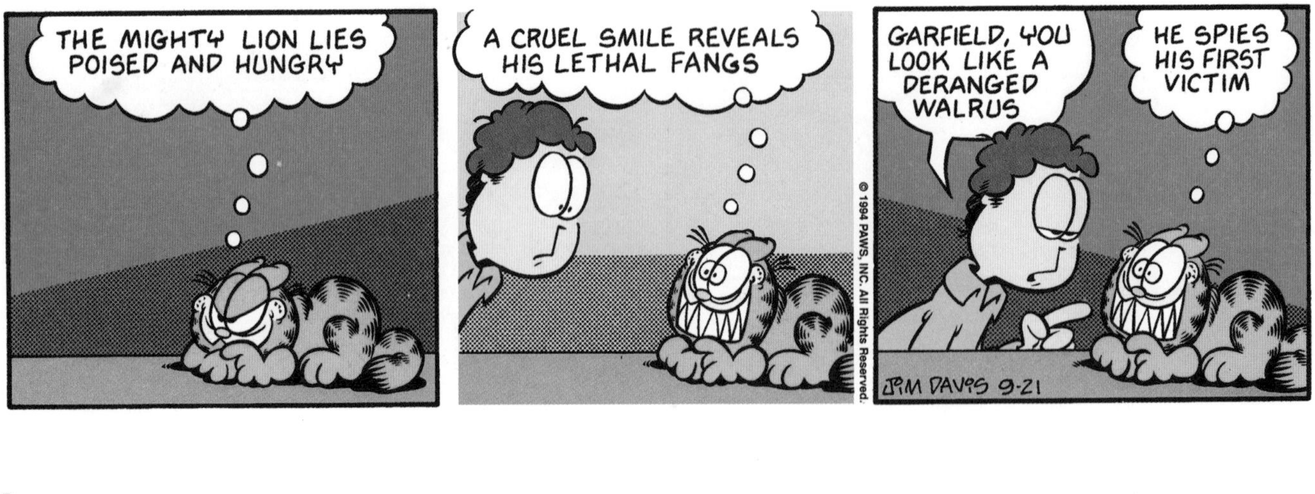
THE MIGHTY LION LIES POISED AND HUNGRY
A CRUEL SMILE REVEALS HIS LETHAL FANGS
GARFIELD, YOU LOOK LIKE A DERANGED WALRUS
HE SPIES HIS FIRST VICTIM
© 1994 PAWS, INC. All Rights Reserved.
JIM DAVIS 9-21

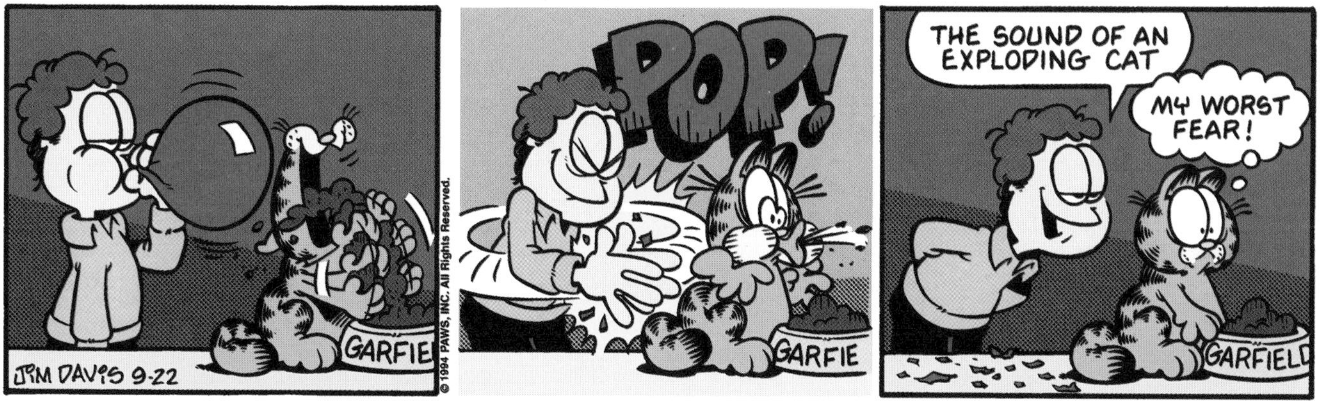
JIM DAVIS 9-22
GARFIE
© 1994 PAWS, INC. All Rights Reserved.
POP!
GARFIE
THE SOUND OF AN EXPLODING CAT
MY WORST FEAR!
GARFIELD

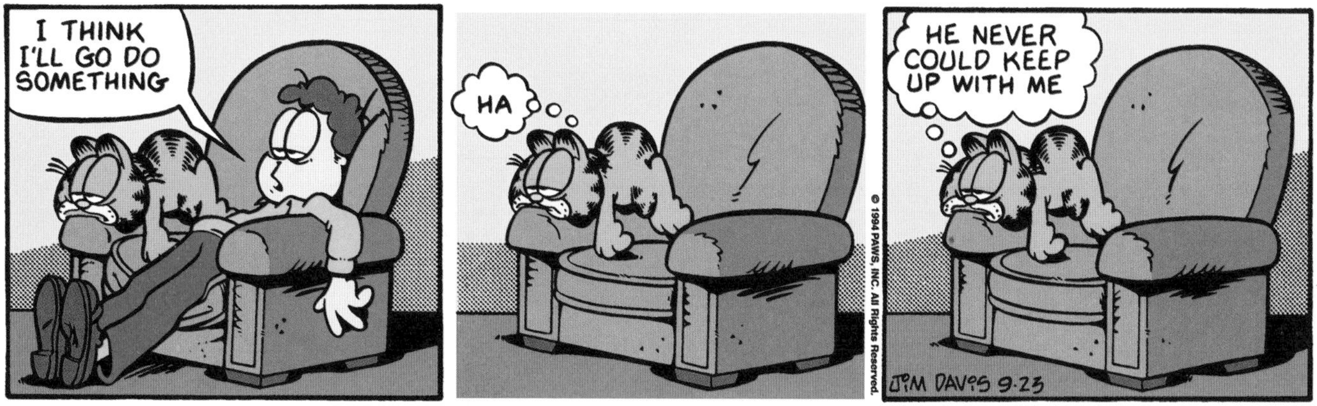
I THINK I'LL GO DO SOMETHING
HA
© 1994 PAWS, INC. All Rights Reserved.
HE NEVER COULD KEEP UP WITH ME
JIM DAVIS 9-23

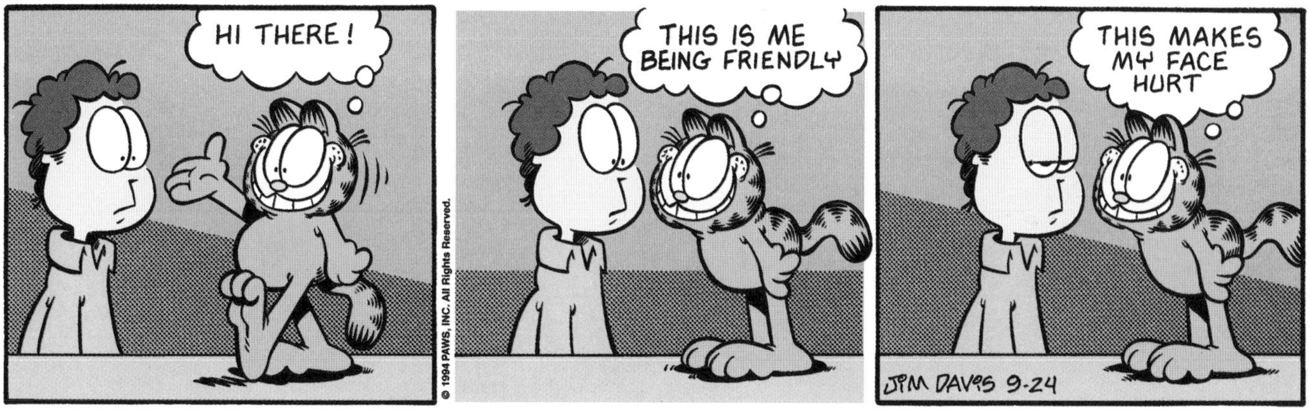
HI THERE!
© 1994 PAWS, INC. All Rights Reserved.
THIS IS ME BEING FRIENDLY
THIS MAKES MY FACE HURT
JIM DAVIS 9-24

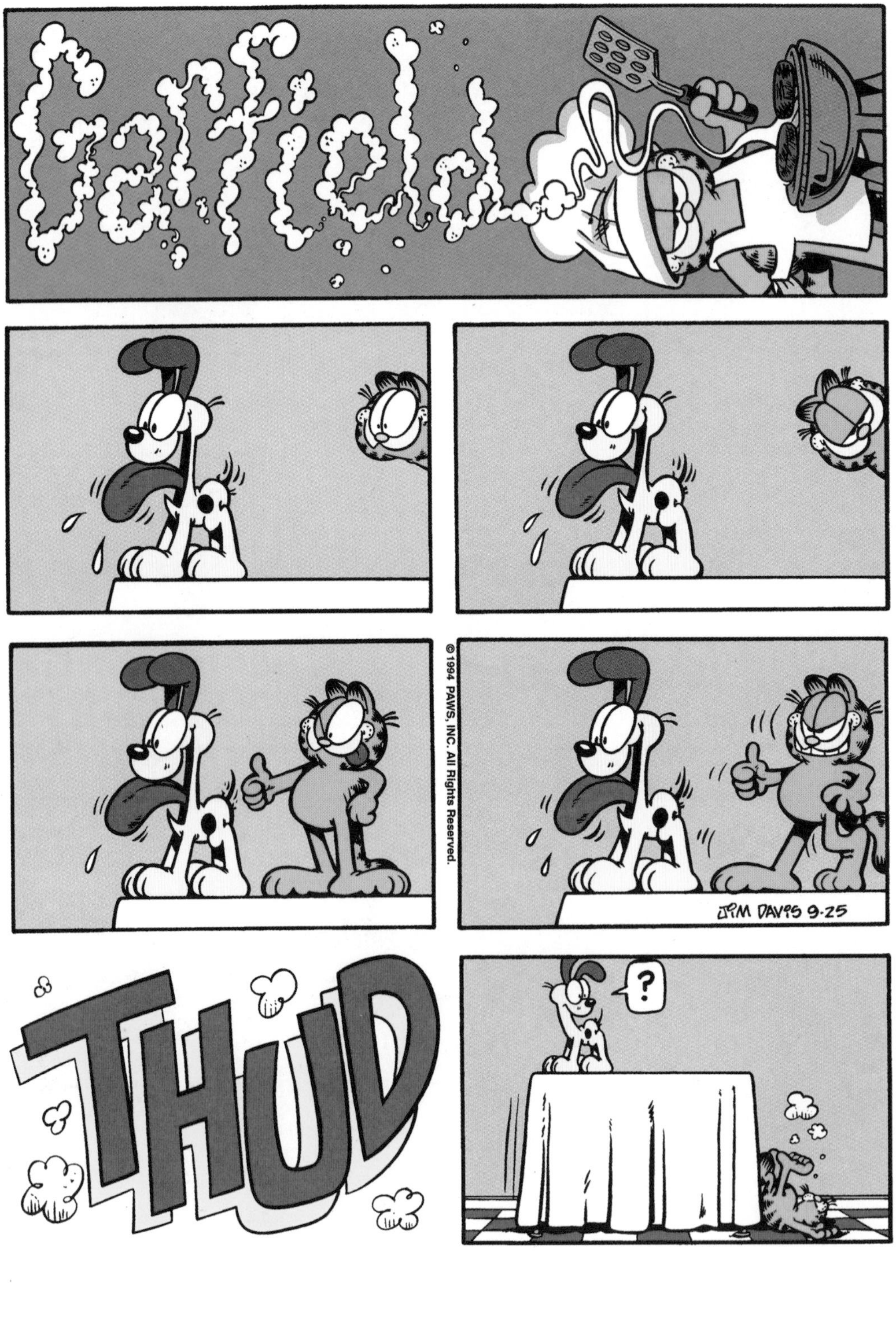
Garfield
© 1994 PAWS, INC. All Rights Reserved.
JIM DAVIS 9-25
THUD
?

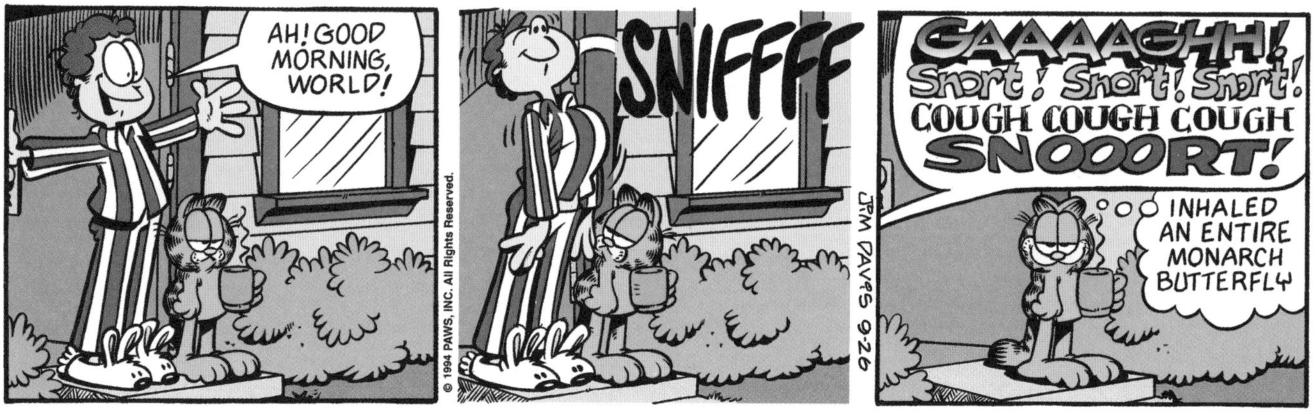
AH! GOOD MORNING, WORLD!
© 1994 PAWS, INC. All Rights Reserved.
SNIFFFF
JIM DAVIS 9-26
GAAAAGHH!
Snort! Snort! Snort!
COUGH COUGH COUGH
SNOOORT!
INHALED AN ENTIRE MONARCH BUTTERFLY

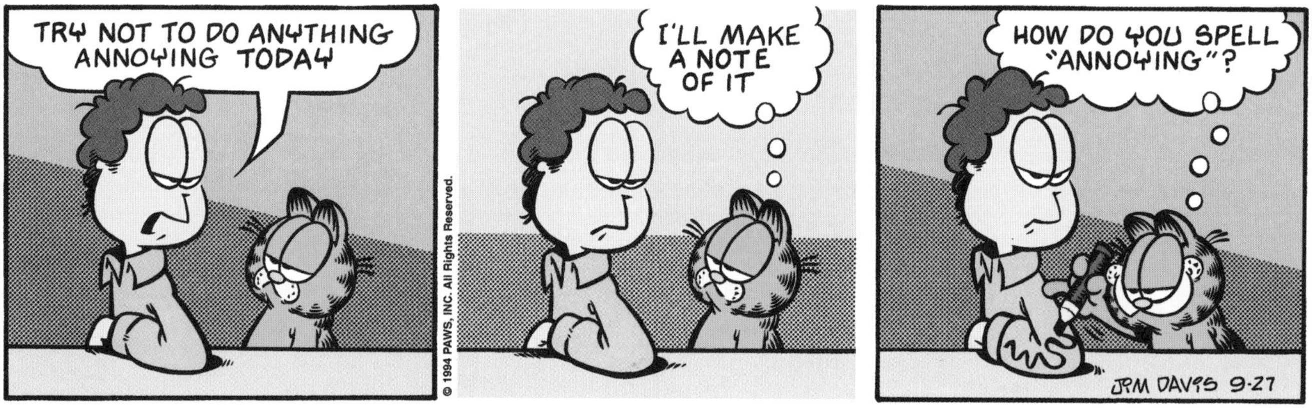
TRY NOT TO DO ANYTHING ANNOYING TODAY
© 1994 PAWS, INC. All Rights Reserved.
I'LL MAKE A NOTE OF IT
HOW DO YOU SPELL "ANNOYING"?
JIM DAVIS 9-27

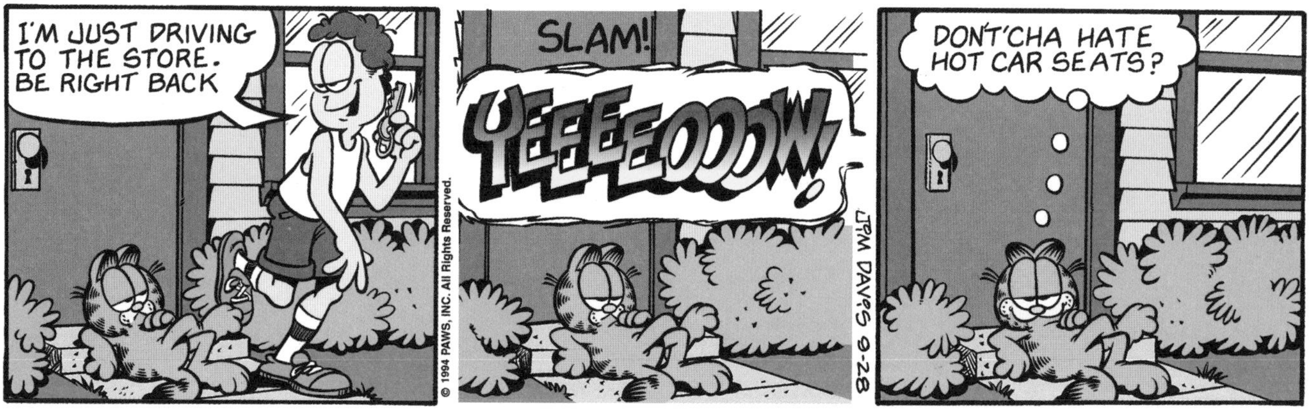
I'M JUST DRIVING TO THE STORE. BE RIGHT BACK
© 1994 PAWS, INC. All Rights Reserved.
SLAM!
YEEEEOOOW!
JIM DAVIS 9-28
DON'T'CHA HATE HOT CAR SEATS?

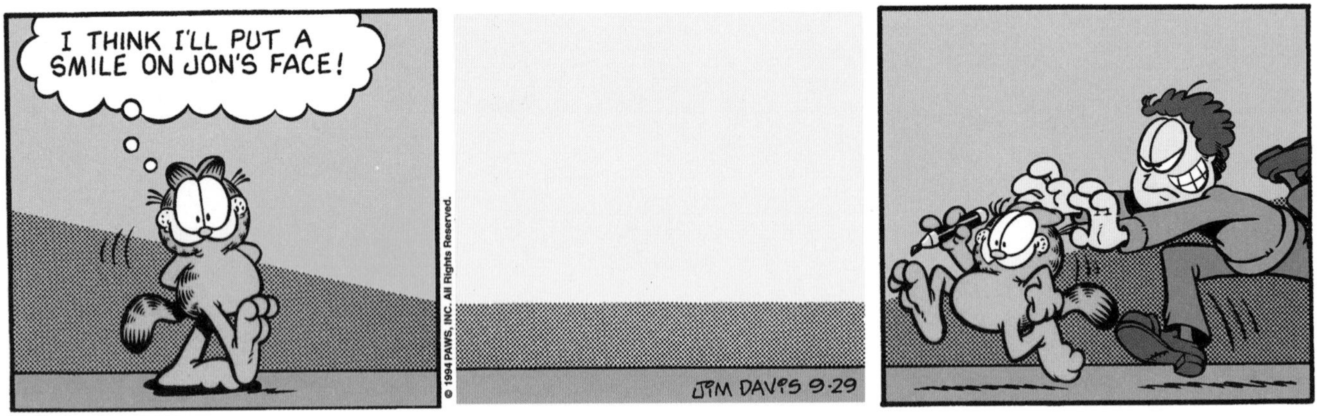
I THINK I'LL PUT A SMILE ON JON'S FACE!
© 1994 PAWS, INC. All Rights Reserved.
JIM DAVIS 9-29

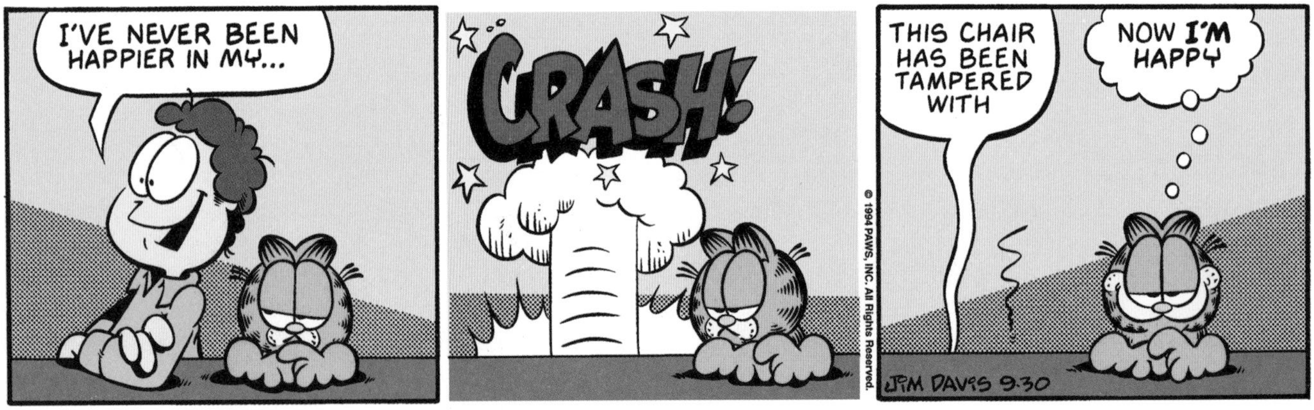
I'VE NEVER BEEN HAPPIER IN MY...
CRASH!
THIS CHAIR HAS BEEN TAMPERED WITH
NOW I'M HAPPY
© 1994 PAWS, INC. All Rights Reserved.
JIM DAVIS 9-30

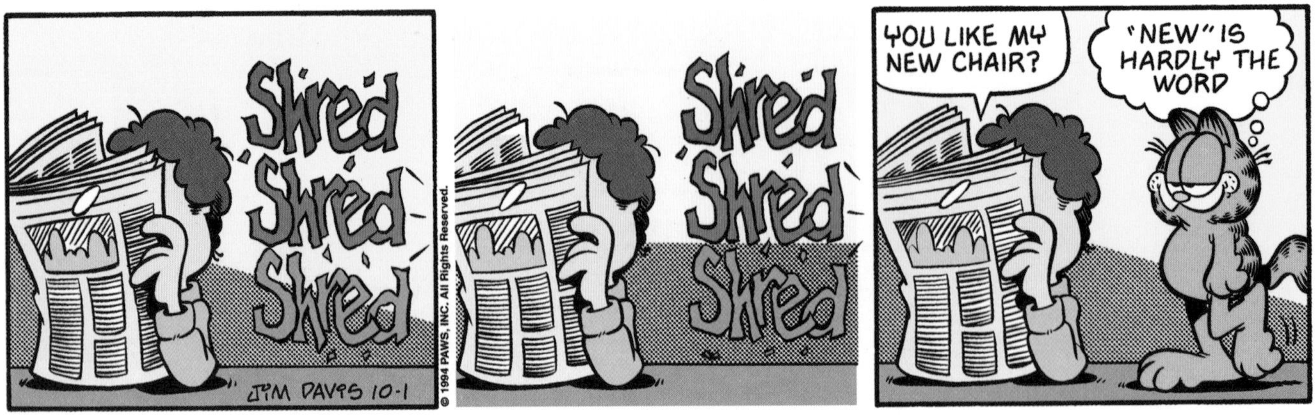
Shred Shred Shred
JIM DAVIS 10-1
© 1994 PAWS, INC. All Rights Reserved.
Shred Shred Shred
YOU LIKE MY NEW CHAIR?
"NEW" IS HARDLY THE WORD

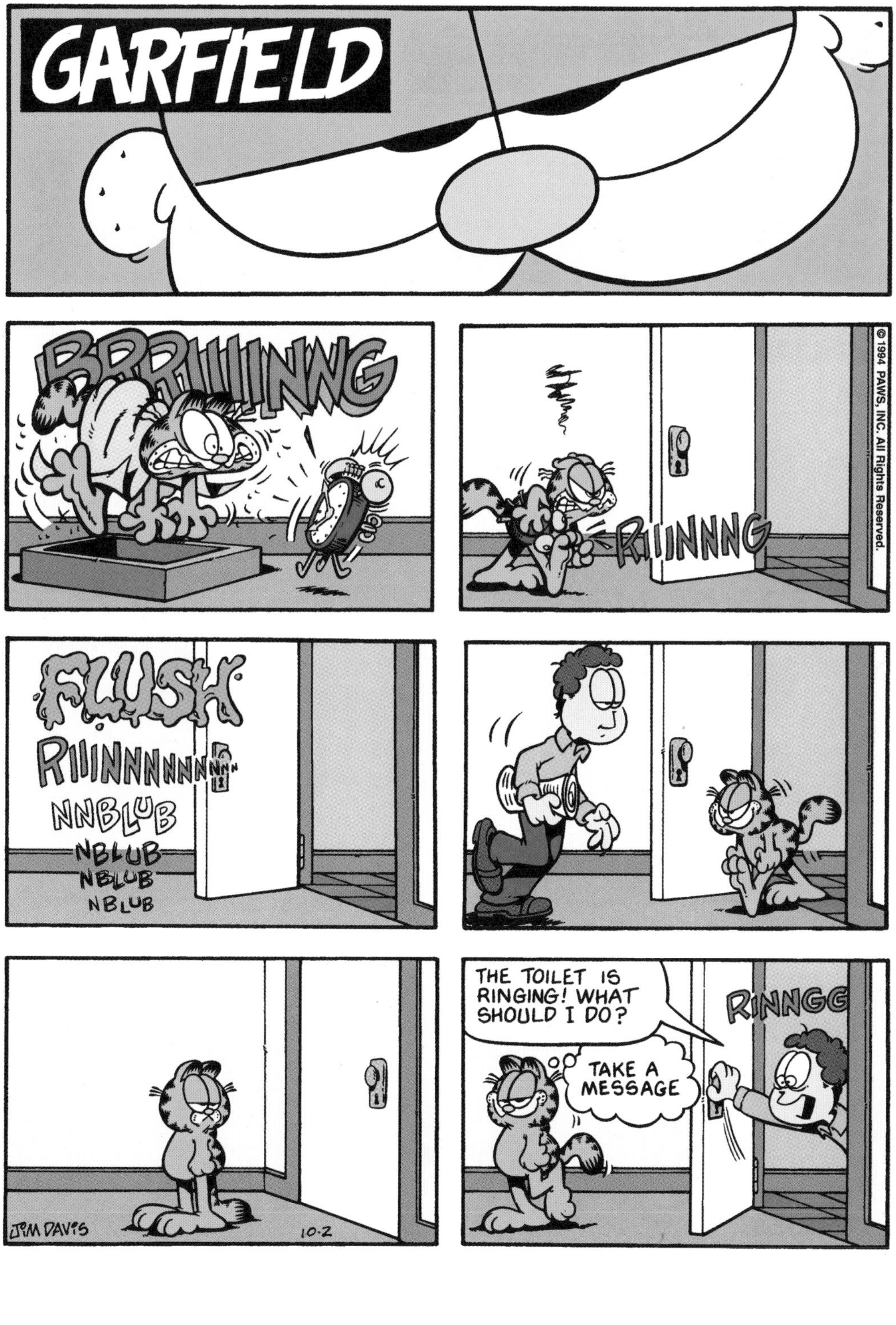
GARFIELD
BRRIIIIINNG
RIIINNNG
© 1994 PAWS, INC. All Rights Reserved.
FLUSH
RIIINNNNNNNN
NNBLUB
NBLUB
NBLUB
NBLUB
THE TOILET IS RINGING! WHAT SHOULD I DO?
RINNGG
TAKE A MESSAGE
JIM DAVIS
10-2

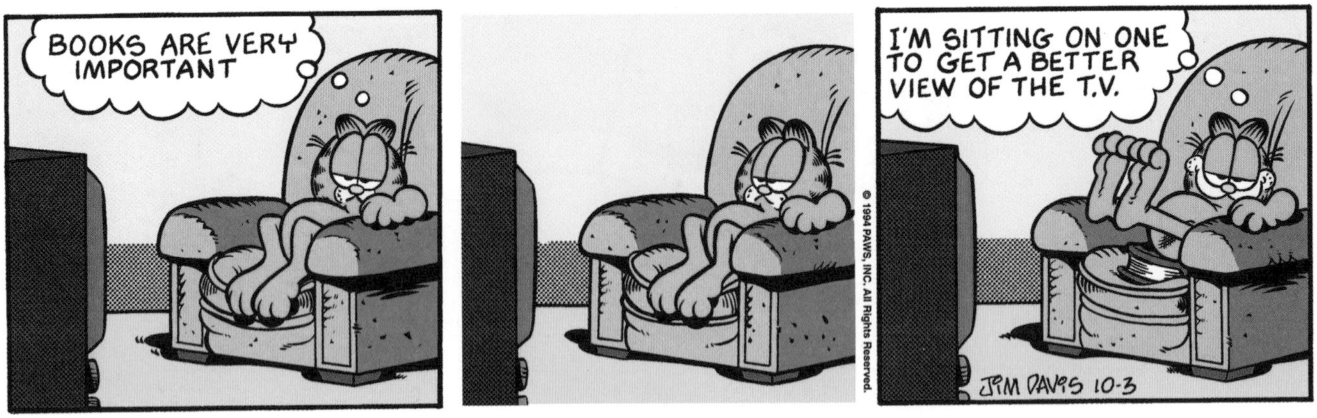
BOOKS ARE VERY IMPORTANT
I'M SITTING ON ONE TO GET A BETTER VIEW OF THE T.V.
© 1994 PAWS, INC. All Rights Reserved.
JIM DAVIS 10-3

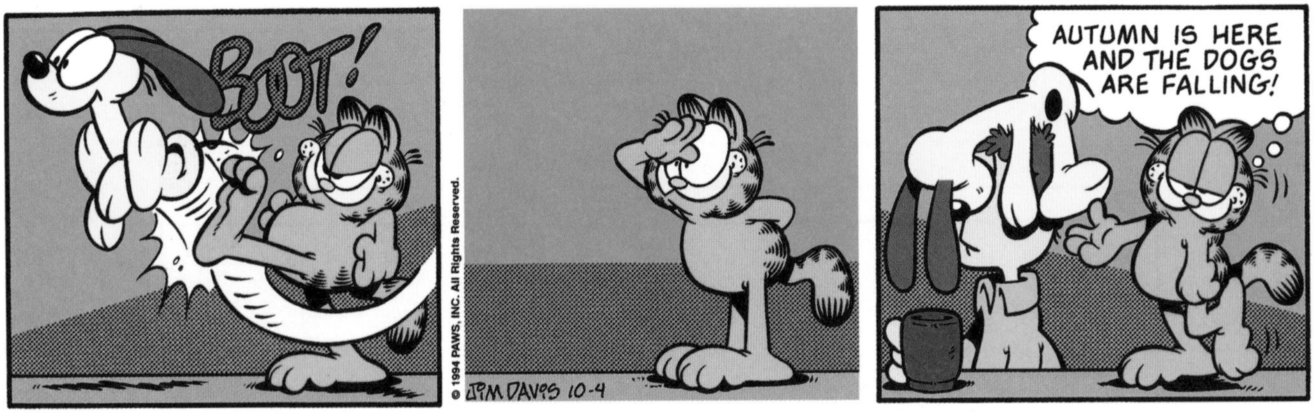
BOOT!
AUTUMN IS HERE AND THE DOGS ARE FALLING!
© 1994 PAWS, INC. All Rights Reserved.
JIM DAVIS 10-4

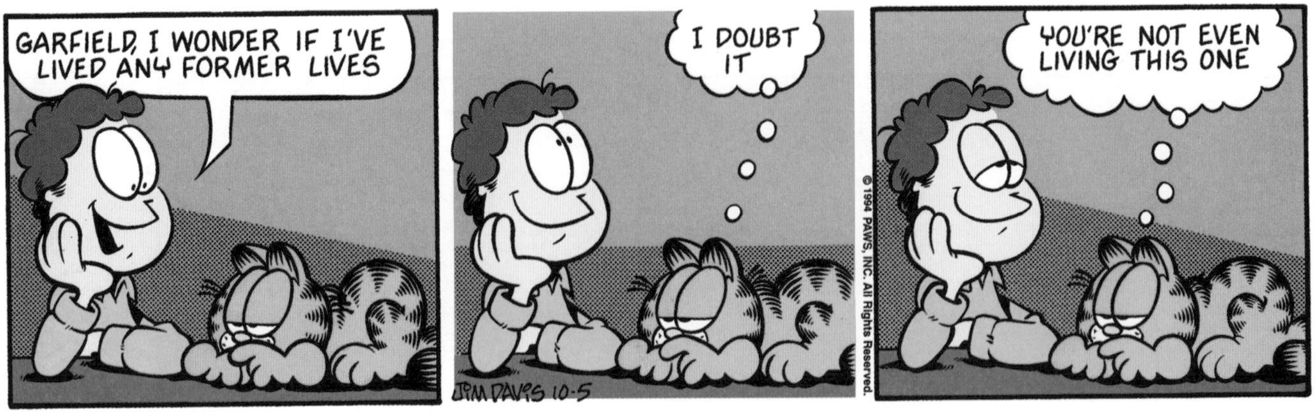
GARFIELD, I WONDER IF I'VE LIVED ANY FORMER LIVES
I DOUBT IT
YOU'RE NOT EVEN LIVING THIS ONE
© 1994 PAWS, INC. All Rights Reserved.
JIM DAVIS 10-5

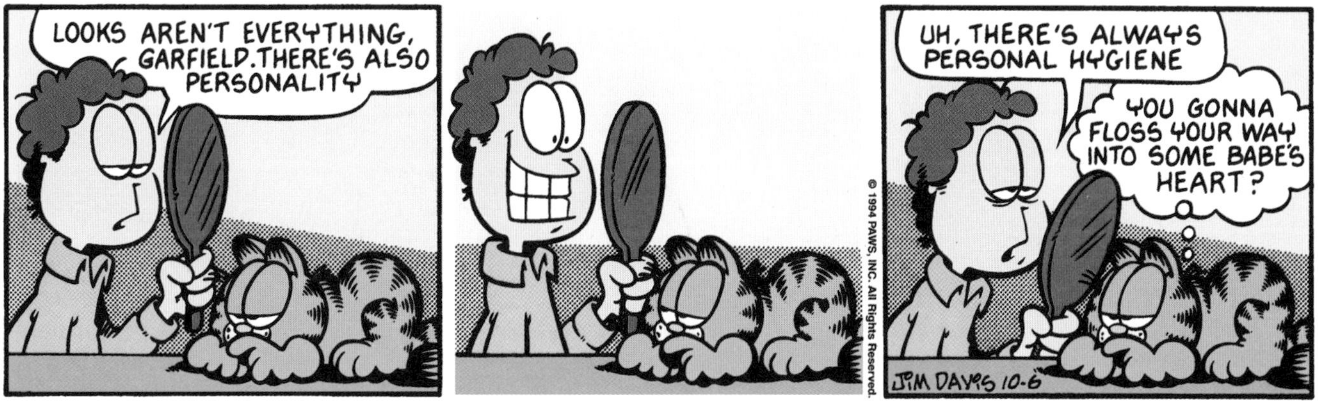
LOOKS AREN'T EVERYTHING, GARFIELD. THERE'S ALSO PERSONALITY
UH, THERE'S ALWAYS PERSONAL HYGIENE
YOU GONNA FLOSS YOUR WAY INTO SOME BABE'S HEART?
© 1994 PAWS, INC. All Rights Reserved.
JIM DAVIS 10-6

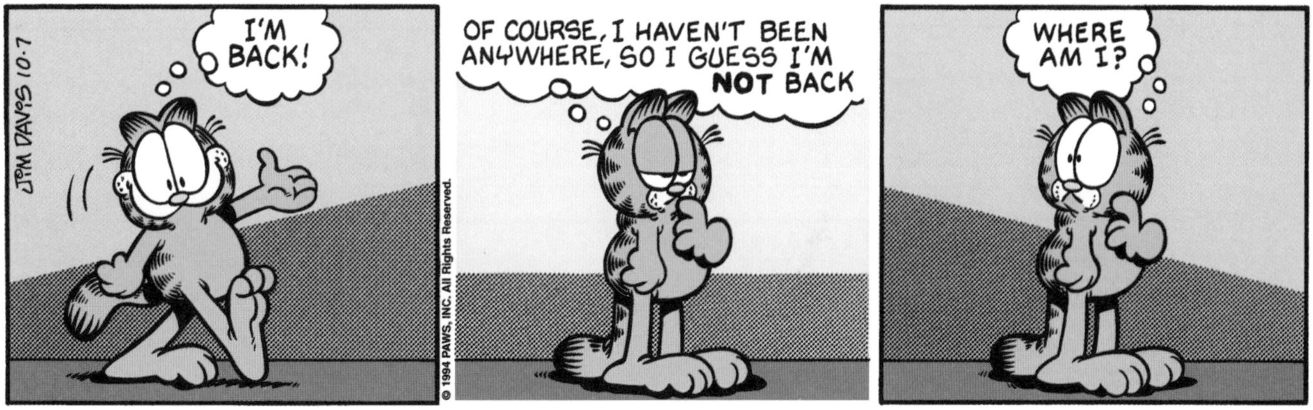
JIM DAVIS 10-7
I'M BACK!
© 1994 PAWS, INC. All Rights Reserved.
OF COURSE, I HAVEN'T BEEN ANYWHERE, SO I GUESS I'M **NOT** BACK
WHERE AM I?

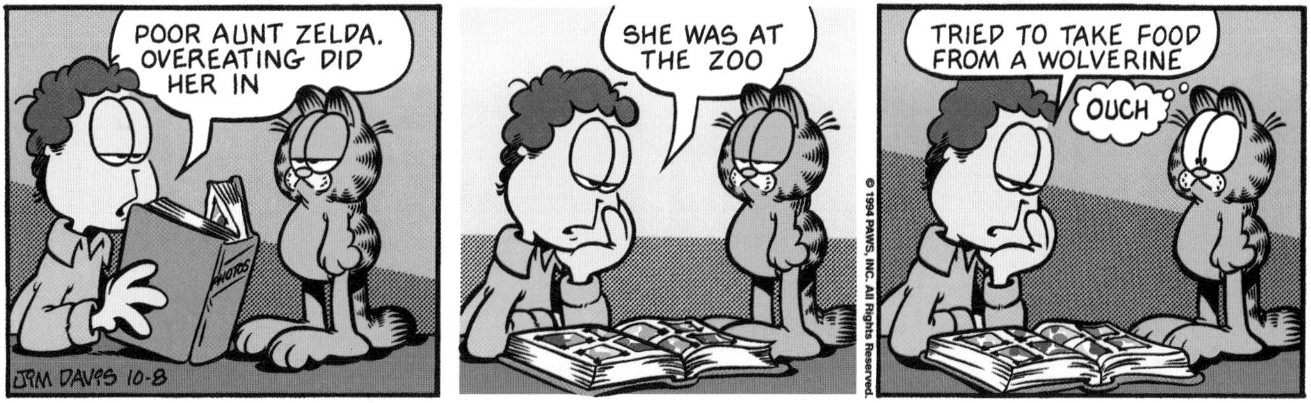
POOR AUNT ZELDA. OVEREATING DID HER IN
PHOTOS
JIM DAVIS 10-8
SHE WAS AT THE ZOO
© 1994 PAWS, INC. All Rights Reserved.
TRIED TO TAKE FOOD FROM A WOLVERINE
OUCH

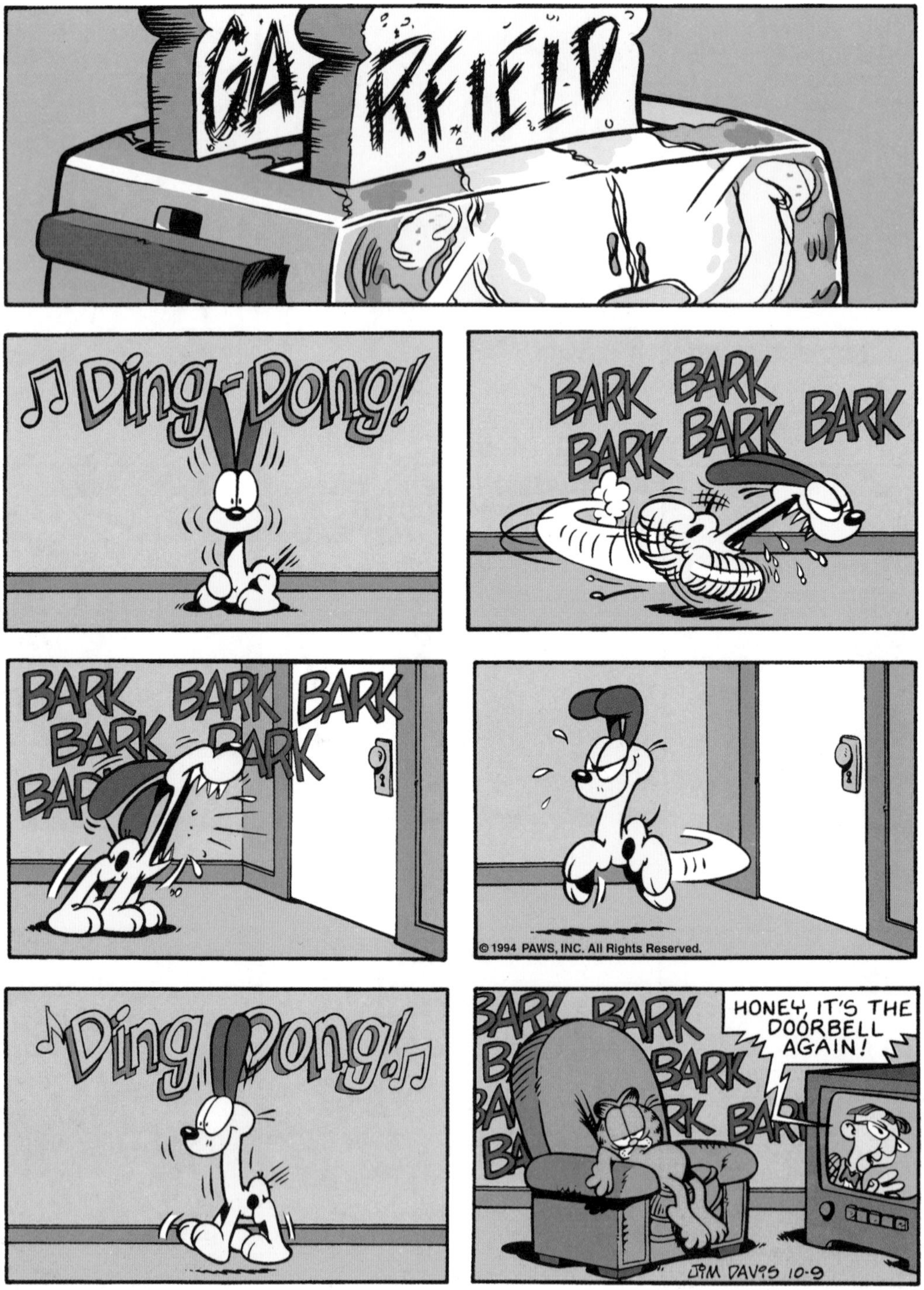
GARFIELD
♫ Ding-Dong!
BARK BARK
BARK BARK BARK
BARK BARK BARK
BARK
BARK
© 1994 PAWS, INC. All Rights Reserved.
♪ Ding Dong! ♫
BARK BARK
BARK
HONEY, IT'S THE DOORBELL AGAIN!
JIM DAVIS 10-9

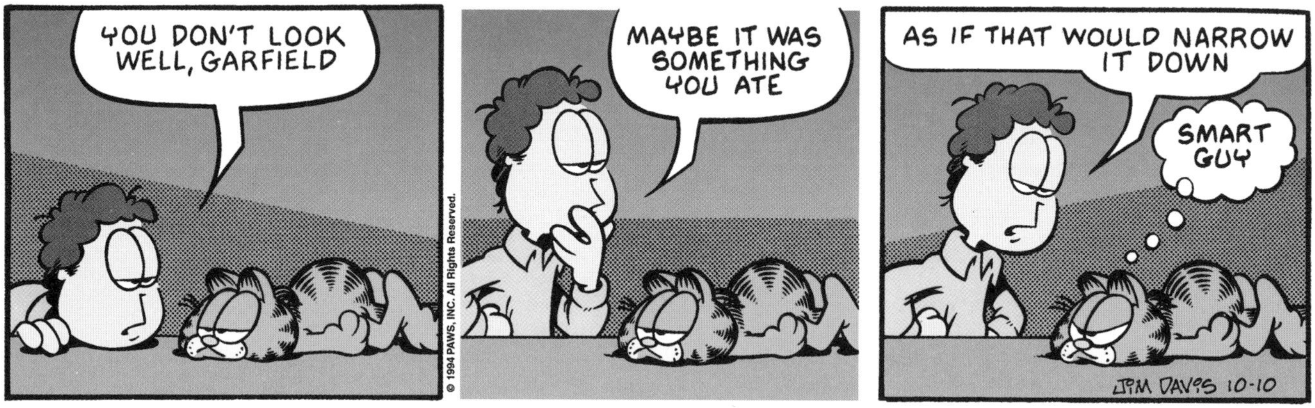
YOU DON'T LOOK WELL, GARFIELD
© 1994 PAWS, INC. All Rights Reserved.
MAYBE IT WAS SOMETHING YOU ATE
AS IF THAT WOULD NARROW IT DOWN
SMART GUY
JIM DAVIS 10-10

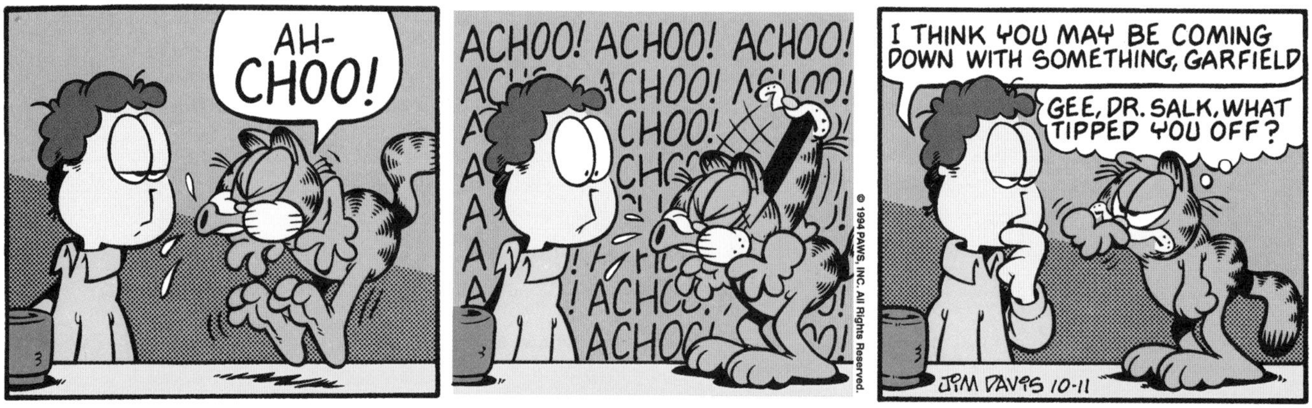
AH-CHOO!
ACHOO! ACHOO! ACHOO!
© 1994 PAWS, INC. All Rights Reserved.
I THINK YOU MAY BE COMING DOWN WITH SOMETHING, GARFIELD
GEE, DR. SALK, WHAT TIPPED YOU OFF?
JIM DAVIS 10-11

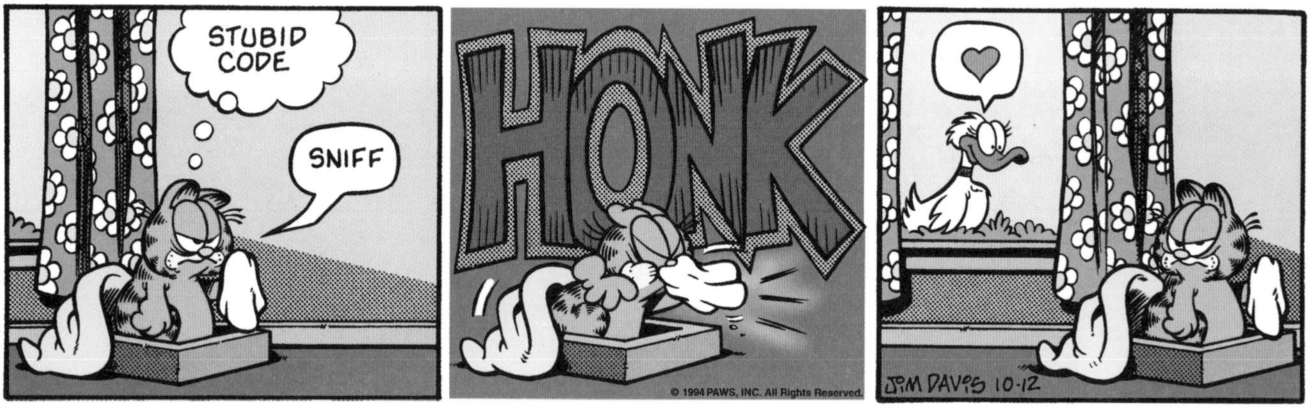
STUBID CODE
SNIFF
HONK
© 1994 PAWS, INC. All Rights Reserved.
JIM DAVIS 10-12

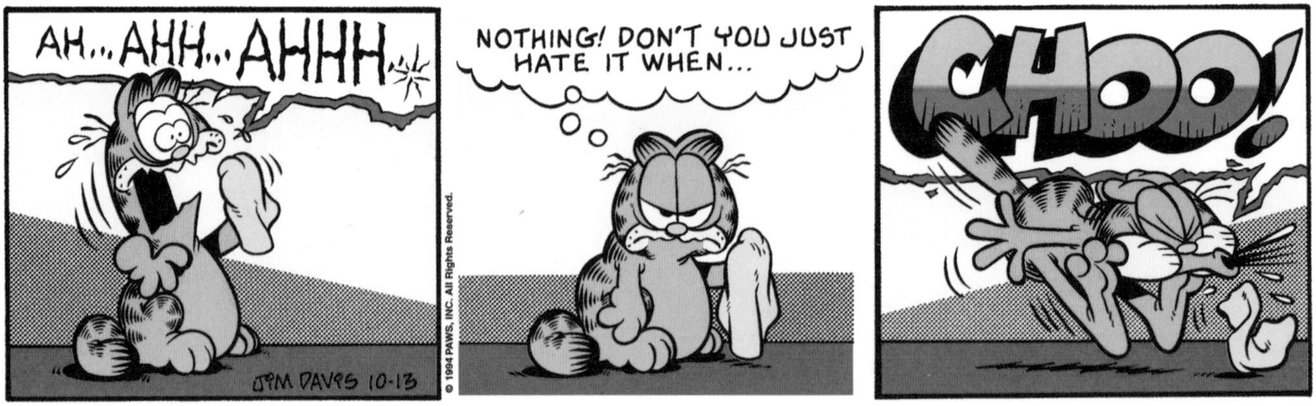
AH...AHH...AHHH
JIM DAVIS 10-13
NOTHING! DON'T YOU JUST HATE IT WHEN...
CHOO!

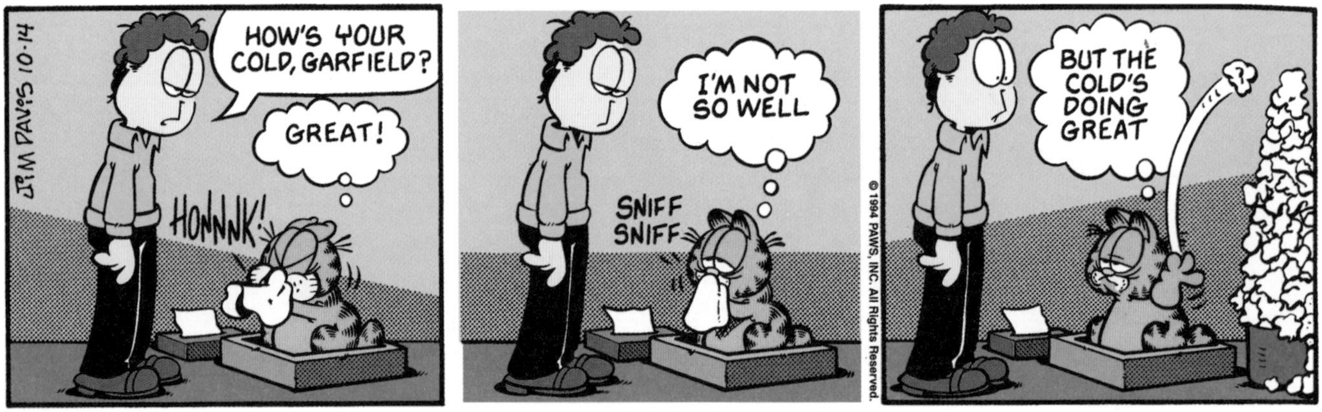
JIM DAVIS 10-14
HOW'S YOUR COLD, GARFIELD?
GREAT!
HONNNK!
I'M NOT SO WELL
SNIFF SNIFF
BUT THE COLD'S DOING GREAT

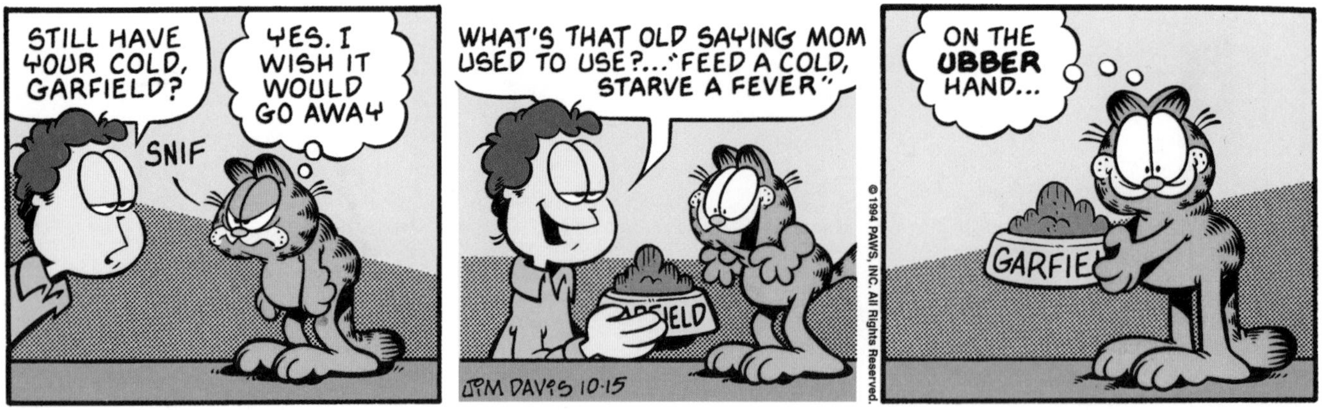
STILL HAVE YOUR COLD, GARFIELD?
YES. I WISH IT WOULD GO AWAY
SNIF
WHAT'S THAT OLD SAYING MOM USED TO USE?..."FEED A COLD, STARVE A FEVER"
JIM DAVIS 10-15
ON THE UBBER HAND...
GARFIE

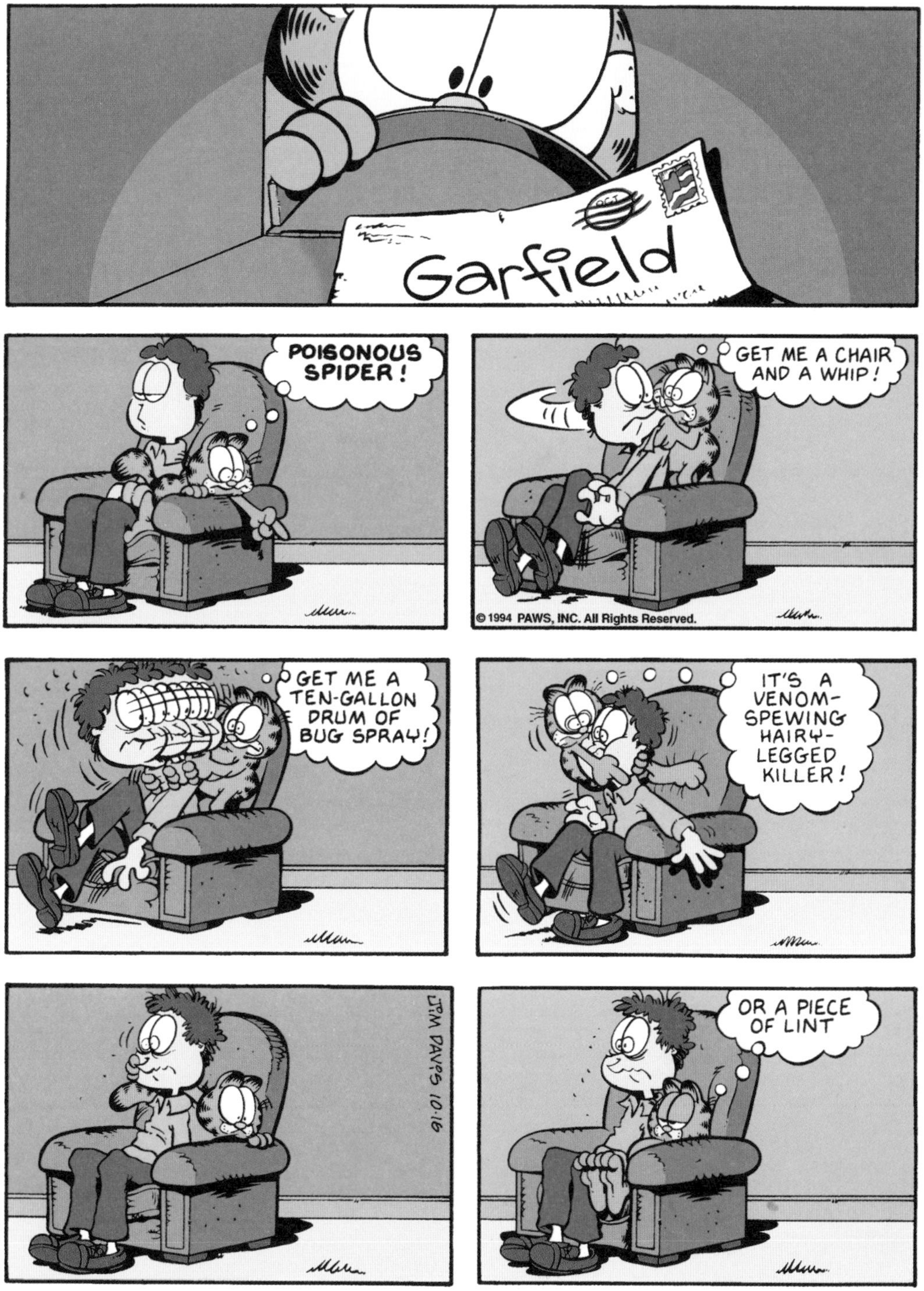
Garfield
POISONOUS SPIDER!
GET ME A CHAIR AND A WHIP!
© 1994 PAWS, INC. All Rights Reserved.
GET ME A TEN-GALLON DRUM OF BUG SPRAY!
IT'S A VENOM-SPEWING HAIRY-LEGGED KILLER!
JIM DAVIS 10-16
OR A PIECE OF LINT

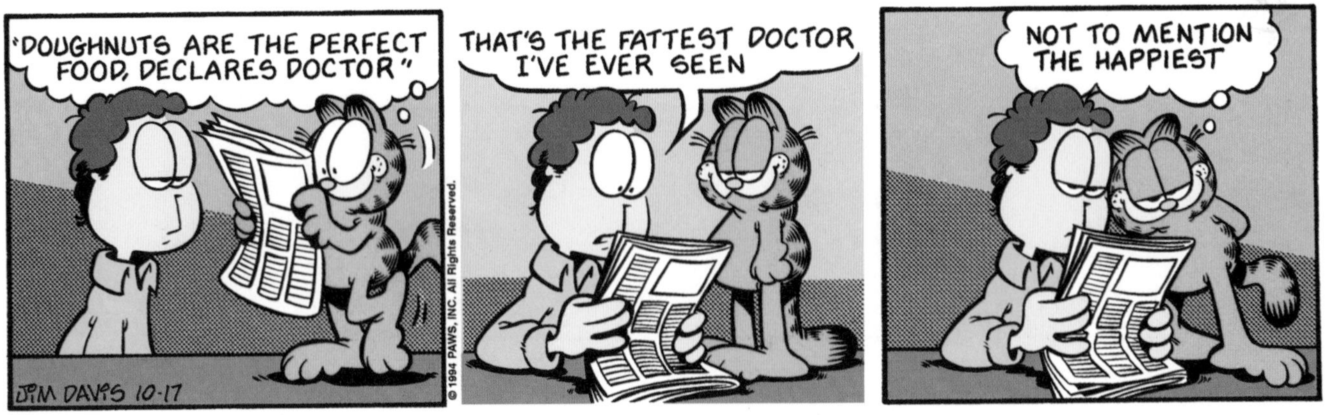
"DOUGHNUTS ARE THE PERFECT FOOD, DECLARES DOCTOR"
JIM DAVIS 10-17
© 1994 PAWS, INC. All Rights Reserved.
THAT'S THE FATTEST DOCTOR I'VE EVER SEEN
NOT TO MENTION THE HAPPIEST

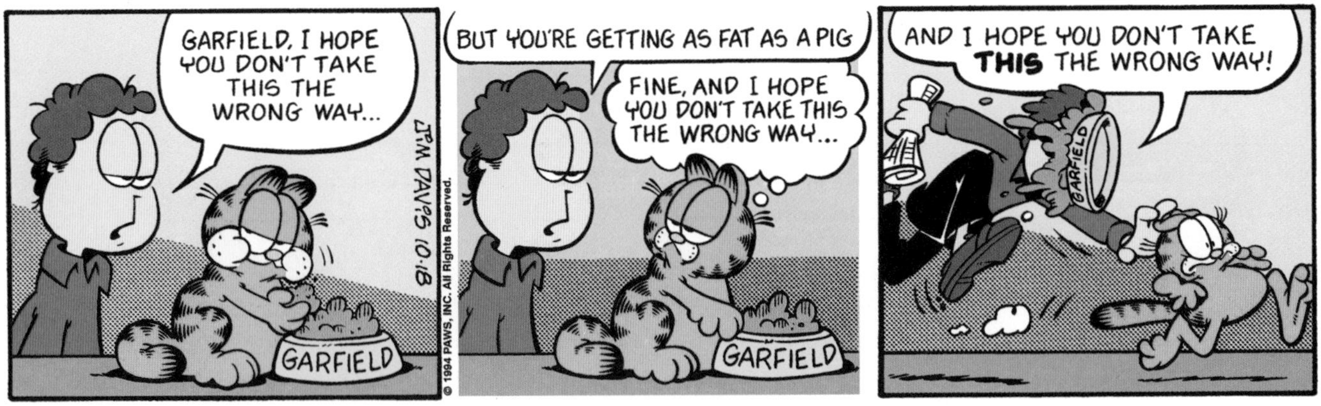
GARFIELD, I HOPE YOU DON'T TAKE THIS THE WRONG WAY...
JIM DAVIS 10-18
© 1994 PAWS, INC. All Rights Reserved.
GARFIELD
BUT YOU'RE GETTING AS FAT AS A PIG
FINE, AND I HOPE YOU DON'T TAKE THIS THE WRONG WAY...
GARFIELD
AND I HOPE YOU DON'T TAKE **THIS** THE WRONG WAY!
GARFIELD

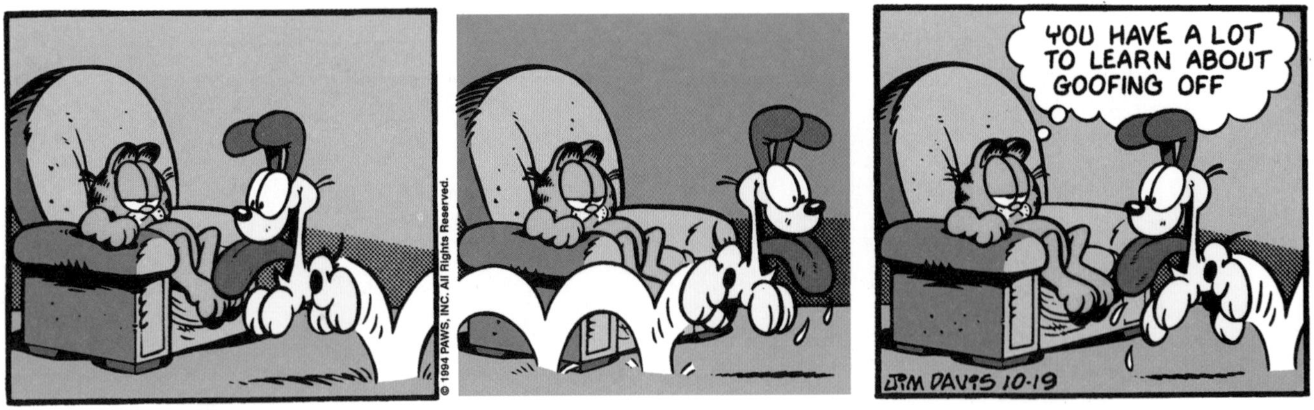
© 1994 PAWS, INC. All Rights Reserved.
YOU HAVE A LOT TO LEARN ABOUT GOOFING OFF
JIM DAVIS 10-19

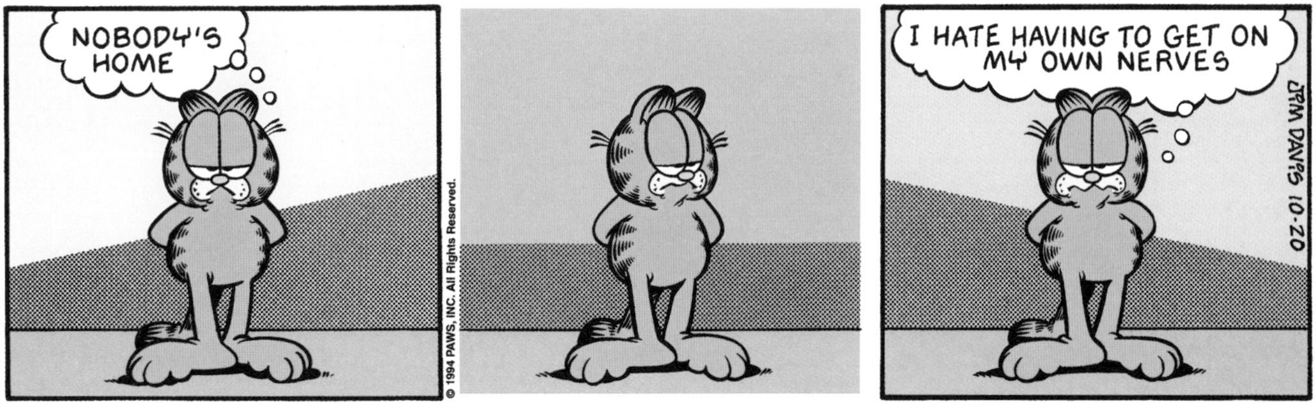
NOBODY'S HOME
© 1994 PAWS, INC. All Rights Reserved.
I HATE HAVING TO GET ON MY OWN NERVES
JIM DAVIS 10-20

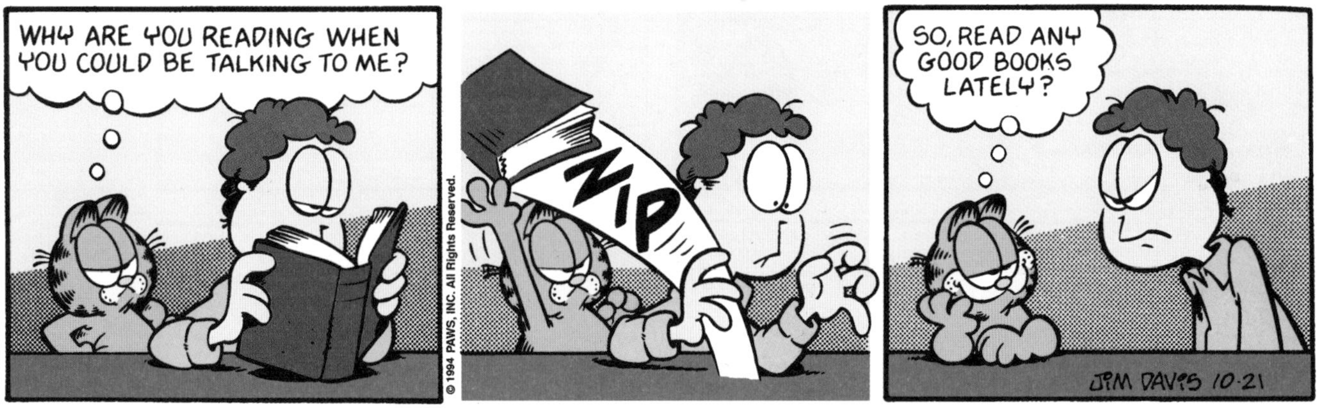
WHY ARE YOU READING WHEN YOU COULD BE TALKING TO ME?
© 1994 PAWS, INC. All Rights Reserved.
RIP
SO, READ ANY GOOD BOOKS LATELY?
JIM DAVIS 10-21

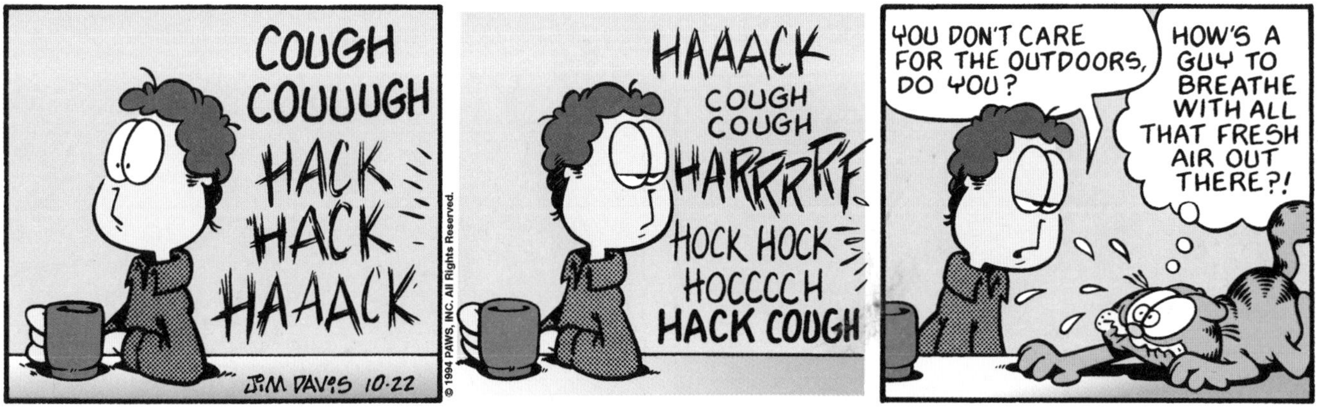
COUGH
COUUUGH
HACK
HACK
HAAACK
JIM DAVIS 10-22
© 1994 PAWS, INC. All Rights Reserved.
HAAACK
COUGH
COUGH
HARRRRF
HOCK HOCK
HOCCCCH
HACK COUGH
YOU DON'T CARE FOR THE OUTDOORS, DO YOU?
HOW'S A GUY TO BREATHE WITH ALL THAT FRESH AIR OUT THERE?!

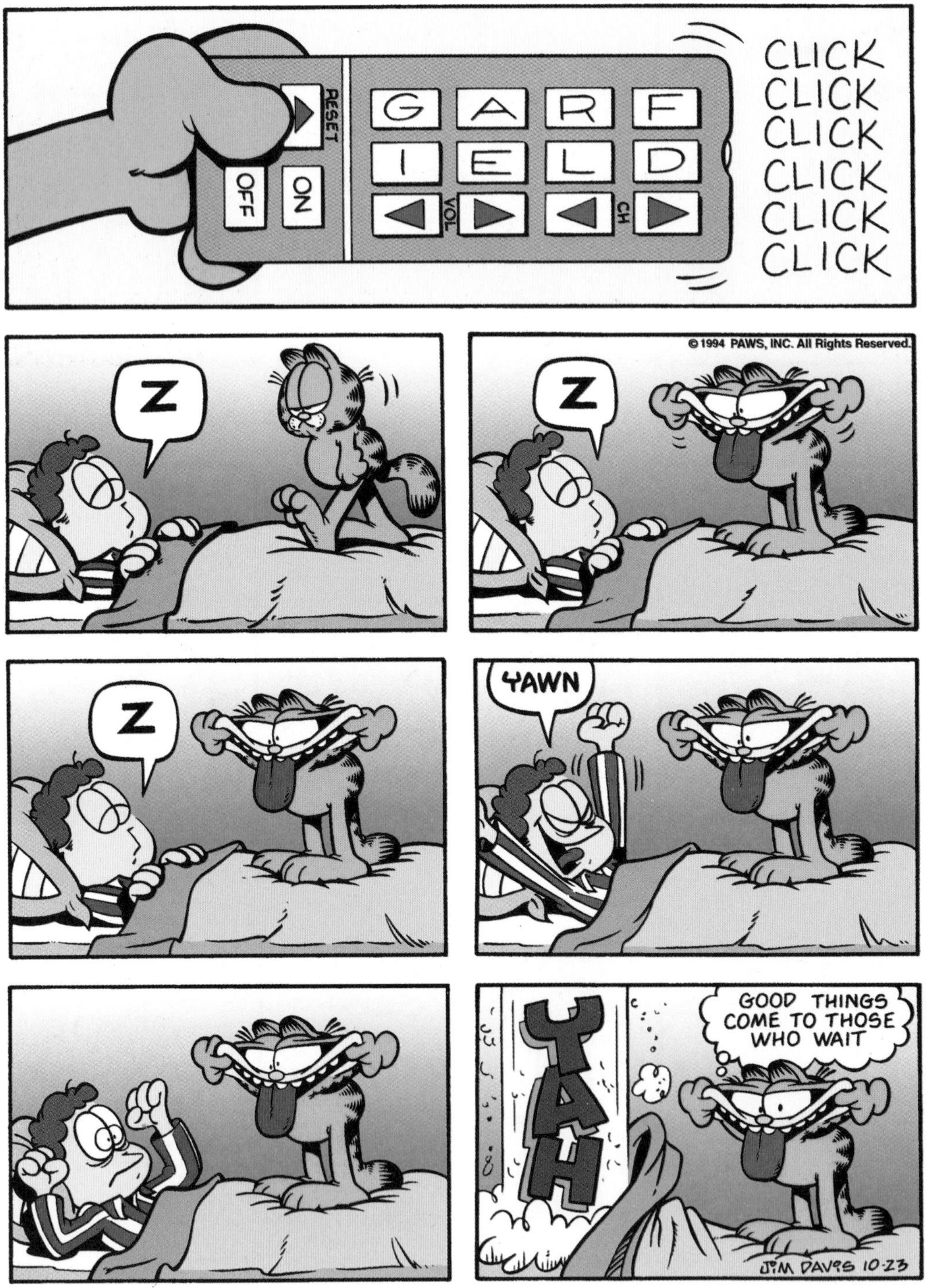
RESET
G A R F
I E L D
OFF
ON
VOL
CH
CLICK
CLICK
CLICK
CLICK
CLICK
CLICK
Z
© 1994 PAWS, INC. All Rights Reserved.
Z
Z
YAWN
YAH
GOOD THINGS COME TO THOSE WHO WAIT
JIM DAVIS 10-23

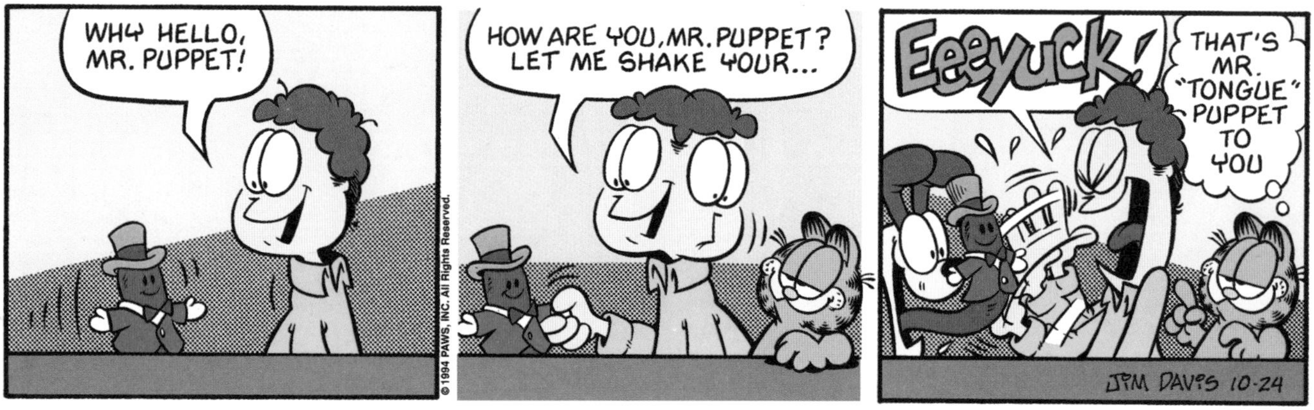
WHY HELLO, MR. PUPPET!
HOW ARE YOU, MR. PUPPET? LET ME SHAKE YOUR...
Eeeyuck!
THAT'S MR. "TONGUE" PUPPET TO YOU
JIM DAVIS 10-24
© 1994 PAWS, INC. All Rights Reserved.

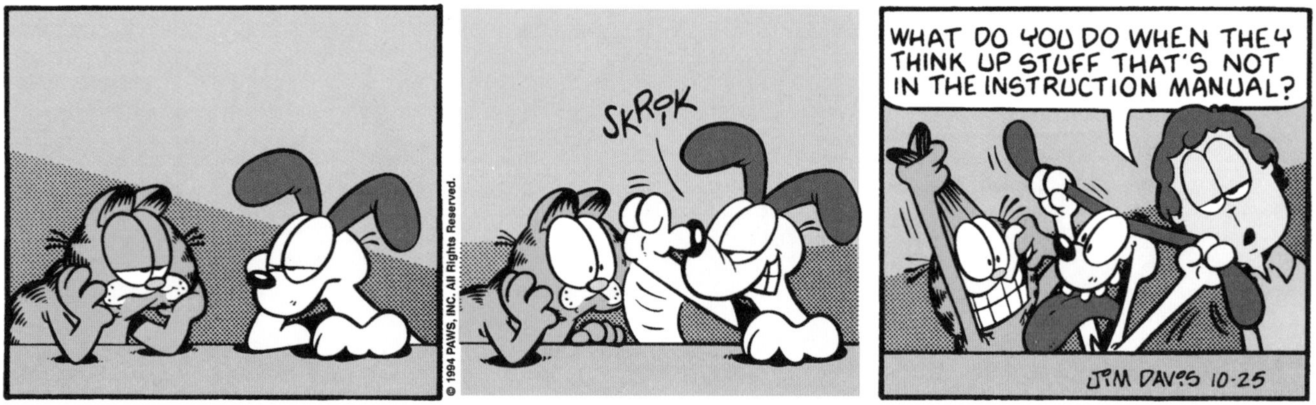
SKRONK
WHAT DO YOU DO WHEN THEY THINK UP STUFF THAT'S NOT IN THE INSTRUCTION MANUAL?
JIM DAVIS 10-25
© 1994 PAWS, INC. All Rights Reserved.

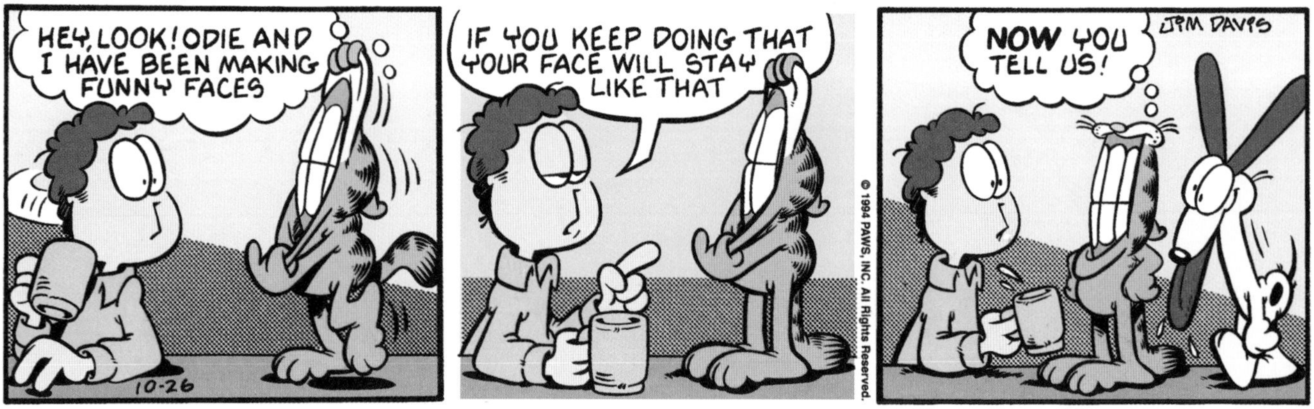
HEY, LOOK! ODIE AND I HAVE BEEN MAKING FUNNY FACES
10-26
IF YOU KEEP DOING THAT YOUR FACE WILL STAY LIKE THAT
NOW YOU TELL US!
JIM DAVIS
© 1994 PAWS, INC. All Rights Reserved.

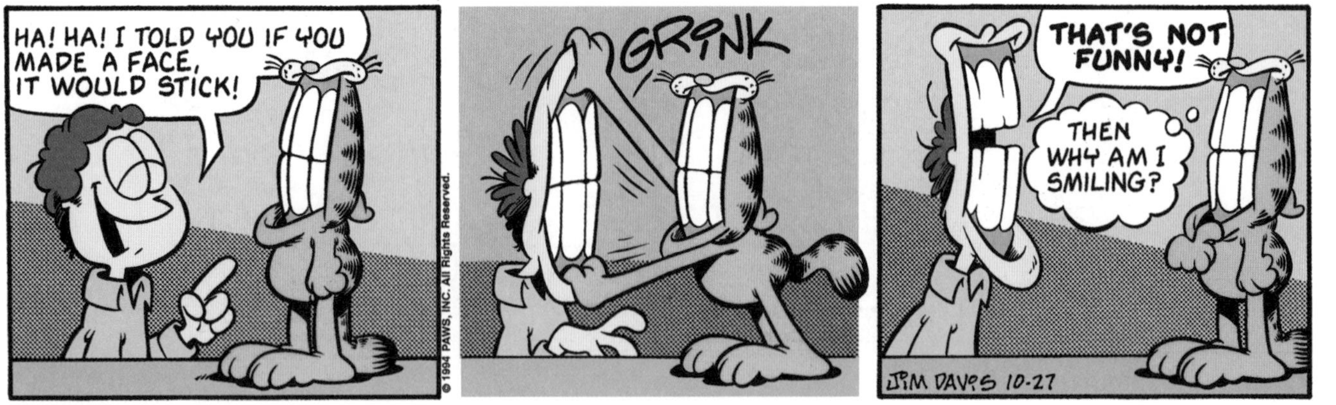
HA! HA! I TOLD YOU IF YOU MADE A FACE, IT WOULD STICK!
© 1994 PAWS, INC. All Rights Reserved.
GRINK
THAT'S NOT FUNNY!
THEN WHY AM I SMILING?
JIM DAVIS 10-27

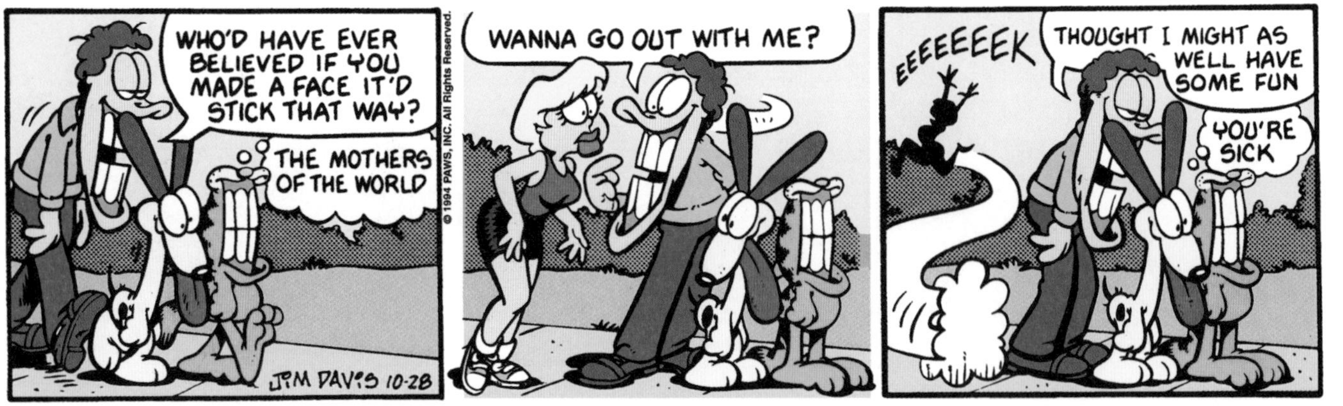
WHO'D HAVE EVER BELIEVED IF YOU MADE A FACE IT'D STICK THAT WAY?
THE MOTHERS OF THE WORLD
JIM DAVIS 10-28
© 1994 PAWS, INC. All Rights Reserved.
WANNA GO OUT WITH ME?
EEEEEEEK
THOUGHT I MIGHT AS WELL HAVE SOME FUN
YOU'RE SICK

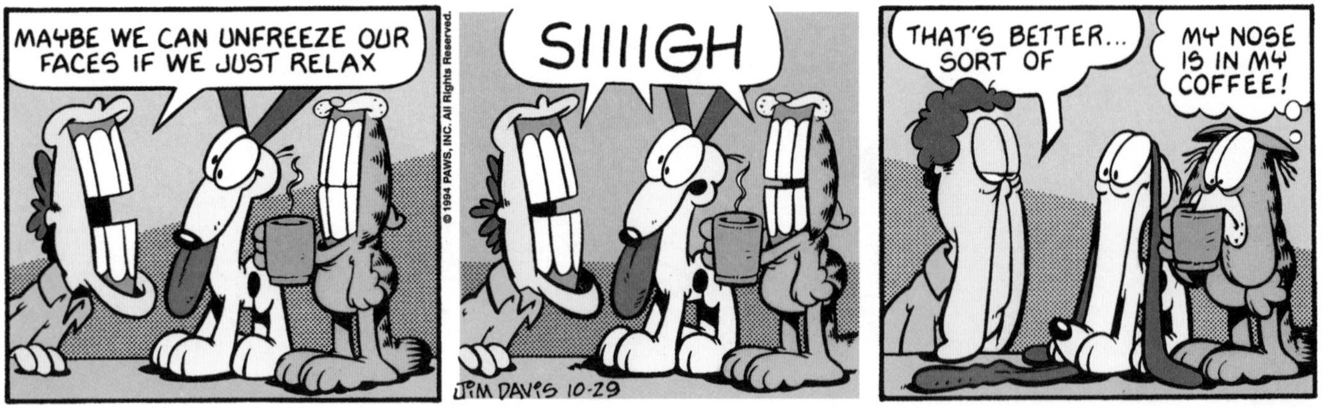
MAYBE WE CAN UNFREEZE OUR FACES IF WE JUST RELAX
© 1994 PAWS, INC. All Rights Reserved.
SIIIIGH
JIM DAVIS 10-29
THAT'S BETTER... SORT OF
MY NOSE IS IN MY COFFEE!

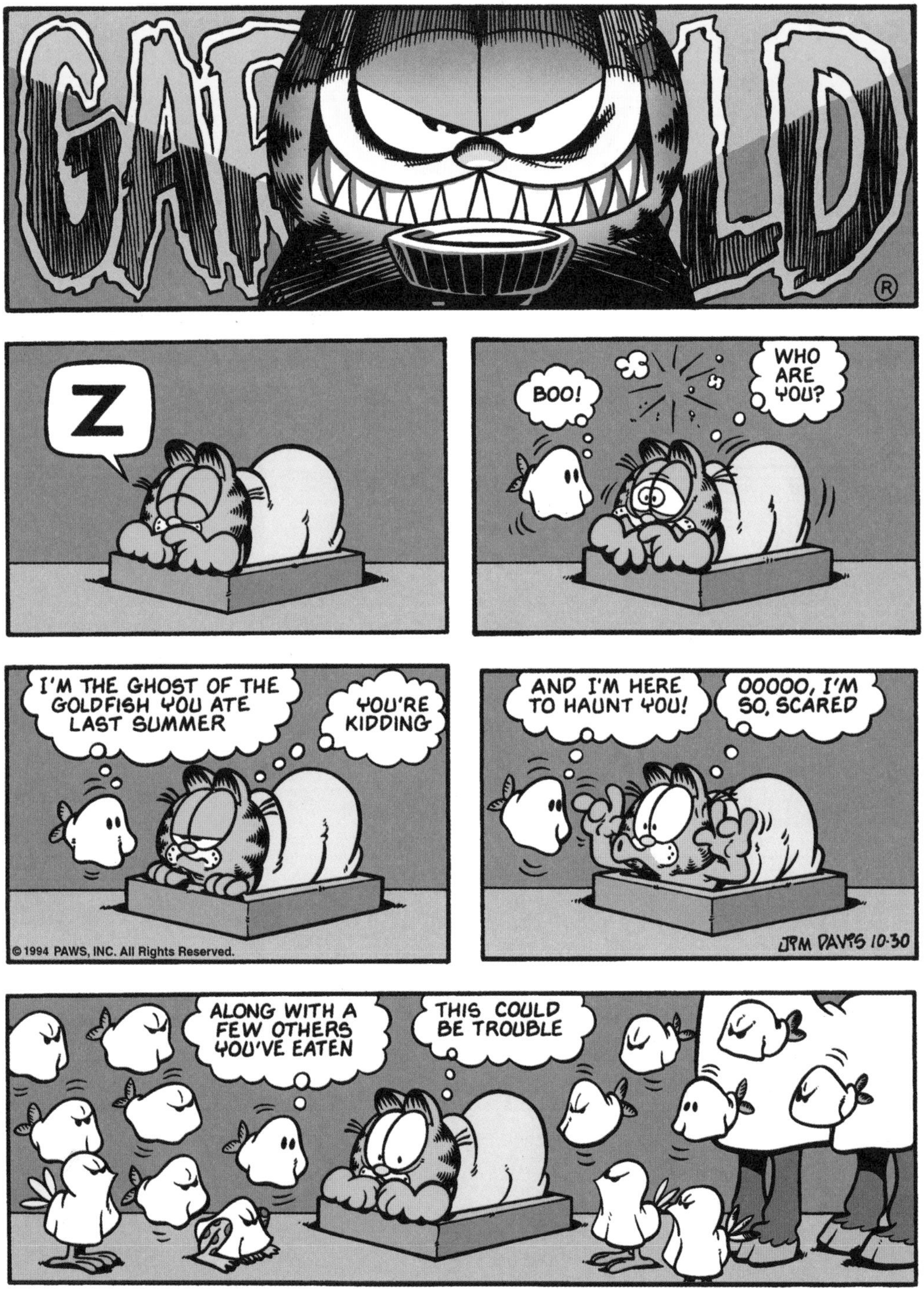
GARFIELD
Z
BOO!
WHO ARE YOU?
I'M THE GHOST OF THE GOLDFISH YOU ATE LAST SUMMER
YOU'RE KIDDING
AND I'M HERE TO HAUNT YOU!
OOOOO, I'M SO, SCARED
© 1994 PAWS, INC. All Rights Reserved.
JIM DAVIS 10-30
ALONG WITH A FEW OTHERS YOU'VE EATEN
THIS COULD BE TROUBLE

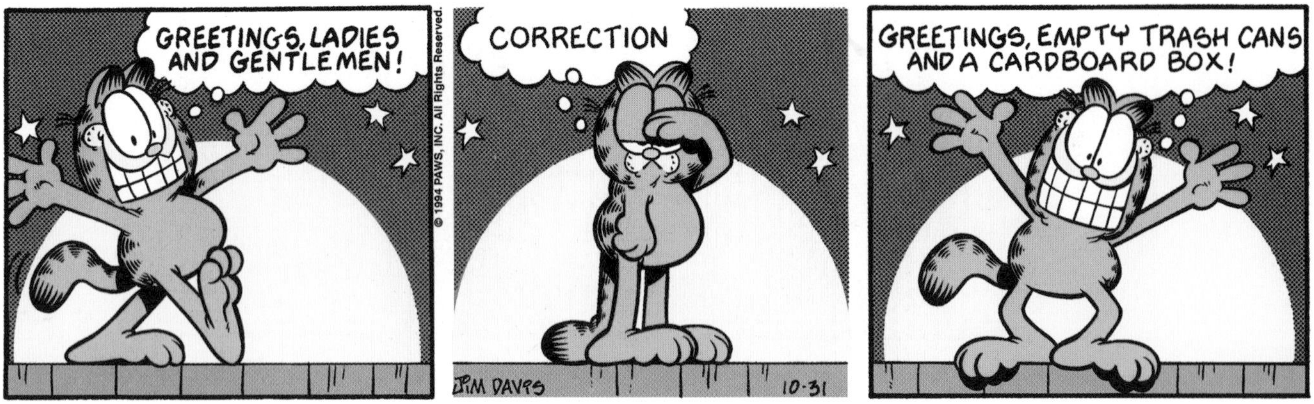
GREETINGS, LADIES AND GENTLEMEN!
© 1994 PAWS, INC. All Rights Reserved.
CORRECTION
GREETINGS, EMPTY TRASH CANS AND A CARDBOARD BOX!
JIM DAVIS 10-31

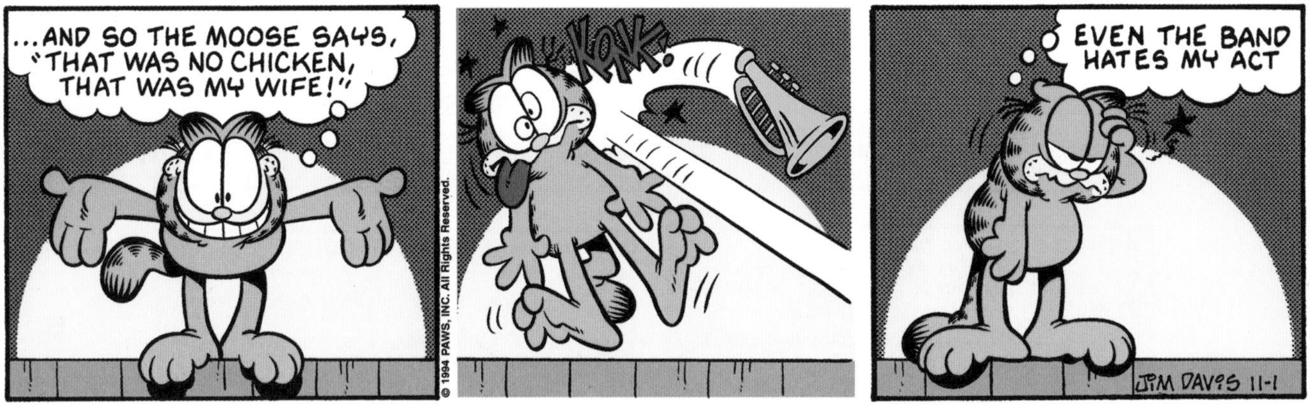
...AND SO THE MOOSE SAYS, "THAT WAS NO CHICKEN, THAT WAS MY WIFE!"
© 1994 PAWS, INC. All Rights Reserved.
KONK!
EVEN THE BAND HATES MY ACT
JIM DAVIS 11-1

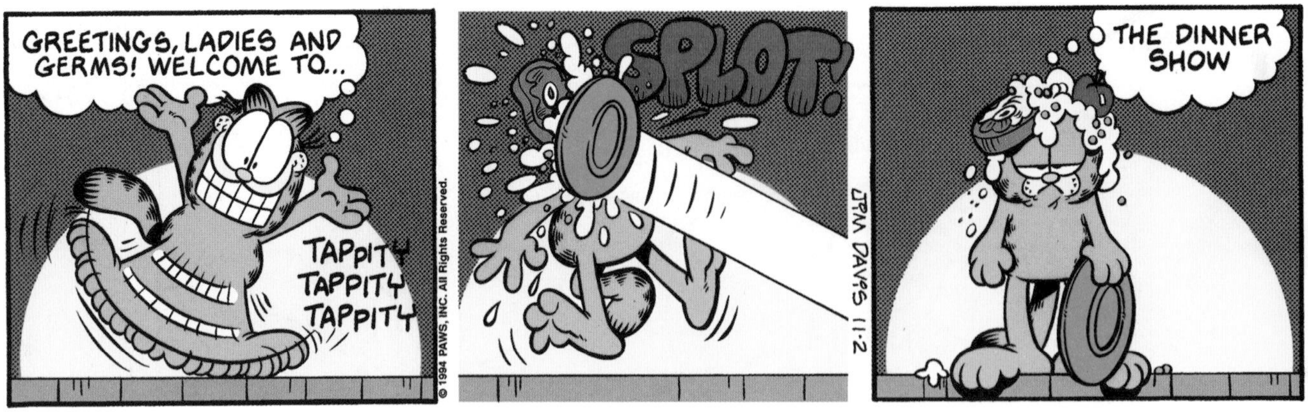
GREETINGS, LADIES AND GERMS! WELCOME TO...
TAPPITY TAPPITY TAPPITY
© 1994 PAWS, INC. All Rights Reserved.
SPLOT!
JIM DAVIS 11-2
THE DINNER SHOW

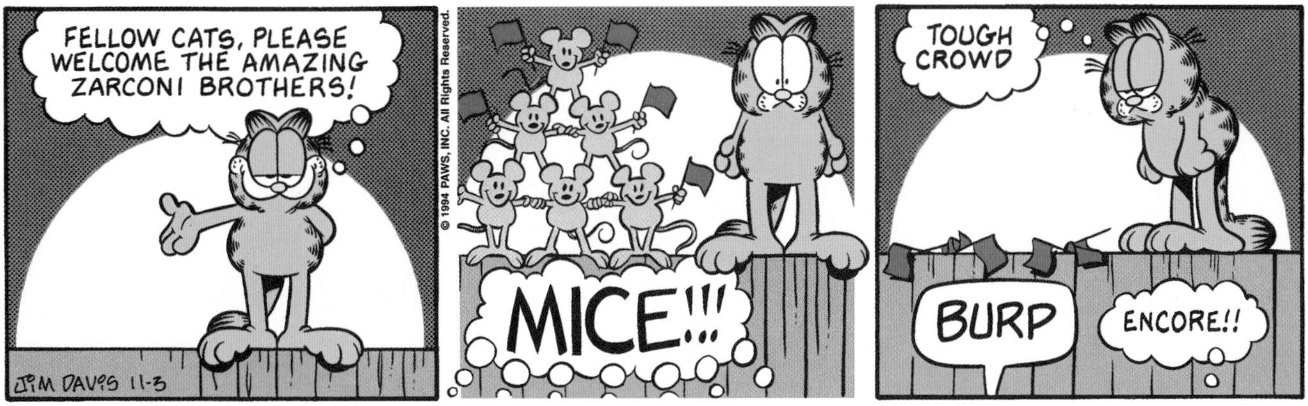
FELLOW CATS, PLEASE WELCOME THE AMAZING ZARCONI BROTHERS!
JIM DAVIS 11-3
© 1994 PAWS, INC. All Rights Reserved.
MICE!!!
TOUGH CROWD
BURP
ENCORE!!

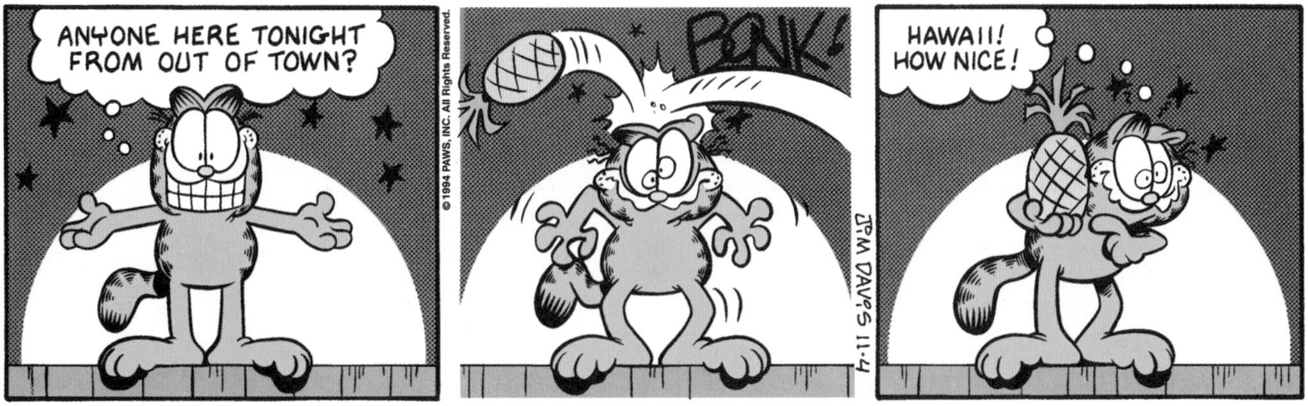
ANYONE HERE TONIGHT FROM OUT OF TOWN?
© 1994 PAWS, INC. All Rights Reserved.
BONK!
JIM DAVIS 11-4
HAWAII! HOW NICE!

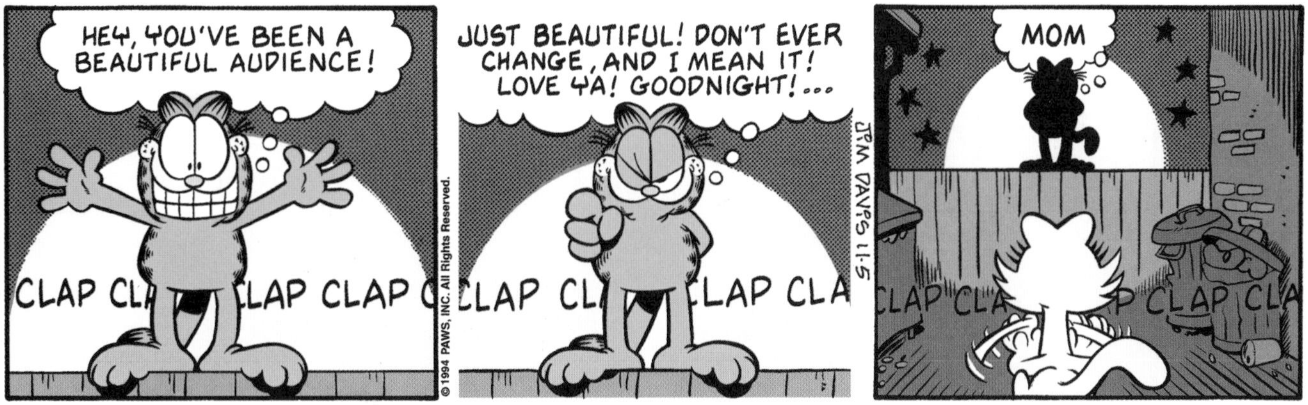
HEY, YOU'VE BEEN A BEAUTIFUL AUDIENCE!
CLAP CLA CLAP CLAP C
© 1994 PAWS, INC. All Rights Reserved.
JUST BEAUTIFUL! DON'T EVER CHANGE, AND I MEAN IT! LOVE YA! GOODNIGHT!...
CLAP CL CLAP CLA
JIM DAVIS 11-5
MOM
CLAP CLA P CLAP CLA

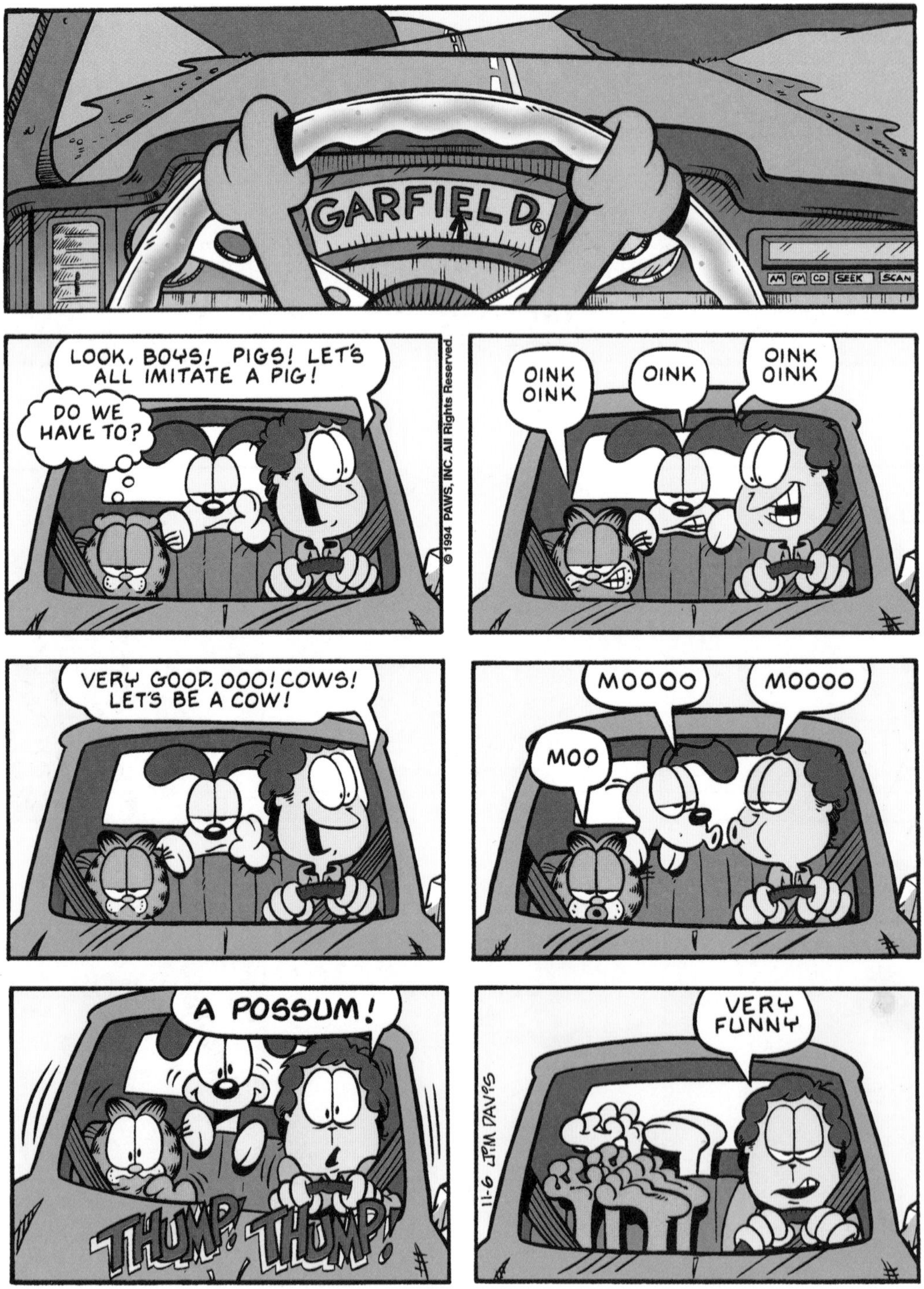
GARFIELD®
AM FM CD SEEK SCAN
LOOK, BOYS! PIGS! LET'S ALL IMITATE A PIG!
DO WE HAVE TO?
© 1994 PAWS, INC. All Rights Reserved.
OINK OINK
OINK
OINK OINK
VERY GOOD. OOO! COWS! LET'S BE A COW!
MOO
MOOOO
MOOOO
A POSSUM!
THUMP! THUMP!
11-6 JIM DAVIS
VERY FUNNY

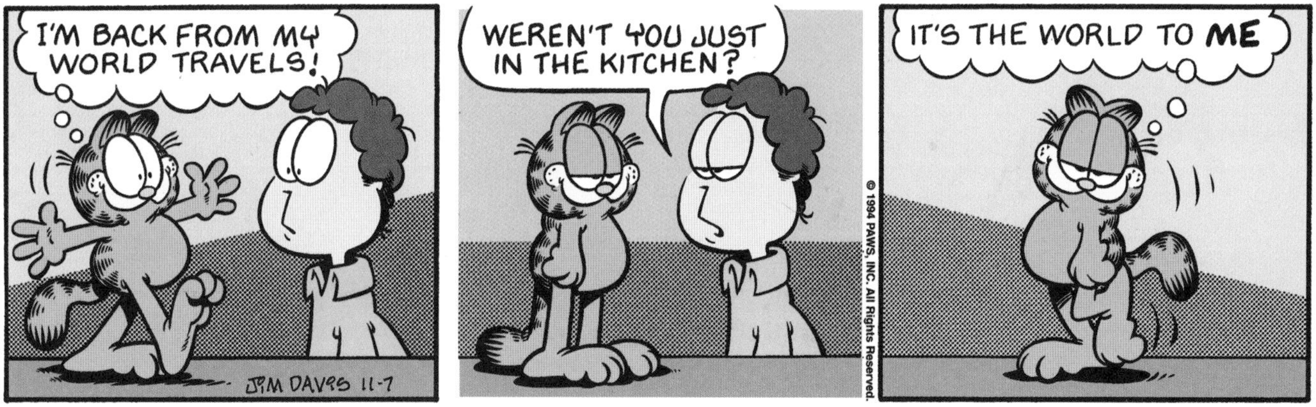
I'M BACK FROM MY WORLD TRAVELS!
JIM DAVIS 11-7
WEREN'T YOU JUST IN THE KITCHEN?
© 1994 PAWS, INC. All Rights Reserved.
IT'S THE WORLD TO **ME**

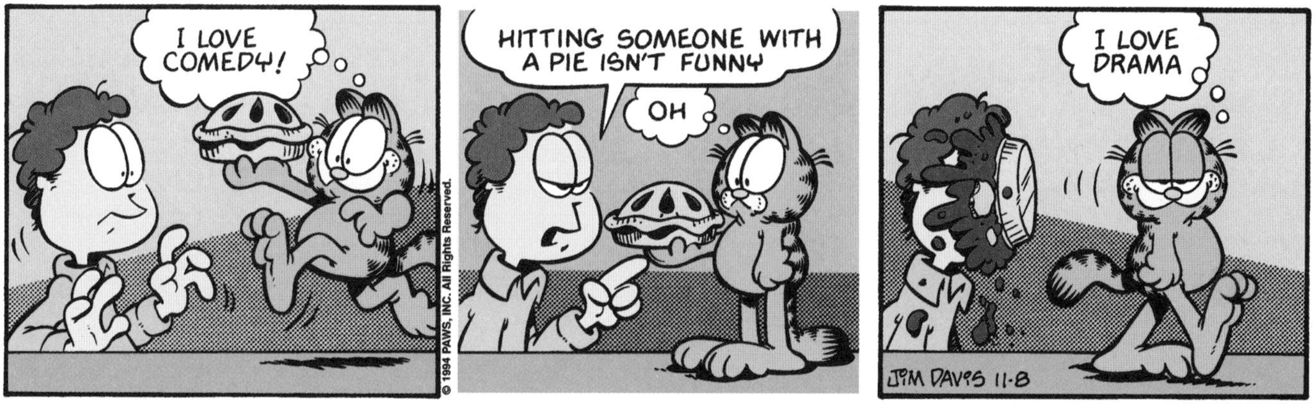
I LOVE COMEDY!
© 1994 PAWS, INC. All Rights Reserved.
HITTING SOMEONE WITH A PIE ISN'T FUNNY
OH
I LOVE DRAMA
JIM DAVIS 11-8

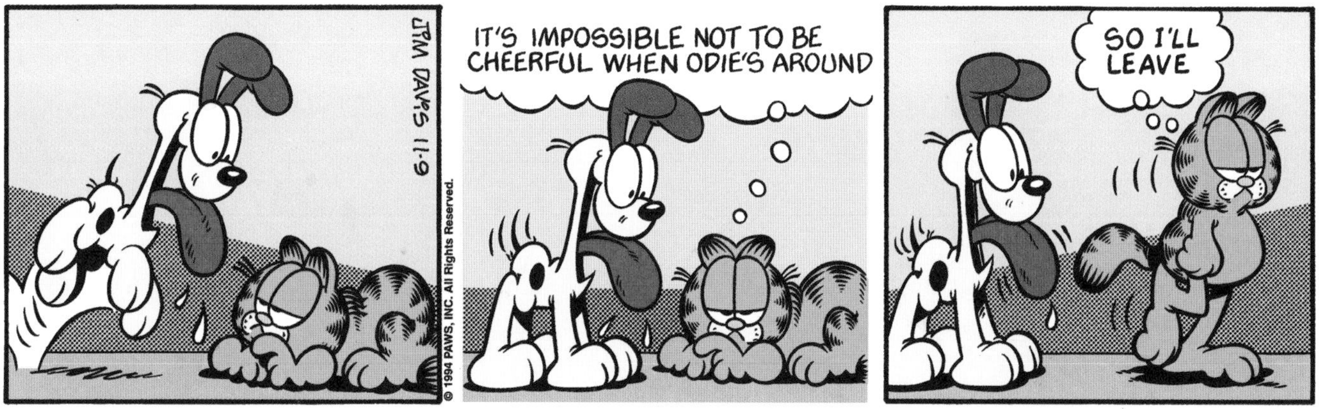
JIM DAVIS 11-9
© 1994 PAWS, INC. All Rights Reserved.
IT'S IMPOSSIBLE NOT TO BE CHEERFUL WHEN ODIE'S AROUND
SO I'LL LEAVE

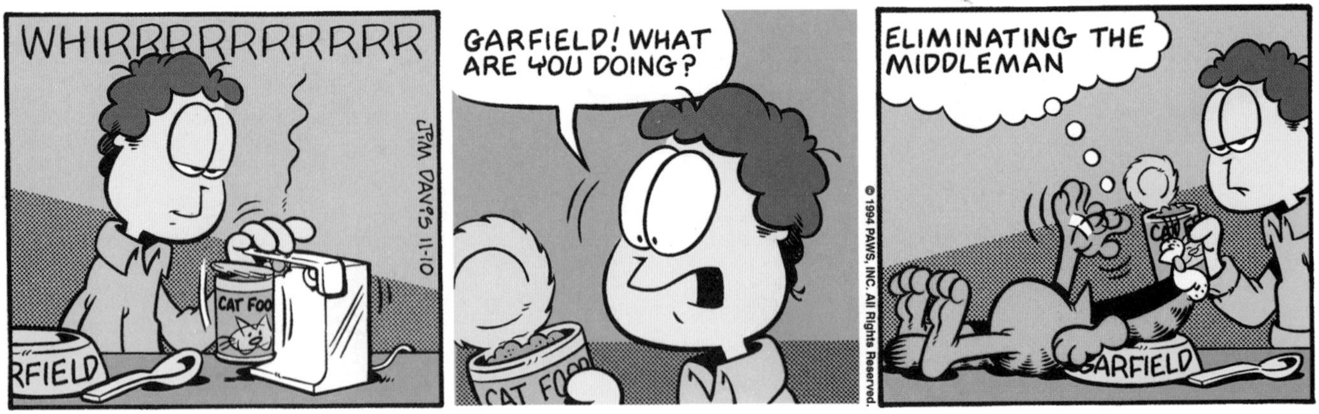
WHIRRRRRRRRRRR
JIM DAVIS 11-10
GARFIELD! WHAT ARE YOU DOING?
ELIMINATING THE MIDDLEMAN
© 1994 PAWS, INC. All Rights Reserved.

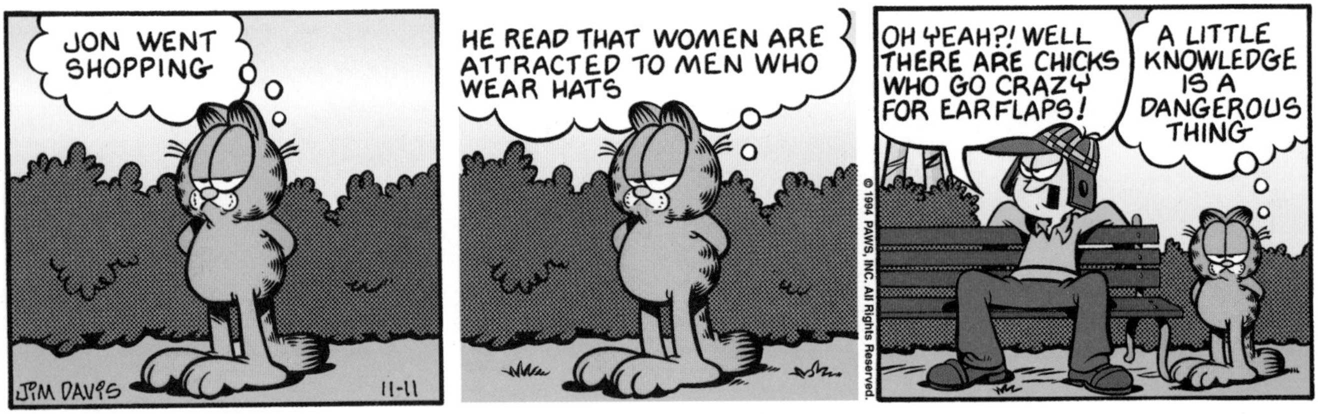
JON WENT SHOPPING
JIM DAVIS 11-11
HE READ THAT WOMEN ARE ATTRACTED TO MEN WHO WEAR HATS
OH YEAH?! WELL THERE ARE CHICKS WHO GO CRAZY FOR EARFLAPS!
A LITTLE KNOWLEDGE IS A DANGEROUS THING
© 1994 PAWS, INC. All Rights Reserved.

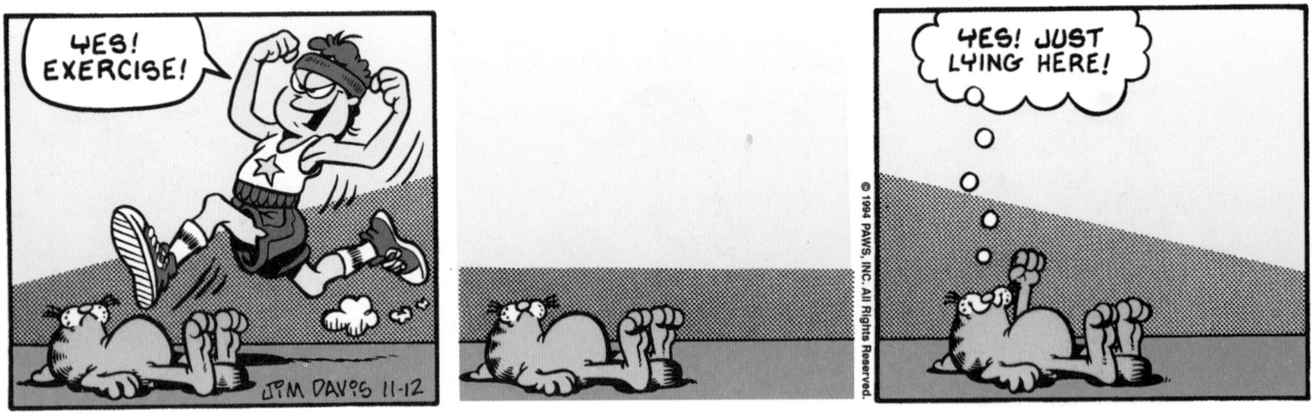
YES! EXERCISE!
JIM DAVIS 11-12
YES! JUST LYING HERE!
© 1994 PAWS, INC. All Rights Reserved.

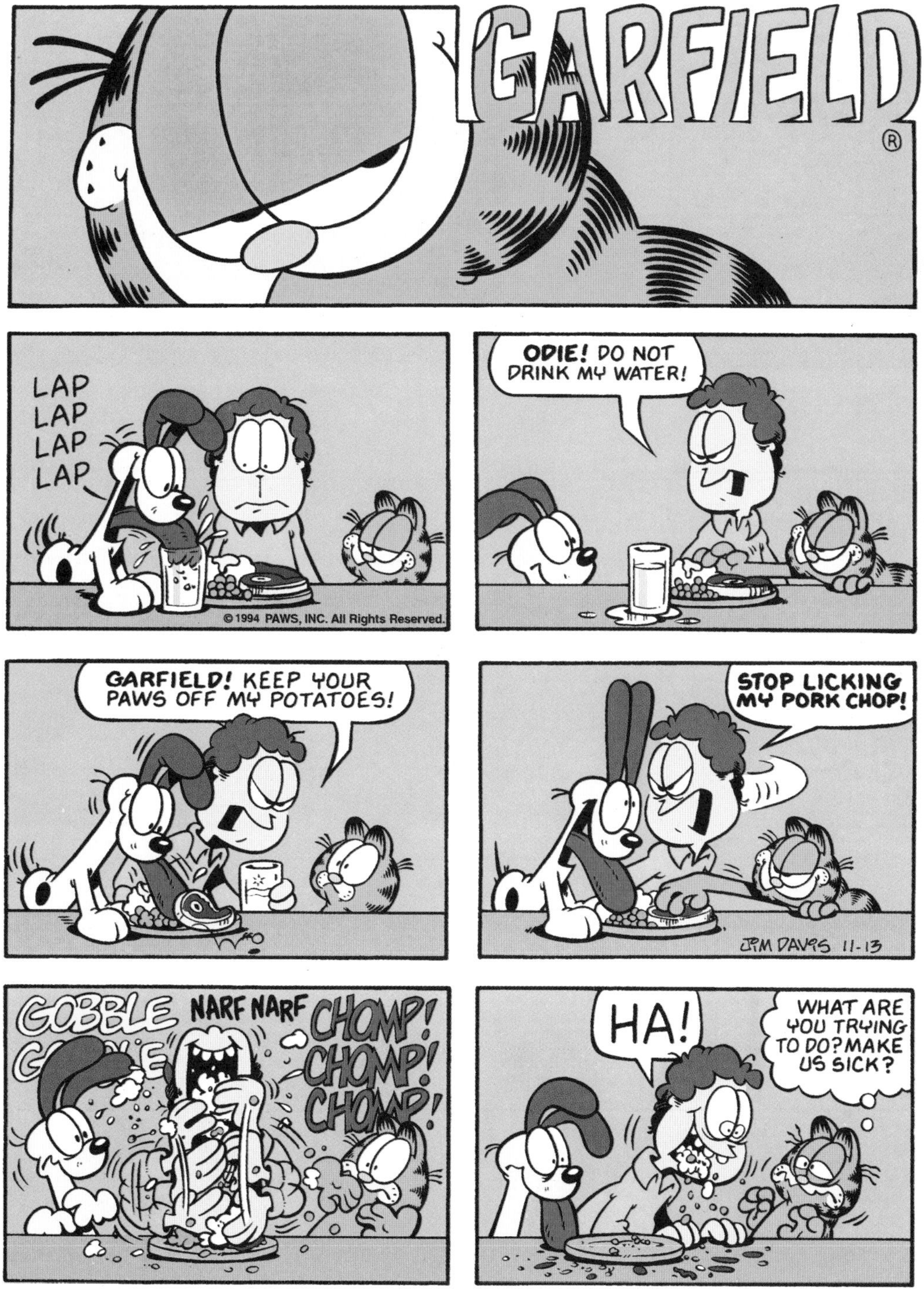
GARFIELD®
LAP LAP LAP LAP
© 1994 PAWS, INC. All Rights Reserved.
ODIE! DO NOT DRINK MY WATER!
GARFIELD! KEEP YOUR PAWS OFF MY POTATOES!
STOP LICKING MY PORK CHOP!
JIM DAVIS 11-13
GOBBLE GOBBLE
NARF NARF
CHOMP! CHOMP! CHOMP!
HA!
WHAT ARE YOU TRYING TO DO? MAKE US SICK?

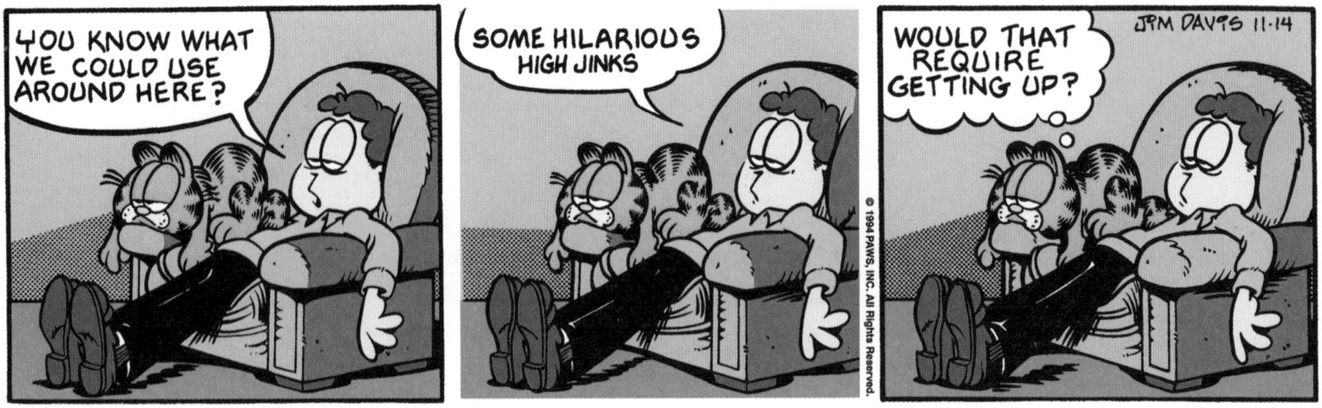
YOU KNOW WHAT WE COULD USE AROUND HERE?
SOME HILARIOUS HIGH JINKS
© 1994 PAWS, INC. All Rights Reserved.
JIM DAVIS 11-14
WOULD THAT REQUIRE GETTING UP?

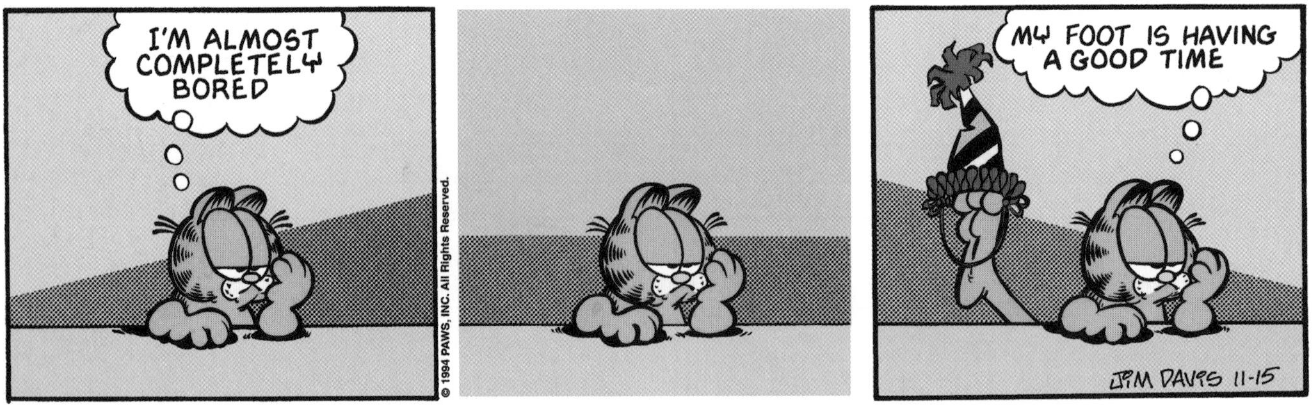
I'M ALMOST COMPLETELY BORED
© 1994 PAWS, INC. All Rights Reserved.
MY FOOT IS HAVING A GOOD TIME
JIM DAVIS 11-15

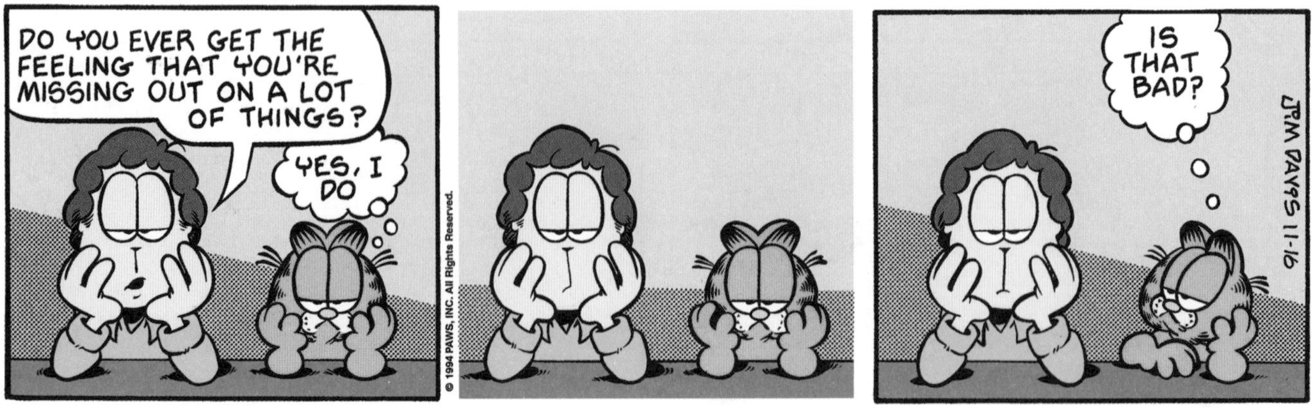
DO YOU EVER GET THE FEELING THAT YOU'RE MISSING OUT ON A LOT OF THINGS?
YES, I DO
© 1994 PAWS, INC. All Rights Reserved.
IS THAT BAD?
JIM DAVIS 11-16

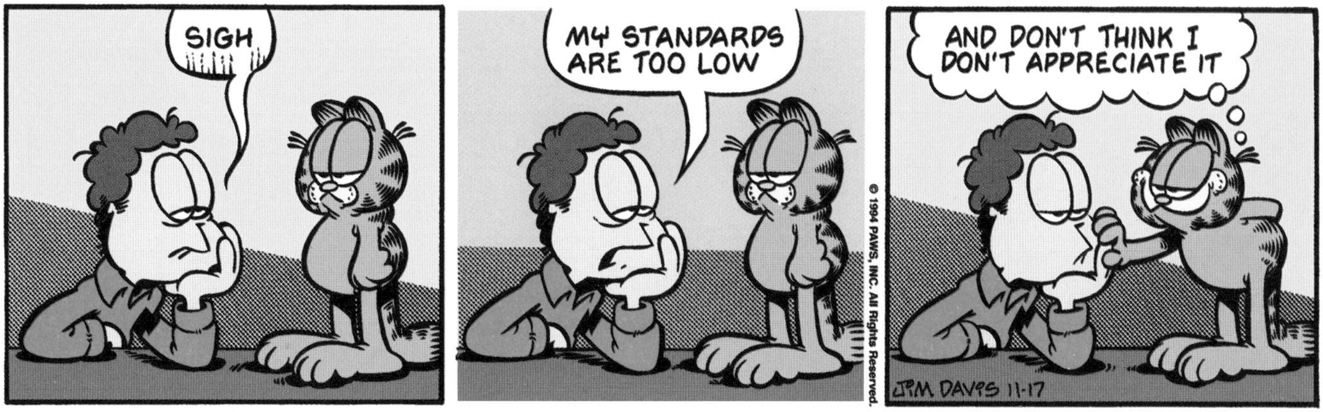
SIGH
MY STANDARDS ARE TOO LOW
© 1994 PAWS, INC. All Rights Reserved.
AND DON'T THINK I DON'T APPRECIATE IT
JIM DAVIS 11-17

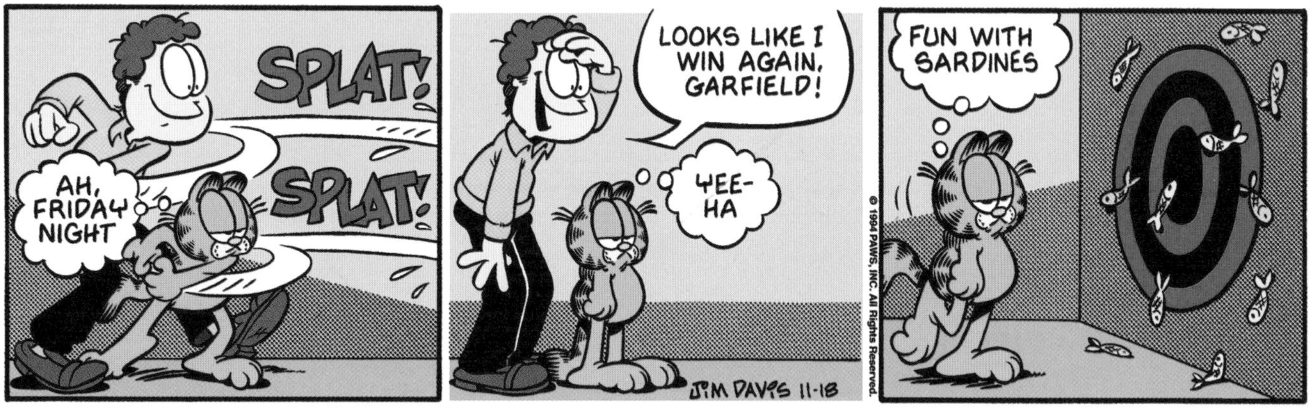
SPLAT!
SPLAT!
AH, FRIDAY NIGHT
LOOKS LIKE I WIN AGAIN, GARFIELD!
YEE-HA
JIM DAVIS 11-18
© 1994 PAWS, INC. All Rights Reserved.
FUN WITH SARDINES

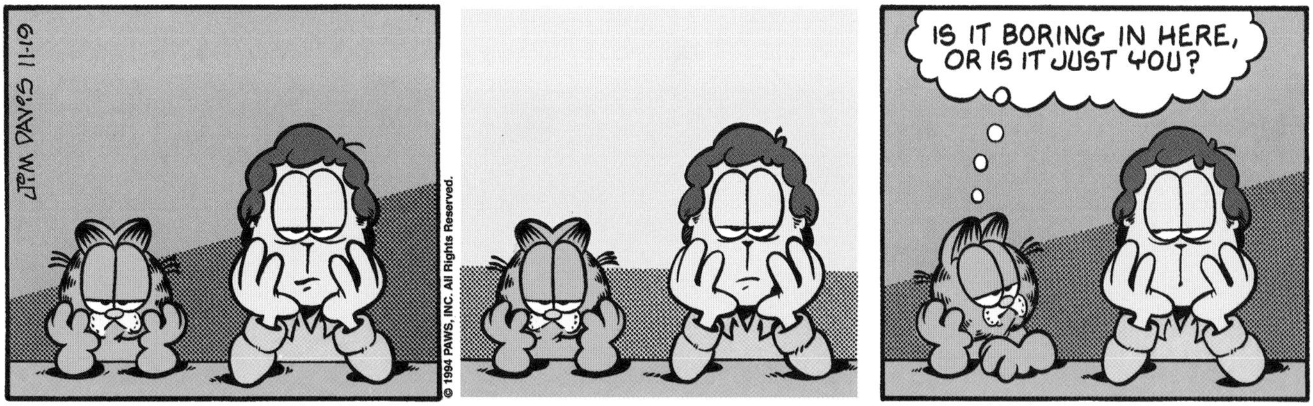
JIM DAVIS 11-19
© 1994 PAWS, INC. All Rights Reserved.
IS IT BORING IN HERE, OR IS IT JUST YOU?

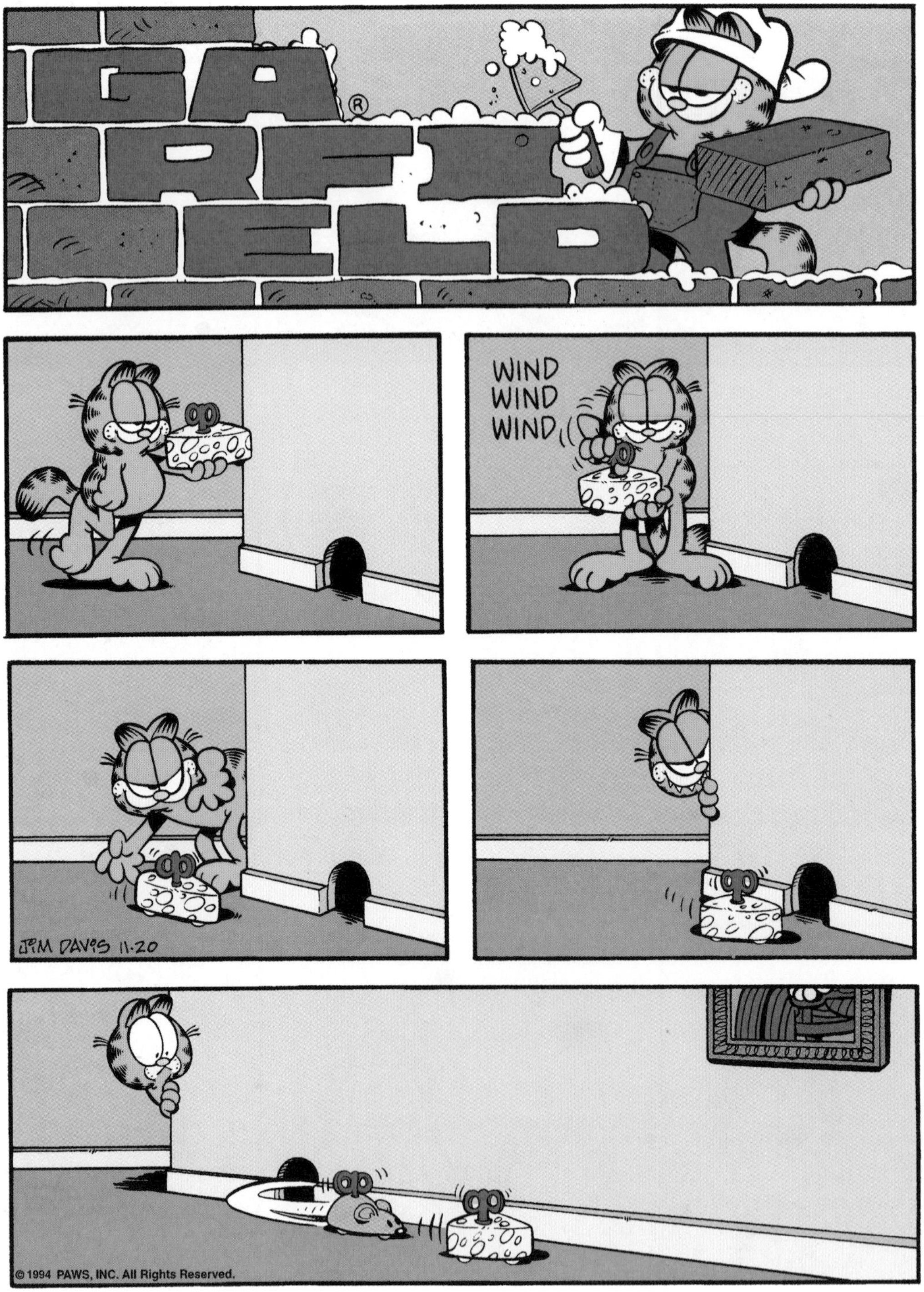
GARFIELD®
WIND
WIND
WIND
JIM DAVIS 11.20
© 1994 PAWS, INC. All Rights Reserved.

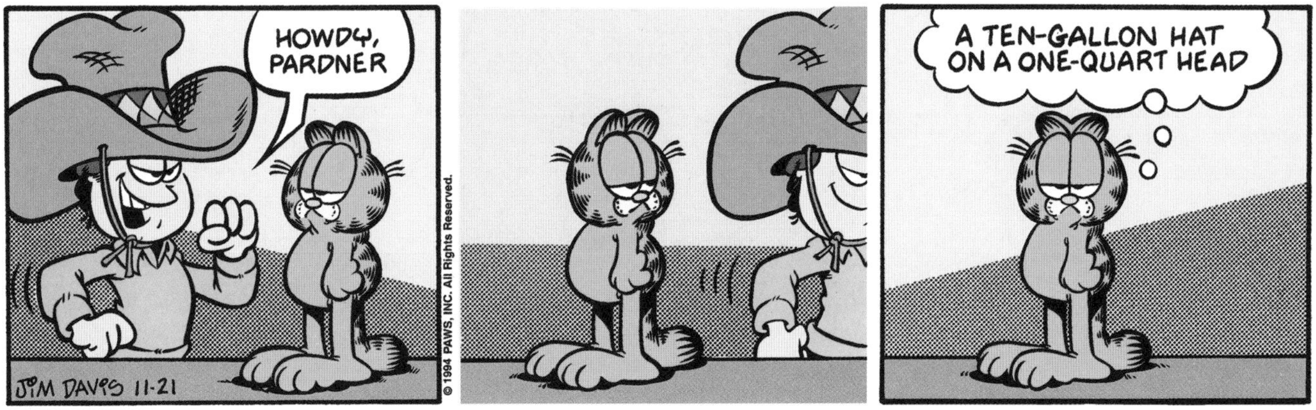
HOWDY, PARDNER
A TEN-GALLON HAT ON A ONE-QUART HEAD
JIM DAVIS 11-21
© 1994 PAWS, INC. All Rights Reserved.

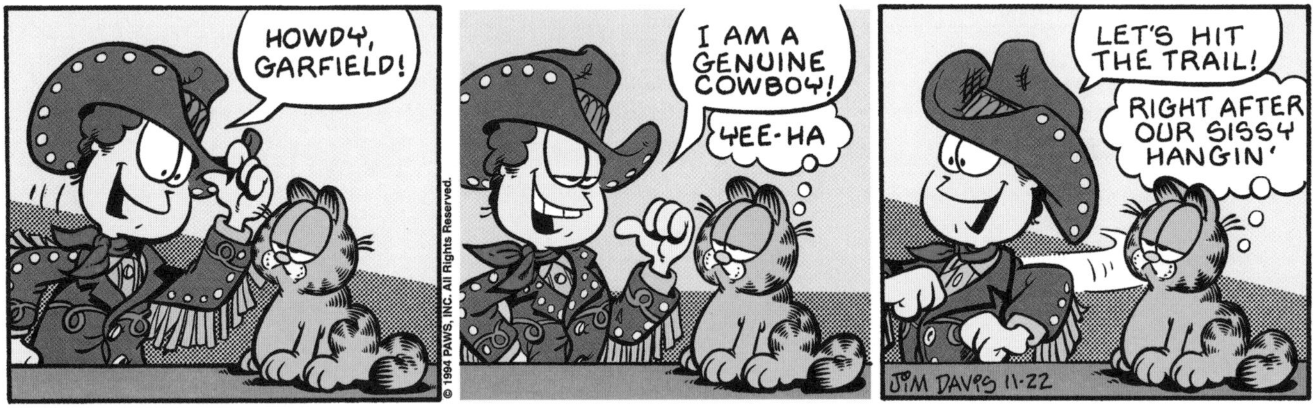
HOWDY, GARFIELD!
I AM A GENUINE COWBOY!
YEE-HA
LET'S HIT THE TRAIL!
RIGHT AFTER OUR SISSY HANGIN'
JIM DAVIS 11-22
© 1994 PAWS, INC. All Rights Reserved.

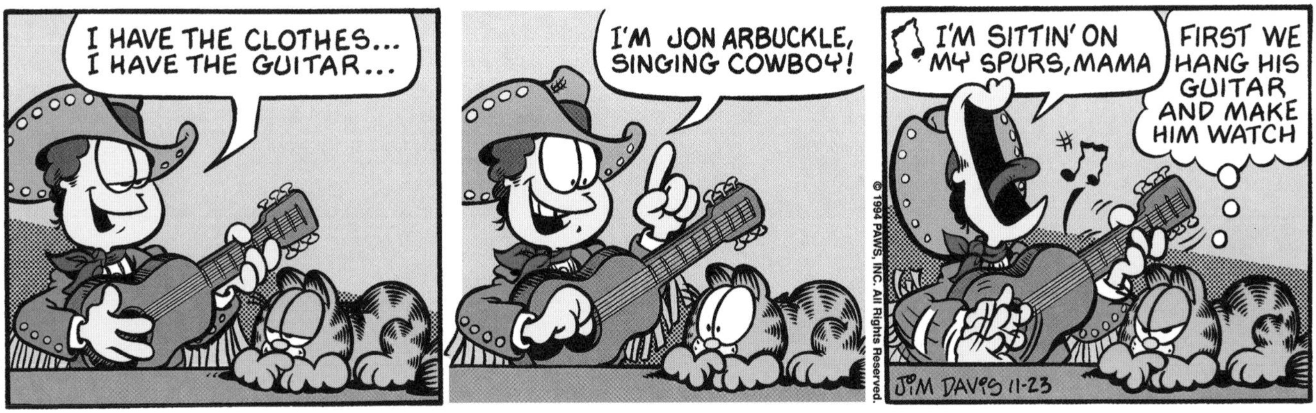
I HAVE THE CLOTHES... I HAVE THE GUITAR...
I'M JON ARBUCKLE, SINGING COWBOY!
I'M SITTIN' ON MY SPURS, MAMA
FIRST WE HANG HIS GUITAR AND MAKE HIM WATCH
JIM DAVIS 11-23
© 1994 PAWS, INC. All Rights Reserved.

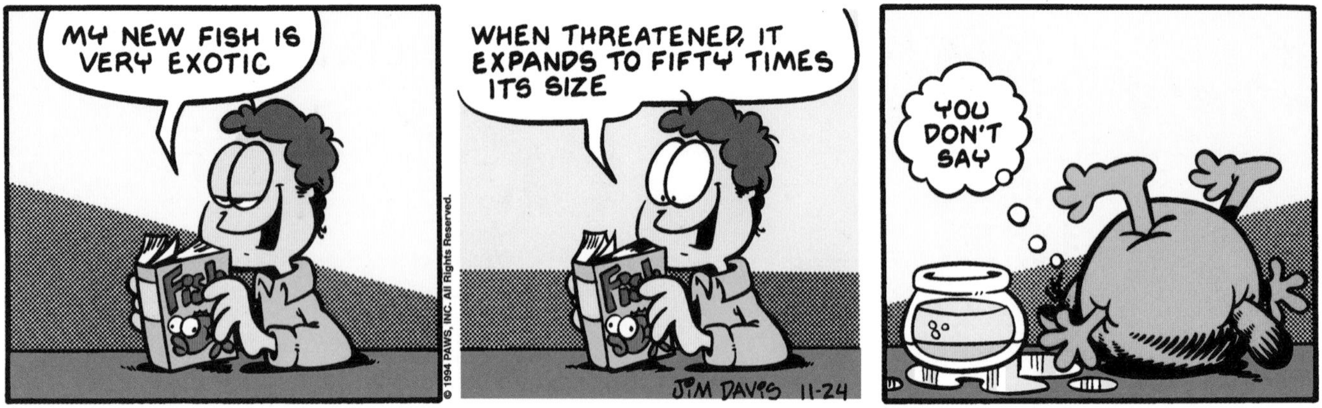
MY NEW FISH IS VERY EXOTIC
WHEN THREATENED, IT EXPANDS TO FIFTY TIMES ITS SIZE
YOU DON'T SAY
© 1994 PAWS, INC. All Rights Reserved.
JIM DAVIS 11-24

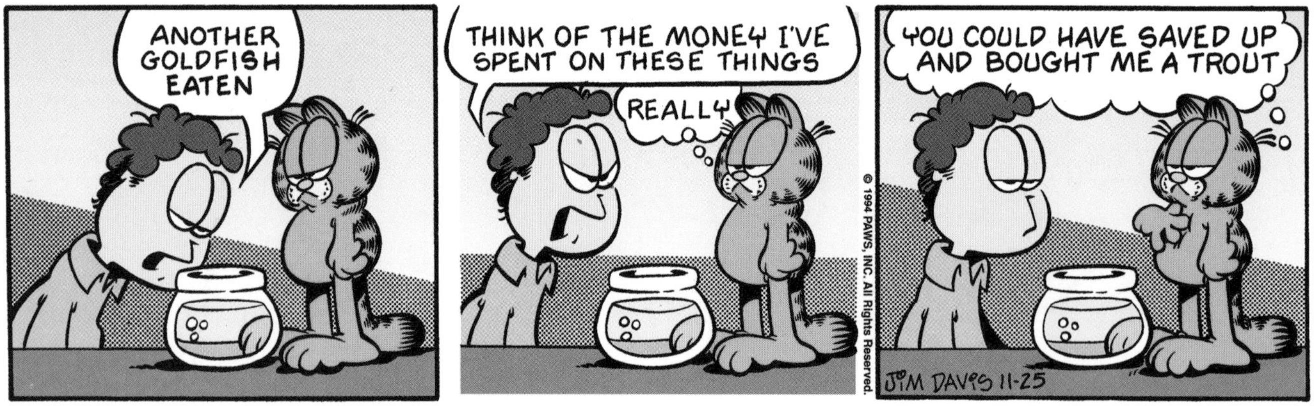
ANOTHER GOLDFISH EATEN
THINK OF THE MONEY I'VE SPENT ON THESE THINGS
REALLY
YOU COULD HAVE SAVED UP AND BOUGHT ME A TROUT
© 1994 PAWS, INC. All Rights Reserved.
JIM DAVIS 11-25

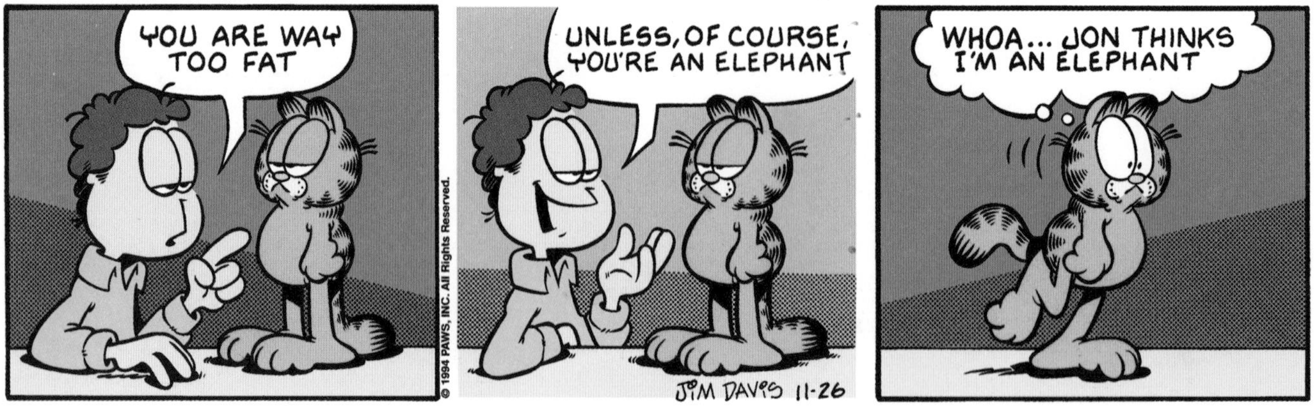
YOU ARE WAY TOO FAT
UNLESS, OF COURSE, YOU'RE AN ELEPHANT
WHOA... JON THINKS I'M AN ELEPHANT
© 1994 PAWS, INC. All Rights Reserved.
JIM DAVIS 11-26

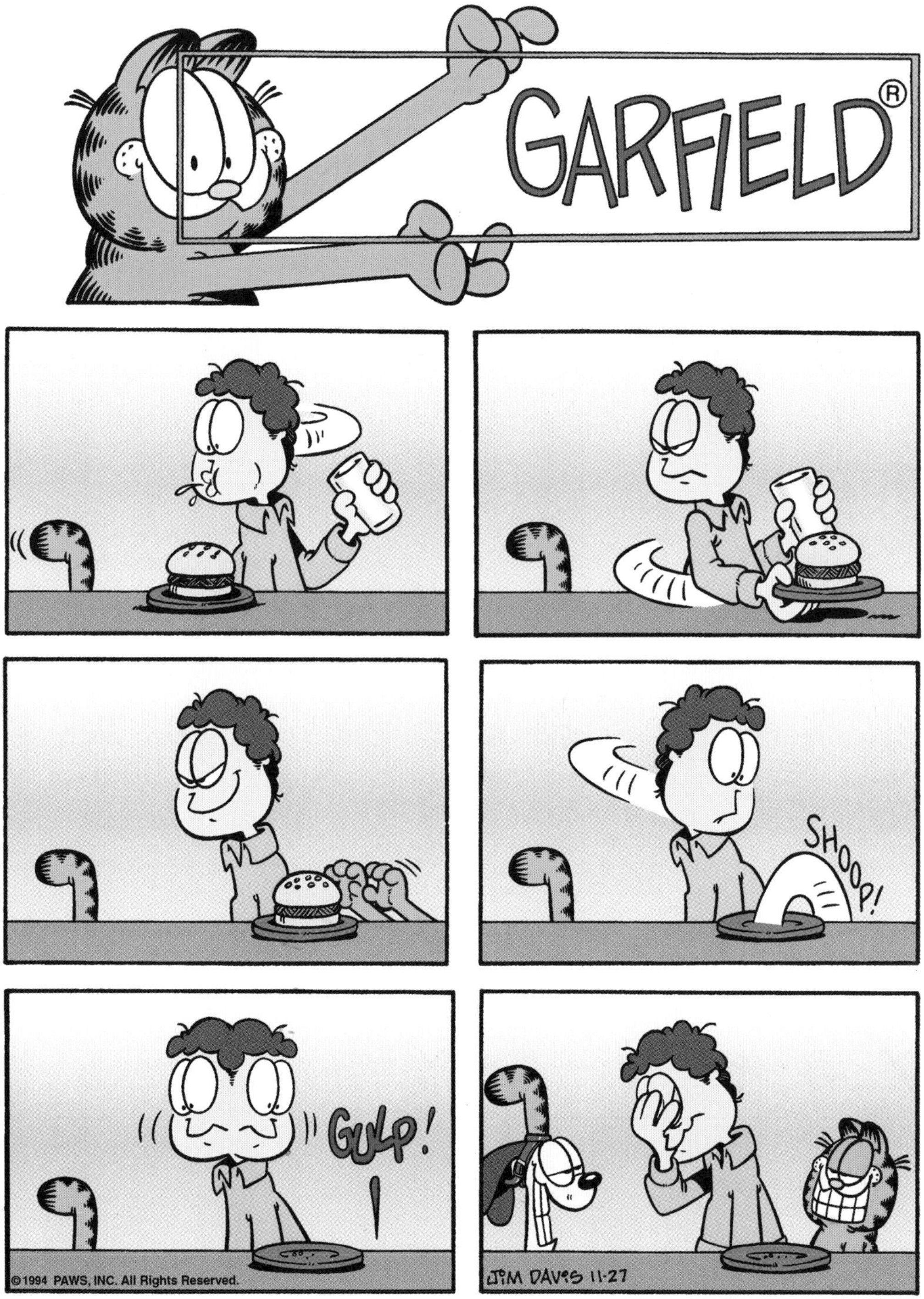
GARFIELD®
SHOOOP!
GULP!
©1994 PAWS, INC. All Rights Reserved.
JIM DAVIS 11-27

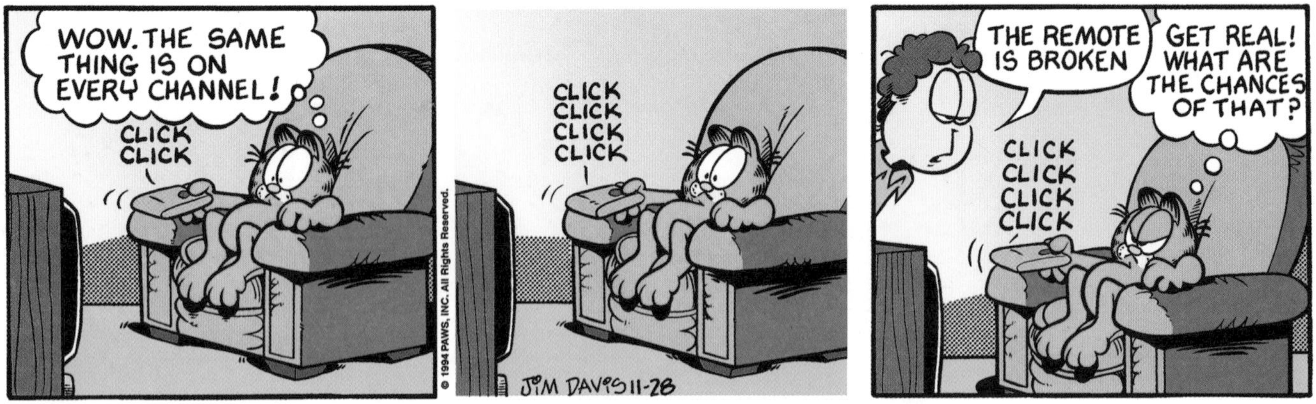
WOW. THE SAME THING IS ON EVERY CHANNEL!
CLICK CLICK
CLICK CLICK CLICK CLICK
© 1994 PAWS, INC. All Rights Reserved.
JIM DAVIS 11-28
THE REMOTE IS BROKEN
GET REAL! WHAT ARE THE CHANCES OF THAT?
CLICK CLICK CLICK CLICK

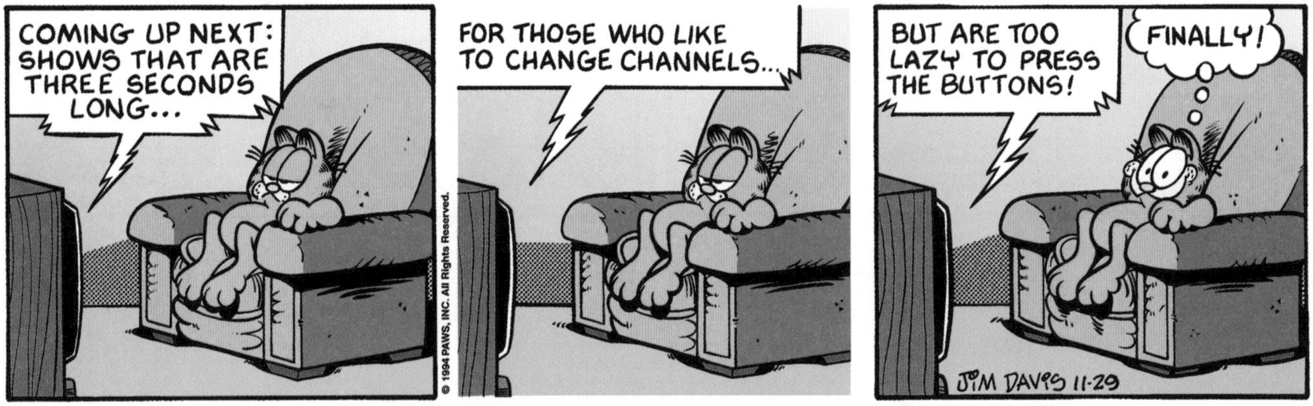
COMING UP NEXT: SHOWS THAT ARE THREE SECONDS LONG...
© 1994 PAWS, INC. All Rights Reserved.
FOR THOSE WHO LIKE TO CHANGE CHANNELS...
BUT ARE TOO LAZY TO PRESS THE BUTTONS!
FINALLY!
JIM DAVIS 11-29

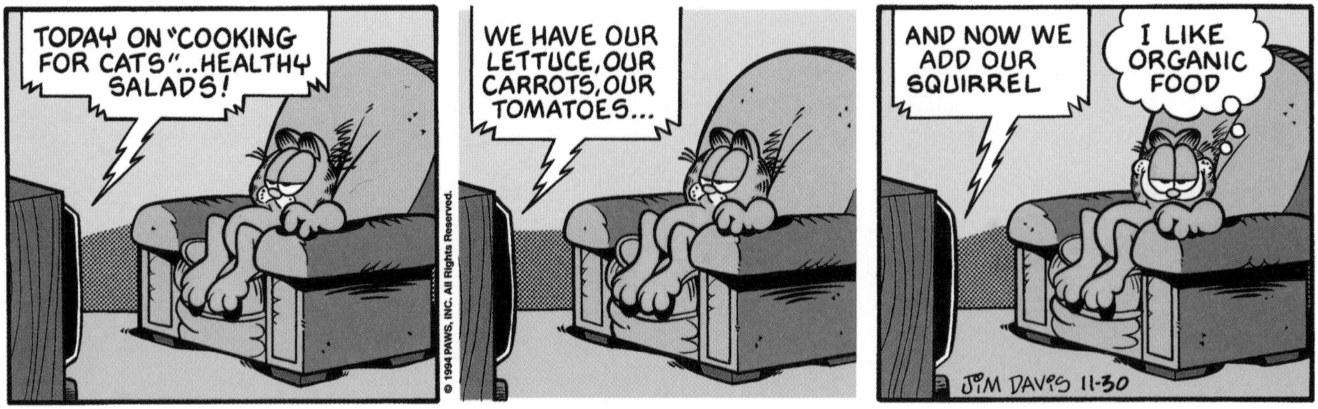
TODAY ON "COOKING FOR CATS"... HEALTHY SALADS!
© 1994 PAWS, INC. All Rights Reserved.
WE HAVE OUR LETTUCE, OUR CARROTS, OUR TOMATOES...
AND NOW WE ADD OUR SQUIRREL
I LIKE ORGANIC FOOD
JIM DAVIS 11-30

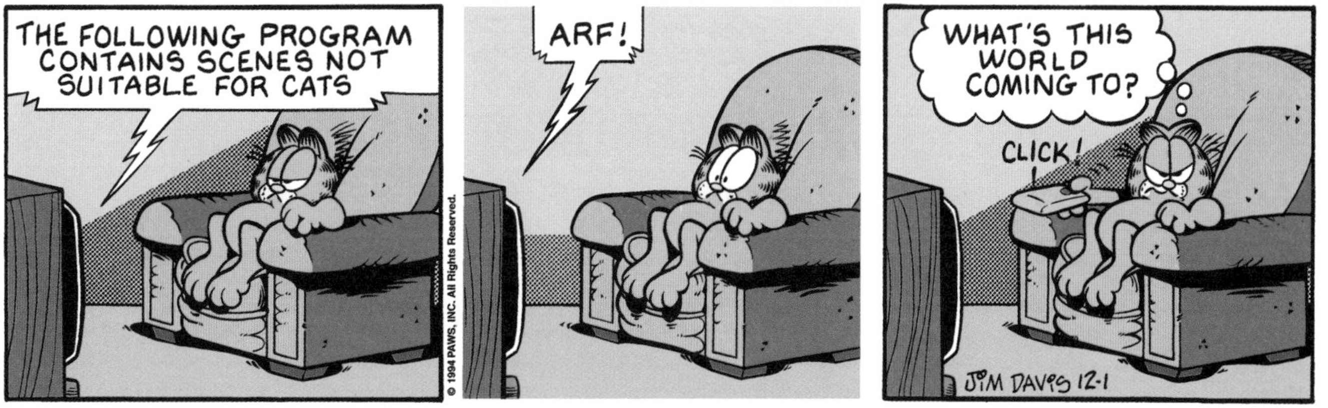
THE FOLLOWING PROGRAM CONTAINS SCENES NOT SUITABLE FOR CATS
© 1994 PAWS, INC. All Rights Reserved.
ARF!
WHAT'S THIS WORLD COMING TO?
CLICK!
JIM DAVIS 12-1

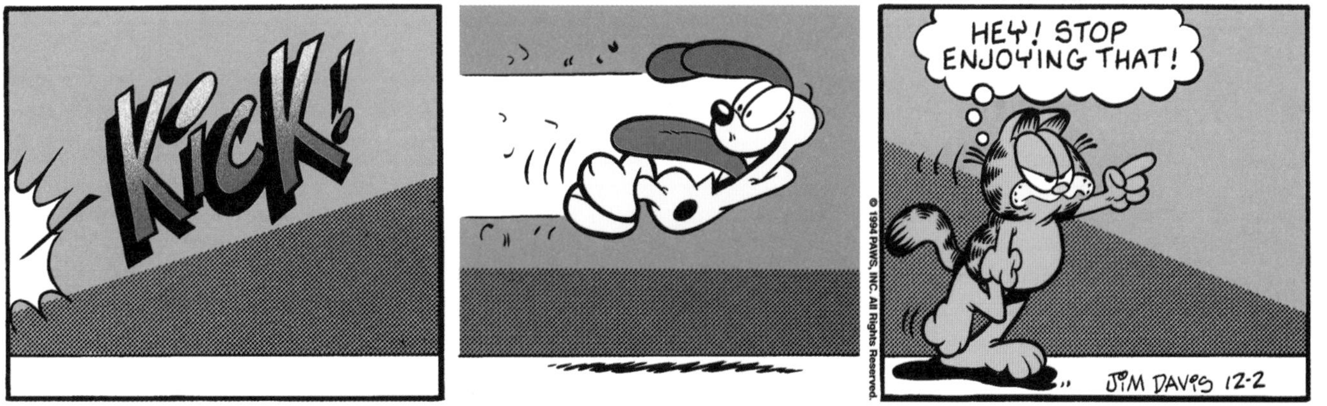
KICK!
© 1994 PAWS, INC. All Rights Reserved.
HEY! STOP ENJOYING THAT!
JIM DAVIS 12-2

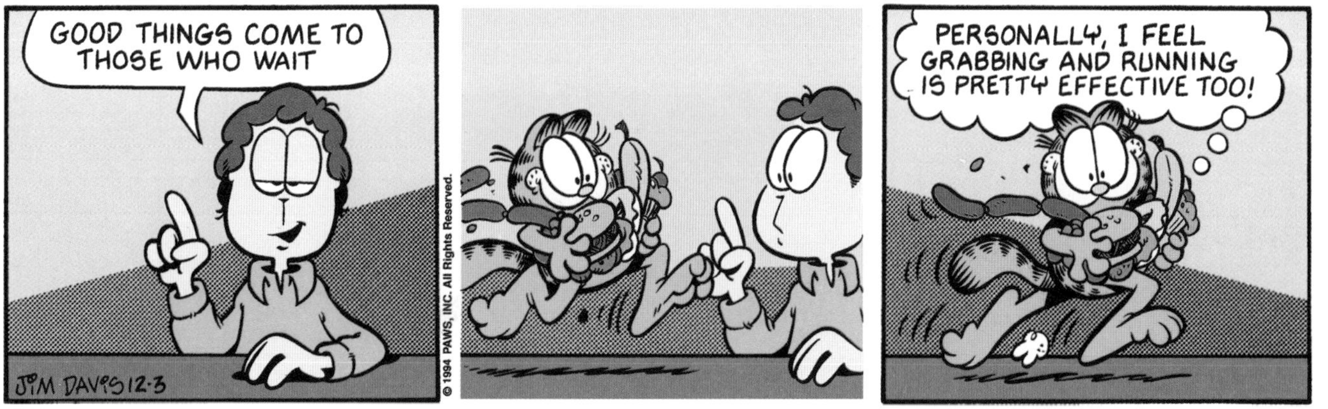
GOOD THINGS COME TO THOSE WHO WAIT
JIM DAVIS 12-3
© 1994 PAWS, INC. All Rights Reserved.
PERSONALLY, I FEEL GRABBING AND RUNNING IS PRETTY EFFECTIVE TOO!

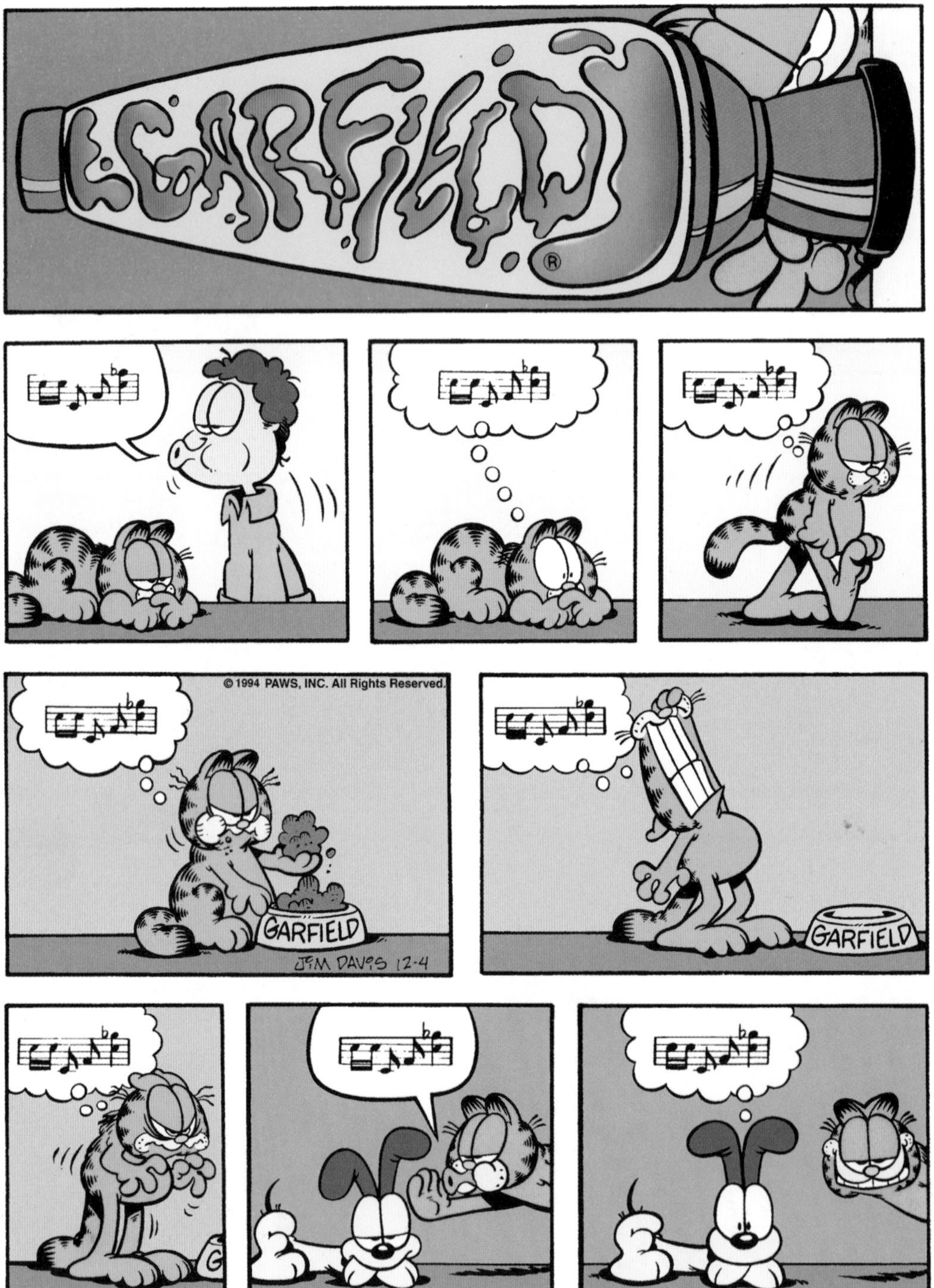
GARFIELD®
© 1994 PAWS, INC. All Rights Reserved.
GARFIELD
JIM DAVIS 12-4
GARFIELD

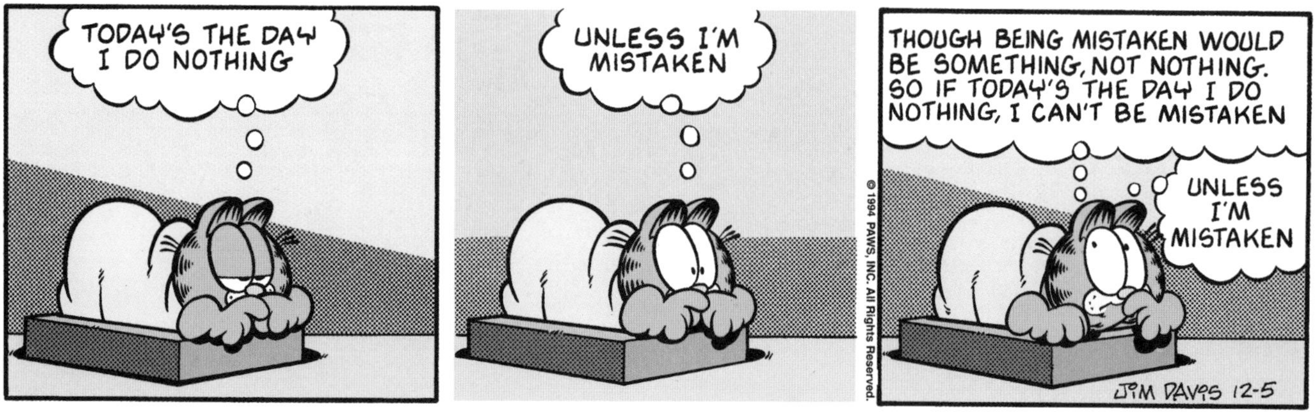
TODAY'S THE DAY I DO NOTHING
UNLESS I'M MISTAKEN
© 1994 PAWS, INC. All Rights Reserved.
THOUGH BEING MISTAKEN WOULD BE SOMETHING, NOT NOTHING. SO IF TODAY'S THE DAY I DO NOTHING, I CAN'T BE MISTAKEN
UNLESS I'M MISTAKEN
JIM DAVIS 12-5

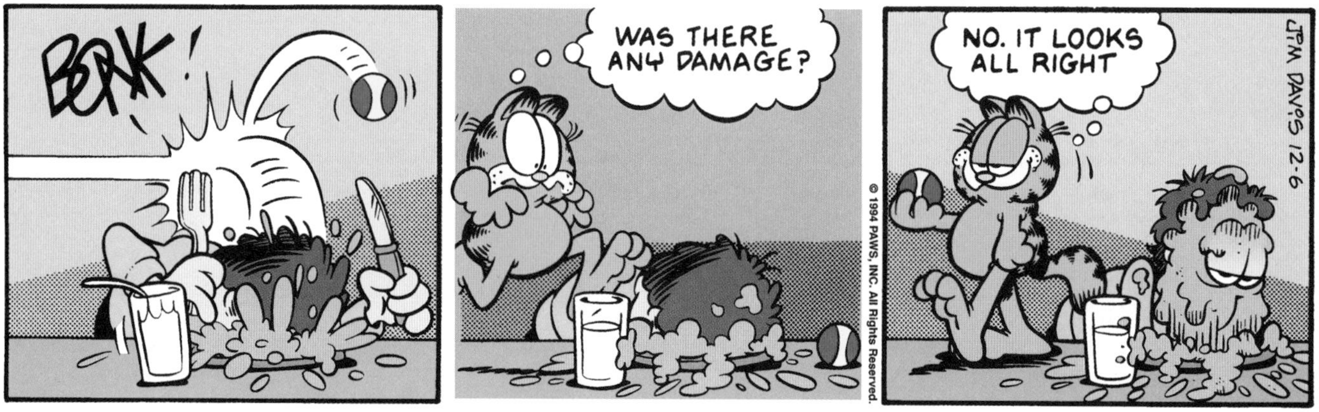
BONK!
WAS THERE ANY DAMAGE?
© 1994 PAWS, INC. All Rights Reserved.
NO. IT LOOKS ALL RIGHT
JIM DAVIS 12-6

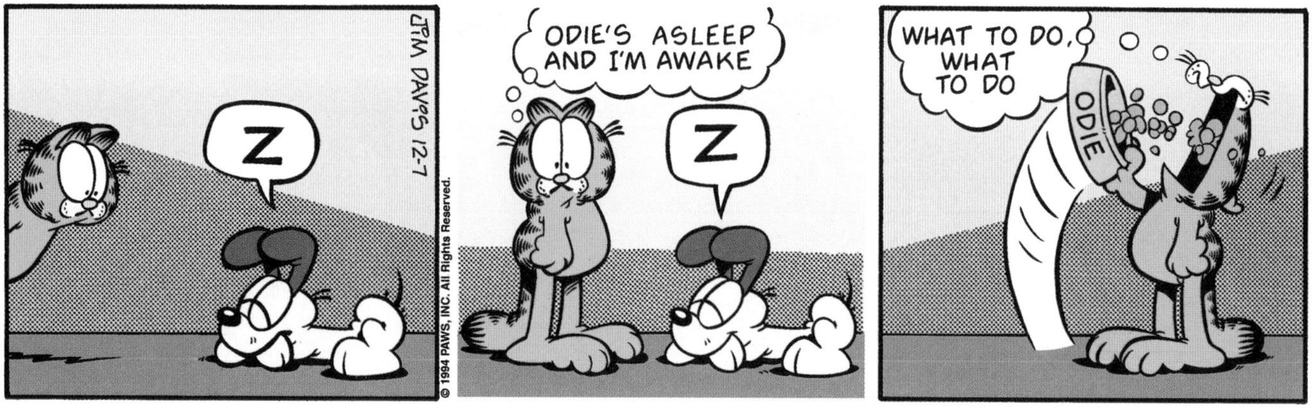
Z
JIM DAVIS 12-7
© 1994 PAWS, INC. All Rights Reserved.
ODIE'S ASLEEP AND I'M AWAKE
Z
WHAT TO DO, WHAT TO DO
ODIE

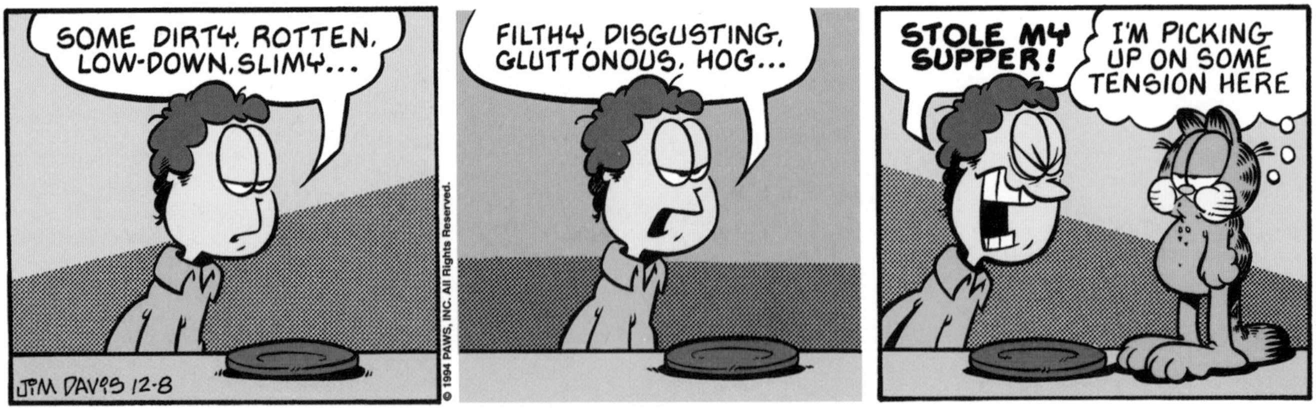
SOME DIRTY, ROTTEN, LOW-DOWN, SLIMY...
JIM DAVIS 12-8
© 1994 PAWS, INC. All Rights Reserved.
FILTHY, DISGUSTING, GLUTTONOUS, HOG...
STOLE MY SUPPER!
I'M PICKING UP ON SOME TENSION HERE

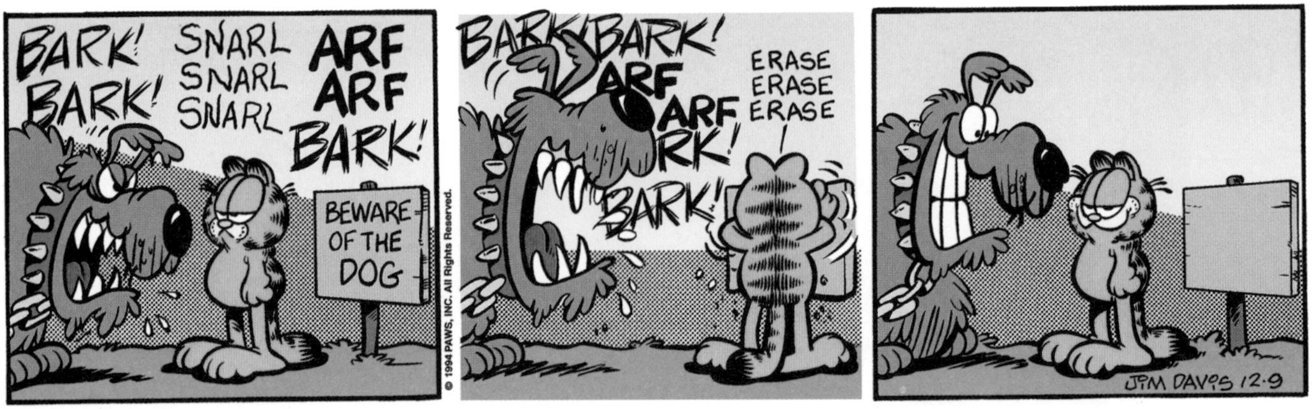
BARK! BARK!
SNARL SNARL SNARL
ARF ARF BARK!
BEWARE OF THE DOG
© 1994 PAWS, INC. All Rights Reserved.
BARK! BARK! ARF ARF BARK!
ERASE ERASE ERASE
JIM DAVIS 12-9

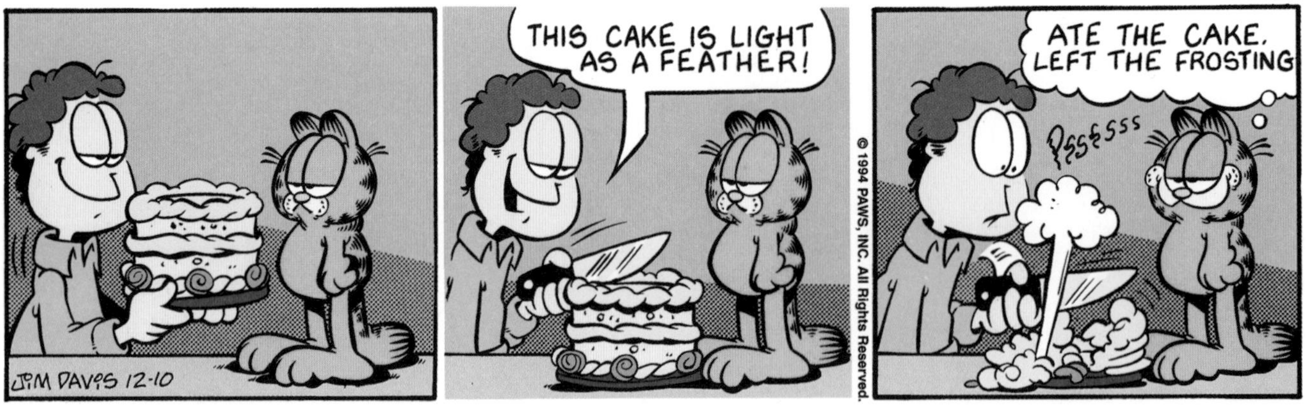
JIM DAVIS 12-10
THIS CAKE IS LIGHT AS A FEATHER!
© 1994 PAWS, INC. All Rights Reserved.
PSSSSSS
ATE THE CAKE. LEFT THE FROSTING

GARFIELD®
THE FIRST SNOWFLAKE!
JON! JON!
© 1994 PAWS, INC. All Rights Reserved.
WIPE WIPE

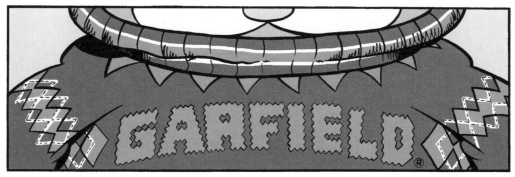

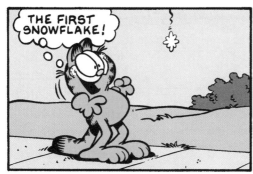

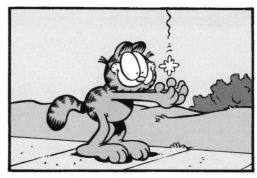

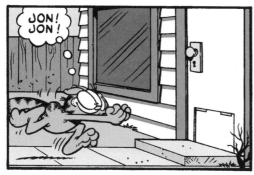

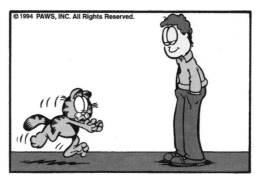

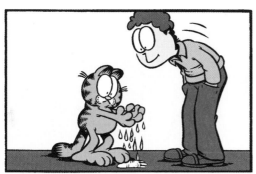

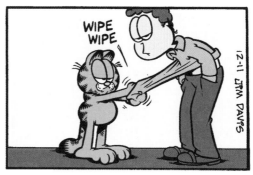

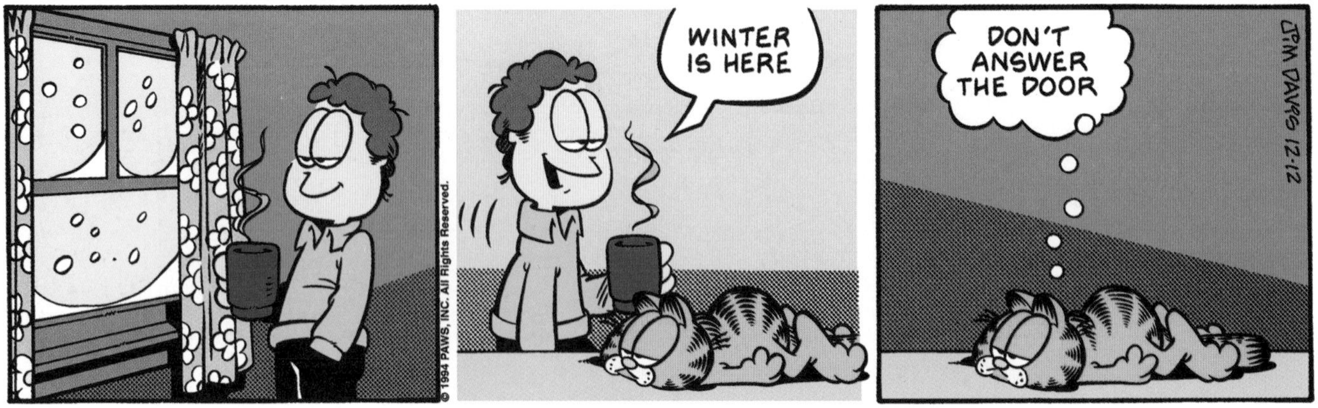
© 1994 PAWS, INC. All Rights Reserved.
WINTER IS HERE
DON'T ANSWER THE DOOR
JIM DAVIS 12-12

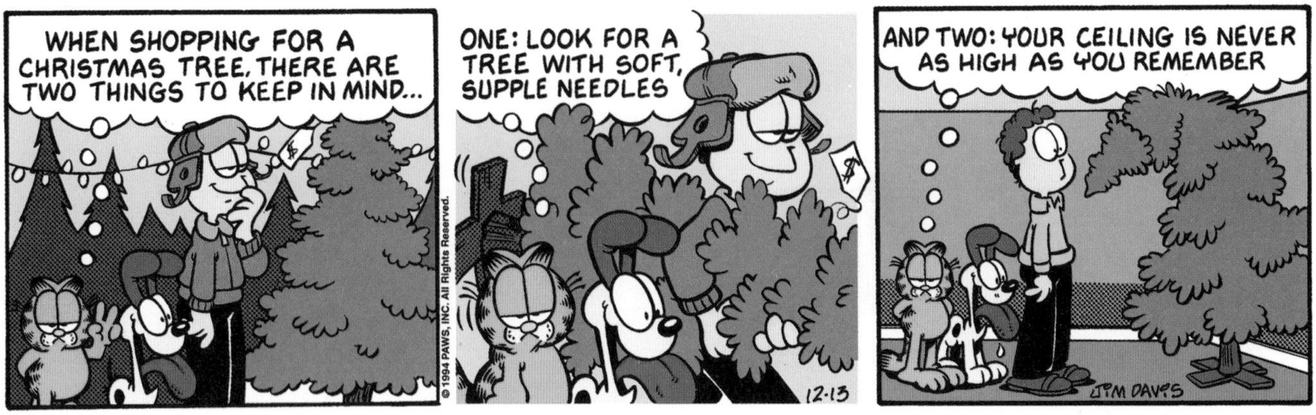
WHEN SHOPPING FOR A CHRISTMAS TREE, THERE ARE TWO THINGS TO KEEP IN MIND...
© 1994 PAWS, INC. All Rights Reserved.
ONE: LOOK FOR A TREE WITH SOFT, SUPPLE NEEDLES
12-13
AND TWO: YOUR CEILING IS NEVER AS HIGH AS YOU REMEMBER
JIM DAVIS

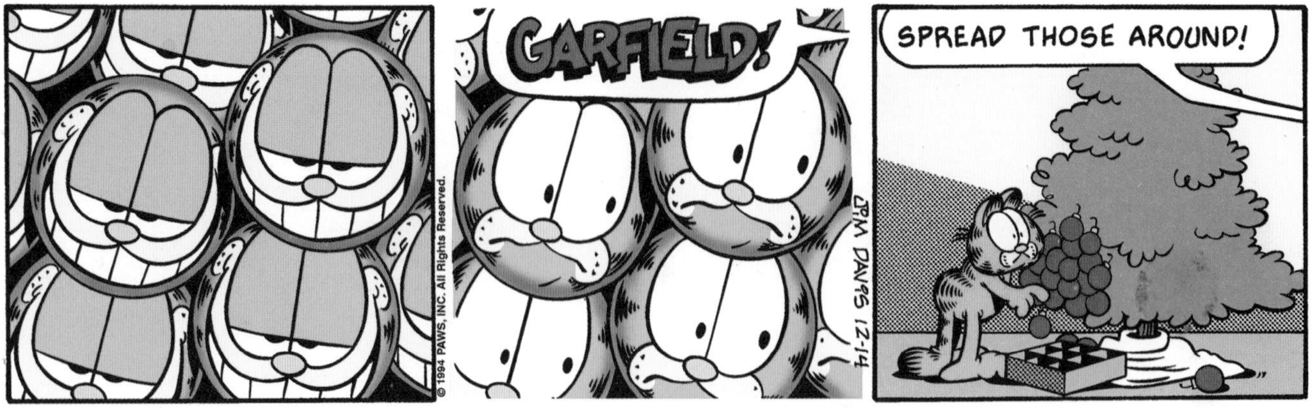
© 1994 PAWS, INC. All Rights Reserved.
GARFIELD!
JIM DAVIS 12-14
SPREAD THOSE AROUND!

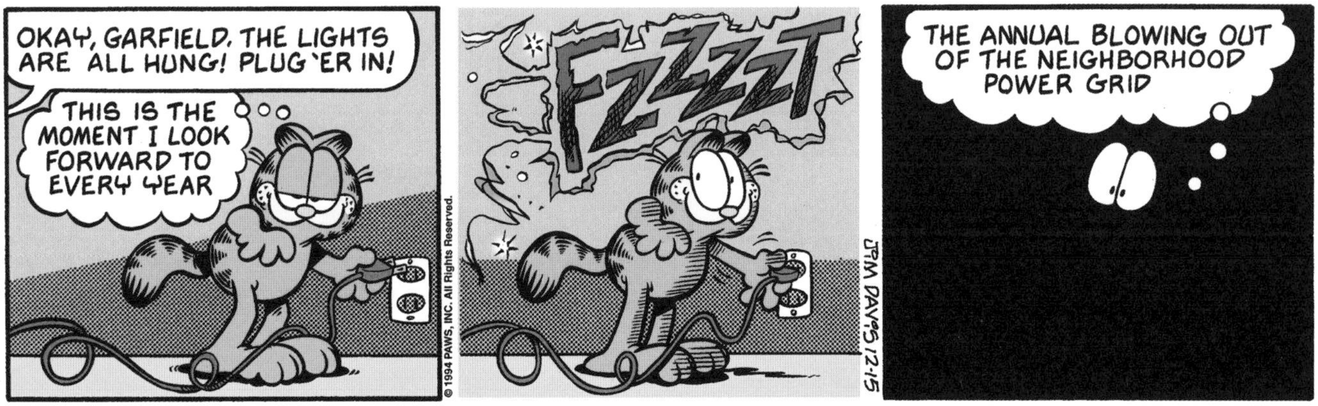
OKAY, GARFIELD. THE LIGHTS ARE ALL HUNG! PLUG 'ER IN!
THIS IS THE MOMENT I LOOK FORWARD TO EVERY YEAR
© 1994 PAWS, INC. All Rights Reserved.
FZZZZT
JIM DAVIS 12-15
THE ANNUAL BLOWING OUT OF THE NEIGHBORHOOD POWER GRID

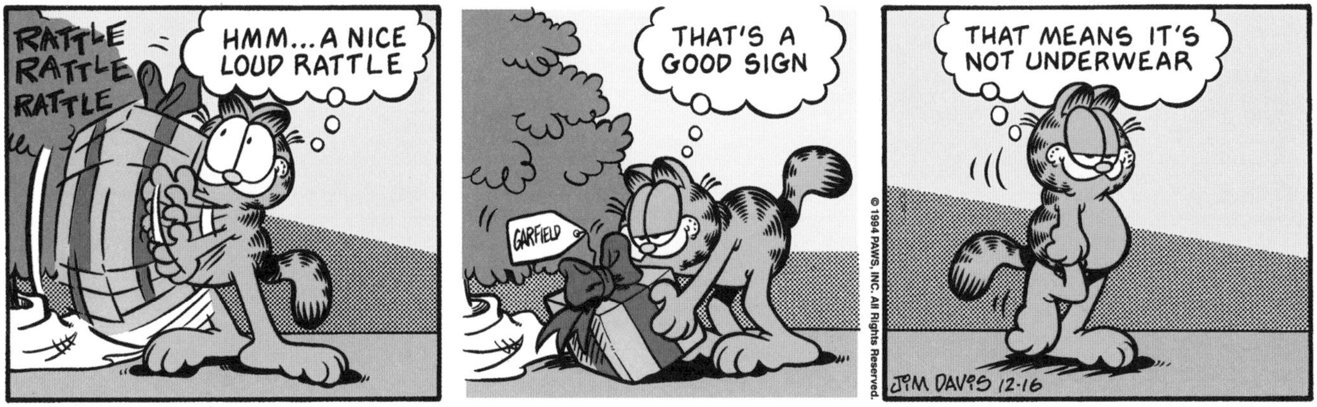
RATTLE RATTLE RATTLE
HMM... A NICE LOUD RATTLE
THAT'S A GOOD SIGN
GARFIELD
© 1994 PAWS, INC. All Rights Reserved.
THAT MEANS IT'S NOT UNDERWEAR
JIM DAVIS 12-16

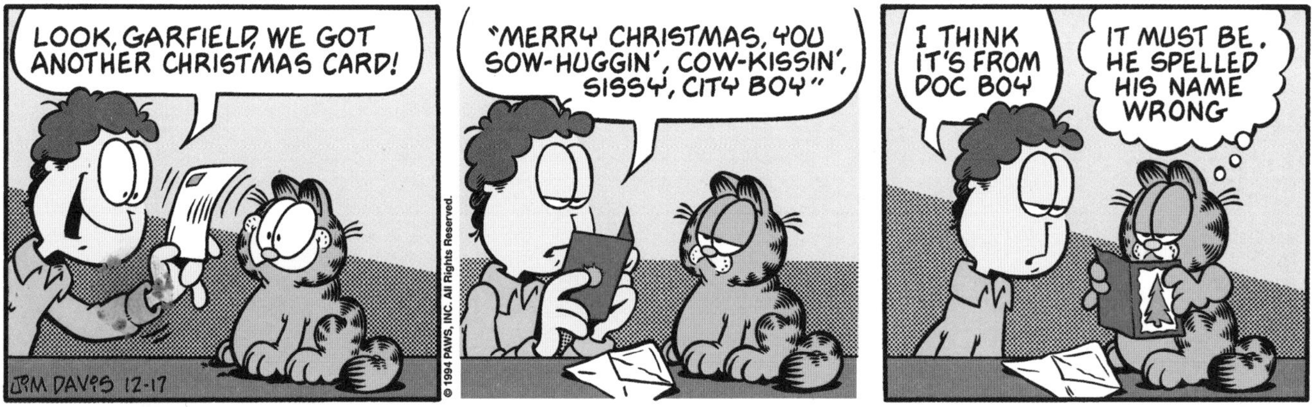
LOOK, GARFIELD, WE GOT ANOTHER CHRISTMAS CARD!
JIM DAVIS 12-17
© 1994 PAWS, INC. All Rights Reserved.
"MERRY CHRISTMAS, YOU SOW-HUGGIN', COW-KISSIN', SISSY, CITY BOY"
I THINK IT'S FROM DOC BOY
IT MUST BE. HE SPELLED HIS NAME WRONG

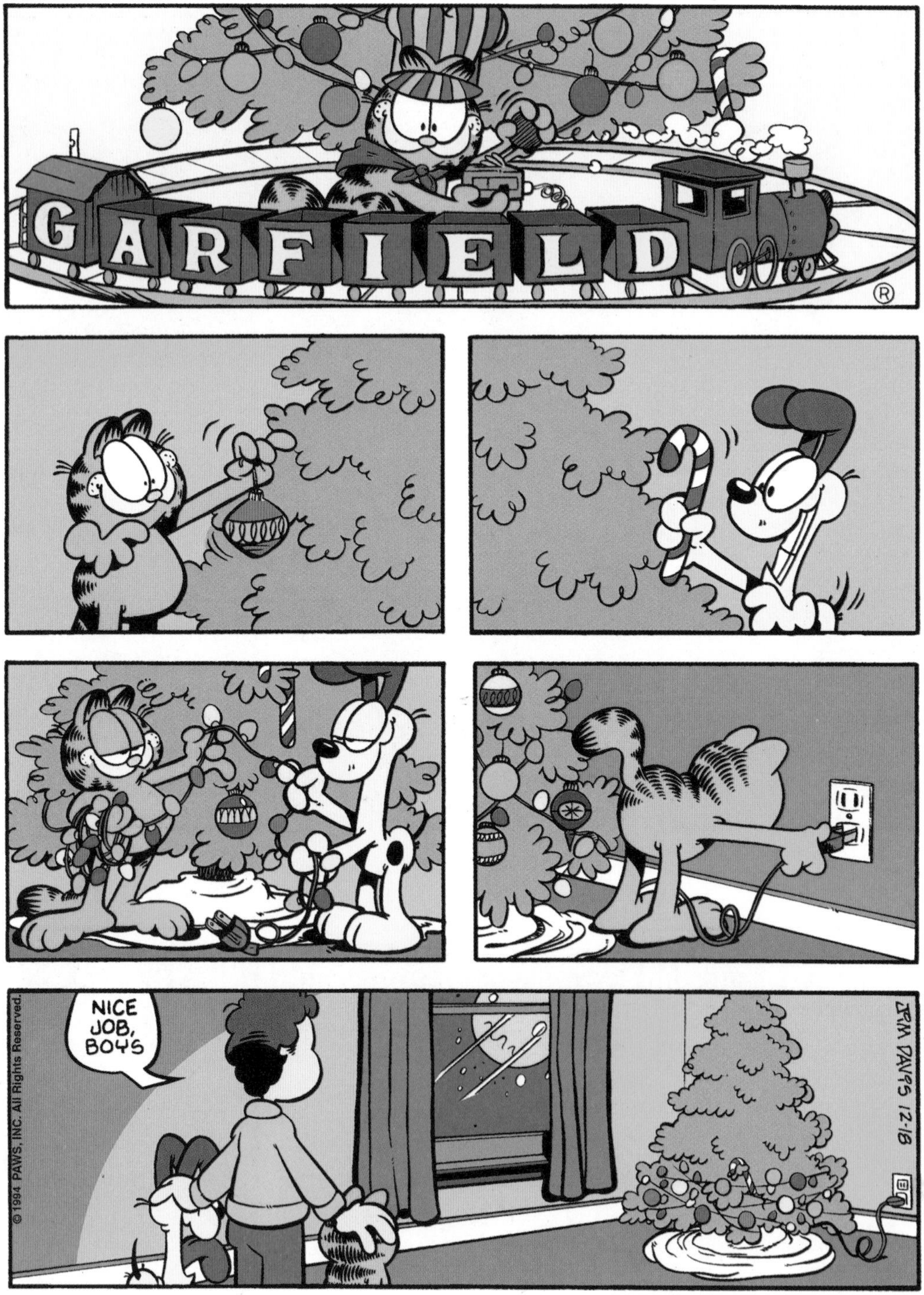
GARFIELD
NICE JOB, BOYS
JPM DAVIS 12-18
©1994 PAWS, INC. All Rights Reserved.

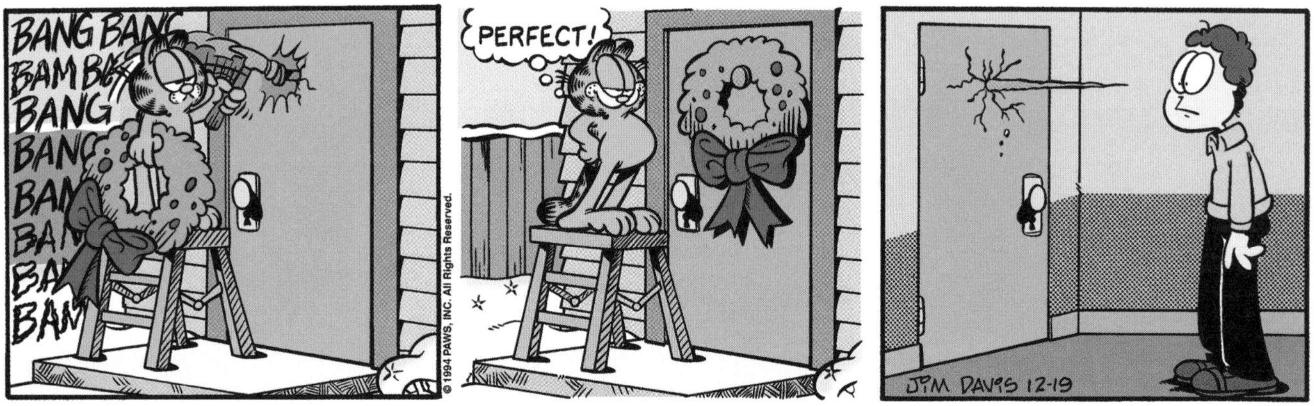

BANG
PERFECT!
© 1994 PAWS, INC. All Rights Reserved.
JIM DAVIS 12-19

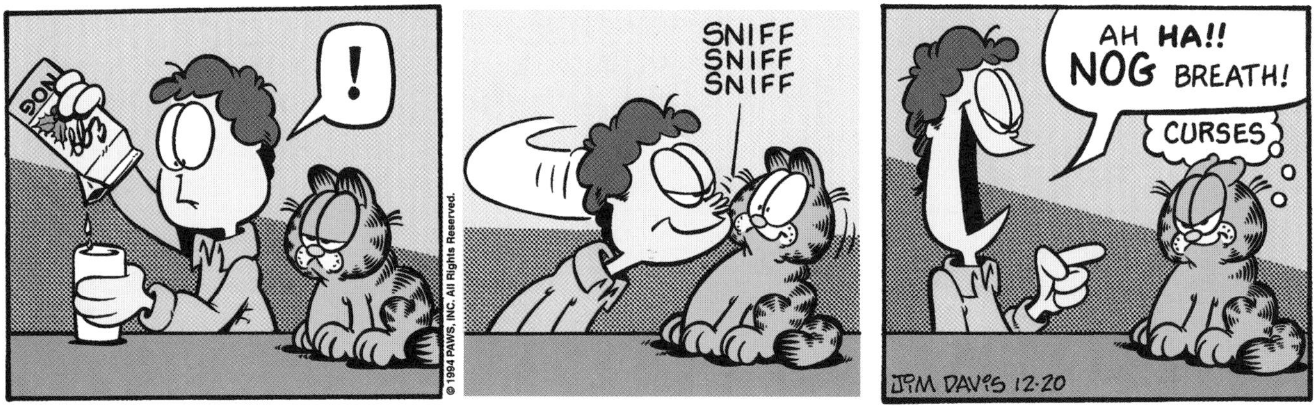

!
SNIFF SNIFF SNIFF
AH **HA!!** **NOG** BREATH!
CURSES
© 1994 PAWS, INC. All Rights Reserved.
JIM DAVIS 12-20

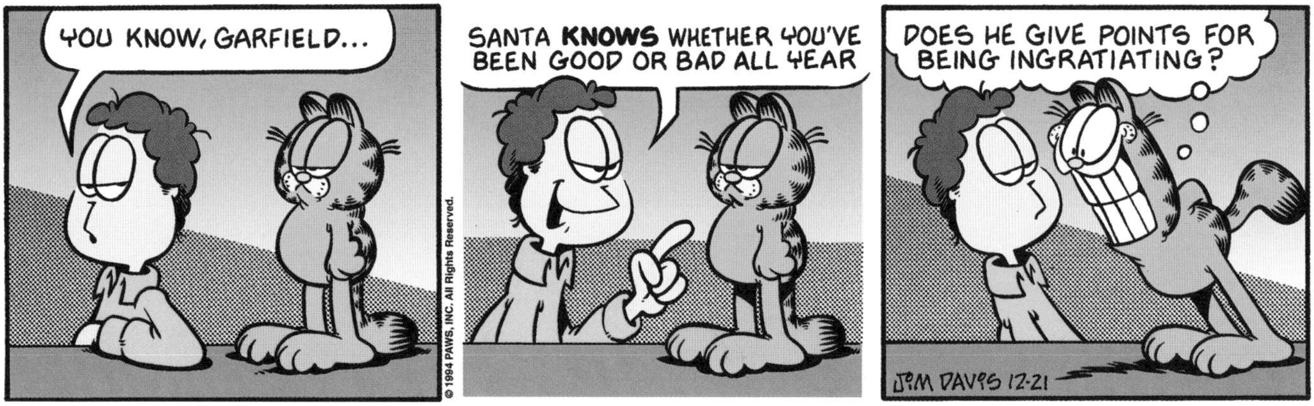

YOU KNOW, GARFIELD...
SANTA **KNOWS** WHETHER YOU'VE BEEN GOOD OR BAD ALL YEAR
DOES HE GIVE POINTS FOR BEING INGRATIATING?
© 1994 PAWS, INC. All Rights Reserved.
JIM DAVIS 12-21

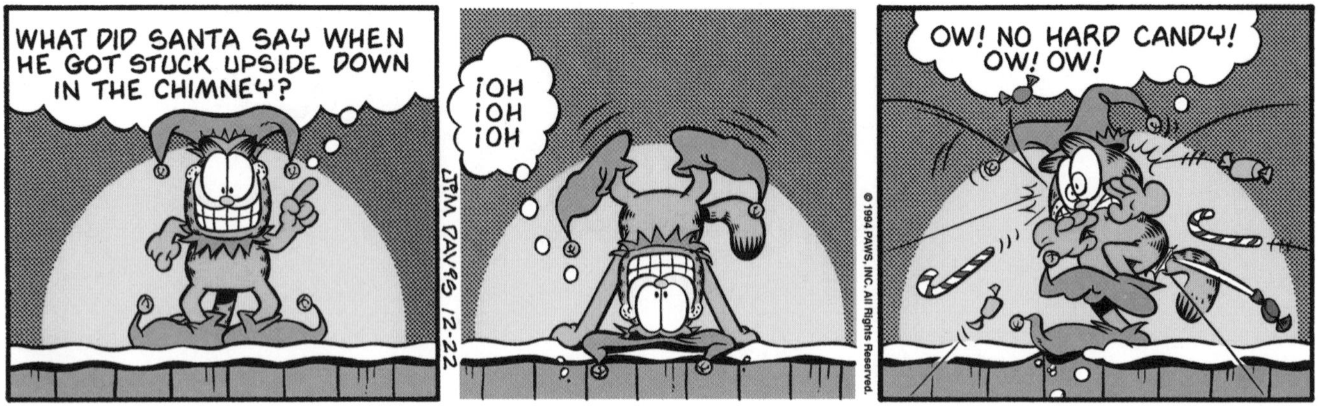
WHAT DID SANTA SAY WHEN HE GOT STUCK UPSIDE DOWN IN THE CHIMNEY?
¡OH
¡OH
¡OH
JIM DAVIS 12-22
© 1994 PAWS, INC. All Rights Reserved.
OW! NO HARD CANDY! OW! OW!

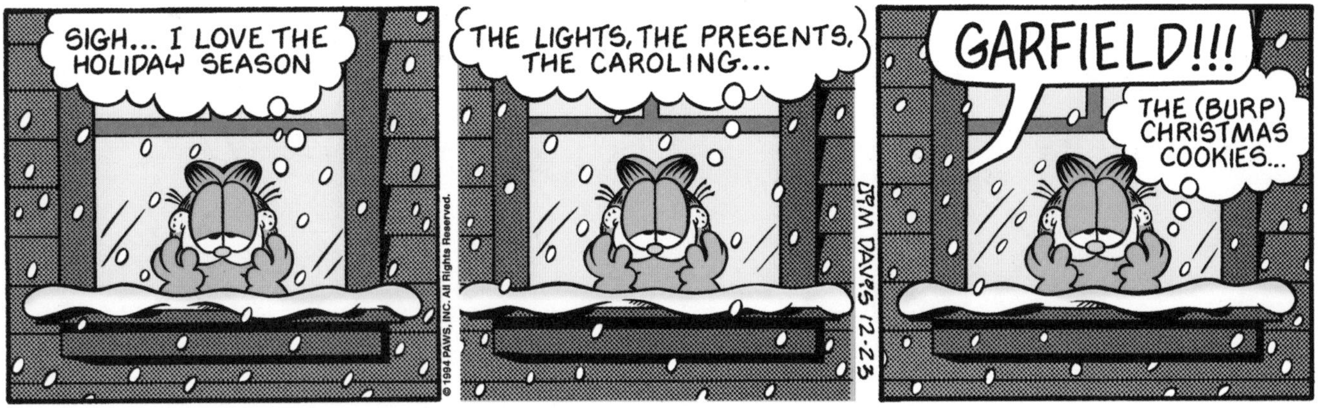
SIGH... I LOVE THE HOLIDAY SEASON
© 1994 PAWS, INC. All Rights Reserved.
THE LIGHTS, THE PRESENTS, THE CAROLING...
JIM DAVIS 12-23
GARFIELD!!!
THE (BURP) CHRISTMAS COOKIES...

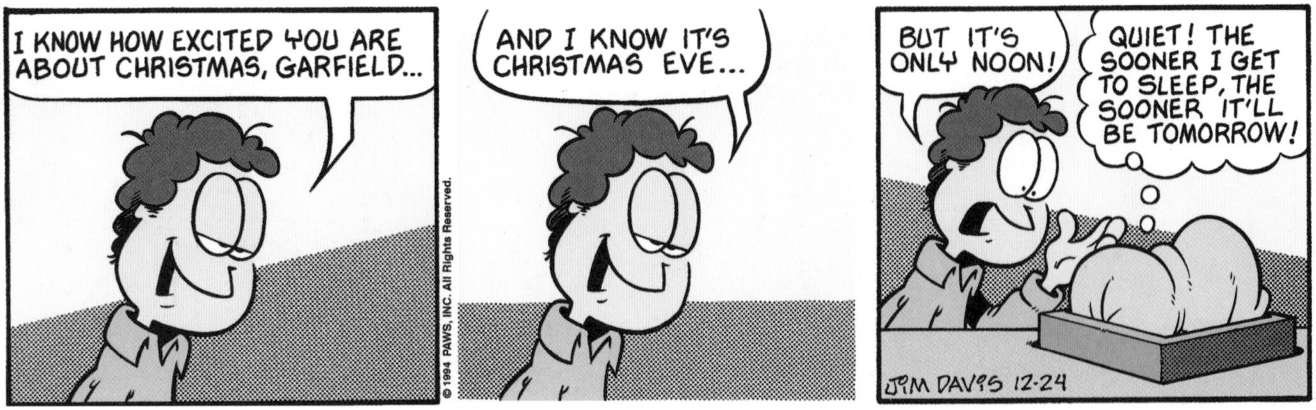
I KNOW HOW EXCITED YOU ARE ABOUT CHRISTMAS, GARFIELD...
© 1994 PAWS, INC. All Rights Reserved.
AND I KNOW IT'S CHRISTMAS EVE...
BUT IT'S ONLY NOON!
QUIET! THE SOONER I GET TO SLEEP, THE SOONER IT'LL BE TOMORROW!
JIM DAVIS 12-24

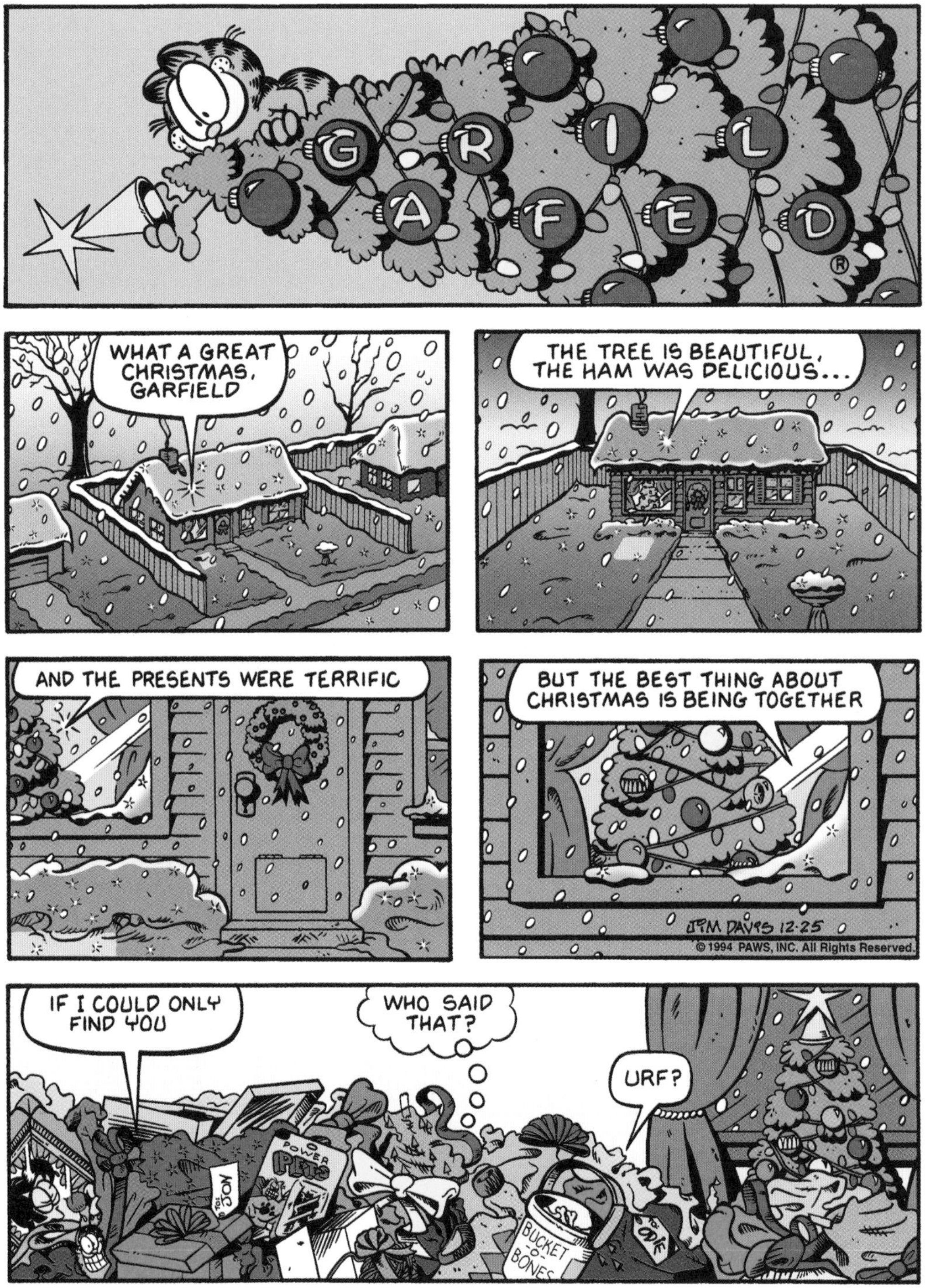
GARFIELD®
WHAT A GREAT CHRISTMAS, GARFIELD
THE TREE IS BEAUTIFUL, THE HAM WAS DELICIOUS...
AND THE PRESENTS WERE TERRIFIC
BUT THE BEST THING ABOUT CHRISTMAS IS BEING TOGETHER
JIM DAVIS 12-25
© 1994 PAWS, INC. All Rights Reserved.
IF I COULD ONLY FIND YOU
WHO SAID THAT?
URF?
TO: JON
POWER PETS
BUCKET -O- BONES
TO: ODIE

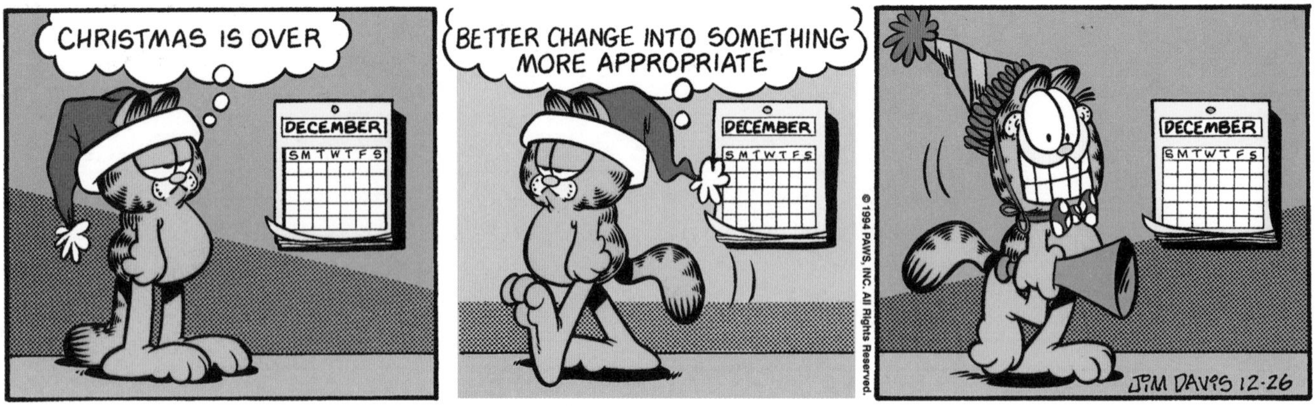
CHRISTMAS IS OVER
DECEMBER
S M T W T F S
BETTER CHANGE INTO SOMETHING MORE APPROPRIATE
DECEMBER
S M T W T F S
© 1994 PAWS, INC. All Rights Reserved.
DECEMBER
S M T W T F S
JIM DAVIS 12-26

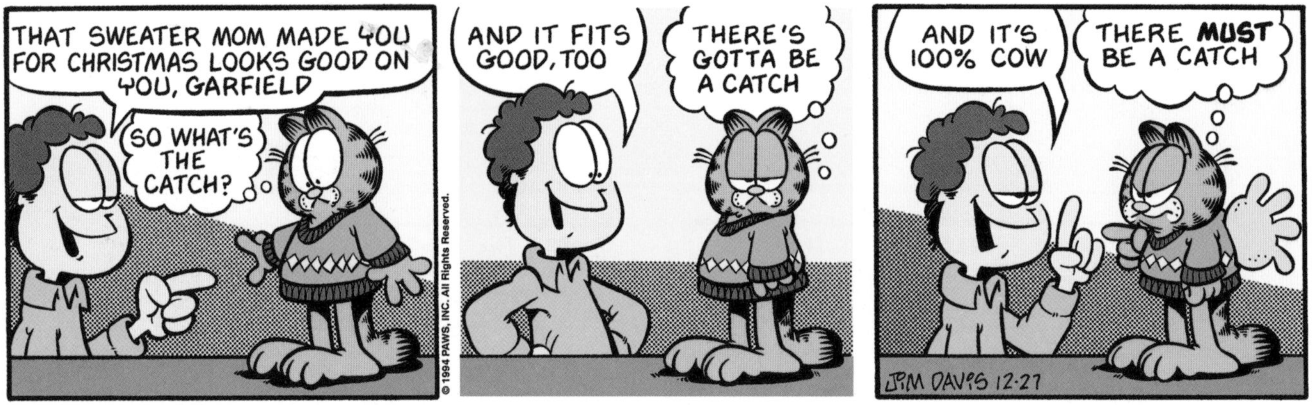
THAT SWEATER MOM MADE YOU FOR CHRISTMAS LOOKS GOOD ON YOU, GARFIELD
SO WHAT'S THE CATCH?
© 1994 PAWS, INC. All Rights Reserved.
AND IT FITS GOOD, TOO
THERE'S GOTTA BE A CATCH
AND IT'S 100% COW
THERE **MUST** BE A CATCH
JIM DAVIS 12-27

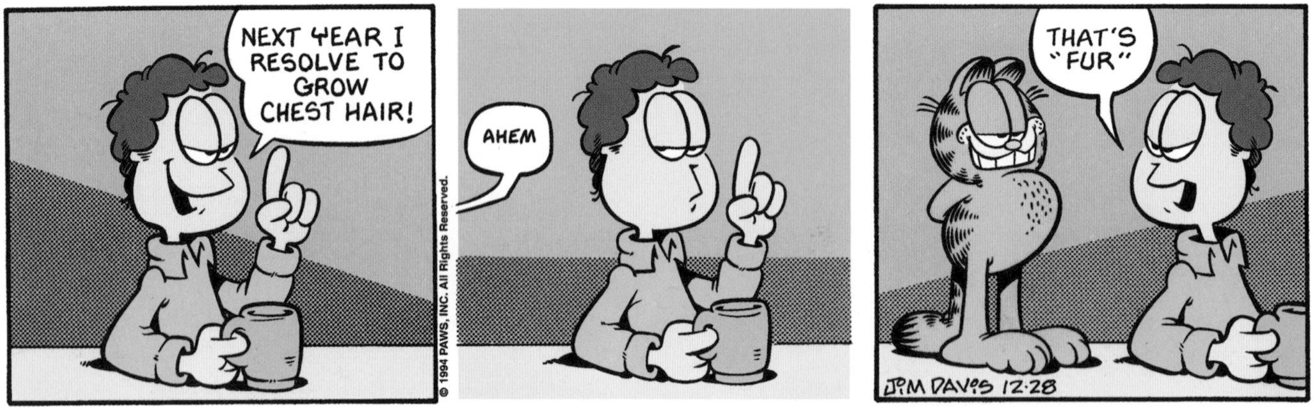
NEXT YEAR I RESOLVE TO GROW CHEST HAIR!
© 1994 PAWS, INC. All Rights Reserved.
AHEM
THAT'S "FUR"
JIM DAVIS 12-28

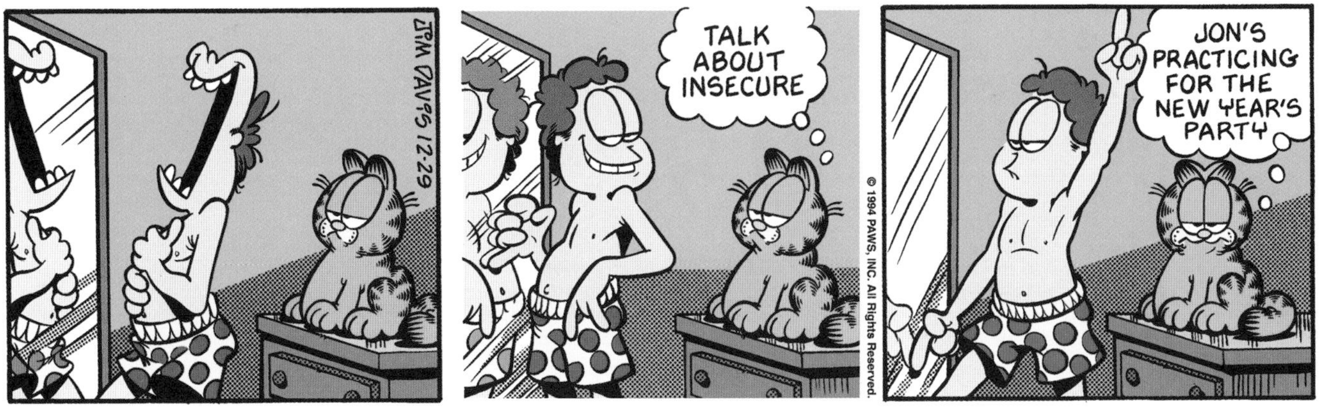
JIM DAVIS 12-29
TALK ABOUT INSECURE
© 1994 PAWS, INC. All Rights Reserved.
JON'S PRACTICING FOR THE NEW YEAR'S PARTY

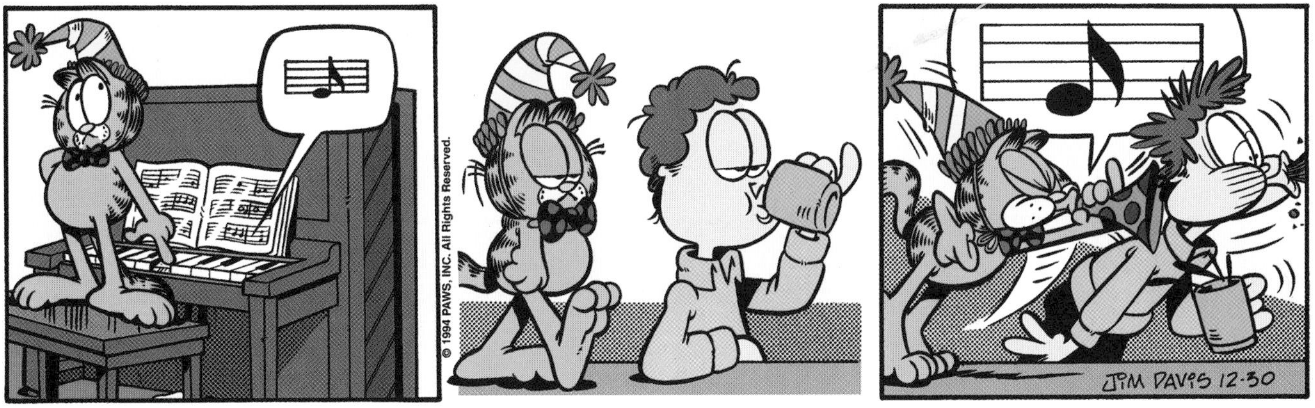
© 1994 PAWS, INC. All Rights Reserved.
JIM DAVIS 12-30

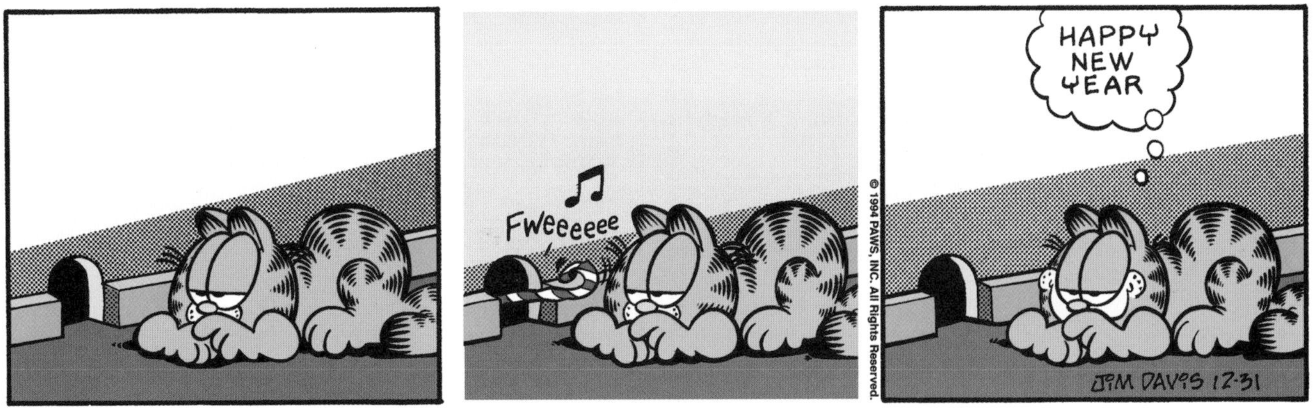
Fweeeeee
© 1994 PAWS, INC. All Rights Reserved.
HAPPY NEW YEAR
JIM DAVIS 12-31

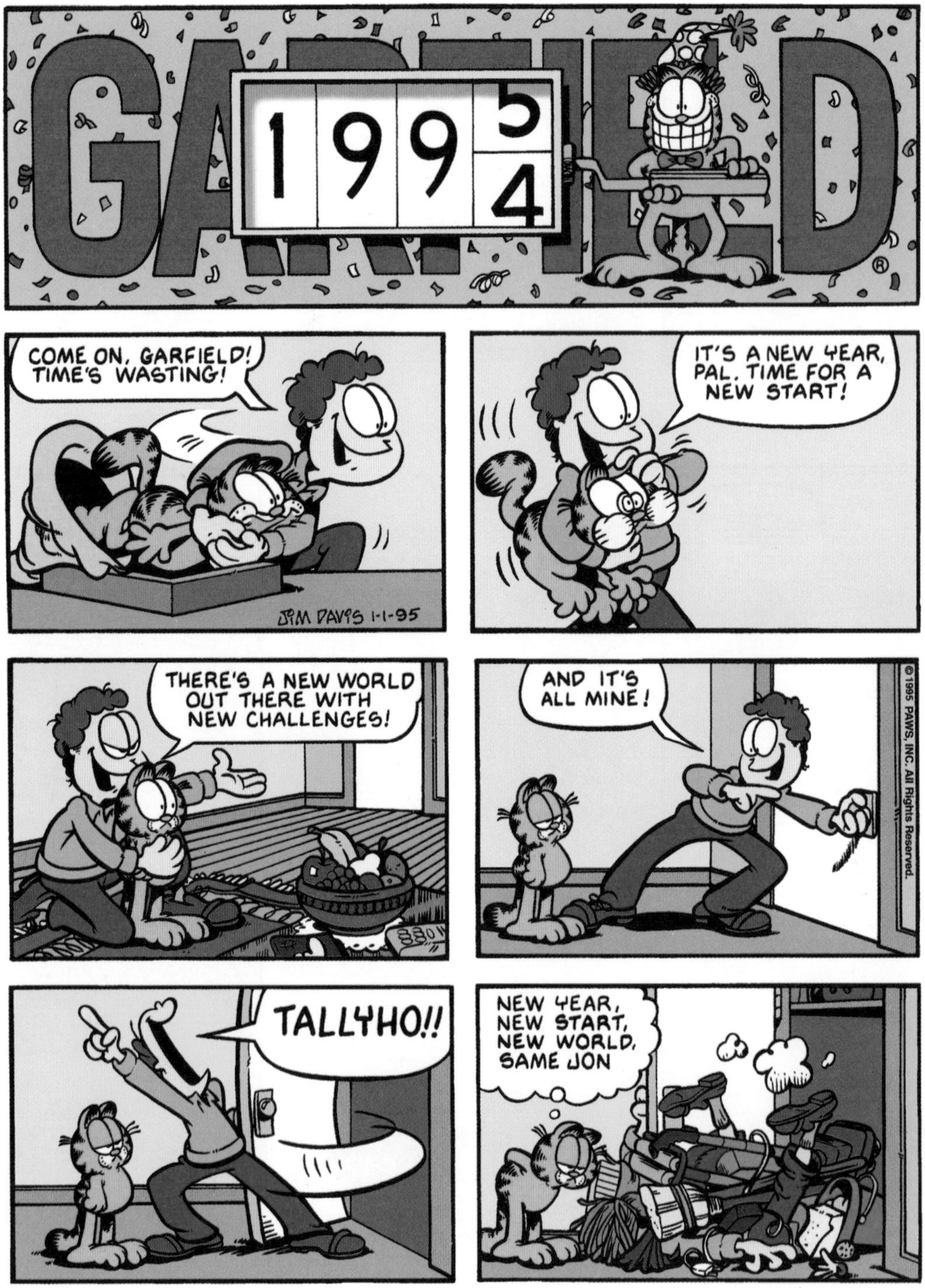
GARFIELD
1995
1994
COME ON, GARFIELD! TIME'S WASTING!
JIM DAVIS 1-1-95
IT'S A NEW YEAR, PAL. TIME FOR A NEW START!
THERE'S A NEW WORLD OUT THERE WITH NEW CHALLENGES!
AND IT'S ALL MINE!
© 1995 PAWS, INC. All Rights Reserved.
TALLYHO!!
NEW YEAR, NEW START, NEW WORLD, SAME JON

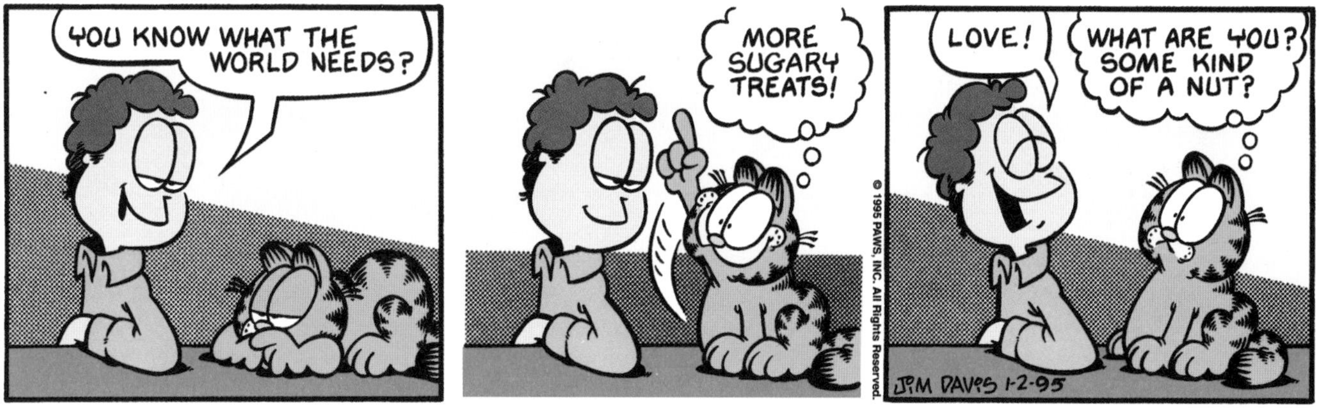
YOU KNOW WHAT THE WORLD NEEDS?
MORE SUGARY TREATS!
© 1995 PAWS, INC. All Rights Reserved.
LOVE!
WHAT ARE YOU? SOME KIND OF A NUT?
JIM DAVIS 1-2-95

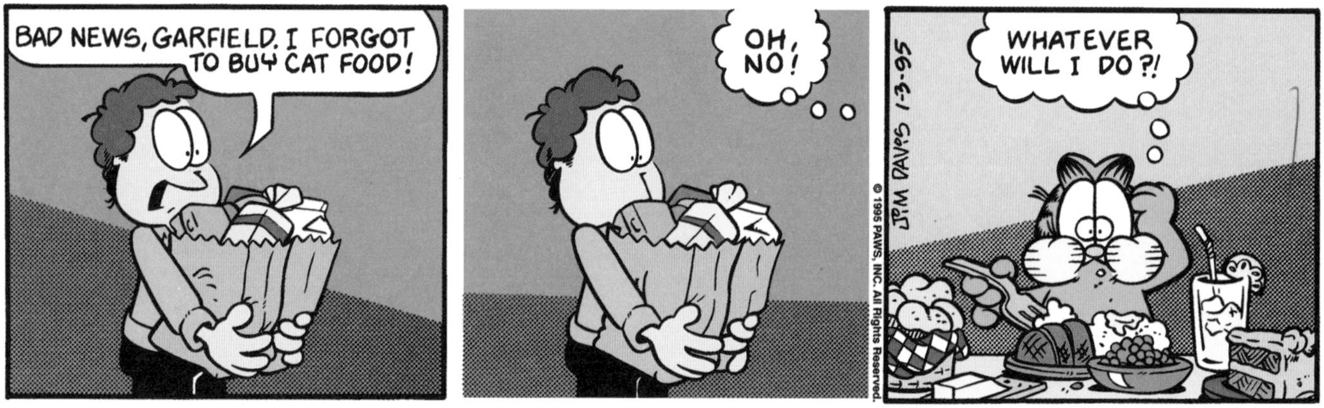
BAD NEWS, GARFIELD. I FORGOT TO BUY CAT FOOD!
OH, NO!
© 1995 PAWS, INC. All Rights Reserved.
JIM DAVIS 1-3-95
WHATEVER WILL I DO?!

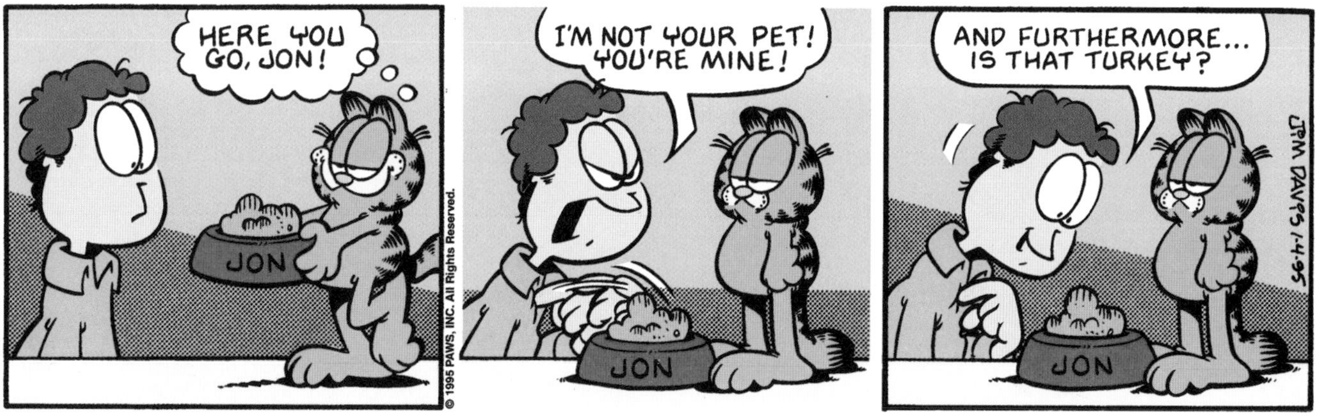
HERE YOU GO, JON!
JON
© 1995 PAWS, INC. All Rights Reserved.
I'M NOT YOUR PET! YOU'RE MINE!
JON
AND FURTHERMORE... IS THAT TURKEY?
JON
JIM DAVIS 1-4-95

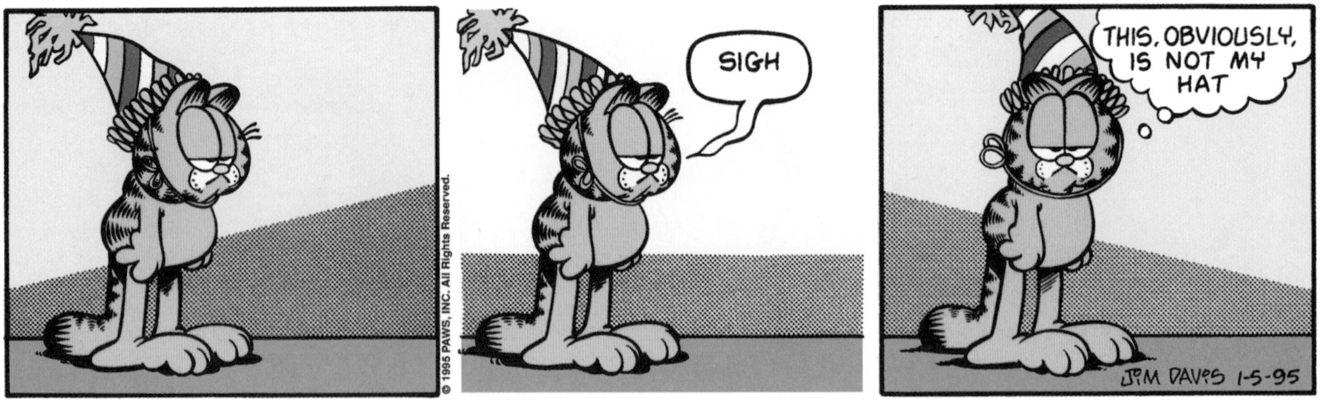
SIGH
THIS, OBVIOUSLY, IS NOT MY HAT

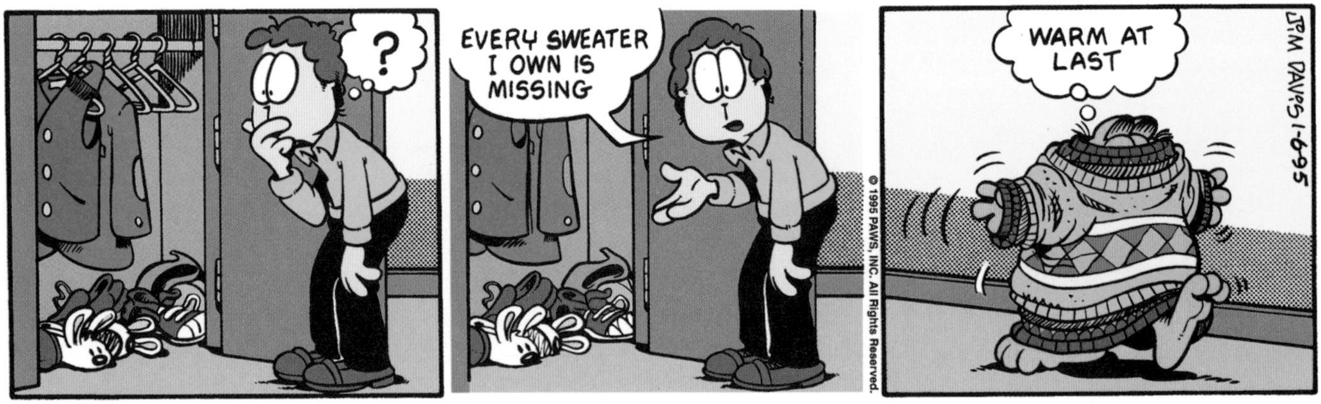
?
EVERY SWEATER I OWN IS MISSING
WARM AT LAST

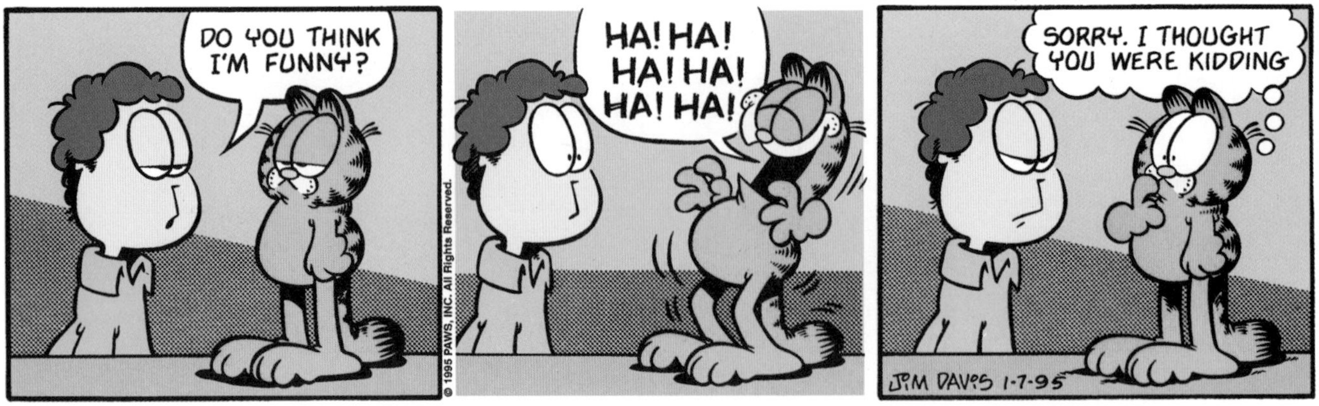
DO YOU THINK I'M FUNNY?
HA! HA! HA! HA! HA! HA!
SORRY. I THOUGHT YOU WERE KIDDING

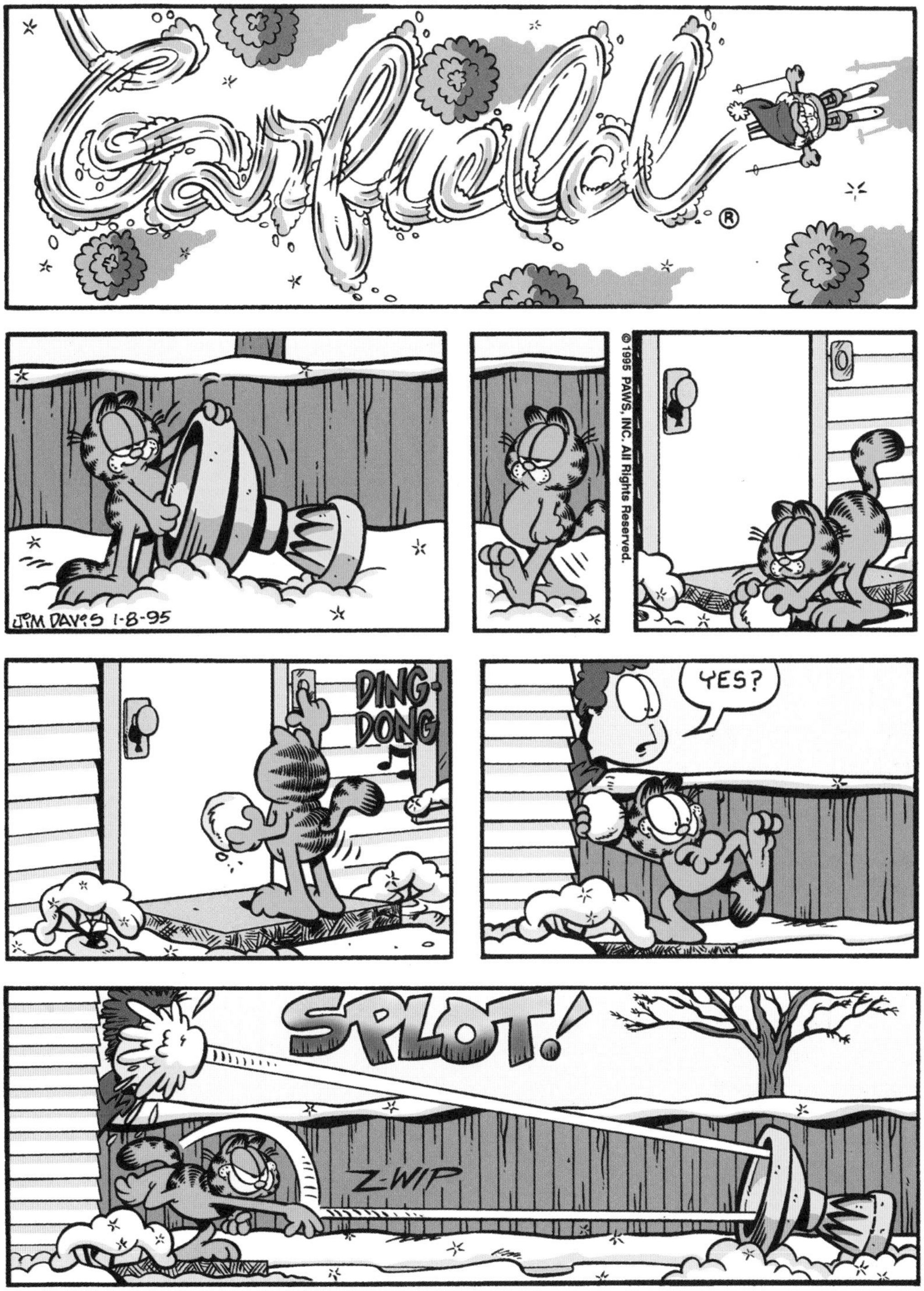
Garfield®
JIM DAVIS 1-8-95
© 1995 PAWS, INC. All Rights Reserved.
DING-DONG
YES?
SPLOT!
Z-WIP

FOUND A SPIDER IN THE FREEZER
© 1995 PAWS, INC. All Rights Reserved.
JIM DAVIS 1-9

SPIDER RACE!
© 1995 PAWS, INC. All Rights Reserved.
WHAP!
THE WINNER!
JIM DAVIS 1-10

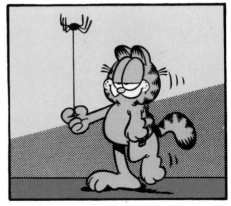

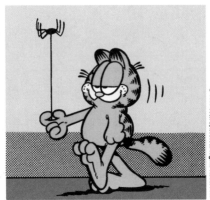

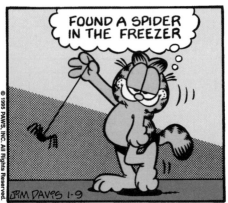

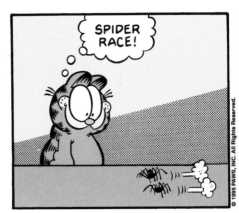

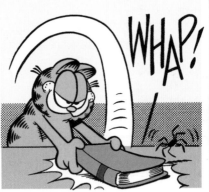

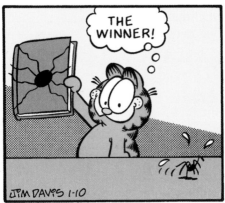

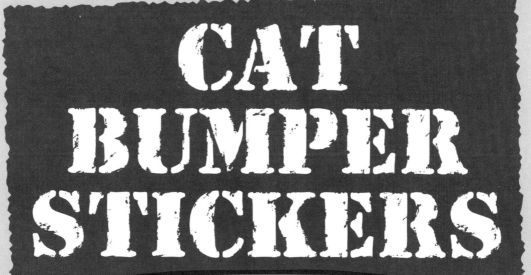

CAT BUMPER STICKERS

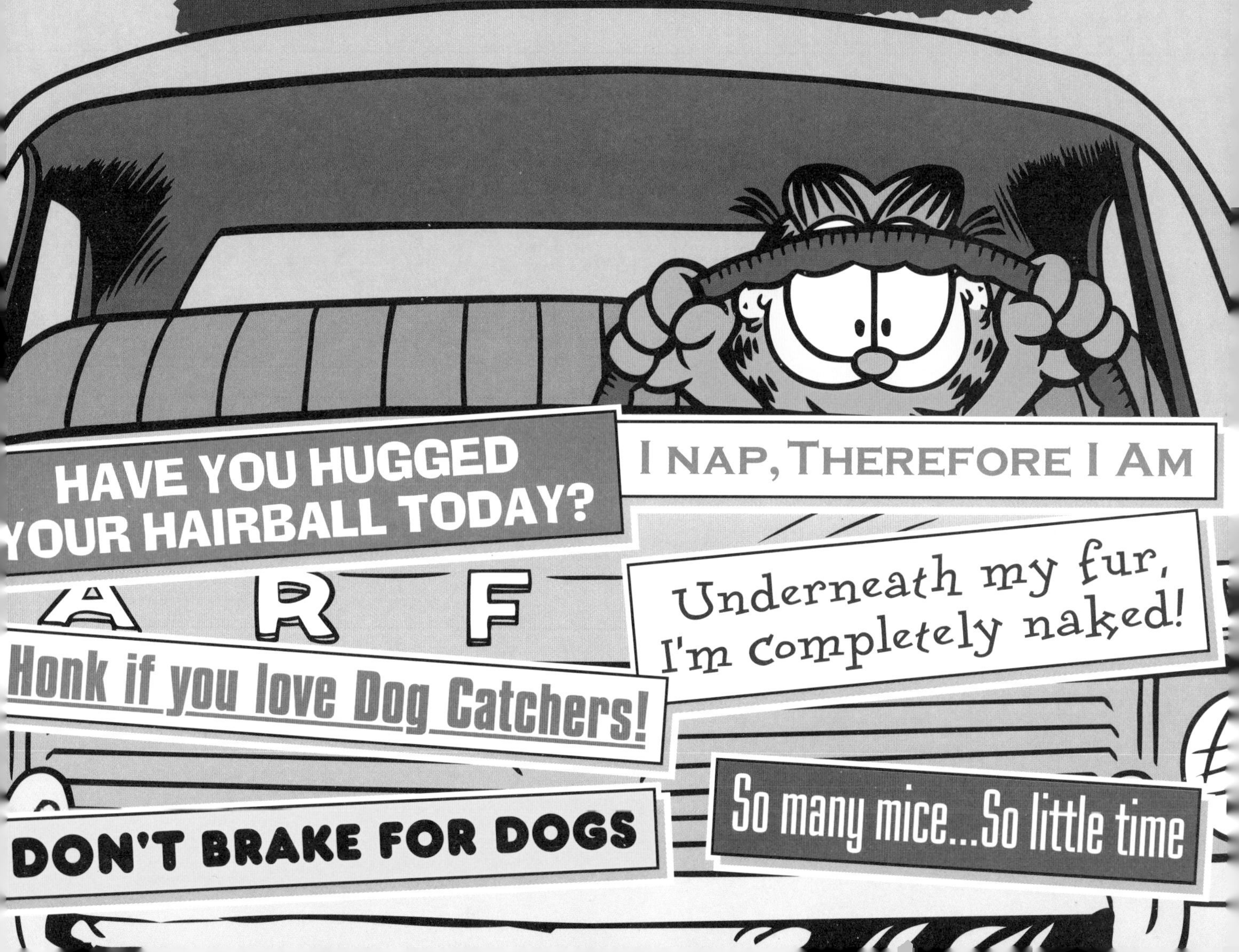
HAVE YOU HUGGED YOUR HAIRBALL TODAY?
I NAP, THEREFORE I AM
A R F
Underneath my fur, I'm completely naked!
Honk if you love Dog Catchers!
So many mice...So little time
DON'T BRAKE FOR DOGS

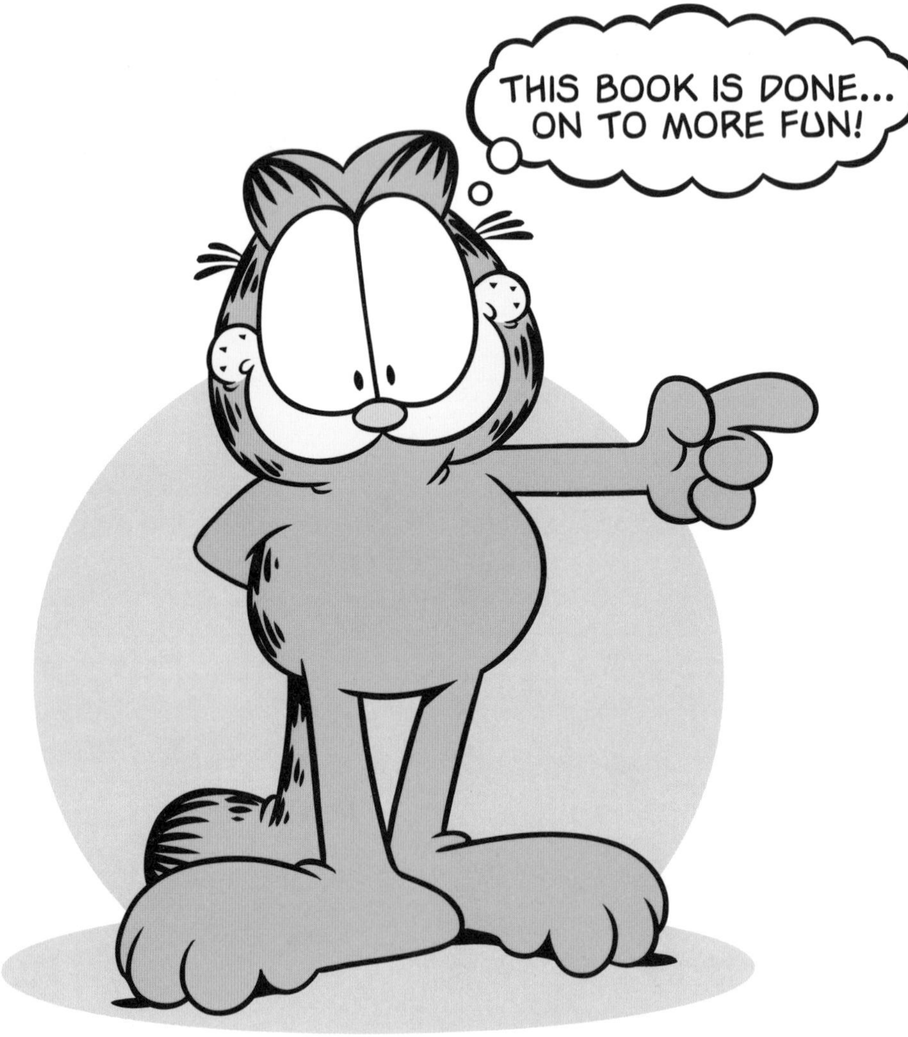
THIS BOOK IS DONE...
ON TO MORE FUN!

Garfield
tons of fun

BY JIM DAVIS

Ballantine Books • New York

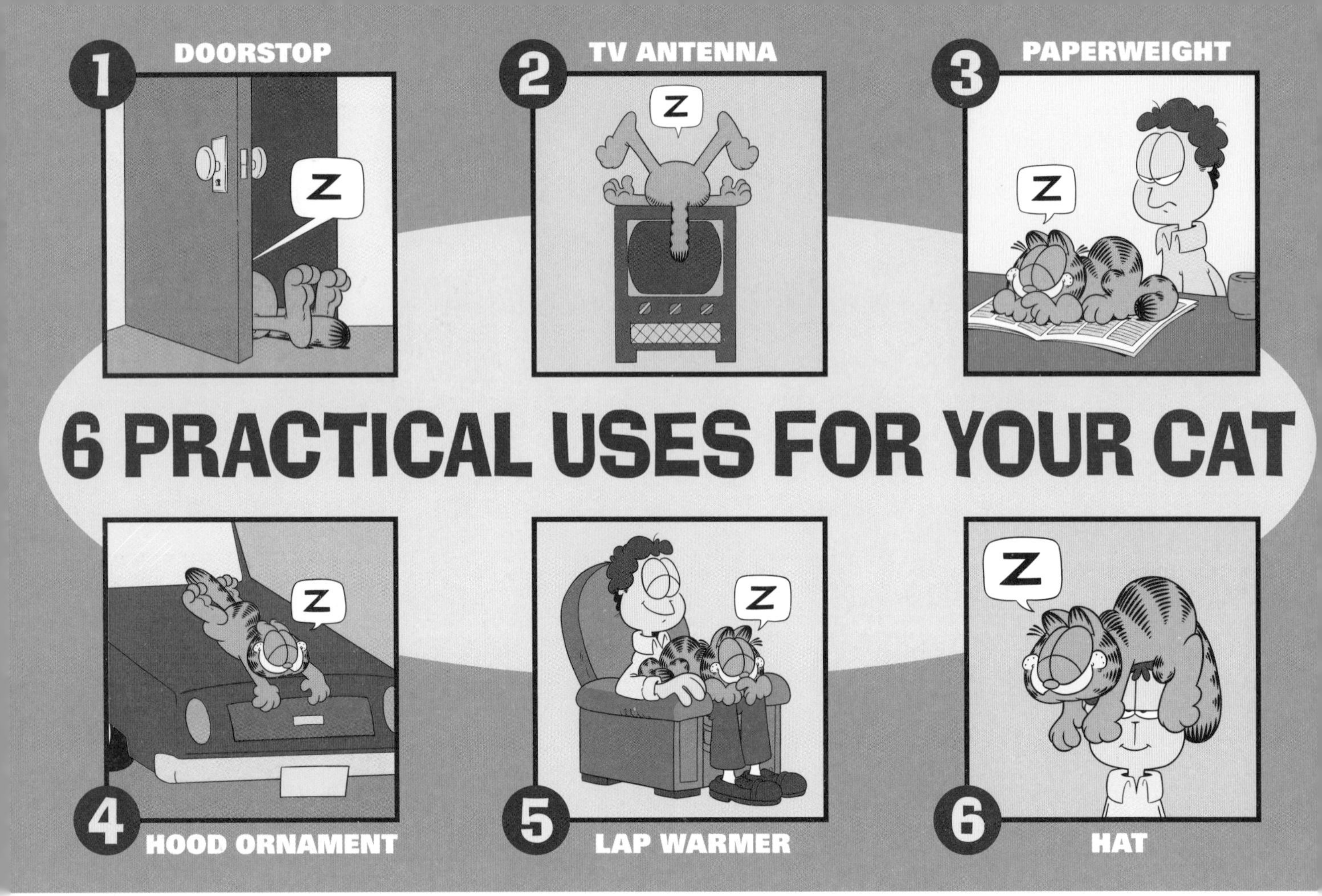
1 DOORSTOP
Z
2 TV ANTENNA
Z
3 PAPERWEIGHT
Z
6 PRACTICAL USES FOR YOUR CAT
Z
4 HOOD ORNAMENT
Z
5 LAP WARMER
Z
6 HAT

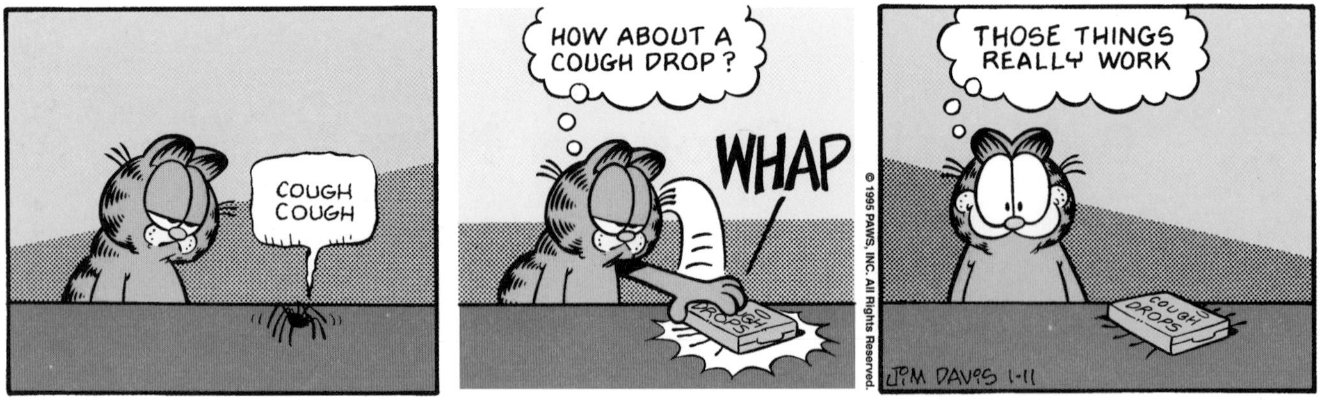
COUGH COUGH
HOW ABOUT A COUGH DROP?
WHAP
© 1995 PAWS, INC. All Rights Reserved.
THOSE THINGS REALLY WORK
COUGH DROPS
JIM DAVIS 1-11

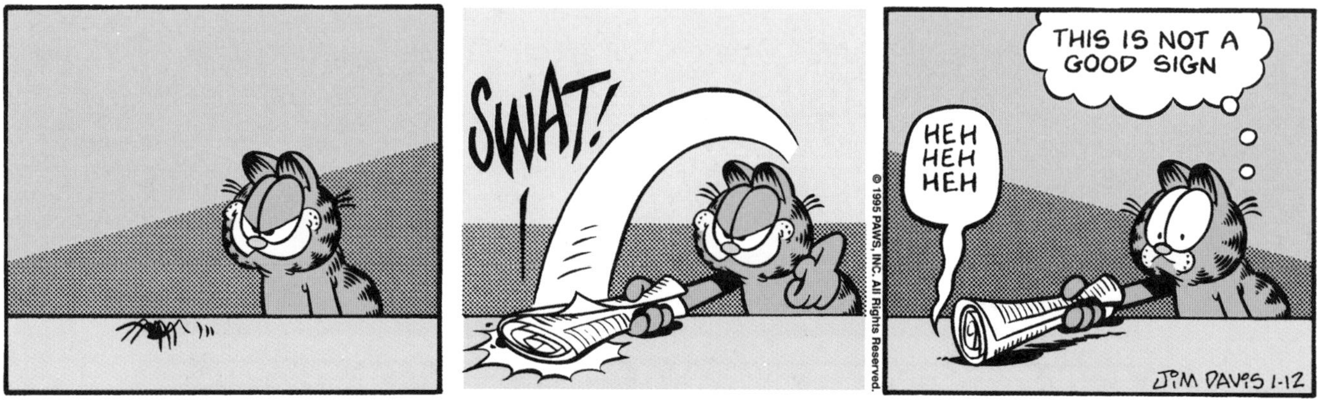
SWAT!
© 1995 PAWS, INC. All Rights Reserved.
HEH HEH HEH
THIS IS NOT A GOOD SIGN
JIM DAVIS 1-12

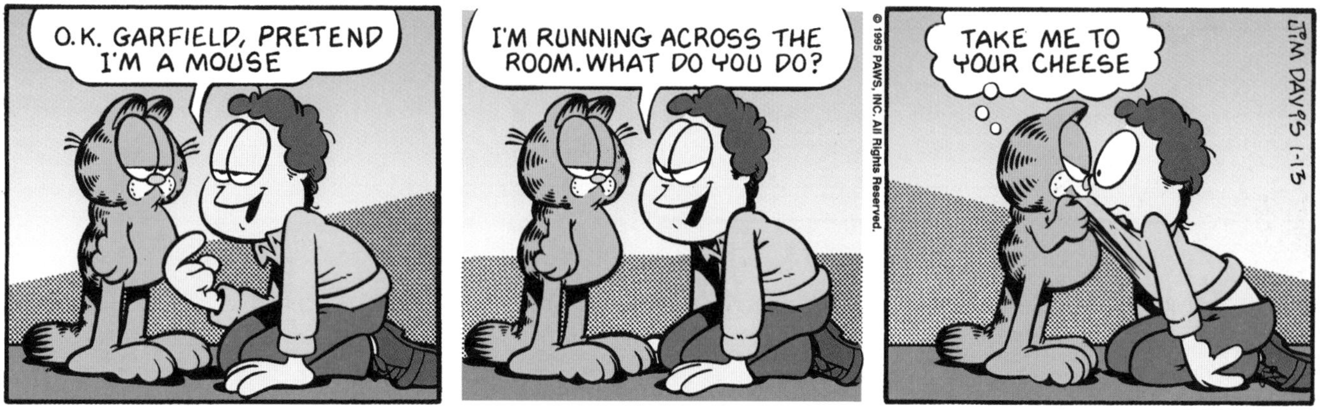
O.K. GARFIELD, PRETEND I'M A MOUSE
I'M RUNNING ACROSS THE ROOM. WHAT DO YOU DO?
© 1995 PAWS, INC. All Rights Reserved.
TAKE ME TO YOUR CHEESE
JIM DAVIS 1-13

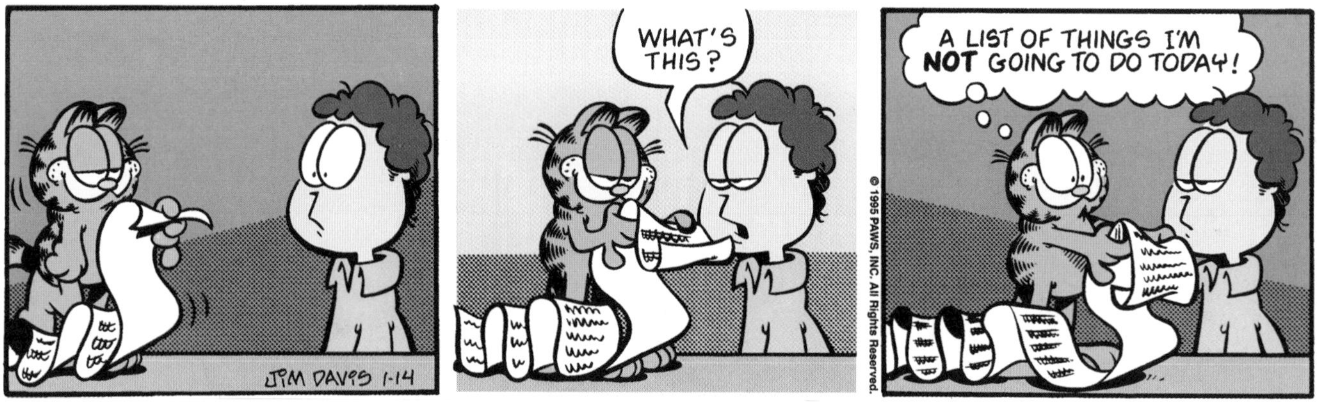
JIM DAVIS 1-14
WHAT'S THIS?
© 1995 PAWS, INC. All Rights Reserved.
A LIST OF THINGS I'M **NOT** GOING TO DO TODAY!

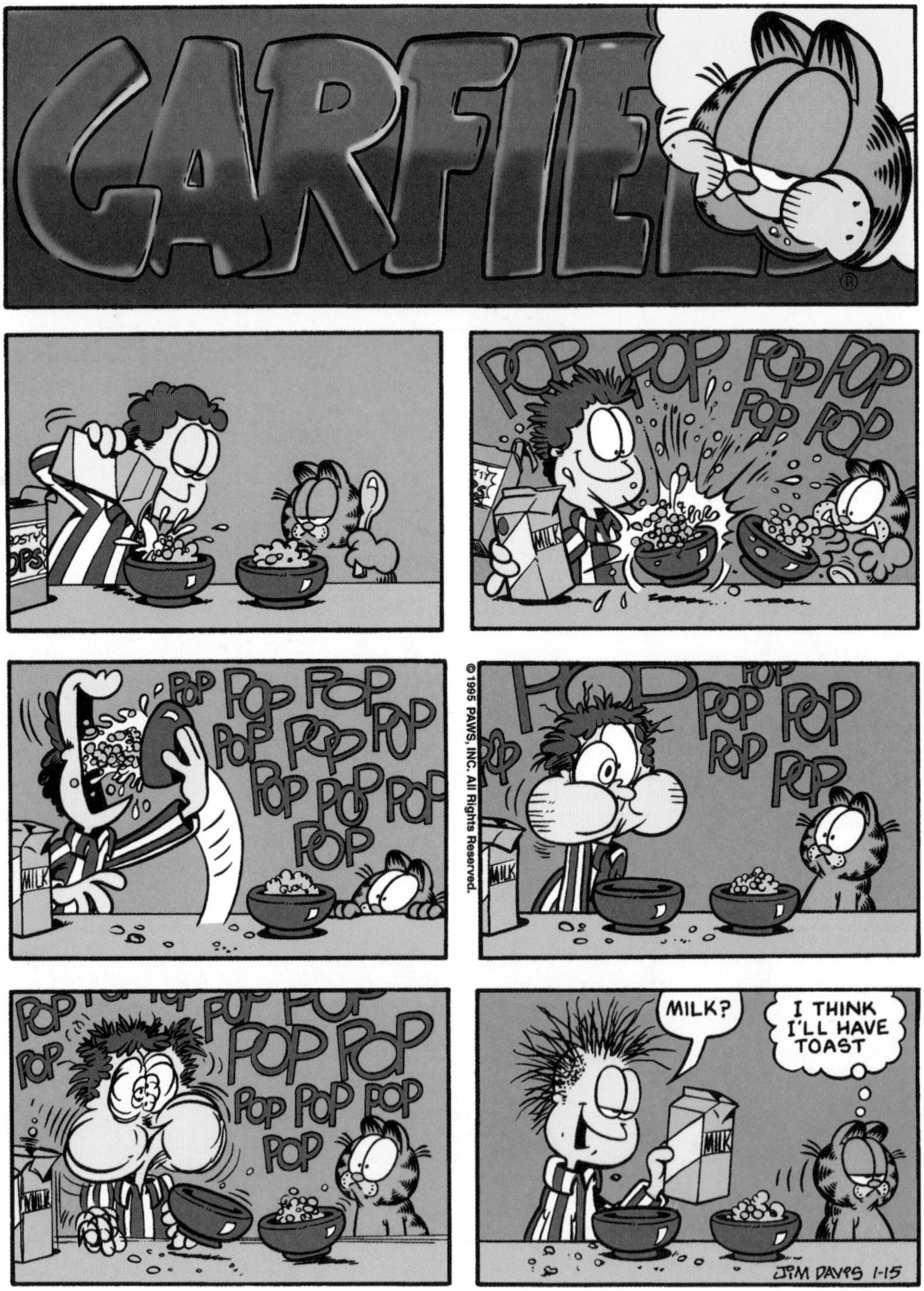
GARFIELD
POP POP POP POP POP POP
MILK
POP POP POP POP POP POP POP POP POP POP
POP POP POP POP POP POP
MILK
POP POP POP POP POP POP POP POP POP
MILK
MILK?
I THINK I'LL HAVE TOAST
MILK
JIM DAVIS 1-15

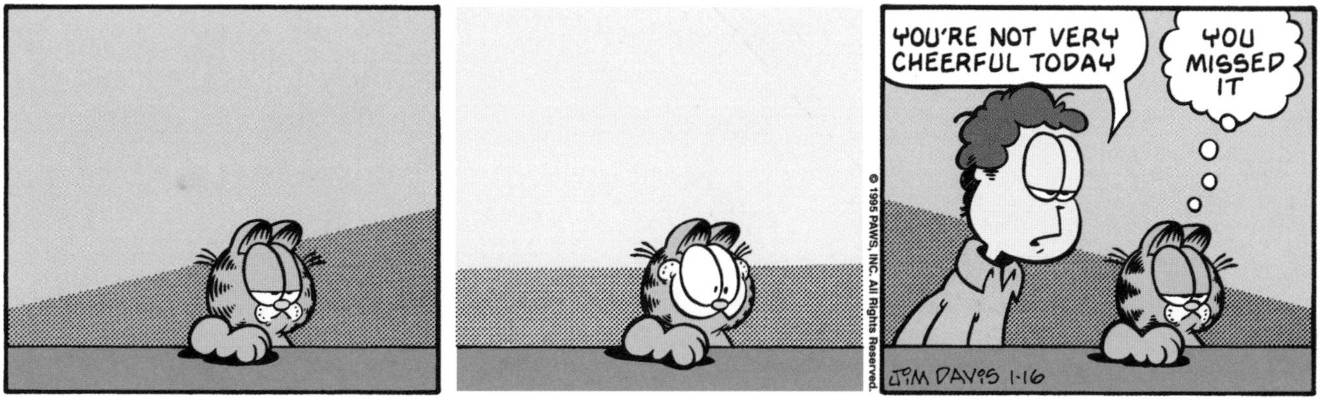
© 1995 PAWS, INC. All Rights Reserved.
YOU'RE NOT VERY CHEERFUL TODAY
YOU MISSED IT
JIM DAVIS 1-16

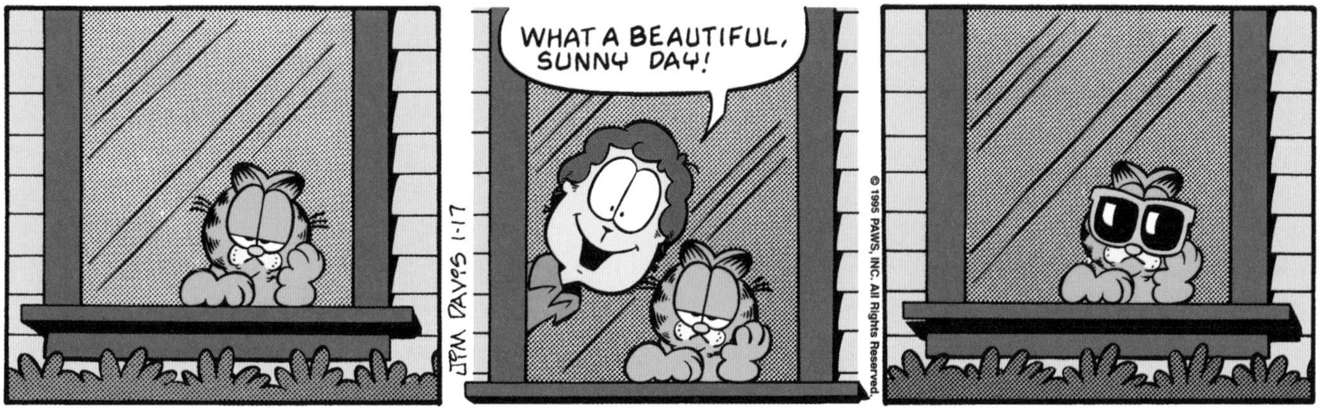
JIM DAVIS 1-17
WHAT A BEAUTIFUL, SUNNY DAY!
© 1995 PAWS, INC. All Rights Reserved.

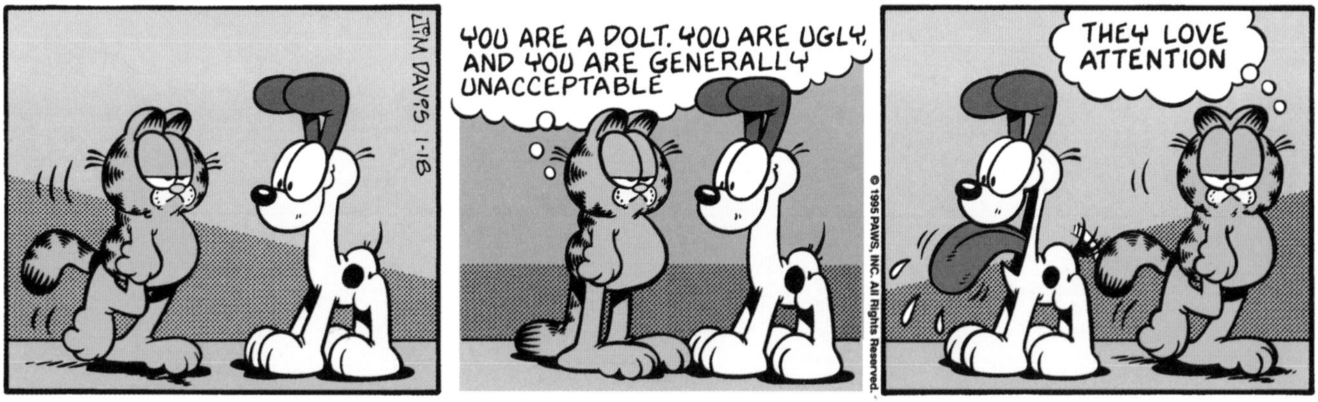
JIM DAVIS 1-18
YOU ARE A DOLT. YOU ARE UGLY, AND YOU ARE GENERALLY UNACCEPTABLE
© 1995 PAWS, INC. All Rights Reserved.
THEY LOVE ATTENTION

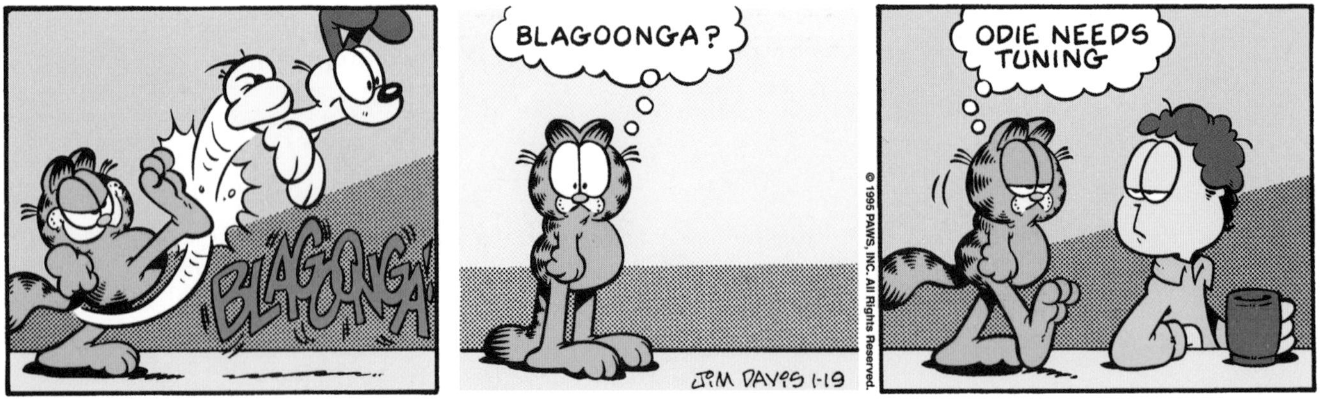
BLAGOONGA!
BLAGOONGA?
JIM DAVIS 1-19
© 1995 PAWS, INC. All Rights Reserved.
ODIE NEEDS TUNING

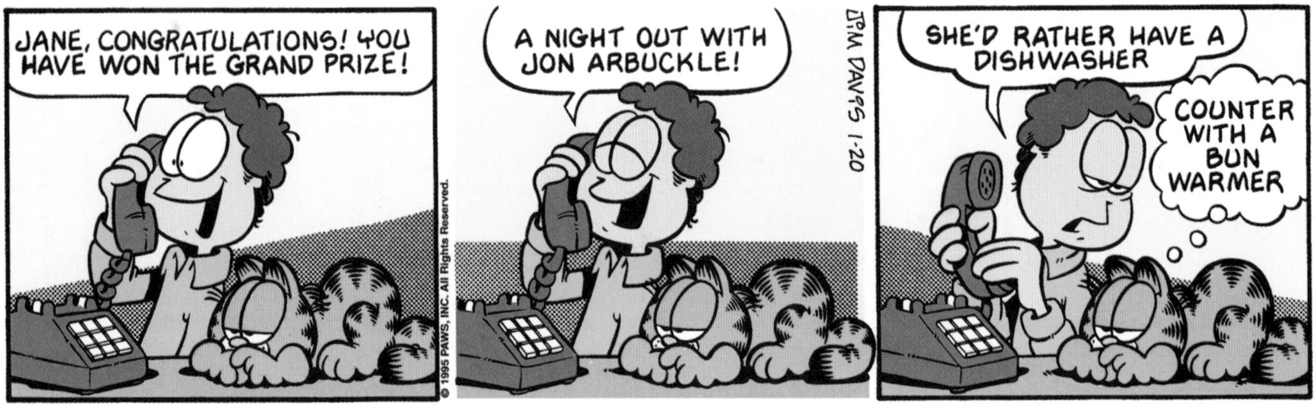
JANE, CONGRATULATIONS! YOU HAVE WON THE GRAND PRIZE!
© 1995 PAWS, INC. All Rights Reserved.
A NIGHT OUT WITH JON ARBUCKLE!
JIM DAVIS 1-20
SHE'D RATHER HAVE A DISHWASHER
COUNTER WITH A BUN WARMER

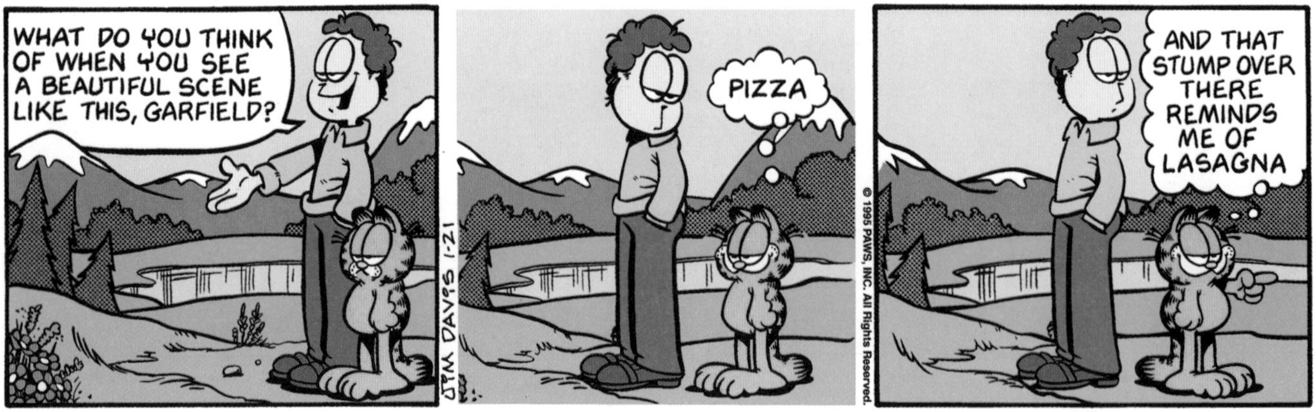
WHAT DO YOU THINK OF WHEN YOU SEE A BEAUTIFUL SCENE LIKE THIS, GARFIELD?
JIM DAVIS 1-21
PIZZA
© 1995 PAWS, INC. All Rights Reserved.
AND THAT STUMP OVER THERE REMINDS ME OF LASAGNA

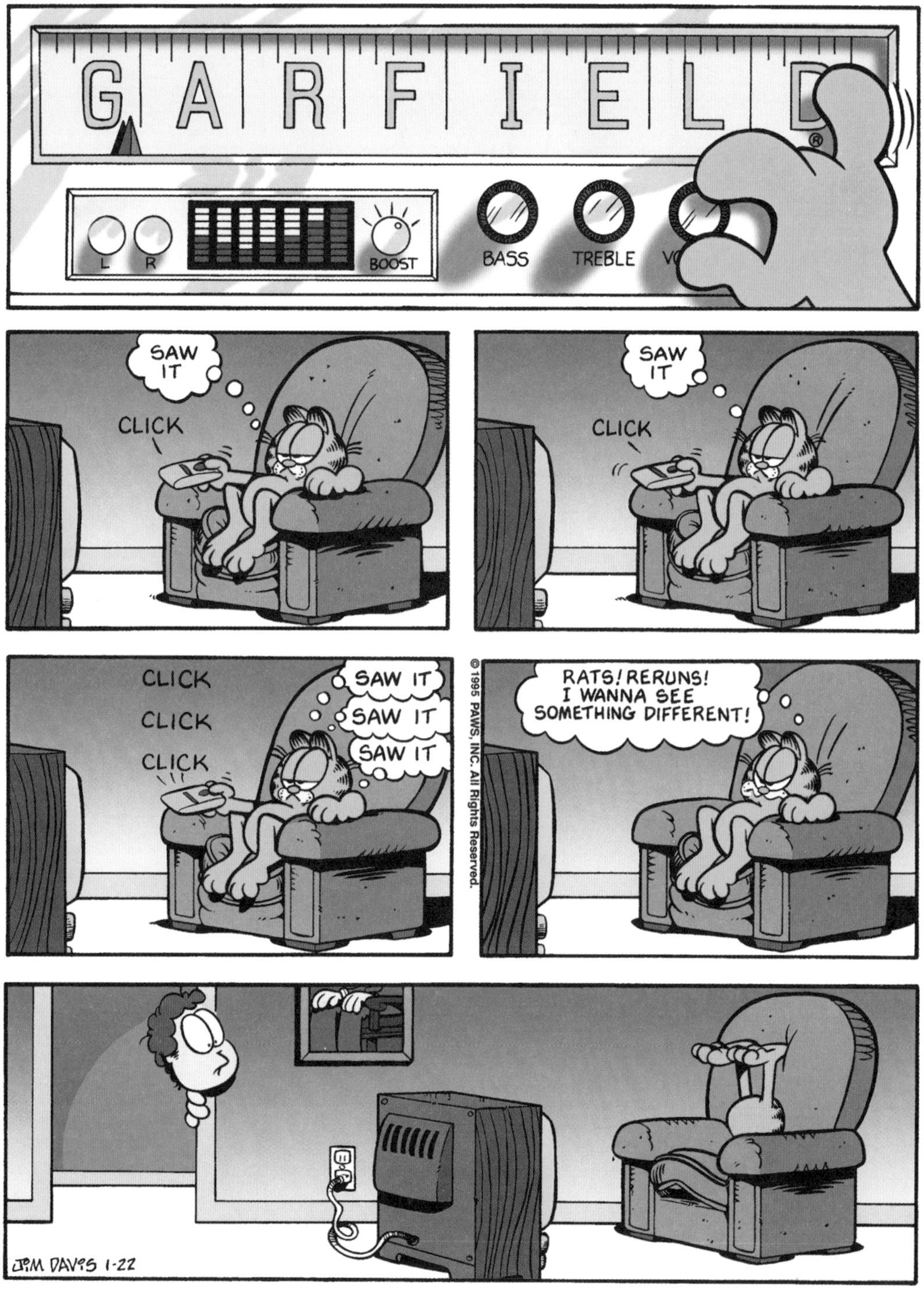
GARFIELD
L
R
BOOST
BASS
TREBLE
SAW IT
CLICK
SAW IT
CLICK
CLICK
CLICK
CLICK
SAW IT
SAW IT
SAW IT
RATS! RERUNS! I WANNA SEE SOMETHING DIFFERENT!
JIM DAVIS 1-22

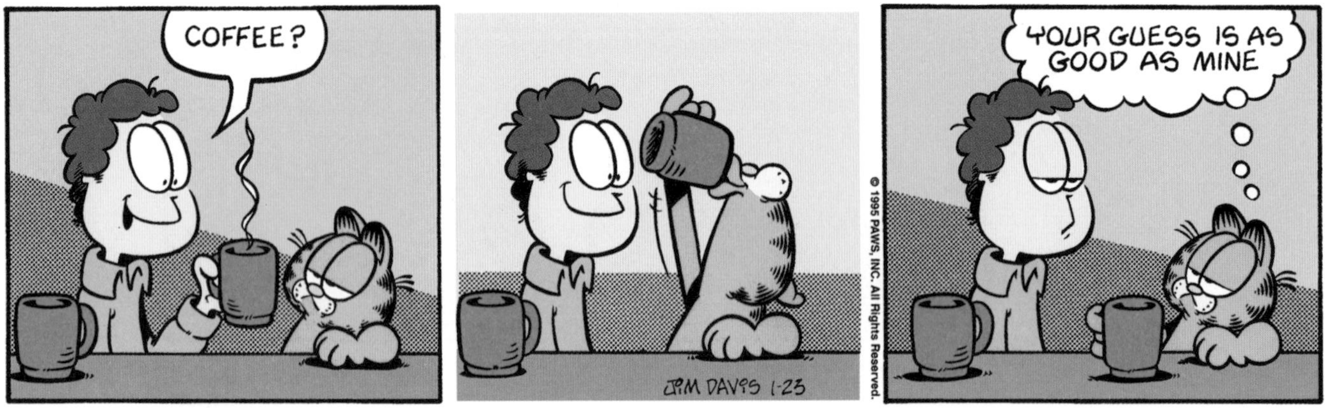
COFFEE?
JIM DAVIS 1-23
© 1995 PAWS, INC. All Rights Reserved.
YOUR GUESS IS AS GOOD AS MINE

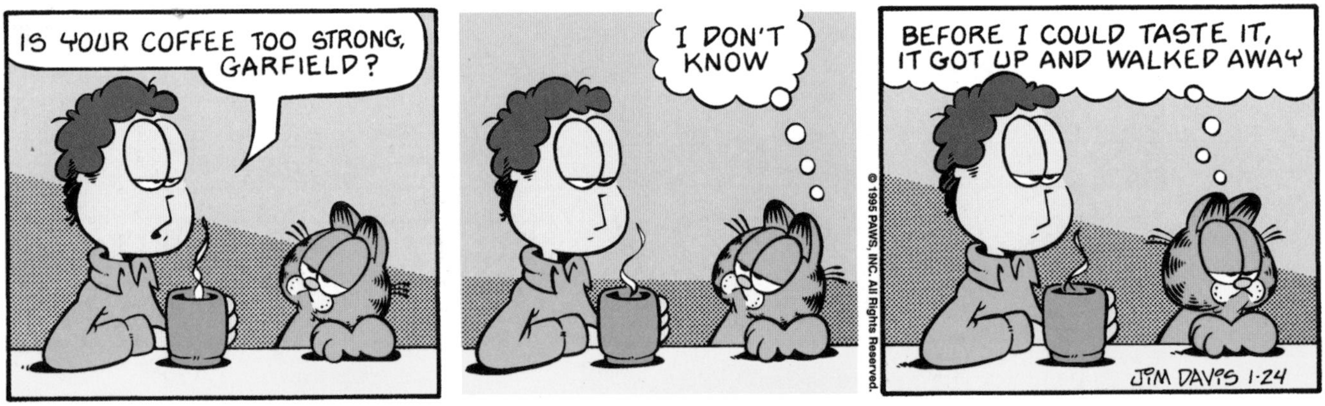
IS YOUR COFFEE TOO STRONG, GARFIELD?
I DON'T KNOW
© 1995 PAWS, INC. All Rights Reserved.
BEFORE I COULD TASTE IT, IT GOT UP AND WALKED AWAY
JIM DAVIS 1-24

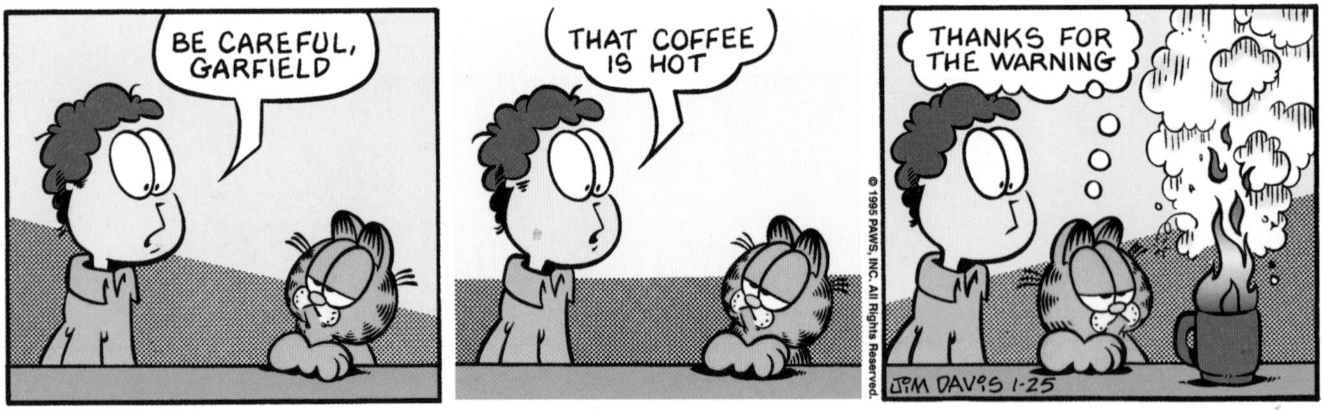
BE CAREFUL, GARFIELD
THAT COFFEE IS HOT
© 1995 PAWS, INC. All Rights Reserved.
THANKS FOR THE WARNING
JIM DAVIS 1-25

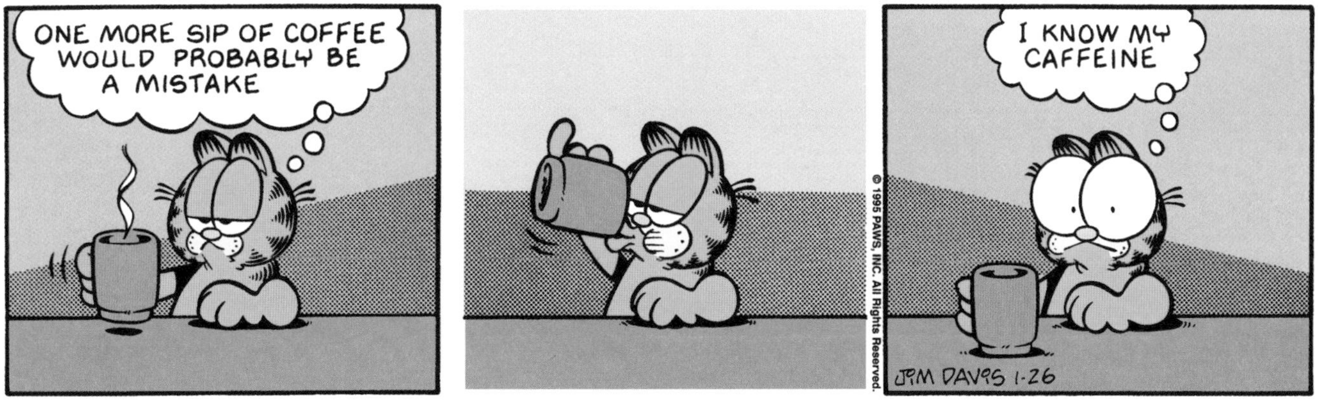
ONE MORE SIP OF COFFEE WOULD PROBABLY BE A MISTAKE
I KNOW MY CAFFEINE
© 1995 PAWS, INC. All Rights Reserved.
JIM DAVIS 1-26

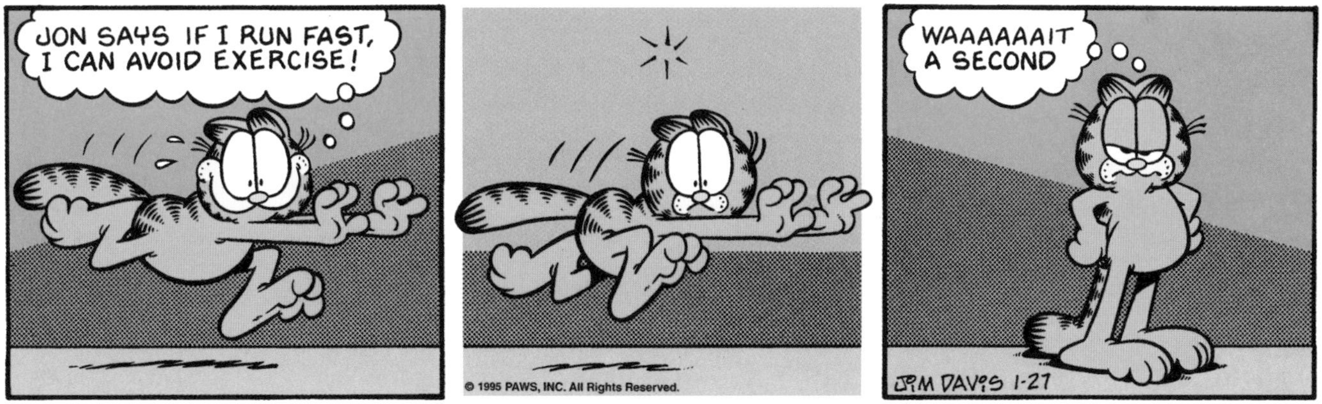
JON SAYS IF I RUN FAST, I CAN AVOID EXERCISE!
© 1995 PAWS, INC. All Rights Reserved.
WAAAAAAIT A SECOND
JIM DAVIS 1-27

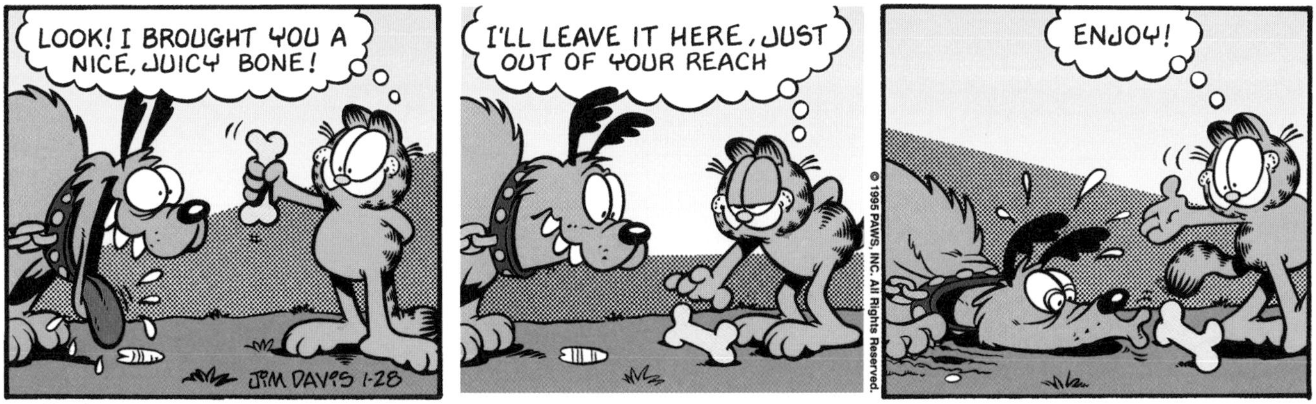
LOOK! I BROUGHT YOU A NICE, JUICY BONE!
JIM DAVIS 1-28
I'LL LEAVE IT HERE, JUST OUT OF YOUR REACH
© 1995 PAWS, INC. All Rights Reserved.
ENJOY!

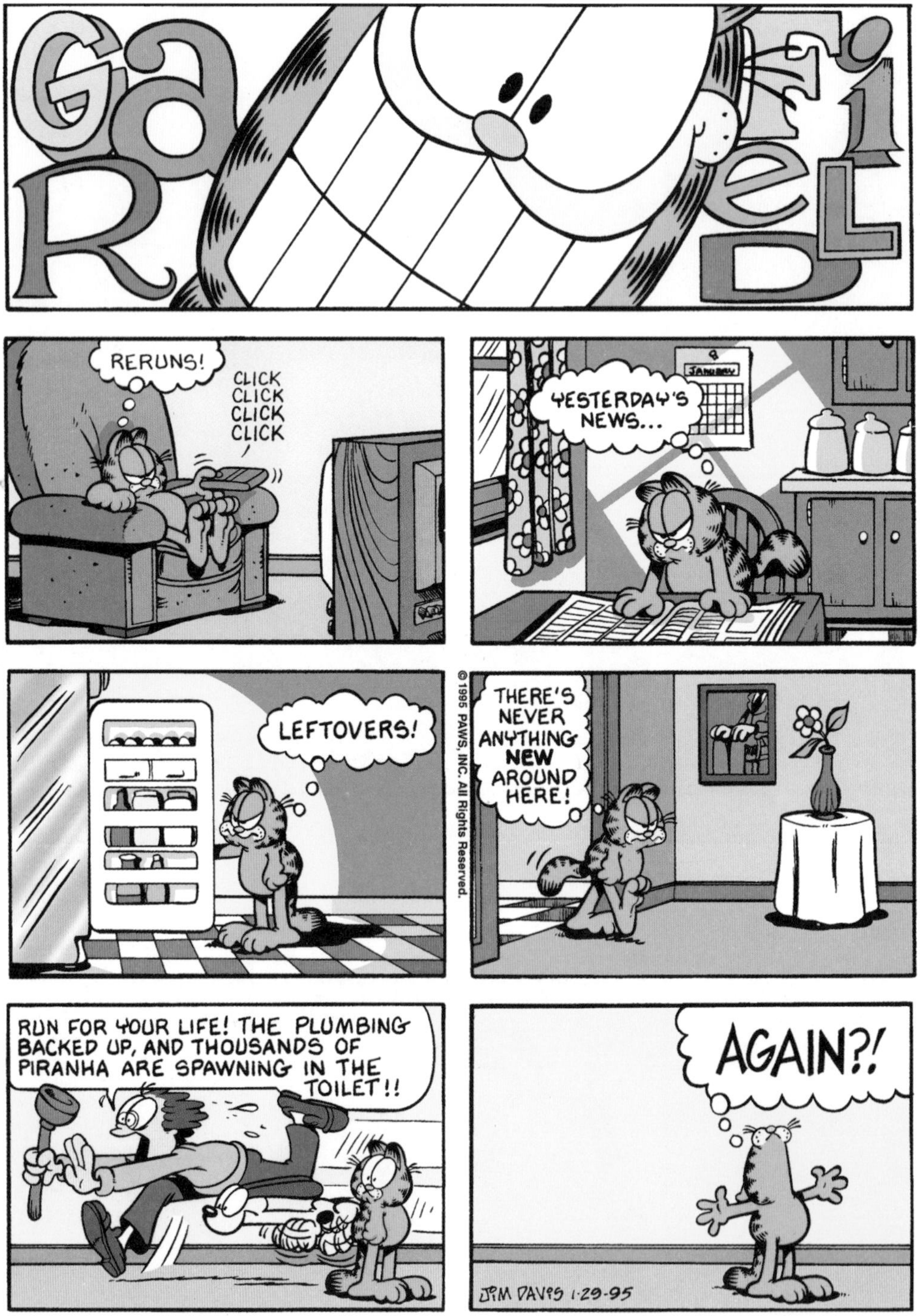
GARFIELD
RERUNS!
CLICK CLICK CLICK CLICK
YESTERDAY'S NEWS...
LEFTOVERS!
THERE'S NEVER ANYTHING **NEW** AROUND HERE!
RUN FOR YOUR LIFE! THE PLUMBING BACKED UP, AND THOUSANDS OF PIRANHA ARE SPAWNING IN THE TOILET!!
AGAIN?!
JIM DAVIS 1-29-95

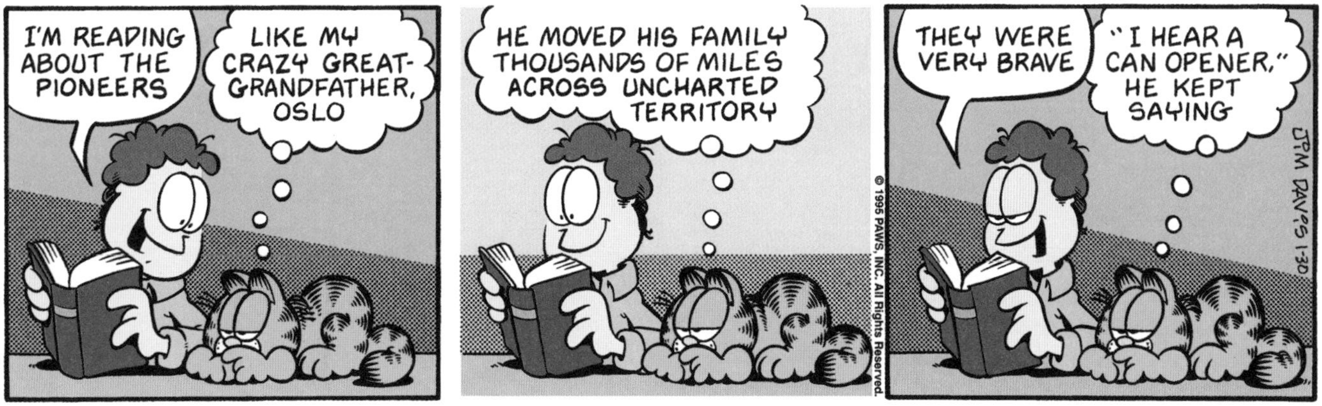
I'M READING ABOUT THE PIONEERS
LIKE MY CRAZY GREAT-GRANDFATHER, OSLO
HE MOVED HIS FAMILY THOUSANDS OF MILES ACROSS UNCHARTED TERRITORY
THEY WERE VERY BRAVE
"I HEAR A CAN OPENER," HE KEPT SAYING
JPM DAVPS 1-30
© 1995 PAWS, INC. All Rights Reserved.

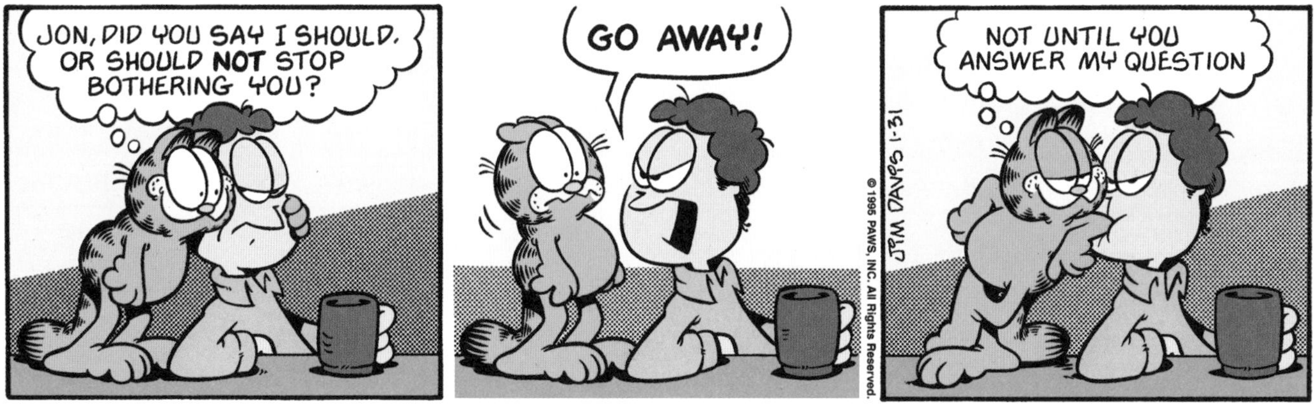
JON, DID YOU SAY I SHOULD, OR SHOULD **NOT** STOP BOTHERING YOU?
GO AWAY!
NOT UNTIL YOU ANSWER MY QUESTION
JPM DAVPS 1-31
© 1995 PAWS, INC. All Rights Reserved.

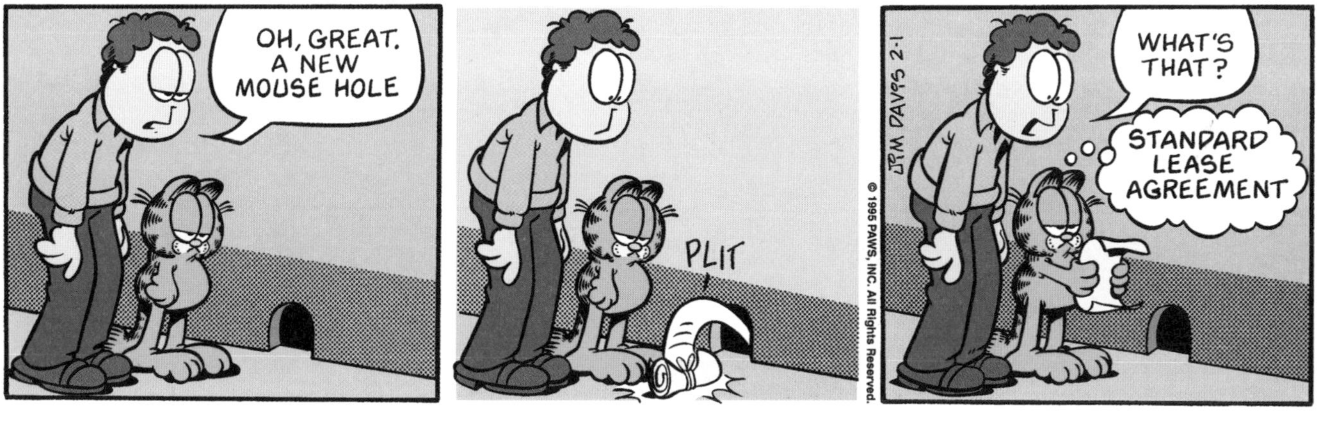
OH, GREAT. A NEW MOUSE HOLE
PLIT
WHAT'S THAT?
STANDARD LEASE AGREEMENT
JPM DAVPS 2-1
© 1995 PAWS, INC. All Rights Reserved.

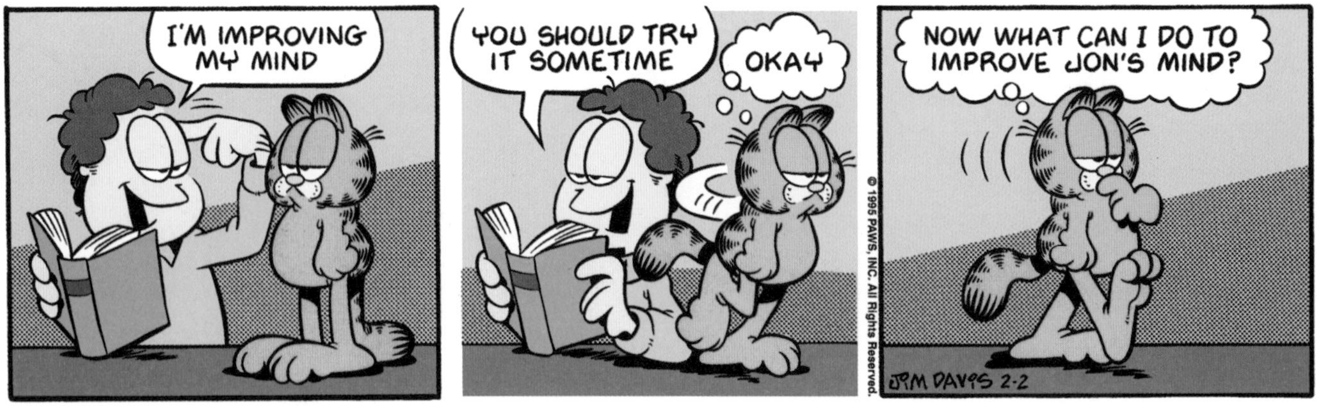
I'M IMPROVING MY MIND
YOU SHOULD TRY IT SOMETIME
OKAY
© 1995 PAWS, INC. All Rights Reserved.
NOW WHAT CAN I DO TO IMPROVE JON'S MIND?
JIM DAVIS 2-2

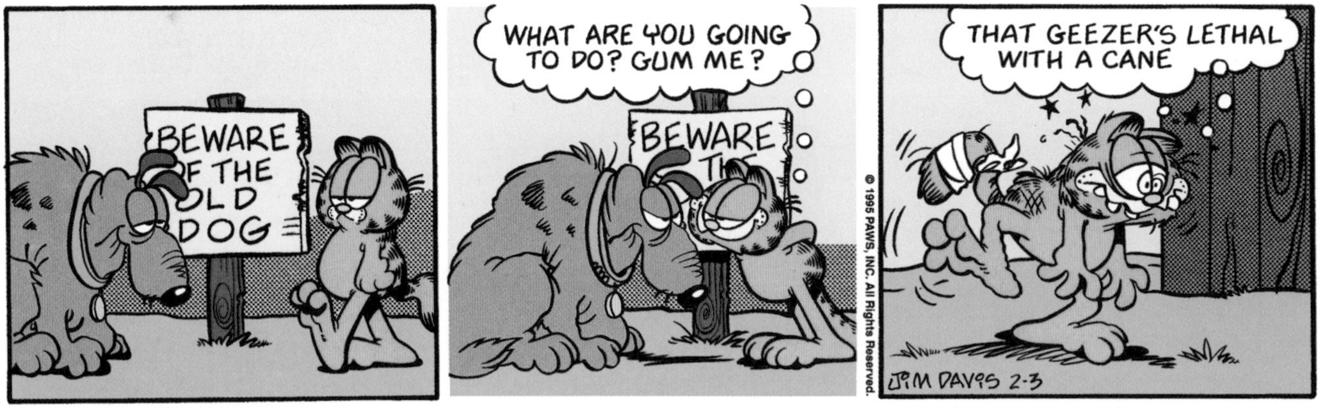
BEWARE OF THE OLD DOG
WHAT ARE YOU GOING TO DO? GUM ME?
BEWARE
© 1995 PAWS, INC. All Rights Reserved.
THAT GEEZER'S LETHAL WITH A CANE
JIM DAVIS 2-3

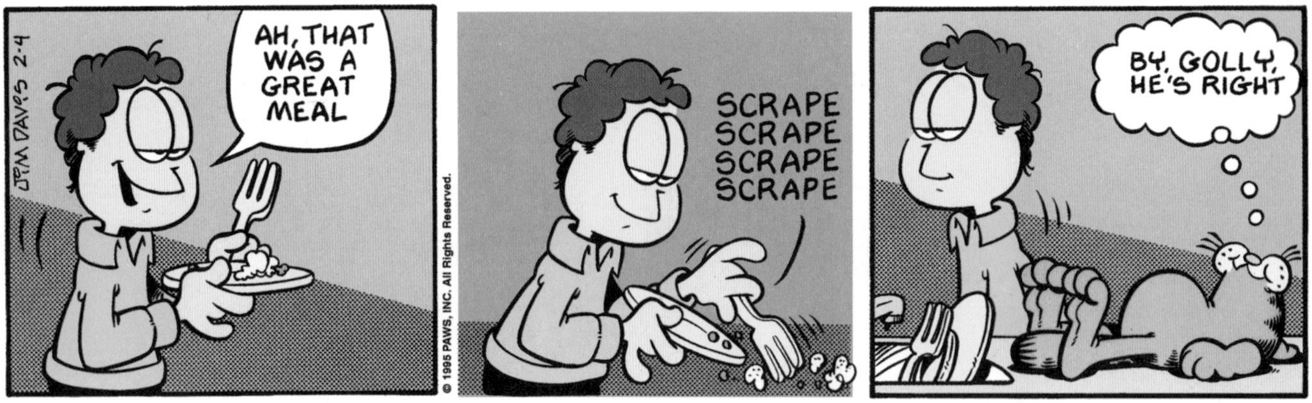
JIM DAVIS 2-4
AH, THAT WAS A GREAT MEAL
© 1995 PAWS, INC. All Rights Reserved.
SCRAPE SCRAPE SCRAPE SCRAPE
BY, GOLLY, HE'S RIGHT

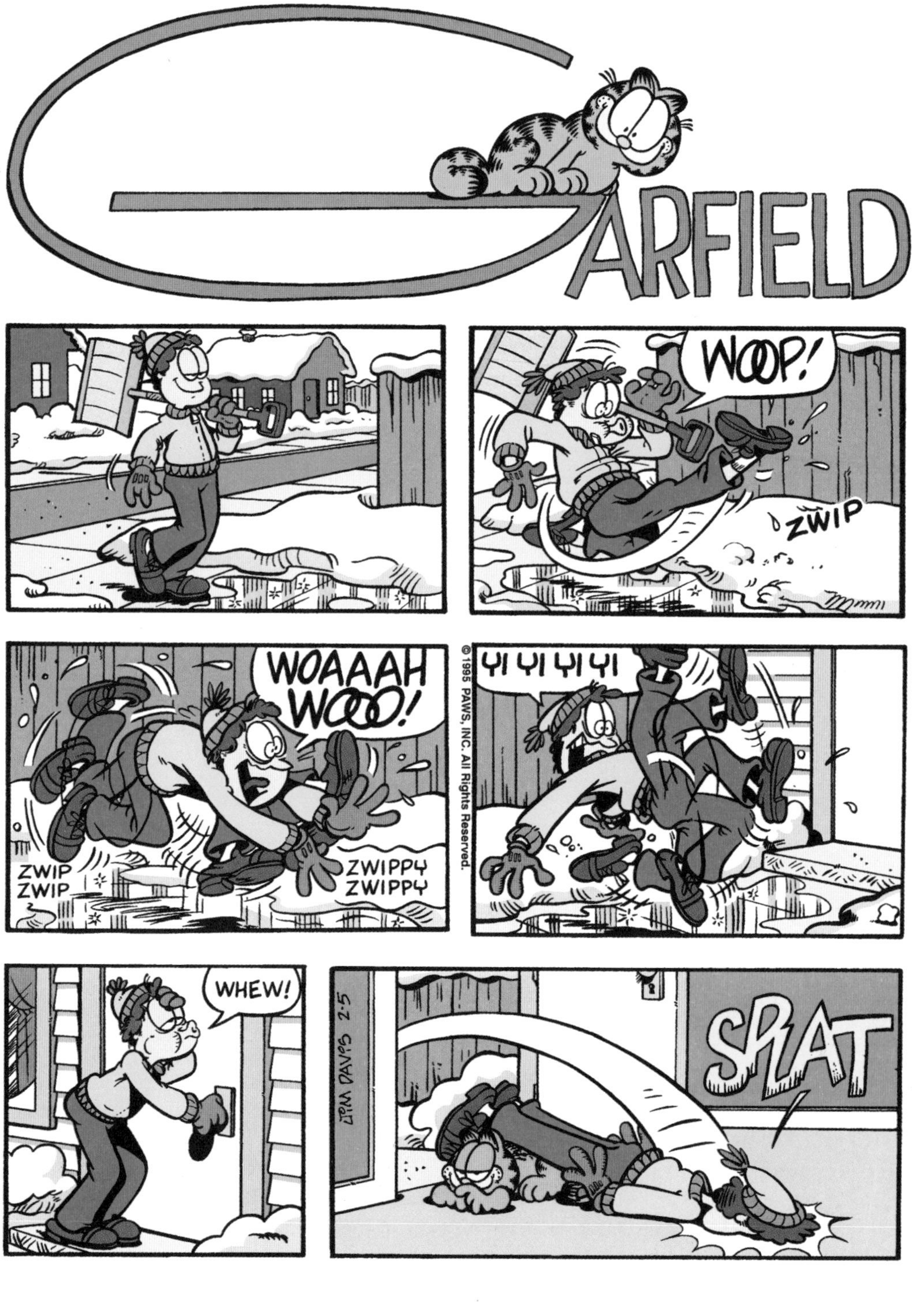
GARFIELD
WOOP!
ZWIP
WOAAAH WOOO!
ZWIP ZWIP
ZWIPPY ZWIPPY
© 1995 PAWS, INC. All Rights Reserved.
YI YI YI YI
WHEW!
JIM DAVIS 2-5
SPLAT

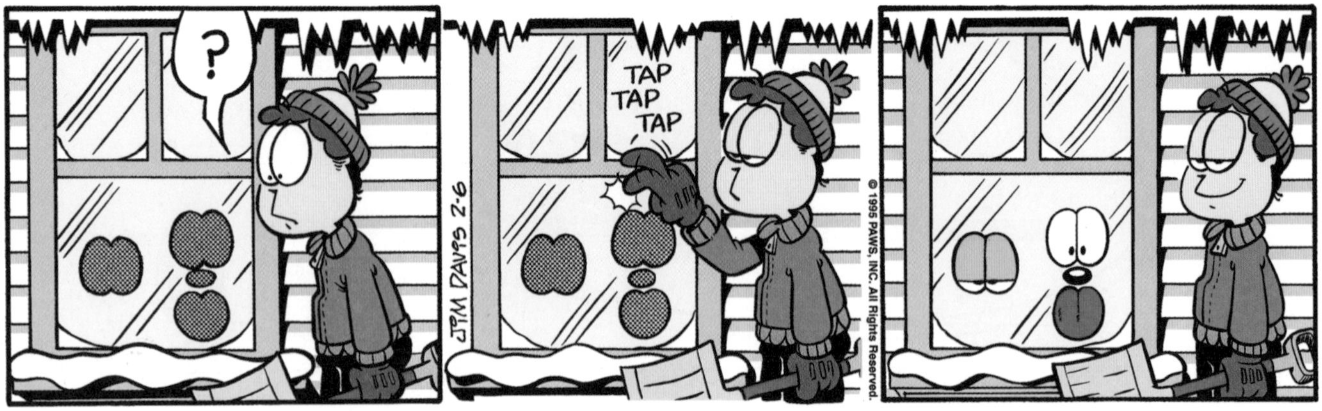
?
JIM DAVIS 2-6
TAP
TAP
TAP
© 1995 PAWS, INC. All Rights Reserved.

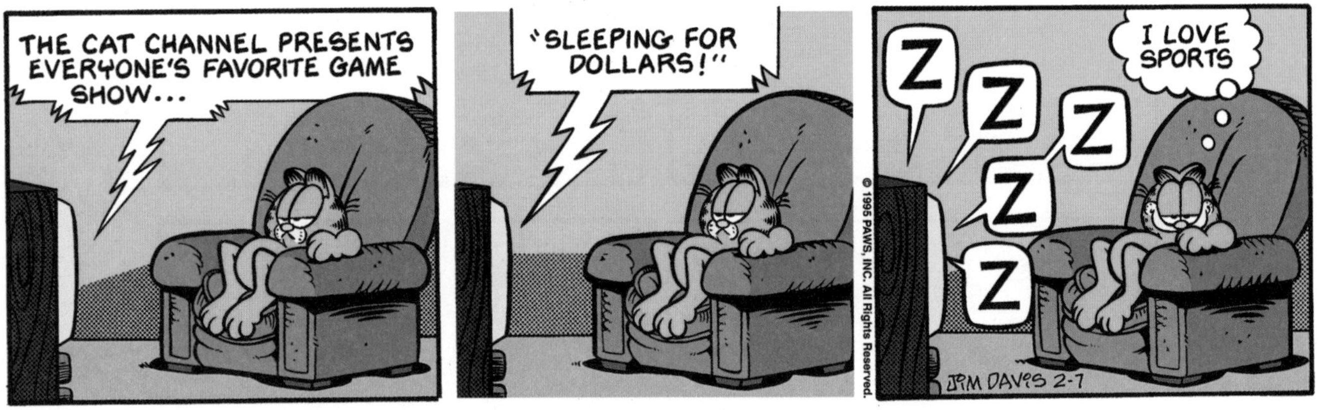
THE CAT CHANNEL PRESENTS EVERYONE'S FAVORITE GAME SHOW...
"SLEEPING FOR DOLLARS!"
© 1995 PAWS, INC. All Rights Reserved.
Z
Z
Z
Z
Z
I LOVE SPORTS
JIM DAVIS 2-7

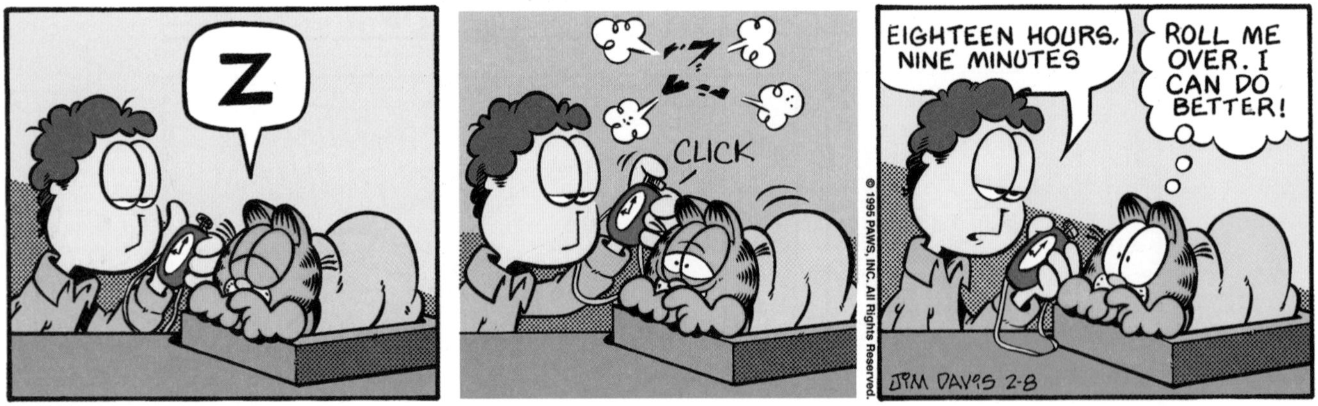
Z
CLICK
© 1995 PAWS, INC. All Rights Reserved.
EIGHTEEN HOURS, NINE MINUTES
ROLL ME OVER. I CAN DO BETTER!
JIM DAVIS 2-8

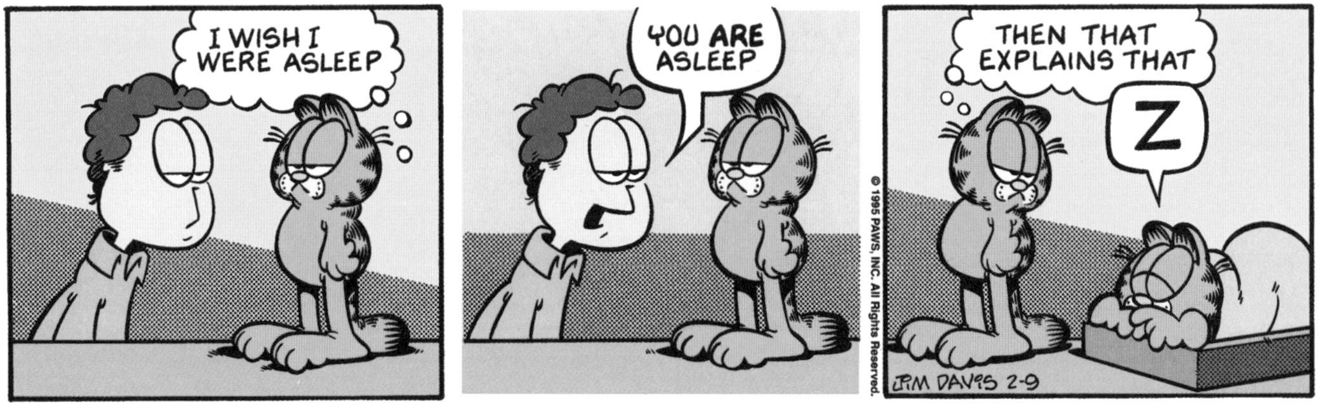
I WISH I WERE ASLEEP
YOU ARE ASLEEP
THEN THAT EXPLAINS THAT
Z
© 1995 PAWS, INC. All Rights Reserved.
JIM DAVIS 2-9

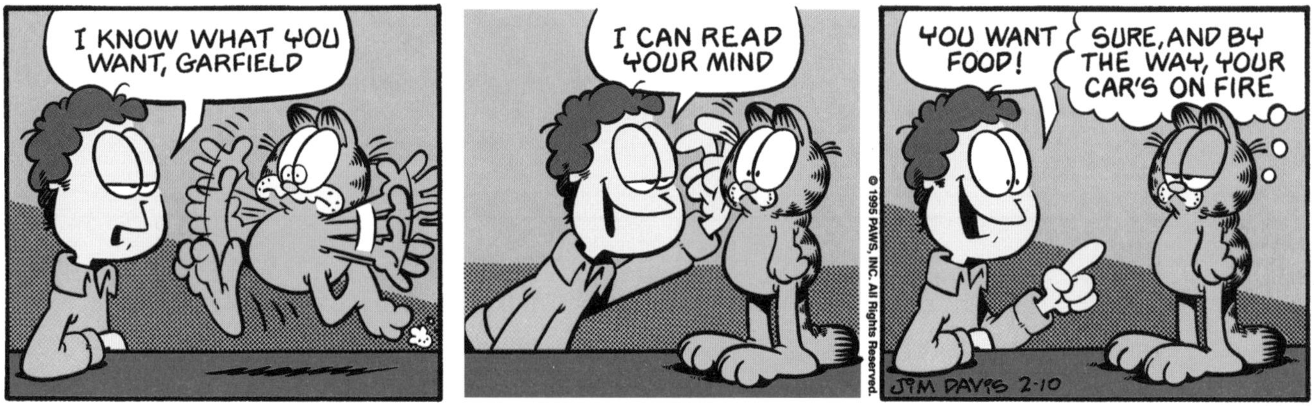
I KNOW WHAT YOU WANT, GARFIELD
I CAN READ YOUR MIND
YOU WANT FOOD!
SURE, AND BY THE WAY, YOUR CAR'S ON FIRE
© 1995 PAWS, INC. All Rights Reserved.
JIM DAVIS 2-10

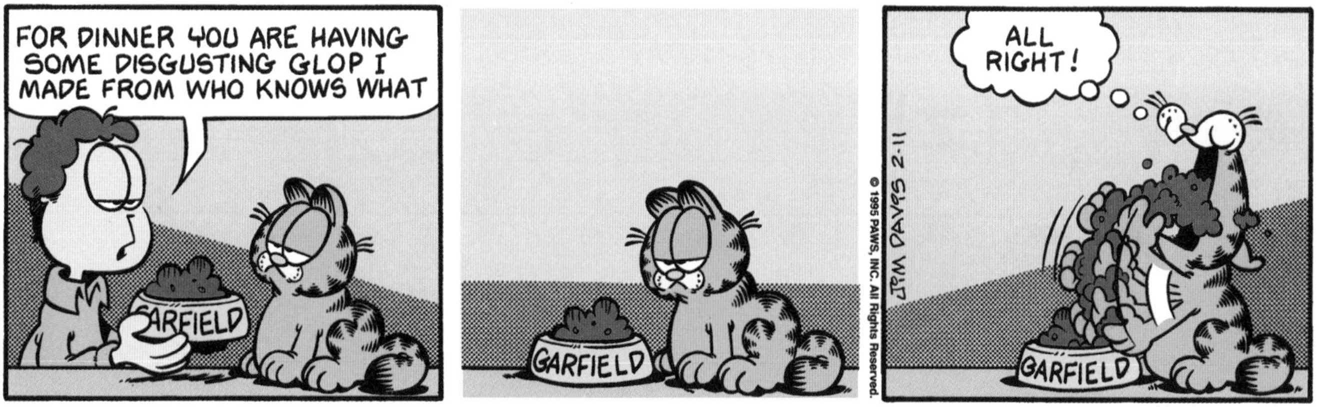
FOR DINNER YOU ARE HAVING SOME DISGUSTING GLOP I MADE FROM WHO KNOWS WHAT
GARFIELD
GARFIELD
© 1995 PAWS, INC. All Rights Reserved.
JIM DAVIS 2-11
ALL RIGHT!
GARFIELD

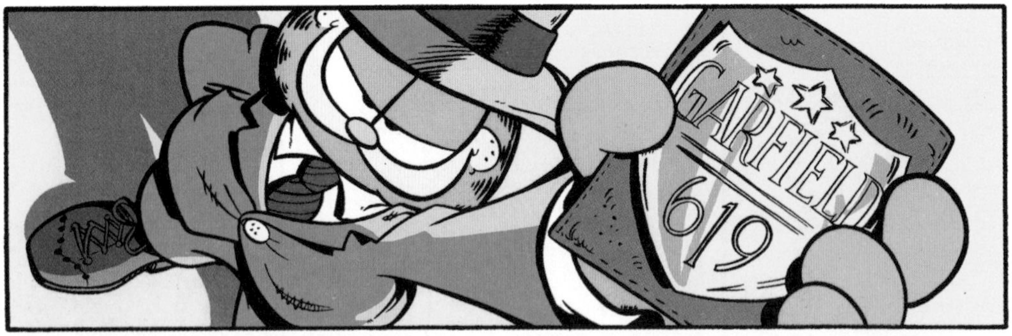
GARFIELD
6/19

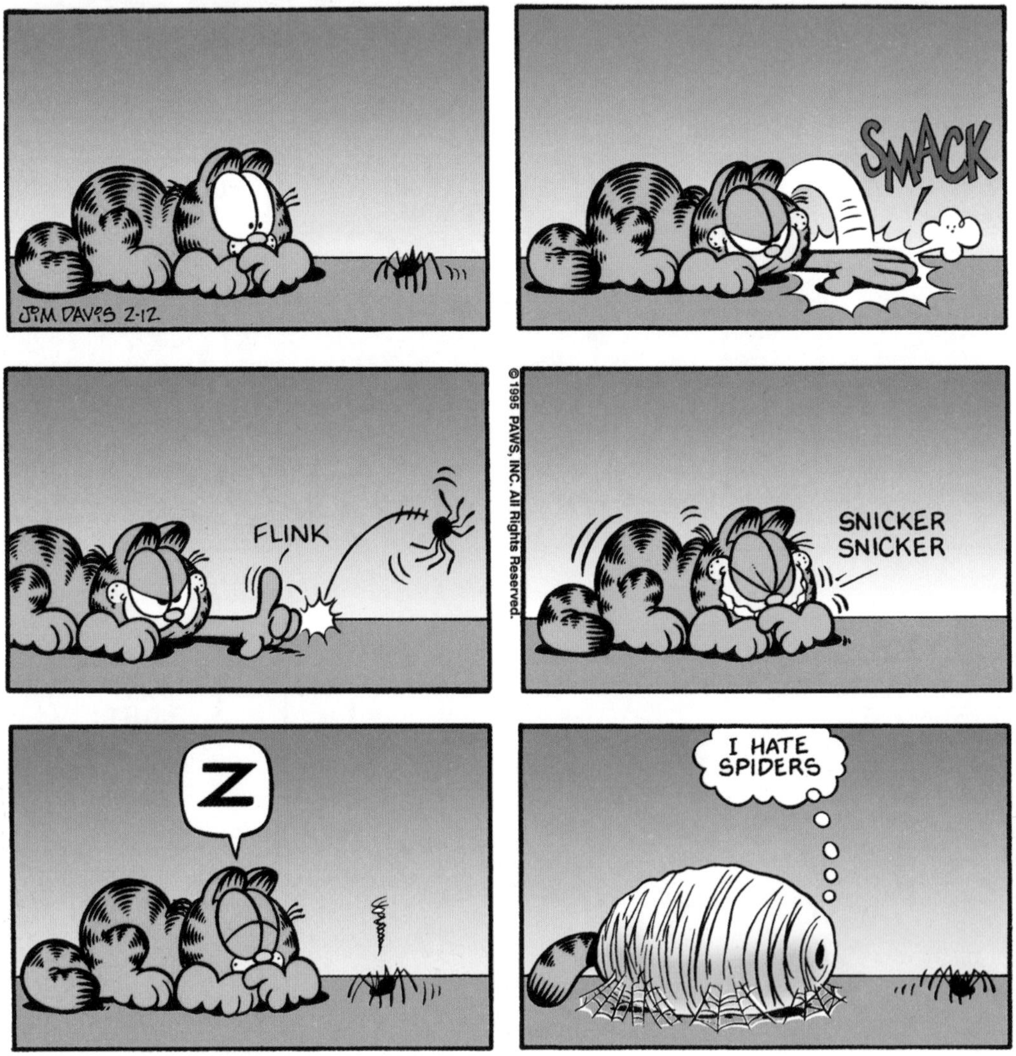
JIM DAVIS 2-12
SMACK
FLINK
SNICKER SNICKER
Z
I HATE SPIDERS

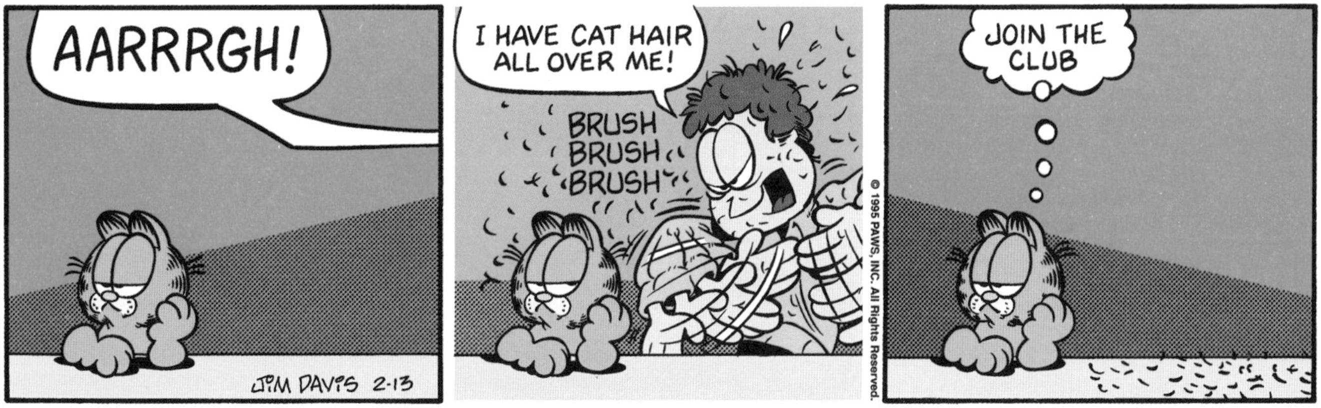
AARRRGH!
JIM DAVIS 2-13
I HAVE CAT HAIR ALL OVER ME!
BRUSH BRUSH BRUSH
© 1995 PAWS, INC. All Rights Reserved.
JOIN THE CLUB

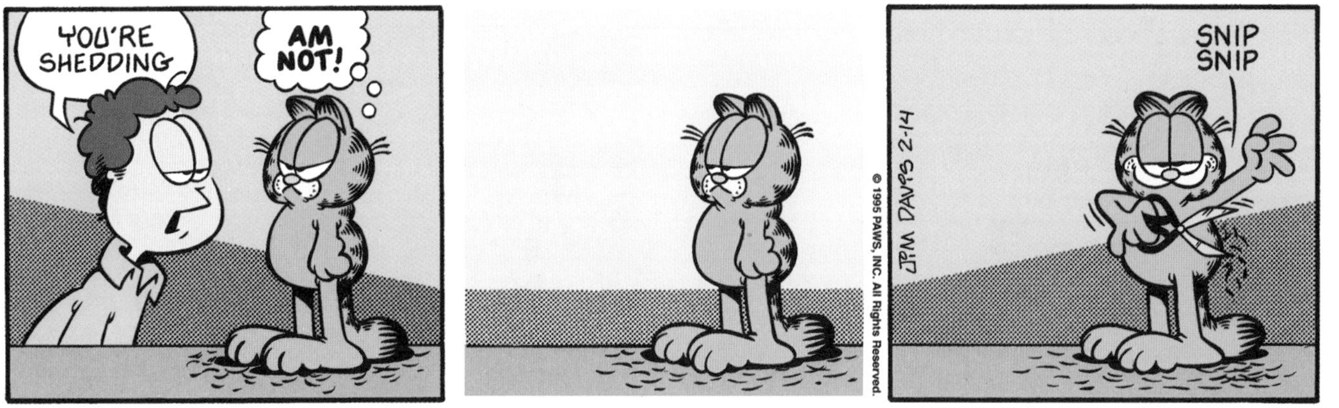
YOU'RE SHEDDING
AM NOT!
© 1995 PAWS, INC. All Rights Reserved.
JIM DAVIS 2-14
SNIP SNIP

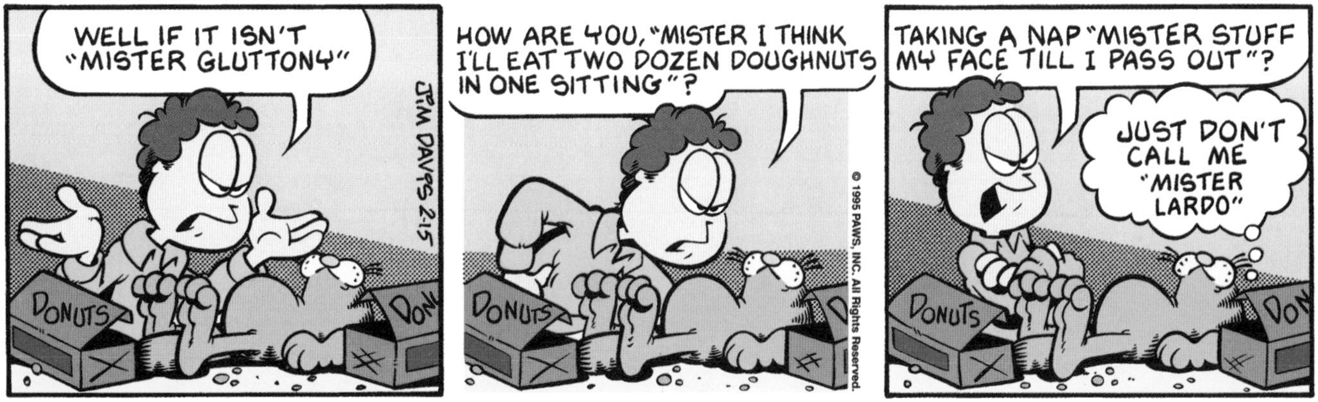
WELL IF IT ISN'T "MISTER GLUTTONY"
JIM DAVIS 2-15
DONUTS
HOW ARE YOU, "MISTER I THINK I'LL EAT TWO DOZEN DOUGHNUTS IN ONE SITTING"?
© 1995 PAWS, INC. All Rights Reserved.
TAKING A NAP "MISTER STUFF MY FACE TILL I PASS OUT"?
JUST DON'T CALL ME "MISTER LARDO"

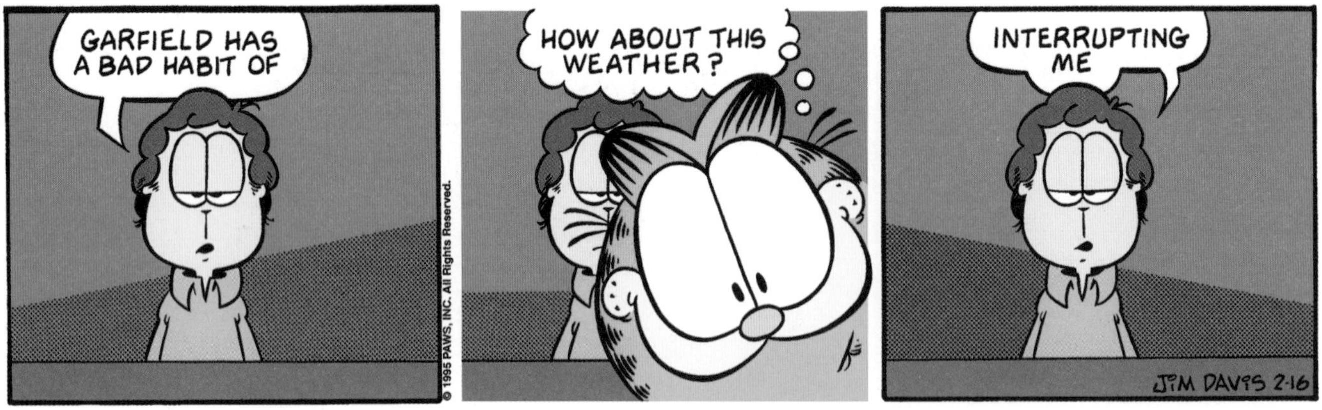
GARFIELD HAS A BAD HABIT OF
HOW ABOUT THIS WEATHER?
INTERRUPTING ME
© 1995 PAWS, INC. All Rights Reserved.
JIM DAVIS 2-16

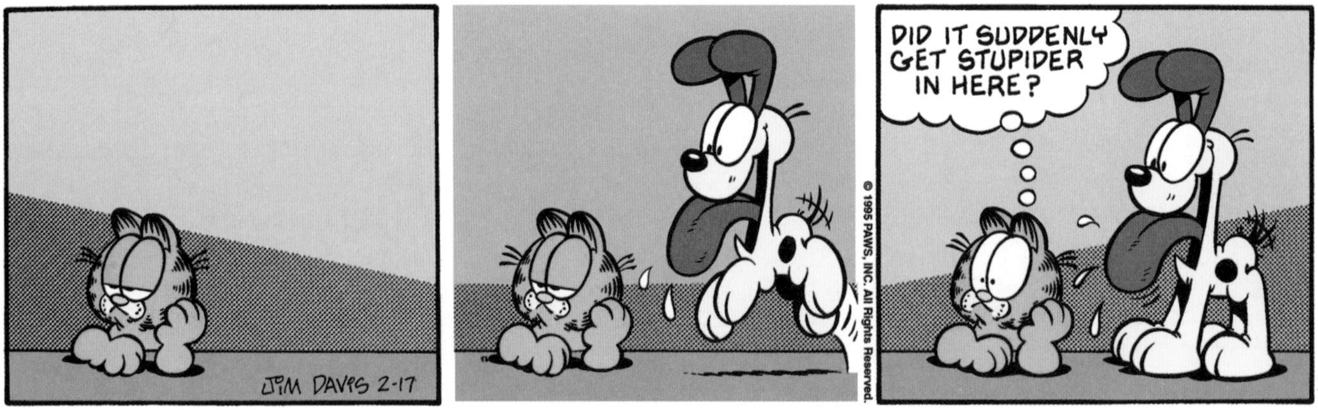
JIM DAVIS 2-17
DID IT SUDDENLY GET STUPIDER IN HERE?
© 1995 PAWS, INC. All Rights Reserved.

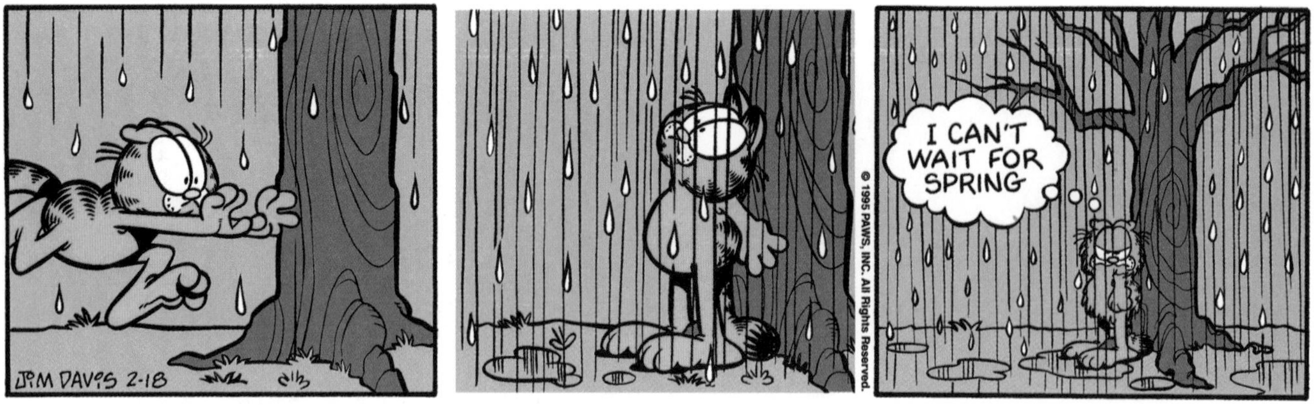
JIM DAVIS 2-18
I CAN'T WAIT FOR SPRING
© 1995 PAWS, INC. All Rights Reserved.

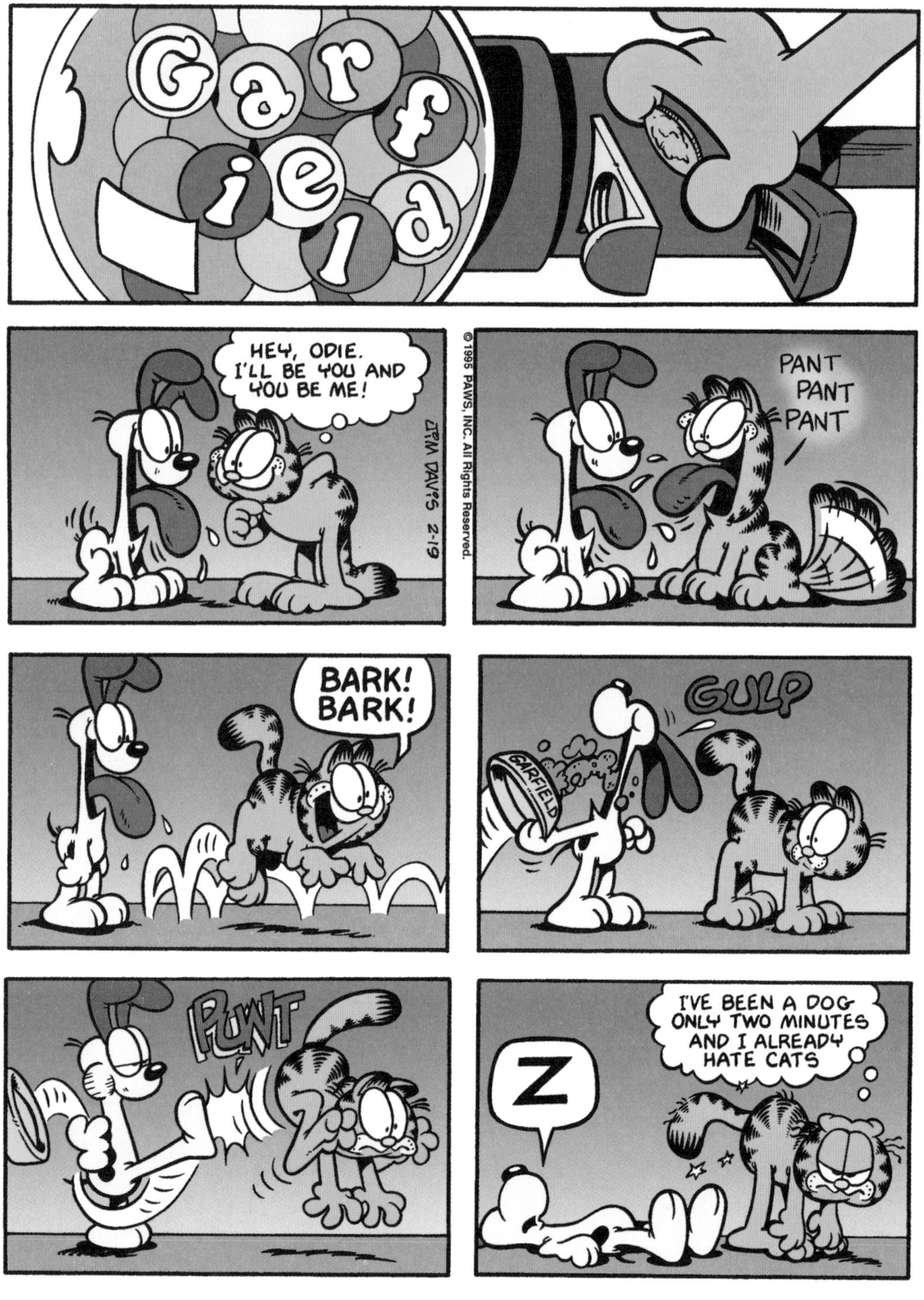

Garfield
HEY, ODIE. I'LL BE YOU AND YOU BE ME!
JPM DAVIS 2-19
© 1995 PAWS, INC. All Rights Reserved.
PANT PANT PANT
BARK! BARK!
GARFIELD
GULP
PUNT
Z
I'VE BEEN A DOG ONLY TWO MINUTES AND I ALREADY HATE CATS

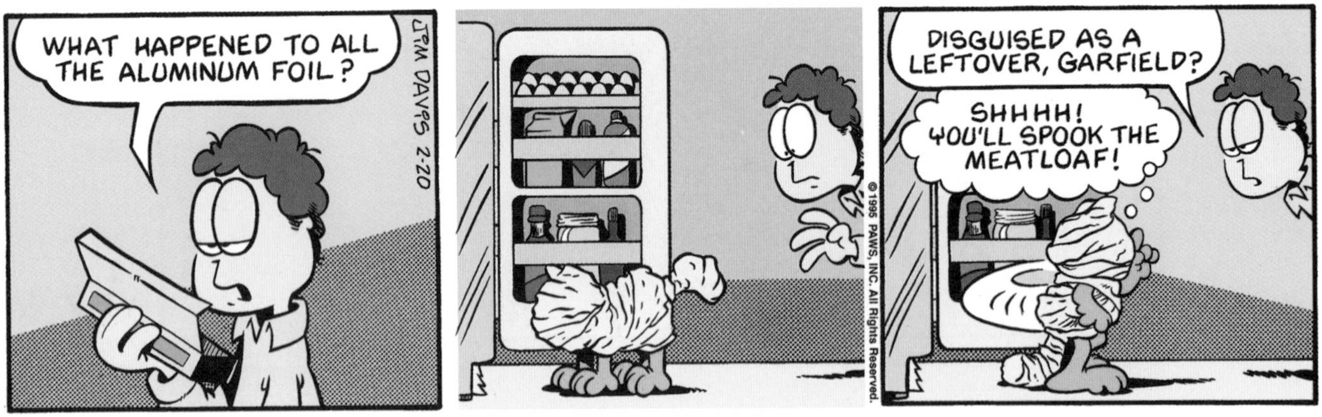
WHAT HAPPENED TO ALL THE ALUMINUM FOIL?
JIM DAVIS 2-20
© 1995 PAWS, INC. All Rights Reserved.
DISGUISED AS A LEFTOVER, GARFIELD?
SHHHH! YOU'LL SPOOK THE MEATLOAF!

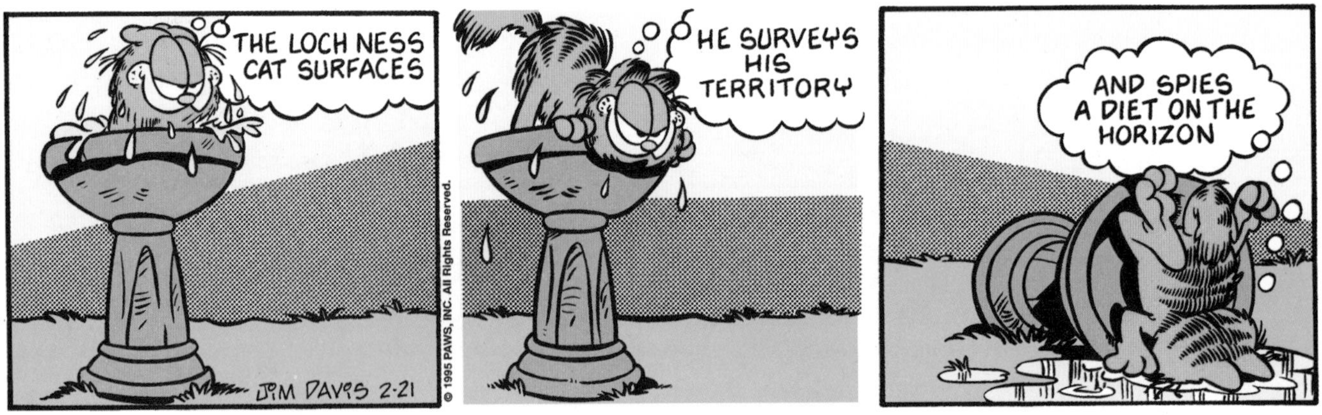
THE LOCH NESS CAT SURFACES
JIM DAVIS 2-21
© 1995 PAWS, INC. All Rights Reserved.
HE SURVEYS HIS TERRITORY
AND SPIES A DIET ON THE HORIZON

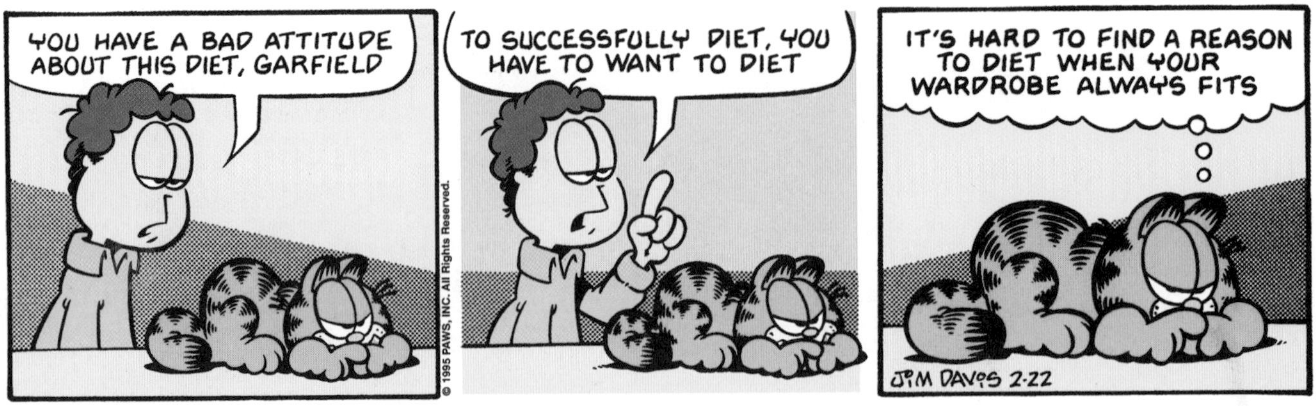
YOU HAVE A BAD ATTITUDE ABOUT THIS DIET, GARFIELD
© 1995 PAWS, INC. All Rights Reserved.
TO SUCCESSFULLY DIET, YOU HAVE TO WANT TO DIET
IT'S HARD TO FIND A REASON TO DIET WHEN YOUR WARDROBE ALWAYS FITS
JIM DAVIS 2-22

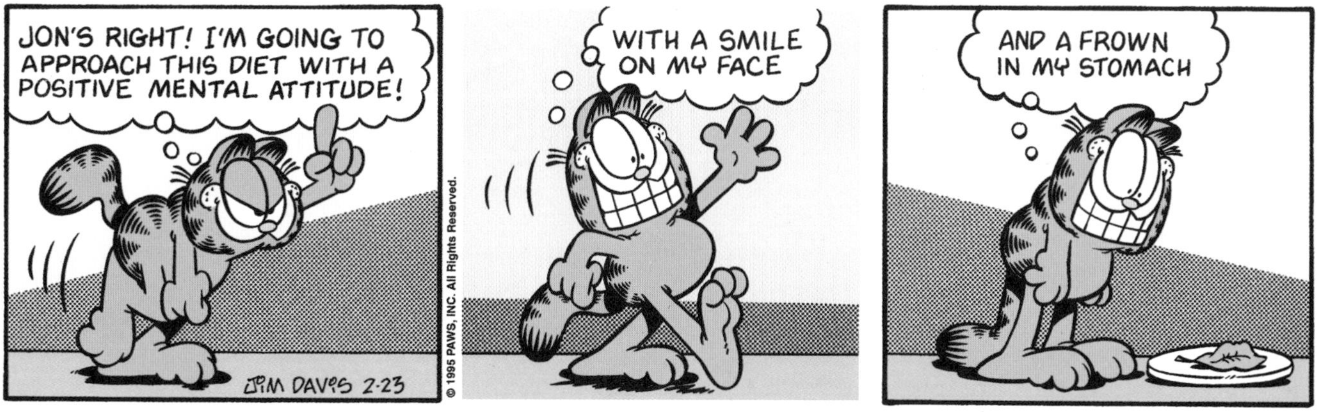
JON'S RIGHT! I'M GOING TO APPROACH THIS DIET WITH A POSITIVE MENTAL ATTITUDE!
JIM DAVIS 2-23
© 1995 PAWS, INC. All Rights Reserved.
WITH A SMILE ON MY FACE
AND A FROWN IN MY STOMACH

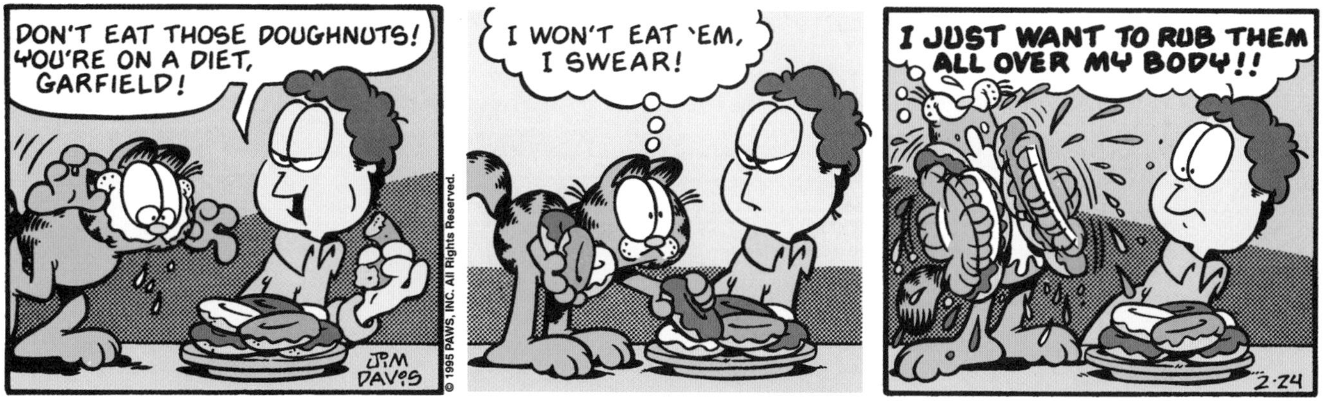
DON'T EAT THOSE DOUGHNUTS! YOU'RE ON A DIET, GARFIELD!
JIM DAVIS
© 1995 PAWS, INC. All Rights Reserved.
I WON'T EAT 'EM, I SWEAR!
I JUST WANT TO RUB THEM ALL OVER MY BODY!!
2-24

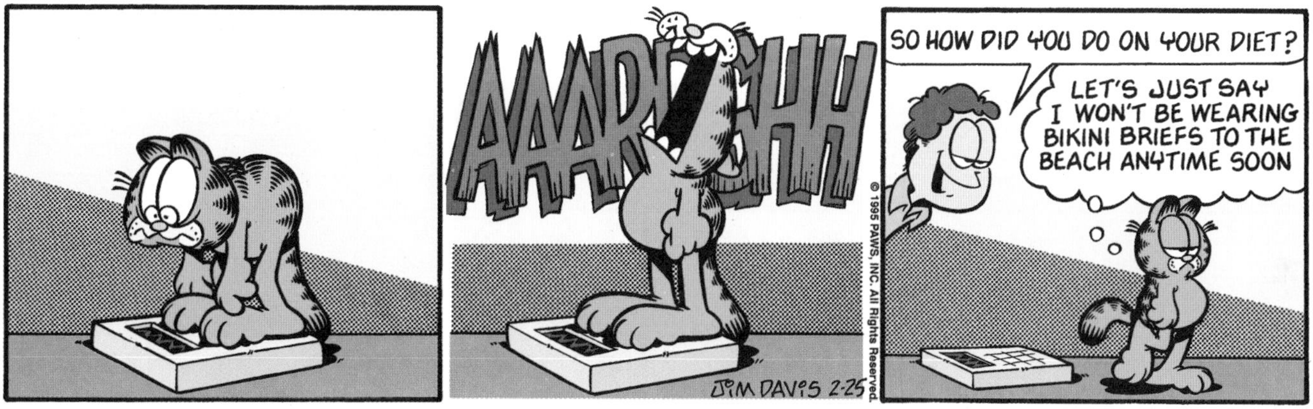
AAARGHH
JIM DAVIS 2-25
© 1995 PAWS, INC. All Rights Reserved.
SO HOW DID YOU DO ON YOUR DIET?
LET'S JUST SAY I WON'T BE WEARING BIKINI BRIEFS TO THE BEACH ANYTIME SOON

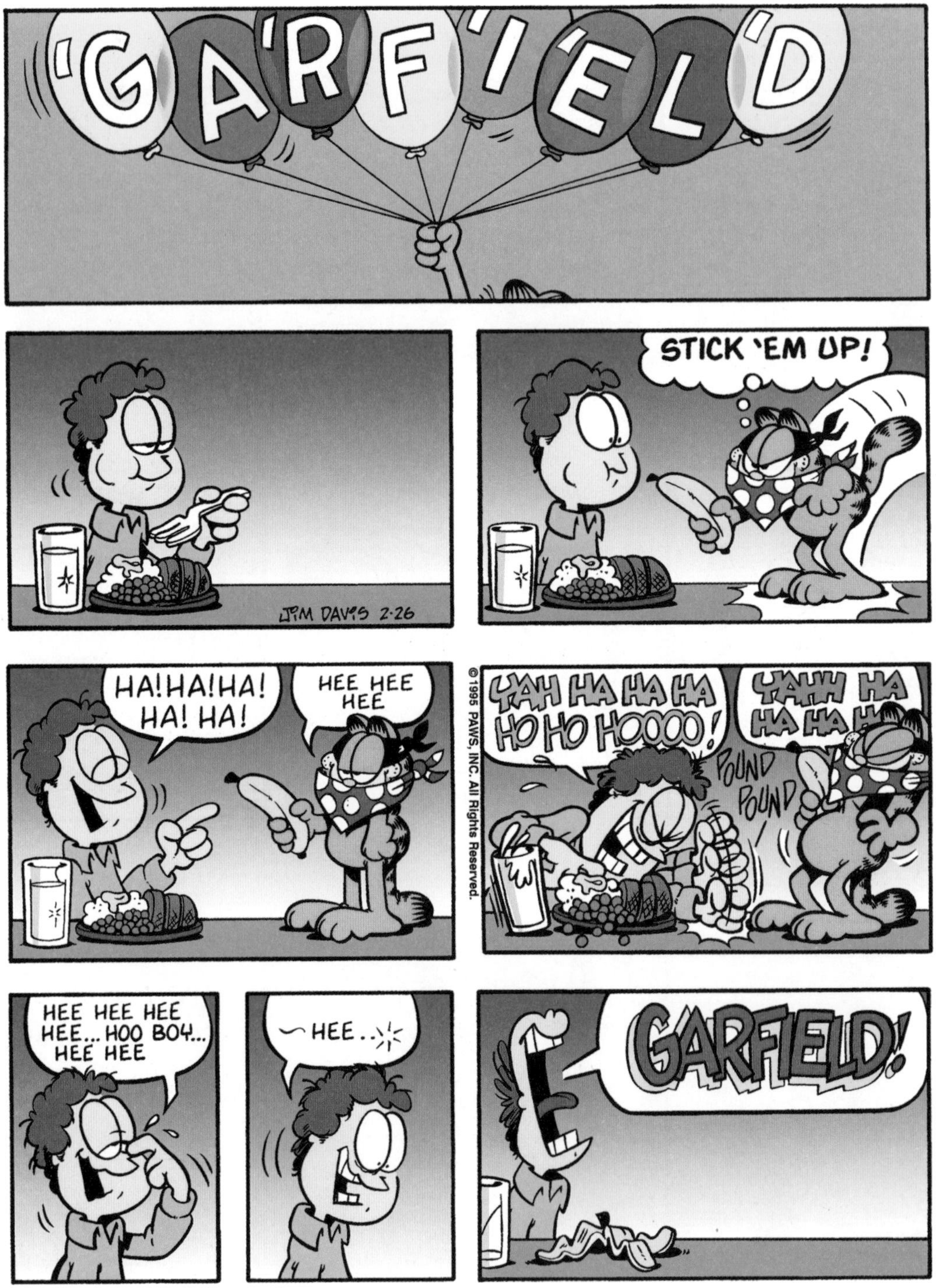
'G'A'R'F'I'E'L'D
JIM DAVIS 2·26
STICK 'EM UP!
HA! HA! HA! HA! HA!
HEE HEE HEE
© 1995 PAWS, INC. All Rights Reserved.
YAH HA HA HA HO HO HOOOO!
YAHH HA HA HA
POUND POUND
HEE HEE HEE HEE... HOO BOY... HEE HEE
HEE..
GARFIELD!

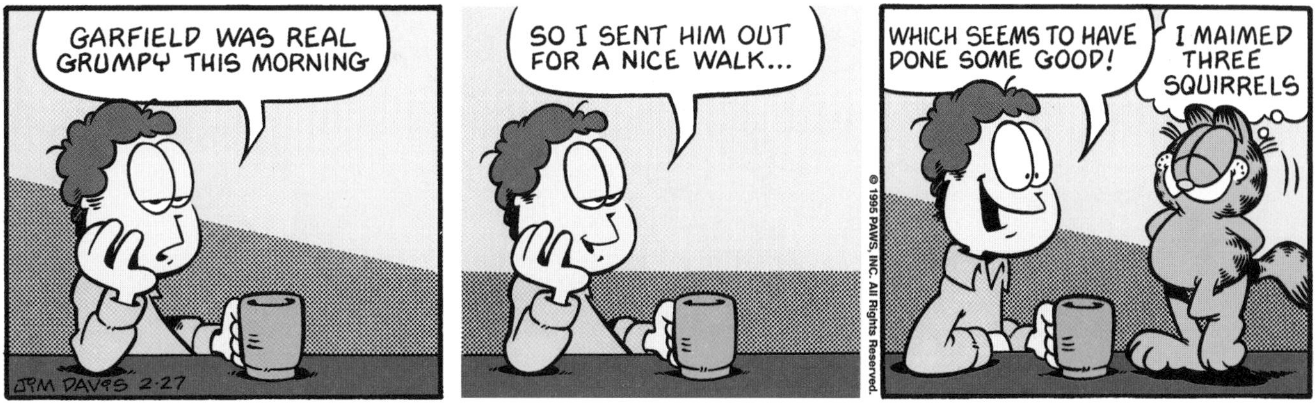
GARFIELD WAS REAL GRUMPY THIS MORNING
JIM DAVIS 2-27
SO I SENT HIM OUT FOR A NICE WALK...
© 1995 PAWS, INC. All Rights Reserved.
WHICH SEEMS TO HAVE DONE SOME GOOD!
I MAIMED THREE SQUIRRELS

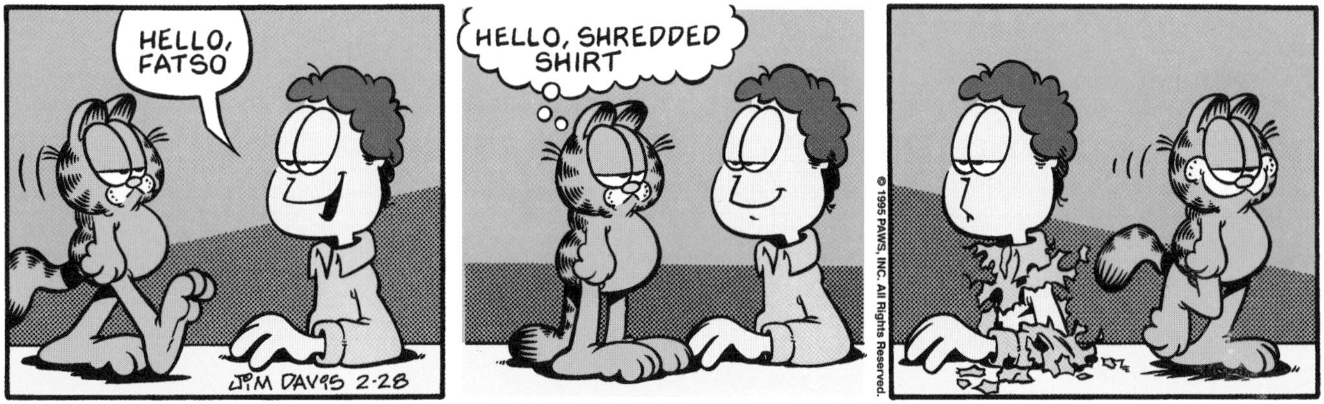
HELLO, FATSO
JIM DAVIS 2-28
HELLO, SHREDDED SHIRT
© 1995 PAWS, INC. All Rights Reserved.

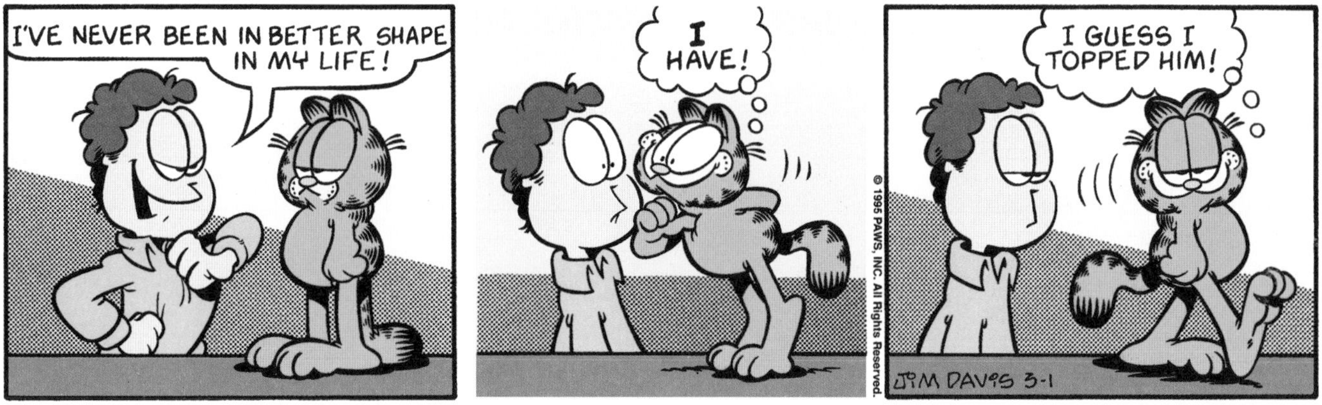
I'VE NEVER BEEN IN BETTER SHAPE IN MY LIFE!
I HAVE!
© 1995 PAWS, INC. All Rights Reserved.
I GUESS I TOPPED HIM!
JIM DAVIS 3-1

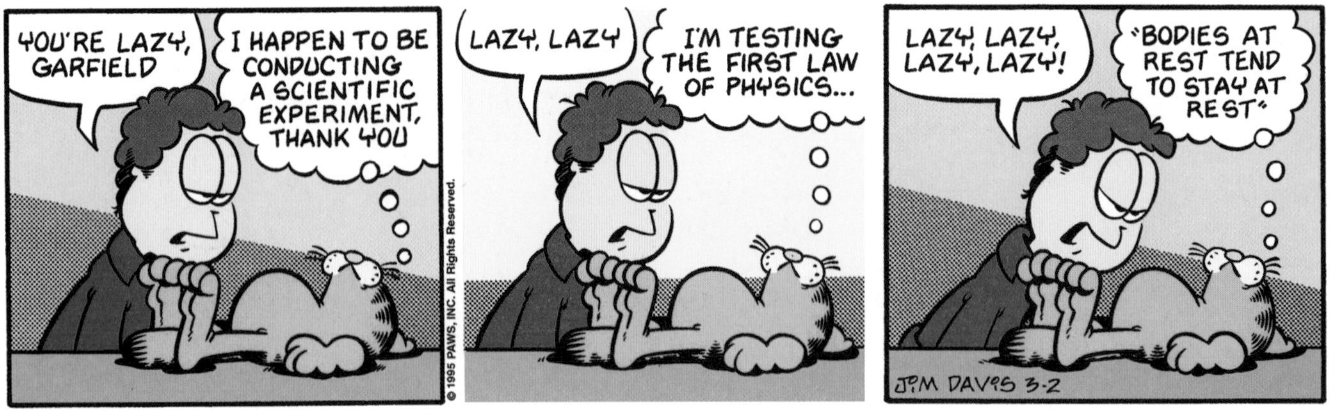
YOU'RE LAZY, GARFIELD
I HAPPEN TO BE CONDUCTING A SCIENTIFIC EXPERIMENT, THANK YOU
LAZY, LAZY
I'M TESTING THE FIRST LAW OF PHYSICS...
LAZY, LAZY, LAZY, LAZY!
"BODIES AT REST TEND TO STAY AT REST"
JIM DAVIS 3-2

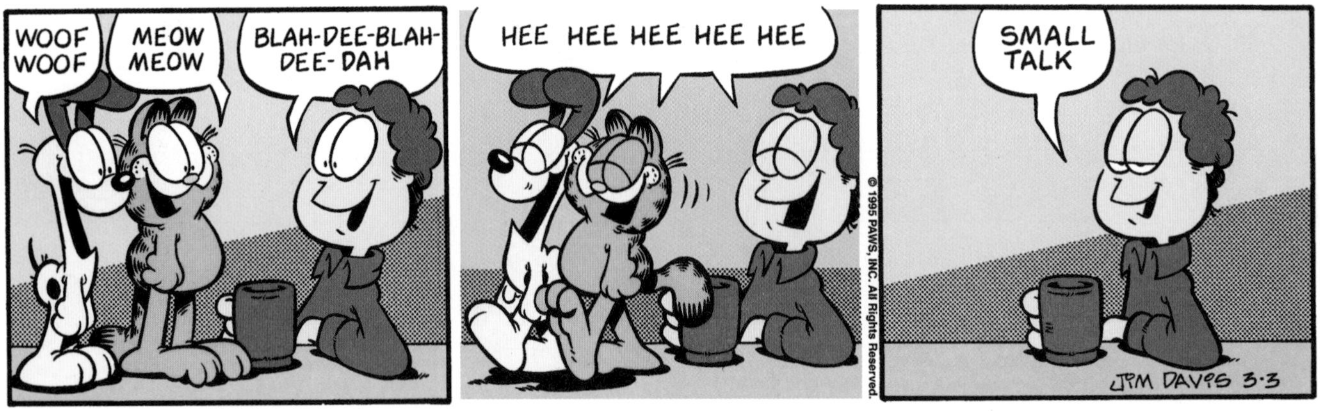
WOOF WOOF
MEOW MEOW
BLAH-DEE-BLAH-DEE-DAH
HEE HEE HEE HEE HEE
SMALL TALK
JIM DAVIS 3-3

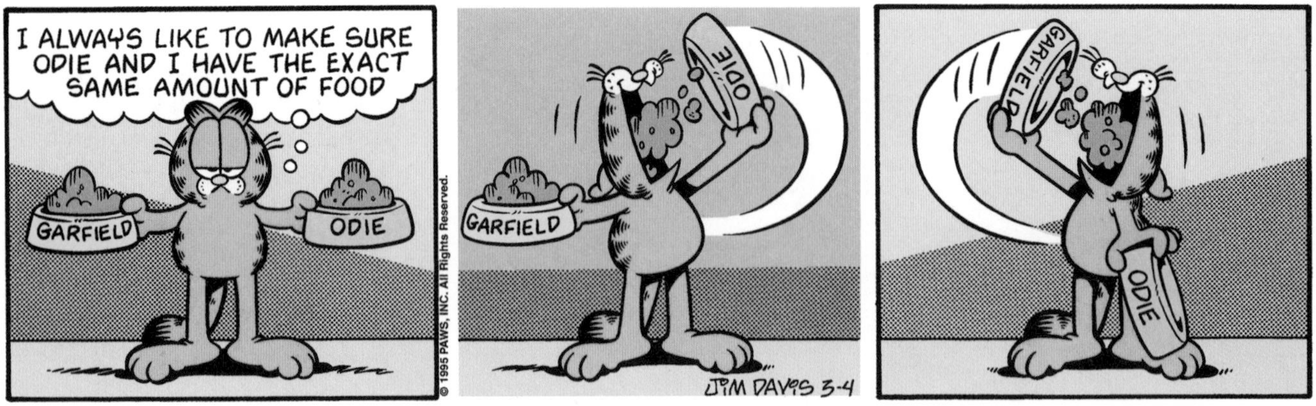
I ALWAYS LIKE TO MAKE SURE ODIE AND I HAVE THE EXACT SAME AMOUNT OF FOOD
GARFIELD
ODIE
GARFIELD
ODIE
JIM DAVIS 3-4
GARFIELD
ODIE

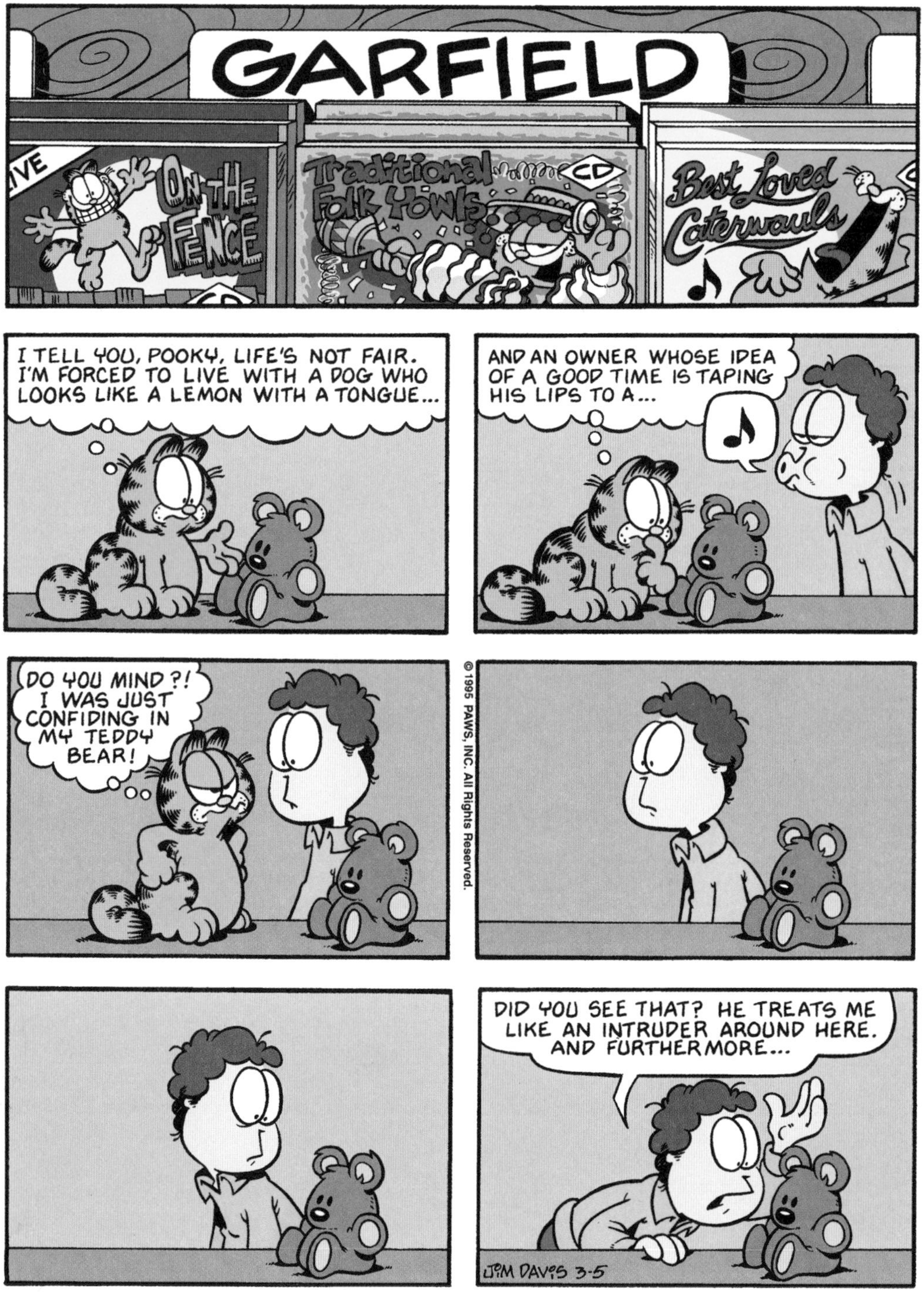
GARFIELD
LIVE
ON THE FENCE
CD
Traditional Folk Yowls
CD
Best Loved Caterwauls
I TELL YOU, POOKY, LIFE'S NOT FAIR. I'M FORCED TO LIVE WITH A DOG WHO LOOKS LIKE A LEMON WITH A TONGUE...
AND AN OWNER WHOSE IDEA OF A GOOD TIME IS TAPING HIS LIPS TO A...
DO YOU MIND?! I WAS JUST CONFIDING IN MY TEDDY BEAR!
DID YOU SEE THAT? HE TREATS ME LIKE AN INTRUDER AROUND HERE. AND FURTHERMORE...
JIM DAVIS 3-5

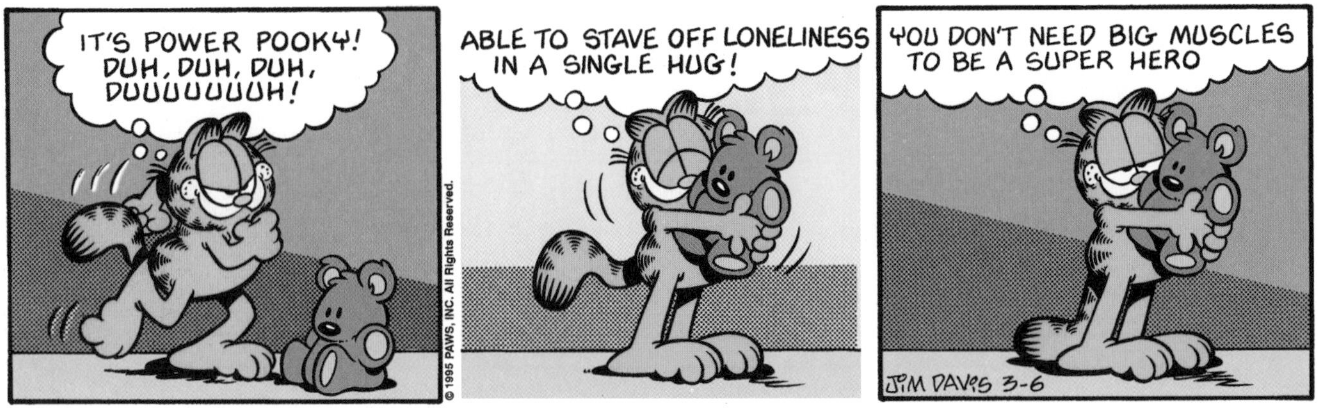
IT'S POWER POOKY! DUH, DUH, DUH, DUUUUUUUH!
ABLE TO STAVE OFF LONELINESS IN A SINGLE HUG!
YOU DON'T NEED BIG MUSCLES TO BE A SUPER HERO
© 1995 PAWS, INC. All Rights Reserved.
JIM DAVIS 3-6

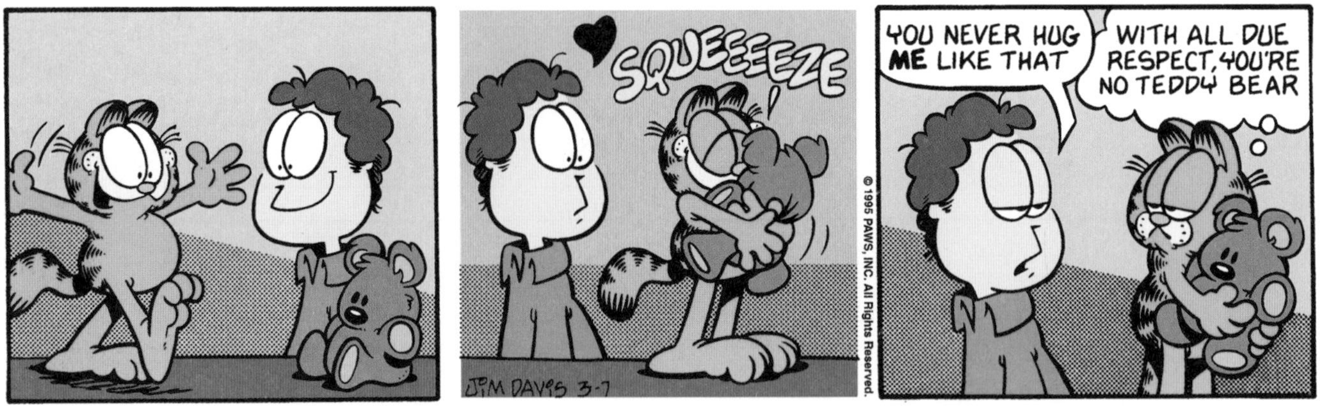
SQUEEEEEZE
JIM DAVIS 3-7
© 1995 PAWS, INC. All Rights Reserved.
YOU NEVER HUG **ME** LIKE THAT
WITH ALL DUE RESPECT, YOU'RE NO TEDDY BEAR

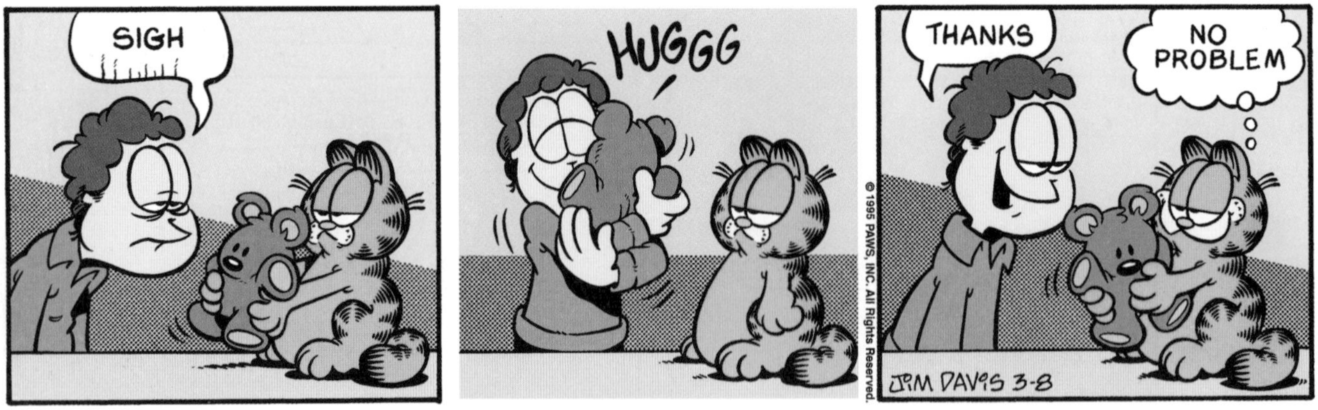
SIGH
HUGGG
© 1995 PAWS, INC. All Rights Reserved.
THANKS
NO PROBLEM
JIM DAVIS 3-8

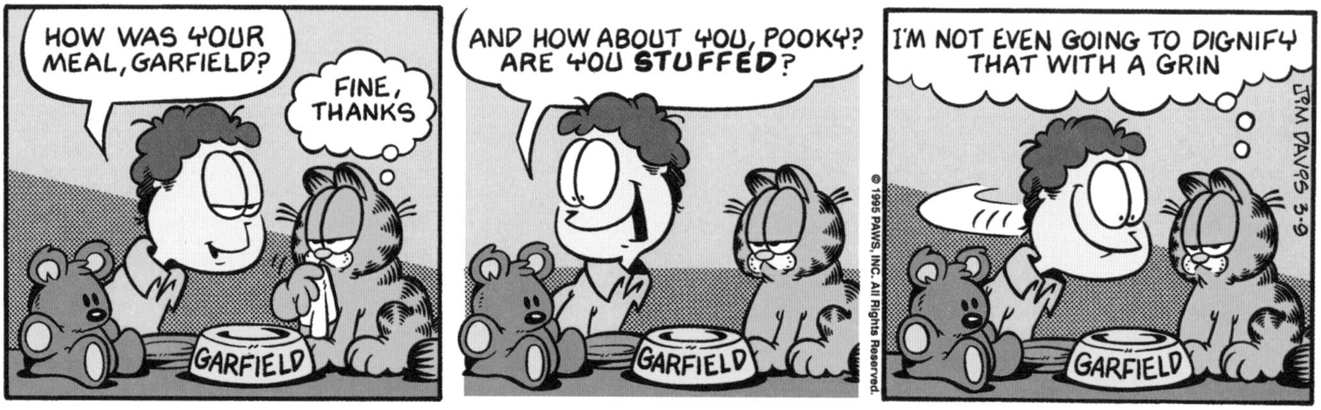
HOW WAS YOUR MEAL, GARFIELD?
FINE, THANKS
AND HOW ABOUT YOU, POOKY? ARE YOU STUFFED?
I'M NOT EVEN GOING TO DIGNIFY THAT WITH A GRIN
GARFIELD
© 1995 PAWS, INC. All Rights Reserved.
JIM DAVIS 3-9

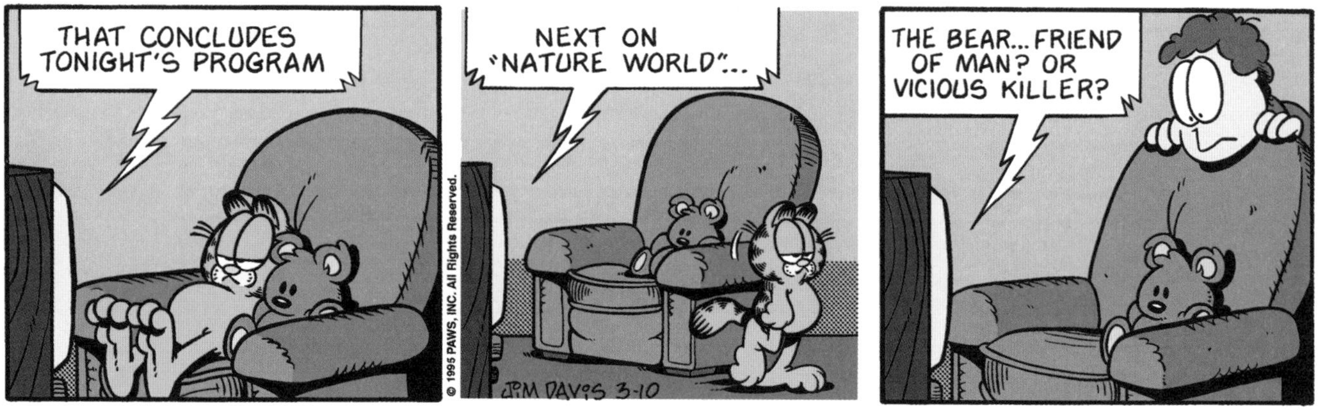
THAT CONCLUDES TONIGHT'S PROGRAM
NEXT ON "NATURE WORLD"...
THE BEAR... FRIEND OF MAN? OR VICIOUS KILLER?
© 1995 PAWS, INC. All Rights Reserved.
JIM DAVIS 3-10

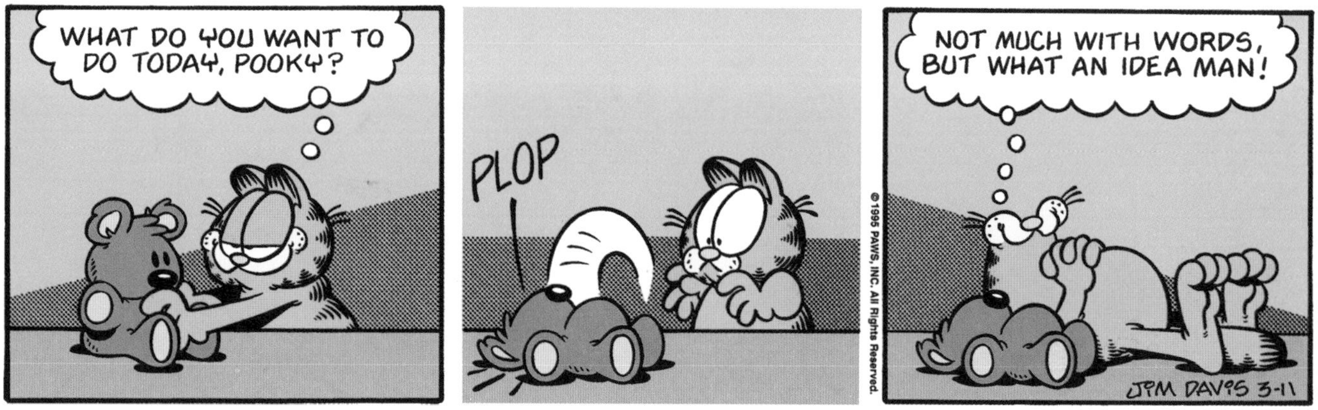
WHAT DO YOU WANT TO DO TODAY, POOKY?
PLOP
NOT MUCH WITH WORDS, BUT WHAT AN IDEA MAN!
© 1995 PAWS, INC. All Rights Reserved.
JIM DAVIS 3-11

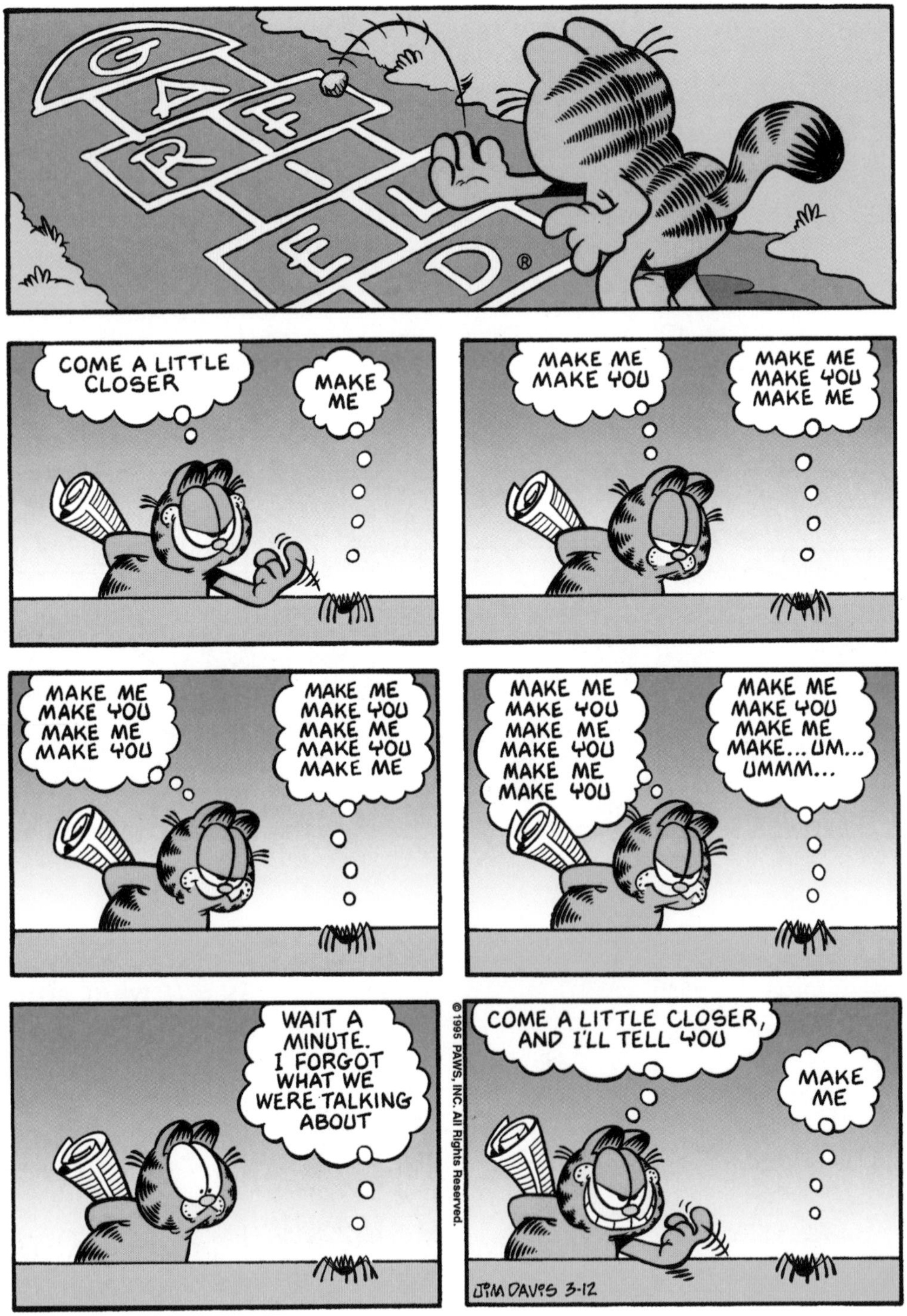
GARFIELD®
COME A LITTLE CLOSER
MAKE ME
MAKE ME MAKE YOU
MAKE ME MAKE YOU MAKE ME
MAKE ME MAKE YOU MAKE ME MAKE YOU
MAKE ME MAKE YOU MAKE ME MAKE YOU MAKE ME
MAKE ME MAKE YOU MAKE ME MAKE YOU MAKE ME MAKE YOU
MAKE ME MAKE YOU MAKE ME MAKE... UM... UMMM...
WAIT A MINUTE. I FORGOT WHAT WE WERE TALKING ABOUT
COME A LITTLE CLOSER, AND I'LL TELL YOU
MAKE ME
JIM DAVIS 3-12

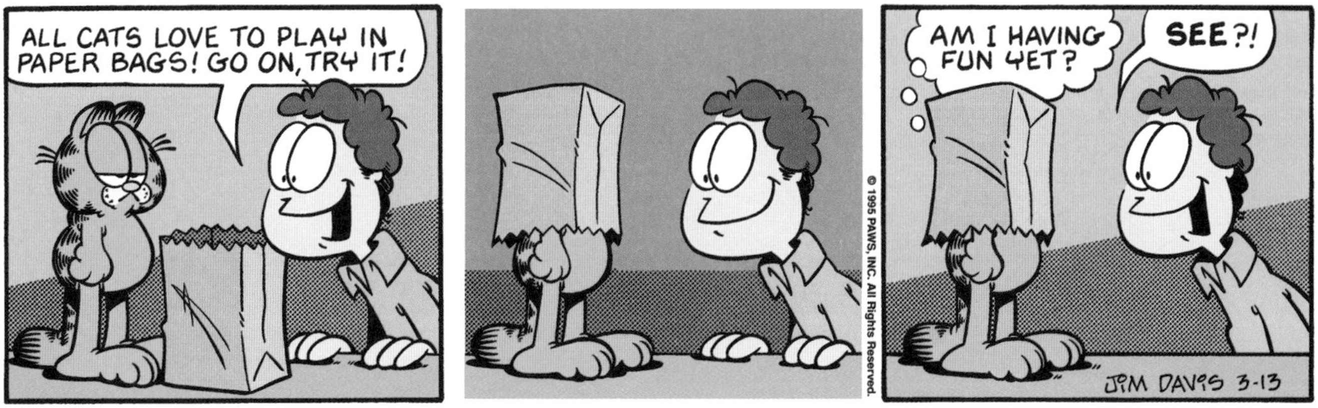
ALL CATS LOVE TO PLAY IN PAPER BAGS! GO ON, TRY IT!
© 1995 PAWS, INC. All Rights Reserved.
AM I HAVING FUN YET?
SEE?!
JIM DAVIS 3-13

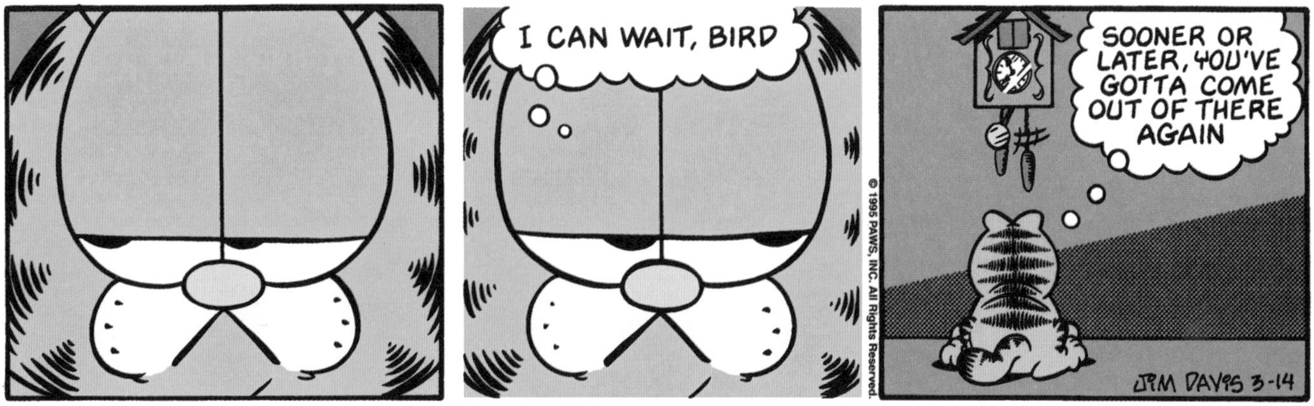
I CAN WAIT, BIRD
© 1995 PAWS, INC. All Rights Reserved.
SOONER OR LATER, YOU'VE GOTTA COME OUT OF THERE AGAIN
JIM DAVIS 3-14

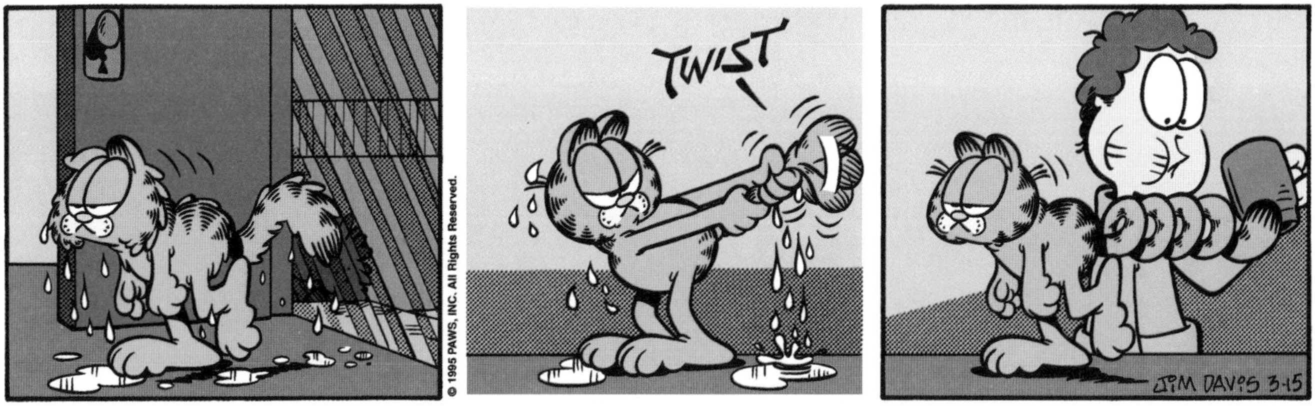
© 1995 PAWS, INC. All Rights Reserved.
TWIST
JIM DAVIS 3-15

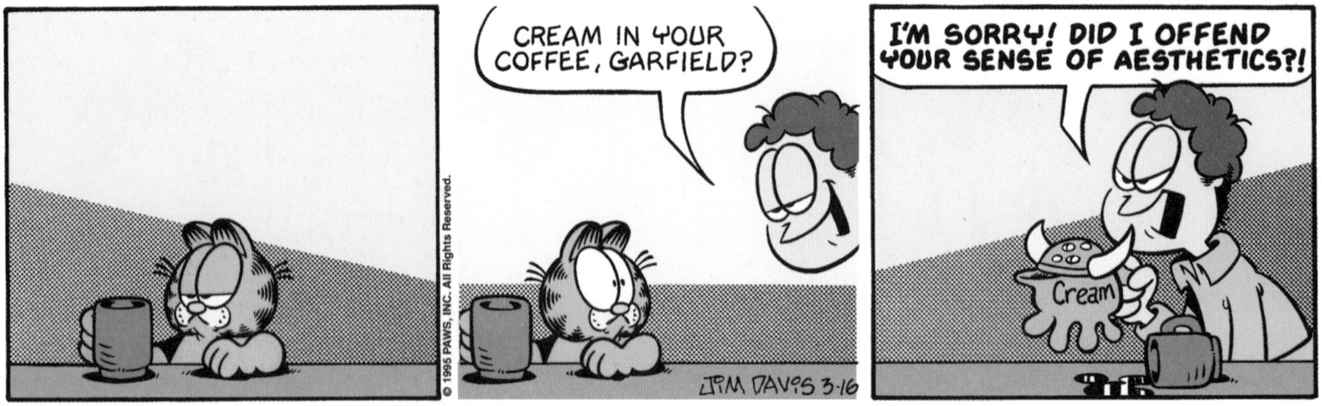
© 1995 PAWS, INC. All Rights Reserved.
CREAM IN YOUR COFFEE, GARFIELD?
JIM DAVIS 3-16
I'M SORRY! DID I OFFEND YOUR SENSE OF AESTHETICS?!
Cream

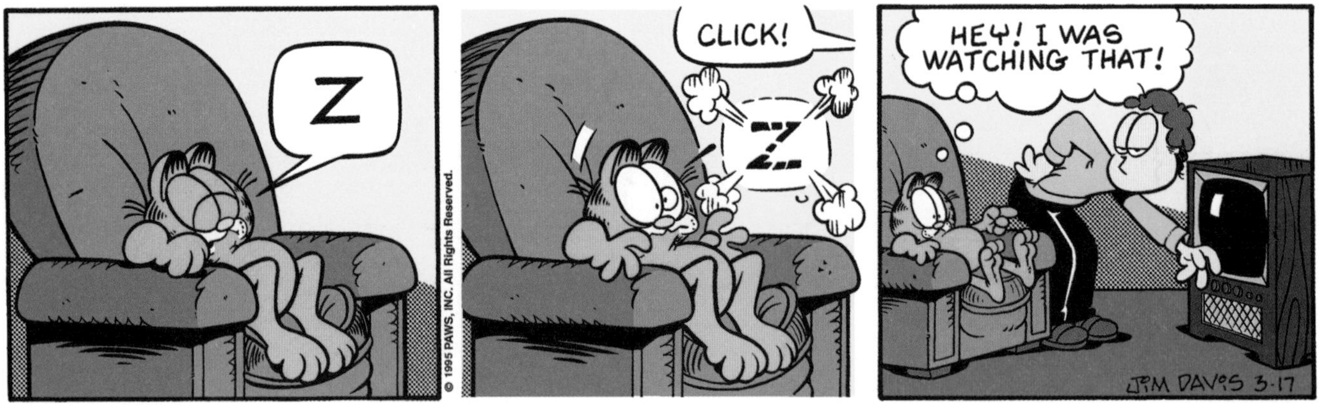
Z
© 1995 PAWS, INC. All Rights Reserved.
CLICK!
HEY! I WAS WATCHING THAT!
JIM DAVIS 3-17

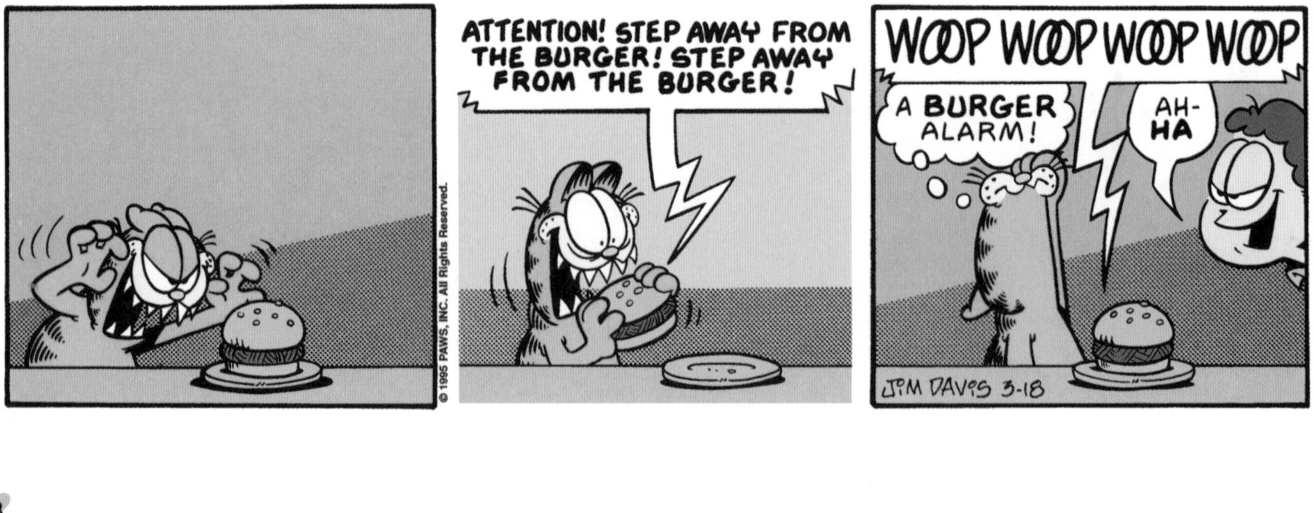
© 1995 PAWS, INC. All Rights Reserved.
ATTENTION! STEP AWAY FROM THE BURGER! STEP AWAY FROM THE BURGER!
WOOP WOOP WOOP WOOP
A BURGER ALARM!
AH-HA
JIM DAVIS 3-18

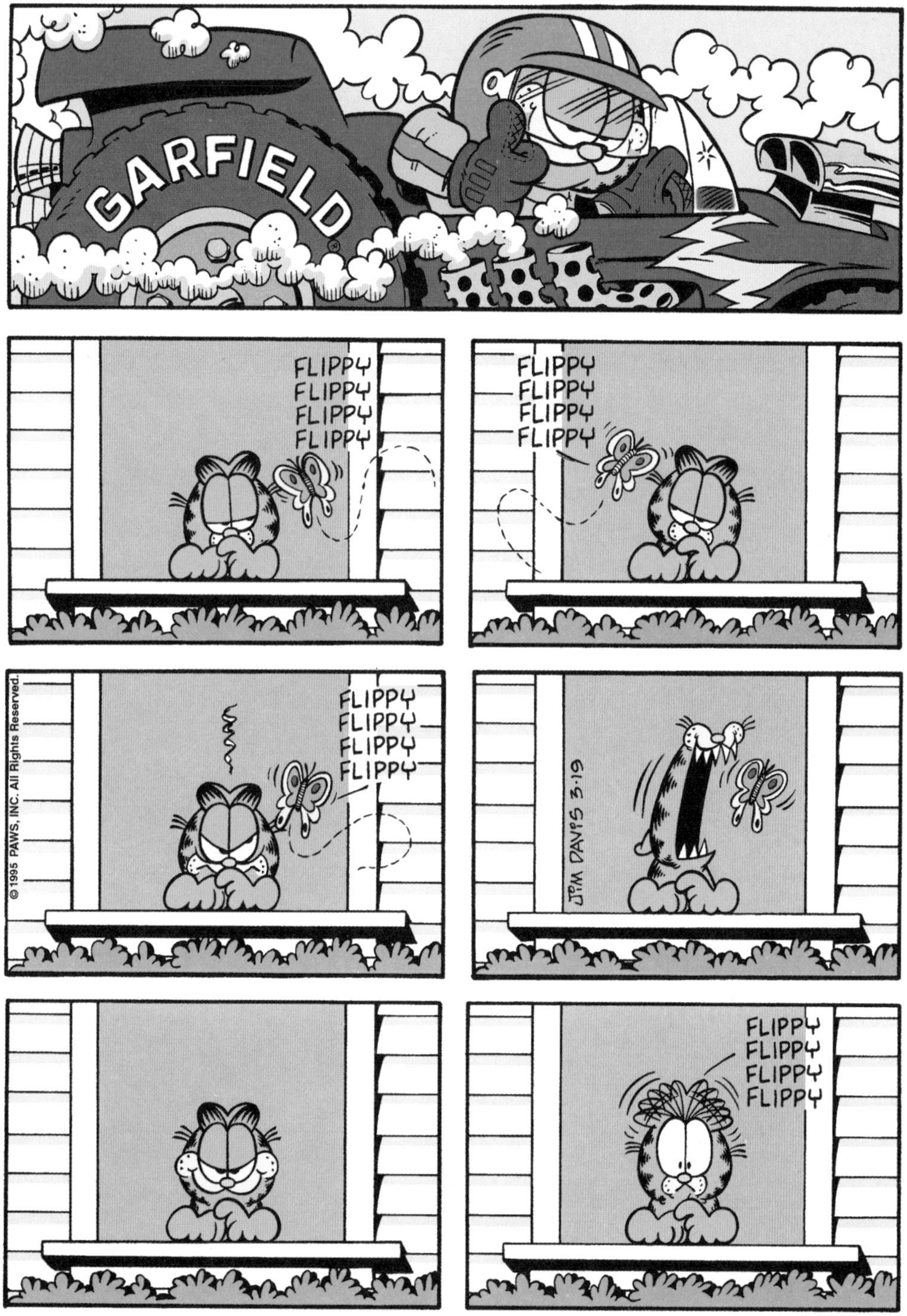
GARFIELD
FLIPPY
FLIPPY
FLIPPY
FLIPPY
FLIPPY
FLIPPY
FLIPPY
FLIPPY
FLIPPY
FLIPPY
FLIPPY
FLIPPY
JPM DAVIS 3-19
FLIPPY
FLIPPY
FLIPPY
FLIPPY

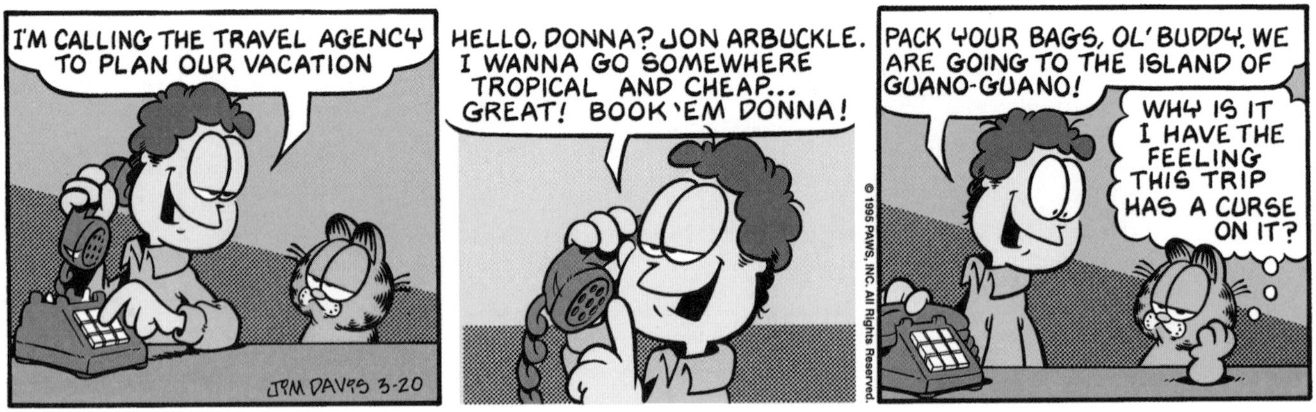
I'M CALLING THE TRAVEL AGENCY TO PLAN OUR VACATION
JIM DAVIS 3-20
HELLO, DONNA? JON ARBUCKLE. I WANNA GO SOMEWHERE TROPICAL AND CHEAP... GREAT! BOOK 'EM DONNA!
© 1995 PAWS, INC. All Rights Reserved.
PACK YOUR BAGS, OL' BUDDY. WE ARE GOING TO THE ISLAND OF GUANO-GUANO!
WHY IS IT I HAVE THE FEELING THIS TRIP HAS A CURSE ON IT?

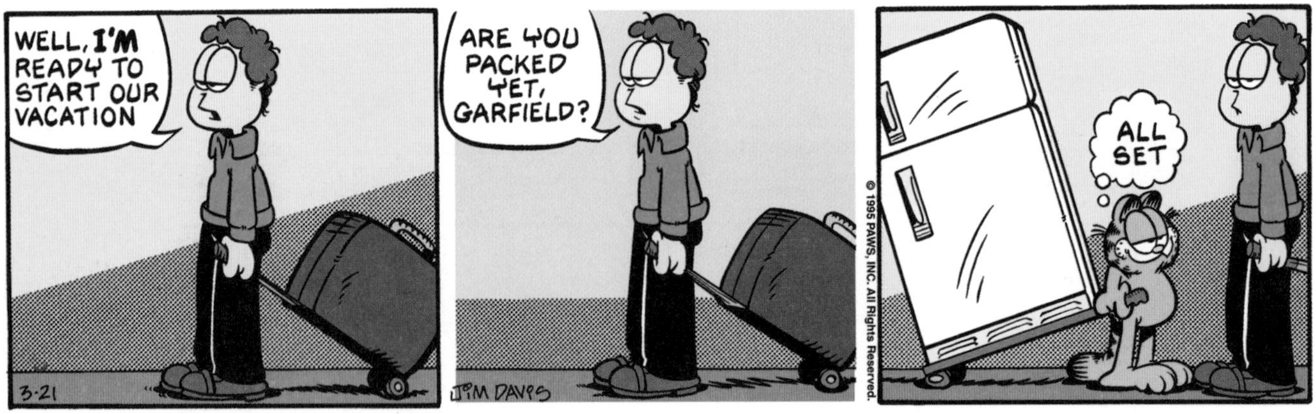
WELL, I'M READY TO START OUR VACATION
3-21
ARE YOU PACKED YET, GARFIELD?
JIM DAVIS
© 1995 PAWS, INC. All Rights Reserved.
ALL SET

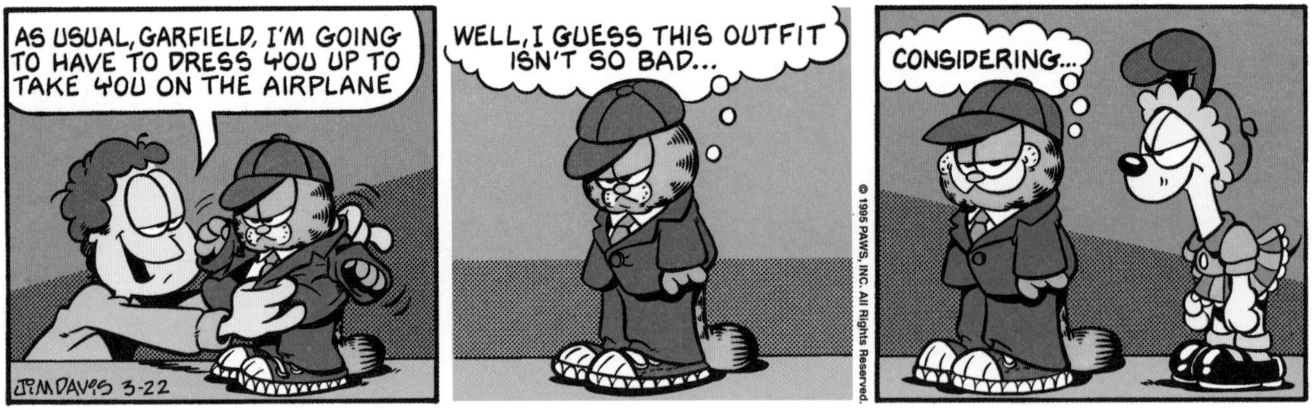
AS USUAL, GARFIELD, I'M GOING TO HAVE TO DRESS YOU UP TO TAKE YOU ON THE AIRPLANE
JIM DAVIS 3-22
WELL, I GUESS THIS OUTFIT ISN'T SO BAD...
© 1995 PAWS, INC. All Rights Reserved.
CONSIDERING...

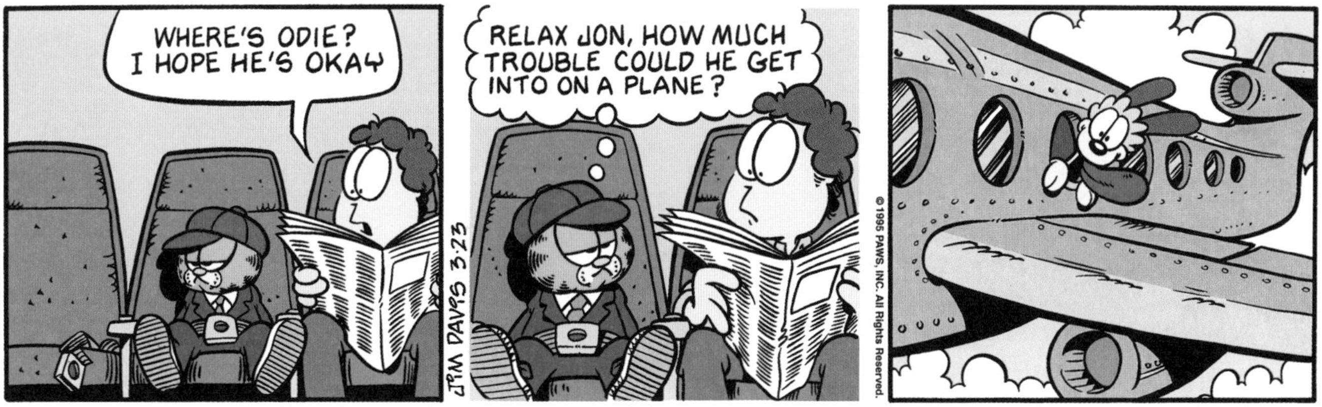
WHERE'S ODIE? I HOPE HE'S OKAY
RELAX JON, HOW MUCH TROUBLE COULD HE GET INTO ON A PLANE?
JPM DAVPS 3-23
© 1995 PAWS, INC. All Rights Reserved.

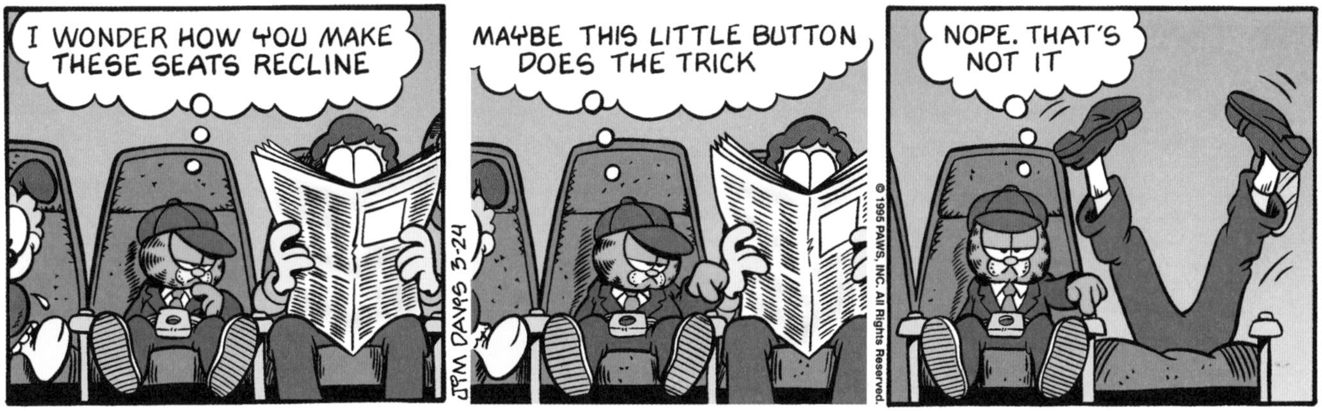
I WONDER HOW YOU MAKE THESE SEATS RECLINE
MAYBE THIS LITTLE BUTTON DOES THE TRICK
NOPE. THAT'S NOT IT
JPM DAVPS 3-24
© 1995 PAWS, INC. All Rights Reserved.

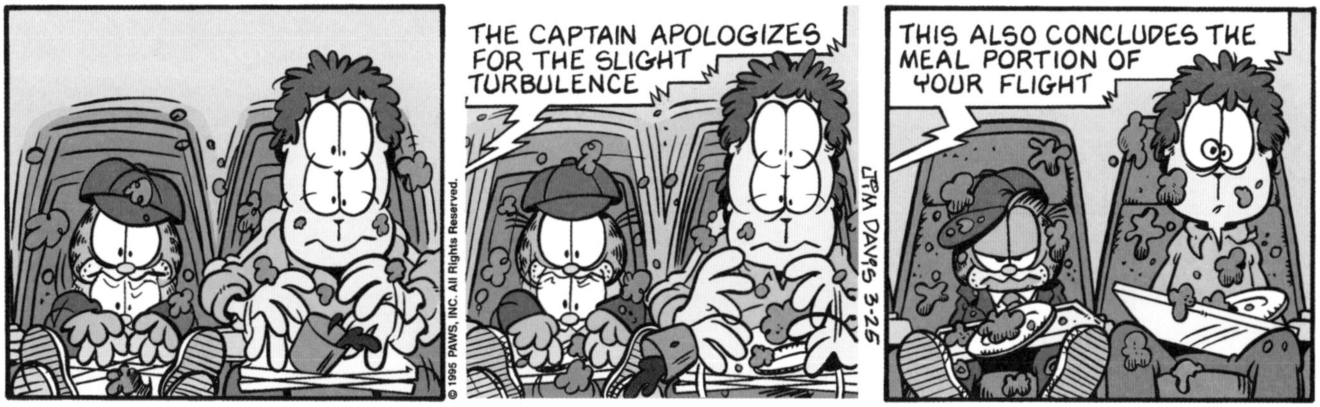
THE CAPTAIN APOLOGIZES FOR THE SLIGHT TURBULENCE
THIS ALSO CONCLUDES THE MEAL PORTION OF YOUR FLIGHT
JPM DAVPS 3-25
© 1995 PAWS, INC. All Rights Reserved.

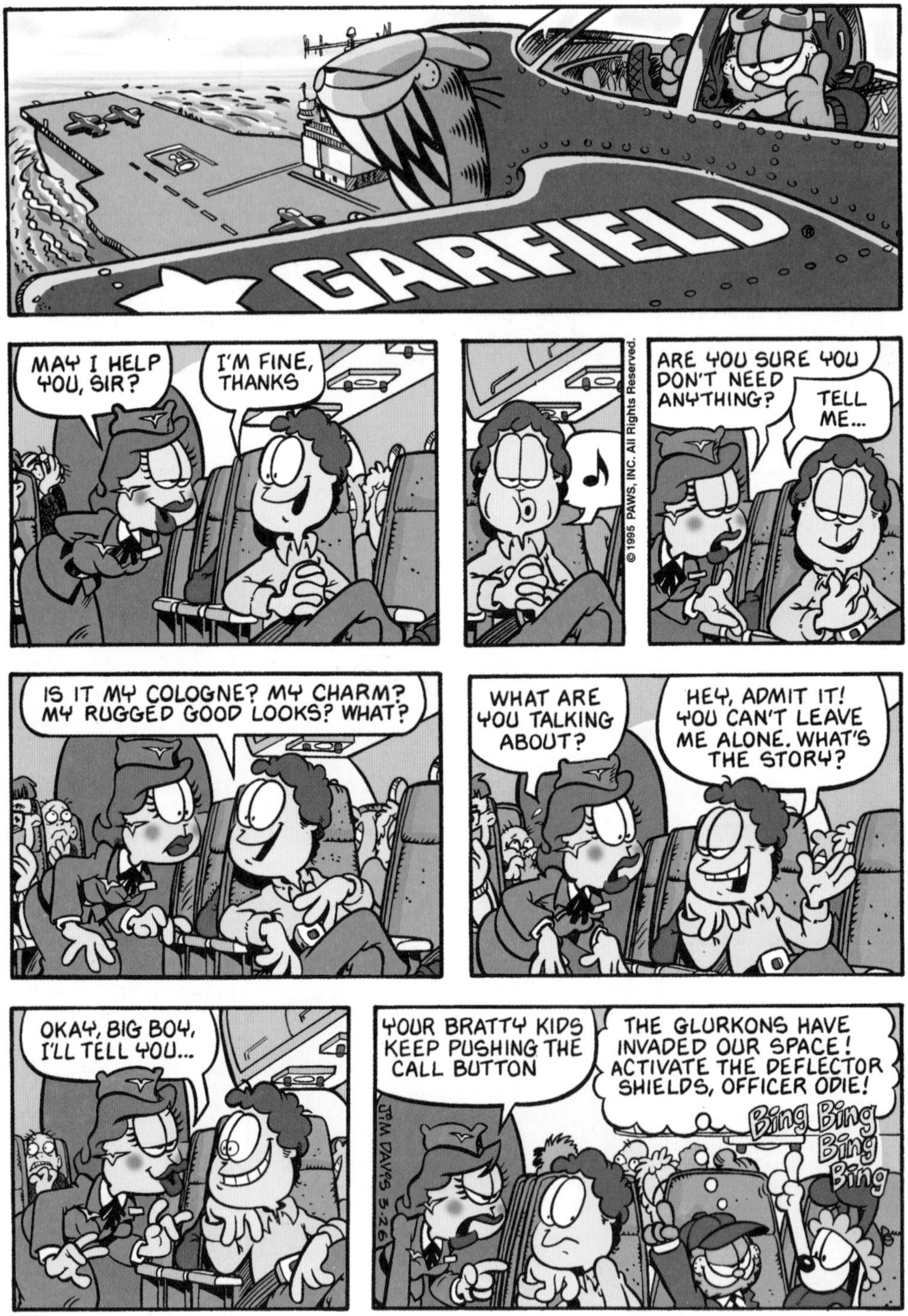
GARFIELD®
MAY I HELP YOU, SIR?
I'M FINE, THANKS
© 1995 PAWS, INC. All Rights Reserved.
ARE YOU SURE YOU DON'T NEED ANYTHING?
TELL ME...
IS IT MY COLOGNE? MY CHARM? MY RUGGED GOOD LOOKS? WHAT?
WHAT ARE YOU TALKING ABOUT?
HEY, ADMIT IT! YOU CAN'T LEAVE ME ALONE. WHAT'S THE STORY?
OKAY, BIG BOY, I'LL TELL YOU...
JIM DAVIS 3-26
YOUR BRATTY KIDS KEEP PUSHING THE CALL BUTTON
THE GLURKONS HAVE INVADED OUR SPACE! ACTIVATE THE DEFLECTOR SHIELDS, OFFICER ODIE!
Bing Bing Bing Bing

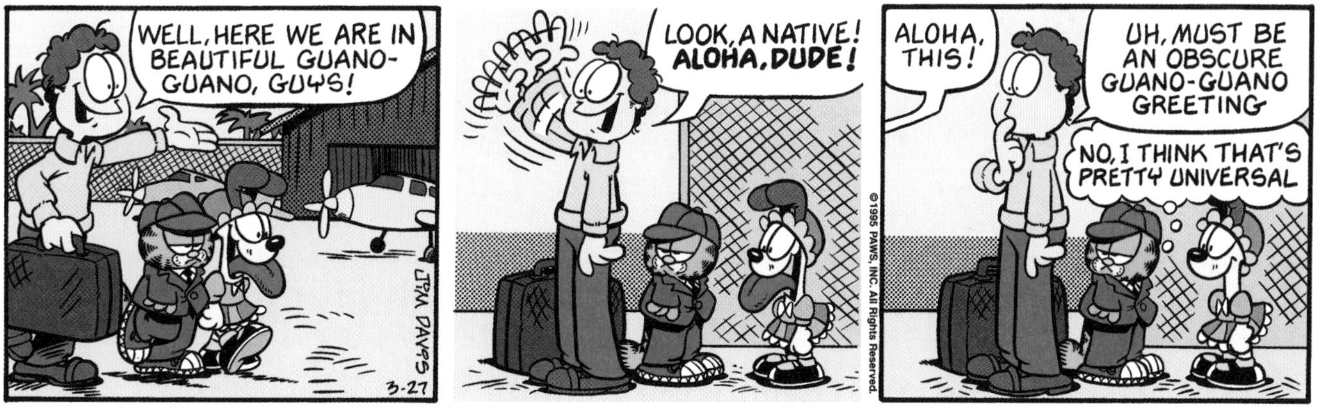
WELL, HERE WE ARE IN BEAUTIFUL GUANO-GUANO, GUYS!
JIM DAVIS
3-27
LOOK, A NATIVE! **ALOHA, DUDE!**
©1995 PAWS, INC. All Rights Reserved.
ALOHA, THIS!
UH, MUST BE AN OBSCURE GUANO-GUANO GREETING
NO, I THINK THAT'S PRETTY UNIVERSAL

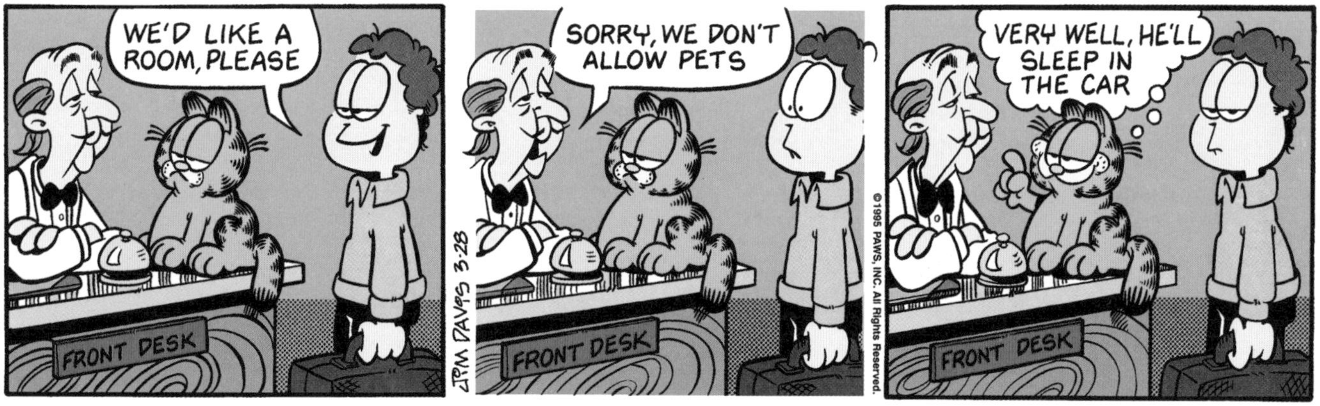
WE'D LIKE A ROOM, PLEASE
FRONT DESK
JIM DAVIS 3-28
SORRY, WE DON'T ALLOW PETS
FRONT DESK
©1995 PAWS, INC. All Rights Reserved.
VERY WELL, HE'LL SLEEP IN THE CAR
FRONT DESK

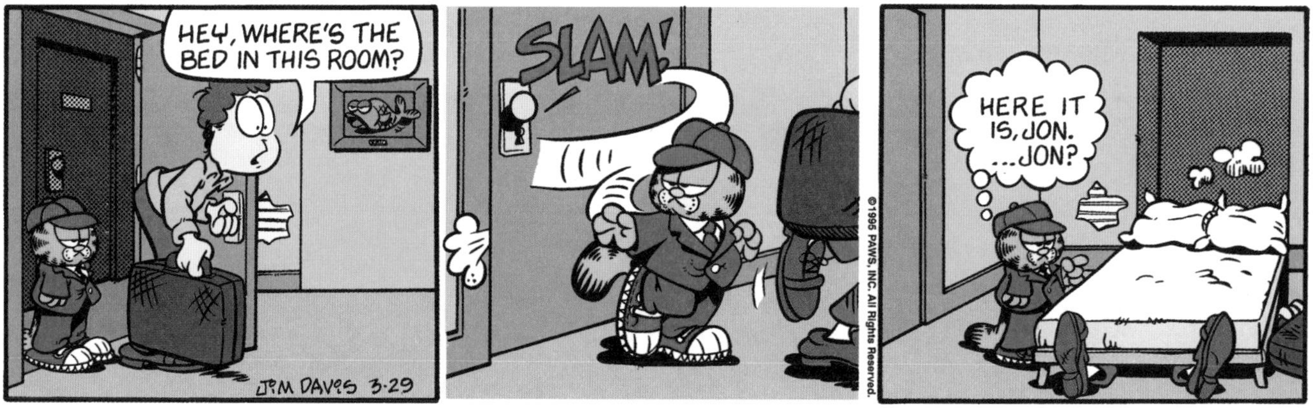
HEY, WHERE'S THE BED IN THIS ROOM?
JIM DAVIS 3-29
SLAM!
©1995 PAWS, INC. All Rights Reserved.
HERE IT IS, JON. ...JON?

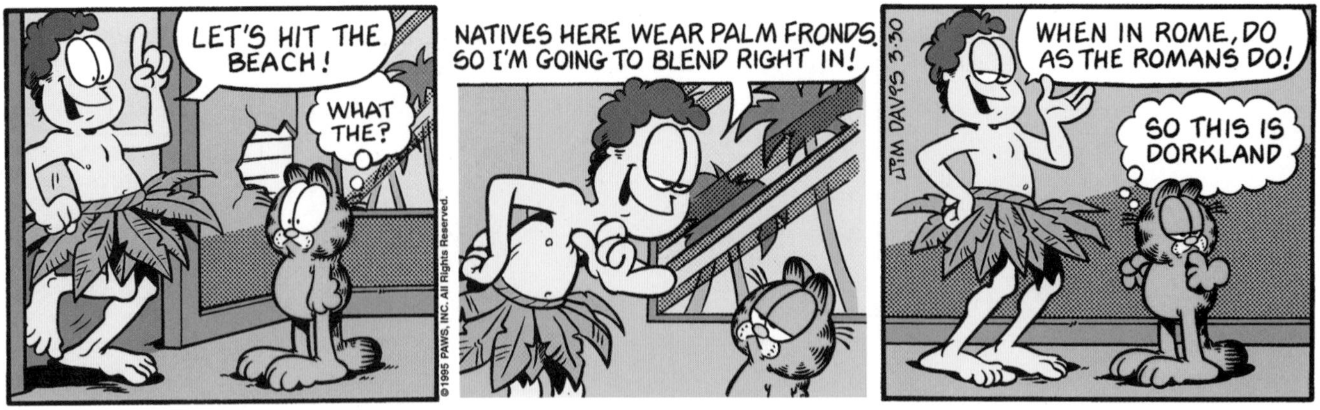
LET'S HIT THE BEACH!
WHAT THE?
©1995 PAWS, INC. All Rights Reserved.
NATIVES HERE WEAR PALM FRONDS, SO I'M GOING TO BLEND RIGHT IN!
JIM DAVIS 3-30
WHEN IN ROME, DO AS THE ROMANS DO!
SO THIS IS DORKLAND

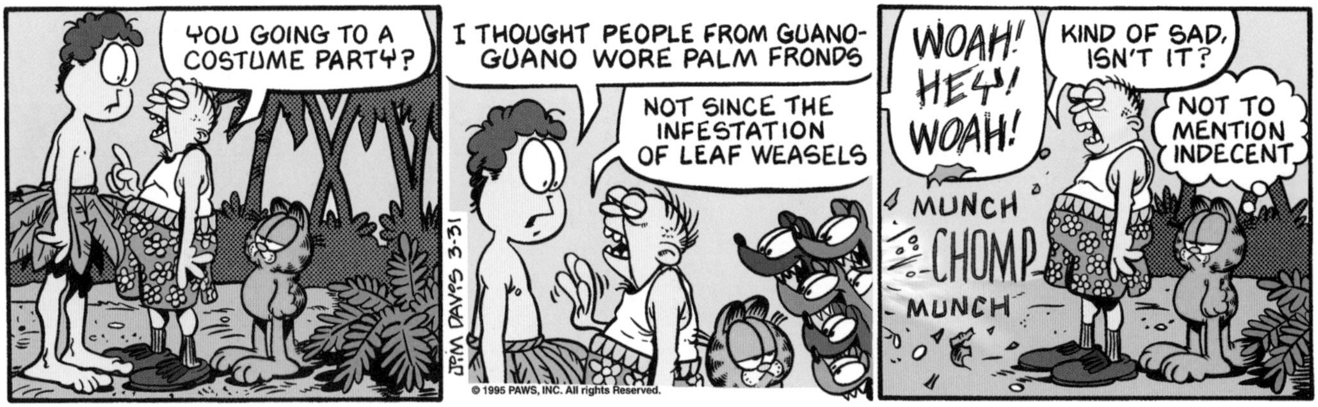
YOU GOING TO A COSTUME PARTY?
JIM DAVIS 3-31
I THOUGHT PEOPLE FROM GUANO-GUANO WORE PALM FRONDS
NOT SINCE THE INFESTATION OF LEAF WEASELS
© 1995 PAWS, INC. All rights Reserved.
WOAH! HEY! WOAH!
KIND OF SAD, ISN'T IT?
NOT TO MENTION INDECENT
MUNCH
CHOMP
MUNCH

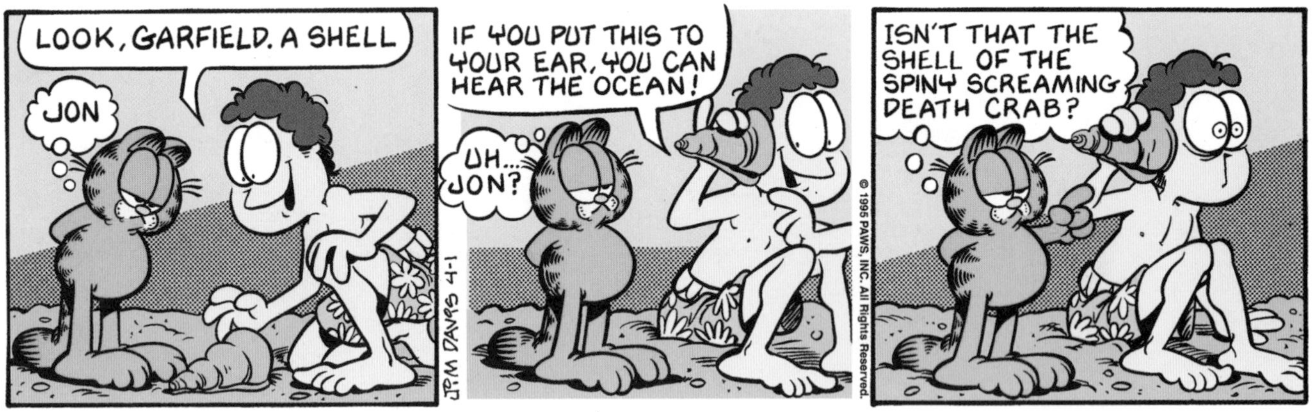
LOOK, GARFIELD. A SHELL
JON
JIM DAVIS 4-1
IF YOU PUT THIS TO YOUR EAR, YOU CAN HEAR THE OCEAN!
UH... JON?
© 1995 PAWS, INC. All Rights Reserved.
ISN'T THAT THE SHELL OF THE SPINY SCREAMING DEATH CRAB?

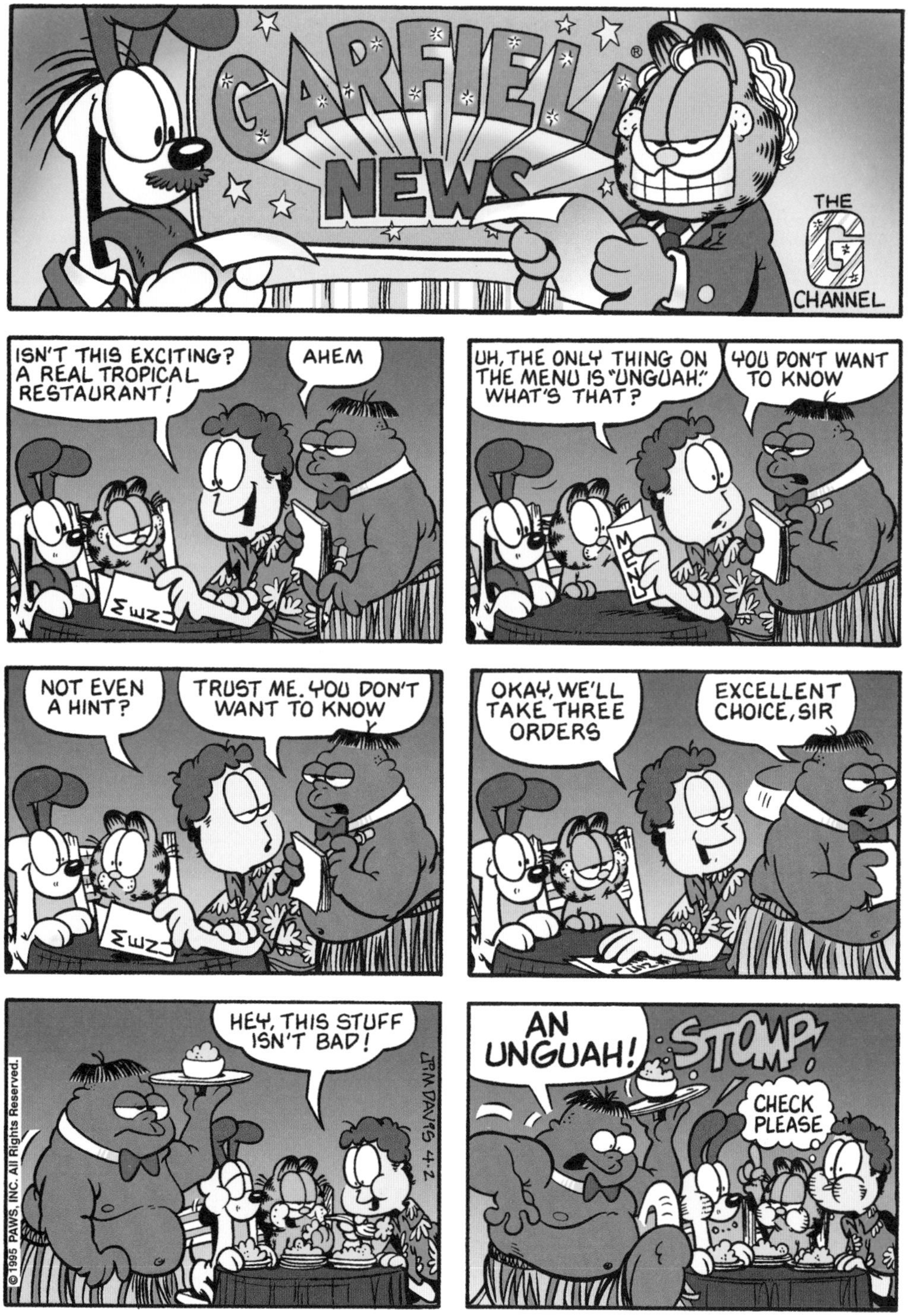
GARFIELD
NEWS
THE G CHANNEL
ISN'T THIS EXCITING? A REAL TROPICAL RESTAURANT!
AHEM
MENU
UH, THE ONLY THING ON THE MENU IS "UNGUAH." WHAT'S THAT?
YOU DON'T WANT TO KNOW
NOT EVEN A HINT?
TRUST ME. YOU DON'T WANT TO KNOW
OKAY, WE'LL TAKE THREE ORDERS
EXCELLENT CHOICE, SIR
HEY, THIS STUFF ISN'T BAD!
© 1995 PAWS, INC. All Rights Reserved.
AN UNGUAH!
STOMP!
CHECK PLEASE

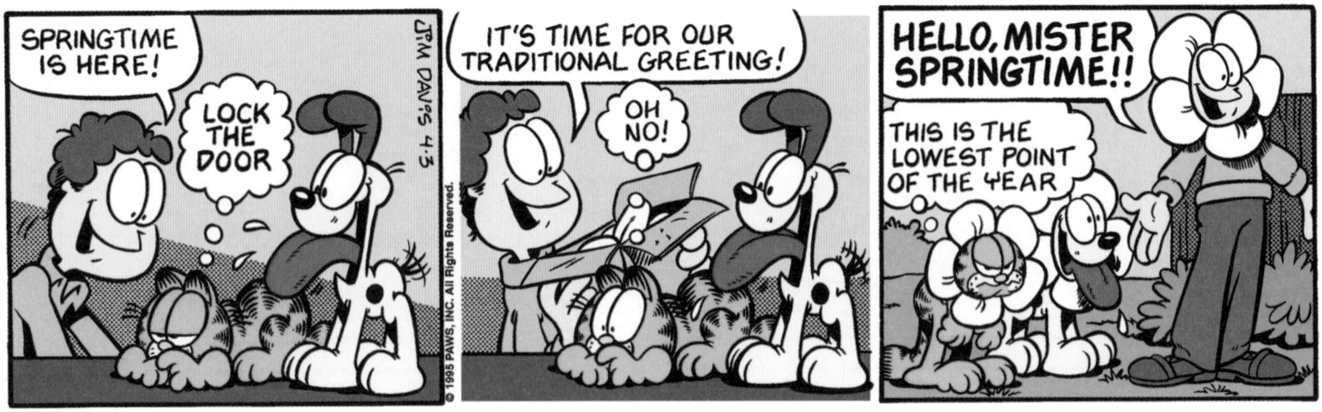
SPRINGTIME IS HERE!
LOCK THE DOOR
JIM DAVIS 4-3
© 1995 PAWS, INC. All Rights Reserved.
IT'S TIME FOR OUR TRADITIONAL GREETING!
OH NO!
HELLO, MISTER SPRINGTIME!!
THIS IS THE LOWEST POINT OF THE YEAR

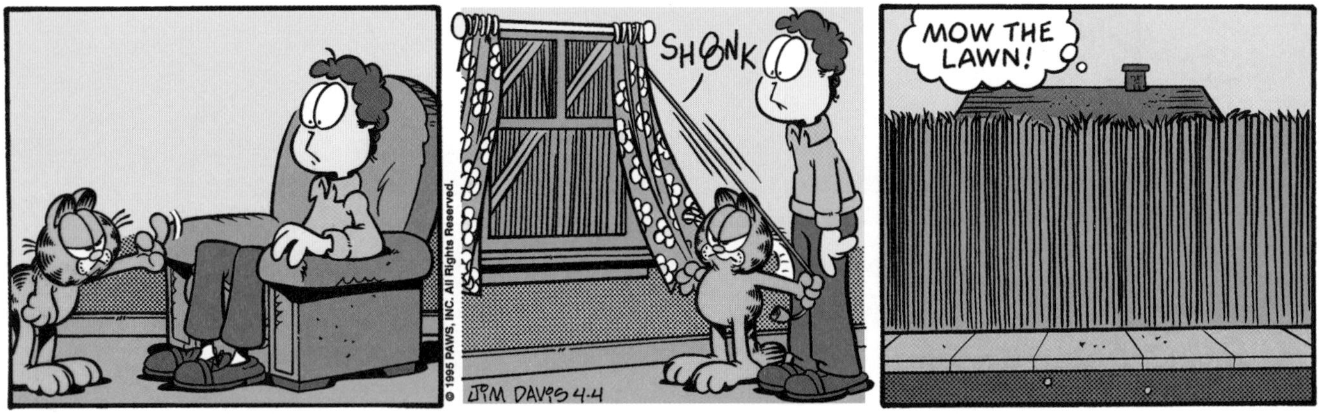
© 1995 PAWS, INC. All Rights Reserved.
JIM DAVIS 4-4
SHOONK
MOW THE LAWN!

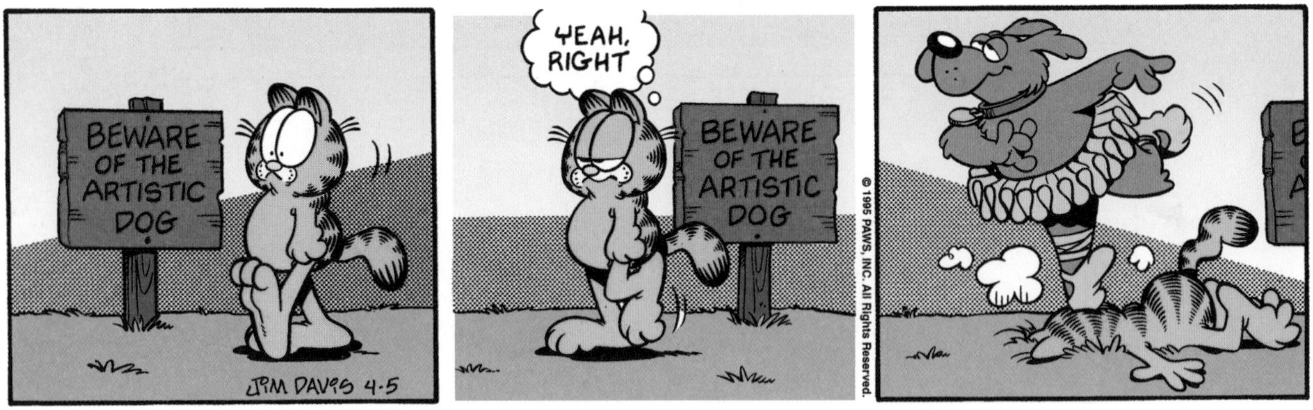
BEWARE OF THE ARTISTIC DOG
JIM DAVIS 4-5
YEAH, RIGHT
BEWARE OF THE ARTISTIC DOG
© 1995 PAWS, INC. All Rights Reserved.

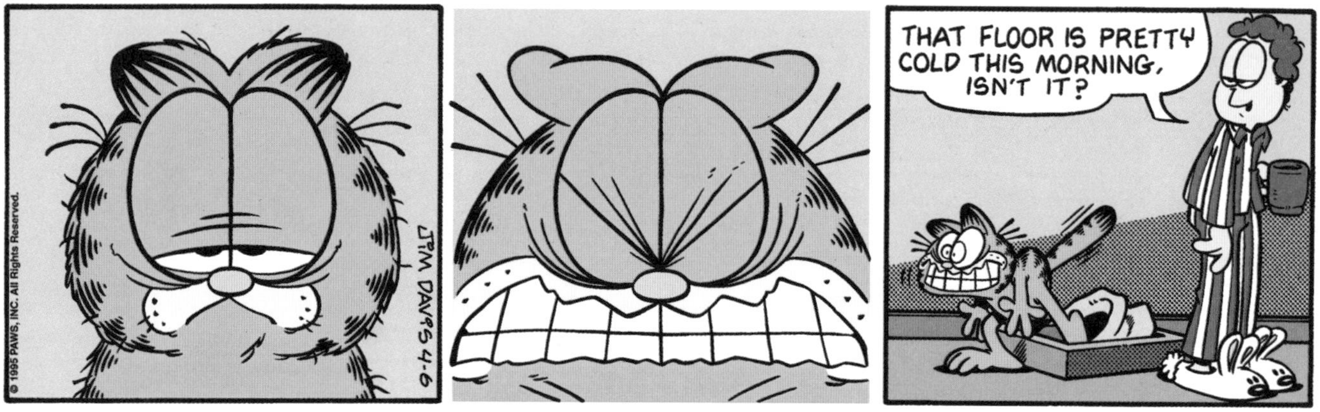
© 1995 PAWS, INC. All Rights Reserved.
JIM DAVIS 4-6
THAT FLOOR IS PRETTY COLD THIS MORNING, ISN'T IT?

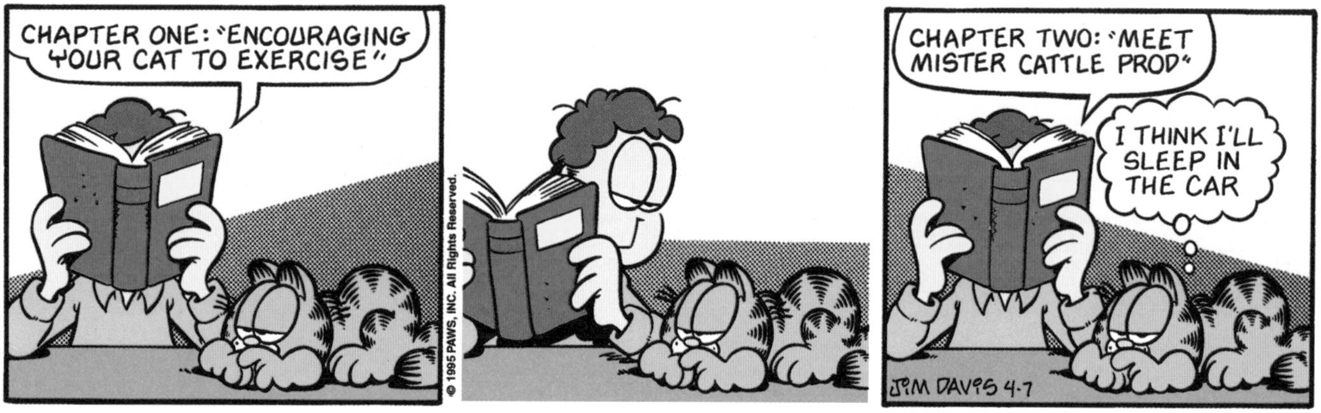
CHAPTER ONE: "ENCOURAGING YOUR CAT TO EXERCISE"
© 1995 PAWS, INC. All Rights Reserved.
CHAPTER TWO: "MEET MISTER CATTLE PROD"
I THINK I'LL SLEEP IN THE CAR
JIM DAVIS 4-7

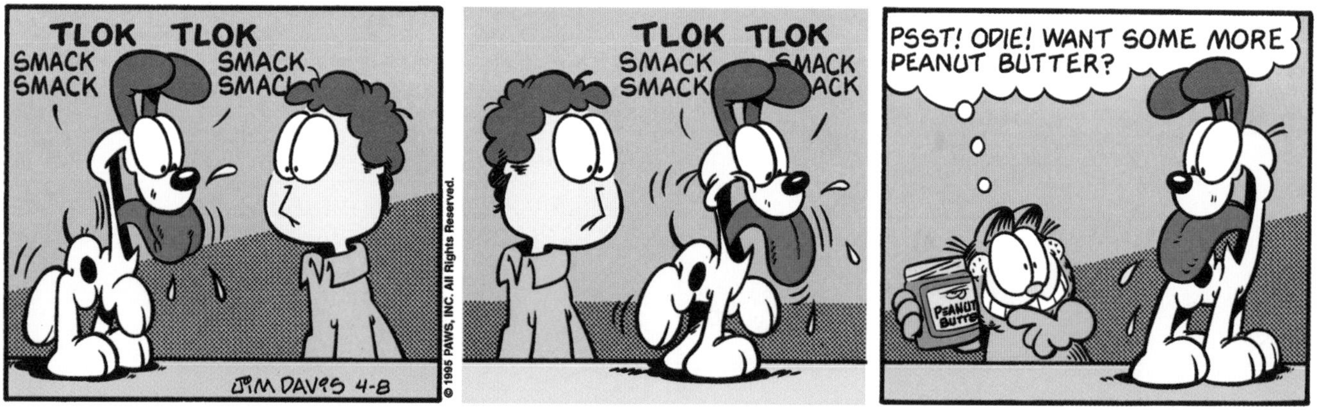
TLOK TLOK
SMACK SMACK
JIM DAVIS 4-8
© 1995 PAWS, INC. All Rights Reserved.
TLOK TLOK
SMACK SMACK
PSST! ODIE! WANT SOME MORE PEANUT BUTTER?

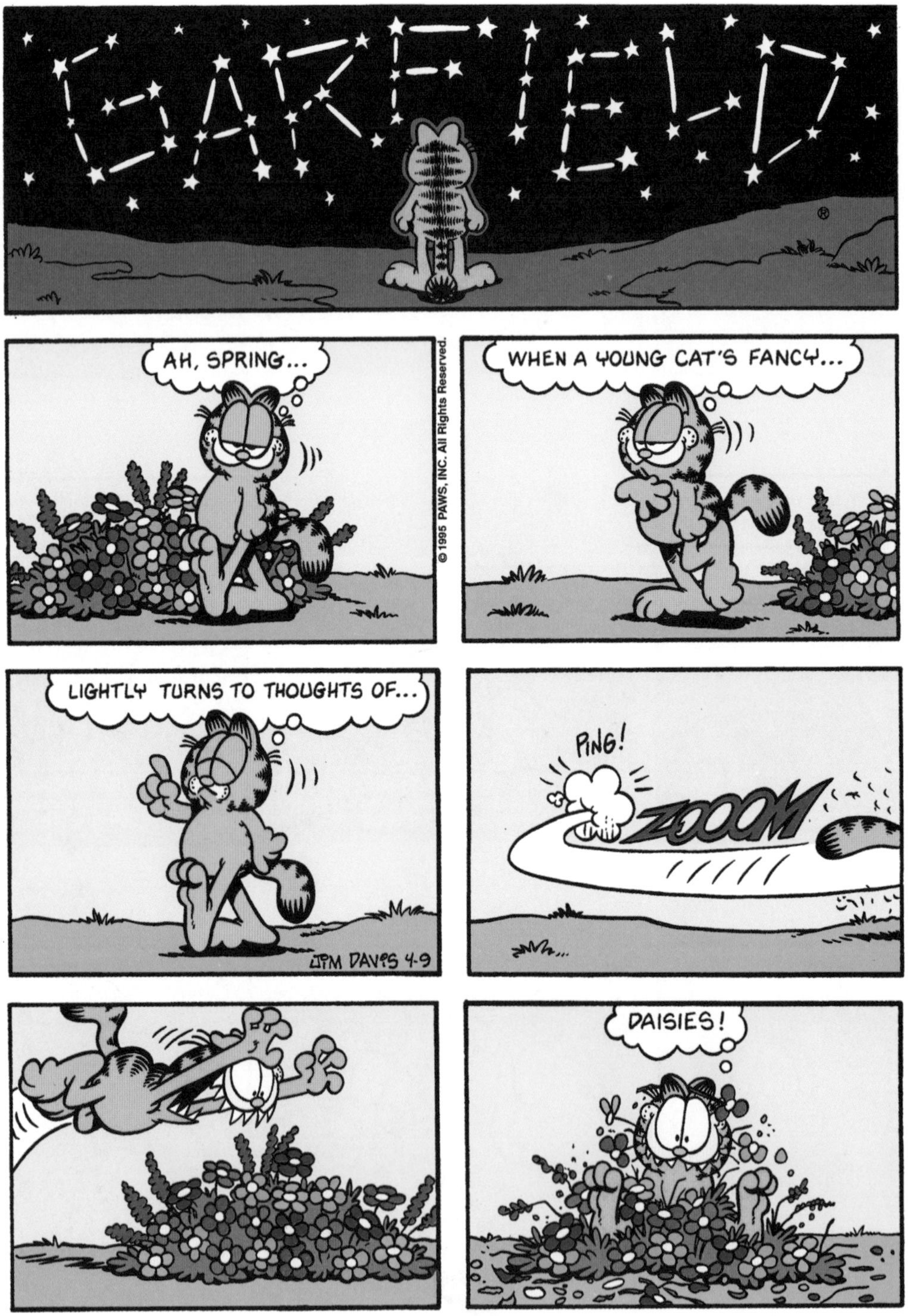
GARFIELD
AH, SPRING...
WHEN A YOUNG CAT'S FANCY...
LIGHTLY TURNS TO THOUGHTS OF...
PING!
ZOOOM
DAISIES!
JIM DAVIS 4-9

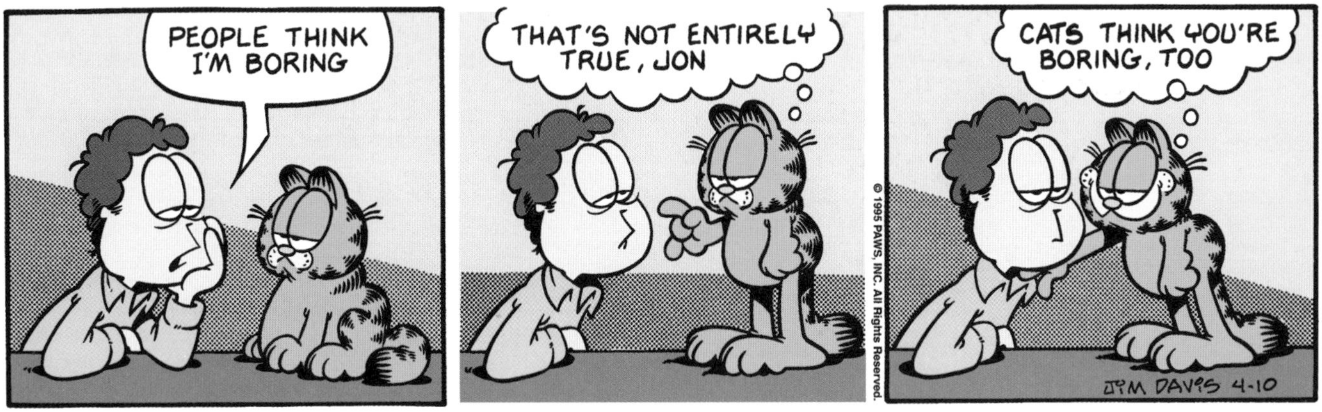
PEOPLE THINK I'M BORING
THAT'S NOT ENTIRELY TRUE, JON
CATS THINK YOU'RE BORING, TOO
JIM DAVIS 4-10

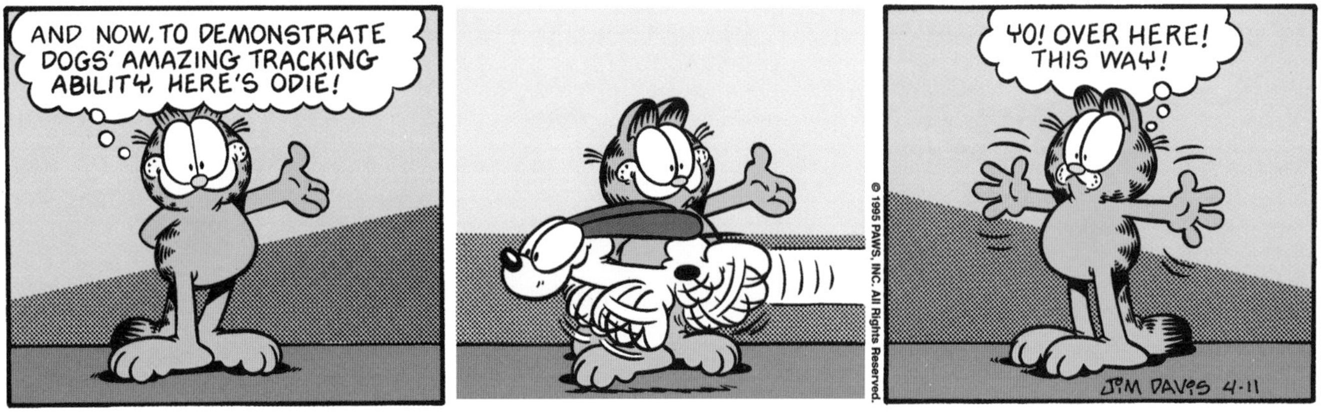
AND NOW, TO DEMONSTRATE DOGS' AMAZING TRACKING ABILITY, HERE'S ODIE!
YO! OVER HERE! THIS WAY!
JIM DAVIS 4-11

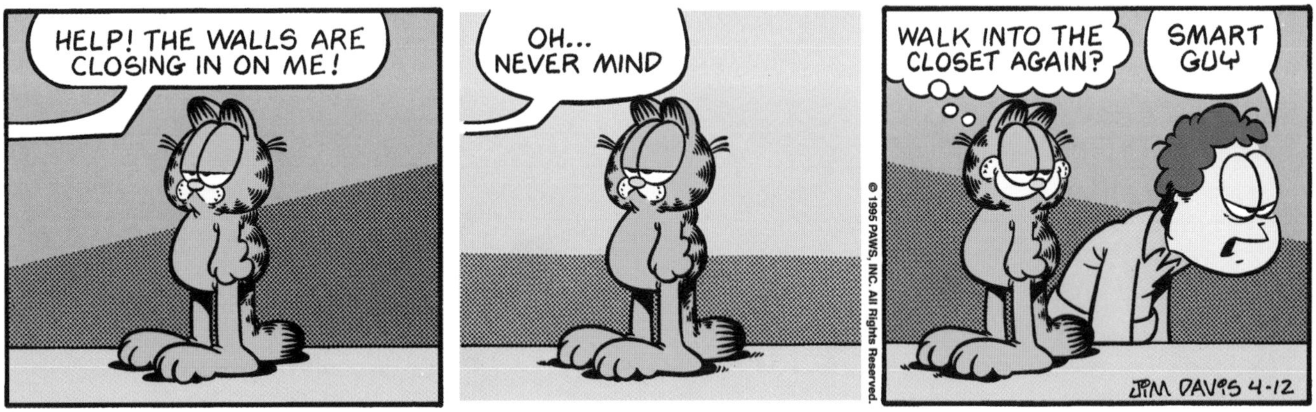
HELP! THE WALLS ARE CLOSING IN ON ME!
OH... NEVER MIND
WALK INTO THE CLOSET AGAIN?
SMART GUY
JIM DAVIS 4-12

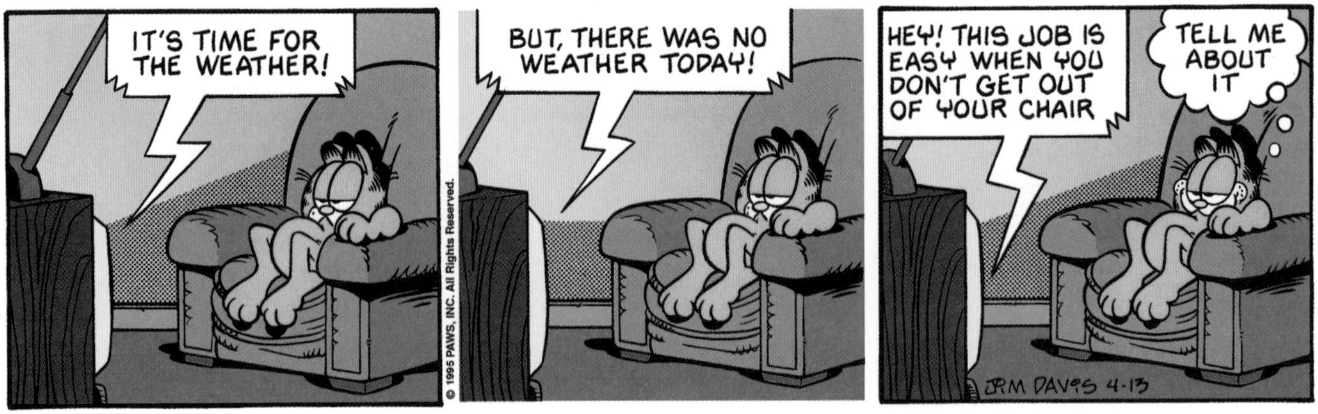
IT'S TIME FOR THE WEATHER!
BUT, THERE WAS NO WEATHER TODAY!
HEY! THIS JOB IS EASY WHEN YOU DON'T GET OUT OF YOUR CHAIR
TELL ME ABOUT IT
© 1995 PAWS, INC. All Rights Reserved.
JIM DAVIS 4-13

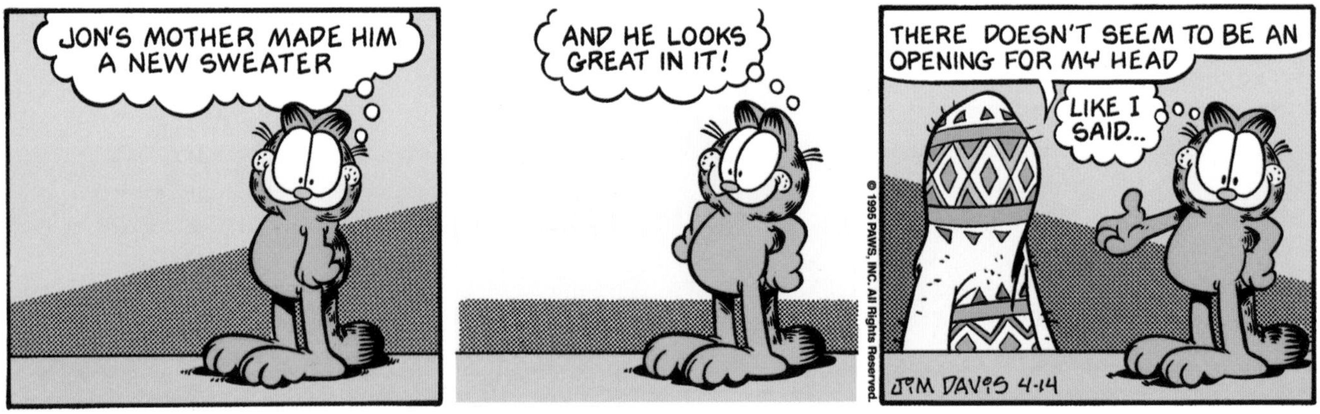
JON'S MOTHER MADE HIM A NEW SWEATER
AND HE LOOKS GREAT IN IT!
THERE DOESN'T SEEM TO BE AN OPENING FOR MY HEAD
LIKE I SAID...
© 1995 PAWS, INC. All Rights Reserved.
JIM DAVIS 4-14

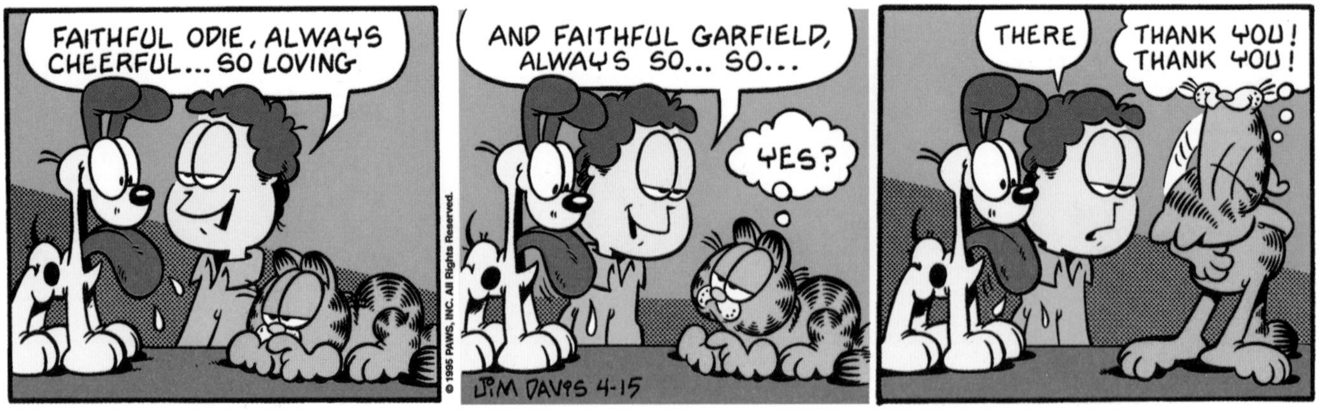
FAITHFUL ODIE, ALWAYS CHEERFUL... SO LOVING
AND FAITHFUL GARFIELD, ALWAYS SO... SO...
YES?
THERE
THANK YOU! THANK YOU!
© 1995 PAWS, INC. All Rights Reserved.
JIM DAVIS 4-15

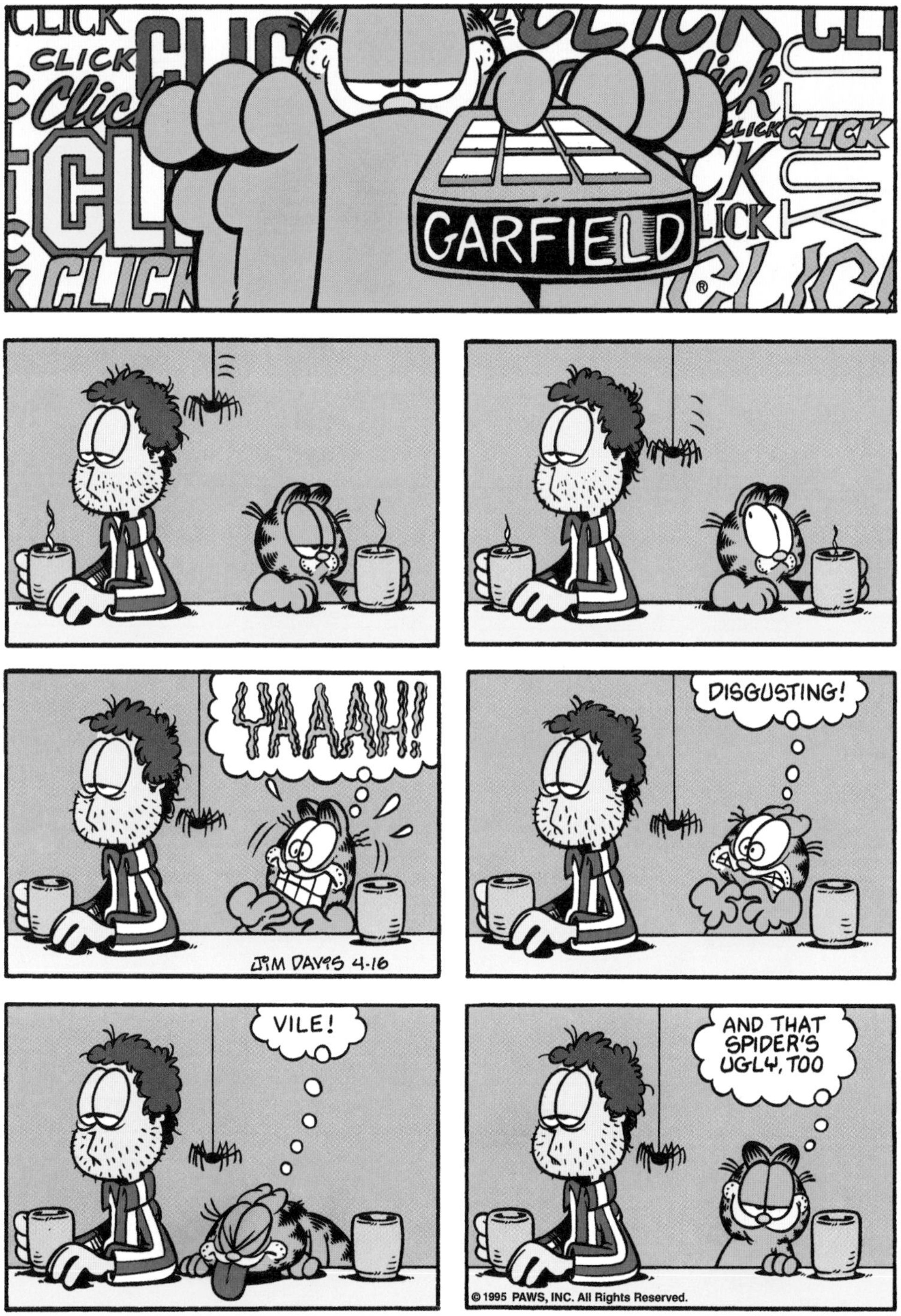
CLICK
GARFIELD
YAAAH!
DISGUSTING!
VILE!
AND THAT SPIDER'S UGLY, TOO
JIM DAVIS 4-16

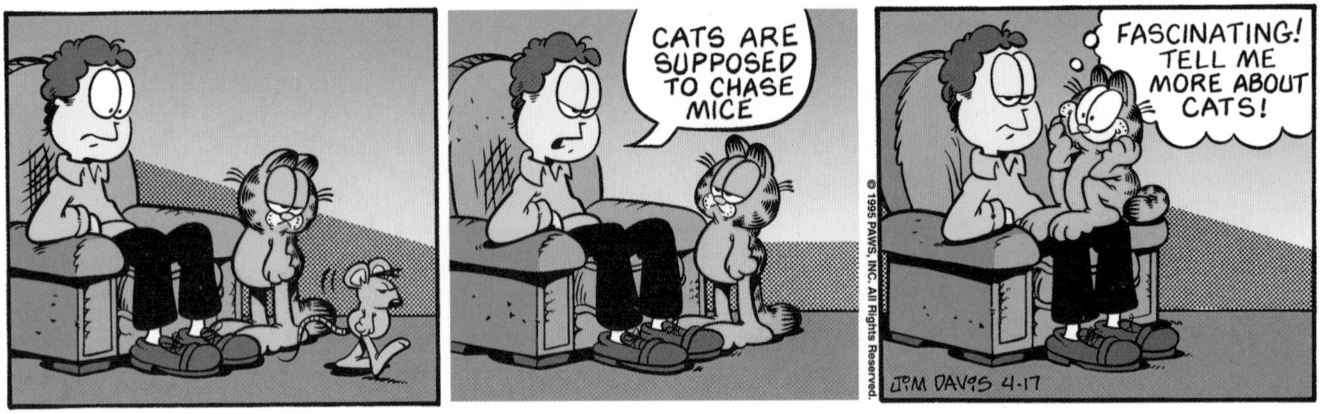
CATS ARE SUPPOSED TO CHASE MICE
FASCINATING! TELL ME MORE ABOUT CATS!
© 1995 PAWS, INC. All Rights Reserved.
JIM DAVIS 4-17

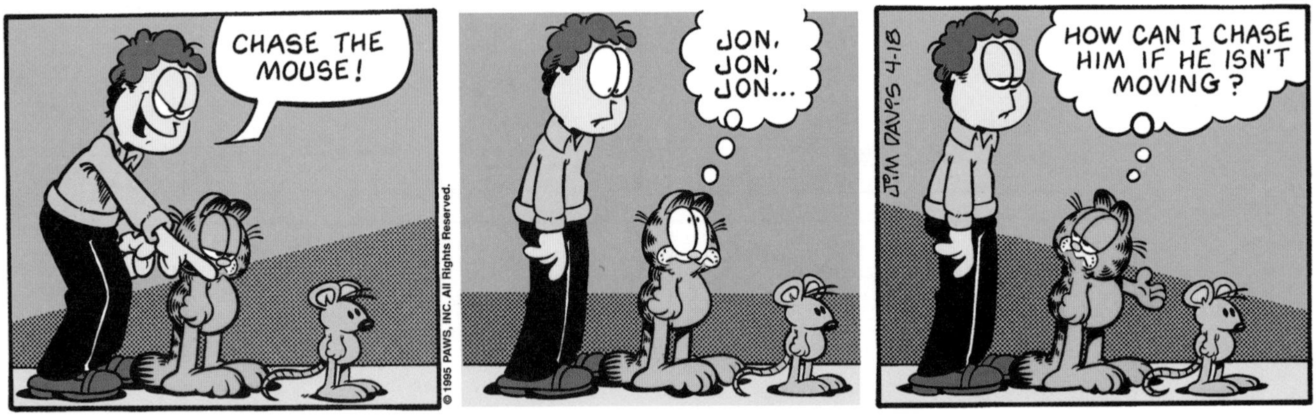
CHASE THE MOUSE!
© 1995 PAWS, INC. All Rights Reserved.
JON, JON, JON...
JIM DAVIS 4-18
HOW CAN I CHASE HIM IF HE ISN'T MOVING?

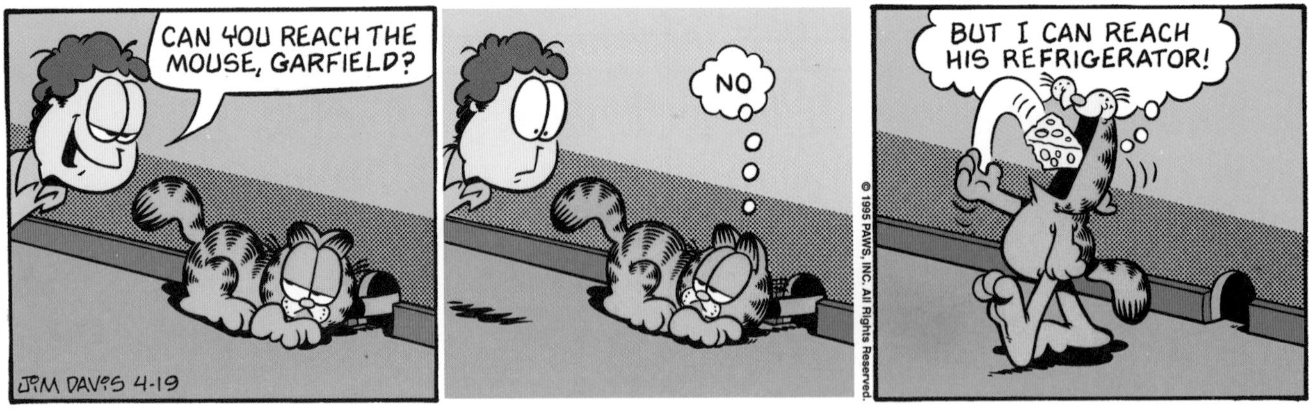
CAN YOU REACH THE MOUSE, GARFIELD?
JIM DAVIS 4-19
NO
© 1995 PAWS, INC. All Rights Reserved.
BUT I CAN REACH HIS REFRIGERATOR!

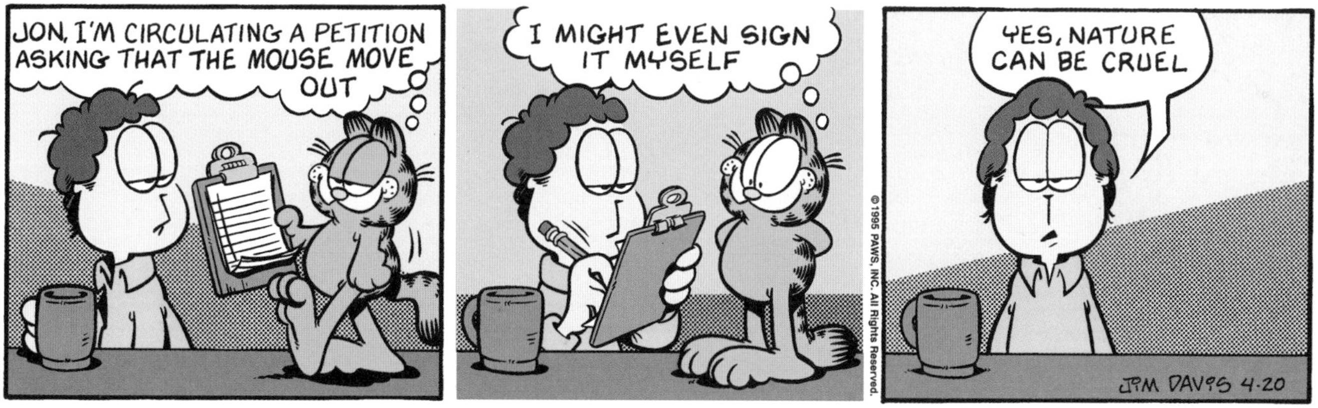
JON, I'M CIRCULATING A PETITION ASKING THAT THE MOUSE MOVE OUT
I MIGHT EVEN SIGN IT MYSELF
YES, NATURE CAN BE CRUEL
© 1995 PAWS, INC. All Rights Reserved.
JIM DAVIS 4-20

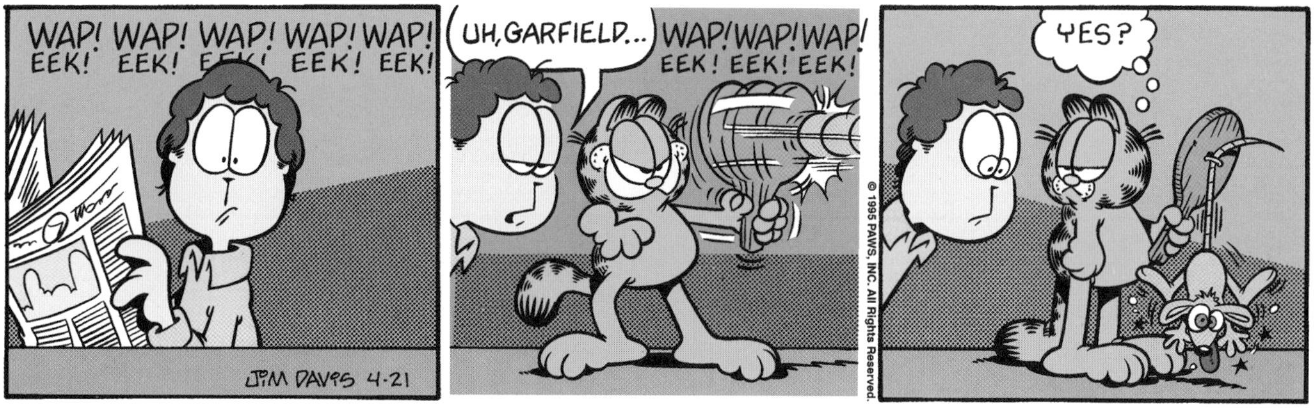
WAP! WAP! WAP! WAP! WAP!
EEK! EEK! EEK! EEK! EEK!
JIM DAVIS 4-21
UH, GARFIELD...
WAP! WAP! WAP!
EEK! EEK! EEK!
© 1995 PAWS, INC. All Rights Reserved.
YES?

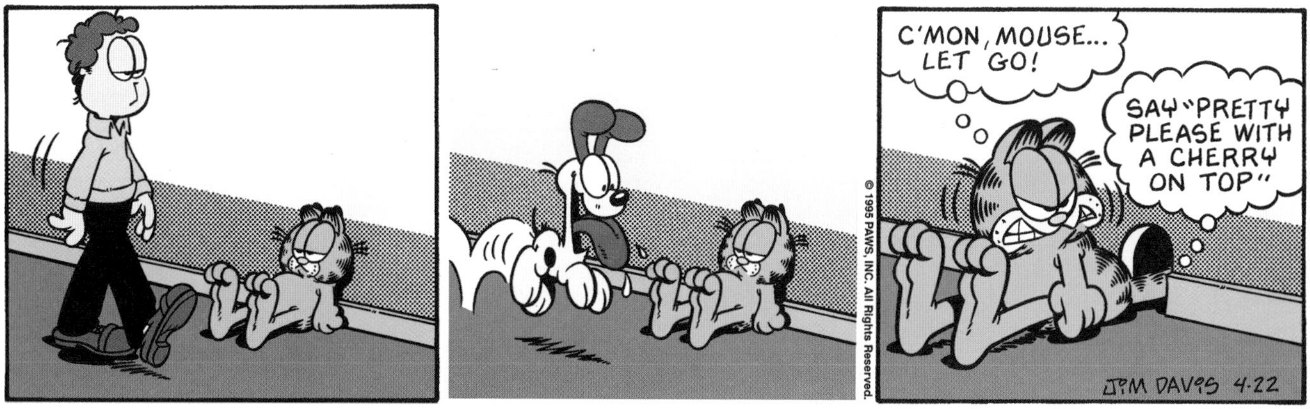
© 1995 PAWS, INC. All Rights Reserved.
C'MON, MOUSE... LET GO!
SAY "PRETTY PLEASE WITH A CHERRY ON TOP"
JIM DAVIS 4-22

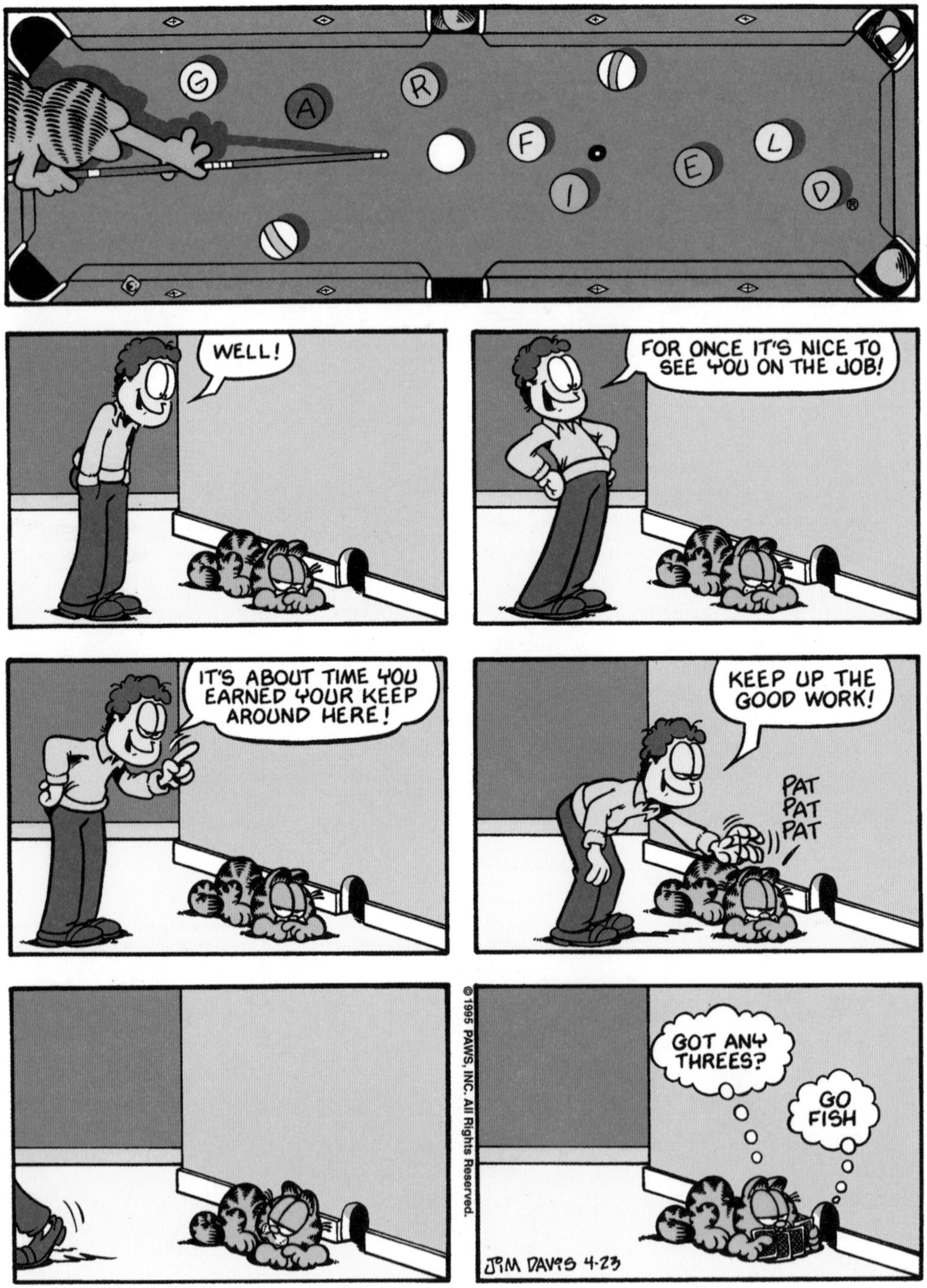
GARFIELD®
WELL!
FOR ONCE IT'S NICE TO SEE YOU ON THE JOB!
IT'S ABOUT TIME YOU EARNED YOUR KEEP AROUND HERE!
KEEP UP THE GOOD WORK!
PAT PAT PAT
GOT ANY THREES?
GO FISH
JIM DAVIS 4-23
© 1995 PAWS, INC. All Rights Reserved.

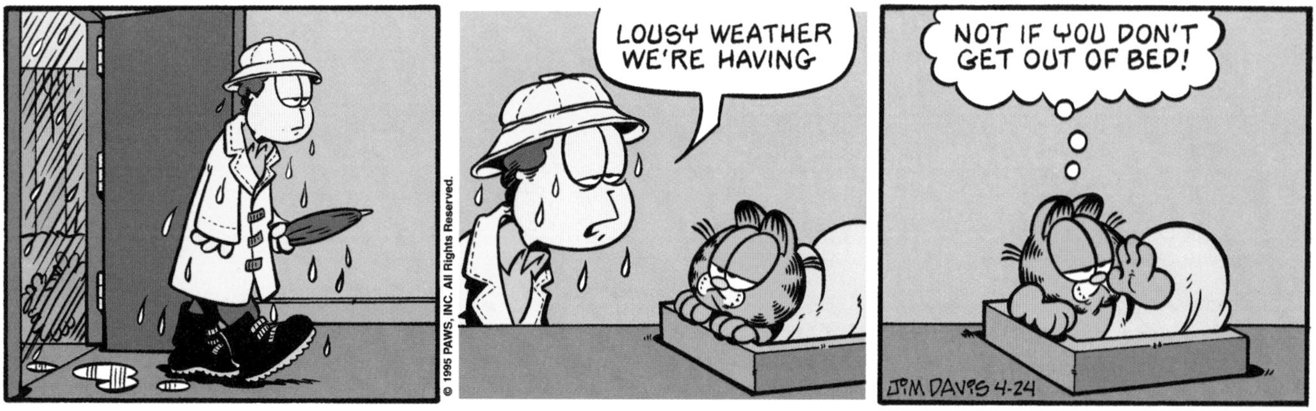
LOUSY WEATHER WE'RE HAVING
NOT IF YOU DON'T GET OUT OF BED!
JIM DAVIS 4-24

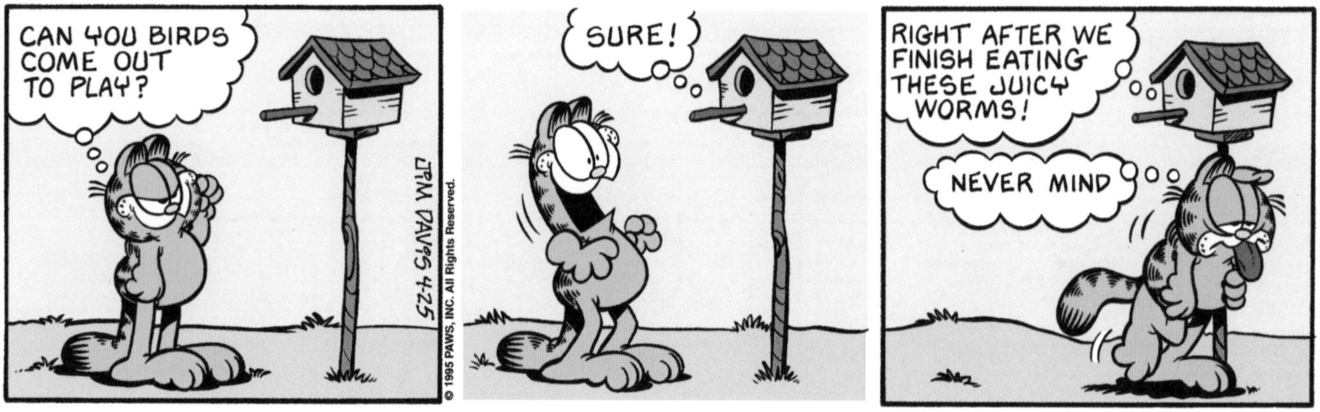
CAN YOU BIRDS COME OUT TO PLAY?
JIM DAVIS 4-25
SURE!
RIGHT AFTER WE FINISH EATING THESE JUICY WORMS!
NEVER MIND

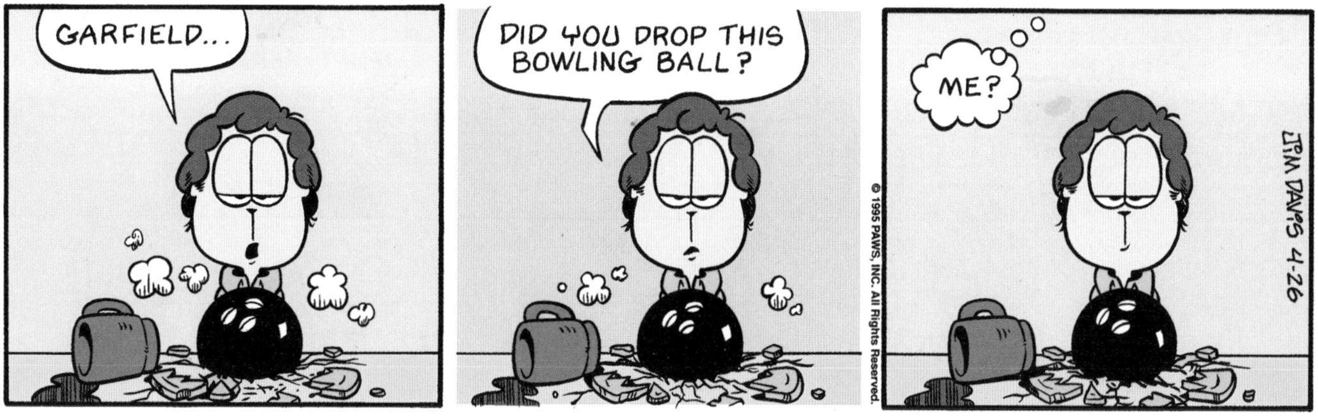
GARFIELD...
DID YOU DROP THIS BOWLING BALL?
ME?
JIM DAVIS 4-26

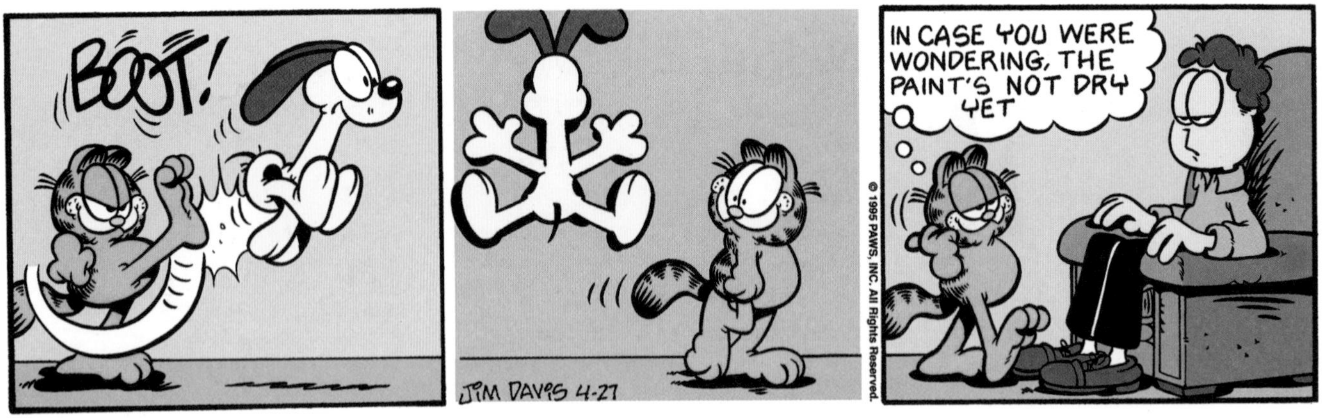
BOOT!
JIM DAVIS 4-27
© 1995 PAWS, INC. All Rights Reserved.
IN CASE YOU WERE WONDERING, THE PAINT'S NOT DRY YET

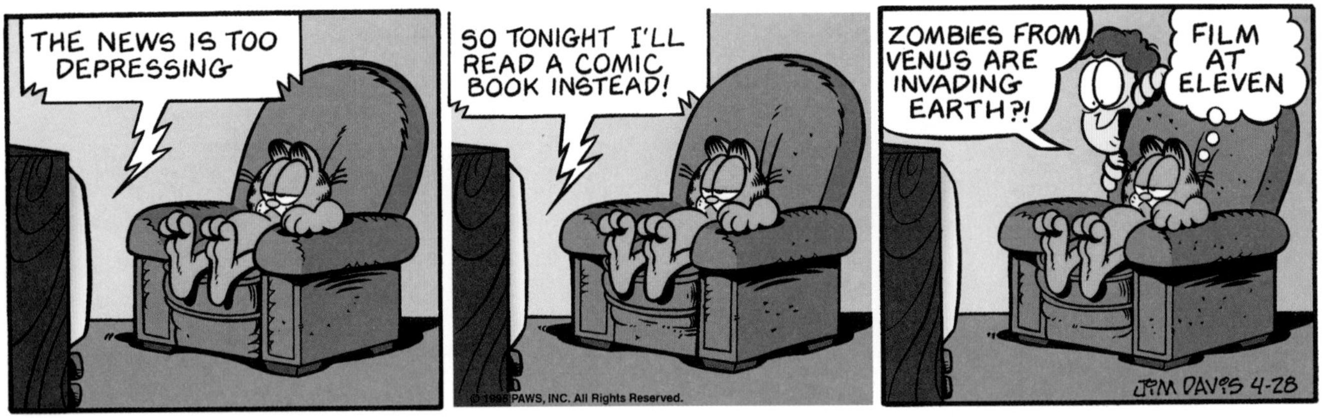
THE NEWS IS TOO DEPRESSING
SO TONIGHT I'LL READ A COMIC BOOK INSTEAD!
© 1995 PAWS, INC. All Rights Reserved.
ZOMBIES FROM VENUS ARE INVADING EARTH?!
FILM AT ELEVEN
JIM DAVIS 4-28

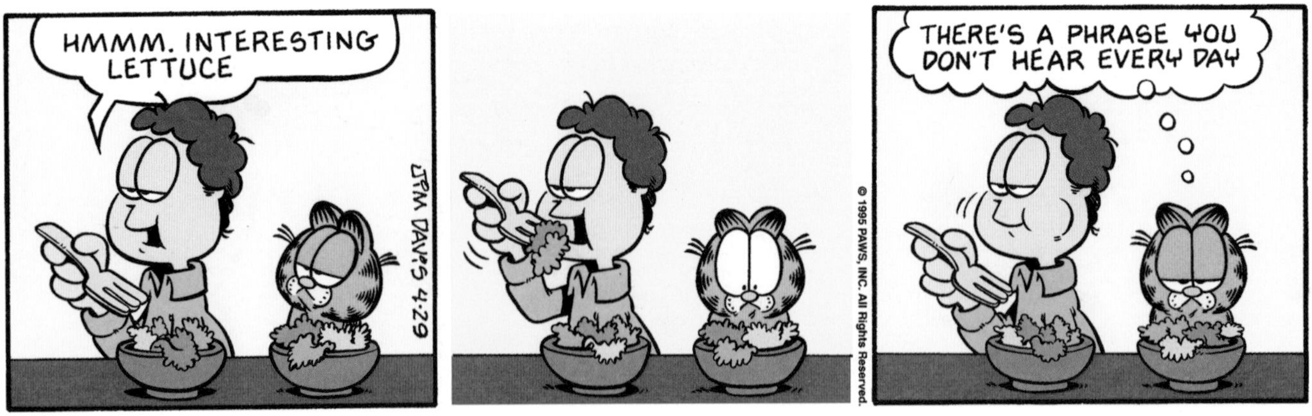
HMMM. INTERESTING LETTUCE
JIM DAVIS 4-29
© 1995 PAWS, INC. All Rights Reserved.
THERE'S A PHRASE YOU DON'T HEAR EVERY DAY

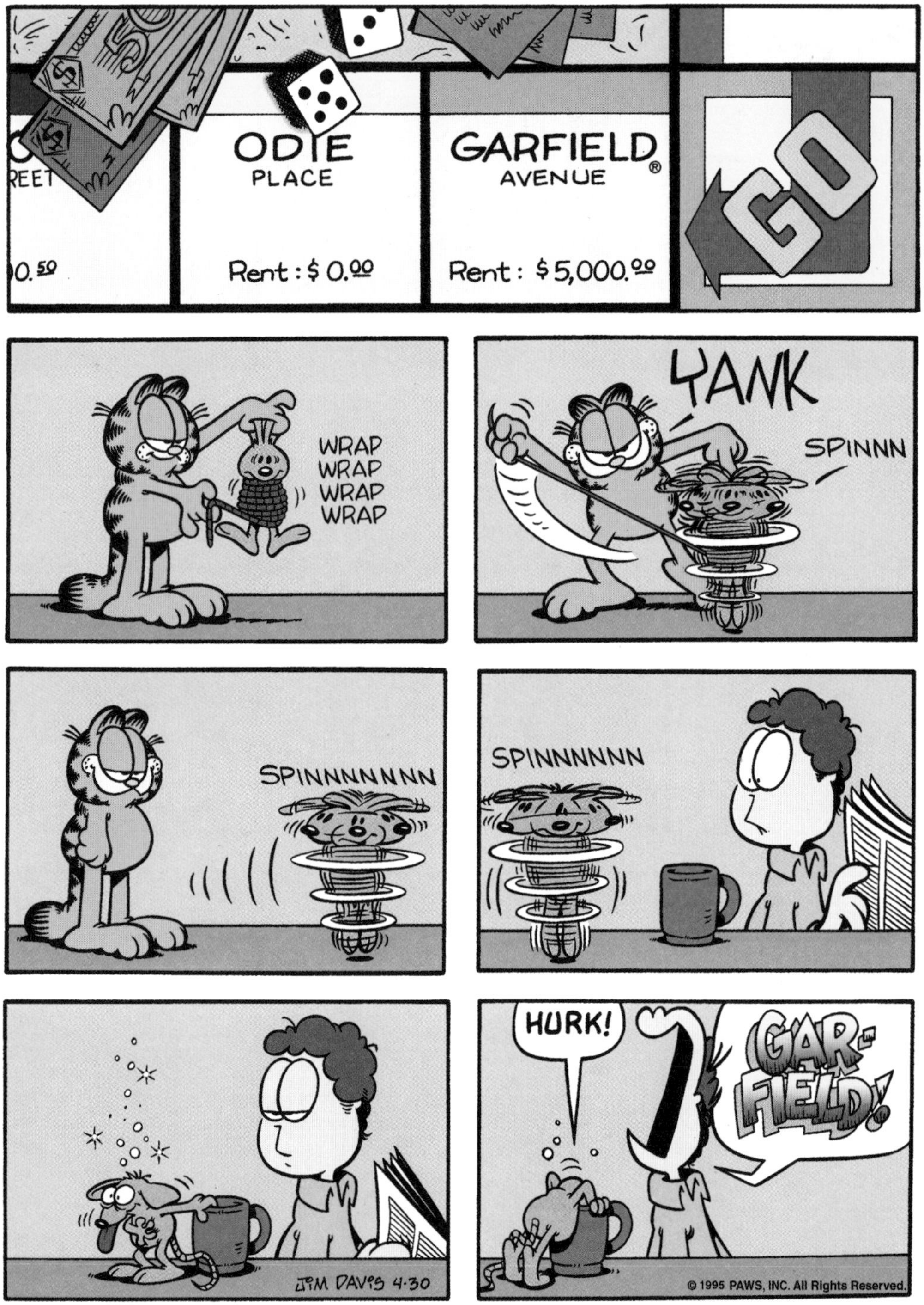
REET
0.50
ODIE
PLACE
Rent: $ 0.00
GARFIELD
AVENUE
Rent: $ 5,000.00
GO
WRAP
WRAP
WRAP
WRAP
YANK
SPINNN
SPINNNNNNNN
SPINNNNNNN
JIM DAVIS 4-30
HURK!
GAR-FIELD!
© 1995 PAWS, INC. All Rights Reserved.

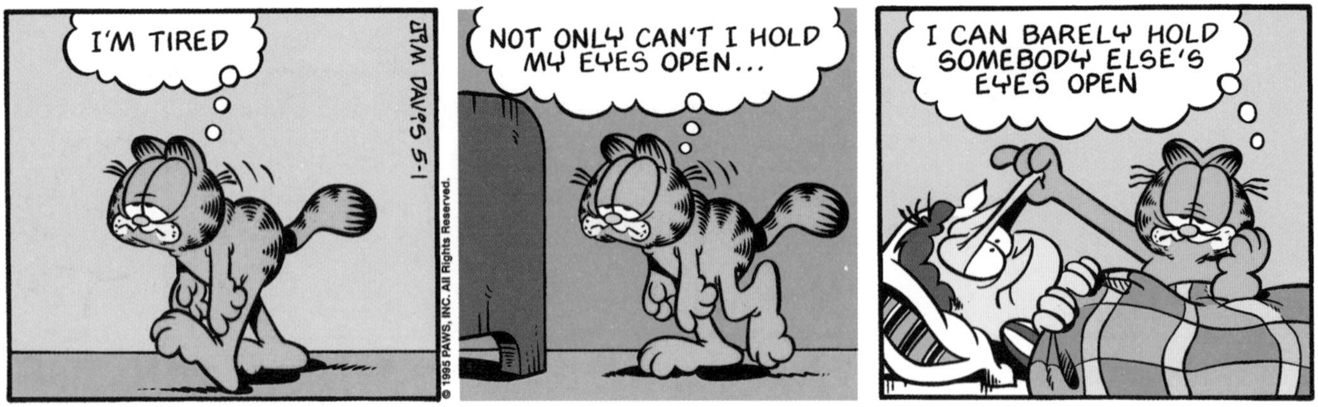
I'M TIRED
JIM DAVIS 5-1
© 1995 PAWS, INC. All Rights Reserved.
NOT ONLY CAN'T I HOLD MY EYES OPEN...
I CAN BARELY HOLD SOMEBODY ELSE'S EYES OPEN

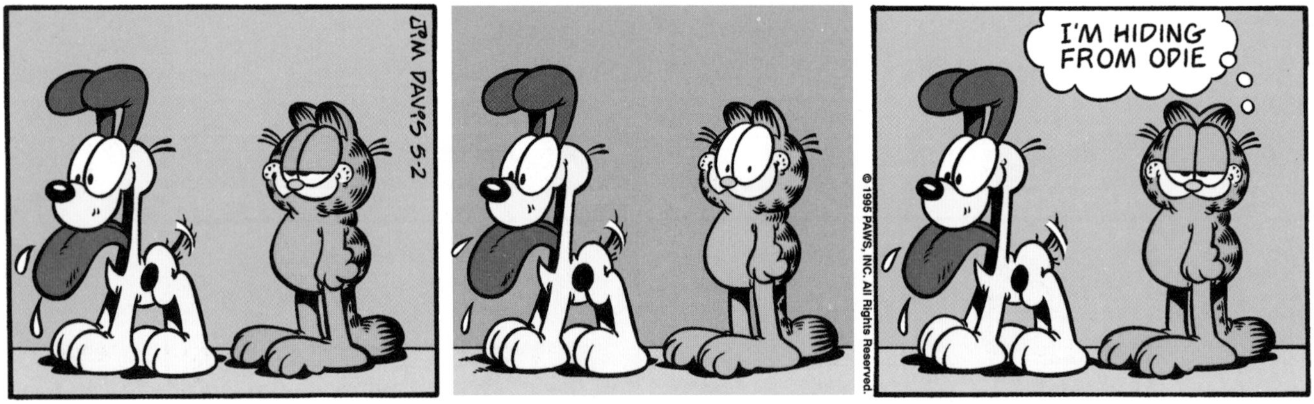
JIM DAVIS 5-2
© 1995 PAWS, INC. All Rights Reserved.
I'M HIDING FROM ODIE

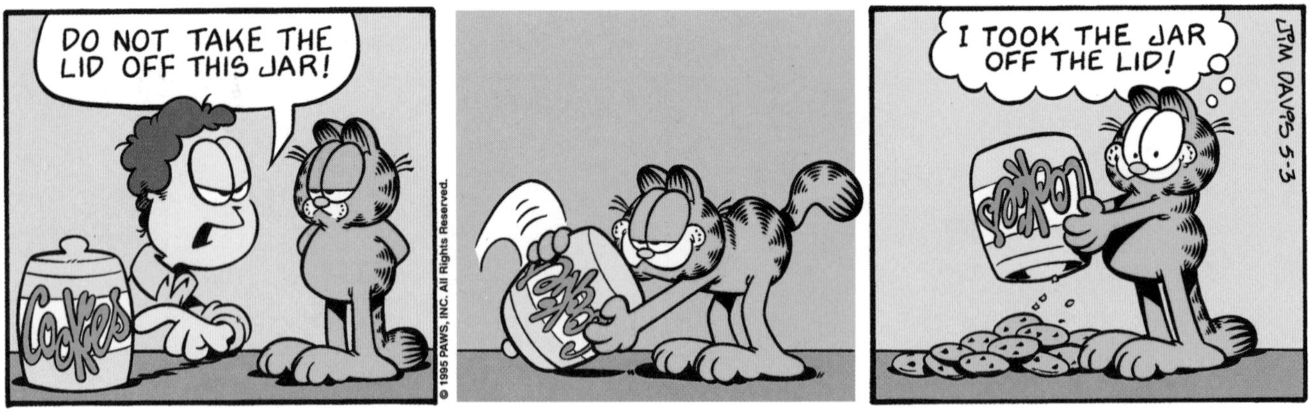
DO NOT TAKE THE LID OFF THIS JAR!
Cookies
© 1995 PAWS, INC. All Rights Reserved.
I TOOK THE JAR OFF THE LID!
JIM DAVIS 5-3

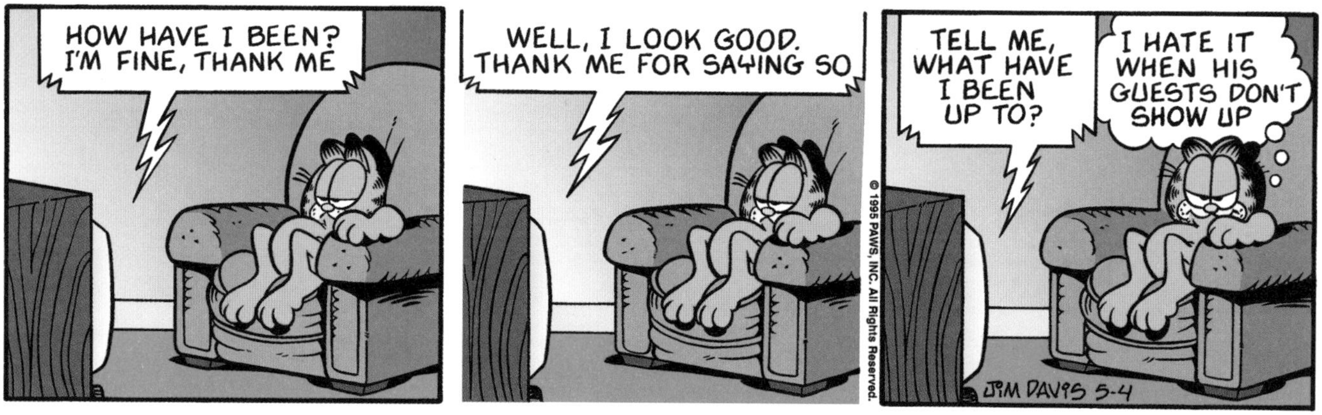
HOW HAVE I BEEN? I'M FINE, THANK ME
WELL, I LOOK GOOD. THANK ME FOR SAYING SO
TELL ME, WHAT HAVE I BEEN UP TO?
I HATE IT WHEN HIS GUESTS DON'T SHOW UP
© 1995 PAWS, INC. All Rights Reserved.
JIM DAVIS 5-4

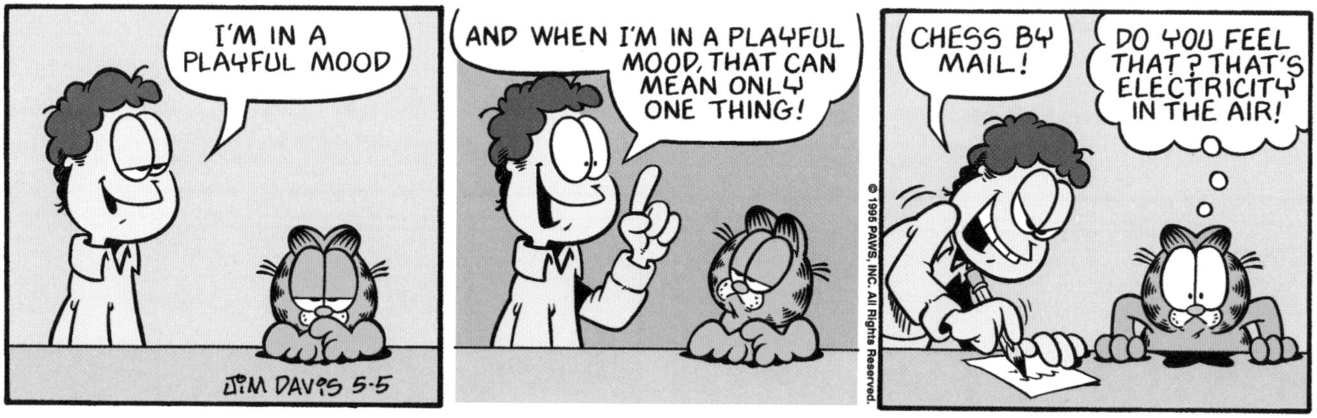
I'M IN A PLAYFUL MOOD
JIM DAVIS 5-5
AND WHEN I'M IN A PLAYFUL MOOD, THAT CAN MEAN ONLY ONE THING!
CHESS BY MAIL!
DO YOU FEEL THAT? THAT'S ELECTRICITY IN THE AIR!
© 1995 PAWS, INC. All Rights Reserved.

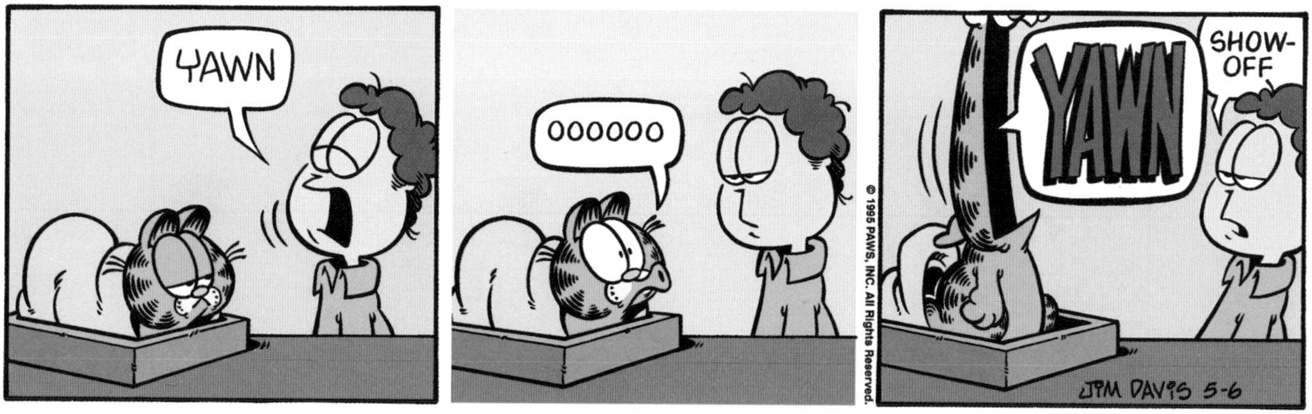
YAWN
OOOOOO
YAWN
SHOW-OFF
© 1995 PAWS, INC. All Rights Reserved.
JIM DAVIS 5-6

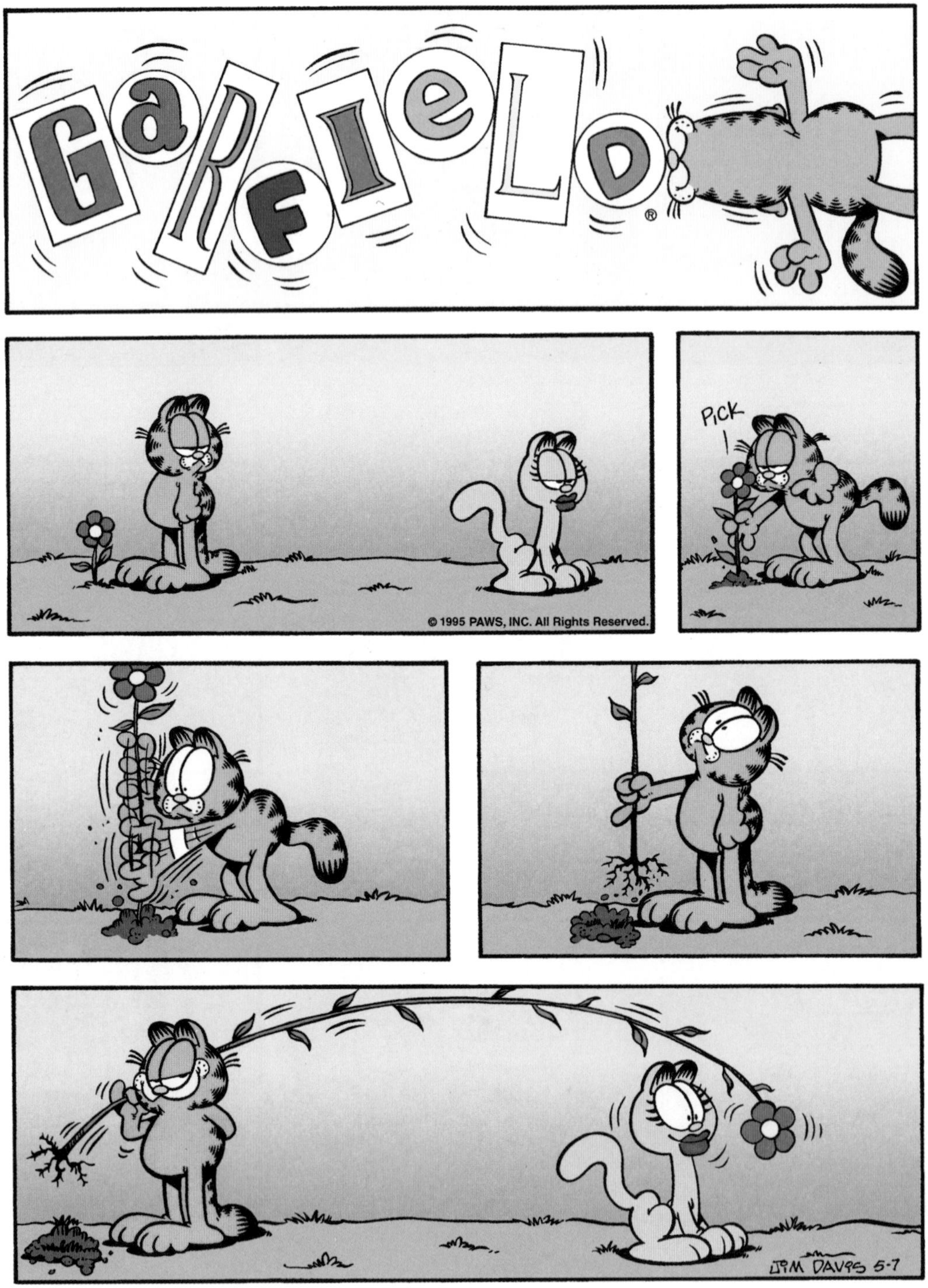
GARFIELD®
PICK
© 1995 PAWS, INC. All Rights Reserved.
JIM DAVIS 5-7

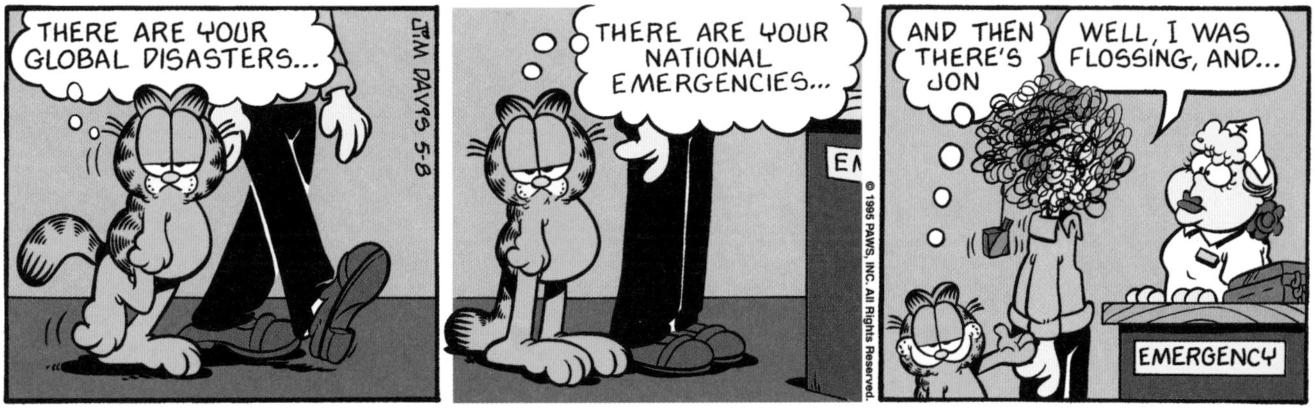
THERE ARE YOUR GLOBAL DISASTERS...
JPM DAVPS 5-8
THERE ARE YOUR NATIONAL EMERGENCIES...
© 1995 PAWS, INC. All Rights Reserved.
AND THEN THERE'S JON
WELL, I WAS FLOSSING, AND...
EMERGENCY

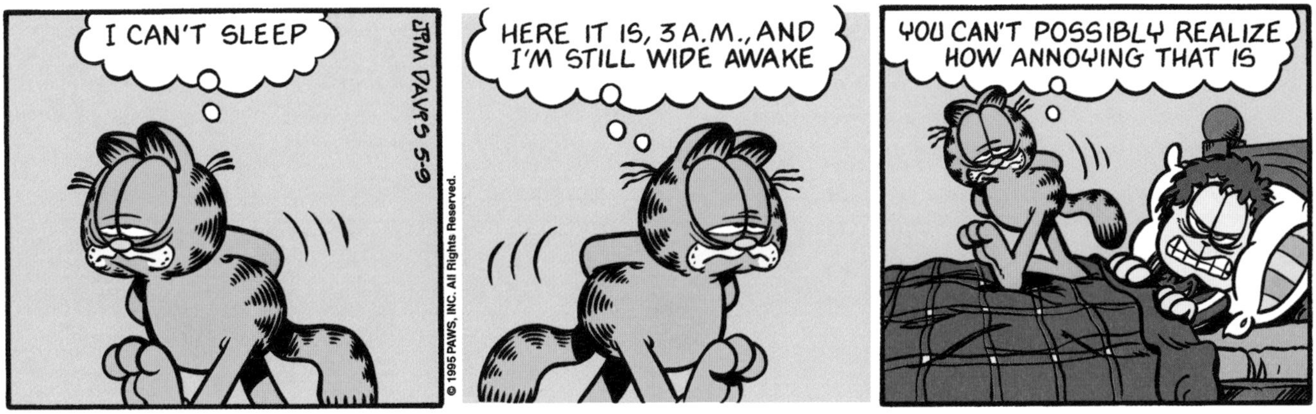
I CAN'T SLEEP
JPM DAVPS 5-9
© 1995 PAWS, INC. All Rights Reserved.
HERE IT IS, 3 A.M., AND I'M STILL WIDE AWAKE
YOU CAN'T POSSIBLY REALIZE HOW ANNOYING THAT IS

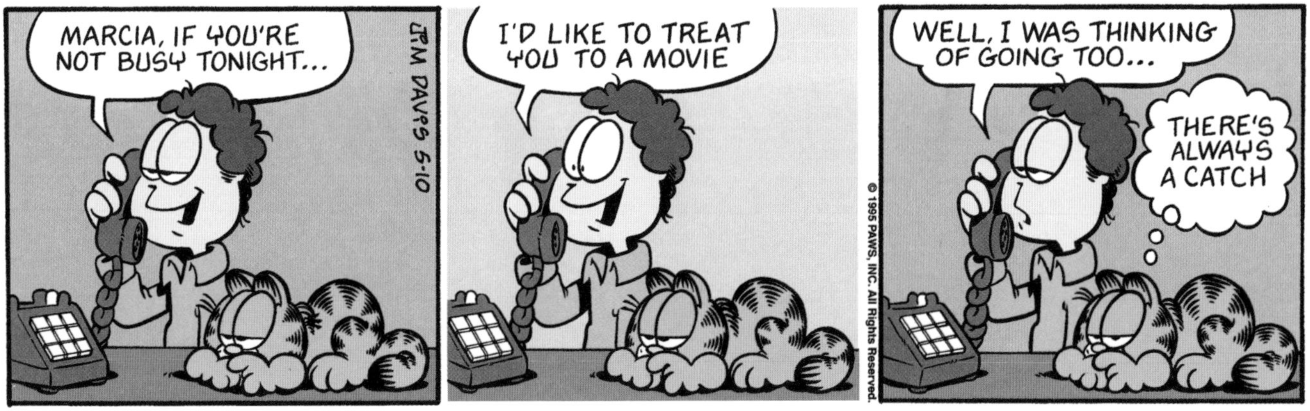
MARCIA, IF YOU'RE NOT BUSY TONIGHT...
JPM DAVPS 5-10
I'D LIKE TO TREAT YOU TO A MOVIE
© 1995 PAWS, INC. All Rights Reserved.
WELL, I WAS THINKING OF GOING TOO...
THERE'S ALWAYS A CATCH

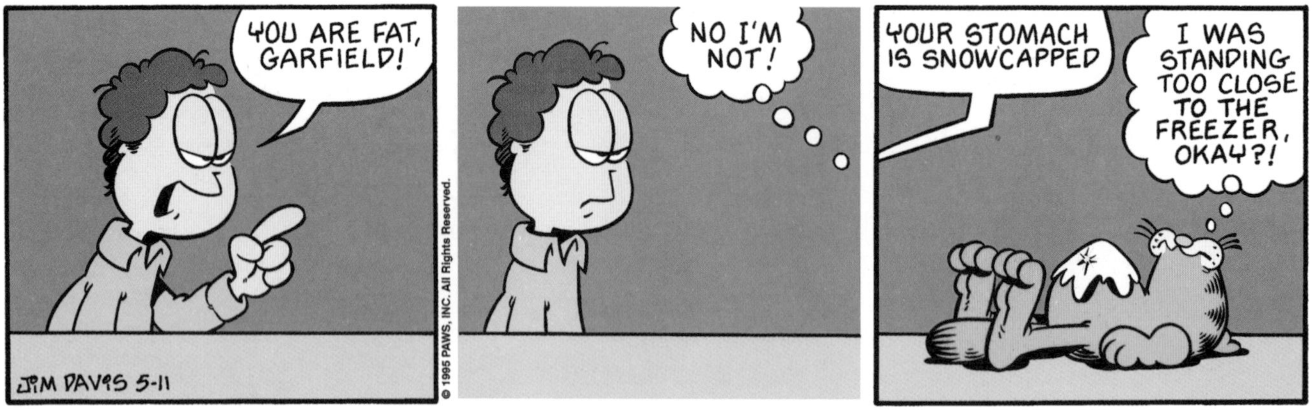
YOU ARE FAT, GARFIELD!
JIM DAVIS 5-11
© 1995 PAWS, INC. All Rights Reserved.
NO I'M NOT!
YOUR STOMACH IS SNOWCAPPED
I WAS STANDING TOO CLOSE TO THE FREEZER, OKAY?!

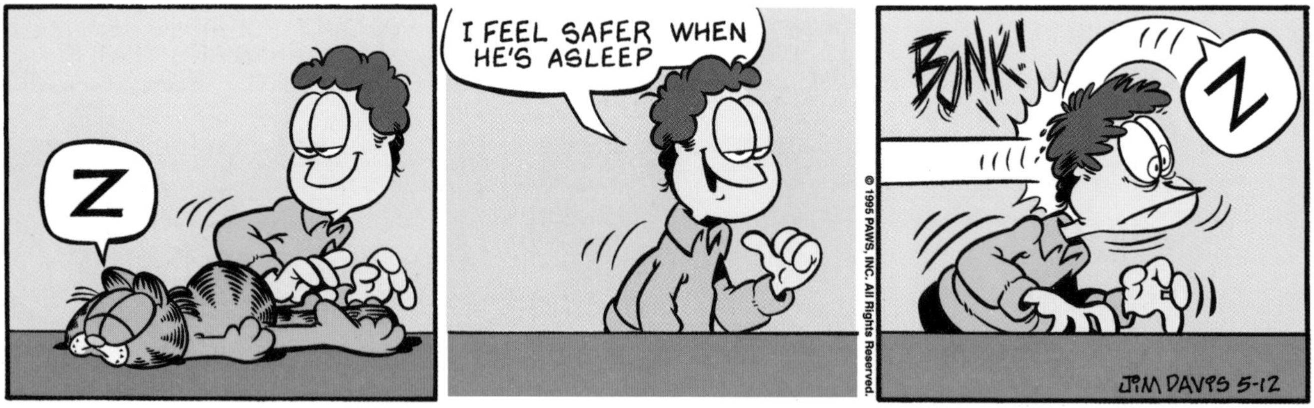
Z
I FEEL SAFER WHEN HE'S ASLEEP
© 1995 PAWS, INC. All Rights Reserved.
BONK!
Z
JIM DAVIS 5-12

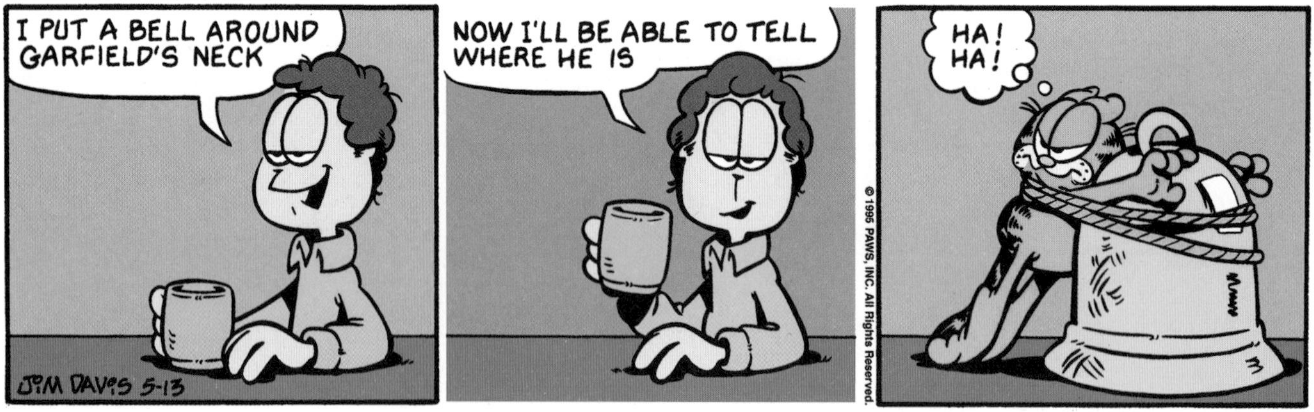
I PUT A BELL AROUND GARFIELD'S NECK
JIM DAVIS 5-13
NOW I'LL BE ABLE TO TELL WHERE HE IS
© 1995 PAWS, INC. All Rights Reserved.
HA! HA!

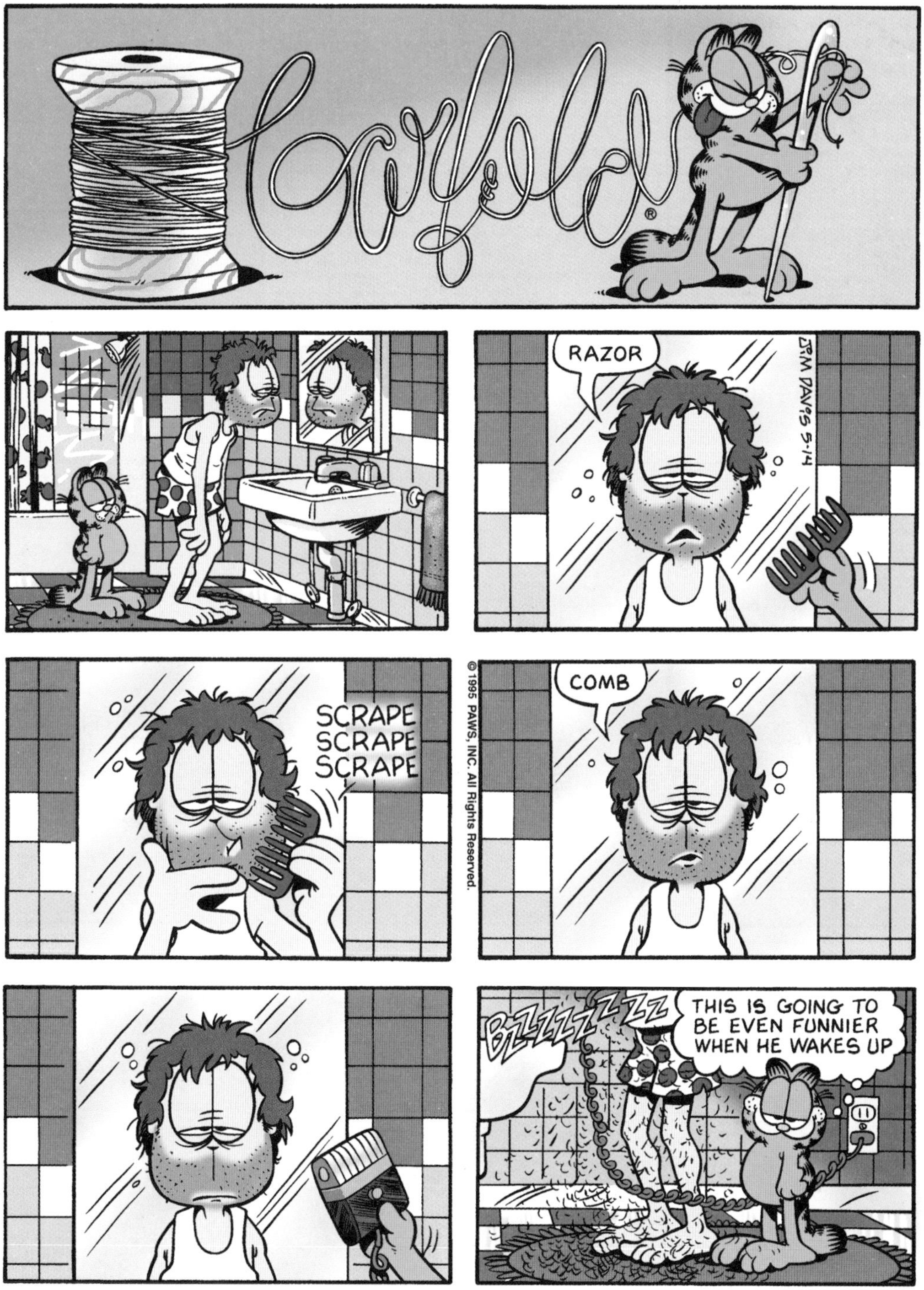
Garfield
JIM DAVIS 5-14
RAZOR
SCRAPE
SCRAPE
SCRAPE
© 1995 PAWS, INC. All Rights Reserved.
COMB
THIS IS GOING TO BE EVEN FUNNIER WHEN HE WAKES UP

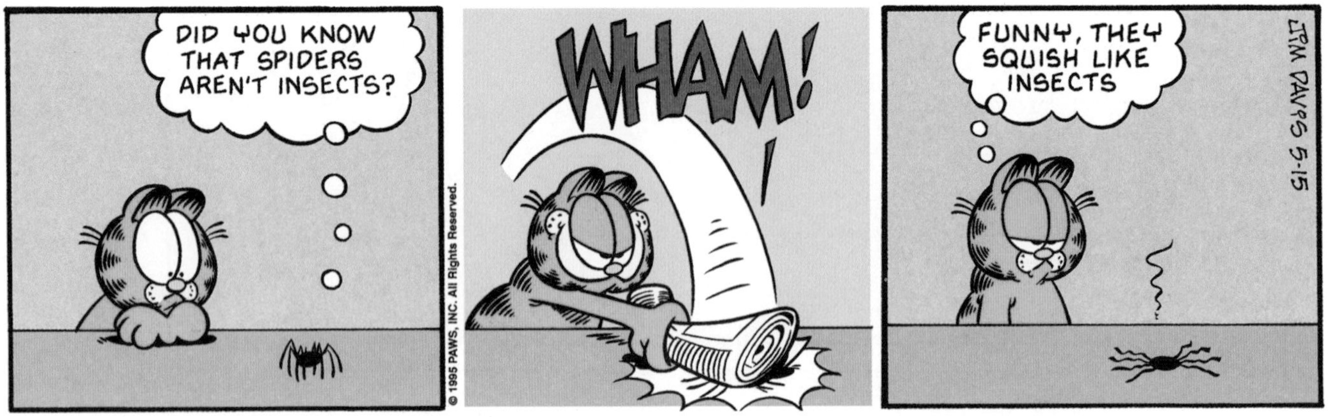
DID YOU KNOW THAT SPIDERS AREN'T INSECTS?
© 1995 PAWS, INC. All Rights Reserved.
WHAM!
FUNNY, THEY SQUISH LIKE INSECTS
JIM DAVIS 5-15

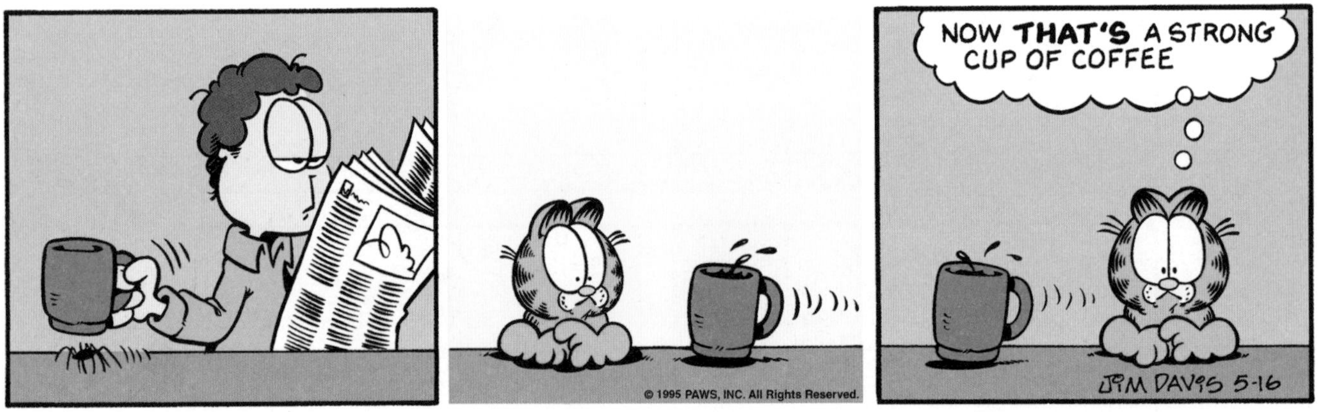
© 1995 PAWS, INC. All Rights Reserved.
NOW THAT'S A STRONG CUP OF COFFEE
JIM DAVIS 5-16

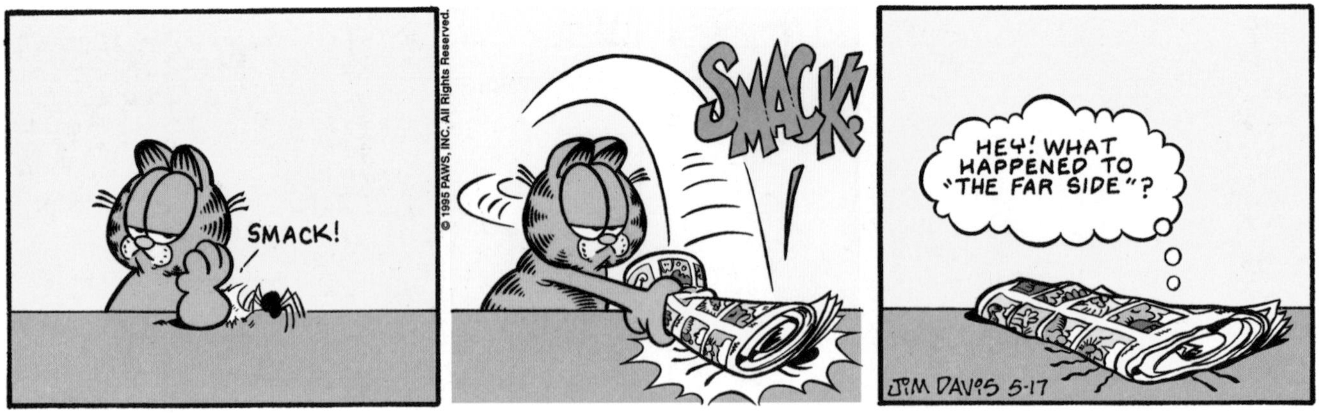
SMACK!
© 1995 PAWS, INC. All Rights Reserved.
SMACK!
HEY! WHAT HAPPENED TO "THE FAR SIDE"?
JIM DAVIS 5-17

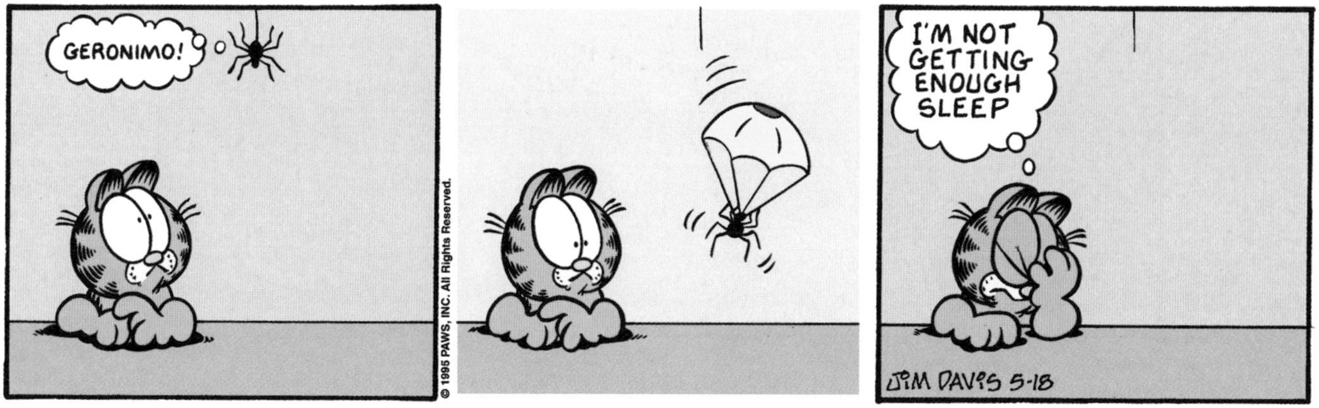
GERONIMO!
© 1995 PAWS, INC. All Rights Reserved.
I'M NOT GETTING ENOUGH SLEEP
JIM DAVIS 5-18

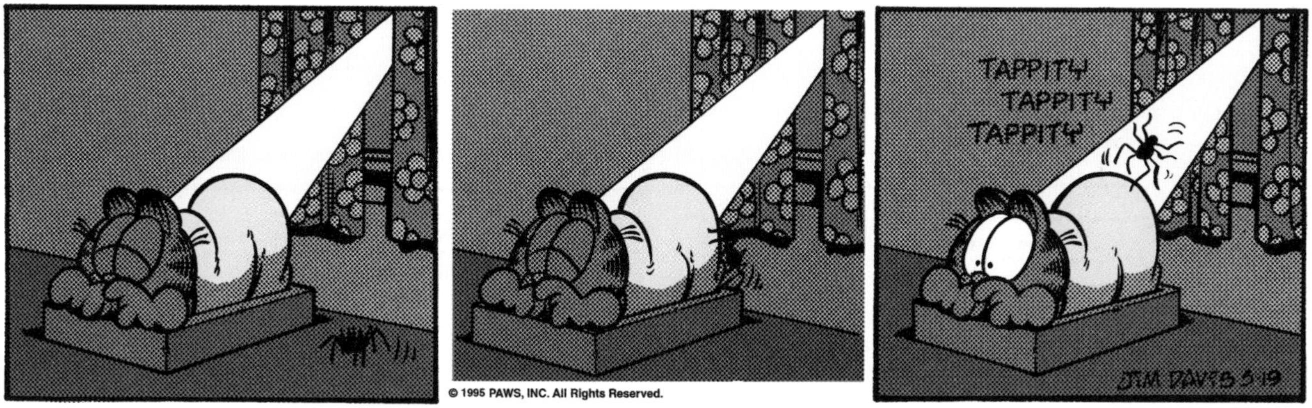
© 1995 PAWS, INC. All Rights Reserved.
TAPPITY TAPPITY TAPPITY
JIM DAVIS 5-19

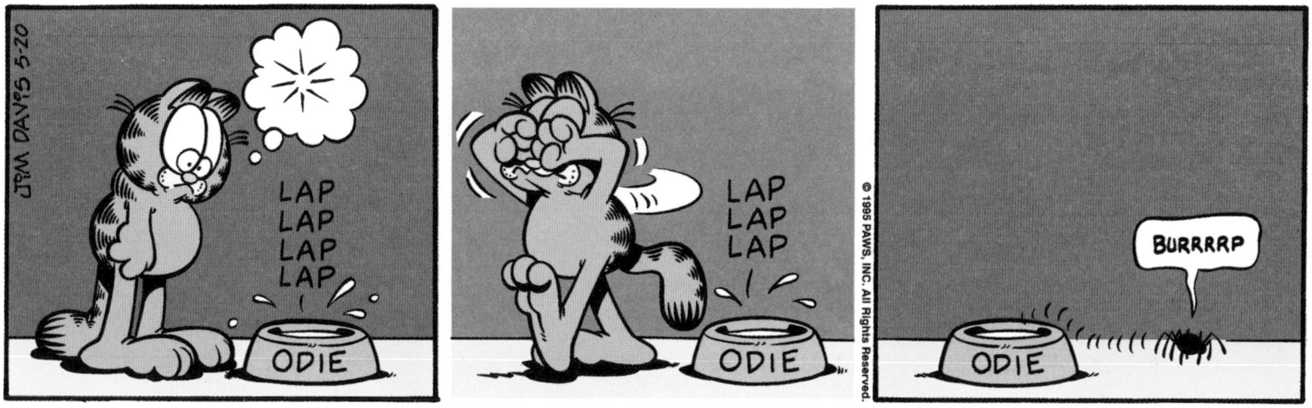
JIM DAVIS 5-20
LAP LAP LAP LAP
ODIE
LAP LAP LAP
ODIE
© 1995 PAWS, INC. All Rights Reserved.
BURRRRP
ODIE

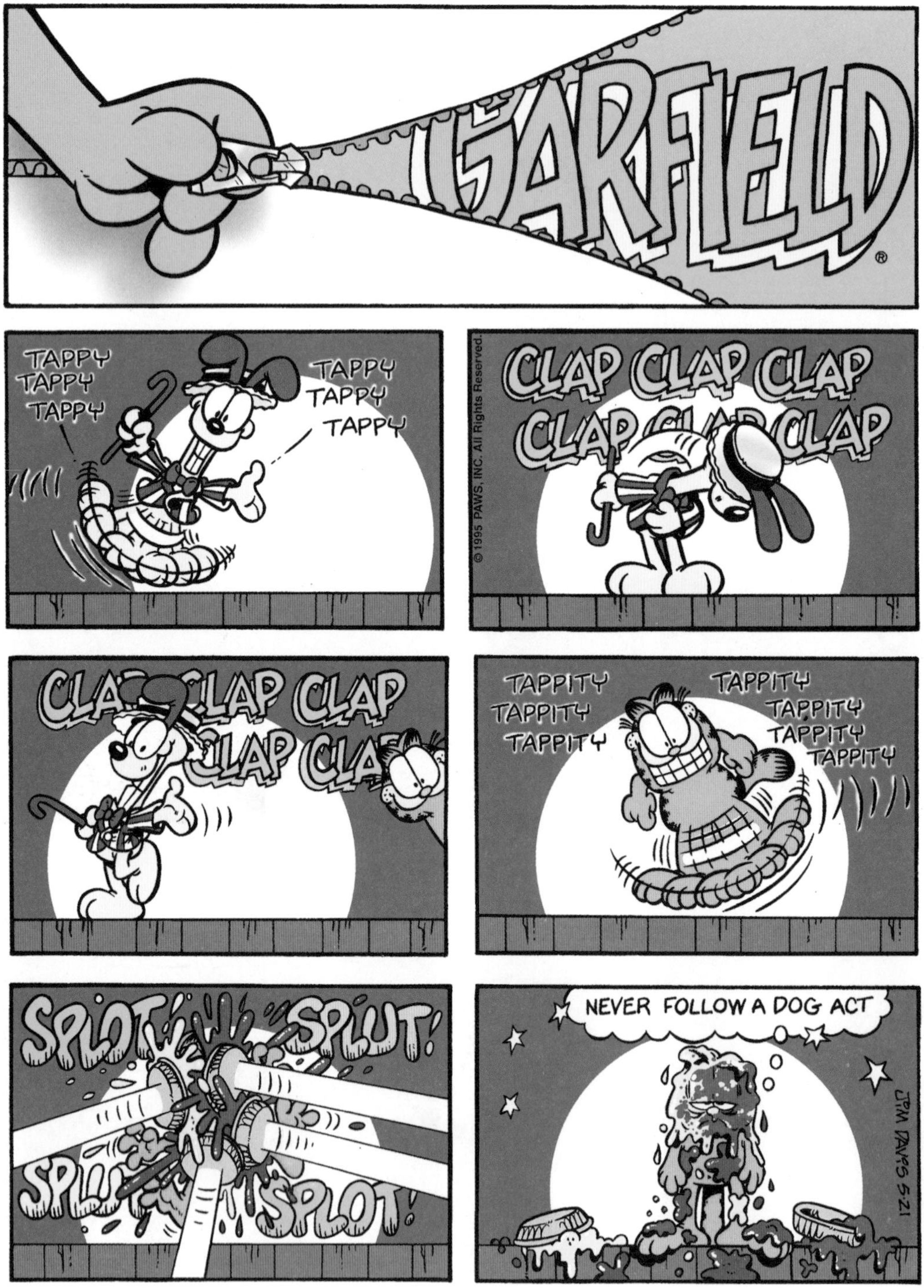
GARFIELD®
TAPPY TAPPY TAPPY
TAPPY TAPPY TAPPY
© 1995 PAWS, INC. All Rights Reserved.
CLAP CLAP CLAP
CLAP CLAP CLAP
TAPPITY TAPPITY TAPPITY
TAPPITY TAPPITY TAPPITY TAPPITY
SPLOT! SPLUT!
SPLOT!
NEVER FOLLOW A DOG ACT
JIM DAVIS 5-21

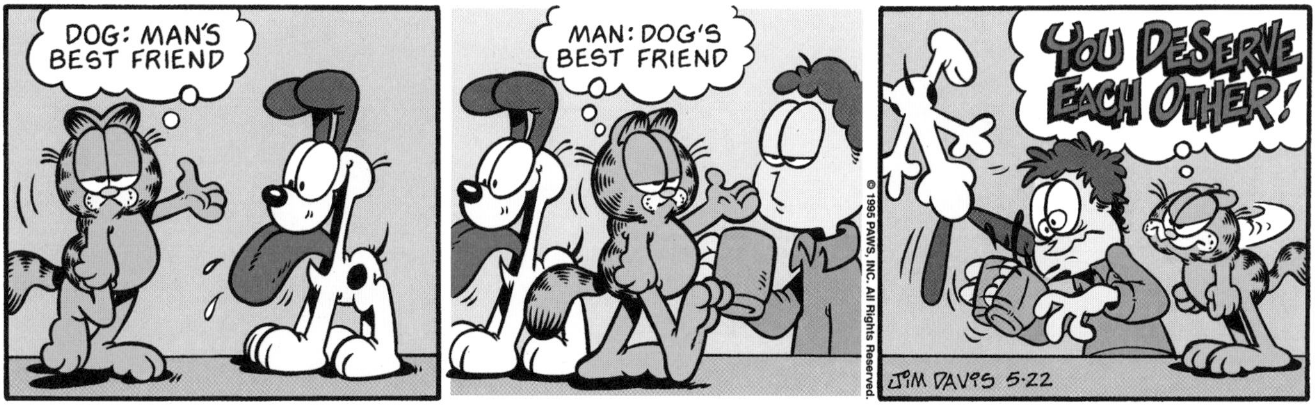
DOG: MAN'S BEST FRIEND
MAN: DOG'S BEST FRIEND
YOU DESERVE EACH OTHER!
© 1995 PAWS, INC. All Rights Reserved.
JIM DAVIS 5-22

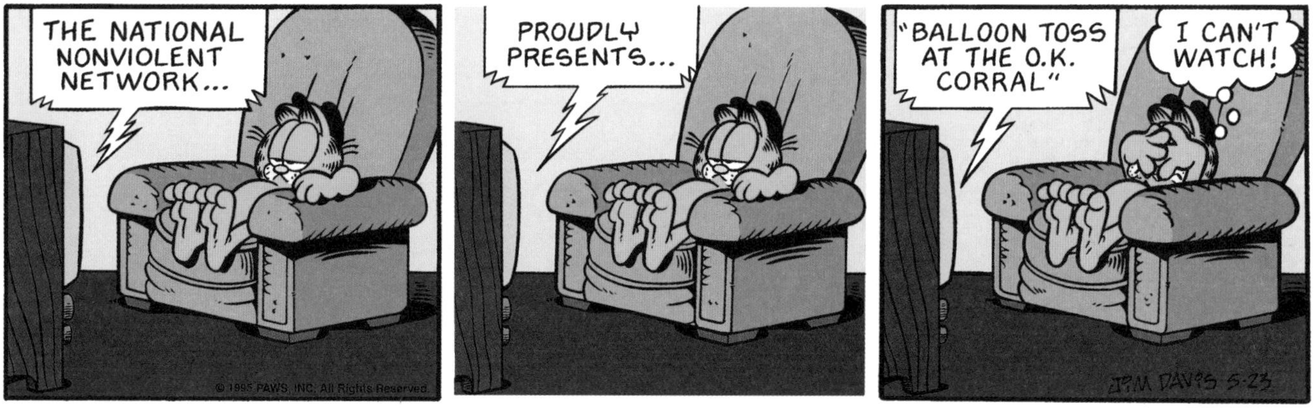
THE NATIONAL NONVIOLENT NETWORK...
PROUDLY PRESENTS...
"BALLOON TOSS AT THE O.K. CORRAL"
I CAN'T WATCH!
© 1995 PAWS, INC. All Rights Reserved.
JIM DAVIS 5-23

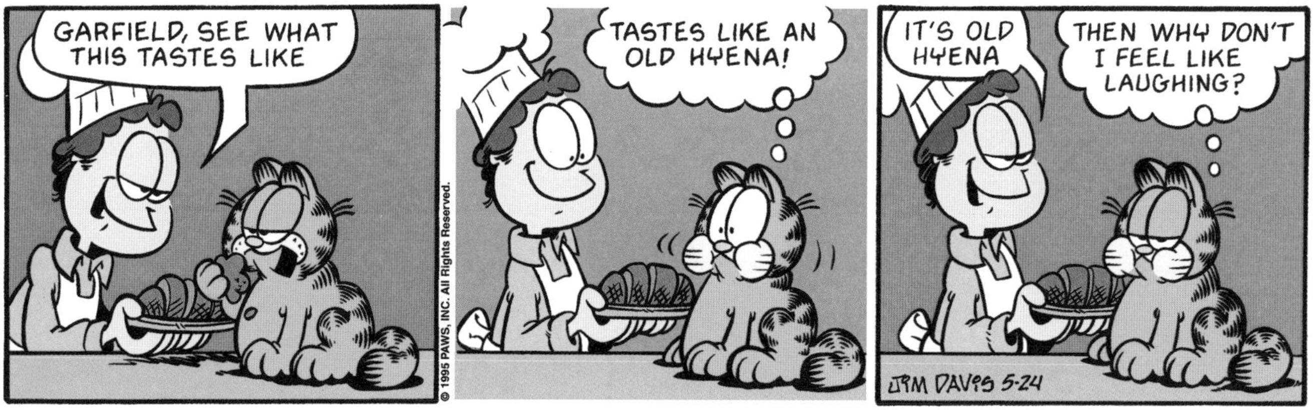
GARFIELD, SEE WHAT THIS TASTES LIKE
TASTES LIKE AN OLD HYENA!
IT'S OLD HYENA
THEN WHY DON'T I FEEL LIKE LAUGHING?
© 1995 PAWS, INC. All Rights Reserved.
JIM DAVIS 5-24

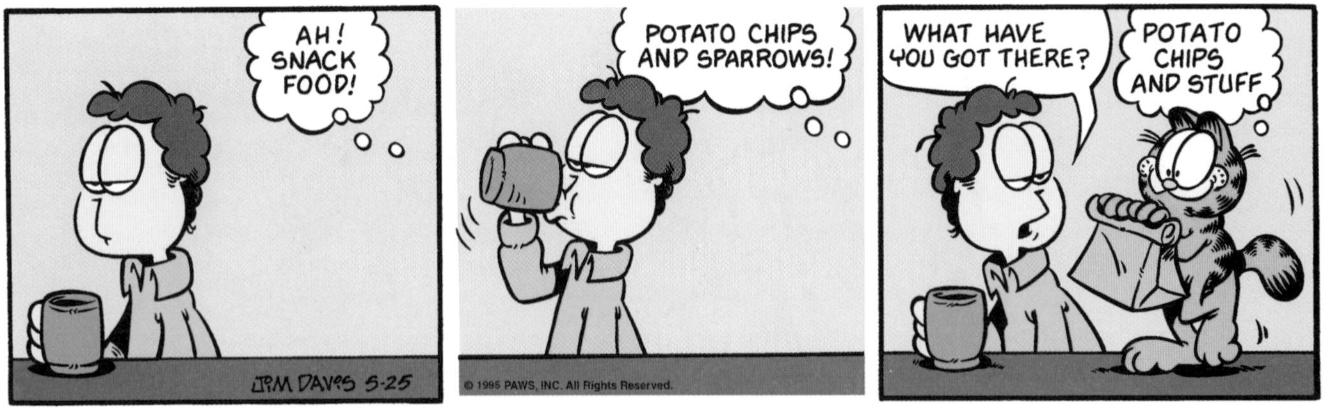
AH! SNACK FOOD!
POTATO CHIPS AND SPARROWS!
WHAT HAVE YOU GOT THERE?
POTATO CHIPS AND STUFF
JIM DAVIS 5-25
© 1995 PAWS, INC. All Rights Reserved.

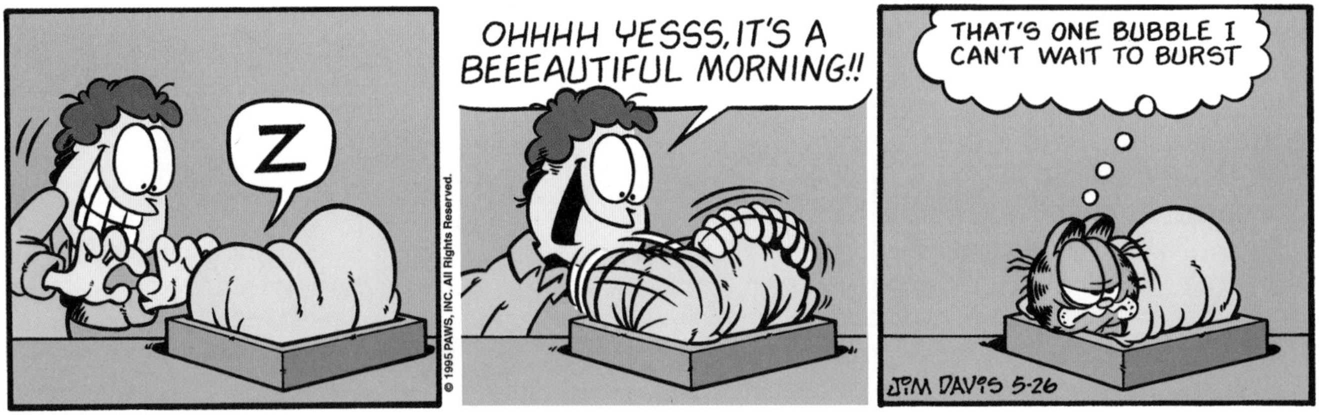
Z
OHHHH YESSS, IT'S A BEEEAUTIFUL MORNING!!
THAT'S ONE BUBBLE I CAN'T WAIT TO BURST
JIM DAVIS 5-26
© 1995 PAWS, INC. All Rights Reserved.

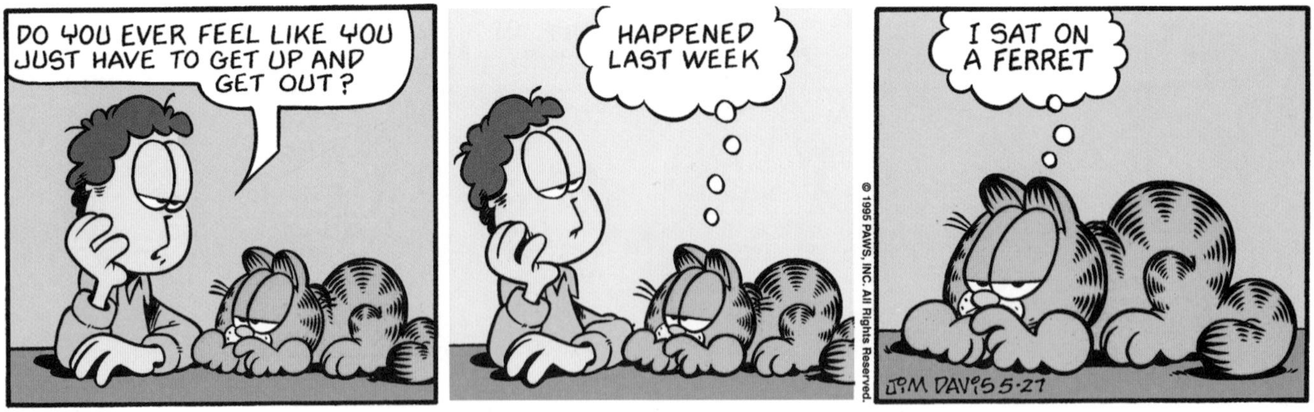
DO YOU EVER FEEL LIKE YOU JUST HAVE TO GET UP AND GET OUT?
HAPPENED LAST WEEK
I SAT ON A FERRET
JIM DAVIS 5-27
© 1995 PAWS, INC. All Rights Reserved.

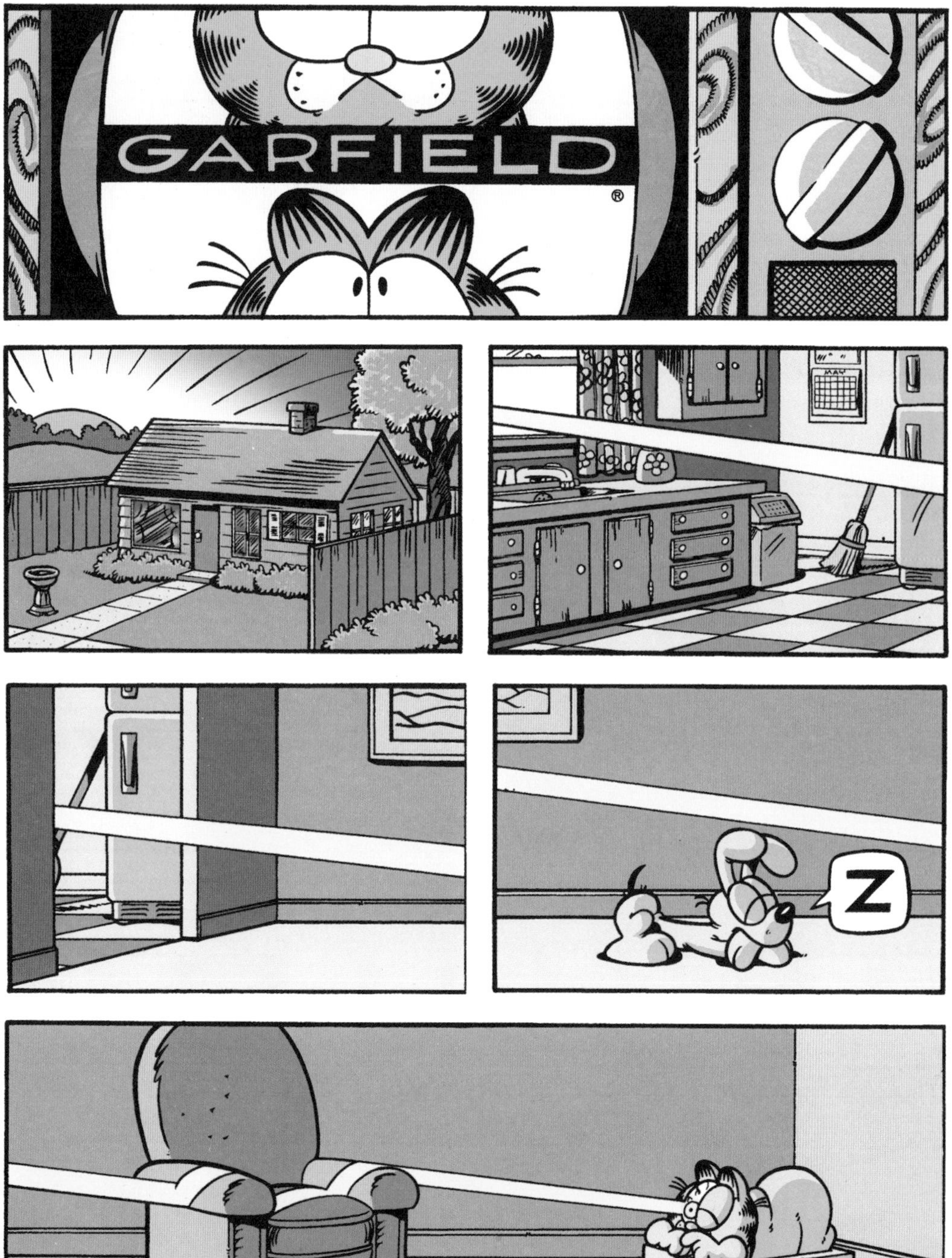
GARFIELD
Z
JIM DAVIS 5-28
© 1995 PAWS, INC. All Rights Reserved.

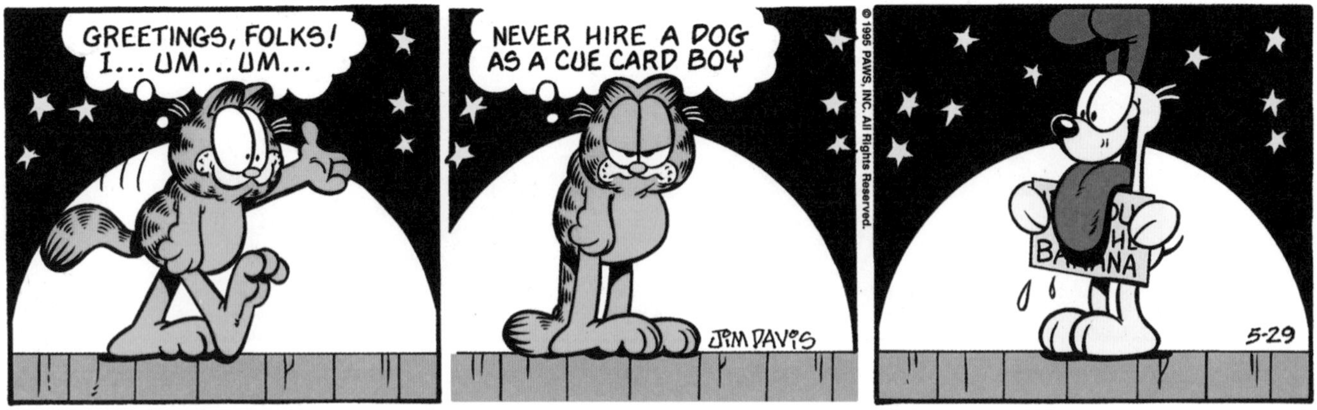
GREETINGS, FOLKS! I... UM... UM...
NEVER HIRE A DOG AS A CUE CARD BOY
JIM DAVIS
© 1995 PAWS, INC. All Rights Reserved.
5-29

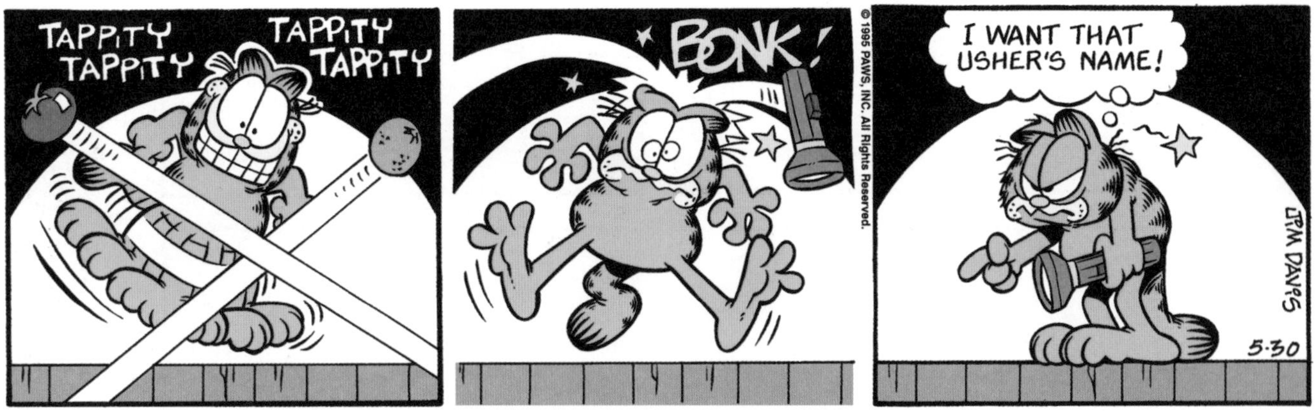
TAPPITY TAPPITY
TAPPITY TAPPITY
BONK!
© 1995 PAWS, INC. All Rights Reserved.
I WANT THAT USHER'S NAME!
JIM DAVIS
5-30

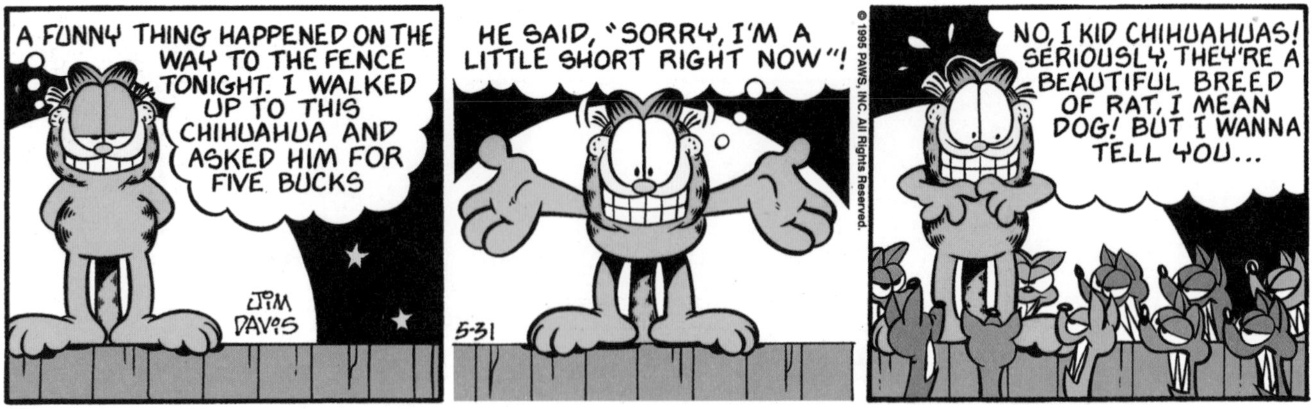
A FUNNY THING HAPPENED ON THE WAY TO THE FENCE TONIGHT. I WALKED UP TO THIS CHIHUAHUA AND ASKED HIM FOR FIVE BUCKS
JIM DAVIS
HE SAID, "SORRY, I'M A LITTLE SHORT RIGHT NOW"!
5-31
© 1995 PAWS, INC. All Rights Reserved.
NO, I KID CHIHUAHUAS! SERIOUSLY, THEY'RE A BEAUTIFUL BREED OF RAT, I MEAN DOG! BUT I WANNA TELL YOU...

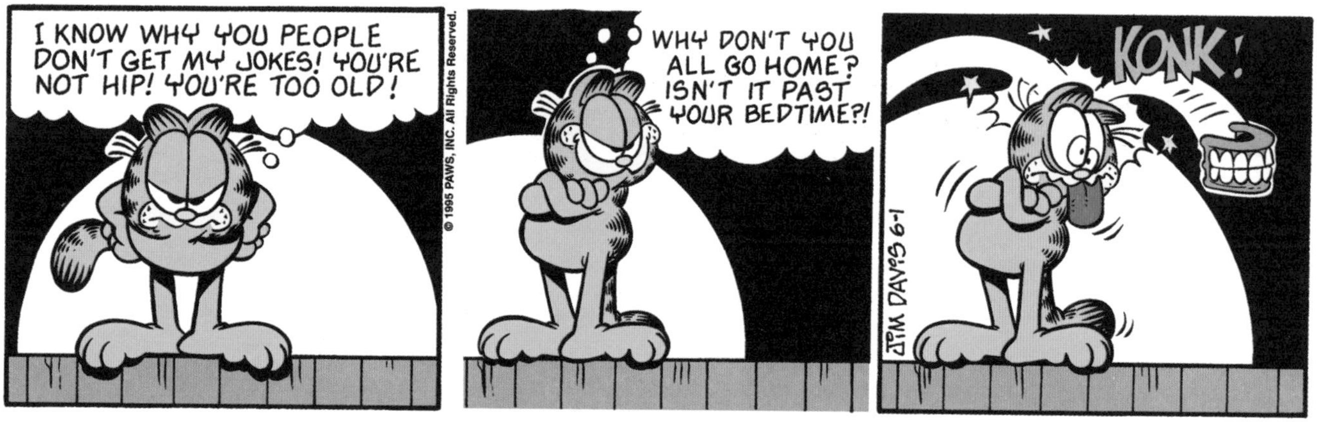
I KNOW WHY YOU PEOPLE DON'T GET MY JOKES! YOU'RE NOT HIP! YOU'RE TOO OLD!
© 1995 PAWS, INC. All Rights Reserved.
WHY DON'T YOU ALL GO HOME? ISN'T IT PAST YOUR BEDTIME?!
KONK!
JIM DAVIS 6-1

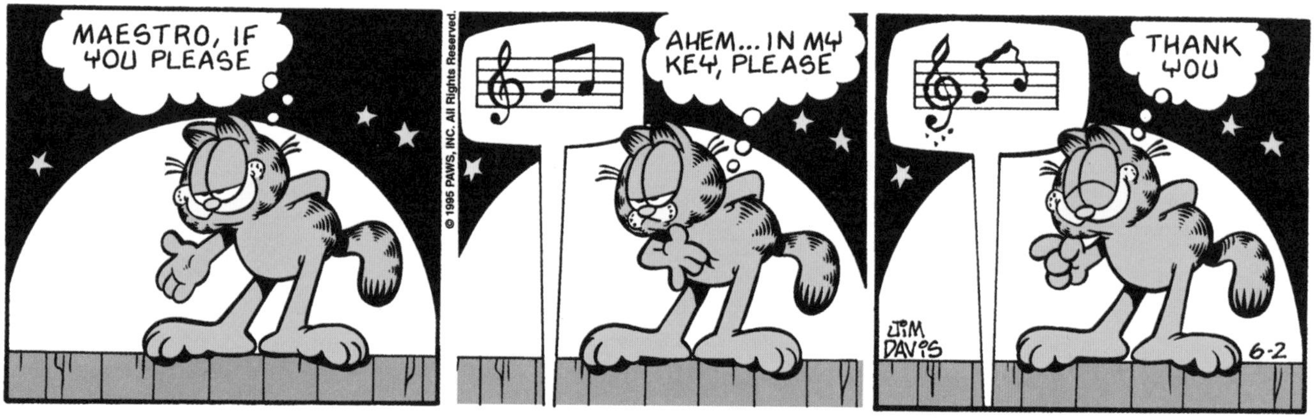
MAESTRO, IF YOU PLEASE
© 1995 PAWS, INC. All Rights Reserved.
AHEM... IN MY KEY, PLEASE
THANK YOU
JIM DAVIS
6-2

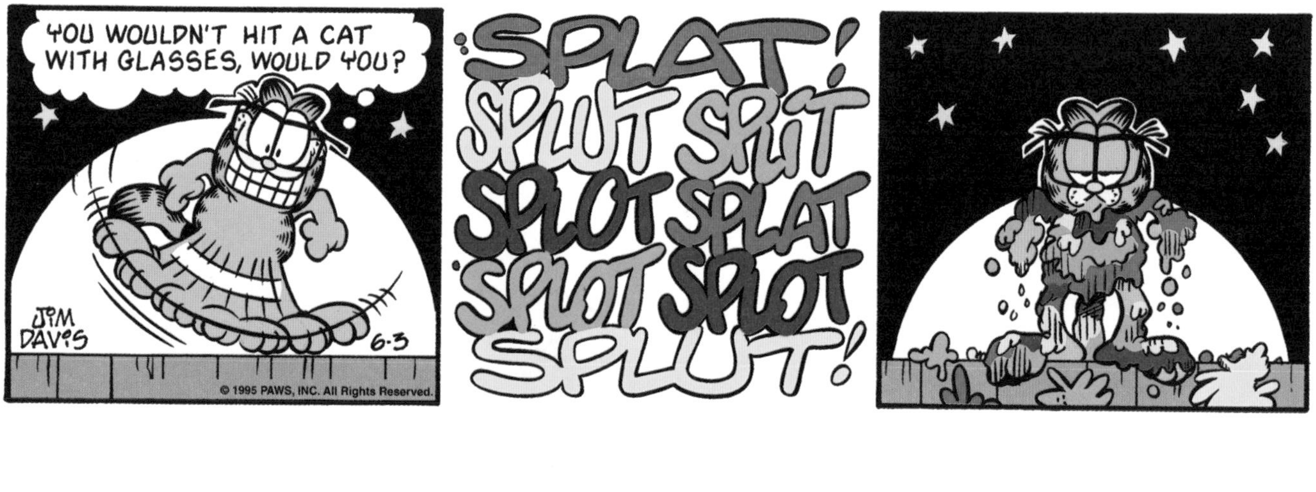
YOU WOULDN'T HIT A CAT WITH GLASSES, WOULD YOU?
JIM DAVIS
6-3
© 1995 PAWS, INC. All Rights Reserved.
SPLAT!
SPLUT SPLIT
SPLOT SPLAT
SPLOT SPLOT
SPLUT!

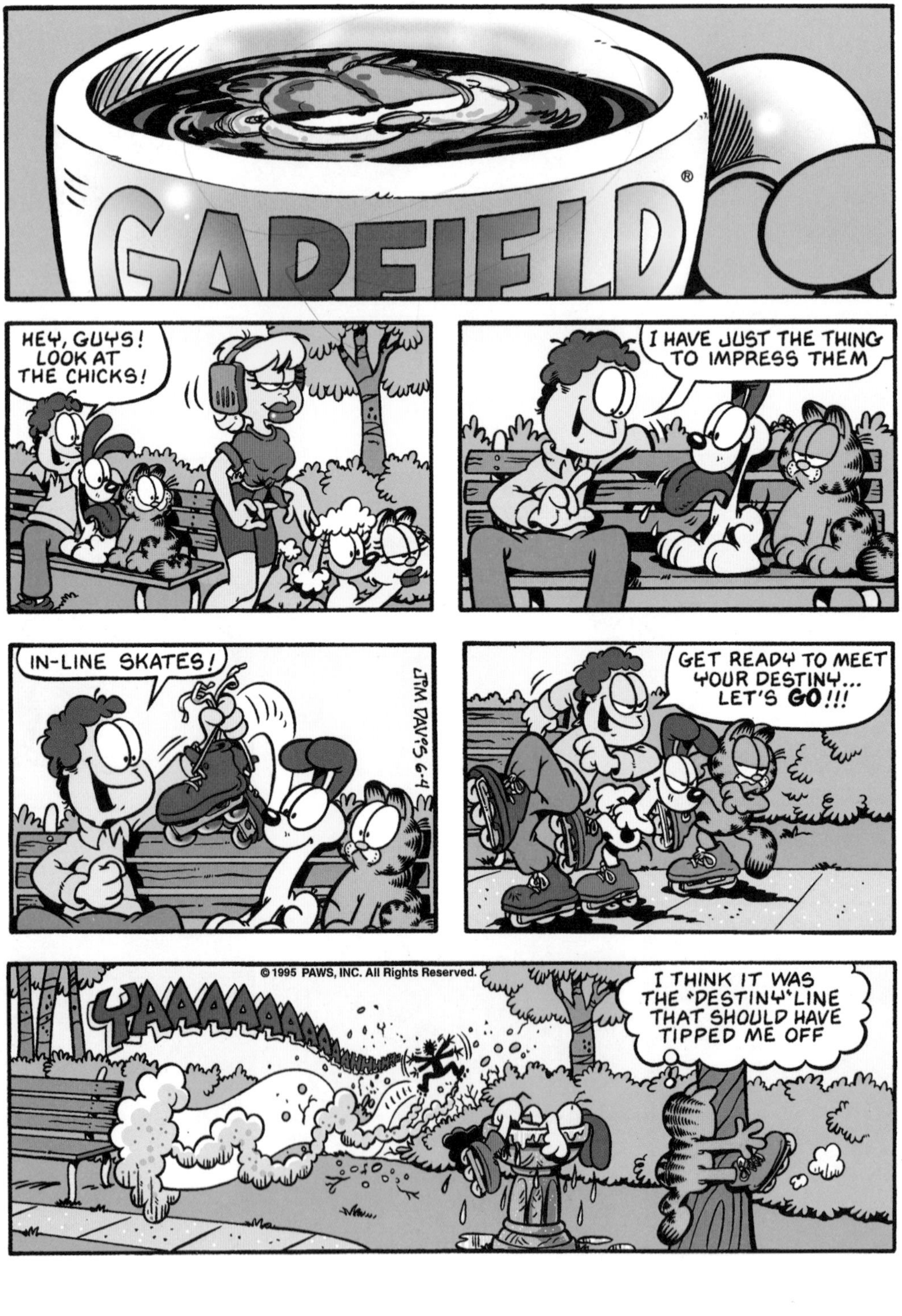
GARFIELD®
HEY, GUYS! LOOK AT THE CHICKS!
I HAVE JUST THE THING TO IMPRESS THEM
IN-LINE SKATES!
JIM DAVIS 6-4
GET READY TO MEET YOUR DESTINY... LET'S GO!!!
© 1995 PAWS, INC. All Rights Reserved.
YAAAAAAAAAAAAAHHHHH
I THINK IT WAS THE "DESTINY" LINE THAT SHOULD HAVE TIPPED ME OFF

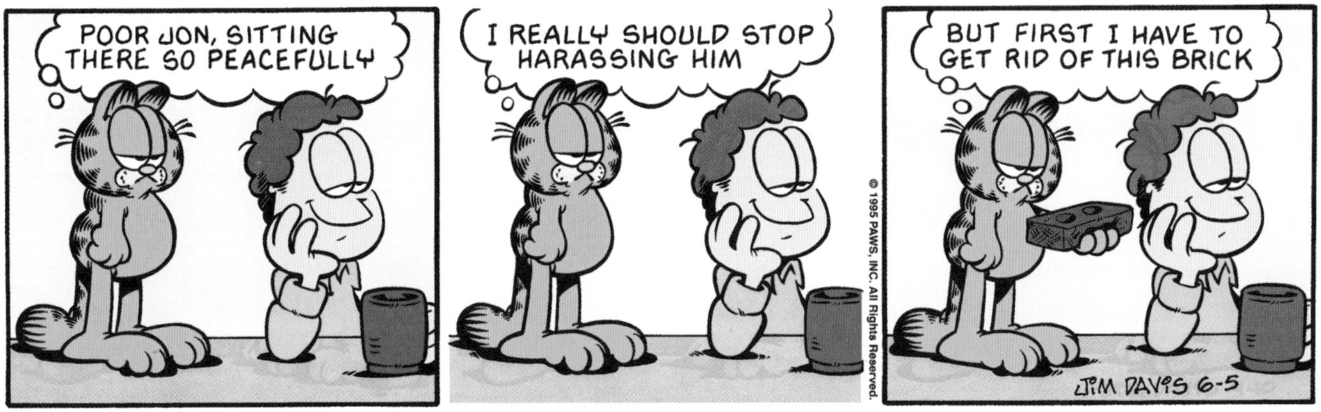
POOR JON, SITTING THERE SO PEACEFULLY
I REALLY SHOULD STOP HARASSING HIM
BUT FIRST I HAVE TO GET RID OF THIS BRICK
JIM DAVIS 6-5

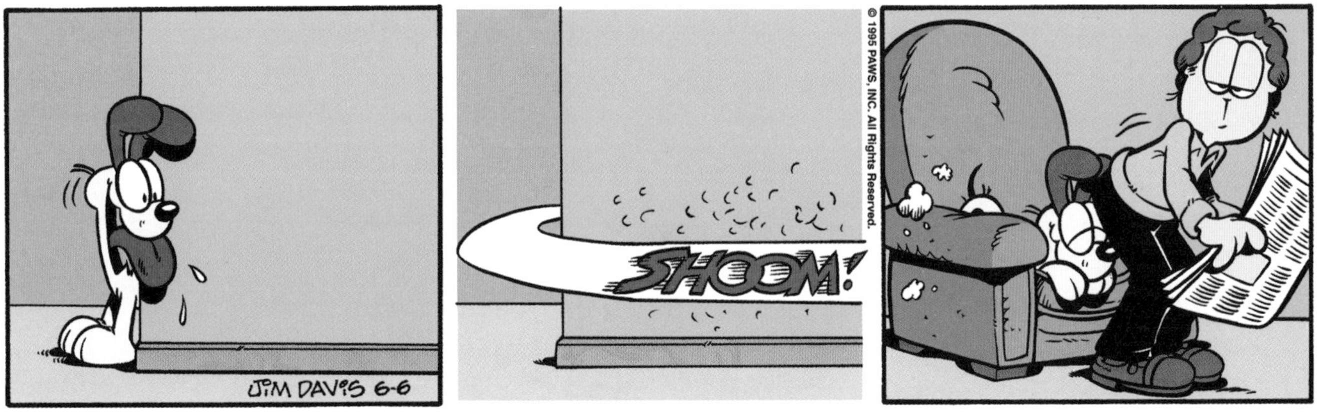
JIM DAVIS 6-6
SHOOM!

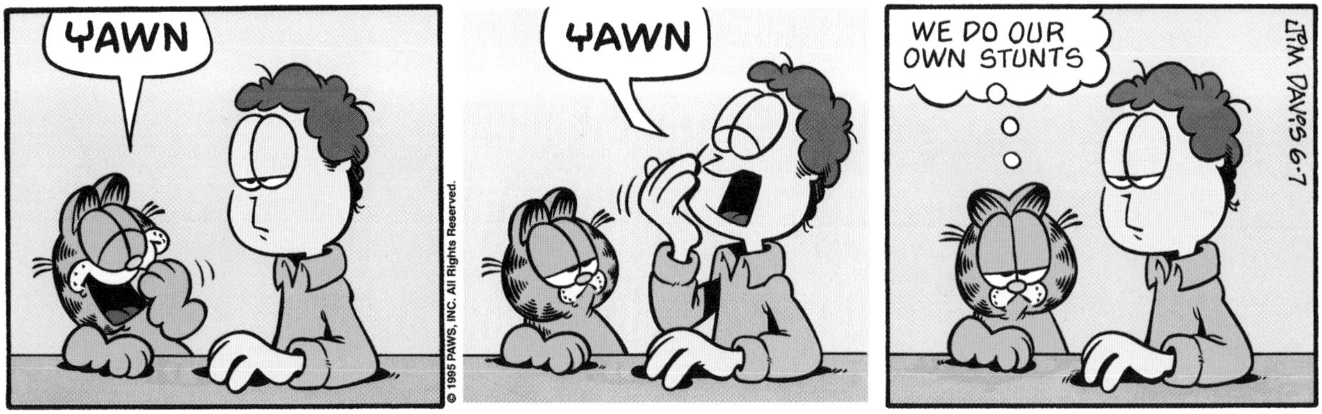
YAWN
YAWN
WE DO OUR OWN STUNTS
JIM DAVIS 6-7

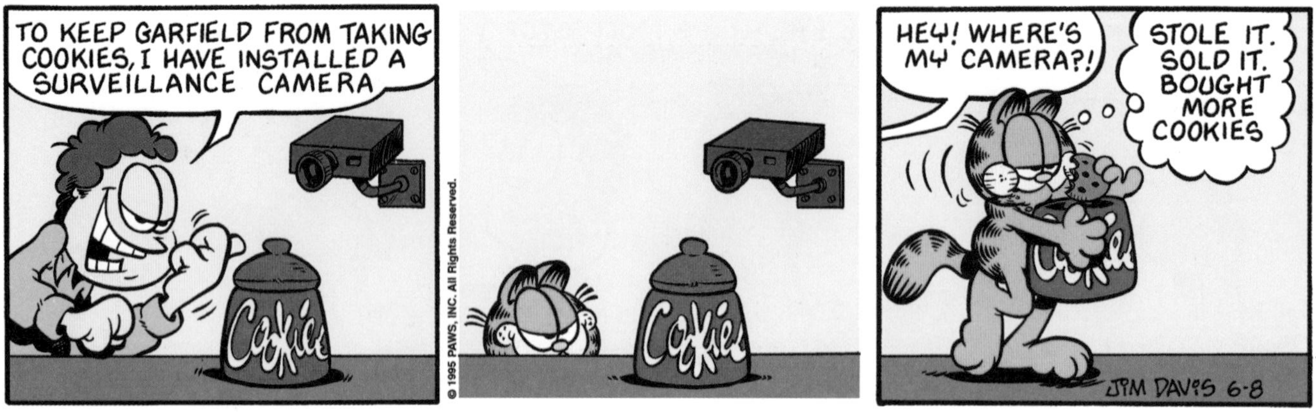
TO KEEP GARFIELD FROM TAKING COOKIES, I HAVE INSTALLED A SURVEILLANCE CAMERA
© 1995 PAWS, INC. All Rights Reserved.
HEY! WHERE'S MY CAMERA?!
STOLE IT. SOLD IT. BOUGHT MORE COOKIES
JIM DAVIS 6-8

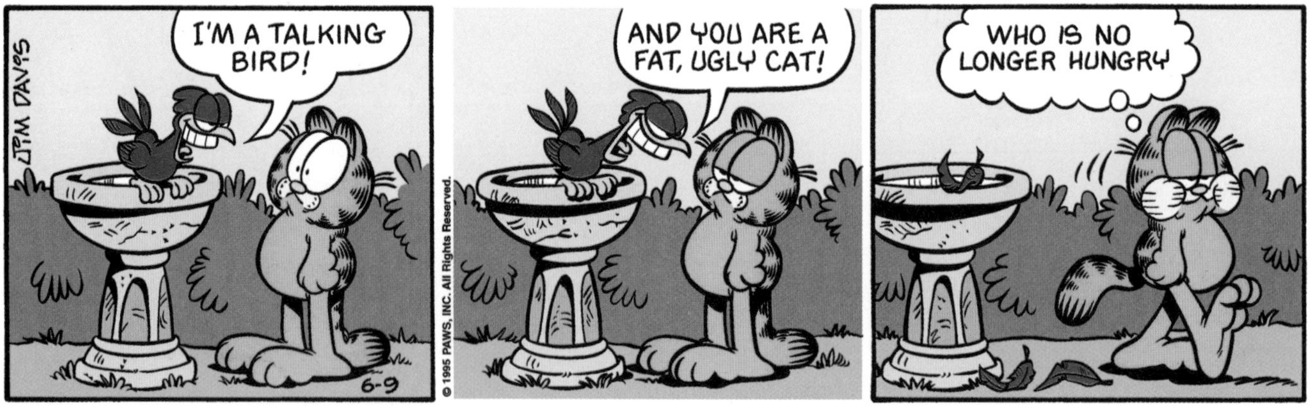
JIM DAVIS
I'M A TALKING BIRD!
6-9
© 1995 PAWS, INC. All Rights Reserved.
AND YOU ARE A FAT, UGLY CAT!
WHO IS NO LONGER HUNGRY

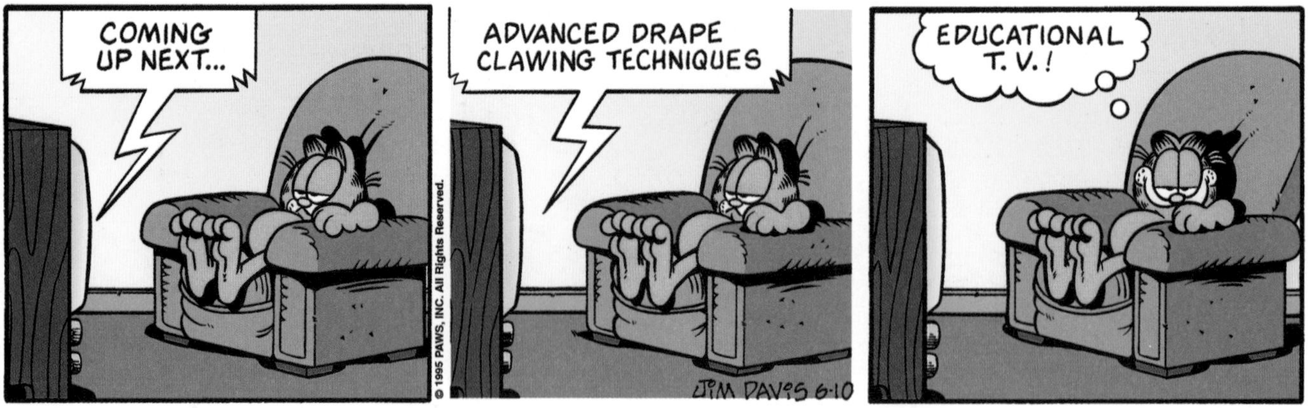
COMING UP NEXT...
© 1995 PAWS, INC. All Rights Reserved.
ADVANCED DRAPE CLAWING TECHNIQUES
JIM DAVIS 6-10
EDUCATIONAL T.V.!

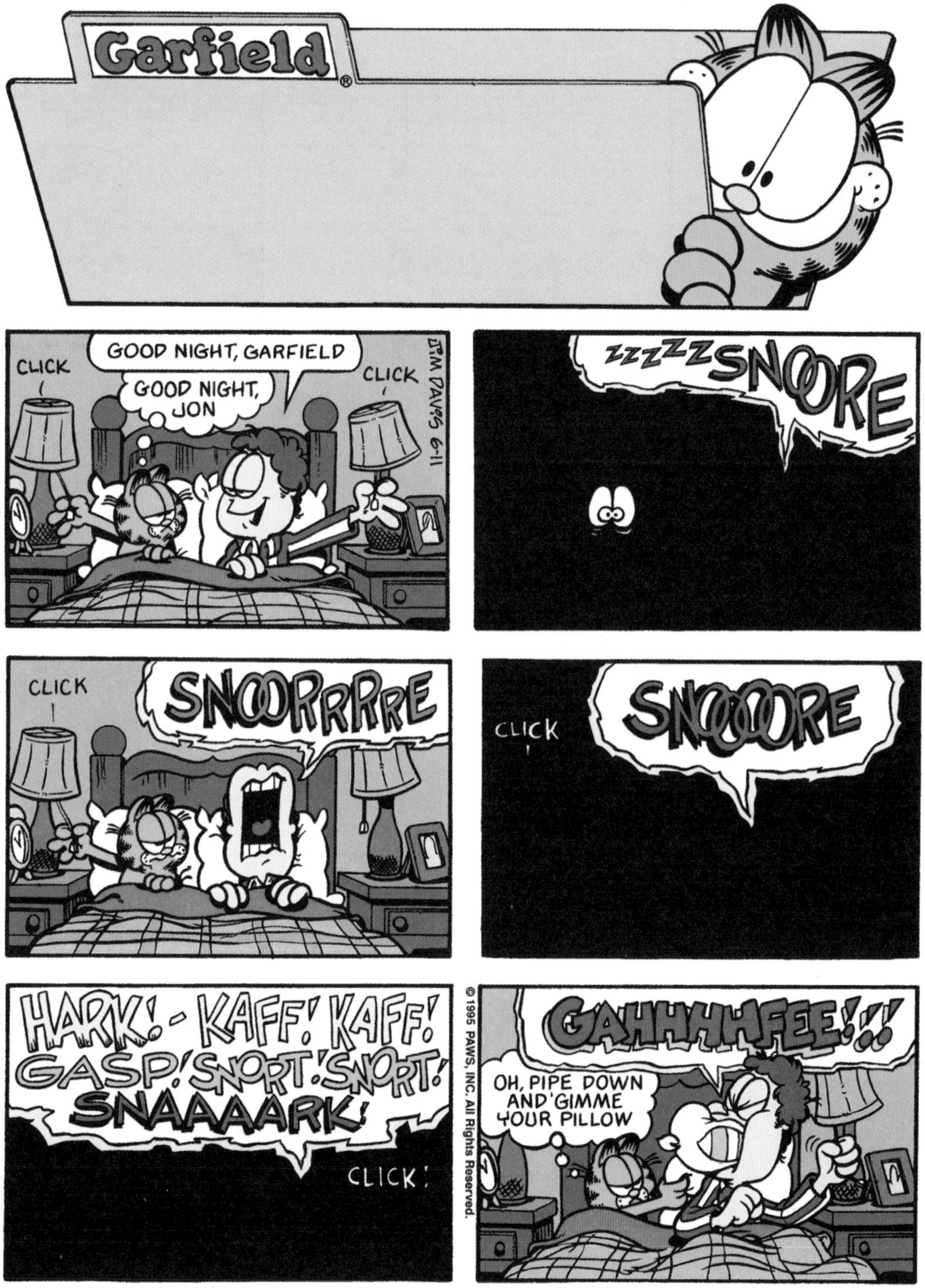
Garfield®
GOOD NIGHT, GARFIELD
GOOD NIGHT, JON
CLICK
CLICK
JIM DAVIS 6-11
ZZZZZSNOORE
CLICK
SNOORRRRRE
CLICK
SNOOOORE
HARK! - KAFF! KAFF!
GASP! SNORT! SNORT!
SNAAAARK!
CLICK!
© 1995 PAWS, INC. All Rights Reserved.
GAHHHHFEE!!!
OH, PIPE DOWN AND GIMME YOUR PILLOW

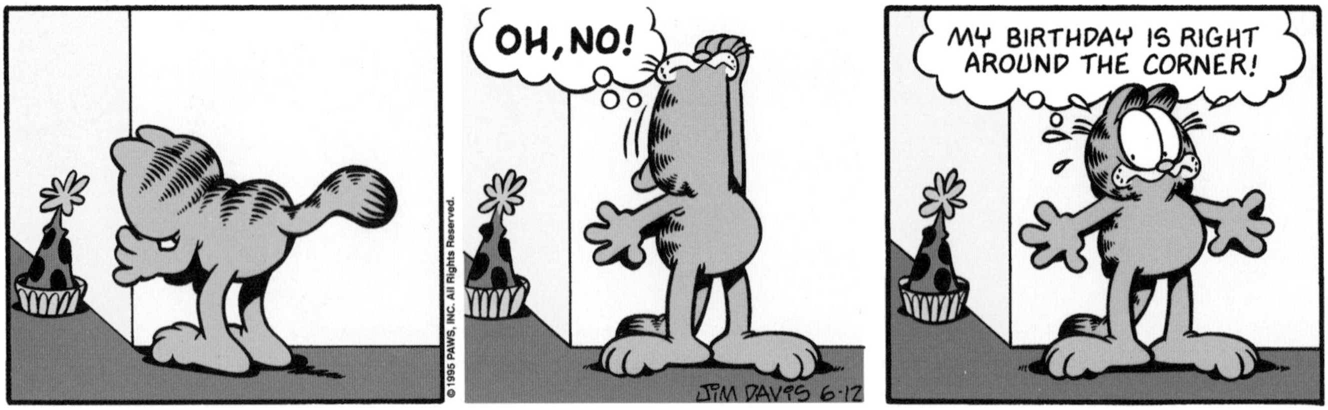
OH, NO!
MY BIRTHDAY IS RIGHT AROUND THE CORNER!
© 1995 PAWS, INC. All Rights Reserved.
JIM DAVIS 6-12

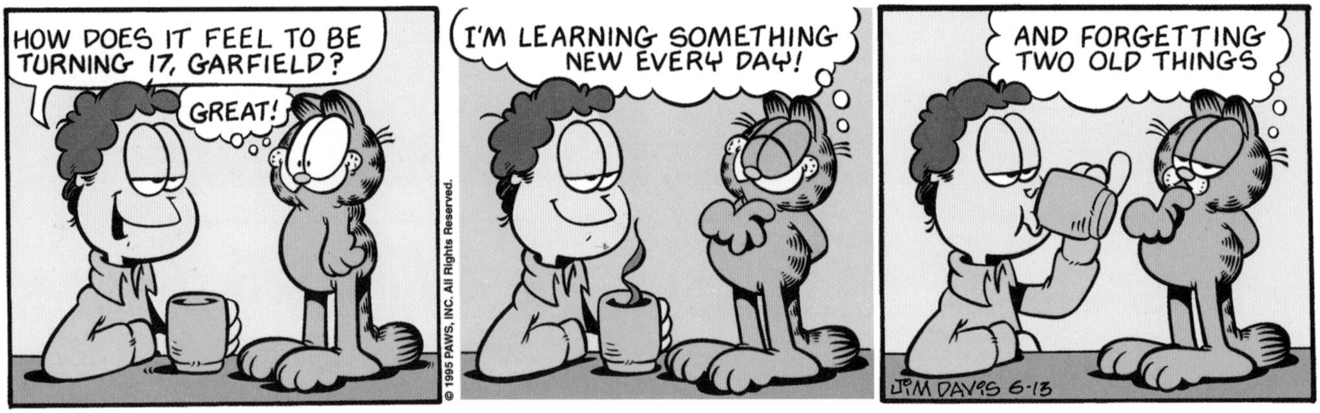
HOW DOES IT FEEL TO BE TURNING 17, GARFIELD?
GREAT!
I'M LEARNING SOMETHING NEW EVERY DAY!
AND FORGETTING TWO OLD THINGS
© 1995 PAWS, INC. All Rights Reserved.
JIM DAVIS 6-13

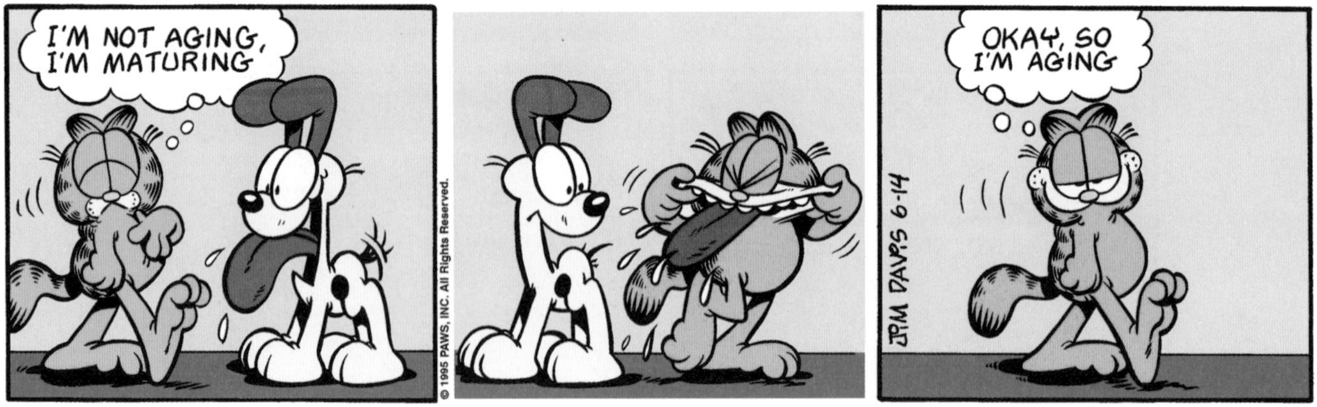
I'M NOT AGING, I'M MATURING
OKAY, SO I'M AGING
© 1995 PAWS, INC. All Rights Reserved.
JIM DAVIS 6-14

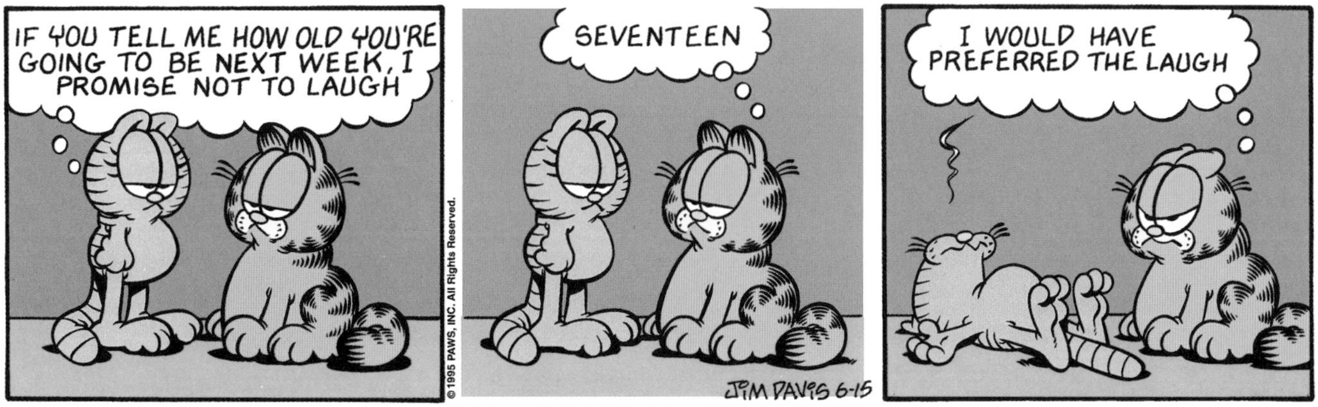
IF YOU TELL ME HOW OLD YOU'RE GOING TO BE NEXT WEEK, I PROMISE NOT TO LAUGH
SEVENTEEN
I WOULD HAVE PREFERRED THE LAUGH
JIM DAVIS 6-15
© 1995 PAWS, INC. All Rights Reserved.

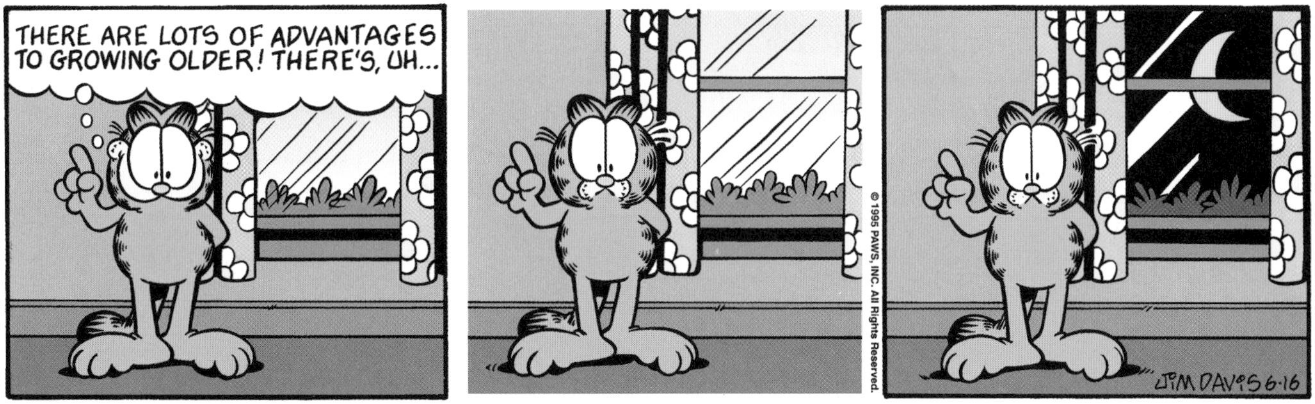
THERE ARE LOTS OF ADVANTAGES TO GROWING OLDER! THERE'S, UH...
JIM DAVIS 6-16
© 1995 PAWS, INC. All Rights Reserved.

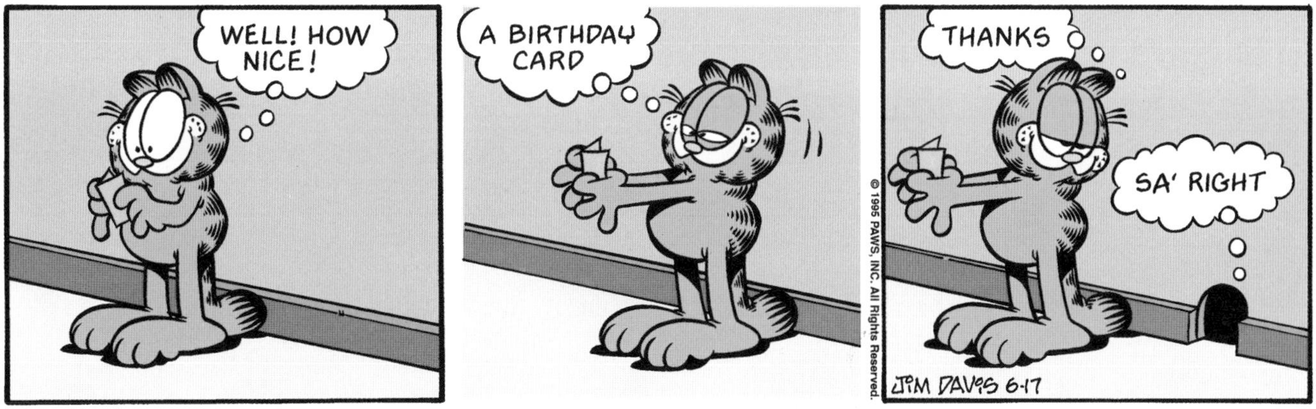
WELL! HOW NICE!
A BIRTHDAY CARD
THANKS
SA' RIGHT
JIM DAVIS 6-17
© 1995 PAWS, INC. All Rights Reserved.

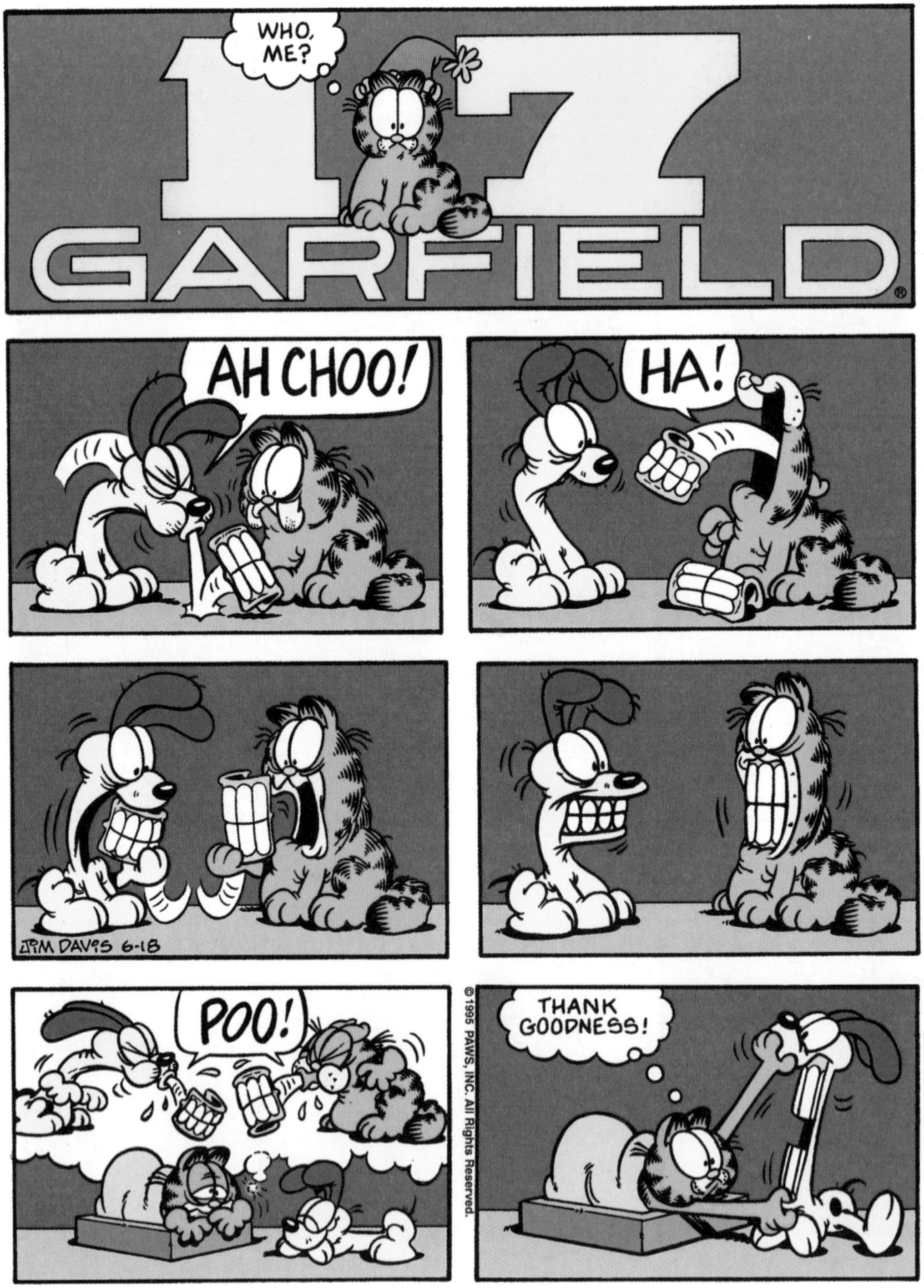
WHO, ME?
GARFIELD
AH CHOO!
HA!
JIM DAVIS 6-18
POO!
THANK GOODNESS!
© 1995 PAWS, INC. All Rights Reserved.

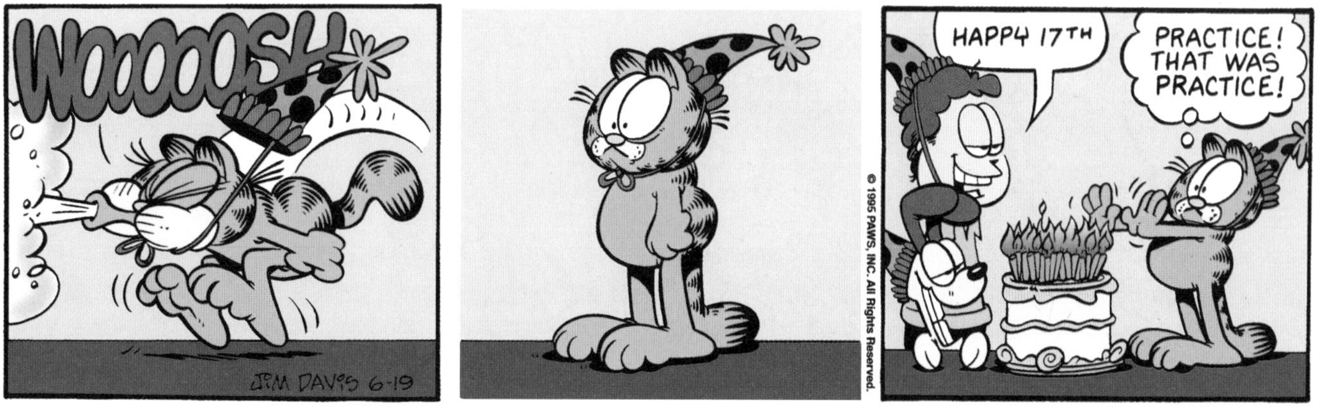
WOOOOOSH
JIM DAVIS 6-19
© 1995 PAWS, INC. All Rights Reserved.
HAPPY 17TH
PRACTICE! THAT WAS PRACTICE!

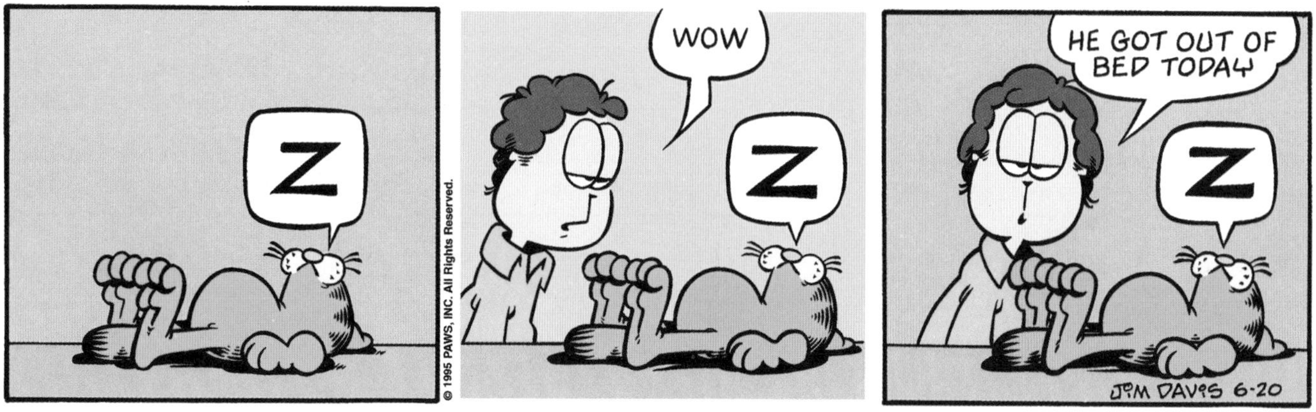
Z
© 1995 PAWS, INC. All Rights Reserved.
WOW
Z
HE GOT OUT OF BED TODAY
Z
JIM DAVIS 6-20

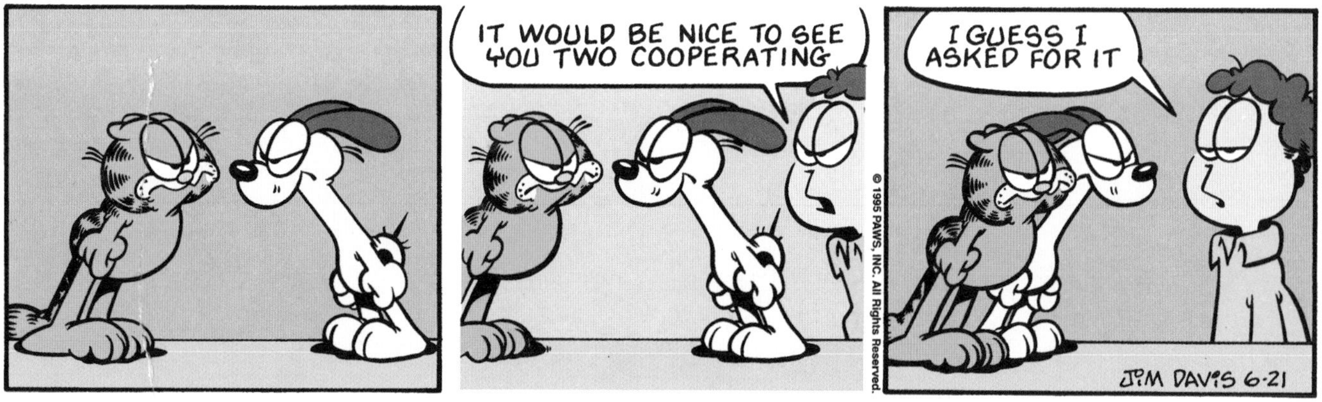
IT WOULD BE NICE TO SEE YOU TWO COOPERATING
© 1995 PAWS, INC. All Rights Reserved.
I GUESS I ASKED FOR IT
JIM DAVIS 6-21

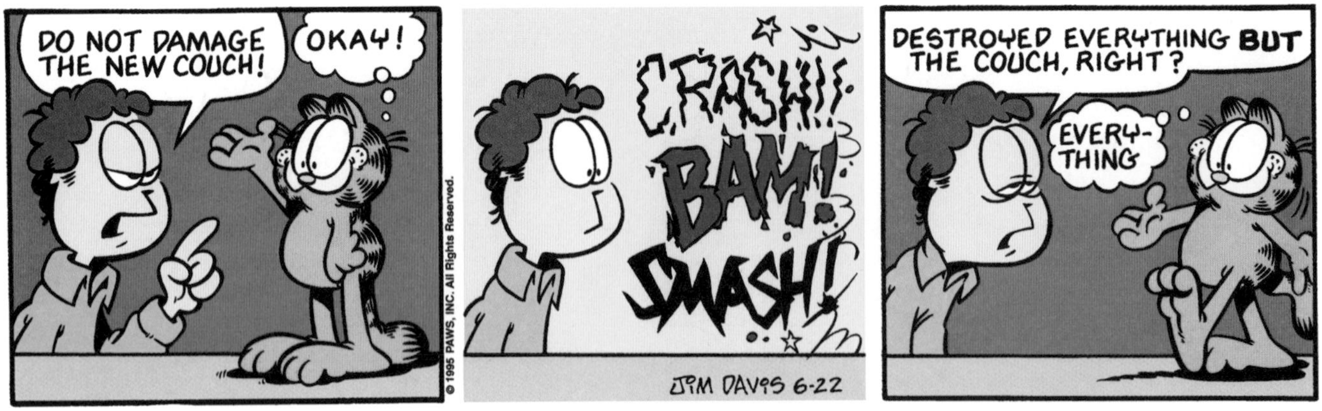
DO NOT DAMAGE THE NEW COUCH!
OKAY!
© 1995 PAWS, INC. All Rights Reserved.
CRASH!!
BAM!
SMASH!
JIM DAVIS 6-22
DESTROYED EVERYTHING BUT THE COUCH, RIGHT?
EVERY-THING

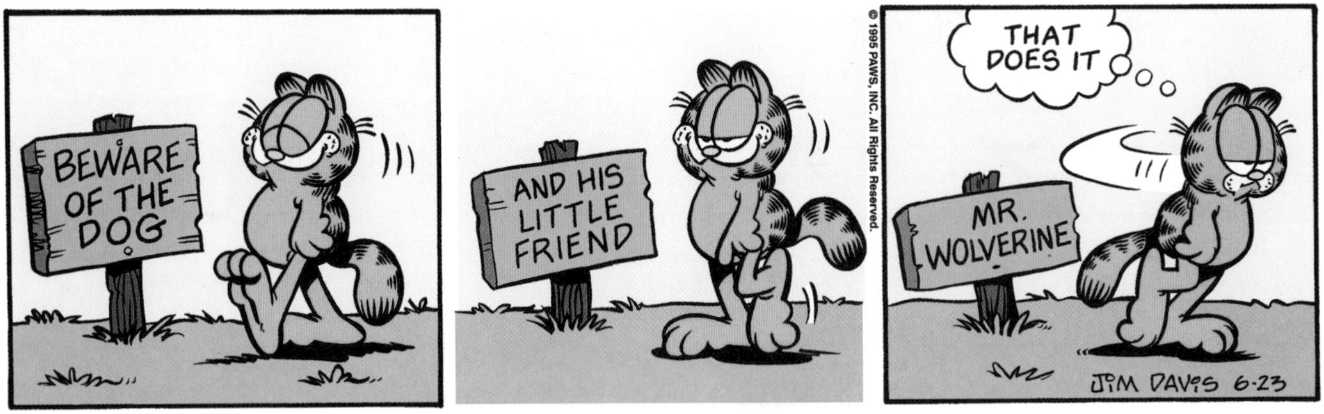
BEWARE OF THE DOG
AND HIS LITTLE FRIEND
© 1995 PAWS, INC. All Rights Reserved.
THAT DOES IT
MR. WOLVERINE
JIM DAVIS 6-23

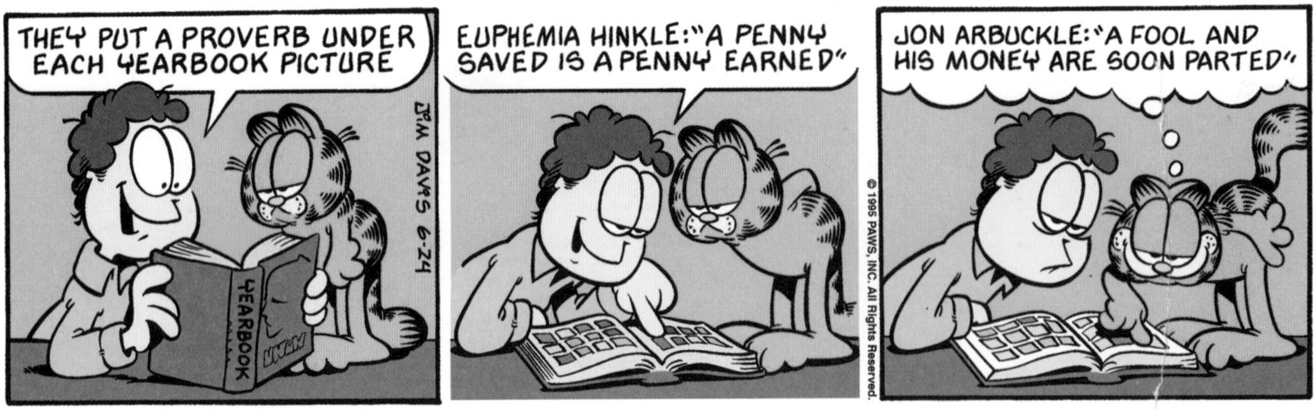
THEY PUT A PROVERB UNDER EACH YEARBOOK PICTURE
YEARBOOK
JIM DAVIS 6-24
EUPHEMIA HINKLE: "A PENNY SAVED IS A PENNY EARNED"
© 1995 PAWS, INC. All Rights Reserved.
JON ARBUCKLE: "A FOOL AND HIS MONEY ARE SOON PARTED"

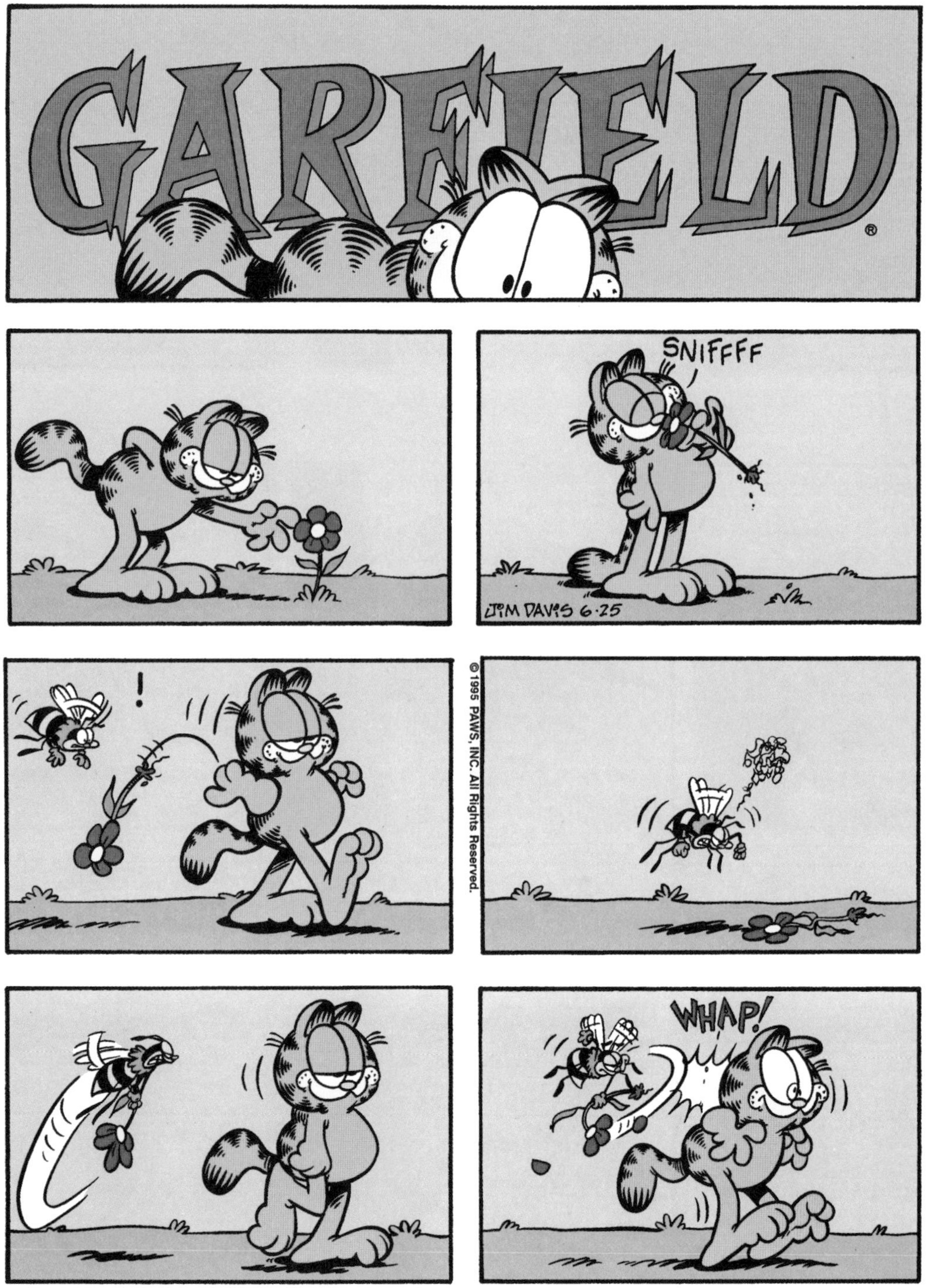
GARFIELD®
SNIFFFF
JIM DAVIS 6-25
© 1995 PAWS, INC. All Rights Reserved.
!
WHAP!

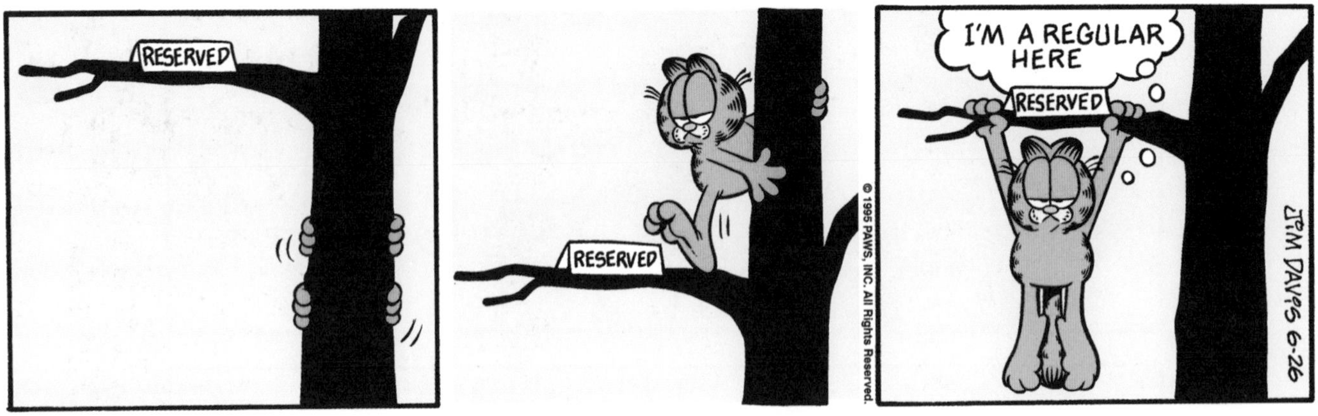
RESERVED
RESERVED
I'M A REGULAR HERE
RESERVED
© 1995 PAWS, INC. All Rights Reserved.
JIM DAVIS 6-26

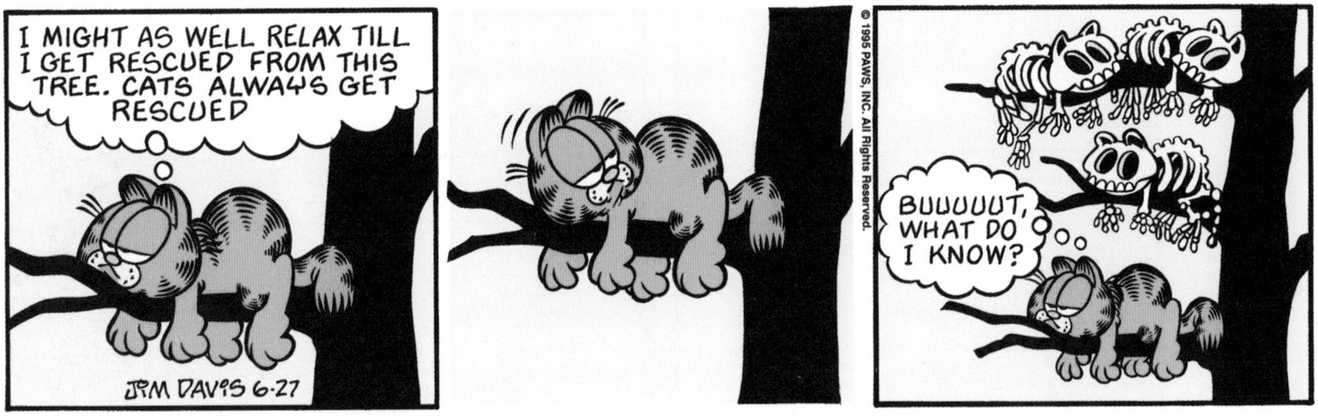
I MIGHT AS WELL RELAX TILL I GET RESCUED FROM THIS TREE. CATS ALWAYS GET RESCUED
JIM DAVIS 6-27
© 1995 PAWS, INC. All Rights Reserved.
BUUUUUT, WHAT DO I KNOW?

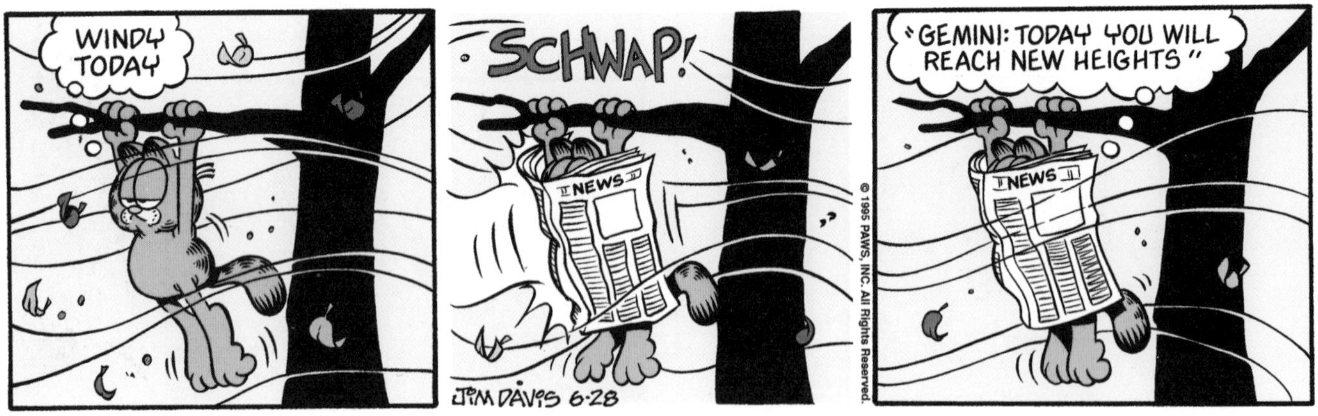
WINDY TODAY
SCHWAP!
NEWS
JIM DAVIS 6-28
© 1995 PAWS, INC. All Rights Reserved.
"GEMINI: TODAY YOU WILL REACH NEW HEIGHTS"
NEWS

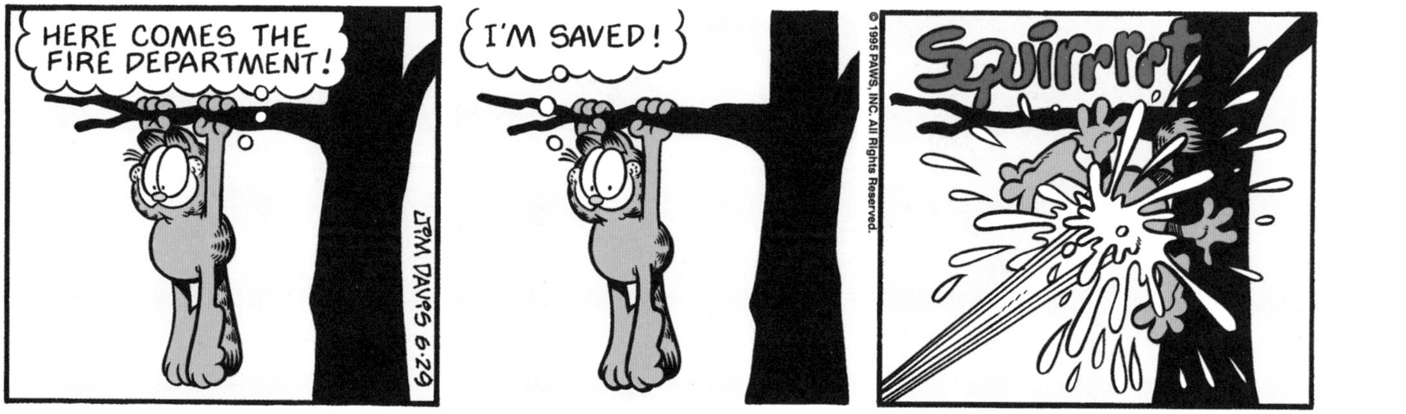
HERE COMES THE FIRE DEPARTMENT!
JIM DAVIS 6-29
I'M SAVED!
© 1995 PAWS, INC. All Rights Reserved.
Squirrrrt

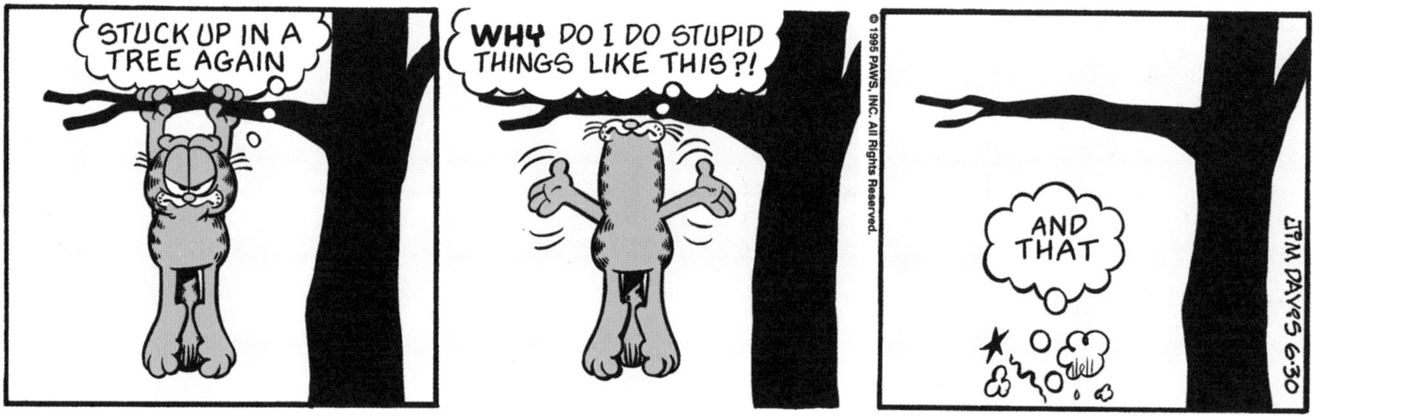
STUCK UP IN A TREE AGAIN
WHY DO I DO STUPID THINGS LIKE THIS?!
© 1995 PAWS, INC. All Rights Reserved.
AND THAT
JIM DAVIS 6-30

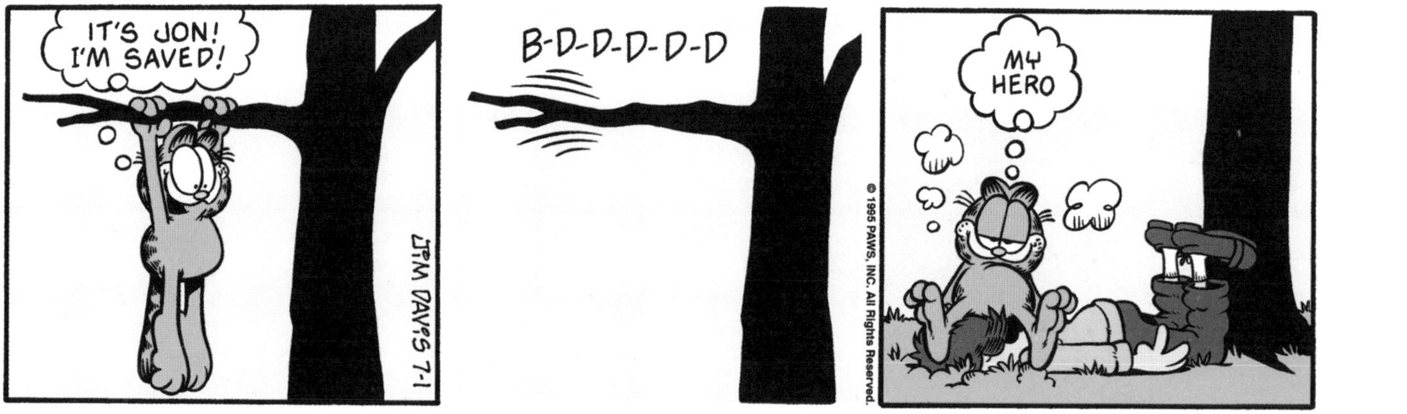
IT'S JON! I'M SAVED!
JIM DAVIS 7-1
B-D-D-D-D-D
© 1995 PAWS, INC. All Rights Reserved.
MY HERO

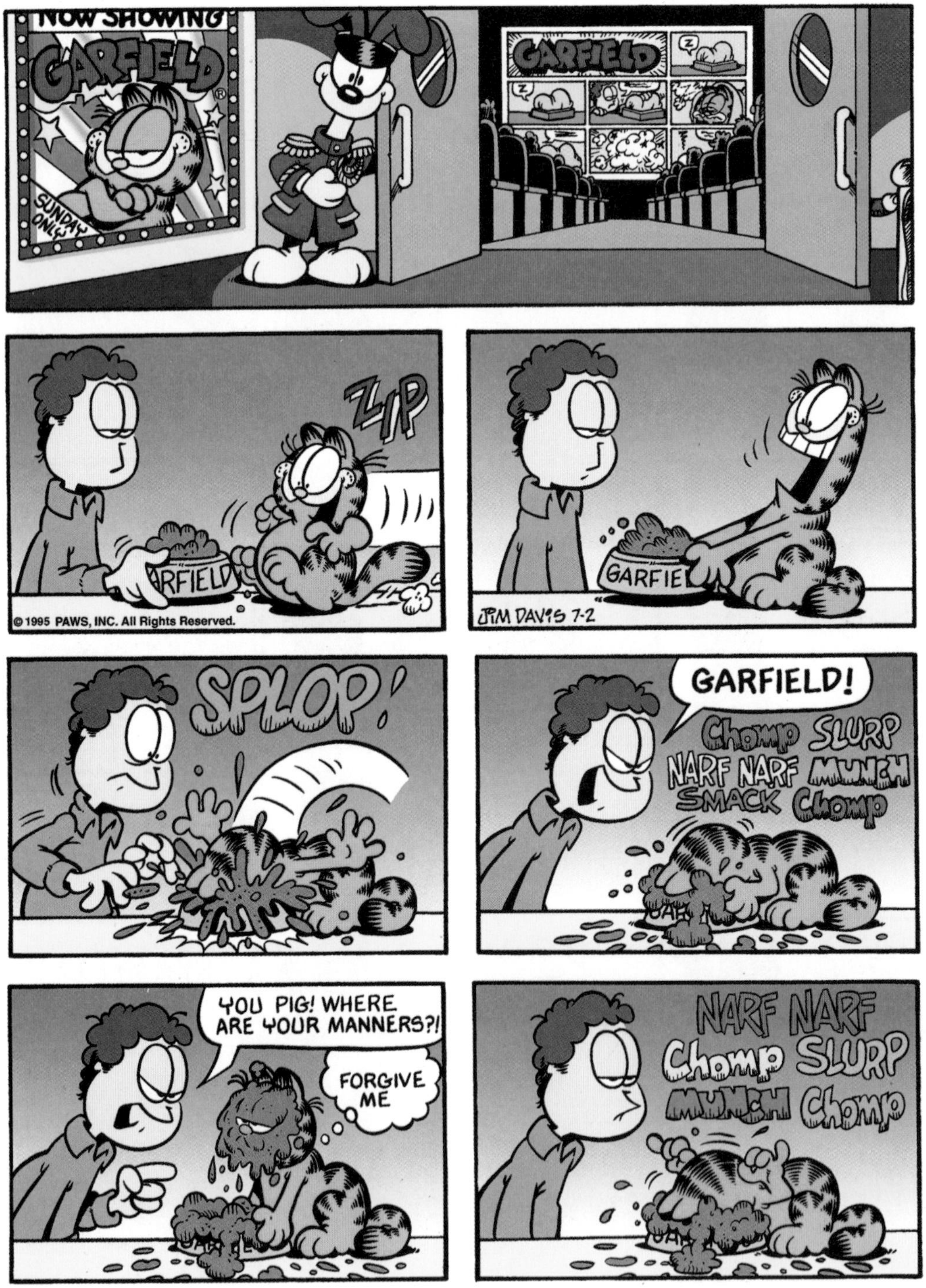
NOW SHOWING
GARFIELD
SUNDAY ONLY
ZIP
© 1995 PAWS, INC. All Rights Reserved.
JIM DAVIS 7-2
SPLOP!
GARFIELD!
Chomp SLURP
NARF NARF MUNCH
SMACK Chomp
YOU PIG! WHERE ARE YOUR MANNERS?!
FORGIVE ME
NARF NARF
Chomp SLURP
MUNCH Chomp

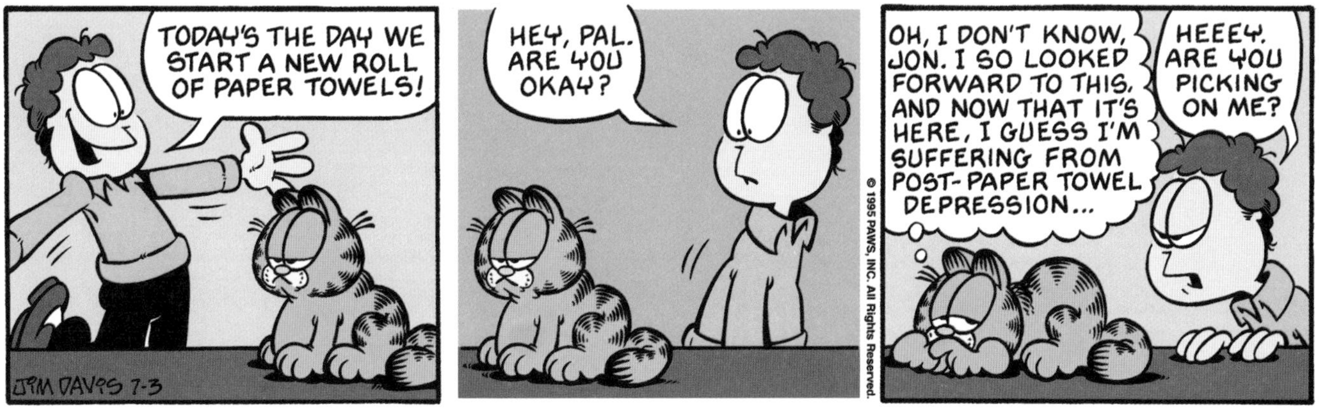
TODAY'S THE DAY WE START A NEW ROLL OF PAPER TOWELS!
JIM DAVIS 7-3
HEY, PAL. ARE YOU OKAY?
© 1995 PAWS, INC. All Rights Reserved.
OH, I DON'T KNOW, JON. I SO LOOKED FORWARD TO THIS, AND NOW THAT IT'S HERE, I GUESS I'M SUFFERING FROM POST-PAPER TOWEL DEPRESSION...
HEEEY. ARE YOU PICKING ON ME?

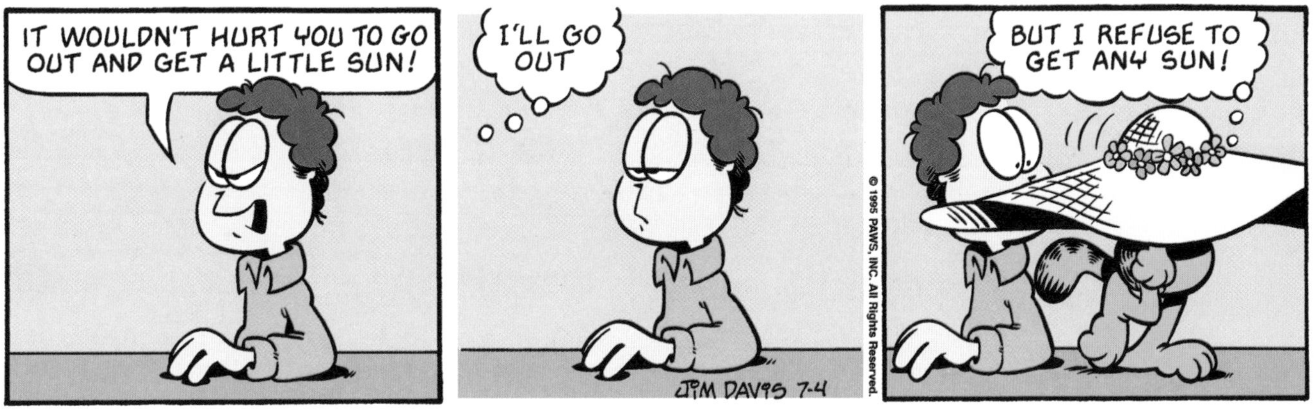
IT WOULDN'T HURT YOU TO GO OUT AND GET A LITTLE SUN!
I'LL GO OUT
JIM DAVIS 7-4
© 1995 PAWS, INC. All Rights Reserved.
BUT I REFUSE TO GET ANY SUN!

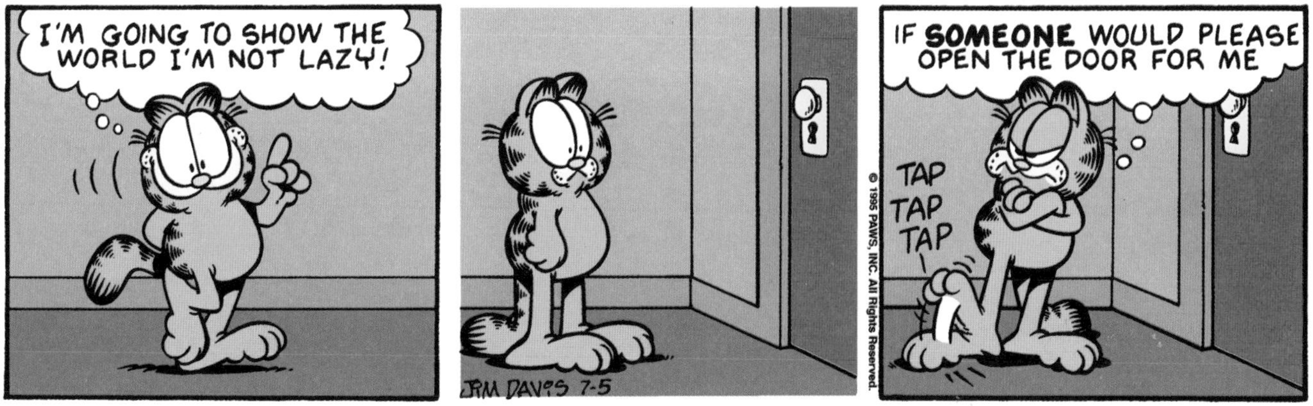
I'M GOING TO SHOW THE WORLD I'M NOT LAZY!
JIM DAVIS 7-5
© 1995 PAWS, INC. All Rights Reserved.
IF SOMEONE WOULD PLEASE OPEN THE DOOR FOR ME
TAP TAP TAP

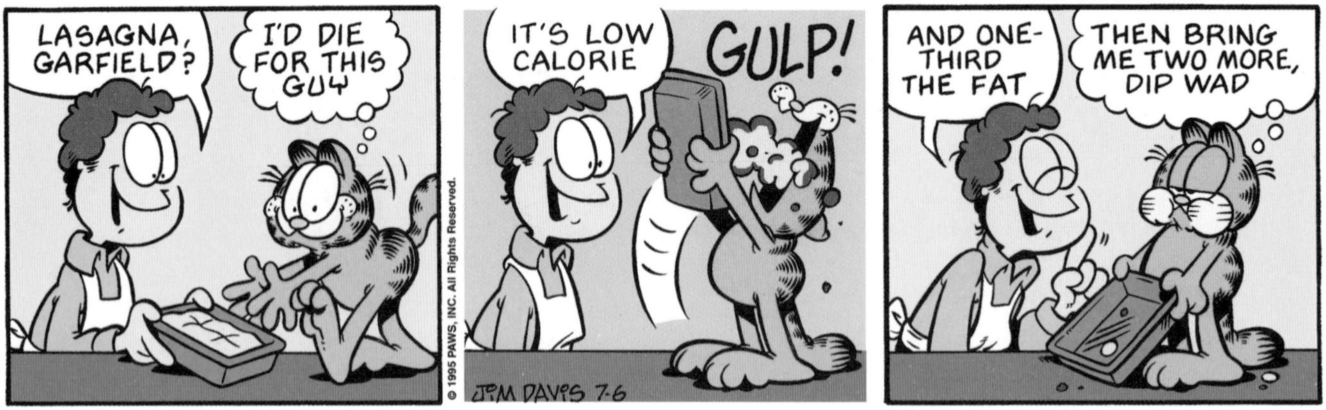
LASAGNA, GARFIELD?
I'D DIE FOR THIS GUY
IT'S LOW CALORIE
GULP!
AND ONE-THIRD THE FAT
THEN BRING ME TWO MORE, DIP WAD
© 1995 PAWS, INC. All Rights Reserved.
JIM DAVIS 7-6

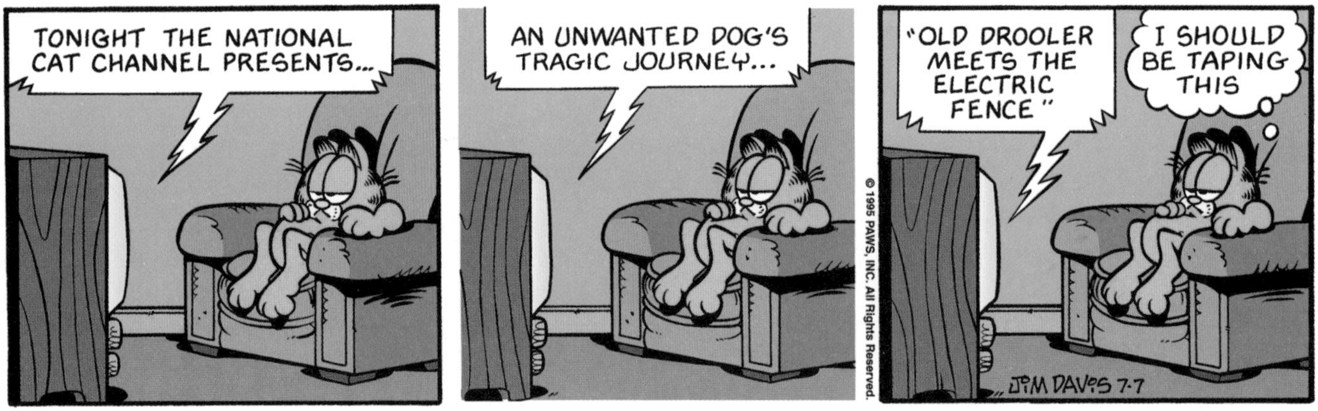
TONIGHT THE NATIONAL CAT CHANNEL PRESENTS...
AN UNWANTED DOG'S TRAGIC JOURNEY...
"OLD DROOLER MEETS THE ELECTRIC FENCE"
I SHOULD BE TAPING THIS
© 1995 PAWS, INC. All Rights Reserved.
JIM DAVIS 7-7

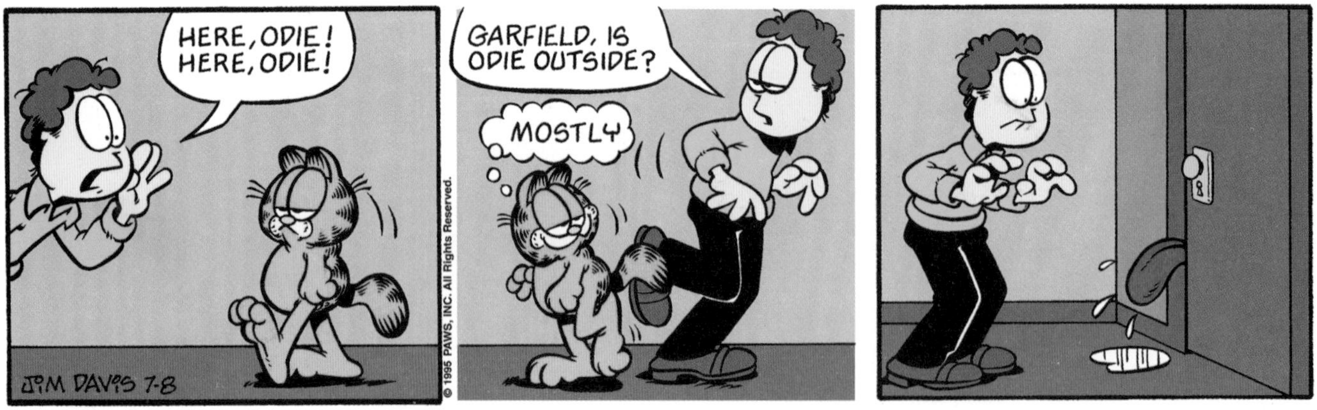
HERE, ODIE! HERE, ODIE!
JIM DAVIS 7-8
© 1995 PAWS, INC. All Rights Reserved.
GARFIELD, IS ODIE OUTSIDE?
MOSTLY

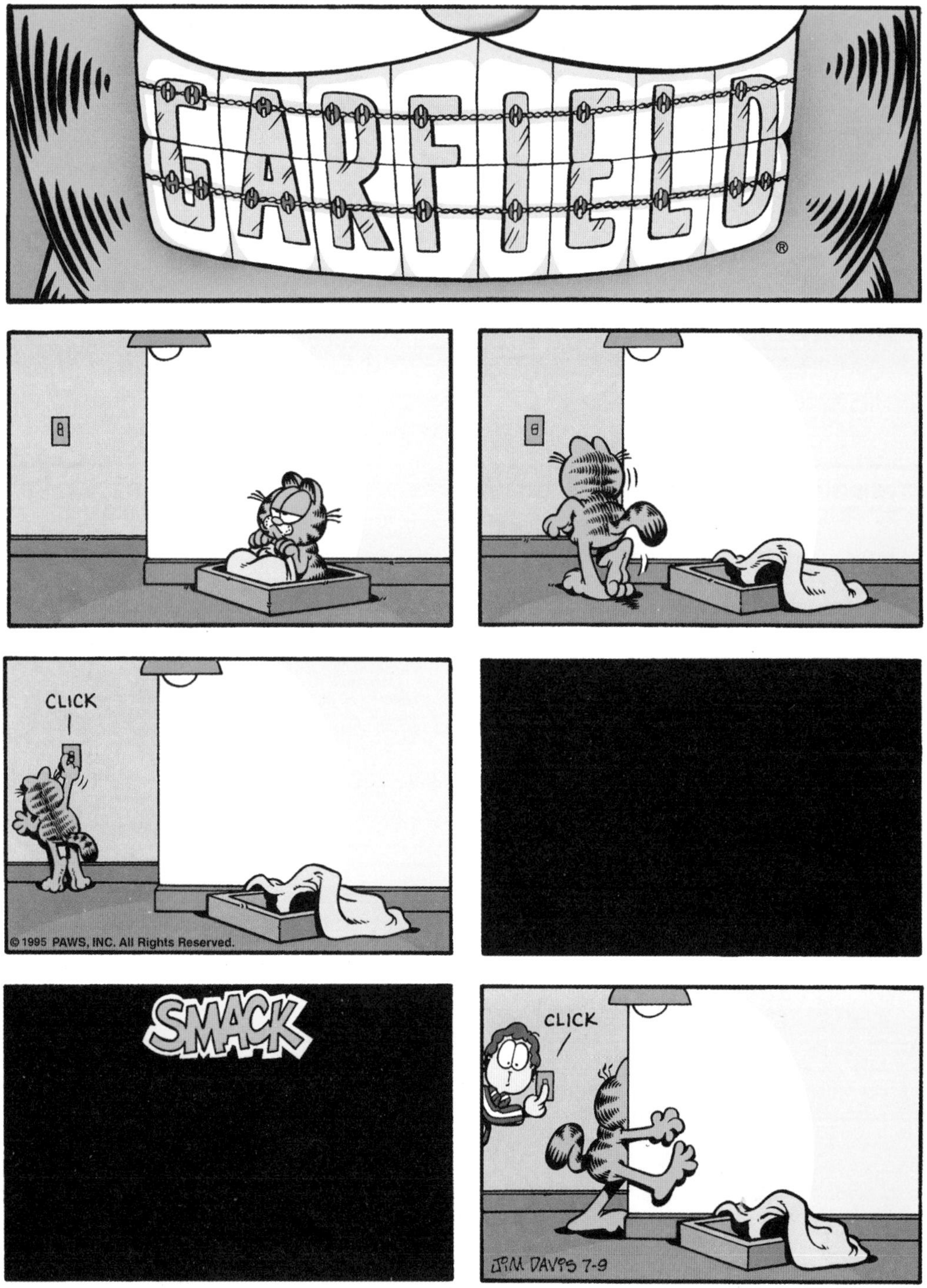

GARFIELD®
CLICK
© 1995 PAWS, INC. All Rights Reserved.
SMACK
CLICK
JIM DAVIS 7-9

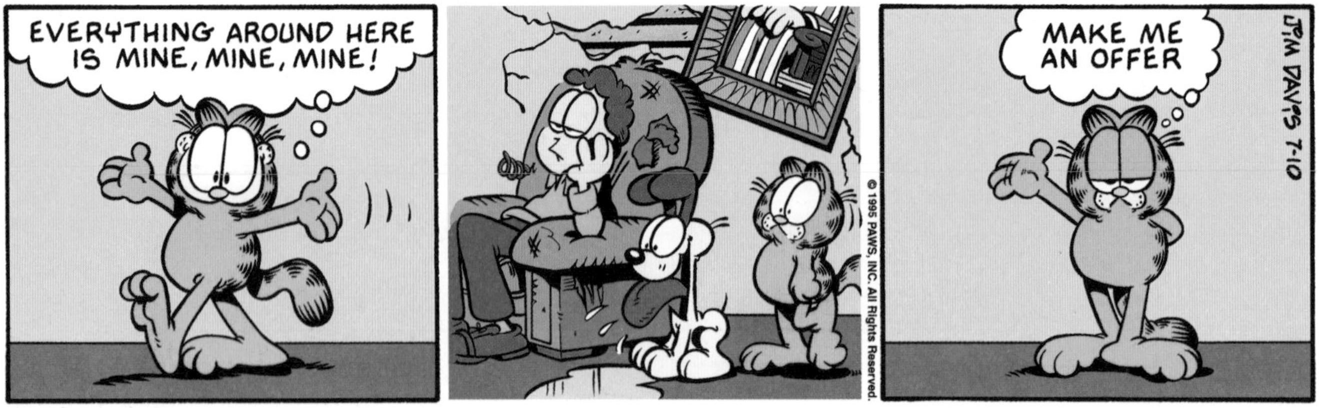
EVERYTHING AROUND HERE IS MINE, MINE, MINE!
© 1995 PAWS, INC. All Rights Reserved.
MAKE ME AN OFFER
JPM DAVIS 7-10

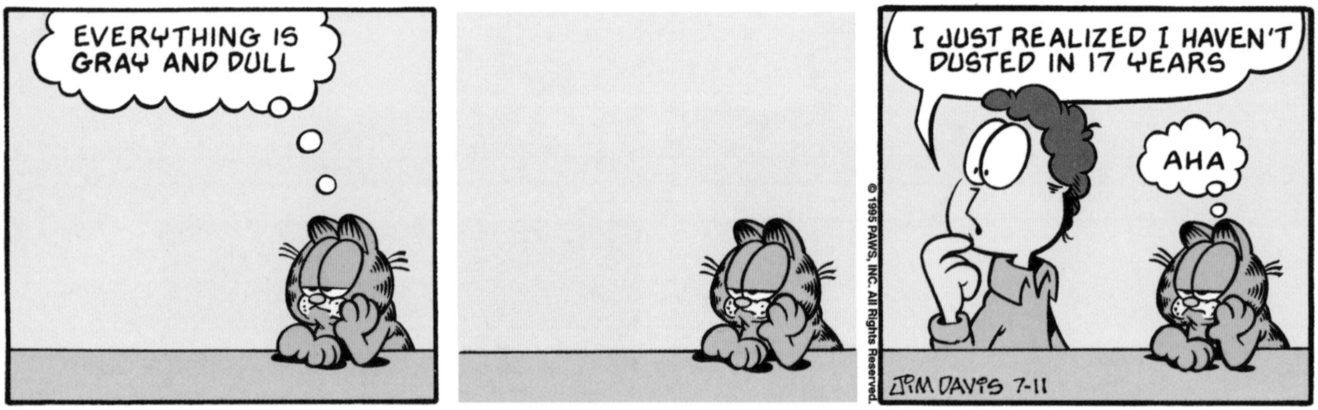
EVERYTHING IS GRAY AND DULL
© 1995 PAWS, INC. All Rights Reserved.
I JUST REALIZED I HAVEN'T DUSTED IN 17 YEARS
AHA
JPM DAVIS 7-11

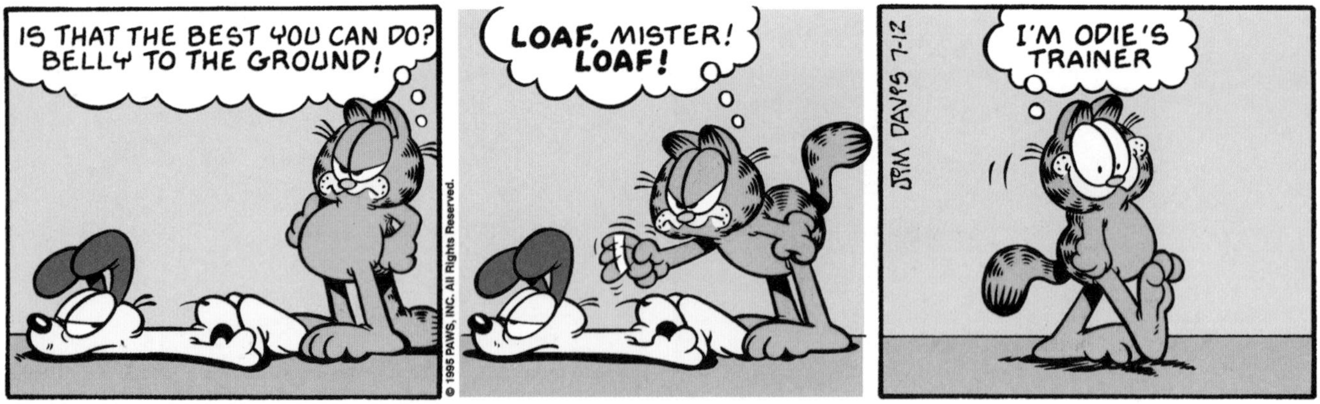
IS THAT THE BEST YOU CAN DO? BELLY TO THE GROUND!
© 1995 PAWS, INC. All Rights Reserved.
LOAF, MISTER! LOAF!
JPM DAVIS 7-12
I'M ODIE'S TRAINER

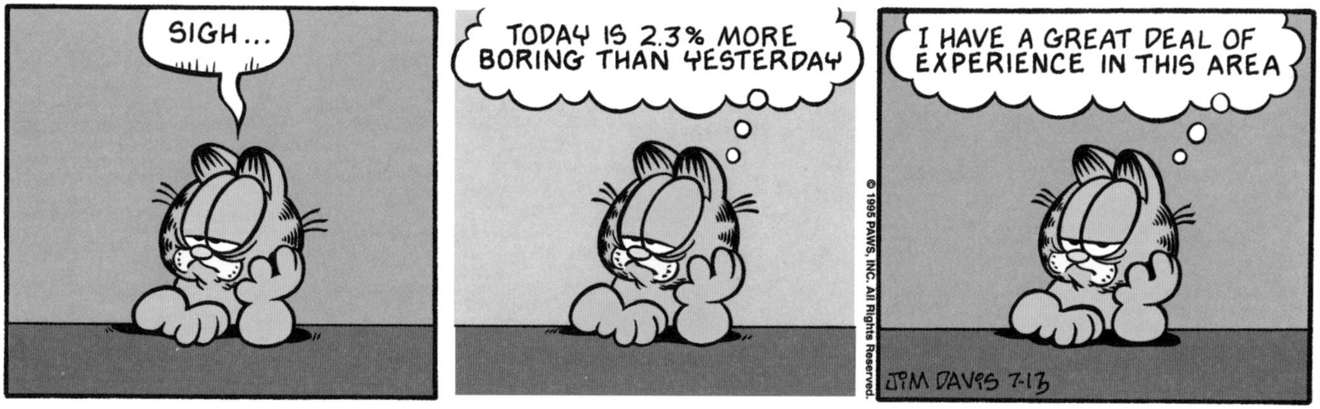
SIGH...
TODAY IS 2.3% MORE BORING THAN YESTERDAY
I HAVE A GREAT DEAL OF EXPERIENCE IN THIS AREA
© 1995 PAWS, INC. All Rights Reserved.
JIM DAVIS 7-13

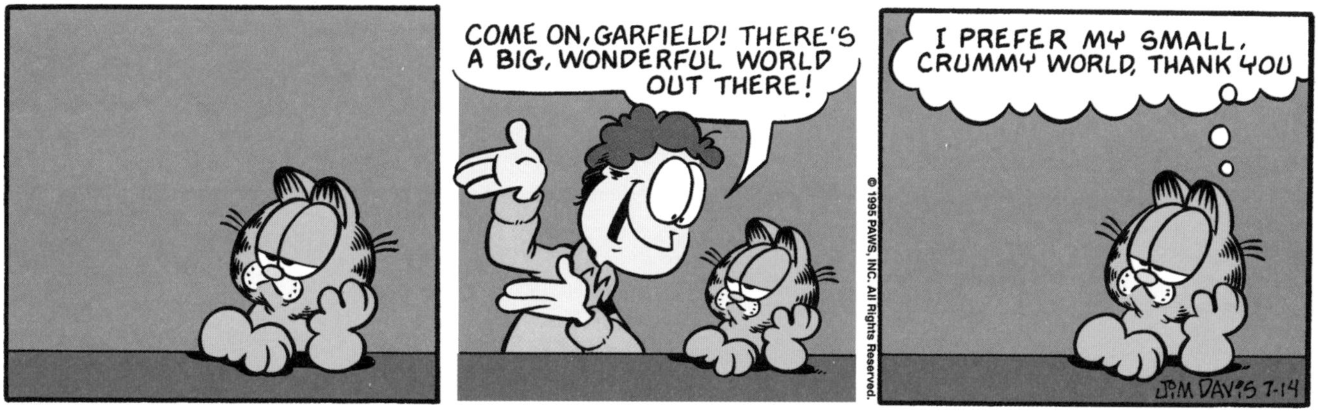
COME ON, GARFIELD! THERE'S A BIG, WONDERFUL WORLD OUT THERE!
I PREFER MY SMALL, CRUMMY WORLD, THANK YOU
© 1995 PAWS, INC. All Rights Reserved.
JIM DAVIS 7-14

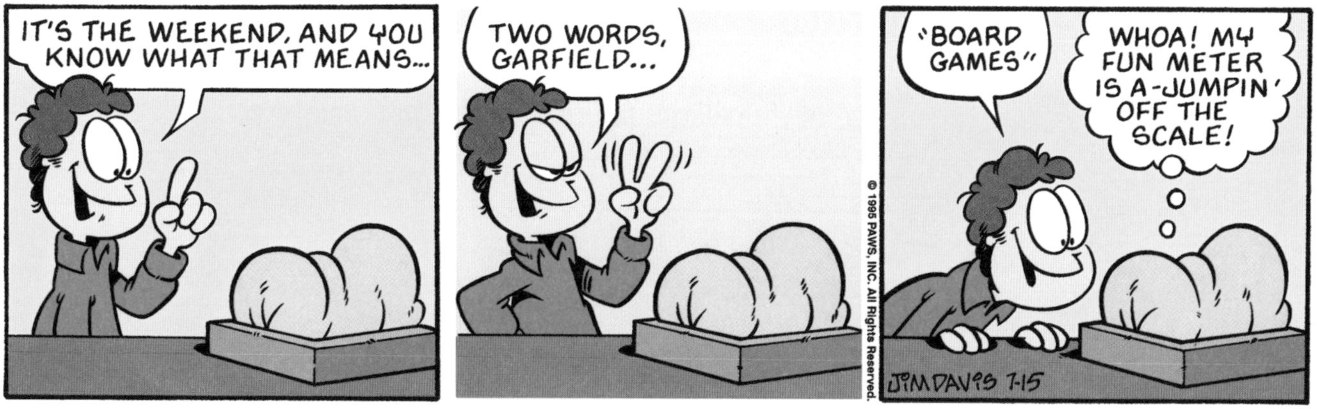
IT'S THE WEEKEND, AND YOU KNOW WHAT THAT MEANS...
TWO WORDS, GARFIELD...
"BOARD GAMES"
WHOA! MY FUN METER IS A-JUMPIN' OFF THE SCALE!
© 1995 PAWS, INC. All Rights Reserved.
JIM DAVIS 7-15

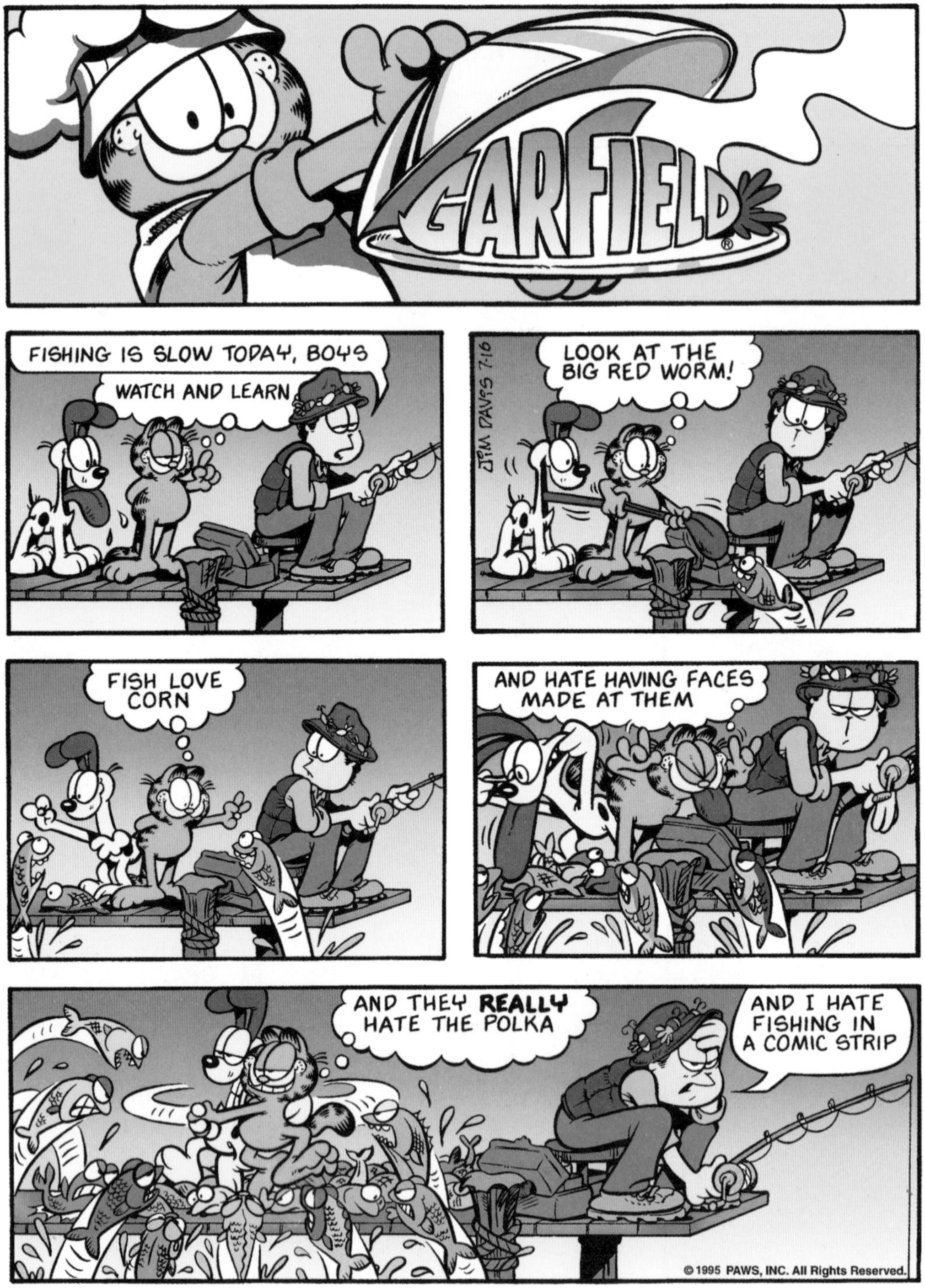
GARFIELD
FISHING IS SLOW TODAY, BOYS
WATCH AND LEARN
JIM DAVIS 7-16
LOOK AT THE BIG RED WORM!
FISH LOVE CORN
AND HATE HAVING FACES MADE AT THEM
AND THEY **REALLY** HATE THE POLKA
AND I HATE FISHING IN A COMIC STRIP
© 1995 PAWS, INC. All Rights Reserved.

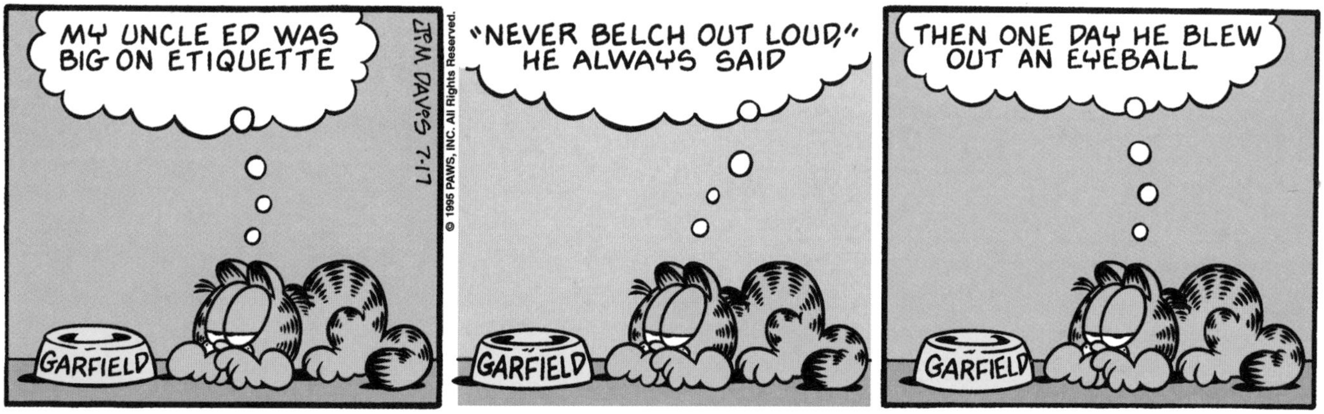
MY UNCLE ED WAS BIG ON ETIQUETTE
GARFIELD
JIM DAVIS 7-17
© 1995 PAWS, INC. All Rights Reserved.
"NEVER BELCH OUT LOUD," HE ALWAYS SAID
GARFIELD
THEN ONE DAY HE BLEW OUT AN EYEBALL
GARFIELD

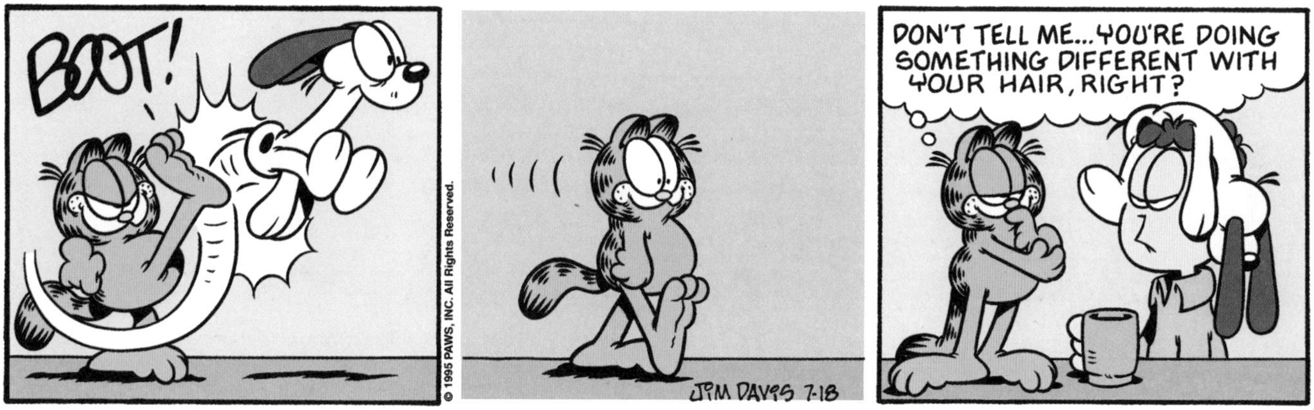
BOOT!
© 1995 PAWS, INC. All Rights Reserved.
JIM DAVIS 7-18
DON'T TELL ME...YOU'RE DOING SOMETHING DIFFERENT WITH YOUR HAIR, RIGHT?

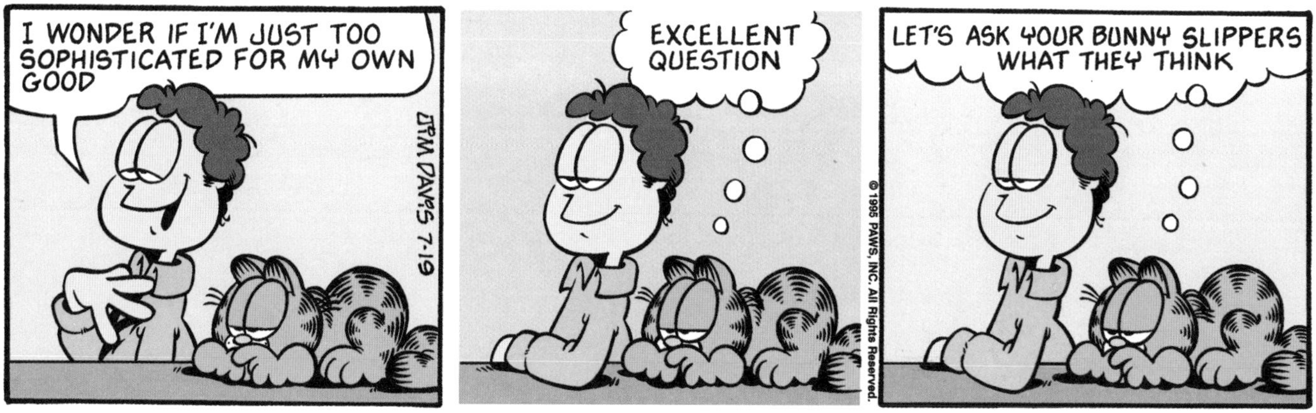
I WONDER IF I'M JUST TOO SOPHISTICATED FOR MY OWN GOOD
JIM DAVIS 7-19
EXCELLENT QUESTION
© 1995 PAWS, INC. All Rights Reserved.
LET'S ASK YOUR BUNNY SLIPPERS WHAT THEY THINK

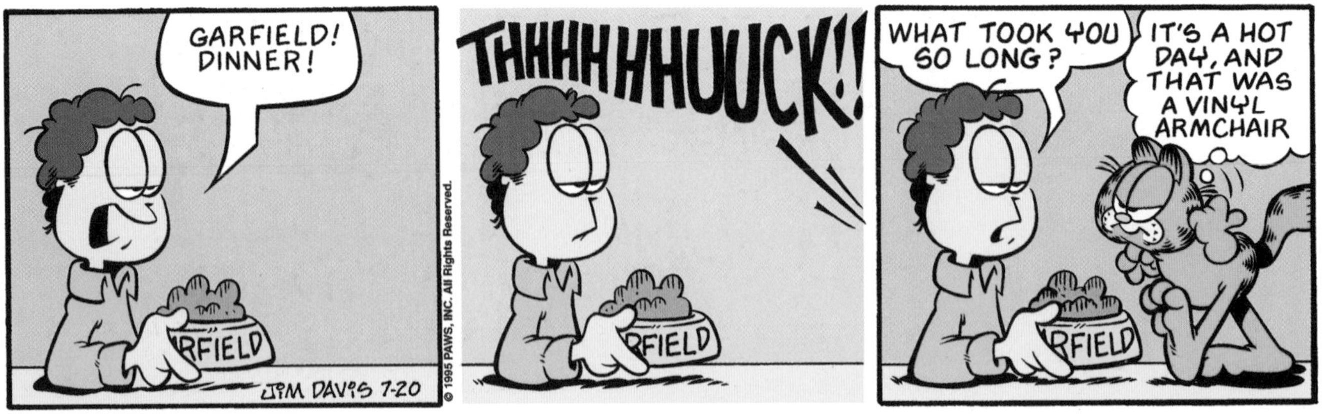
GARFIELD! DINNER!
JIM DAVIS 7-20
© 1995 PAWS, INC. All Rights Reserved.
THHHHHHUUCK!!
WHAT TOOK YOU SO LONG?
IT'S A HOT DAY, AND THAT WAS A VINYL ARMCHAIR

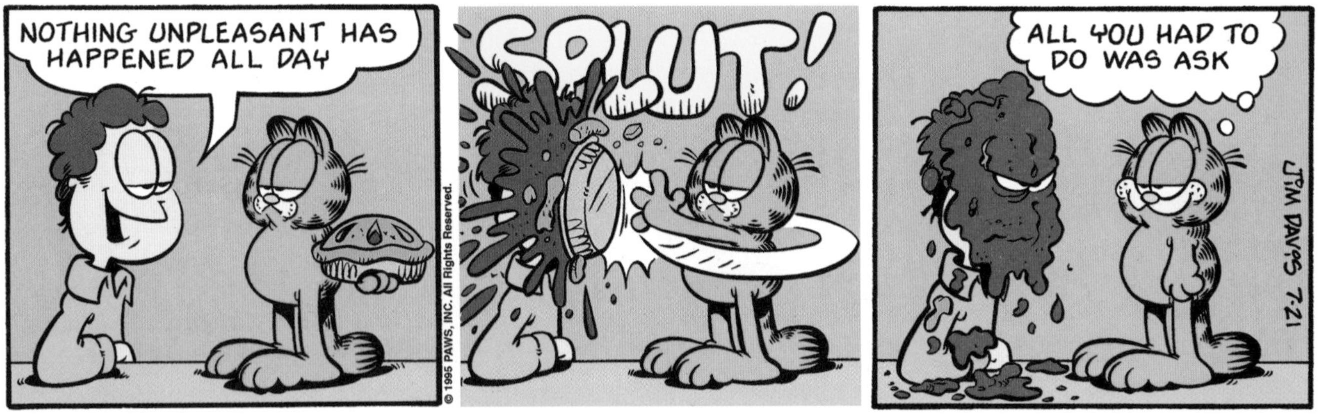
NOTHING UNPLEASANT HAS HAPPENED ALL DAY
© 1995 PAWS, INC. All Rights Reserved.
SPLUT!
ALL YOU HAD TO DO WAS ASK
JIM DAVIS 7-21

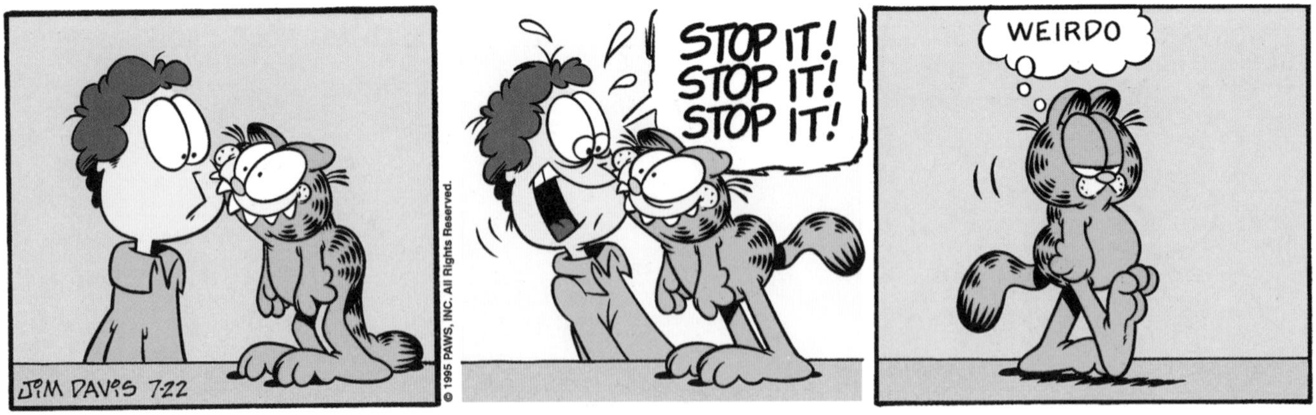
JIM DAVIS 7-22
© 1995 PAWS, INC. All Rights Reserved.
STOP IT! STOP IT! STOP IT!
WEIRDO

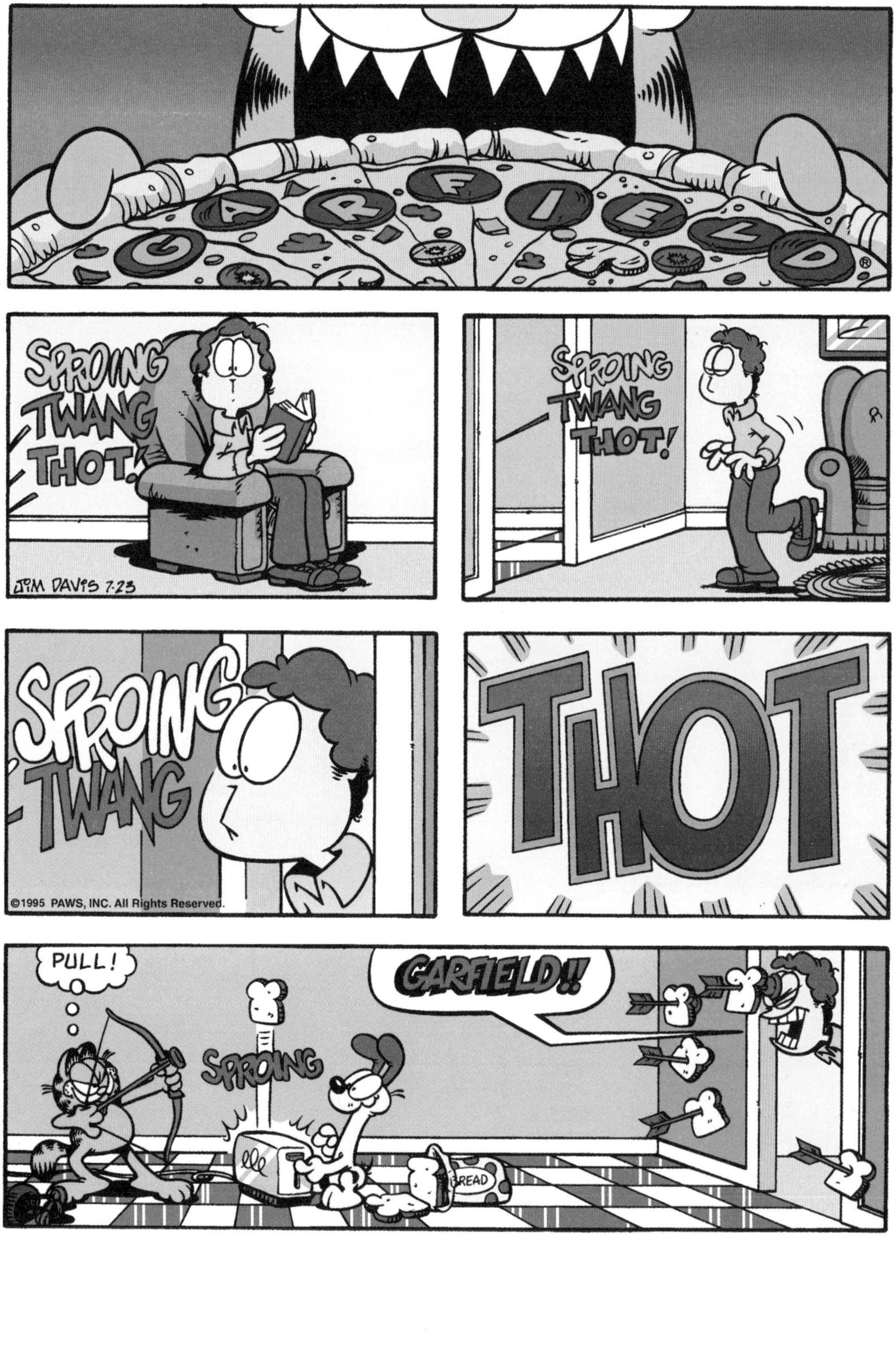
GARFIELD®
SPROING
TWANG
THOT!
JIM DAVIS 7-23
SPROING
TWANG
THOT!
SPROING
TWANG
©1995 PAWS, INC. All Rights Reserved.
THOT
PULL!
GARFIELD!!
SPROING
BREAD

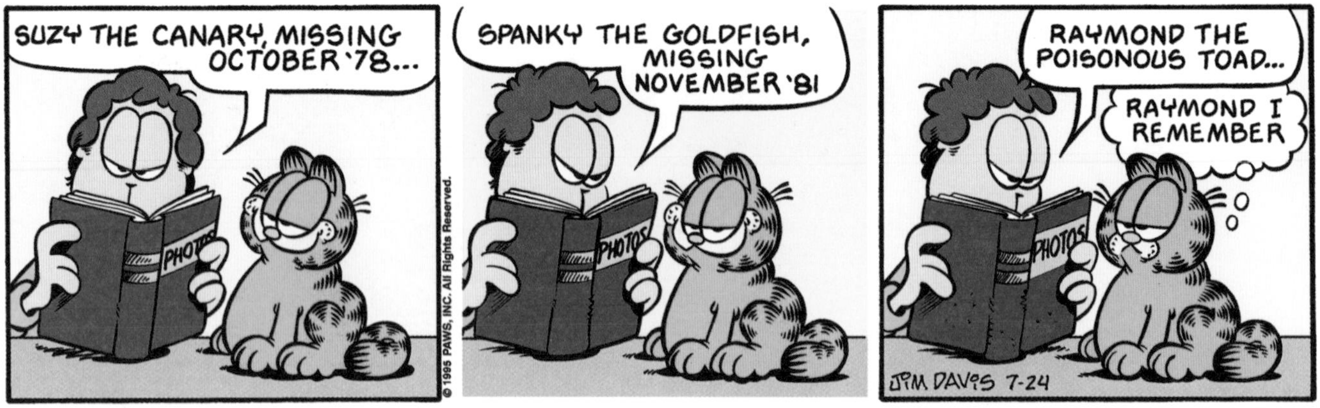
SUZY THE CANARY, MISSING OCTOBER '78...
SPANKY THE GOLDFISH, MISSING NOVEMBER '81
RAYMOND THE POISONOUS TOAD...
RAYMOND I REMEMBER
PHOTOS
JIM DAVIS 7-24
© 1995 PAWS, INC. All Rights Reserved.

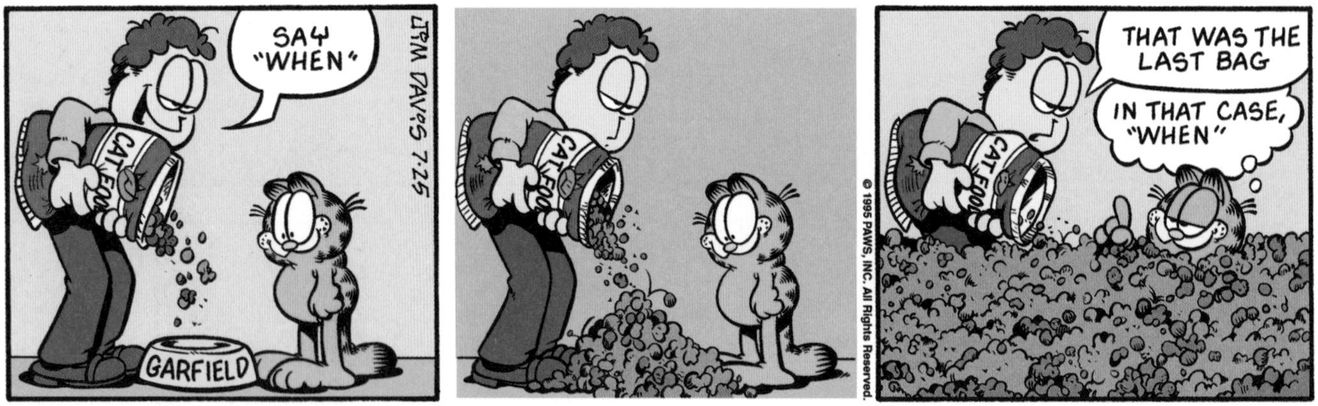
SAY "WHEN"
CAT FOOD
GARFIELD
THAT WAS THE LAST BAG
IN THAT CASE, "WHEN"
JIM DAVIS 7-25
© 1995 PAWS, INC. All Rights Reserved.

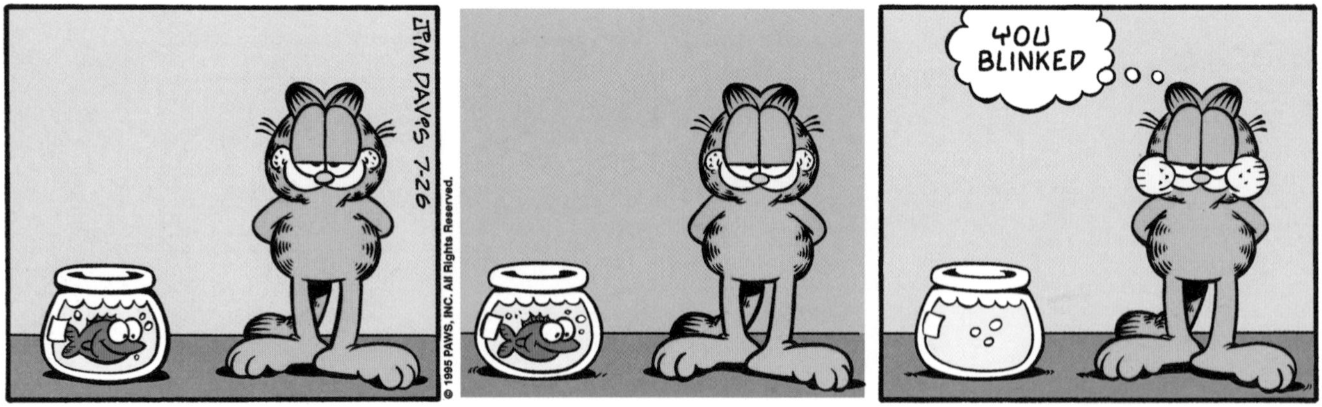
YOU BLINKED
JIM DAVIS 7-26
© 1995 PAWS, INC. All Rights Reserved.

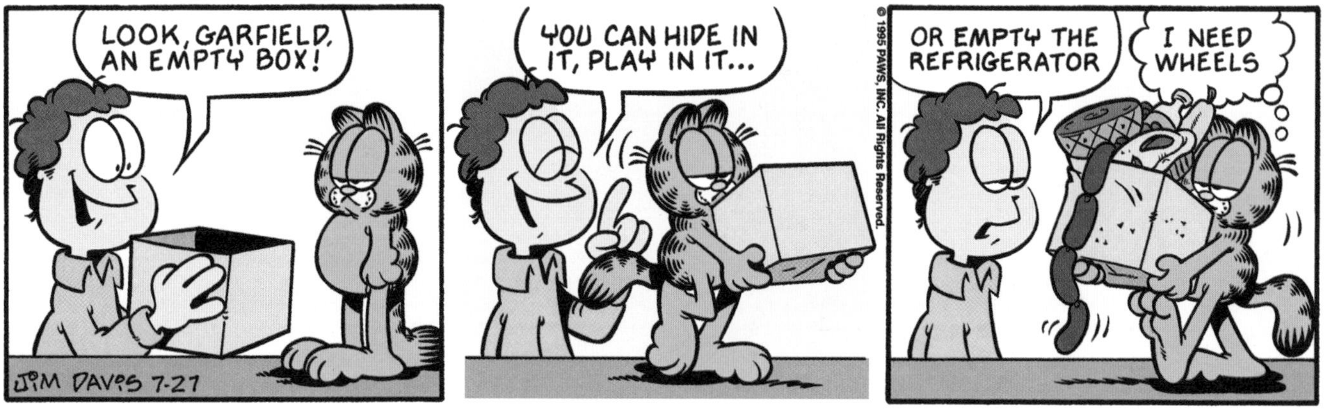
LOOK, GARFIELD, AN EMPTY BOX!
JIM DAVIS 7-27
YOU CAN HIDE IN IT, PLAY IN IT...
© 1995 PAWS, INC. All Rights Reserved.
OR EMPTY THE REFRIGERATOR
I NEED WHEELS

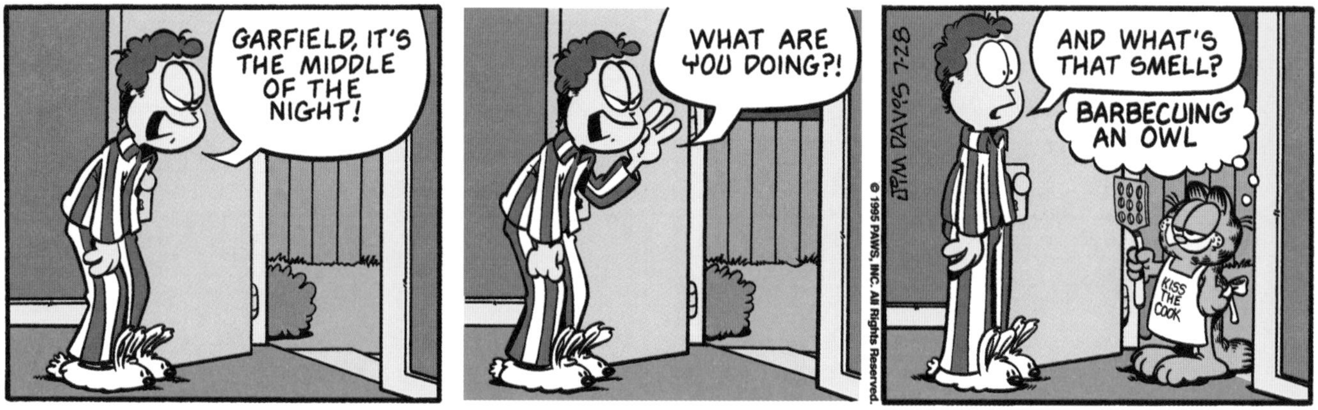
GARFIELD, IT'S THE MIDDLE OF THE NIGHT!
WHAT ARE YOU DOING?!
JIM DAVIS 7-28
© 1995 PAWS, INC. All Rights Reserved.
AND WHAT'S THAT SMELL?
BARBECUING AN OWL
KISS THE COOK

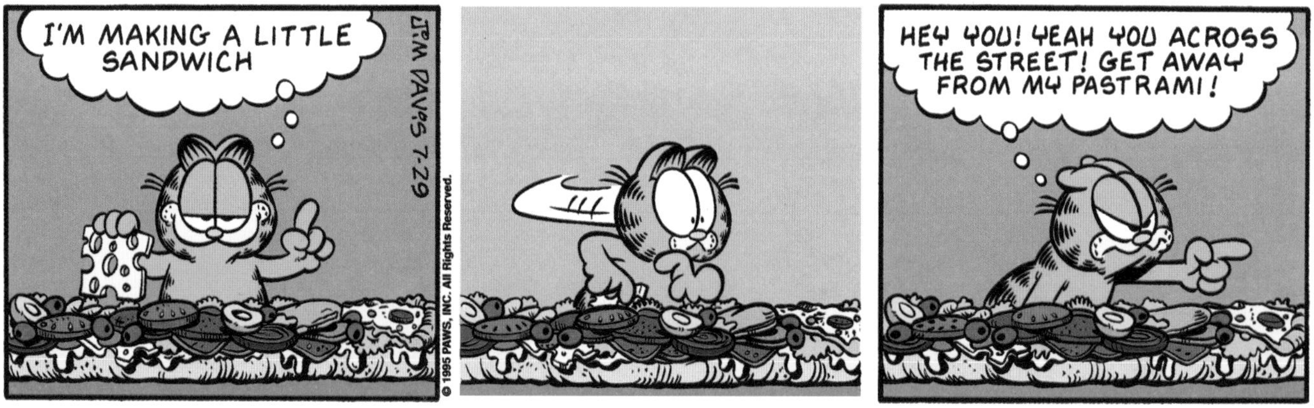
I'M MAKING A LITTLE SANDWICH
JIM DAVIS 7-29
© 1995 PAWS, INC. All Rights Reserved.
HEY YOU! YEAH YOU ACROSS THE STREET! GET AWAY FROM MY PASTRAMI!

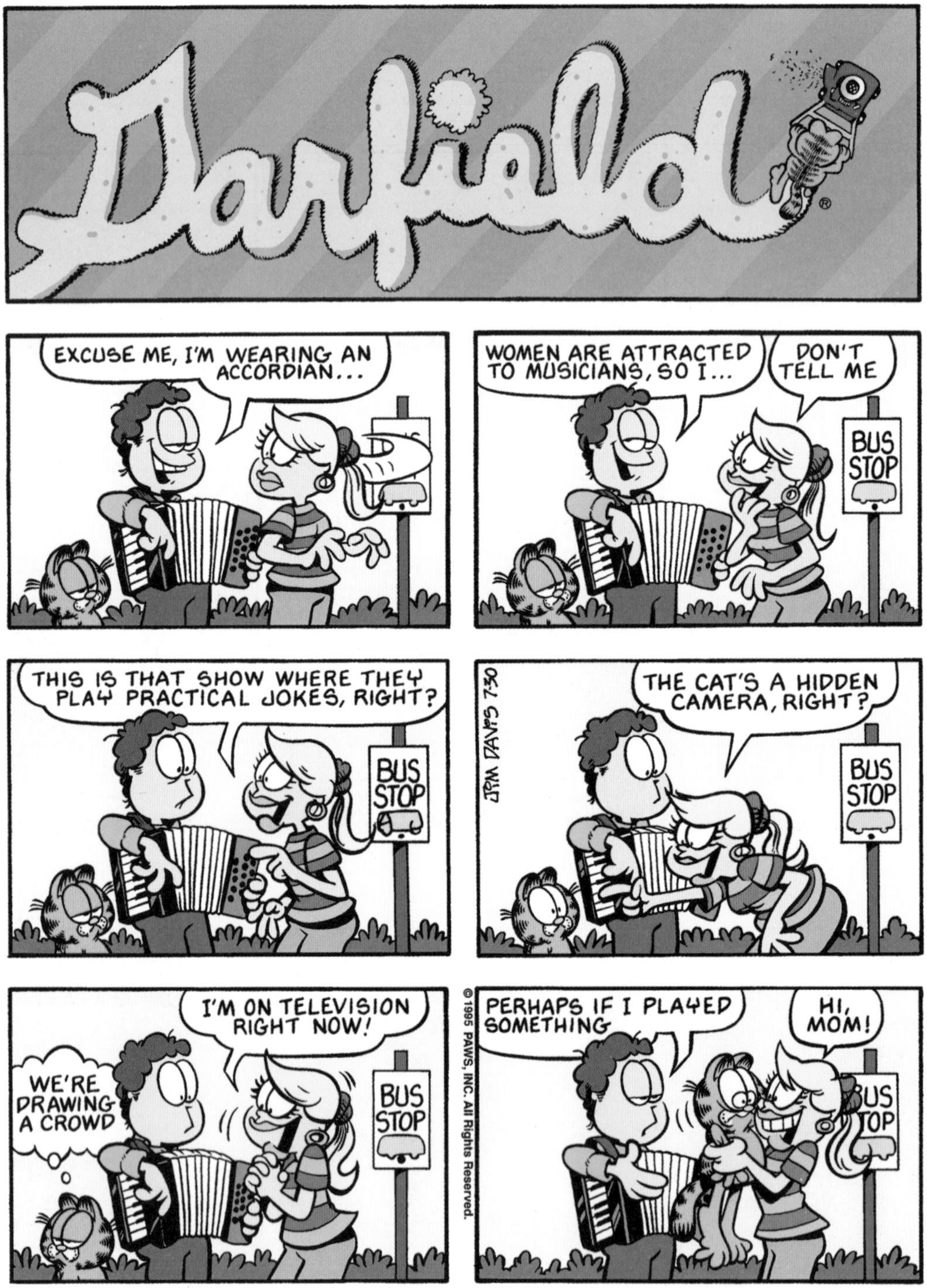
Garfield
EXCUSE ME, I'M WEARING AN ACCORDIAN...
WOMEN ARE ATTRACTED TO MUSICIANS, SO I...
DON'T TELL ME
BUS STOP
THIS IS THAT SHOW WHERE THEY PLAY PRACTICAL JOKES, RIGHT?
BUS STOP
JIM DAVIS 7-30
THE CAT'S A HIDDEN CAMERA, RIGHT?
BUS STOP
I'M ON TELEVISION RIGHT NOW!
WE'RE DRAWING A CROWD
BUS STOP
© 1995 PAWS, INC. All Rights Reserved.
PERHAPS IF I PLAYED SOMETHING
HI, MOM!
BUS STOP

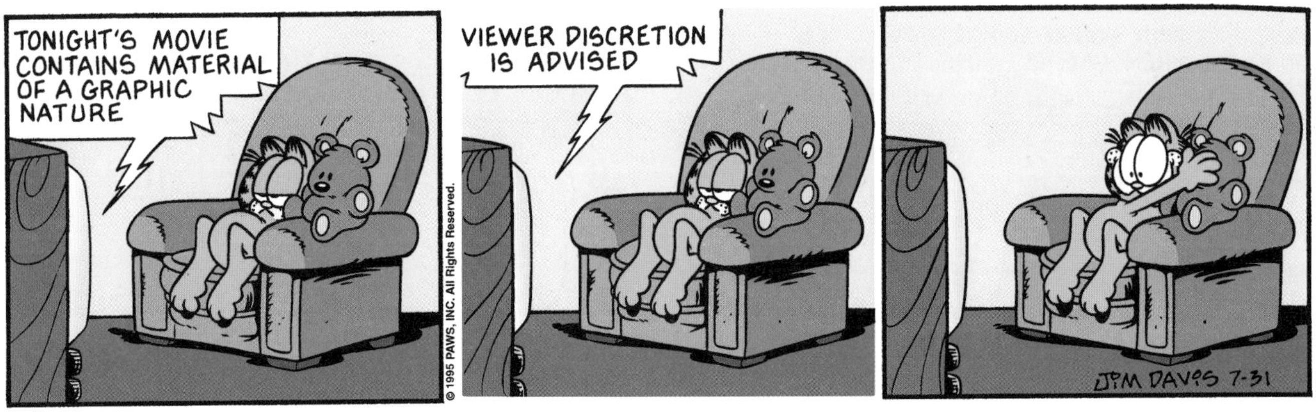
TONIGHT'S MOVIE CONTAINS MATERIAL OF A GRAPHIC NATURE
© 1995 PAWS, INC. All Rights Reserved.
VIEWER DISCRETION IS ADVISED
JIM DAVIS 7-31

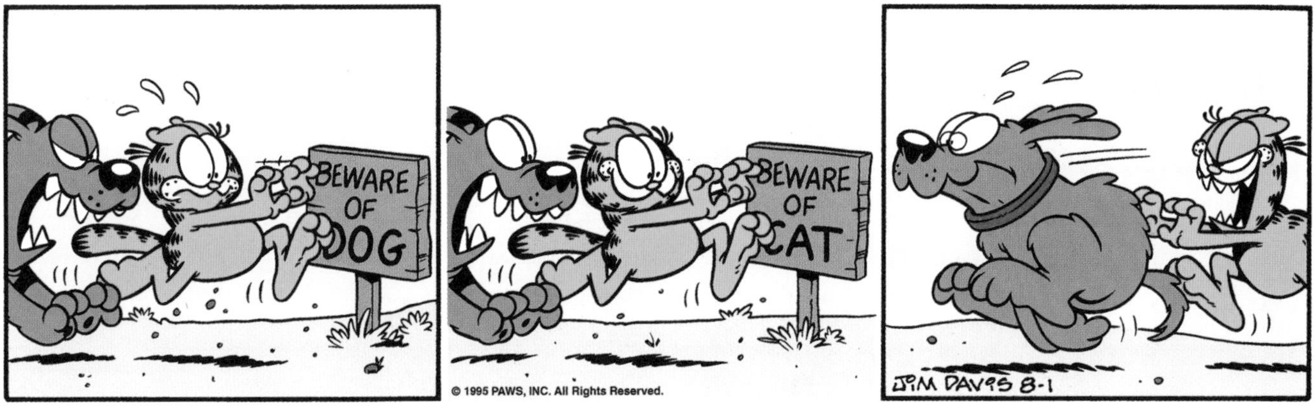
BEWARE OF DOG
BEWARE OF CAT
© 1995 PAWS, INC. All Rights Reserved.
JIM DAVIS 8-1

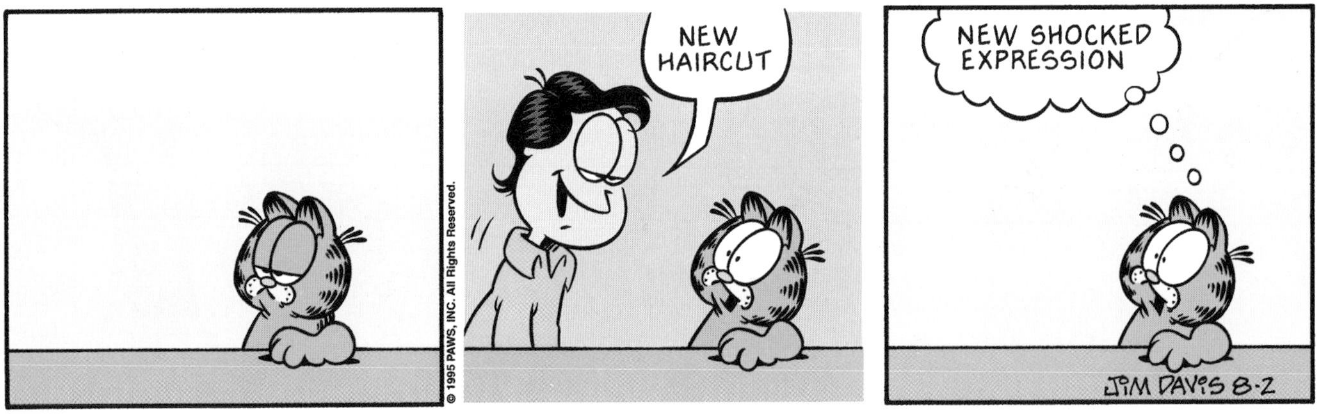
© 1995 PAWS, INC. All Rights Reserved.
NEW HAIRCUT
NEW SHOCKED EXPRESSION
JIM DAVIS 8-2

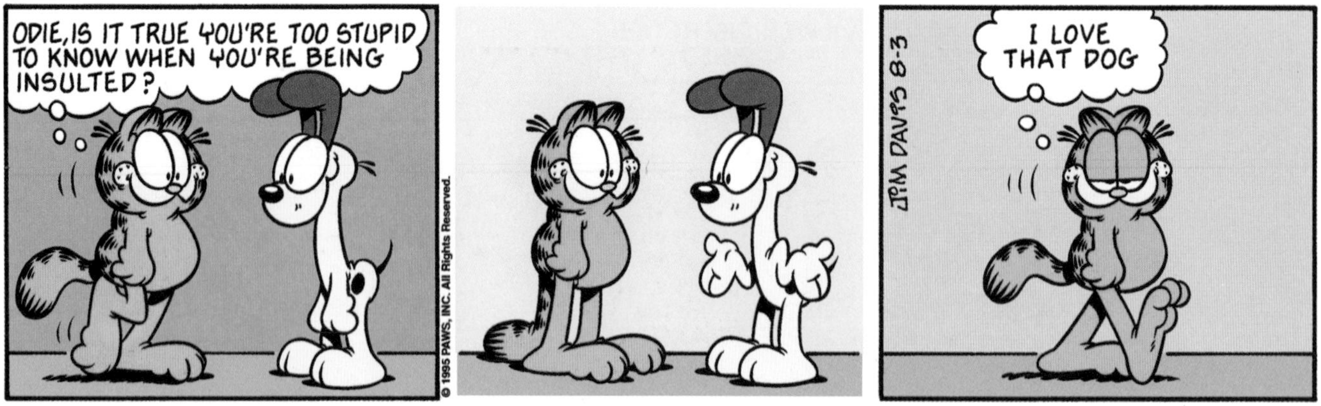
ODIE, IS IT TRUE YOU'RE TOO STUPID TO KNOW WHEN YOU'RE BEING INSULTED?
© 1995 PAWS, INC. All Rights Reserved.
JIM DAVIS 8-3
I LOVE THAT DOG

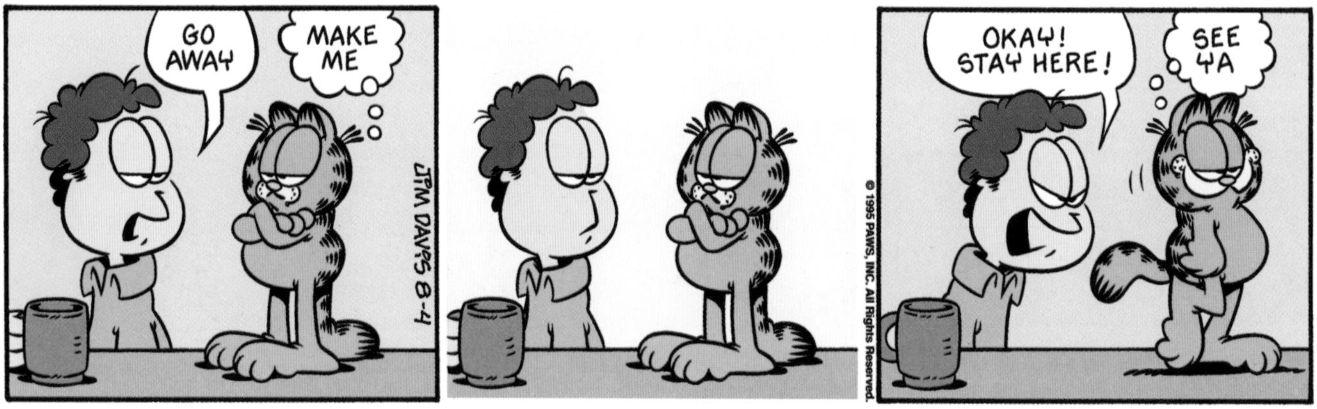
GO AWAY
MAKE ME
JIM DAVIS 8-4
© 1995 PAWS, INC. All Rights Reserved.
OKAY! STAY HERE!
SEE YA

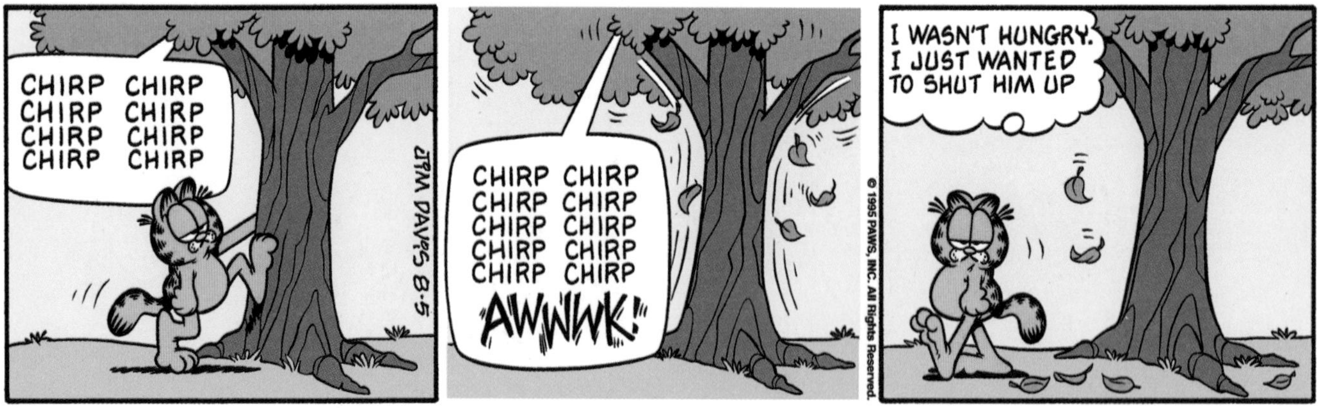
CHIRP CHIRP CHIRP CHIRP CHIRP CHIRP CHIRP CHIRP
JIM DAVIS 8-5
CHIRP CHIRP CHIRP CHIRP CHIRP CHIRP CHIRP CHIRP CHIRP CHIRP
AWWWK!
© 1995 PAWS, INC. All Rights Reserved.
I WASN'T HUNGRY. I JUST WANTED TO SHUT HIM UP

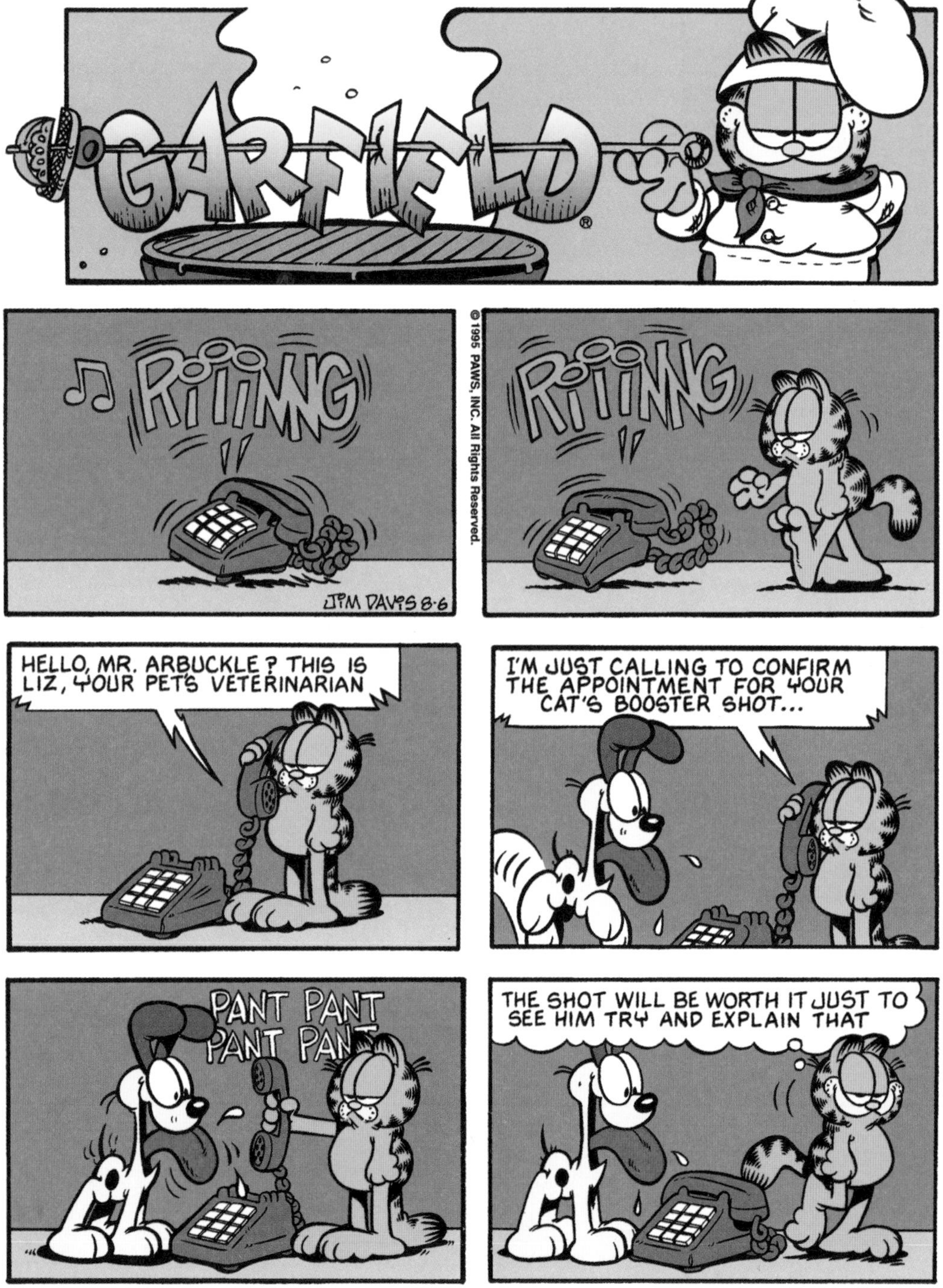
GARFIELD®
© 1995 PAWS, INC. All Rights Reserved.
ROOOOING
JIM DAVIS 8-6
RIIINNG
HELLO, MR. ARBUCKLE? THIS IS LIZ, YOUR PET'S VETERINARIAN
I'M JUST CALLING TO CONFIRM THE APPOINTMENT FOR YOUR CAT'S BOOSTER SHOT...
PANT PANT PANT PANT
THE SHOT WILL BE WORTH IT JUST TO SEE HIM TRY AND EXPLAIN THAT

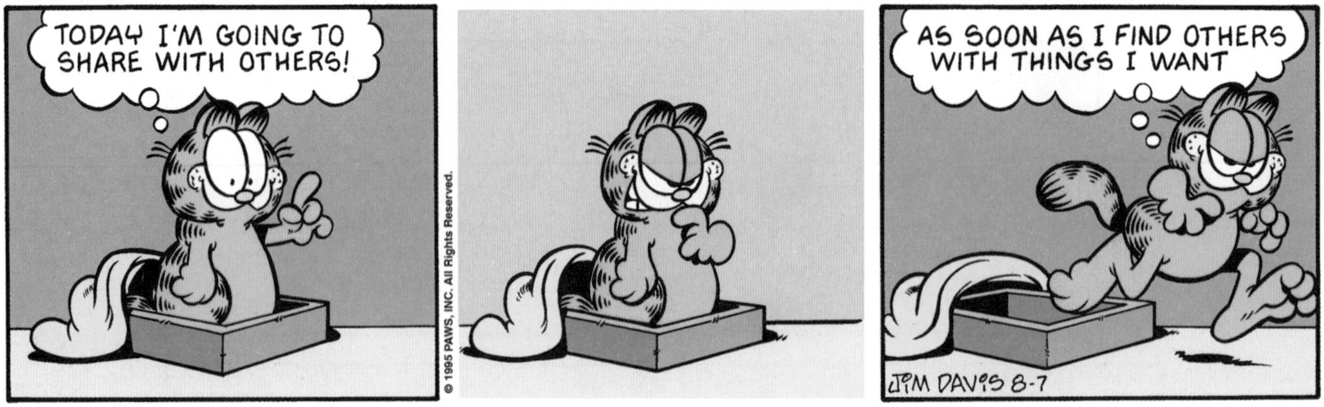
TODAY I'M GOING TO SHARE WITH OTHERS!
AS SOON AS I FIND OTHERS WITH THINGS I WANT
JIM DAVIS 8-7
© 1995 PAWS, INC. All Rights Reserved.

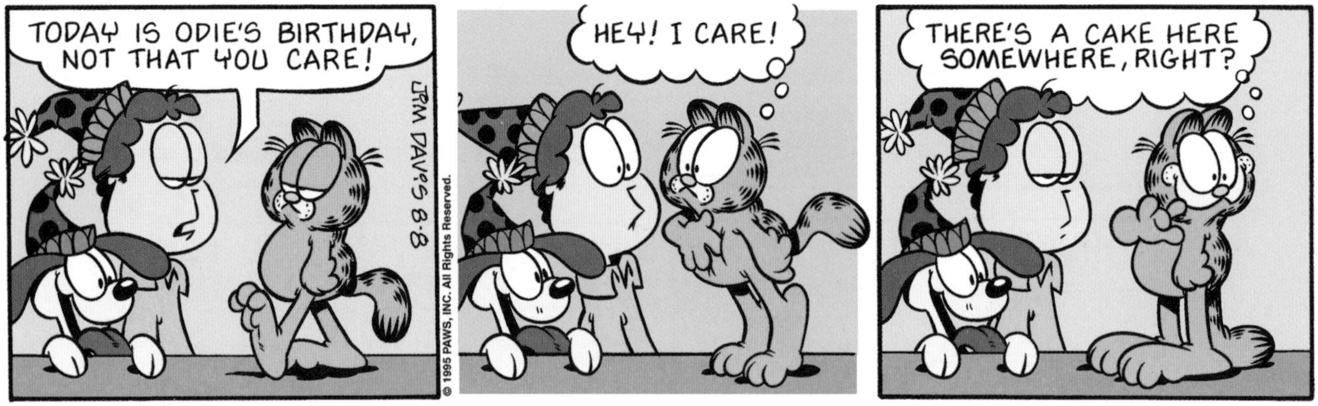
TODAY IS ODIE'S BIRTHDAY, NOT THAT YOU CARE!
JIM DAVIS 8-8
HEY! I CARE!
THERE'S A CAKE HERE SOMEWHERE, RIGHT?
© 1995 PAWS, INC. All Rights Reserved.

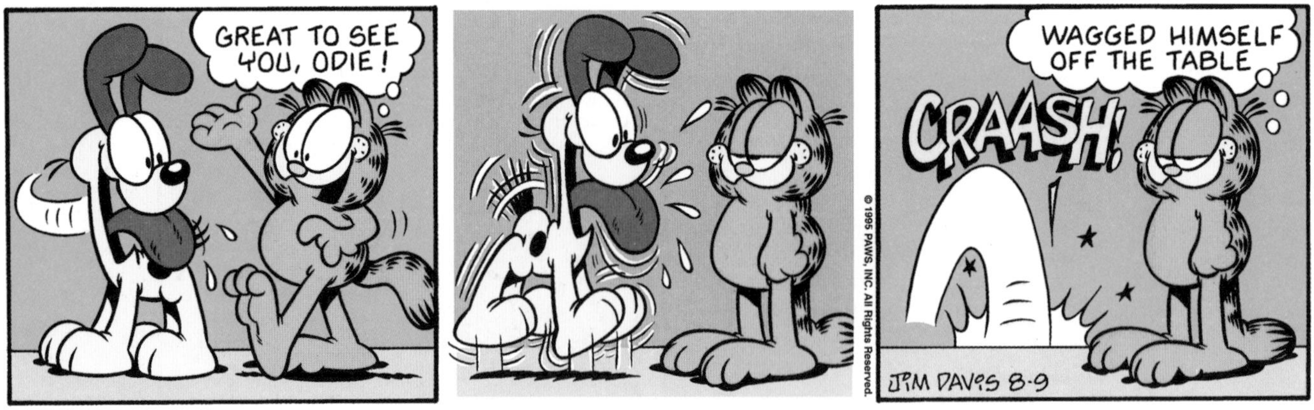
GREAT TO SEE YOU, ODIE!
WAGGED HIMSELF OFF THE TABLE
CRAASH!
JIM DAVIS 8-9
© 1995 PAWS, INC. All Rights Reserved.

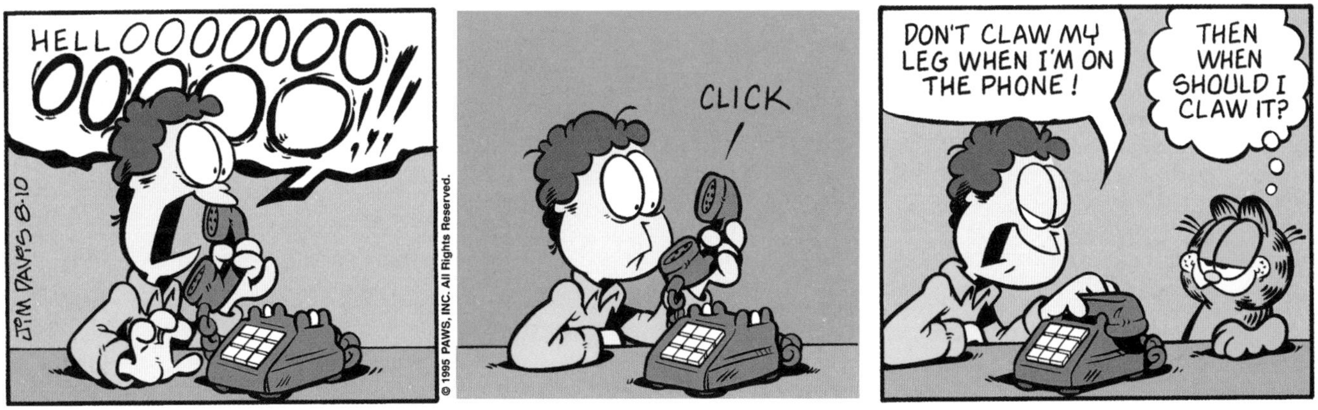
HELLOOOOOOOOOOOOO!!!
JIM DAVIS 8-10
CLICK
© 1995 PAWS, INC. All Rights Reserved.
DON'T CLAW MY LEG WHEN I'M ON THE PHONE!
THEN WHEN SHOULD I CLAW IT?

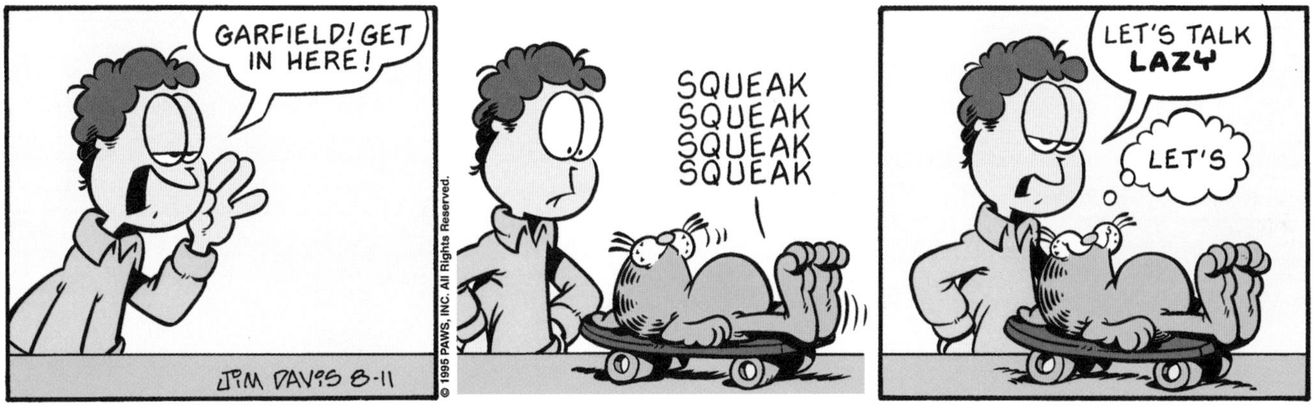
GARFIELD! GET IN HERE!
JIM DAVIS 8-11
© 1995 PAWS, INC. All Rights Reserved.
SQUEAK SQUEAK SQUEAK SQUEAK
LET'S TALK **LAZY**
LET'S

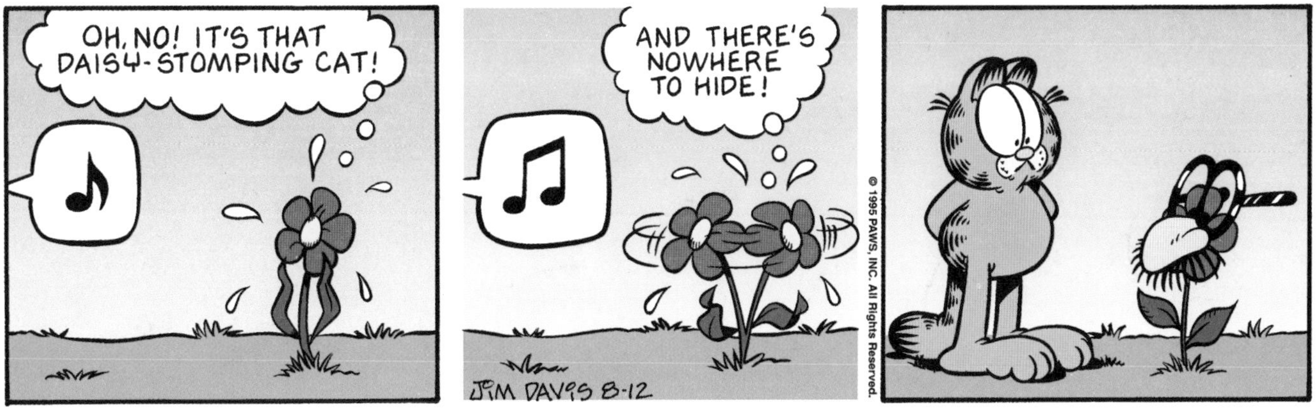
OH, NO! IT'S THAT DAISY-STOMPING CAT!
♪
AND THERE'S NOWHERE TO HIDE!
♫
JIM DAVIS 8-12
© 1995 PAWS, INC. All Rights Reserved.

How lazy *is* Garfield?

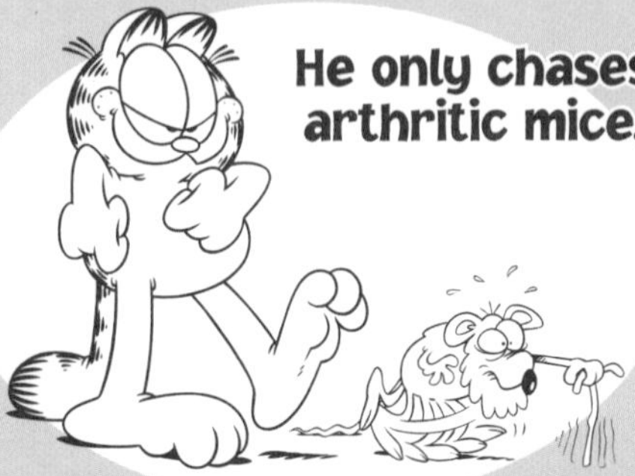

He only chases arthritic mice.

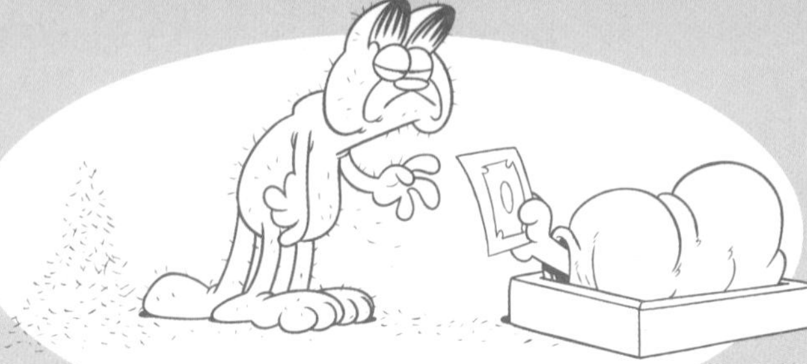

He hired another cat to shed for him.

Garfield is sooooo lazy...

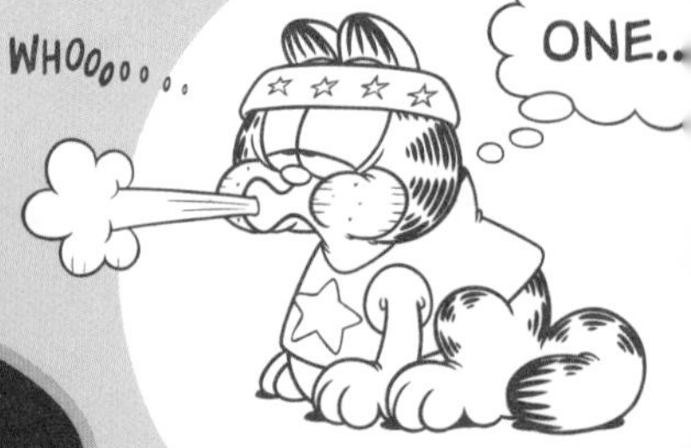
WHOOooo..
ONE..

He thinks breathing is an exercise.

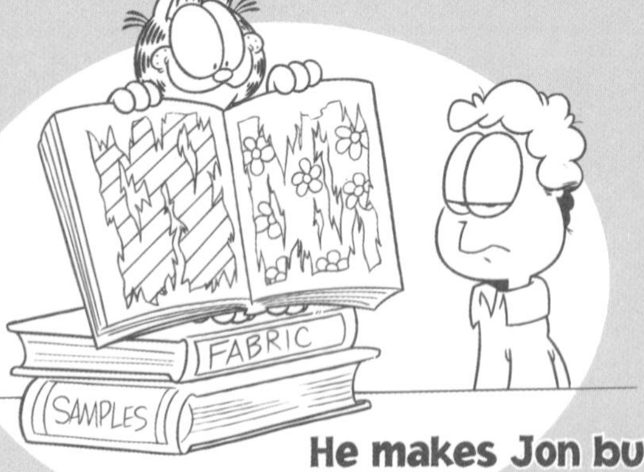
FABRIC
SAMPLES

He makes Jon buy pre-shredded drapes.

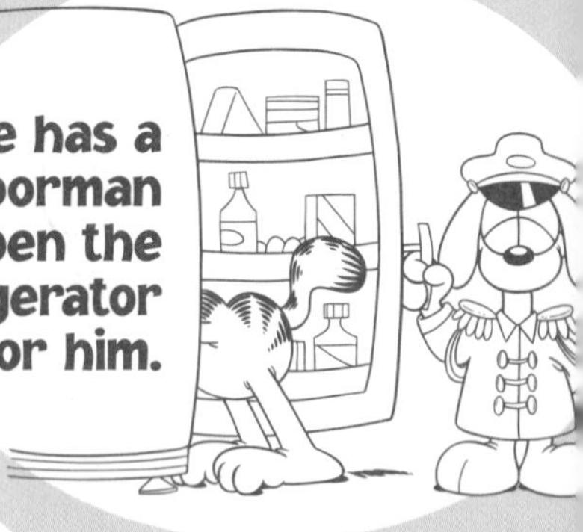

He has a doorman open the refrigerator for him.

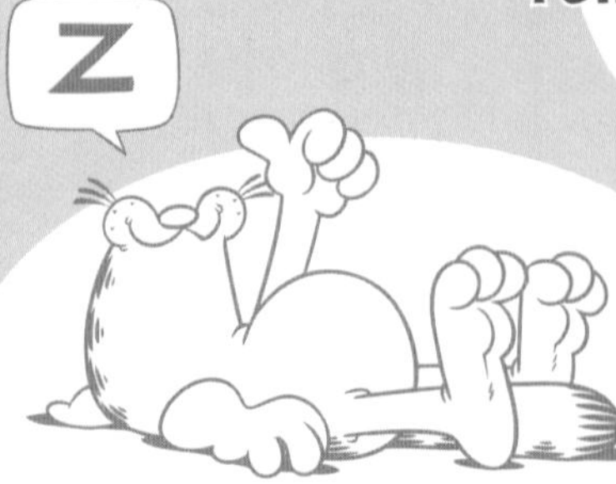
Z

He doesn't walk in his sleep... he hitchhikes.

Garfield

bigger and better

BY JIM DAVIS

Ballantine Books • New York

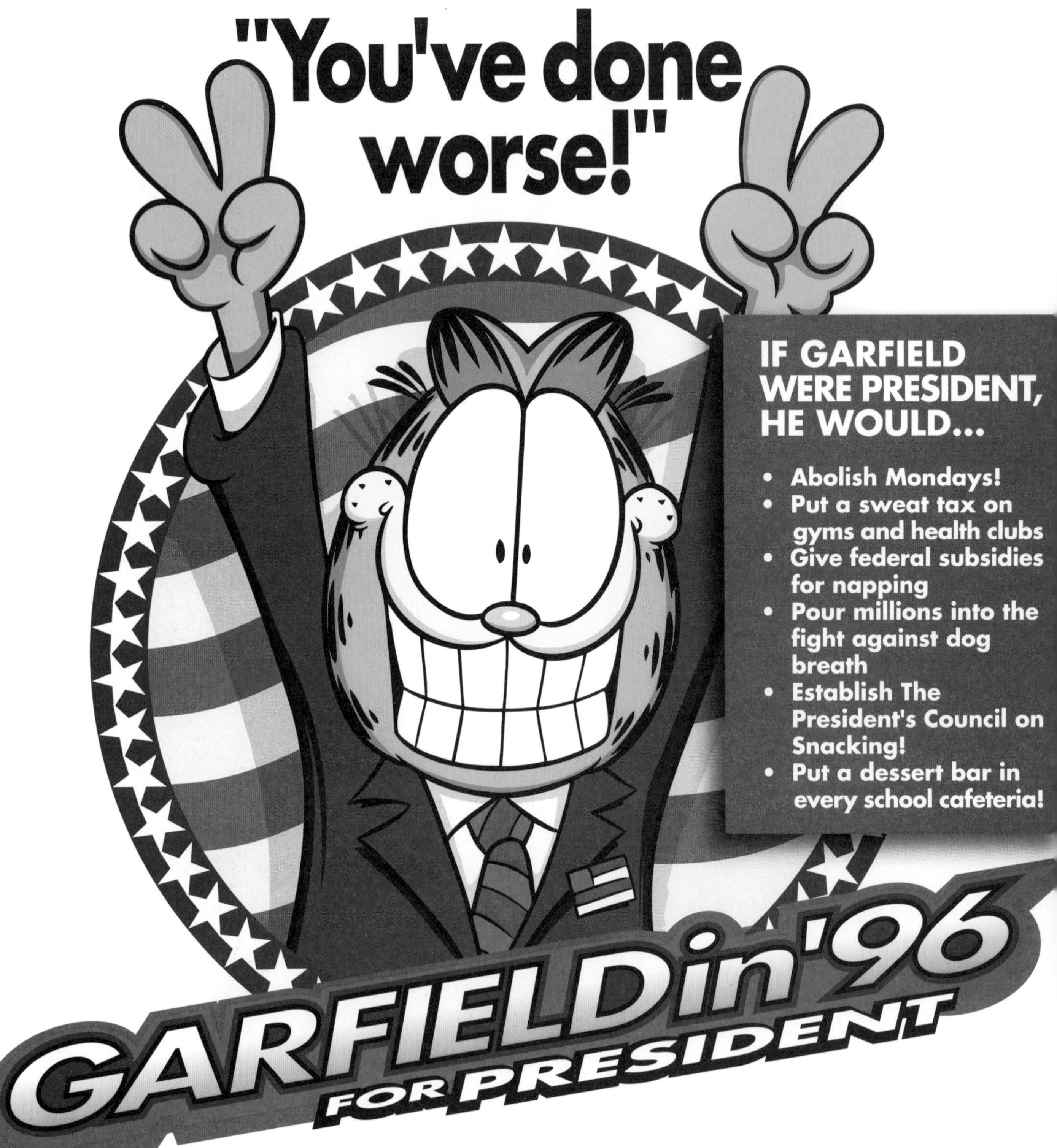
"You've done worse!"
IF GARFIELD WERE PRESIDENT, HE WOULD...
• Abolish Mondays!
• Put a sweat tax on gyms and health clubs
• Give federal subsidies for napping
• Pour millions into the fight against dog breath
• Establish The President's Council on Snacking!
• Put a dessert bar in every school cafeteria!
GARFIELD in '96
FOR PRESIDENT

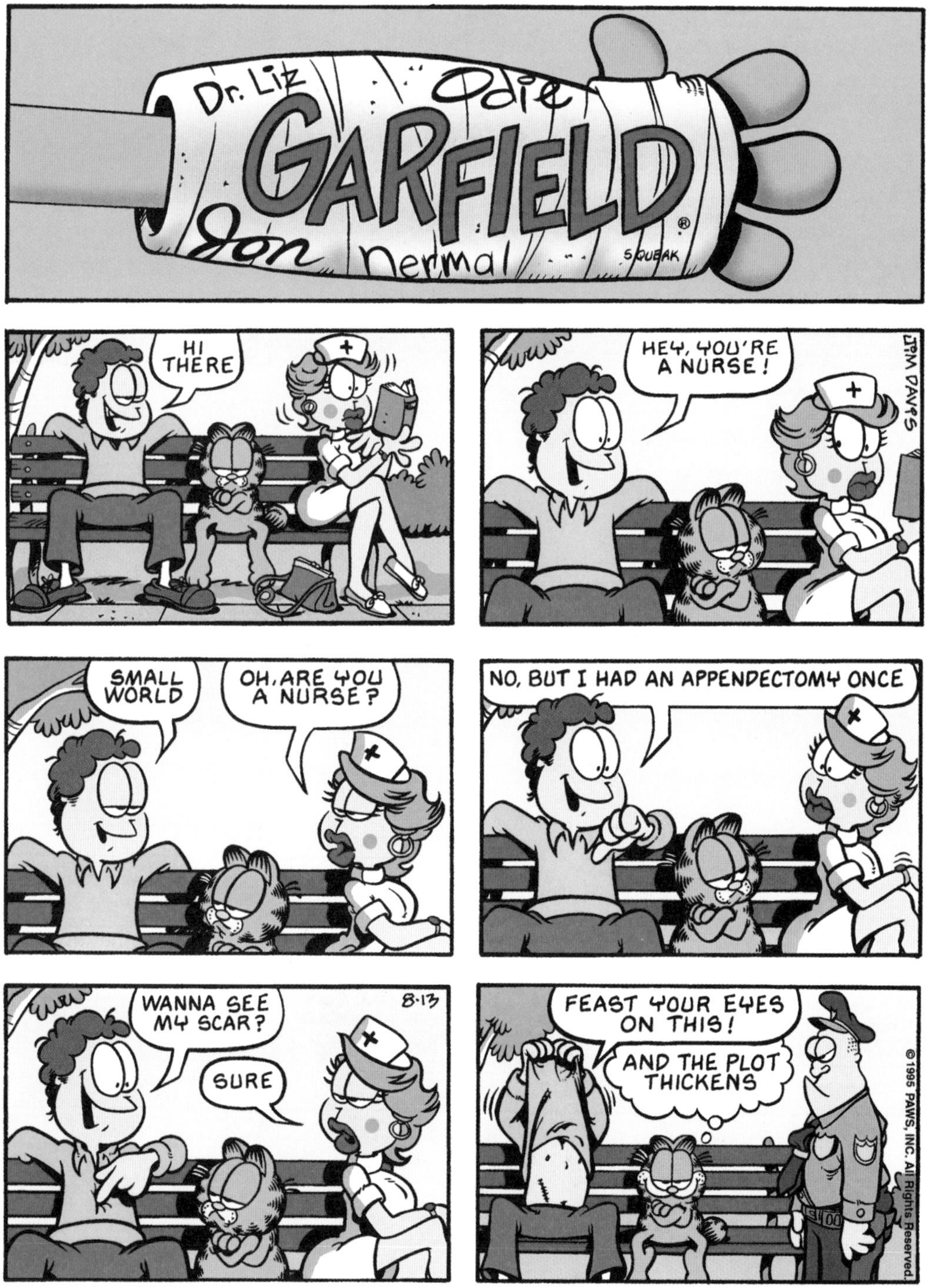
Dr. Liz
Odie
GARFIELD®
Jon
Nermal
SQUEAK
HI THERE
HEY, YOU'RE A NURSE!
JPM DAVIS
SMALL WORLD
OH, ARE YOU A NURSE?
NO, BUT I HAD AN APPENDECTOMY ONCE
WANNA SEE MY SCAR?
8-13
SURE
FEAST YOUR EYES ON THIS!
AND THE PLOT THICKENS
© 1995 PAWS, INC. All Rights Reserved.

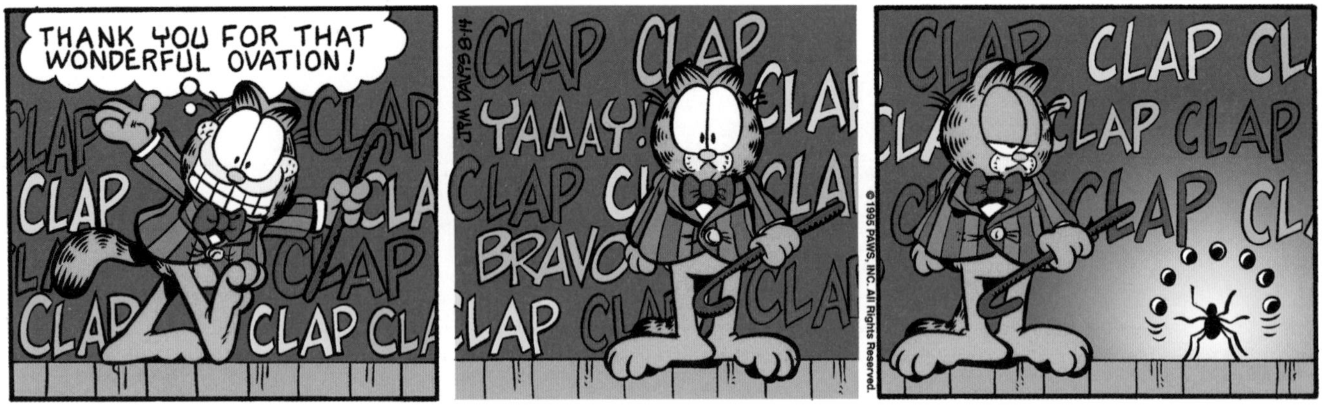
THANK YOU FOR THAT WONDERFUL OVATION!
CLAP CLAP CLAP CLAP
YAAAY!
BRAVO
CLAP CLAP CLAP CLAP
JIM DAVIS 8-14
© 1995 PAWS, INC. All Rights Reserved.

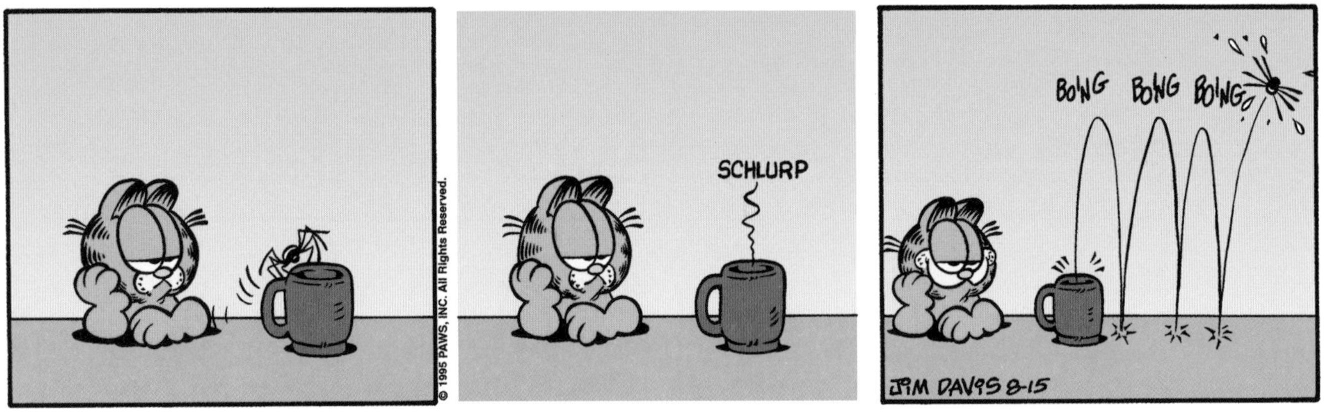
© 1995 PAWS, INC. All Rights Reserved.
SCHLURP
BOING BOING BOING
JIM DAVIS 8-15

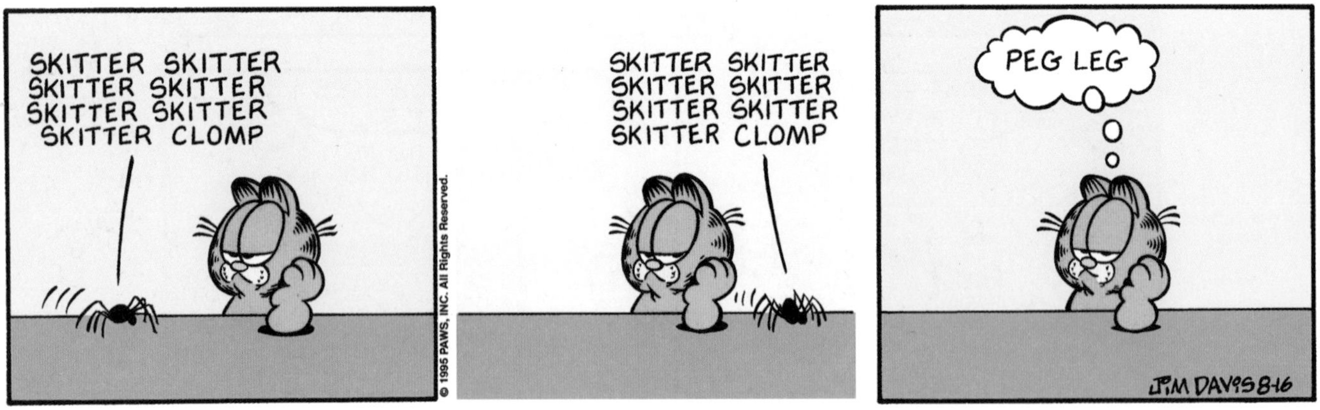
SKITTER SKITTER SKITTER SKITTER SKITTER SKITTER SKITTER CLOMP
© 1995 PAWS, INC. All Rights Reserved.
SKITTER SKITTER SKITTER SKITTER SKITTER SKITTER SKITTER CLOMP
PEG LEG
JIM DAVIS 8-16

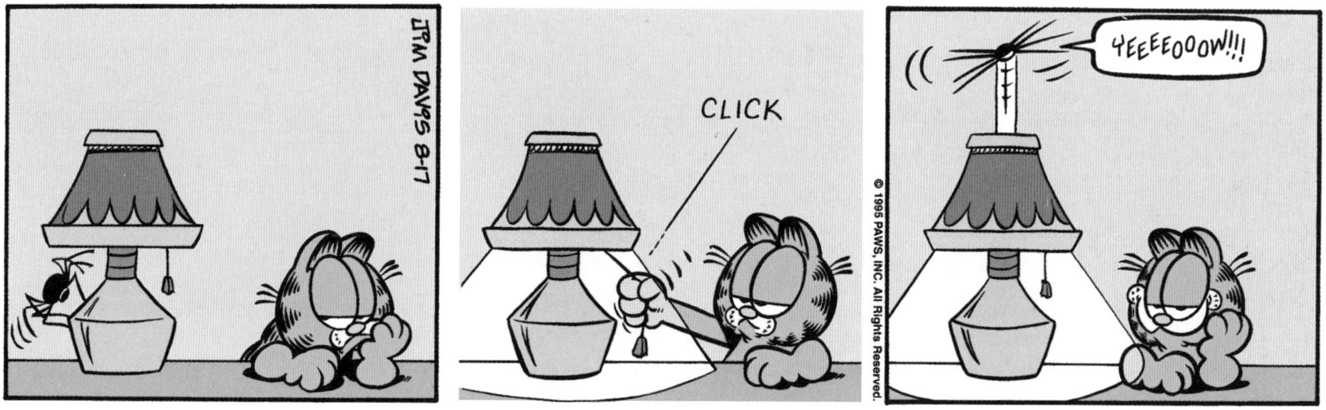
JIM DAVIS 8-17
CLICK
YEEEEOOOW!!!
© 1995 PAWS, INC. All Rights Reserved.

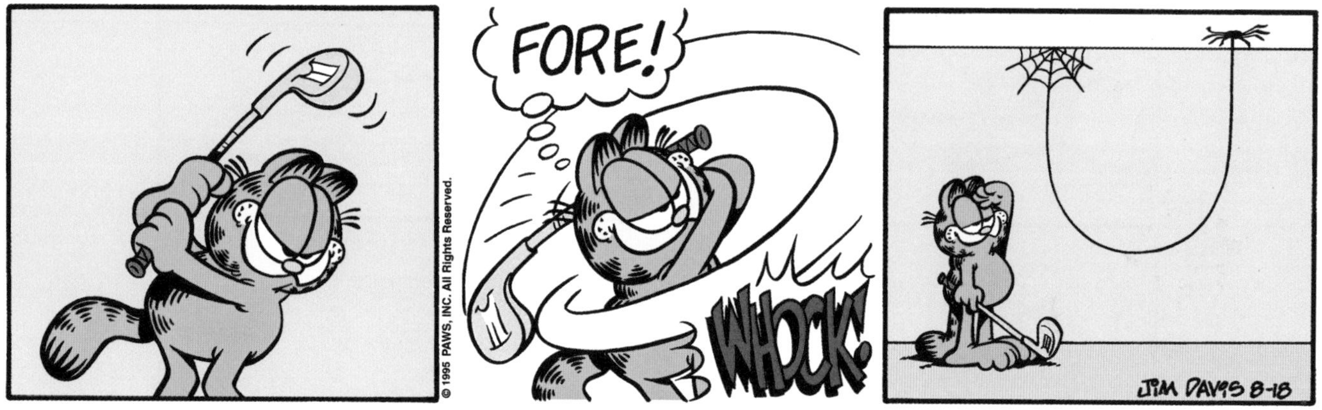
© 1995 PAWS, INC. All Rights Reserved.
FORE!
WHOCK!
JIM DAVIS 8-18

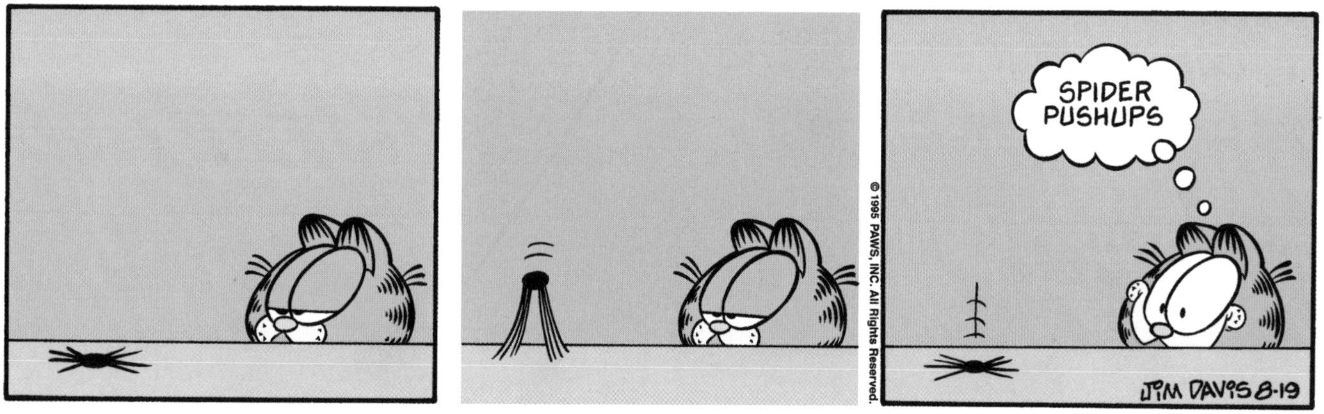
© 1995 PAWS, INC. All Rights Reserved.
SPIDER PUSHUPS
JIM DAVIS 8-19

GARFIELD®
© 1995 PAWS, INC. All Rights Reserved.
TUCK TUCK TUCK TUCK TUCK TUCK TUCK
TUCK TUCK TUCK PAT PAT PAT PAT PAT PAT PAT
FLUFF FLUFF FLUFF FLUFF FLUFF FLUFF
Z
JIM DAVIS 8-20

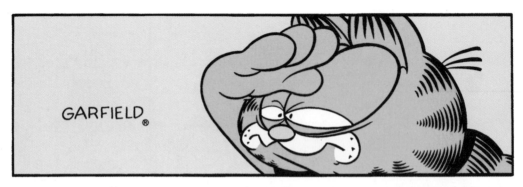

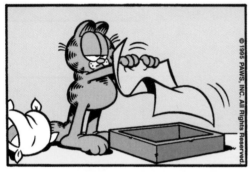

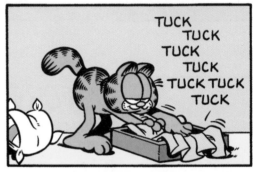

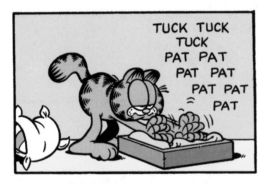

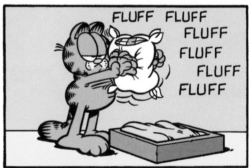

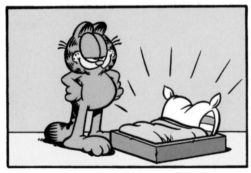

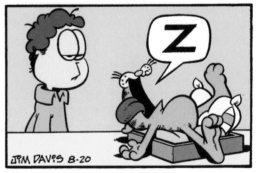

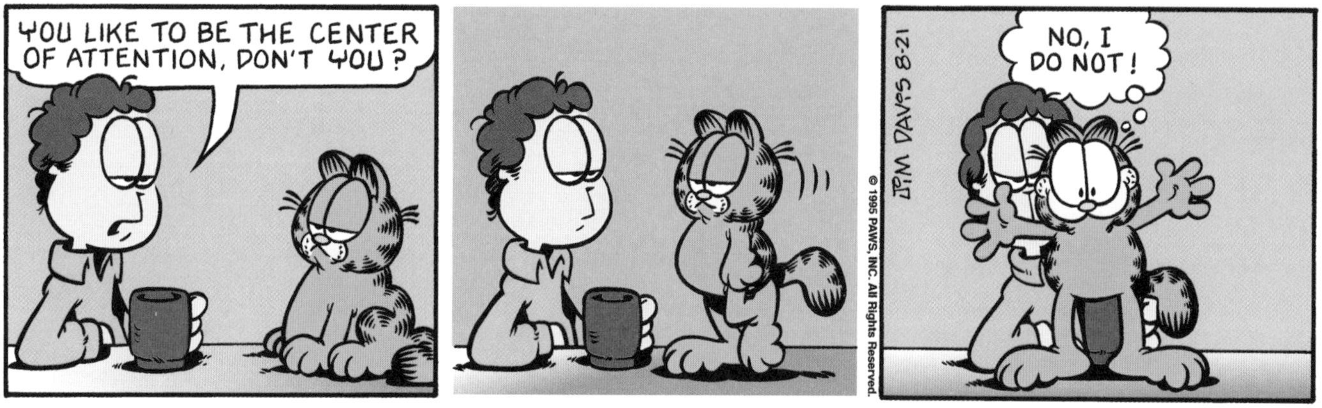
YOU LIKE TO BE THE CENTER OF ATTENTION, DON'T YOU?
NO, I DO NOT!
JIM DAVIS 8-21
© 1995 PAWS, INC. All Rights Reserved.

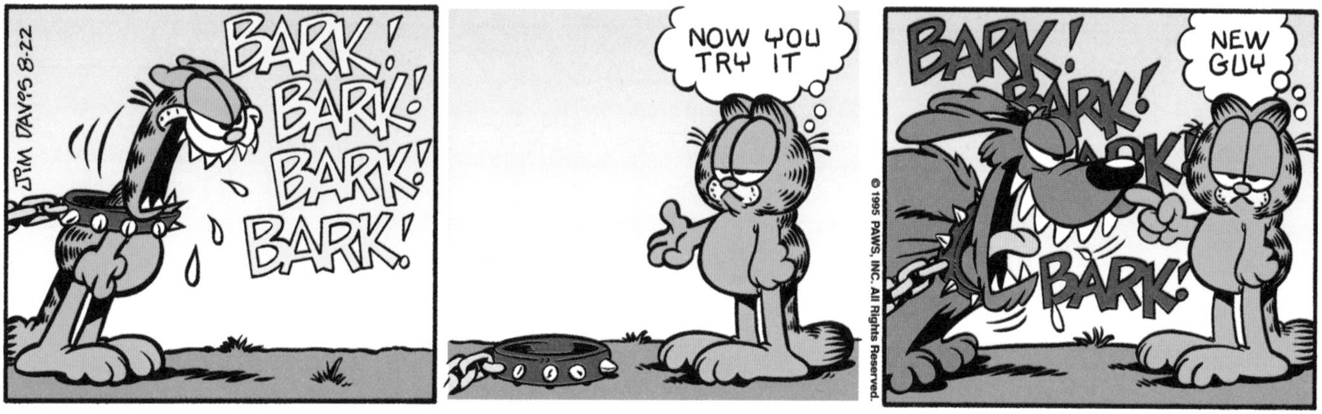
JIM DAVIS 8-22
BARK! BARK! BARK! BARK!
NOW YOU TRY IT
BARK! BARK! BARK! BARK!
NEW GUY
© 1995 PAWS, INC. All Rights Reserved.

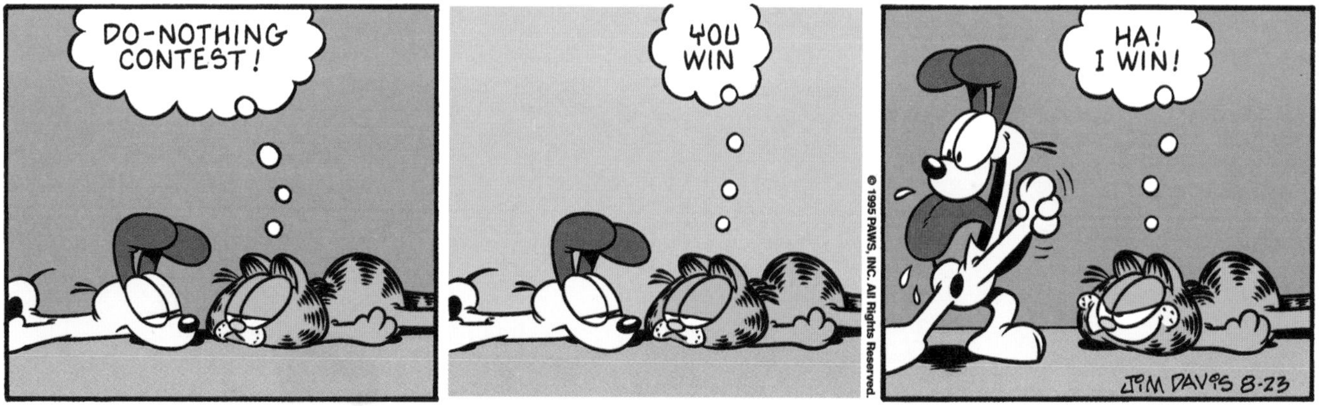
DO-NOTHING CONTEST!
YOU WIN
HA! I WIN!
JIM DAVIS 8-23
© 1995 PAWS, INC. All Rights Reserved.

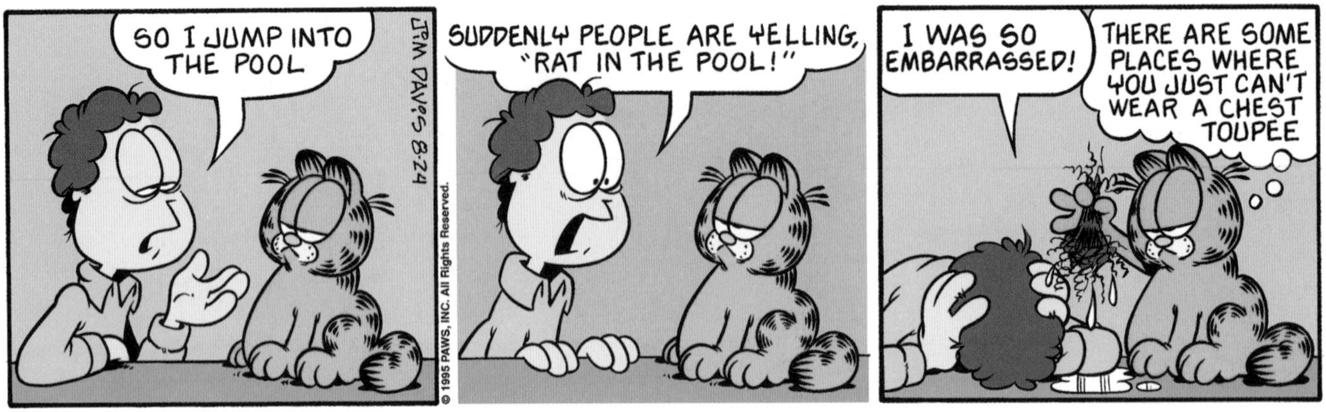
SO I JUMP INTO THE POOL
JIM DAVIS 8-24
© 1995 PAWS, INC. All Rights Reserved.
SUDDENLY PEOPLE ARE YELLING, "RAT IN THE POOL!"
I WAS SO EMBARRASSED!
THERE ARE SOME PLACES WHERE YOU JUST CAN'T WEAR A CHEST TOUPEE

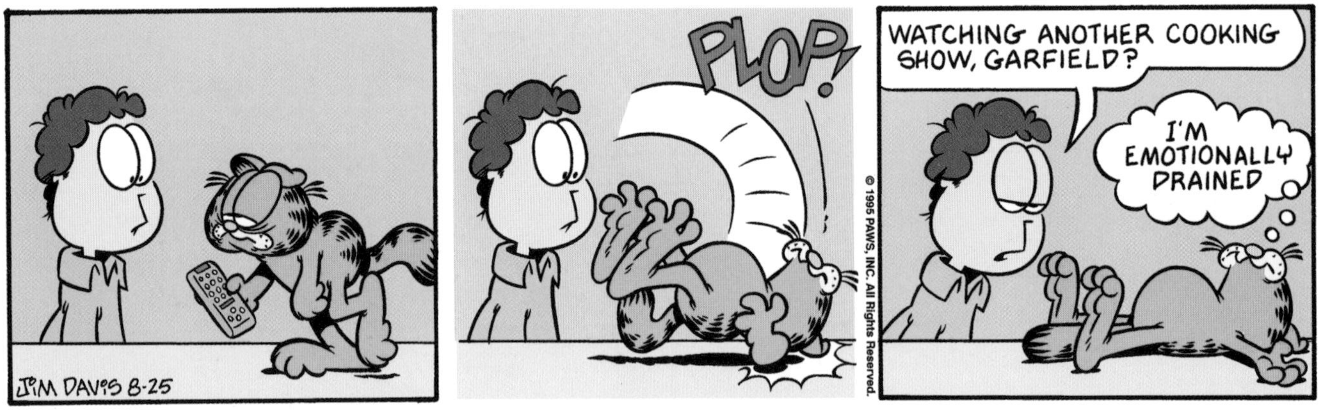
JIM DAVIS 8-25
PLOP!
© 1995 PAWS, INC. All Rights Reserved.
WATCHING ANOTHER COOKING SHOW, GARFIELD?
I'M EMOTIONALLY DRAINED

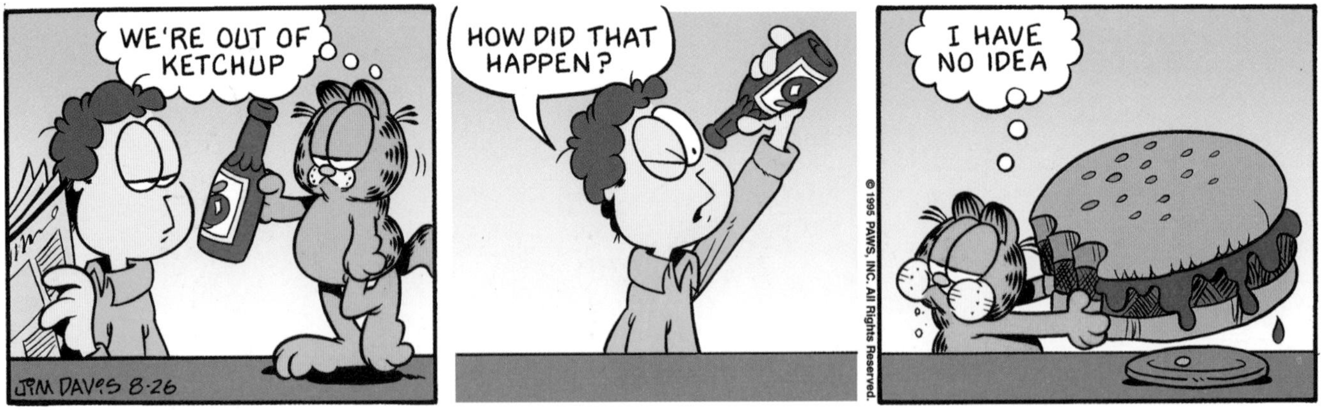
WE'RE OUT OF KETCHUP
JIM DAVIS 8-26
HOW DID THAT HAPPEN?
© 1995 PAWS, INC. All Rights Reserved.
I HAVE NO IDEA

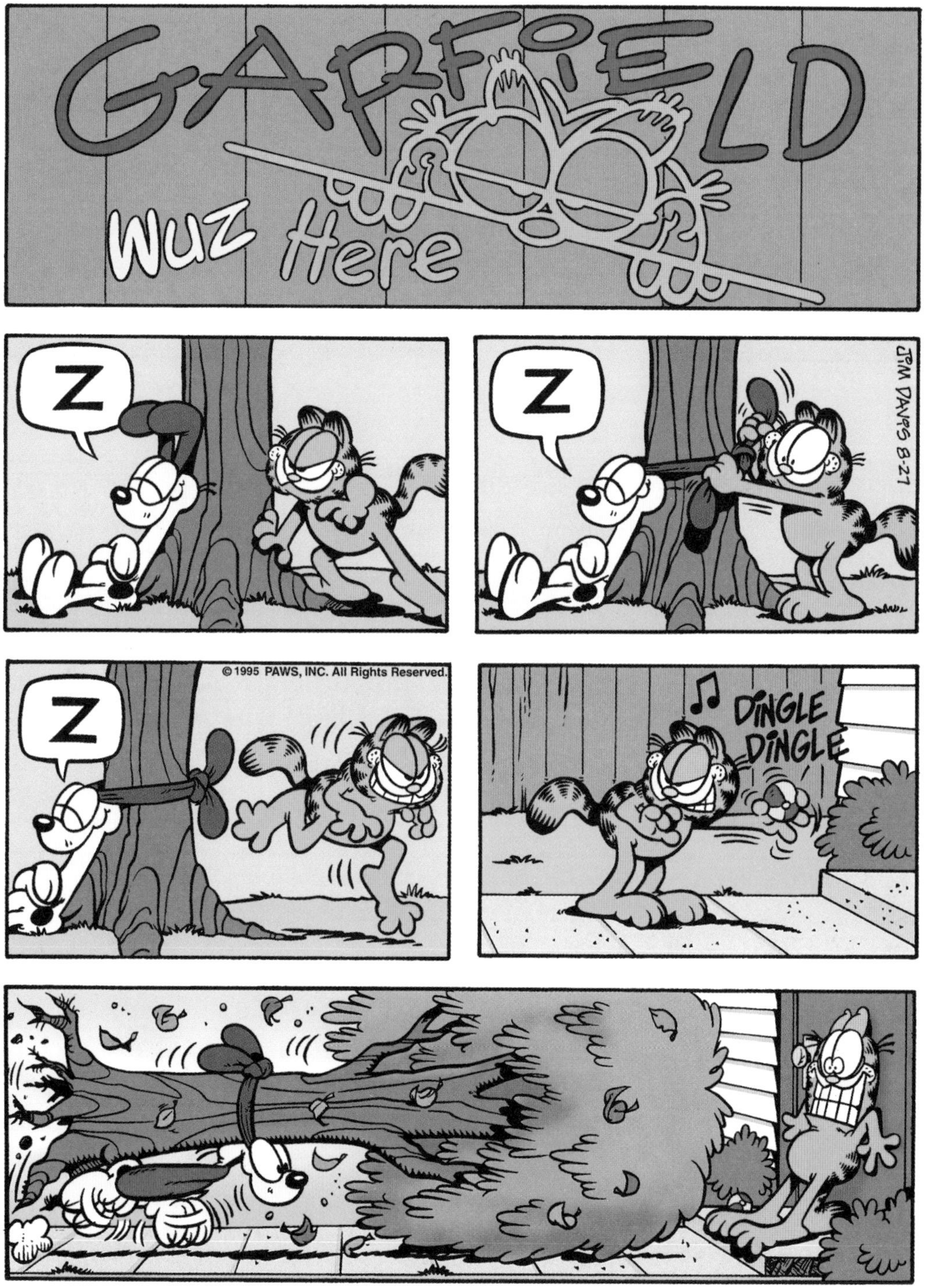
GARFIELD
Wuz Here
Z
Z
JIM DAVIS 8-27
Z
© 1995 PAWS, INC. All Rights Reserved.
DINGLE DINGLE

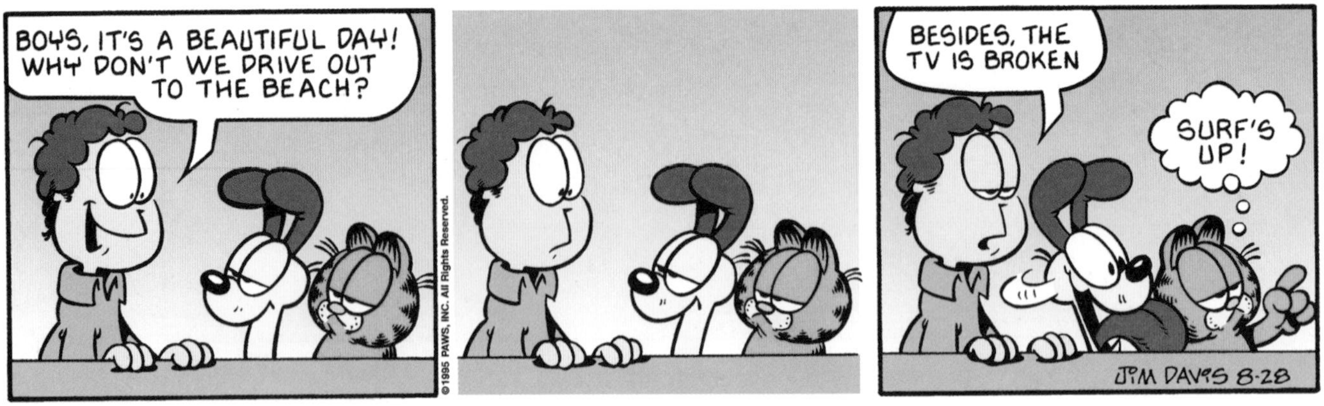
BOYS, IT'S A BEAUTIFUL DAY! WHY DON'T WE DRIVE OUT TO THE BEACH?
BESIDES, THE TV IS BROKEN
SURF'S UP!
JIM DAVIS 8-28
©1995 PAWS, INC. All Rights Reserved.

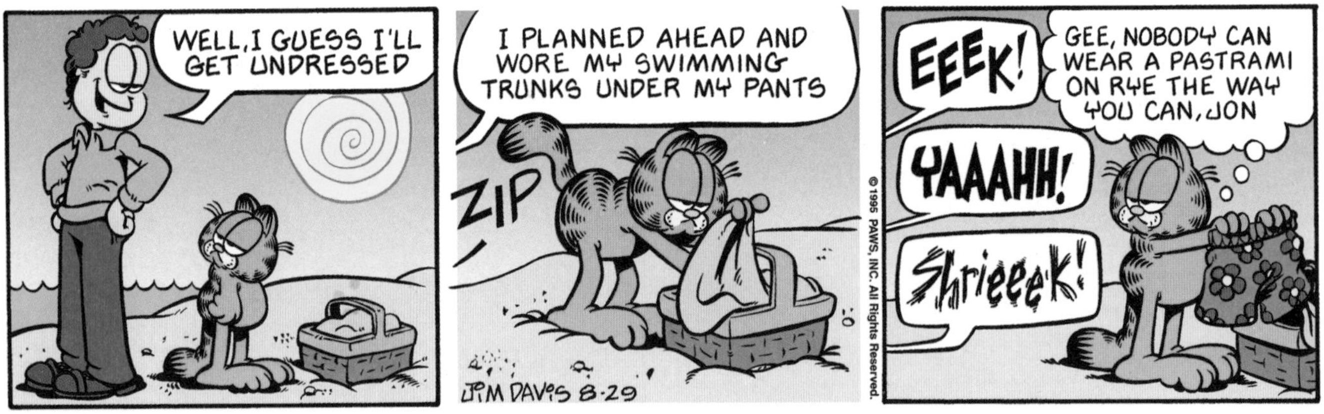
WELL, I GUESS I'LL GET UNDRESSED
I PLANNED AHEAD AND WORE MY SWIMMING TRUNKS UNDER MY PANTS
ZIP
JIM DAVIS 8-29
EEEK!
YAAAHH!
Shrieeek!
GEE, NOBODY CAN WEAR A PASTRAMI ON RYE THE WAY YOU CAN, JON
© 1995 PAWS, INC. All Rights Reserved.

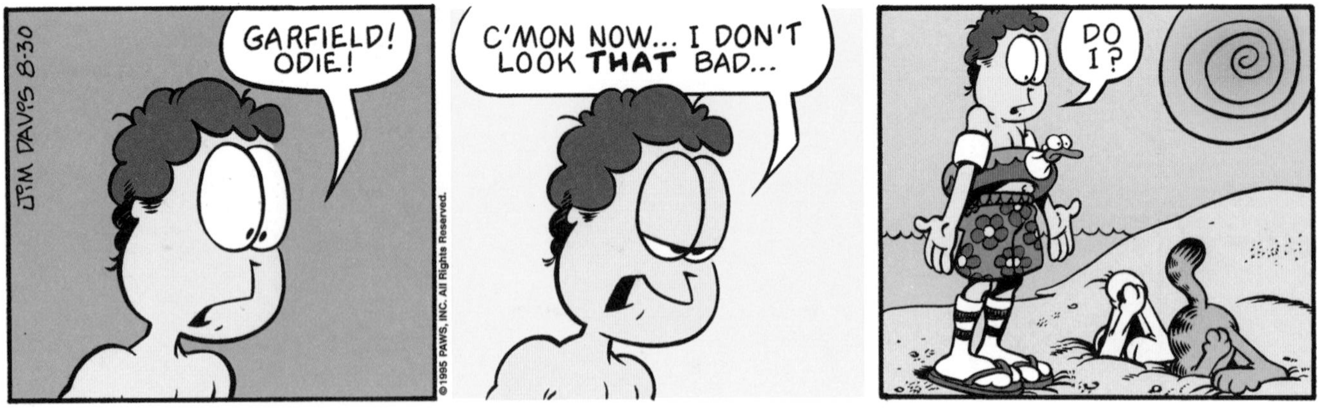
JIM DAVIS 8-30
GARFIELD! ODIE!
C'MON NOW... I DON'T LOOK THAT BAD...
DO I?
©1995 PAWS, INC. All Rights Reserved.

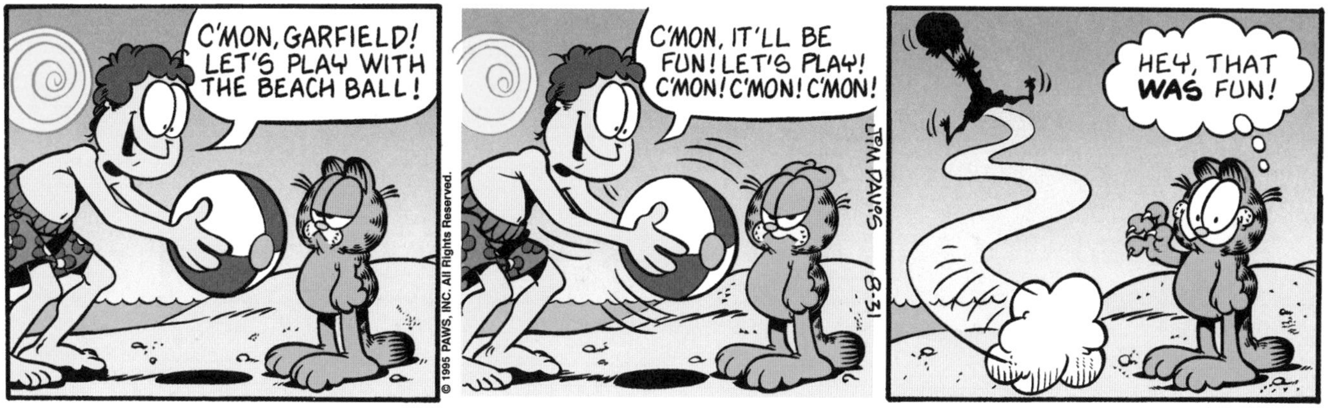
C'MON, GARFIELD! LET'S PLAY WITH THE BEACH BALL!
© 1995 PAWS, INC. All Rights Reserved.
C'MON, IT'LL BE FUN! LET'S PLAY! C'MON! C'MON! C'MON!
JIM DAVIS 8-31
HEY, THAT **WAS** FUN!

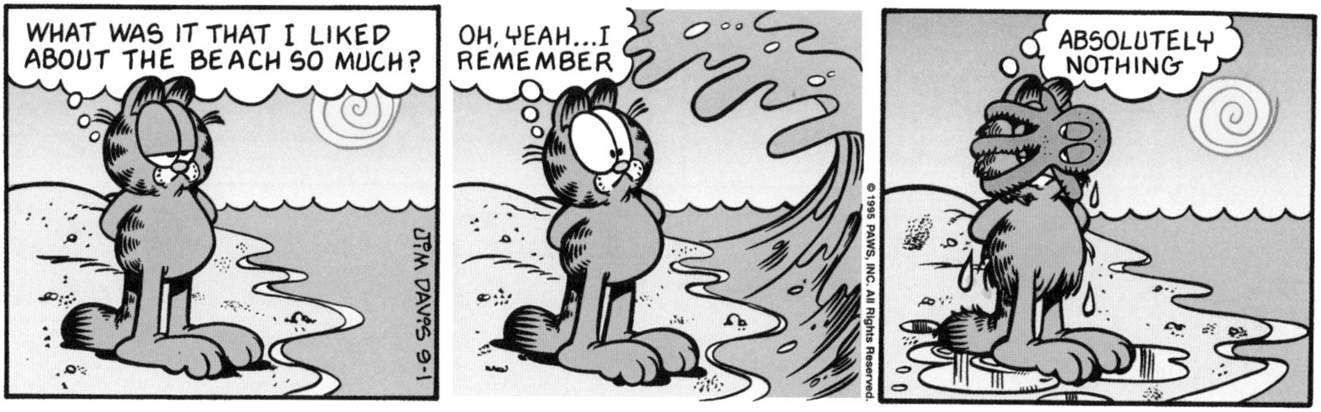
WHAT WAS IT THAT I LIKED ABOUT THE BEACH SO MUCH?
JIM DAVIS 9-1
OH, YEAH...I REMEMBER
© 1995 PAWS, INC. All Rights Reserved.
ABSOLUTELY NOTHING

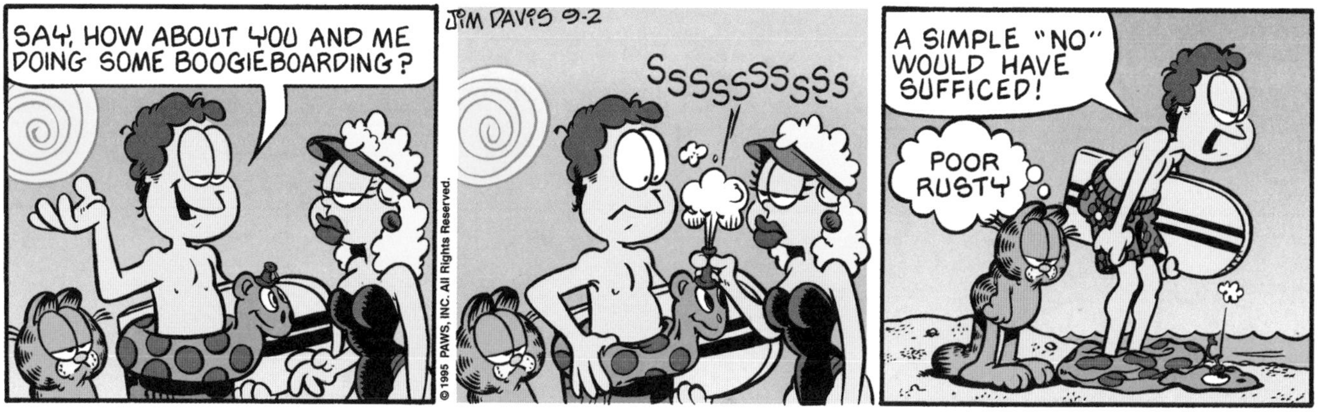
SAY, HOW ABOUT YOU AND ME DOING SOME BOOGIEBOARDING?
© 1995 PAWS, INC. All Rights Reserved.
JIM DAVIS 9-2
SSSSSSSSSS
A SIMPLE "NO" WOULD HAVE SUFFICED!
POOR RUSTY

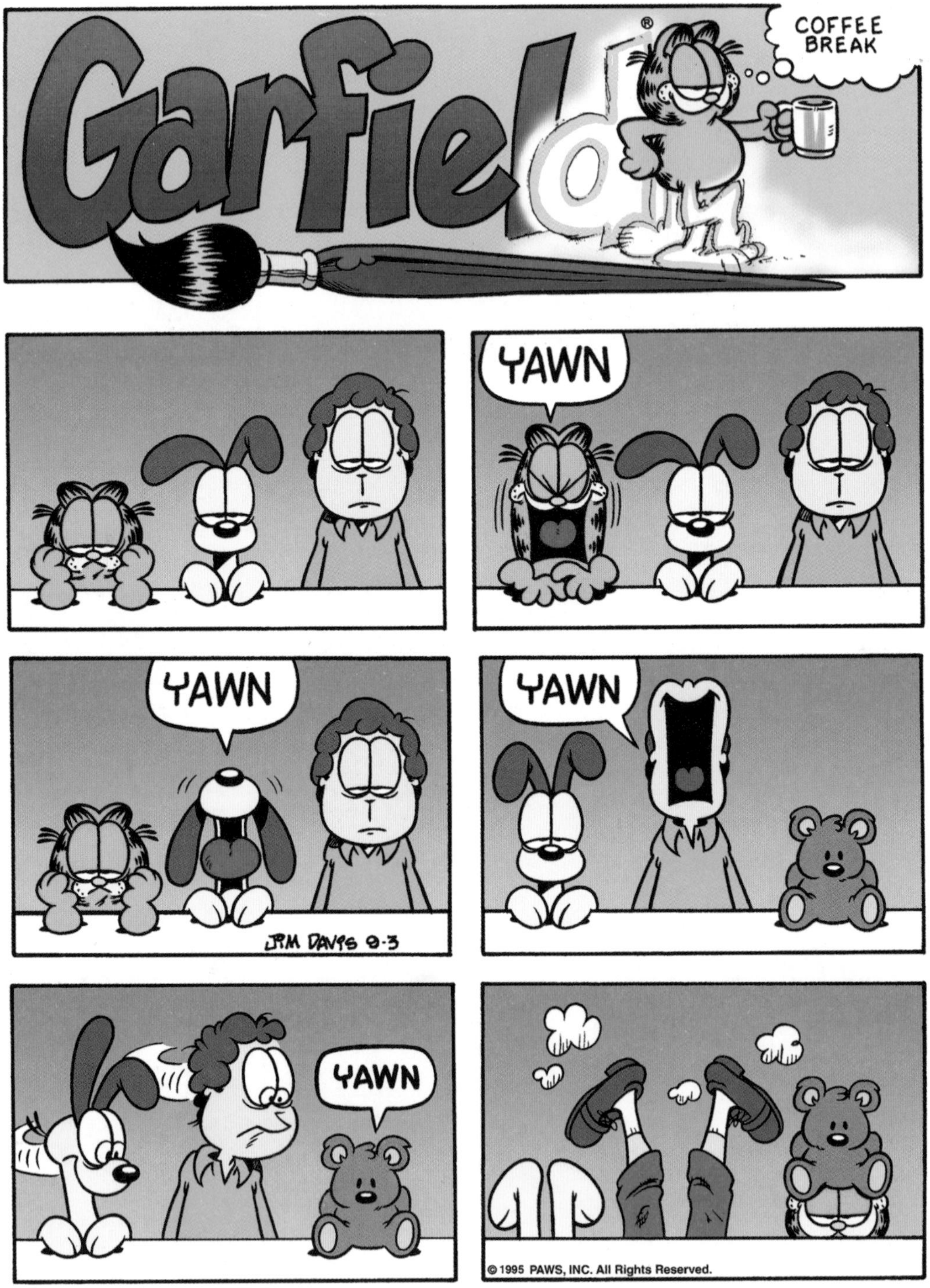
Garfield®
COFFEE BREAK
YAWN
YAWN
JIM DAVIS 9-3
YAWN
YAWN
© 1995 PAWS, INC. All Rights Reserved.

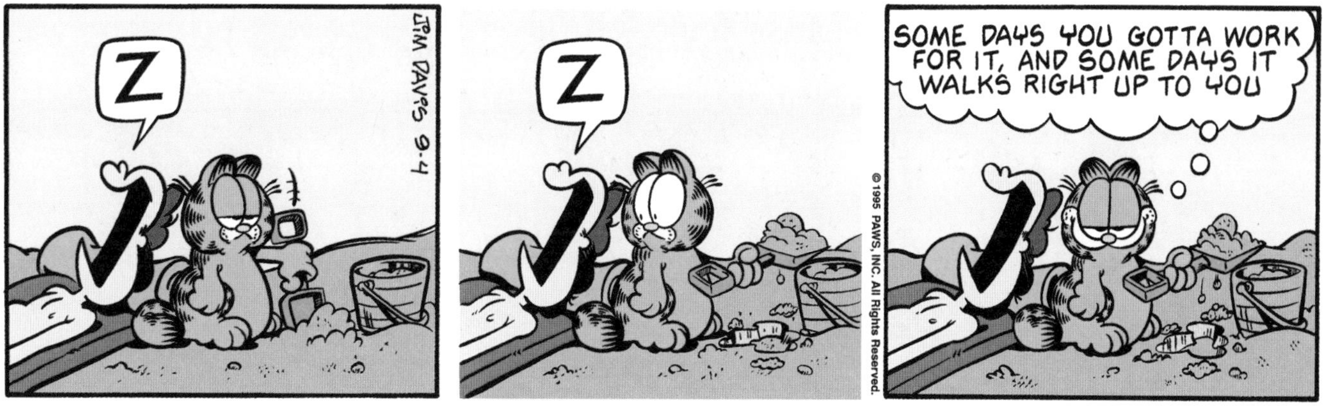
Z
JIM DAVIS 9-4
Z
SOME DAYS YOU GOTTA WORK FOR IT, AND SOME DAYS IT WALKS RIGHT UP TO YOU
© 1995 PAWS, INC. All Rights Reserved.

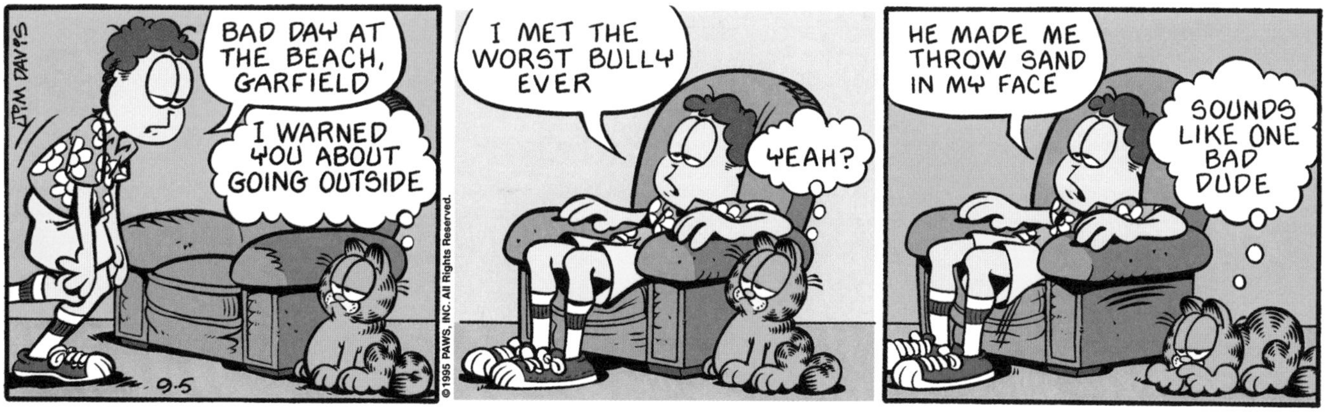
JIM DAVIS 9-5
BAD DAY AT THE BEACH, GARFIELD
I WARNED YOU ABOUT GOING OUTSIDE
© 1995 PAWS, INC. All Rights Reserved.
I MET THE WORST BULLY EVER
YEAH?
HE MADE ME THROW SAND IN MY FACE
SOUNDS LIKE ONE BAD DUDE

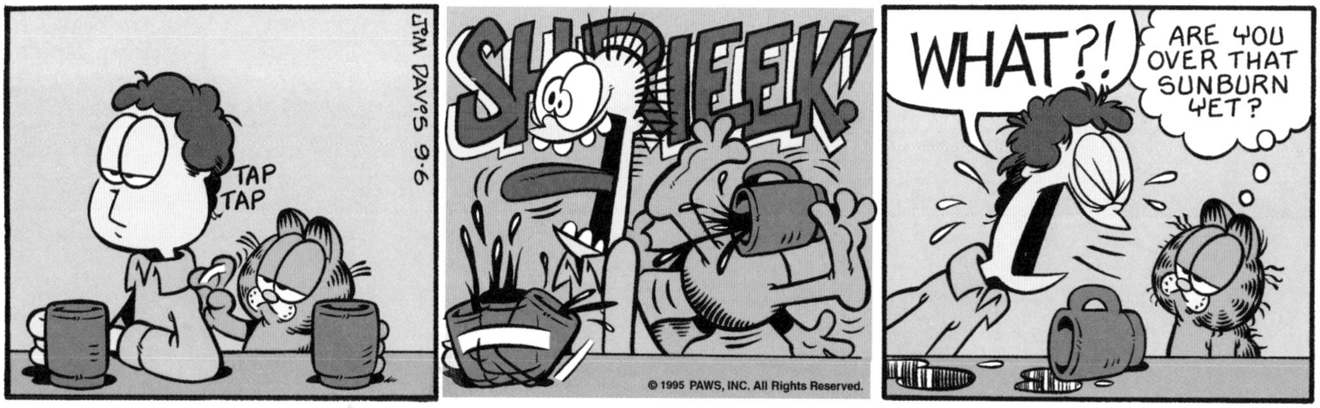
JIM DAVIS 9-6
TAP TAP
SHRIEEK!
© 1995 PAWS, INC. All Rights Reserved.
WHAT?!
ARE YOU OVER THAT SUNBURN YET?

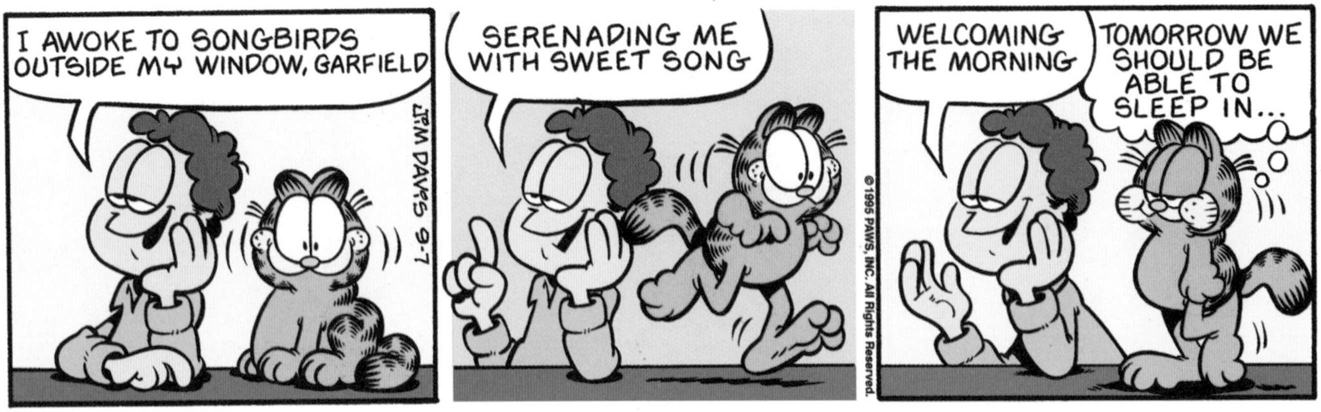
I AWOKE TO SONGBIRDS OUTSIDE MY WINDOW, GARFIELD
JIM DAVIS 9-7
SERENADING ME WITH SWEET SONG
© 1995 PAWS, INC. All Rights Reserved.
WELCOMING THE MORNING
TOMORROW WE SHOULD BE ABLE TO SLEEP IN...

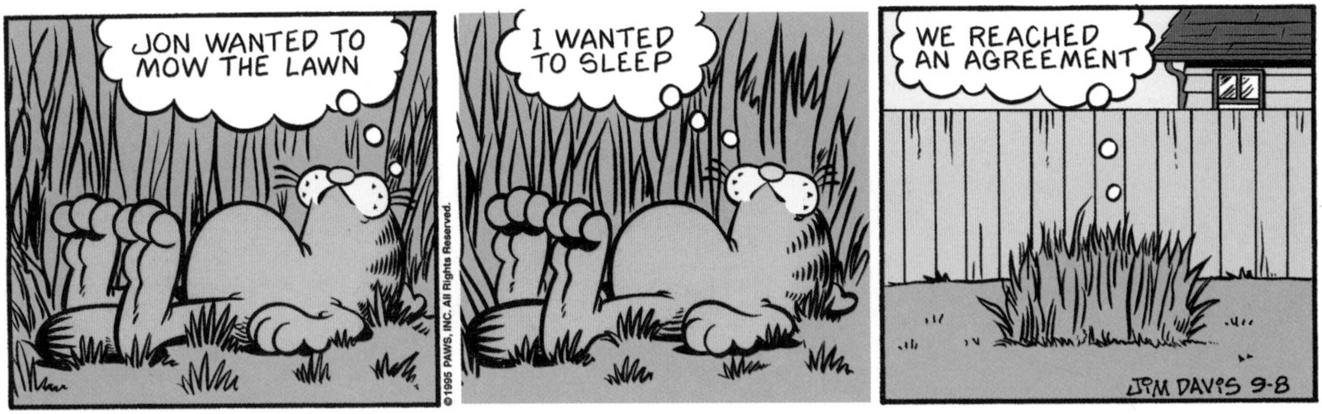
JON WANTED TO MOW THE LAWN
© 1995 PAWS, INC. All Rights Reserved.
I WANTED TO SLEEP
WE REACHED AN AGREEMENT
JIM DAVIS 9-8

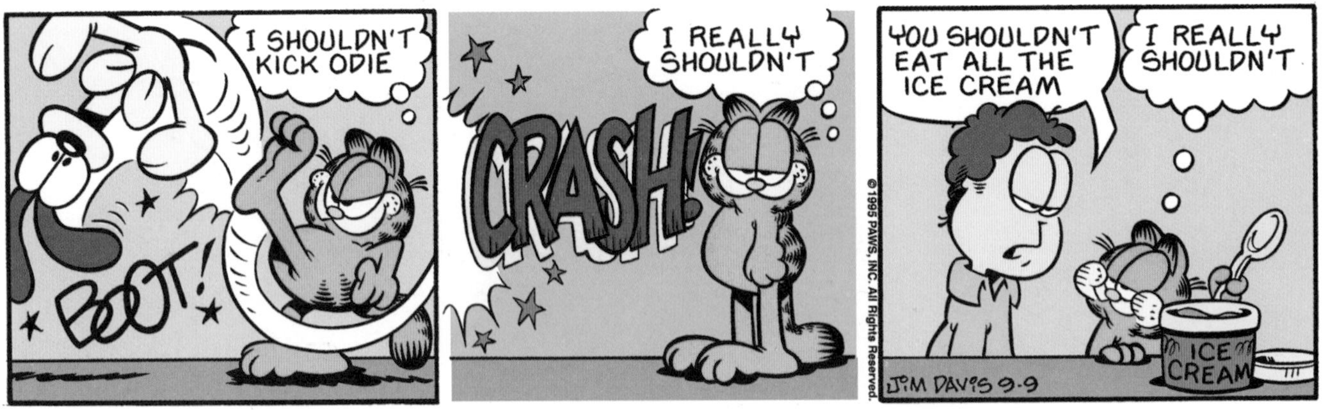
I SHOULDN'T KICK ODIE
BOOT!
CRASH!
I REALLY SHOULDN'T
© 1995 PAWS, INC. All Rights Reserved.
YOU SHOULDN'T EAT ALL THE ICE CREAM
I REALLY SHOULDN'T
ICE CREAM
JIM DAVIS 9-9

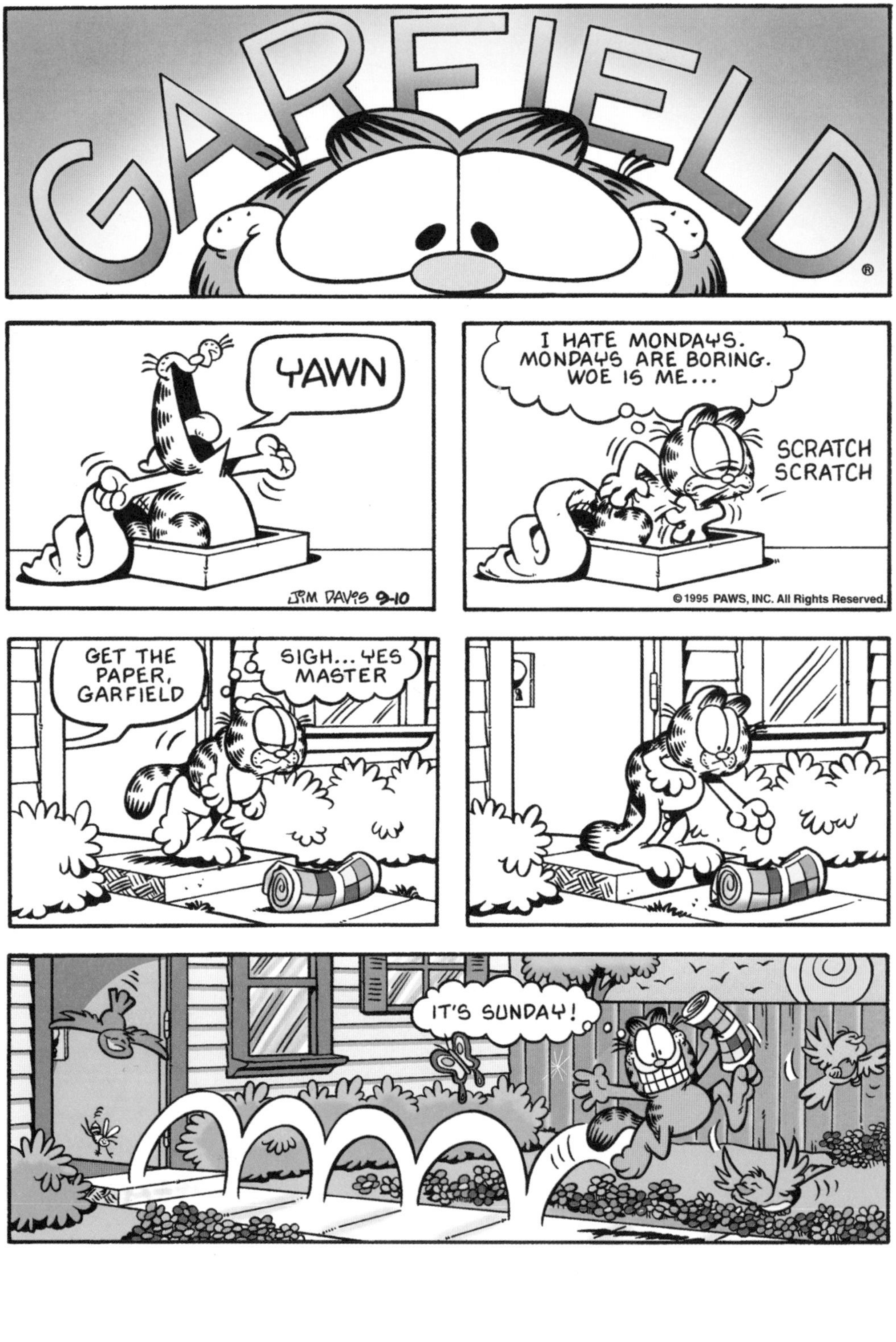
GARFIELD®
YAWN
JIM DAVIS 9-10
I HATE MONDAYS. MONDAYS ARE BORING. WOE IS ME...
SCRATCH SCRATCH
© 1995 PAWS, INC. All Rights Reserved.
GET THE PAPER, GARFIELD
SIGH... YES MASTER
IT'S SUNDAY!

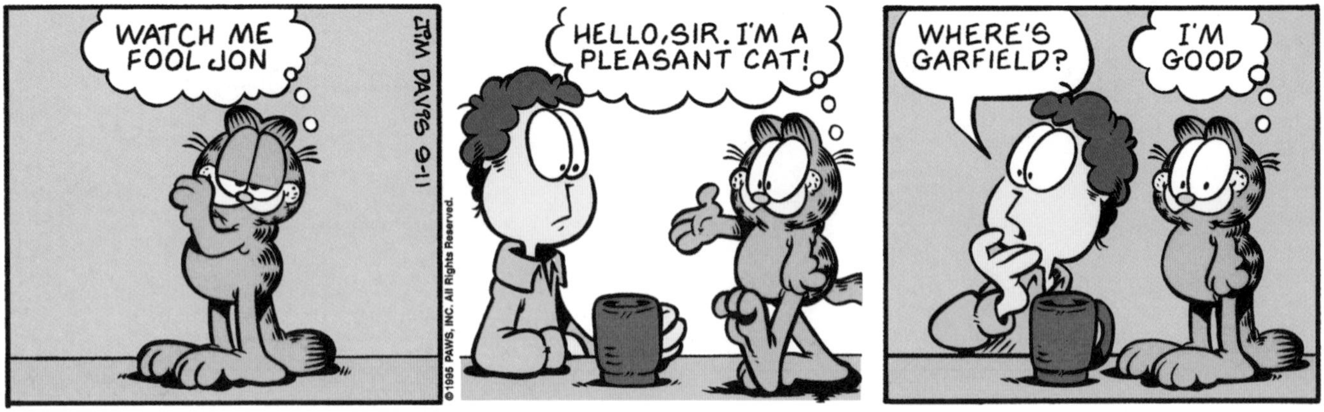
WATCH ME FOOL JON
JIM DAVIS 9-11
© 1995 PAWS, INC. All Rights Reserved.
HELLO, SIR. I'M A PLEASANT CAT!
WHERE'S GARFIELD?
I'M GOOD

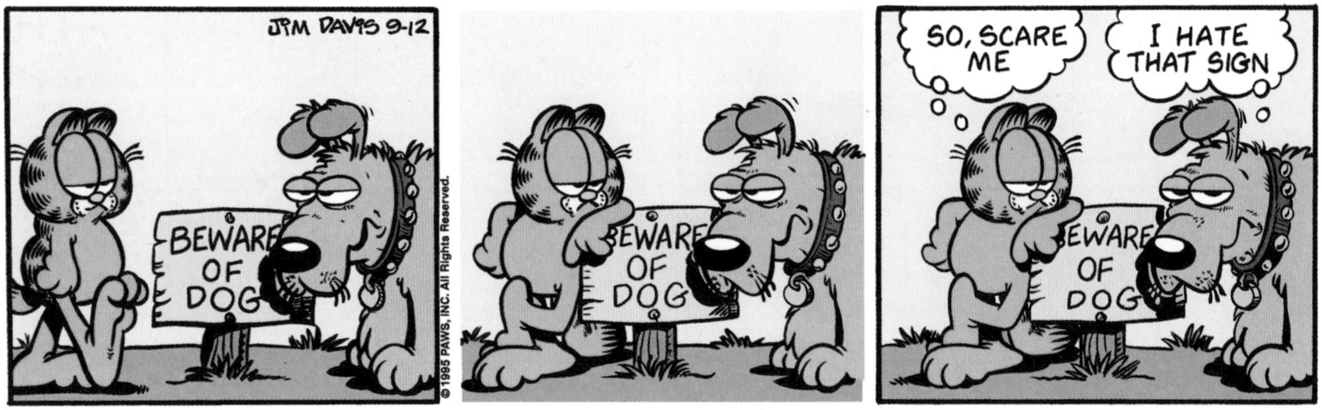
JIM DAVIS 9-12
BEWARE OF DOG
© 1995 PAWS, INC. All Rights Reserved.
SO, SCARE ME
I HATE THAT SIGN

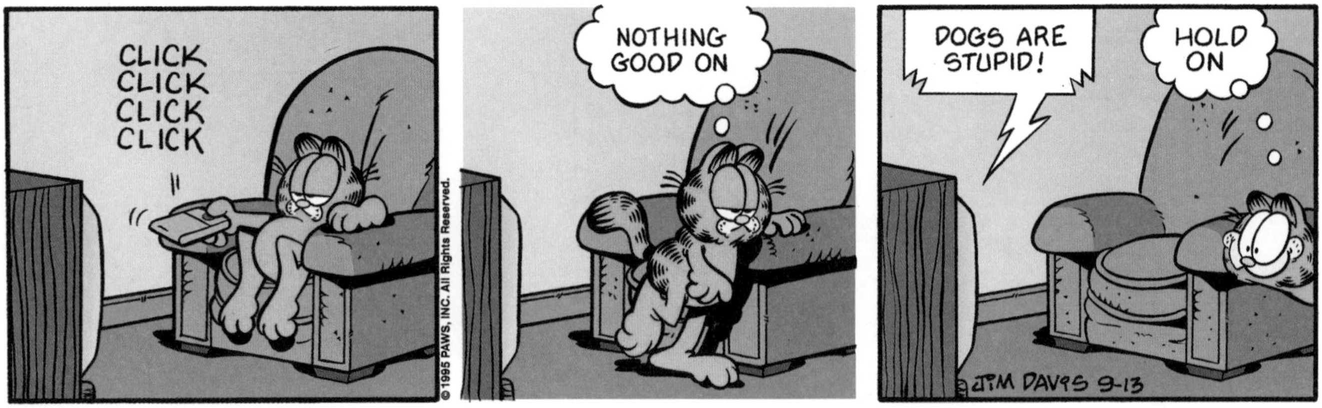
CLICK CLICK CLICK CLICK
© 1995 PAWS, INC. All Rights Reserved.
NOTHING GOOD ON
DOGS ARE STUPID!
HOLD ON
JIM DAVIS 9-13

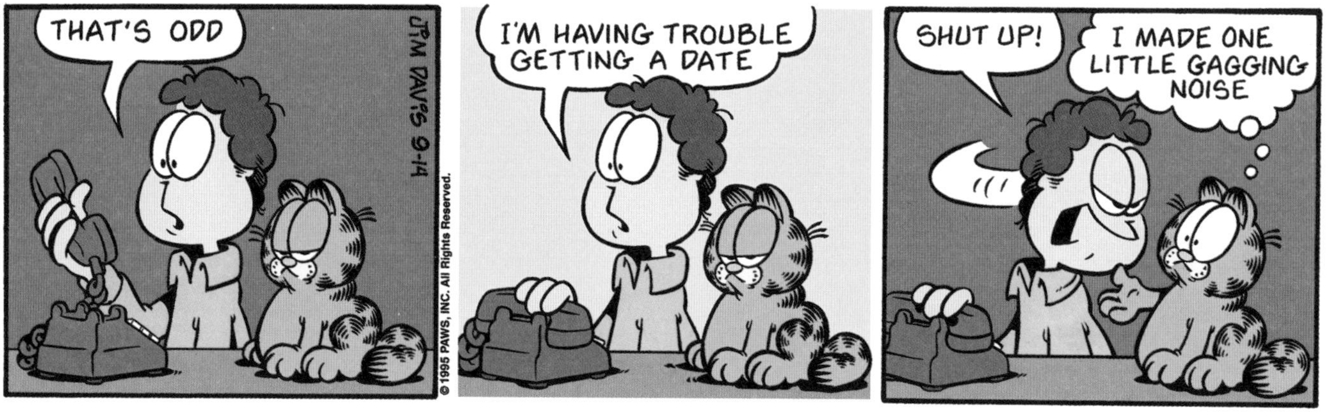
THAT'S ODD
JIM DAVIS 9-14
© 1995 PAWS, INC. All Rights Reserved.
I'M HAVING TROUBLE GETTING A DATE
SHUT UP!
I MADE ONE LITTLE GAGGING NOISE

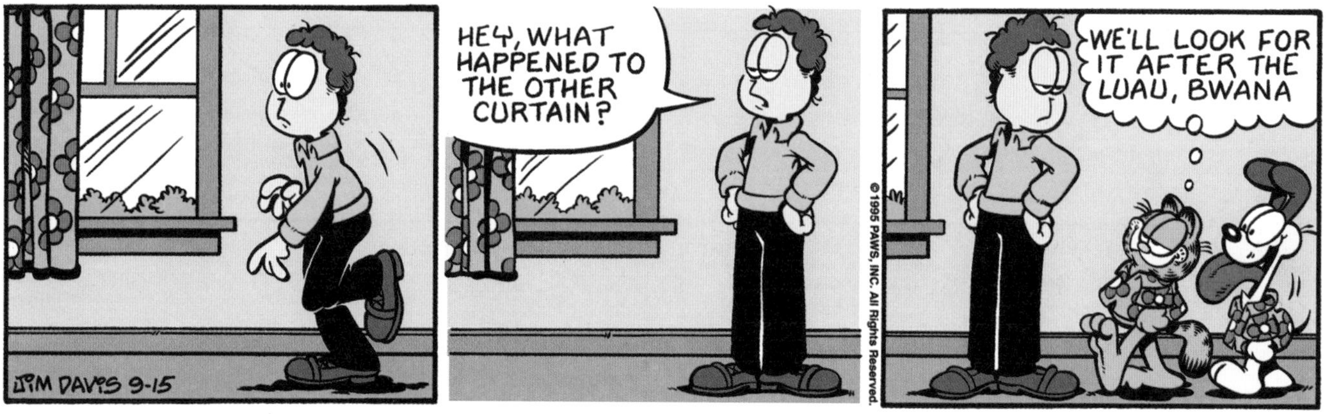
JIM DAVIS 9-15
HEY, WHAT HAPPENED TO THE OTHER CURTAIN?
© 1995 PAWS, INC. All Rights Reserved.
WE'LL LOOK FOR IT AFTER THE LUAU, BWANA

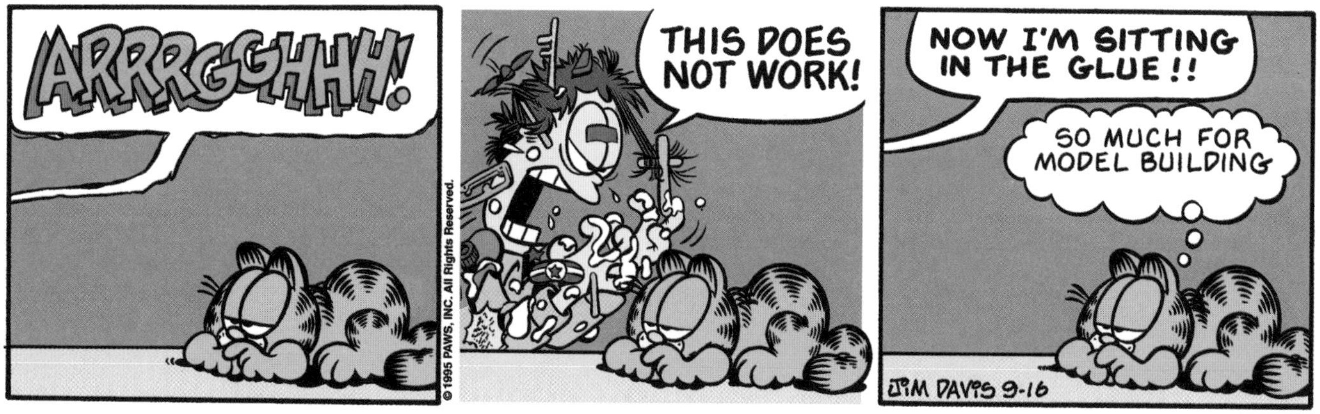
ARRRGGHHH!
© 1995 PAWS, INC. All Rights Reserved.
THIS DOES NOT WORK!
NOW I'M SITTING IN THE GLUE!!
SO MUCH FOR MODEL BUILDING
JIM DAVIS 9-16

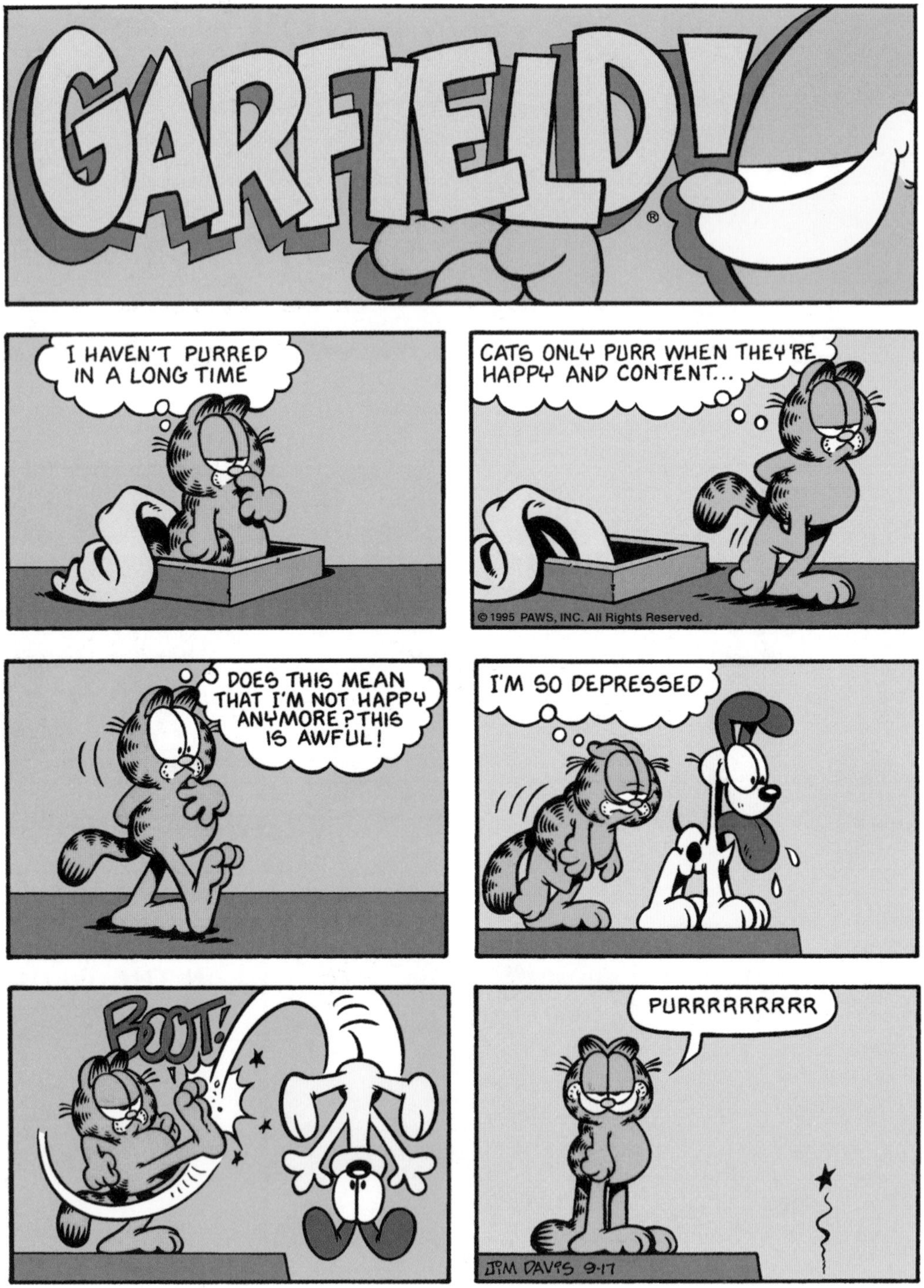
GARFIELD!®
I HAVEN'T PURRED IN A LONG TIME
CATS ONLY PURR WHEN THEY'RE HAPPY AND CONTENT...
© 1995 PAWS, INC. All Rights Reserved.
DOES THIS MEAN THAT I'M NOT HAPPY ANYMORE? THIS IS AWFUL!
I'M SO DEPRESSED
BOOT!
PURRRRRRRRR
JIM DAVIS 9-17

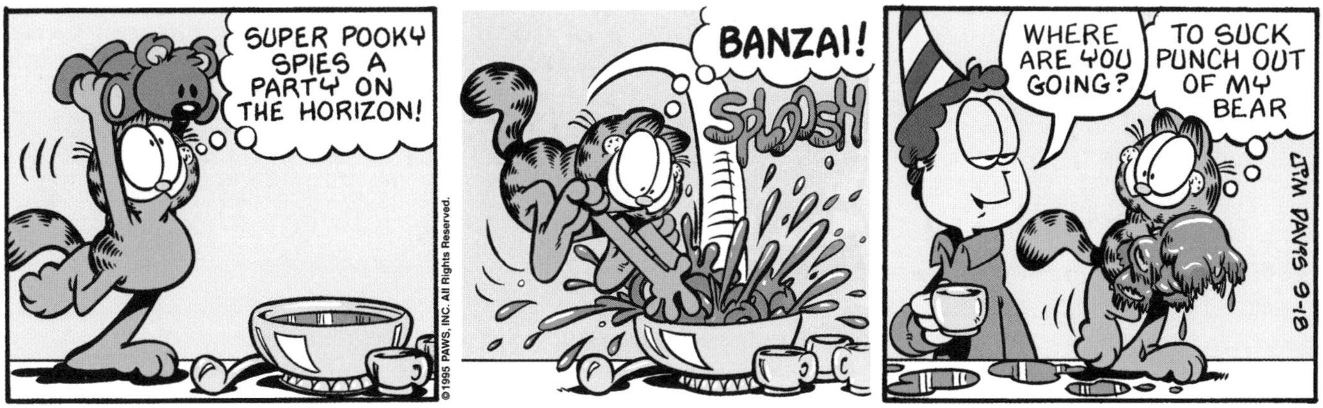
SUPER POOKY SPIES A PARTY ON THE HORIZON!
©1995 PAWS, INC. All Rights Reserved.
BANZAI!
SPLOOSH
WHERE ARE YOU GOING?
TO SUCK PUNCH OUT OF MY BEAR
JIM DAVIS 9-18

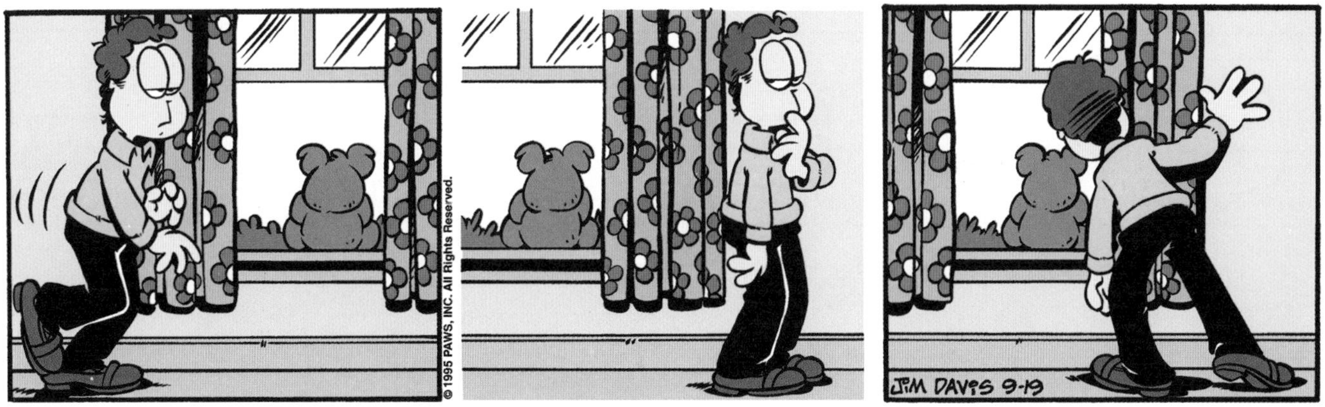
©1995 PAWS, INC. All Rights Reserved.
JIM DAVIS 9-19

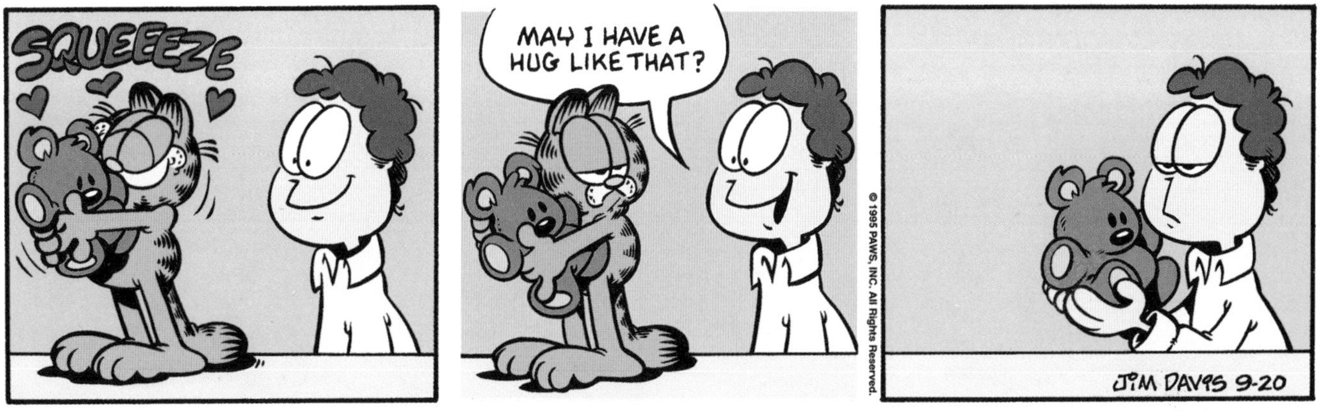
SQUEEEEZE
MAY I HAVE A HUG LIKE THAT?
©1995 PAWS, INC. All Rights Reserved.
JIM DAVIS 9-20

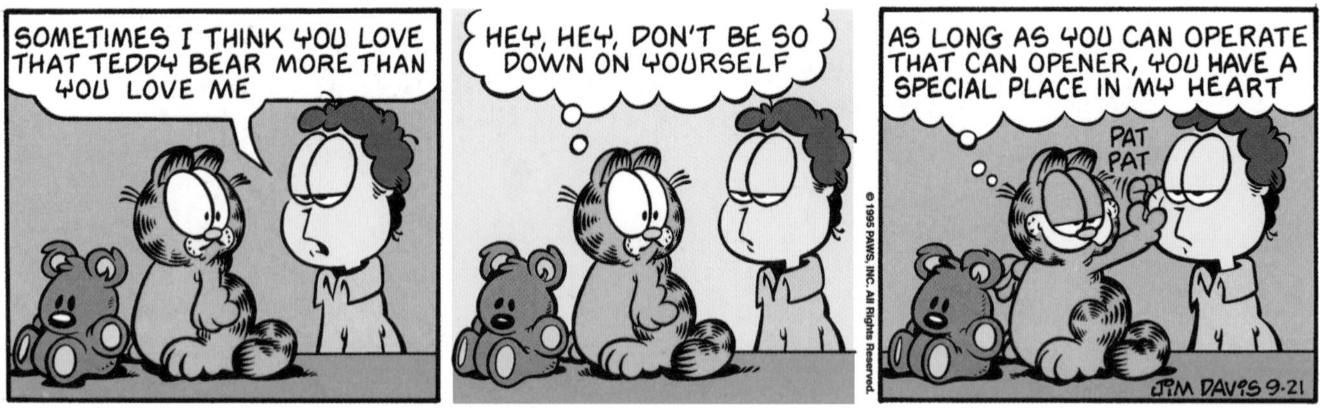
SOMETIMES I THINK YOU LOVE THAT TEDDY BEAR MORE THAN YOU LOVE ME
HEY, HEY, DON'T BE SO DOWN ON YOURSELF
AS LONG AS YOU CAN OPERATE THAT CAN OPENER, YOU HAVE A SPECIAL PLACE IN MY HEART
PAT PAT
JIM DAVIS 9-21
© 1995 PAWS, INC. All Rights Reserved.

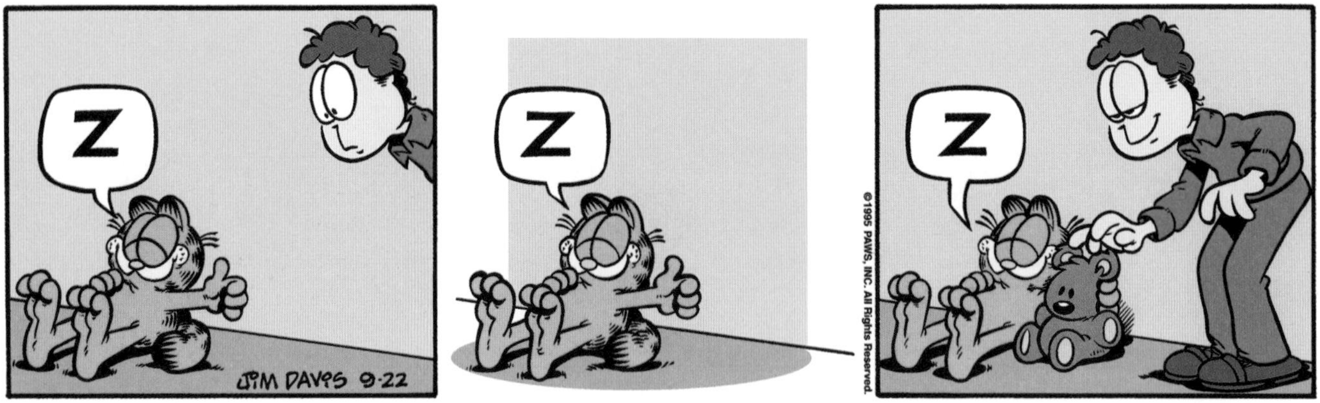
Z
Z
Z
JIM DAVIS 9-22
© 1995 PAWS, INC. All Rights Reserved.

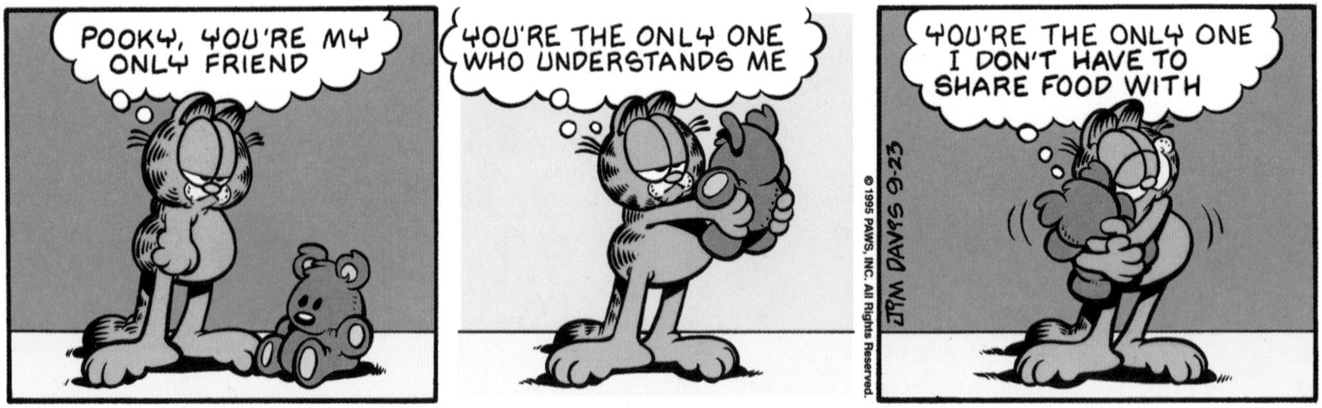
POOKY, YOU'RE MY ONLY FRIEND
YOU'RE THE ONLY ONE WHO UNDERSTANDS ME
YOU'RE THE ONLY ONE I DON'T HAVE TO SHARE FOOD WITH
JIM DAVIS 9-23
© 1995 PAWS, INC. All Rights Reserved.

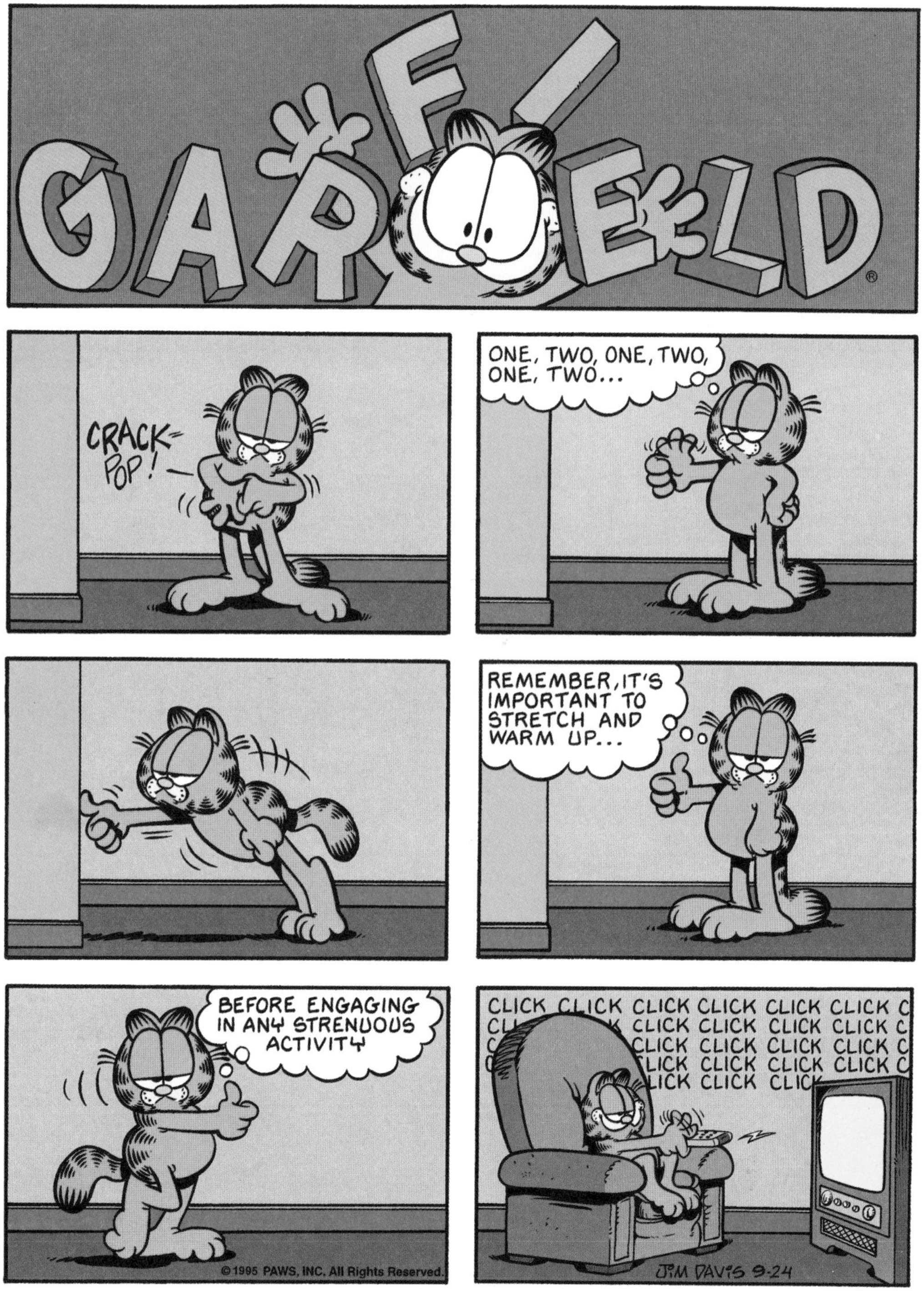
GARFIELD
CRACK POP!
ONE, TWO, ONE, TWO, ONE, TWO...
REMEMBER, IT'S IMPORTANT TO STRETCH AND WARM UP...
BEFORE ENGAGING IN ANY STRENUOUS ACTIVITY
CLICK CLICK CLICK CLICK CLICK CLICK
CLICK CLICK CLICK CLICK
CLICK CLICK CLICK CLICK
CLICK CLICK CLICK
CLICK CLICK
© 1995 PAWS, INC. All Rights Reserved.
JIM DAVIS 9-24

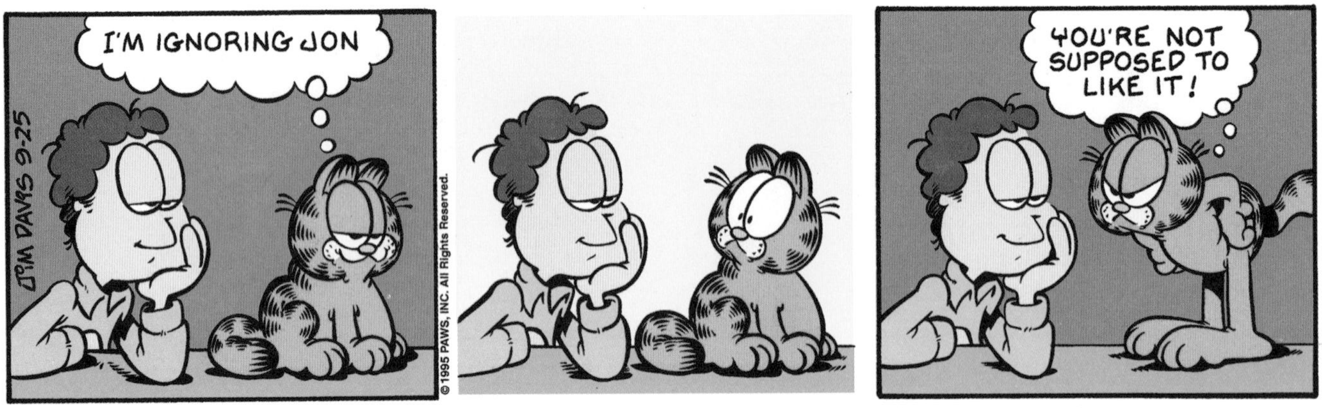
I'M IGNORING JON
JIM DAVIS 9-25
© 1995 PAWS, INC. All Rights Reserved.
YOU'RE NOT SUPPOSED TO LIKE IT!

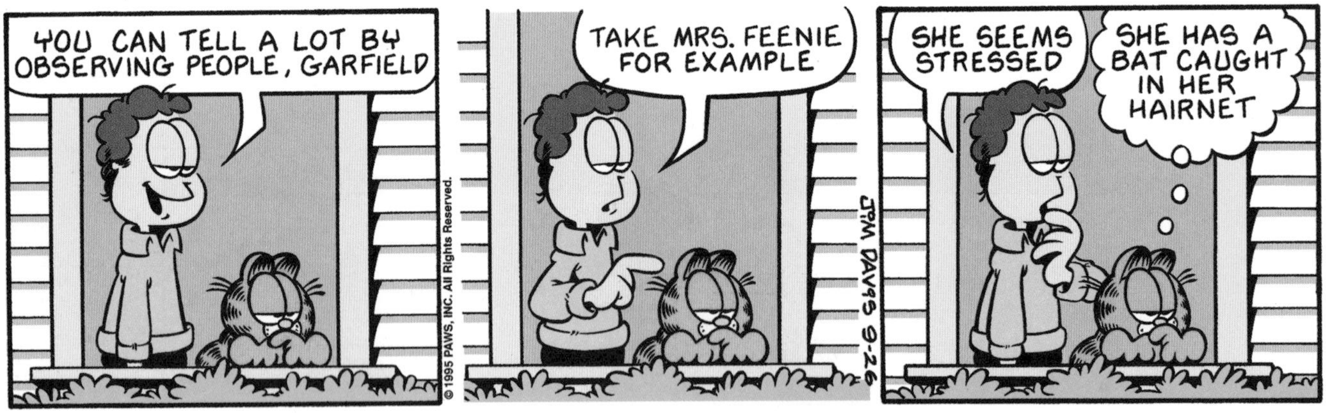
YOU CAN TELL A LOT BY OBSERVING PEOPLE, GARFIELD
© 1995 PAWS, INC. All Rights Reserved.
TAKE MRS. FEENIE FOR EXAMPLE
JIM DAVIS 9-26
SHE SEEMS STRESSED
SHE HAS A BAT CAUGHT IN HER HAIRNET

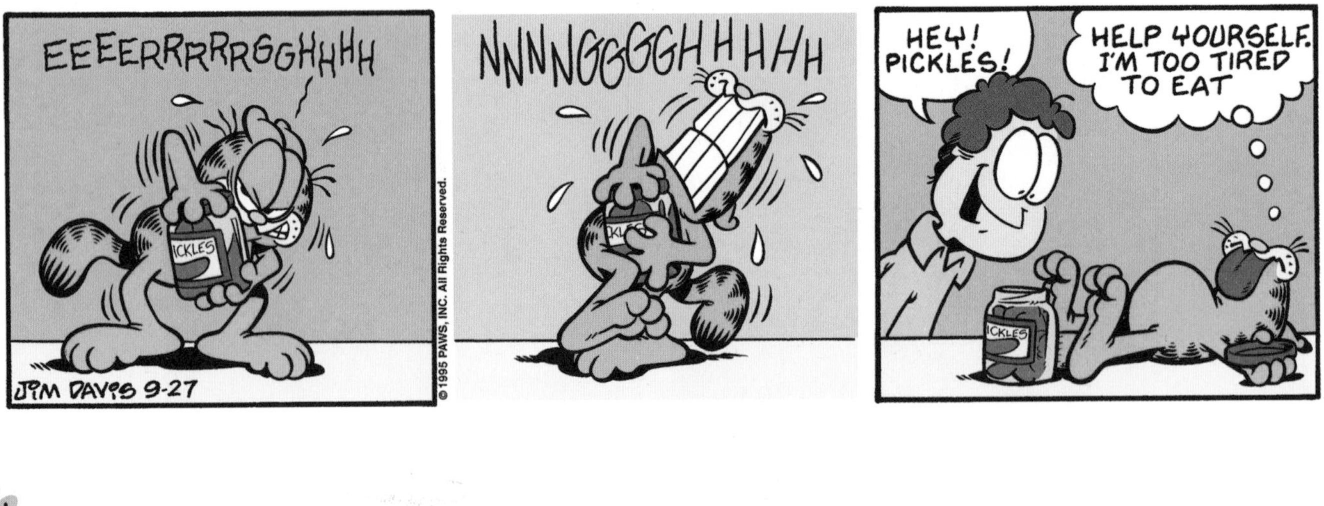
EEEERRRRRGGHHHH
PICKLES
JIM DAVIS 9-27
© 1995 PAWS, INC. All Rights Reserved.
NNNNGGGGHHHHH
HEY! PICKLES!
HELP YOURSELF. I'M TOO TIRED TO EAT

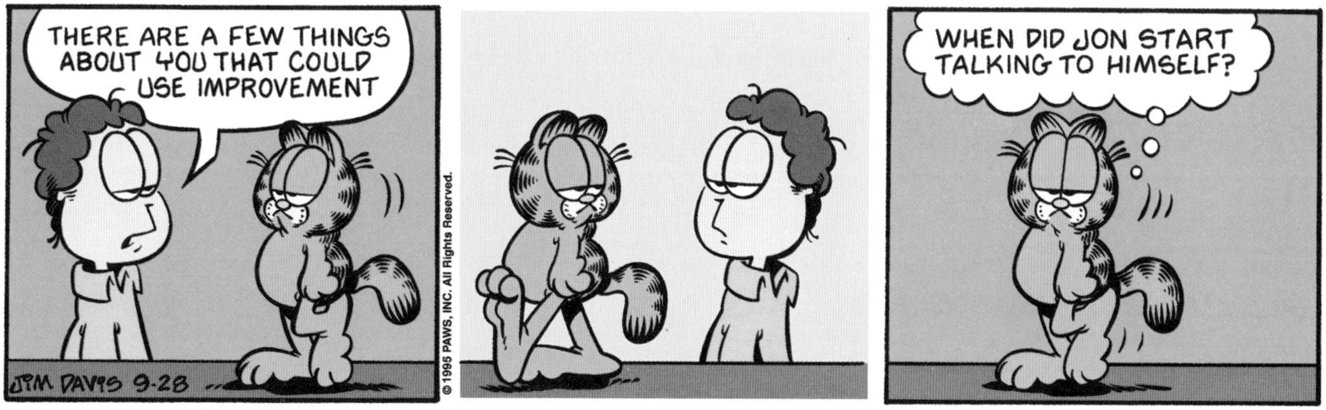
THERE ARE A FEW THINGS ABOUT YOU THAT COULD USE IMPROVEMENT
JIM DAVIS 9-28
© 1995 PAWS, INC. All Rights Reserved.
WHEN DID JON START TALKING TO HIMSELF?

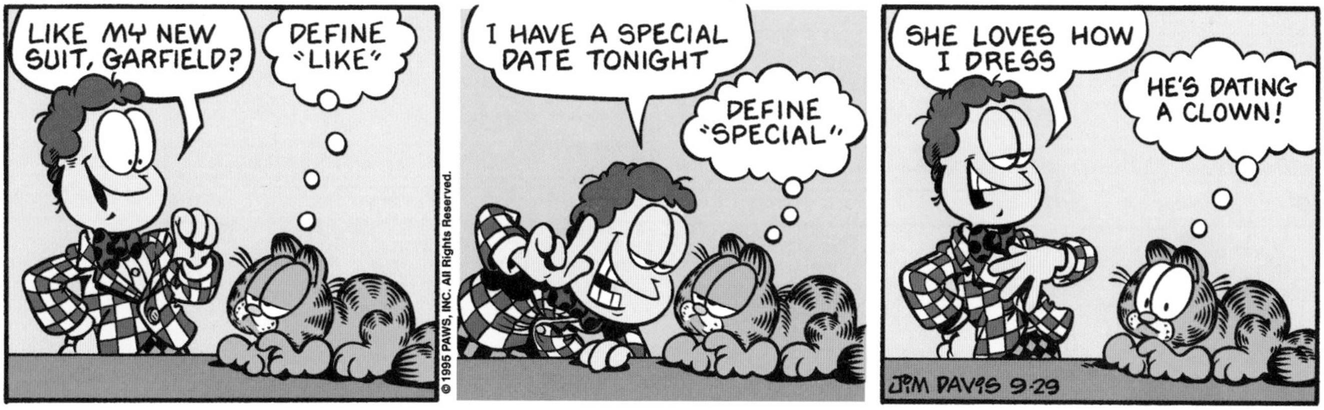
LIKE MY NEW SUIT, GARFIELD?
DEFINE "LIKE"
© 1995 PAWS, INC. All Rights Reserved.
I HAVE A SPECIAL DATE TONIGHT
DEFINE "SPECIAL"
SHE LOVES HOW I DRESS
HE'S DATING A CLOWN!
JIM DAVIS 9-29

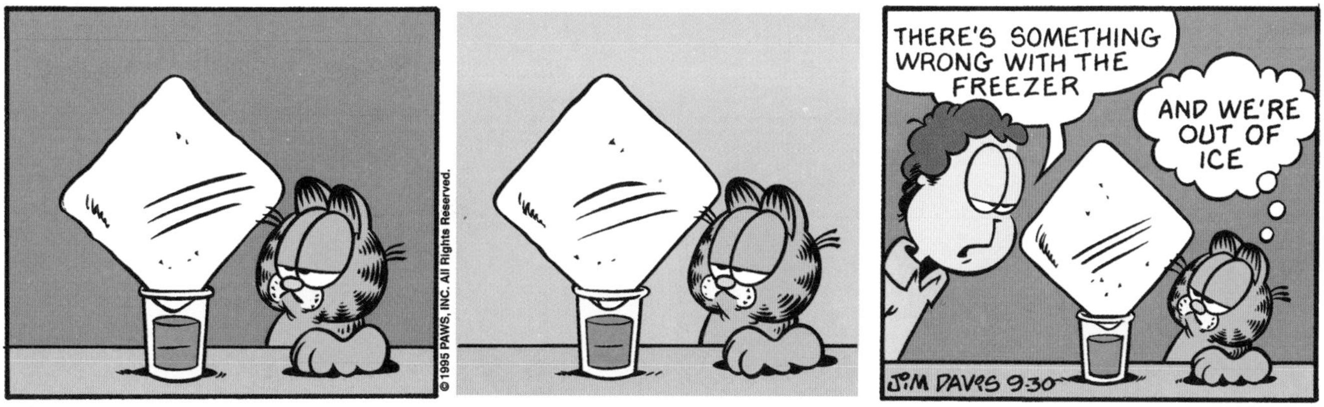
© 1995 PAWS, INC. All Rights Reserved.
THERE'S SOMETHING WRONG WITH THE FREEZER
AND WE'RE OUT OF ICE
JIM DAVIS 9-30

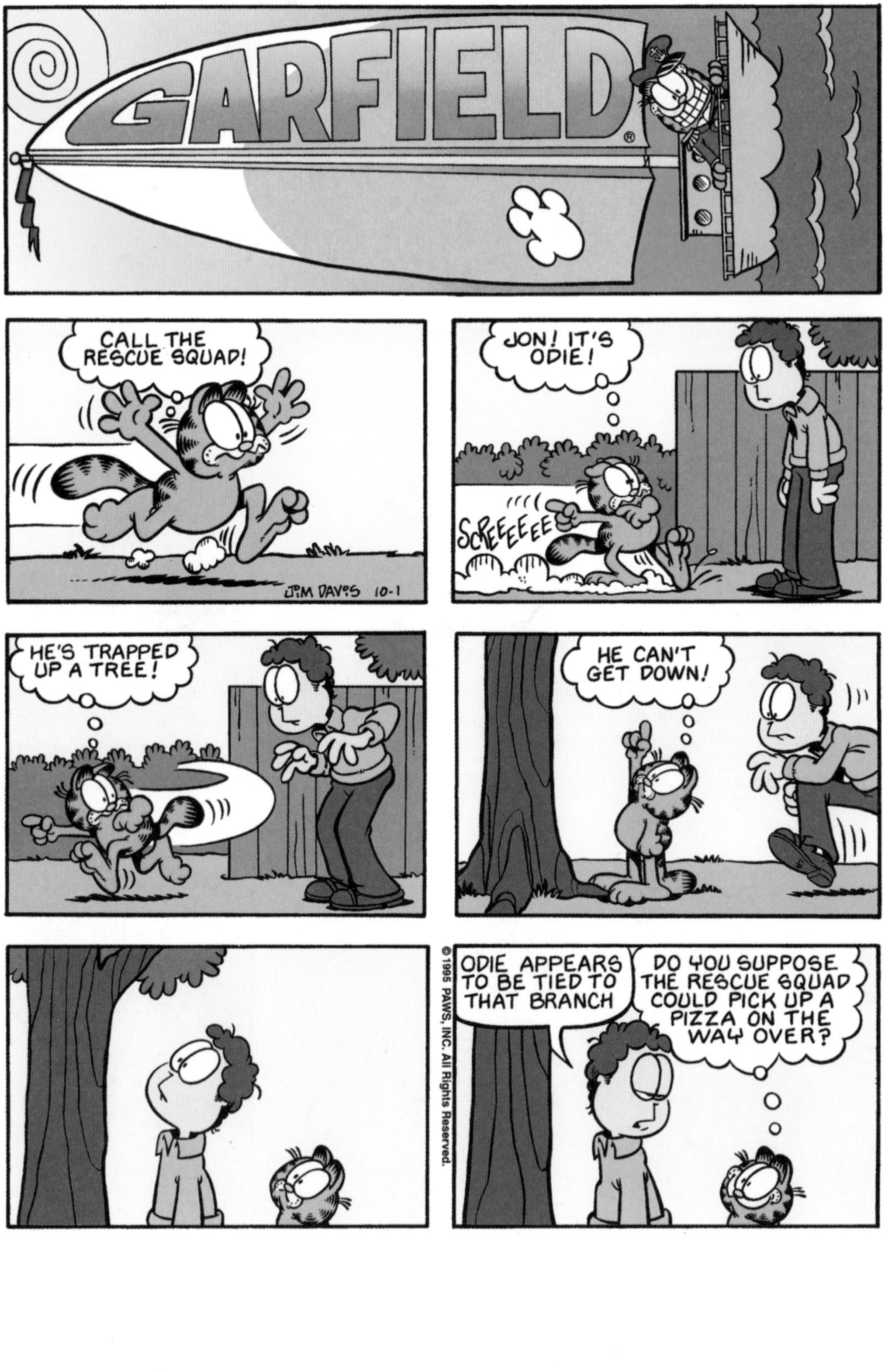
GARFIELD®
CALL THE RESCUE SQUAD!
JIM DAVIS 10-1
JON! IT'S ODIE!
SCREEEEEE
HE'S TRAPPED UP A TREE!
HE CAN'T GET DOWN!
ODIE APPEARS TO BE TIED TO THAT BRANCH
DO YOU SUPPOSE THE RESCUE SQUAD COULD PICK UP A PIZZA ON THE WAY OVER?

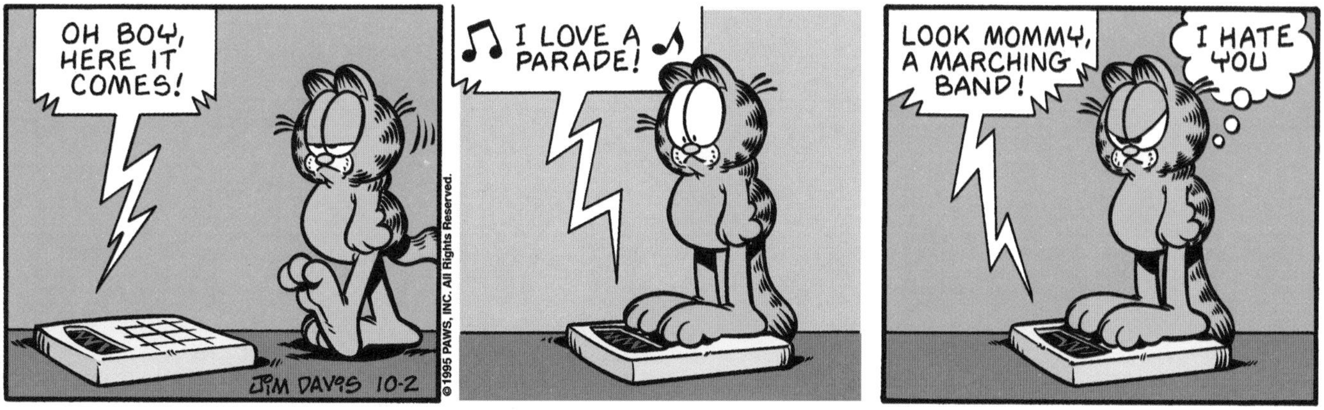
OH BOY, HERE IT COMES!
JIM DAVIS 10-2
© 1995 PAWS, INC. All Rights Reserved.
I LOVE A PARADE!
LOOK MOMMY, A MARCHING BAND!
I HATE YOU

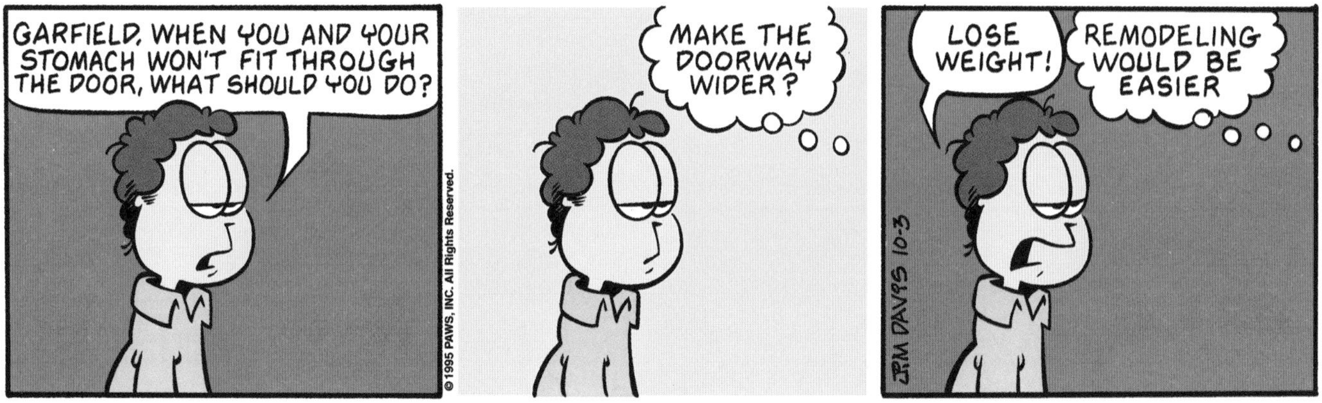
GARFIELD, WHEN YOU AND YOUR STOMACH WON'T FIT THROUGH THE DOOR, WHAT SHOULD YOU DO?
© 1995 PAWS, INC. All Rights Reserved.
MAKE THE DOORWAY WIDER?
LOSE WEIGHT!
REMODELING WOULD BE EASIER
JIM DAVIS 10-3

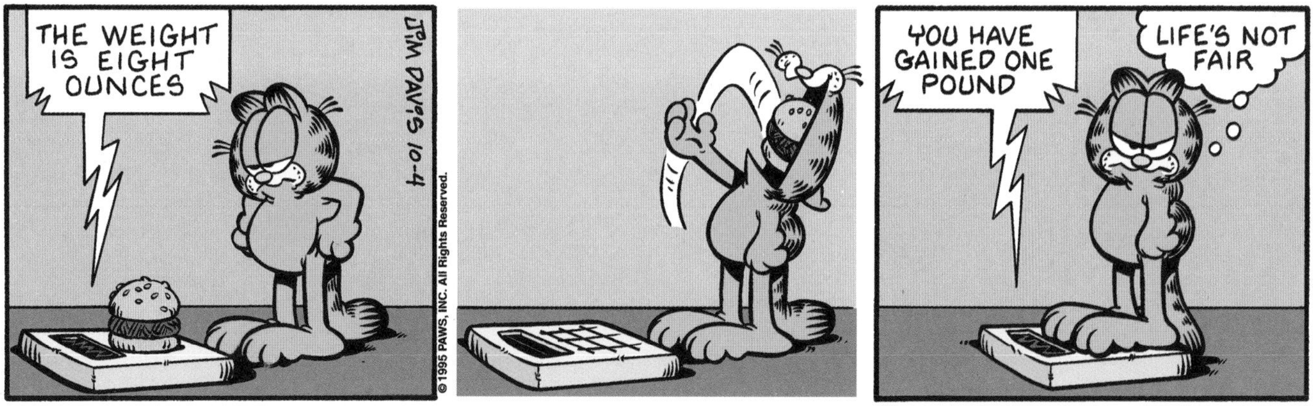
THE WEIGHT IS EIGHT OUNCES
JIM DAVIS 10-4
© 1995 PAWS, INC. All Rights Reserved.
YOU HAVE GAINED ONE POUND
LIFE'S NOT FAIR

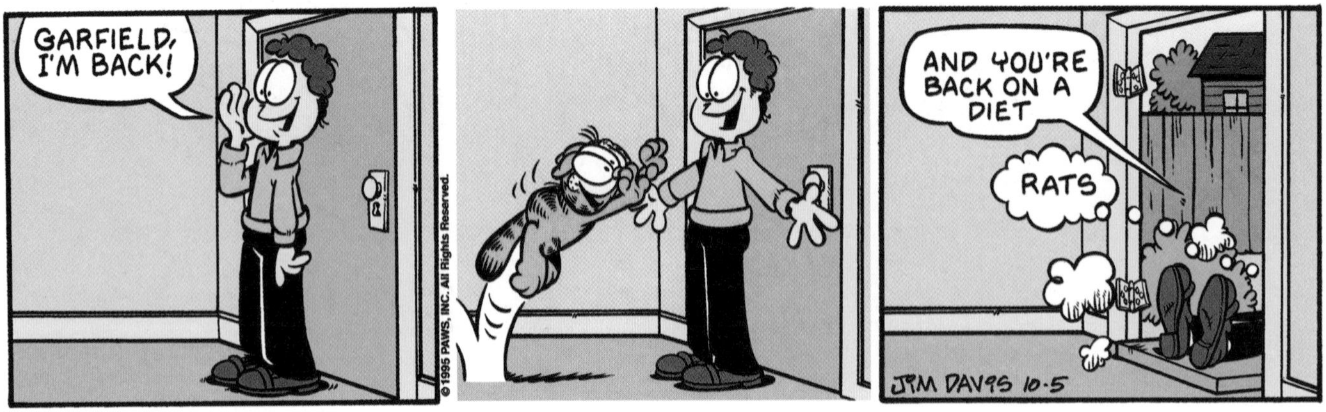
GARFIELD, I'M BACK!
©1995 PAWS, INC. All Rights Reserved.
AND YOU'RE BACK ON A DIET
RATS
JIM DAVIS 10-5

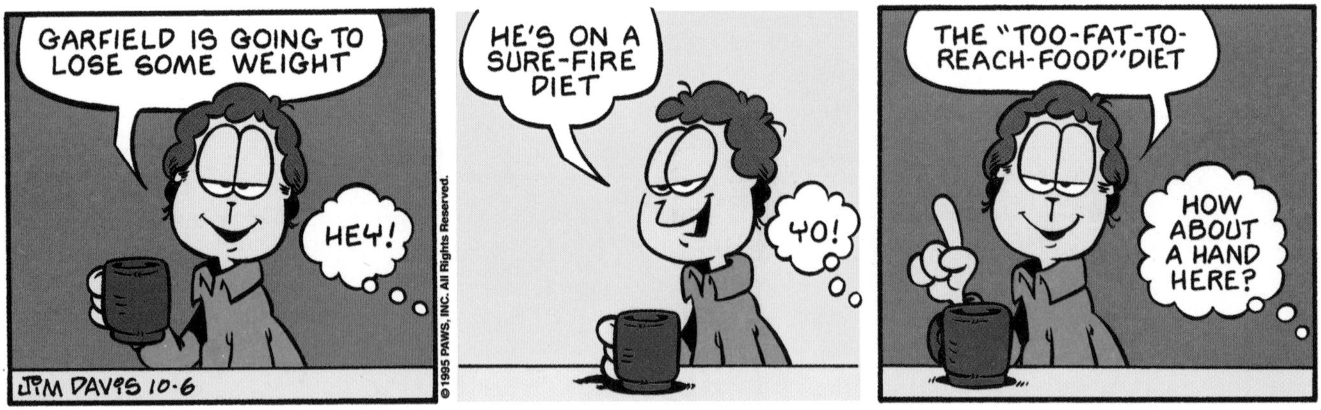
GARFIELD IS GOING TO LOSE SOME WEIGHT
HEY!
JIM DAVIS 10-6
©1995 PAWS, INC. All Rights Reserved.
HE'S ON A SURE-FIRE DIET
YO!
THE "TOO-FAT-TO-REACH-FOOD" DIET
HOW ABOUT A HAND HERE?

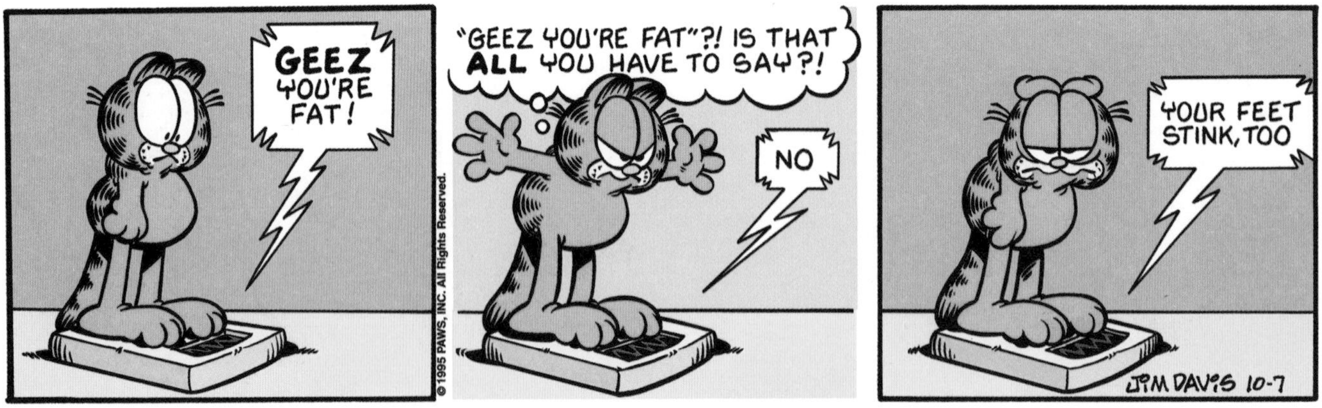
GEEZ YOU'RE FAT!
©1995 PAWS, INC. All Rights Reserved.
"GEEZ YOU'RE FAT"?! IS THAT ALL YOU HAVE TO SAY?!
NO
YOUR FEET STINK, TOO
JIM DAVIS 10-7

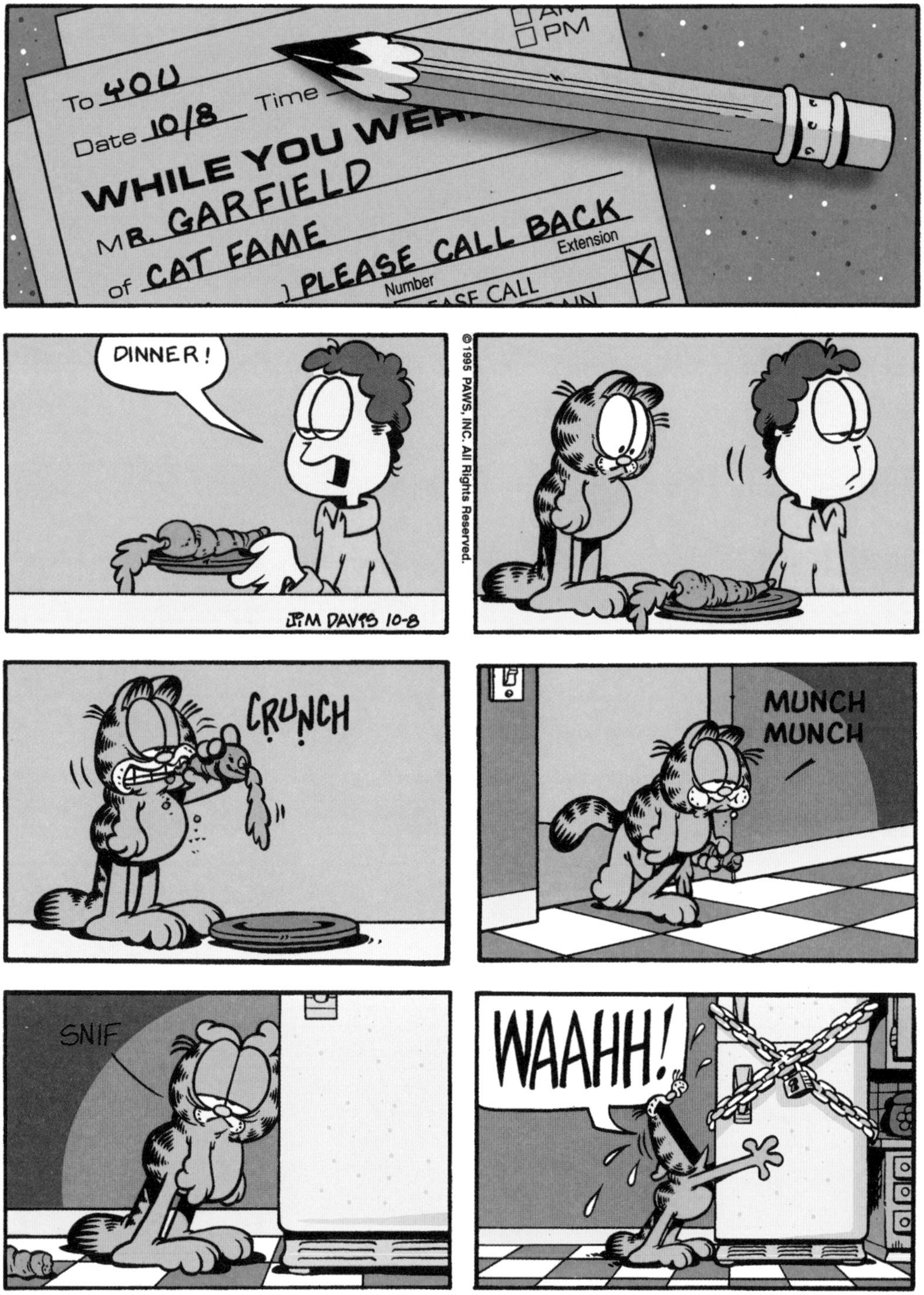
To YOU
Date 10/8 Time
AM
PM
WHILE YOU WER
MR. GARFIELD
of CAT FAME
PLEASE CALL BACK
Number
Extension
DINNER!
JIM DAVIS 10-8
CRUNCH
MUNCH MUNCH
SNIF
WAAHH!

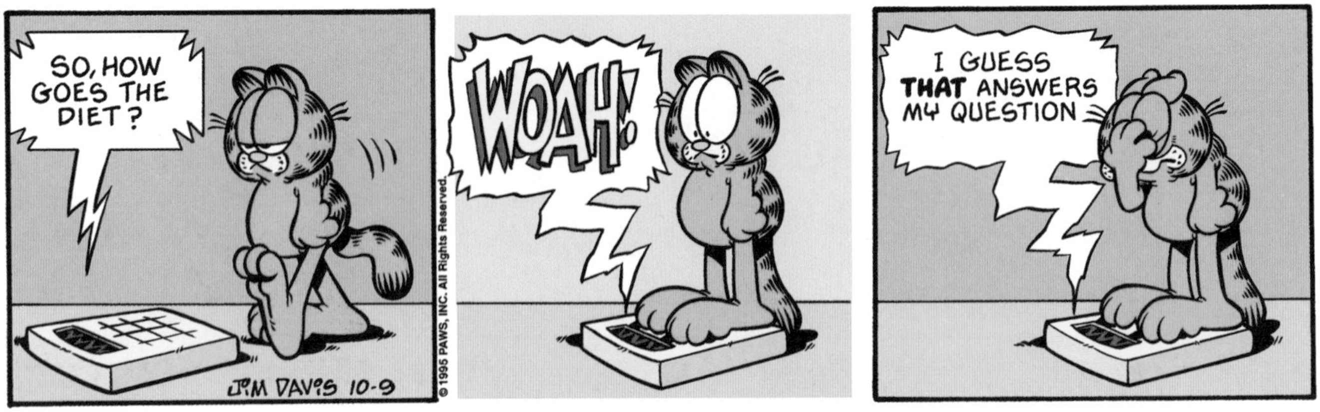
SO, HOW GOES THE DIET?
JIM DAVIS 10-9
© 1995 PAWS, INC. All Rights Reserved.
WOAH!
I GUESS **THAT** ANSWERS MY QUESTION

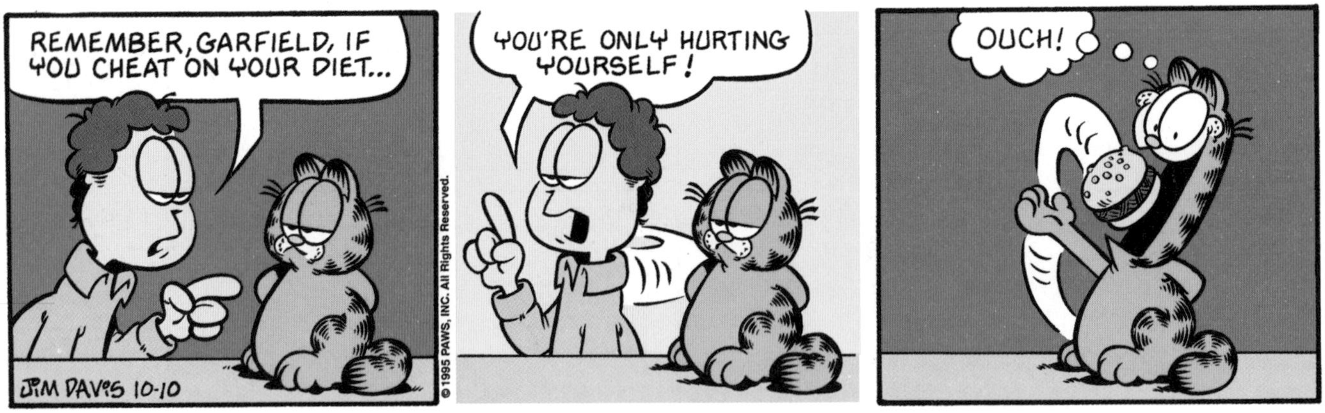
REMEMBER, GARFIELD, IF YOU CHEAT ON YOUR DIET...
JIM DAVIS 10-10
© 1995 PAWS, INC. All Rights Reserved.
YOU'RE ONLY HURTING YOURSELF!
OUCH!

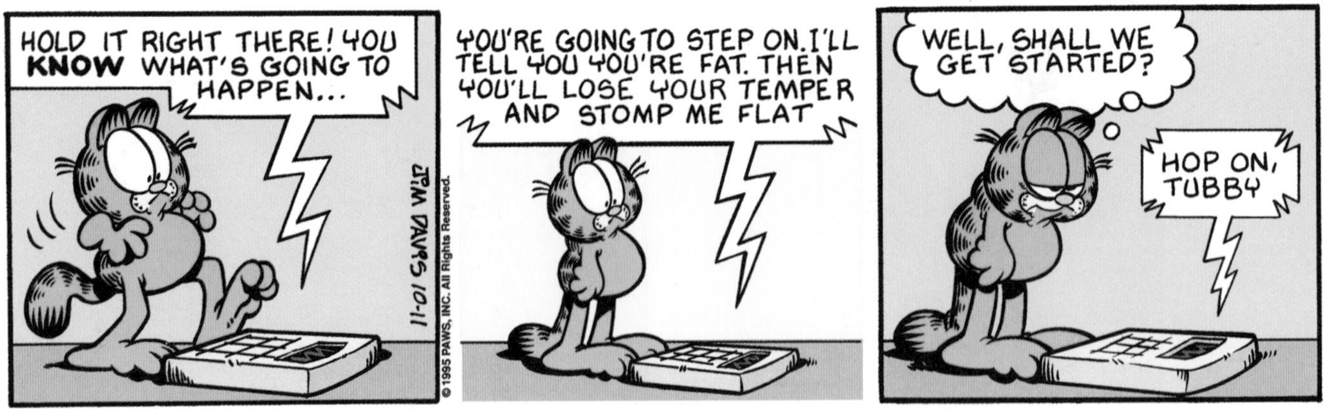
HOLD IT RIGHT THERE! YOU **KNOW** WHAT'S GOING TO HAPPEN...
JIM DAVIS 10-11
© 1995 PAWS, INC. All Rights Reserved.
YOU'RE GOING TO STEP ON. I'LL TELL YOU YOU'RE FAT. THEN YOU'LL LOSE YOUR TEMPER AND STOMP ME FLAT
WELL, SHALL WE GET STARTED?
HOP ON, TUBBY

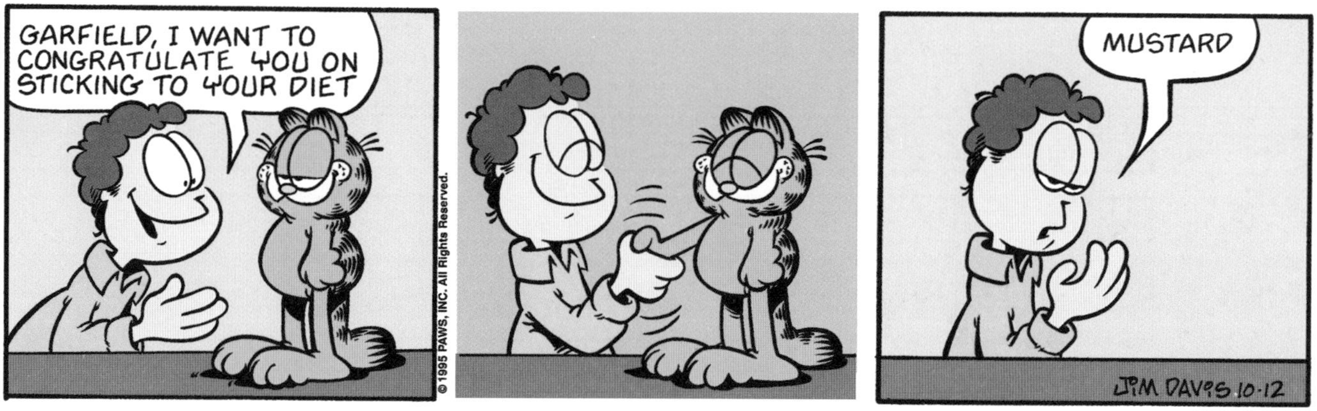
GARFIELD, I WANT TO CONGRATULATE YOU ON STICKING TO YOUR DIET
© 1995 PAWS, INC. All Rights Reserved.
MUSTARD
JIM DAVIS 10-12

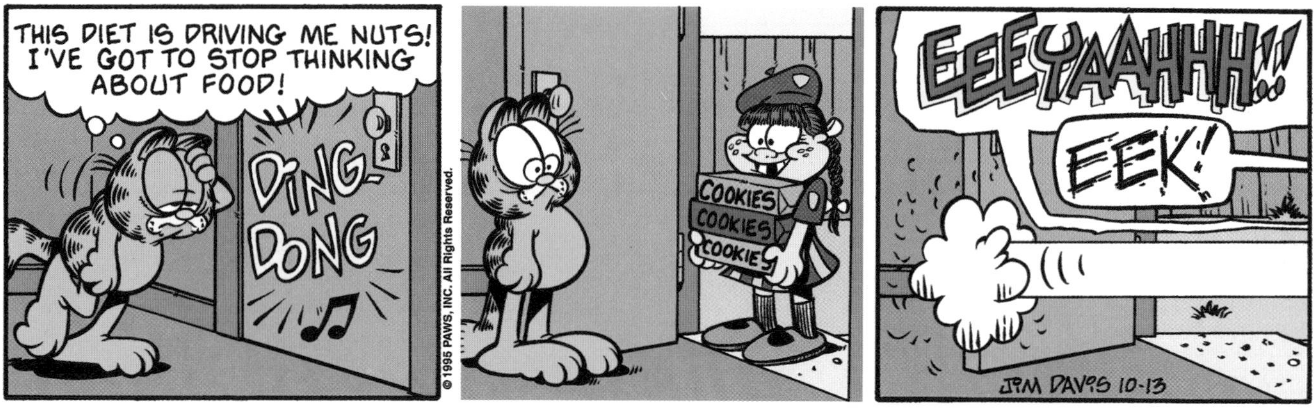
THIS DIET IS DRIVING ME NUTS! I'VE GOT TO STOP THINKING ABOUT FOOD!
DING-DONG
© 1995 PAWS, INC. All Rights Reserved.
COOKIES
COOKIES
COOKIES
EEEYAAHHH!!
EEK!
JIM DAVIS 10-13

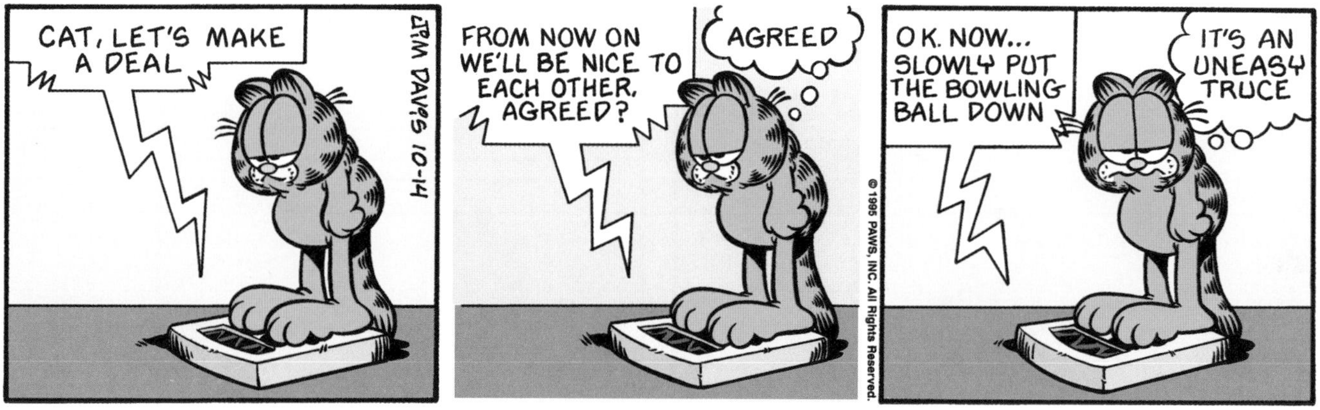
CAT, LET'S MAKE A DEAL
JIM DAVIS 10-14
FROM NOW ON WE'LL BE NICE TO EACH OTHER, AGREED?
AGREED
© 1995 PAWS, INC. All Rights Reserved.
O.K. NOW... SLOWLY PUT THE BOWLING BALL DOWN
IT'S AN UNEASY TRUCE

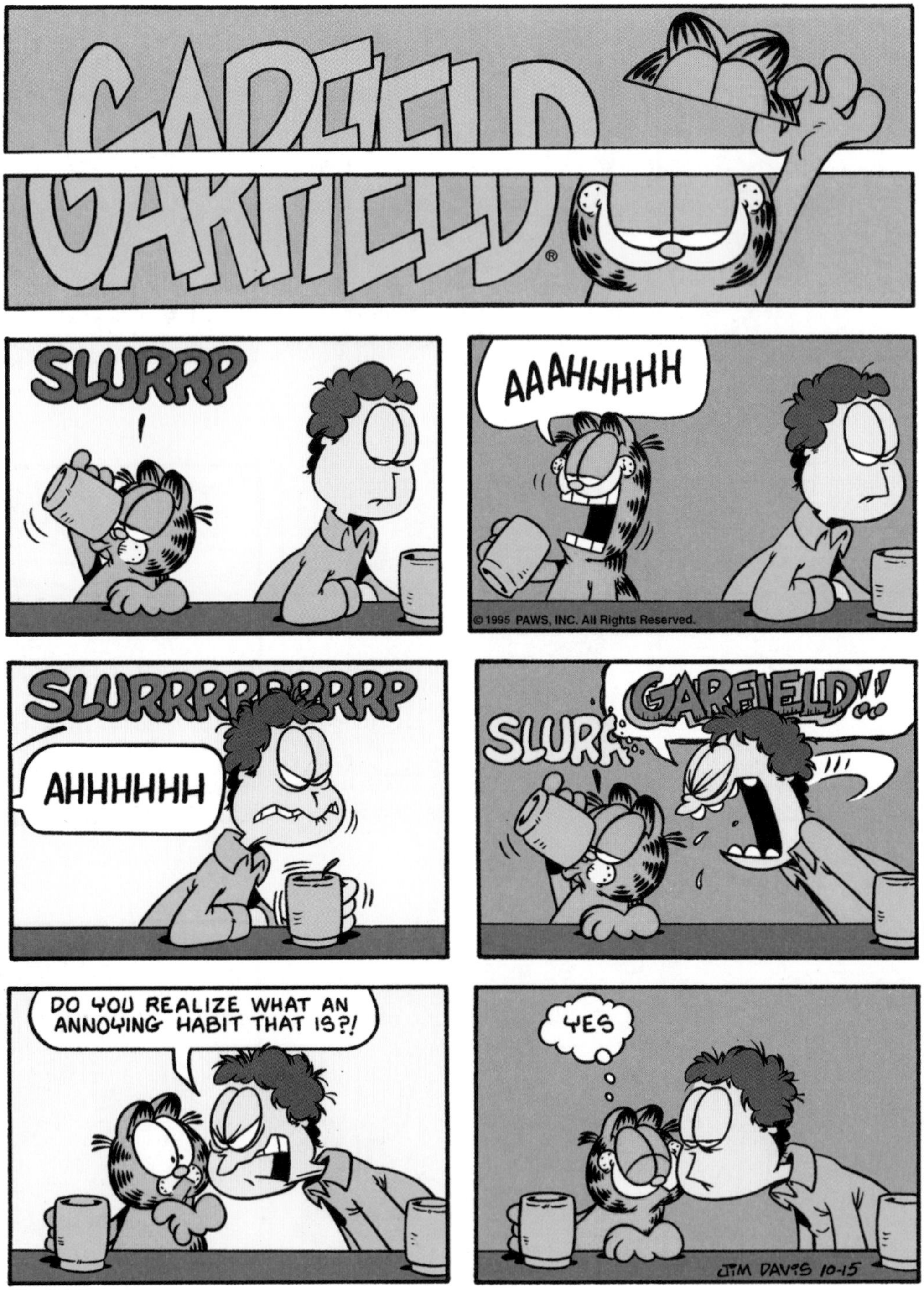
GARFIELD
GARFIELD®
SLURRP
AAAHHHHH
© 1995 PAWS, INC. All Rights Reserved.
SLURRRRRRRRP
AHHHHHH
SLURR
GARFIELD!!
DO YOU REALIZE WHAT AN ANNOYING HABIT THAT IS?!
YES
JIM DAVIS 10-15

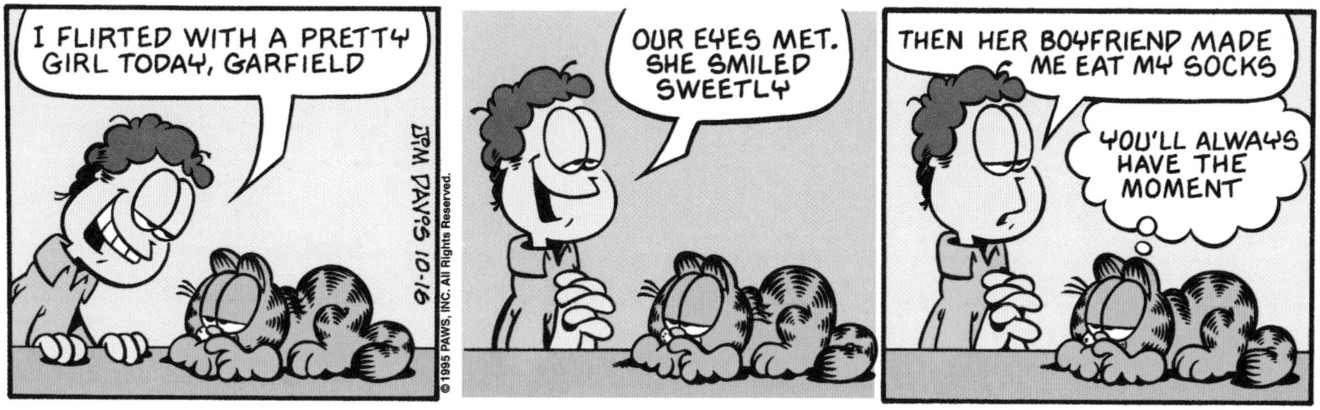
I FLIRTED WITH A PRETTY GIRL TODAY, GARFIELD
JIM DAVIS 10-16
© 1995 PAWS, INC. All Rights Reserved.
OUR EYES MET. SHE SMILED SWEETLY
THEN HER BOYFRIEND MADE ME EAT MY SOCKS
YOU'LL ALWAYS HAVE THE MOMENT

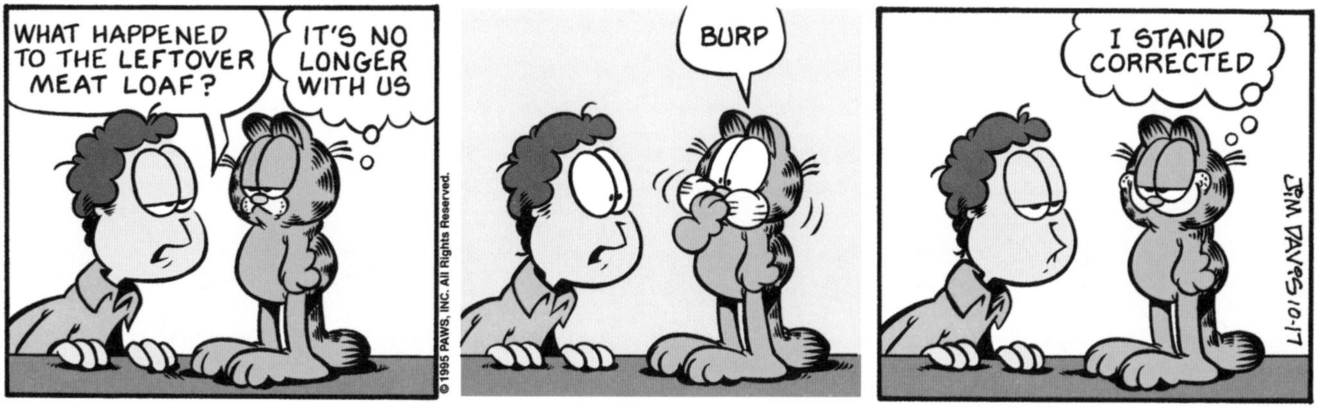
WHAT HAPPENED TO THE LEFTOVER MEAT LOAF?
IT'S NO LONGER WITH US
© 1995 PAWS, INC. All Rights Reserved.
BURP
I STAND CORRECTED
JIM DAVIS 10-17

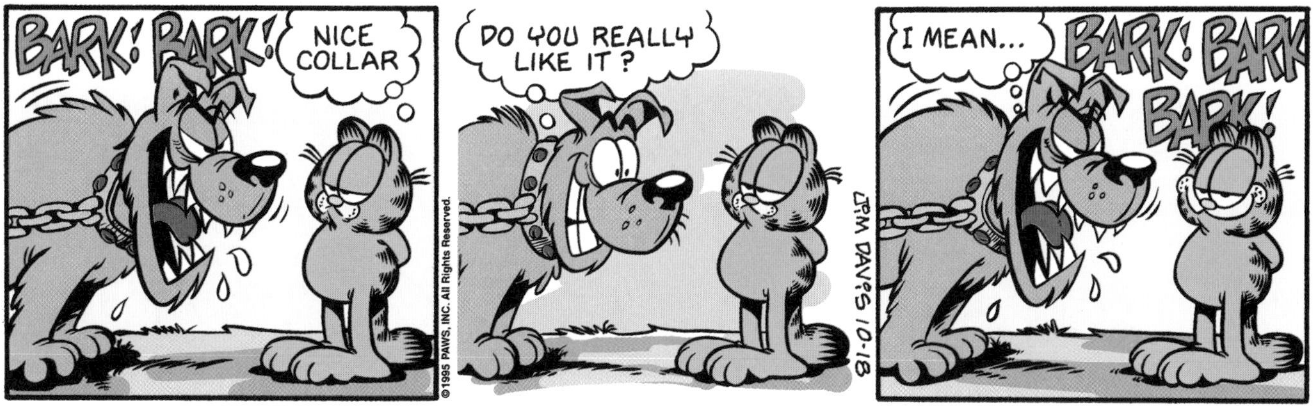
BARK! BARK!
NICE COLLAR
© 1995 PAWS, INC. All Rights Reserved.
DO YOU REALLY LIKE IT?
JIM DAVIS 10-18
I MEAN...
BARK! BARK
BARK!

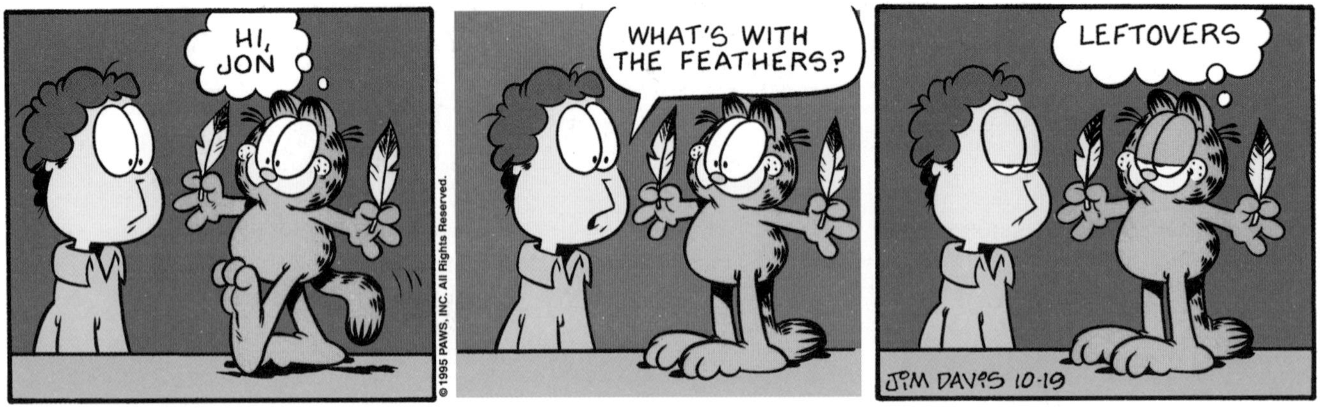
HI, JON
WHAT'S WITH THE FEATHERS?
LEFTOVERS
© 1995 PAWS, INC. All Rights Reserved.
JIM DAVIS 10-19

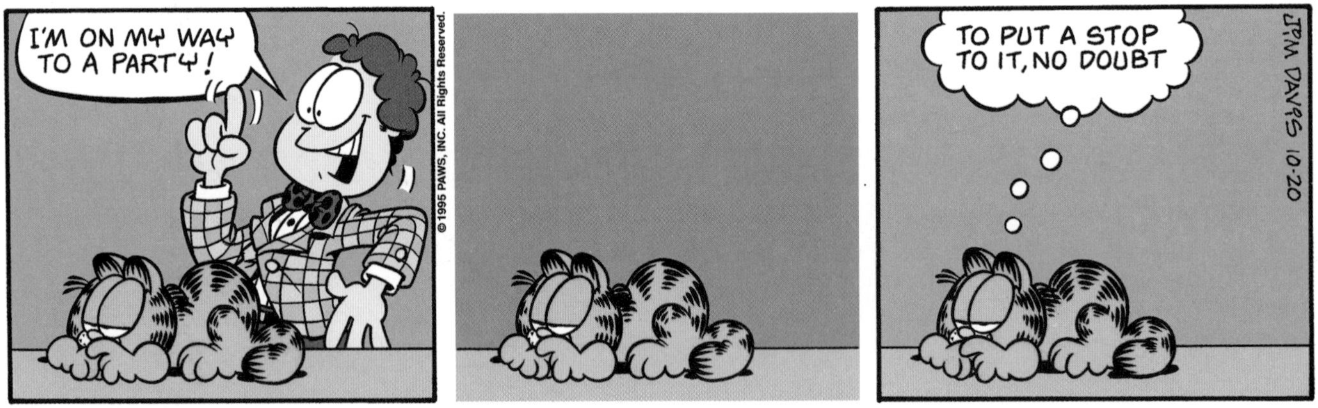
I'M ON MY WAY TO A PARTY!
TO PUT A STOP TO IT, NO DOUBT
© 1995 PAWS, INC. All Rights Reserved.
JIM DAVIS 10-20

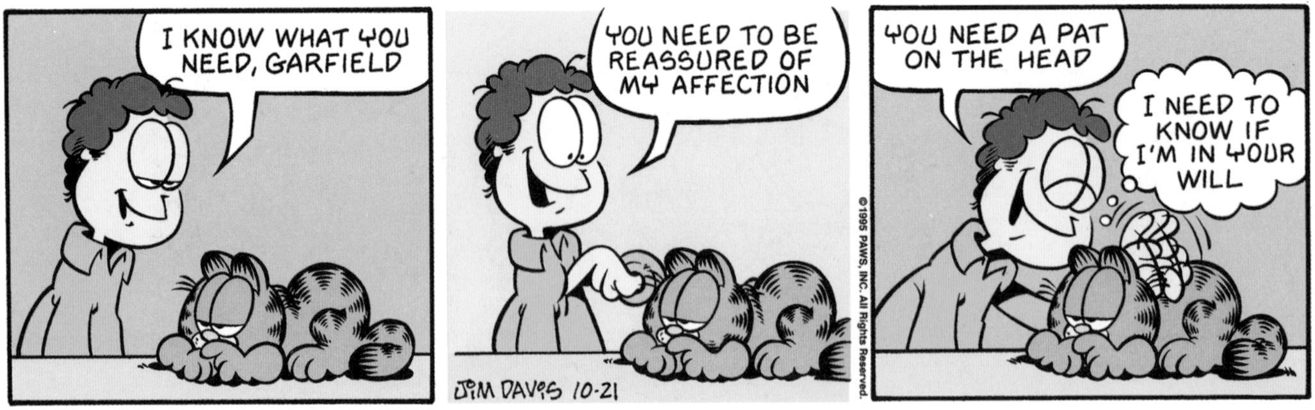
I KNOW WHAT YOU NEED, GARFIELD
YOU NEED TO BE REASSURED OF MY AFFECTION
YOU NEED A PAT ON THE HEAD
I NEED TO KNOW IF I'M IN YOUR WILL
© 1995 PAWS, INC. All Rights Reserved.
JIM DAVIS 10-21

GARFIELD
RIGHT THIS WAY, MY DEAR
WHAT'S GOING ON HERE?! YOU PROMISED ME A SHOW AND DINNER!
YES, I DID
HERE'S YOUR SHOW
TAPPITY TAPPITY TAPPITY TAPPITY
SPLUT!
©1995 PAWS, INC. All Rights Reserved.
AND HERE'S YOUR DINNER
JIM DAVIS 10-22

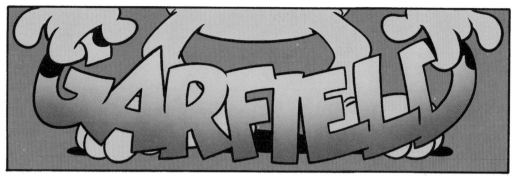

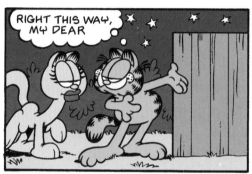

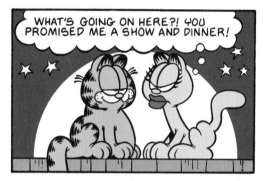

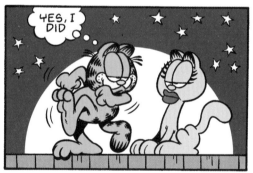

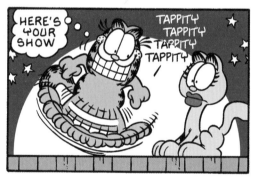

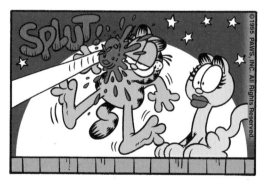

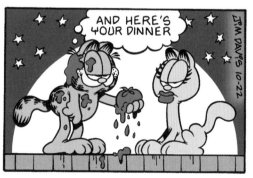

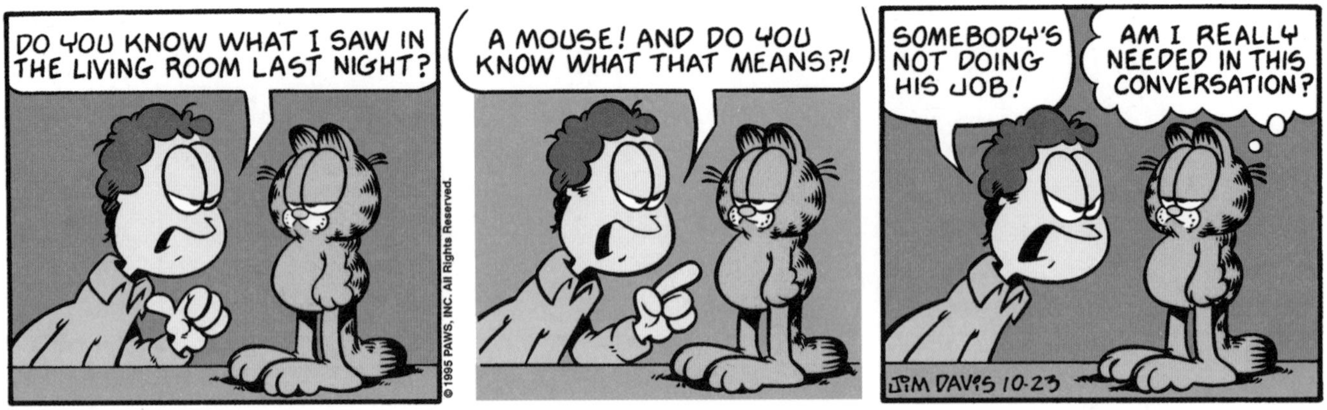
DO YOU KNOW WHAT I SAW IN THE LIVING ROOM LAST NIGHT?
A MOUSE! AND DO YOU KNOW WHAT THAT MEANS?!
SOMEBODY'S NOT DOING HIS JOB!
AM I REALLY NEEDED IN THIS CONVERSATION?
© 1995 PAWS, INC. All Rights Reserved.
JIM DAVIS 10-23

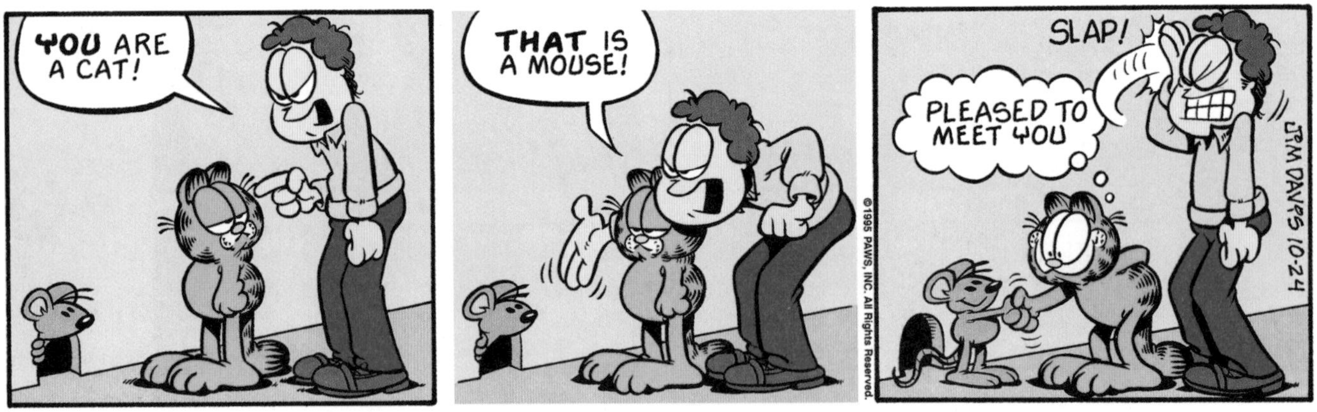
YOU ARE A CAT!
THAT IS A MOUSE!
PLEASED TO MEET YOU
SLAP!
© 1995 PAWS, INC. All Rights Reserved.
JIM DAVIS 10-24

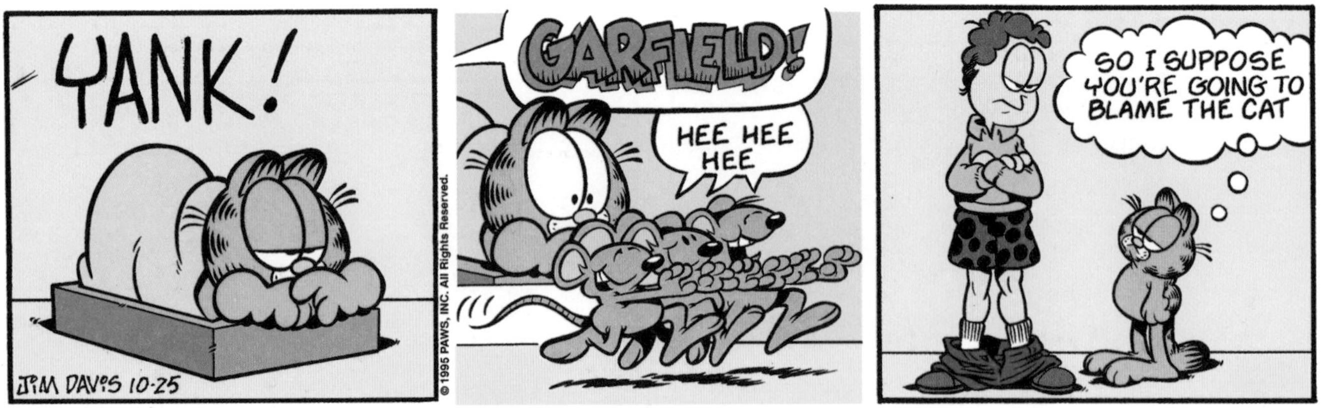
YANK!
GARFIELD!
HEE HEE HEE
SO I SUPPOSE YOU'RE GOING TO BLAME THE CAT
© 1995 PAWS, INC. All Rights Reserved.
JIM DAVIS 10-25

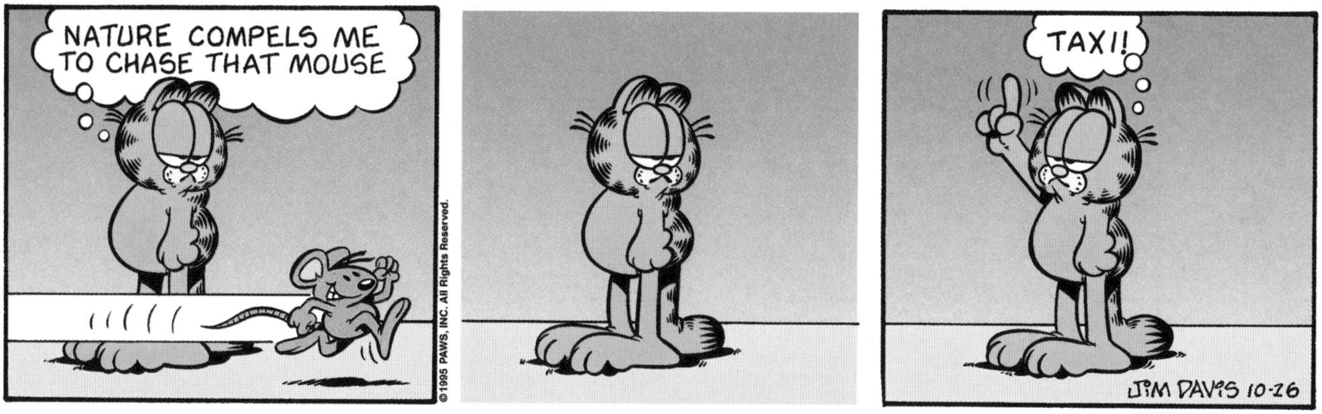

NATURE COMPELS ME TO CHASE THAT MOUSE
TAXI!
JIM DAVIS 10-26
© 1995 PAWS, INC. All Rights Reserved.

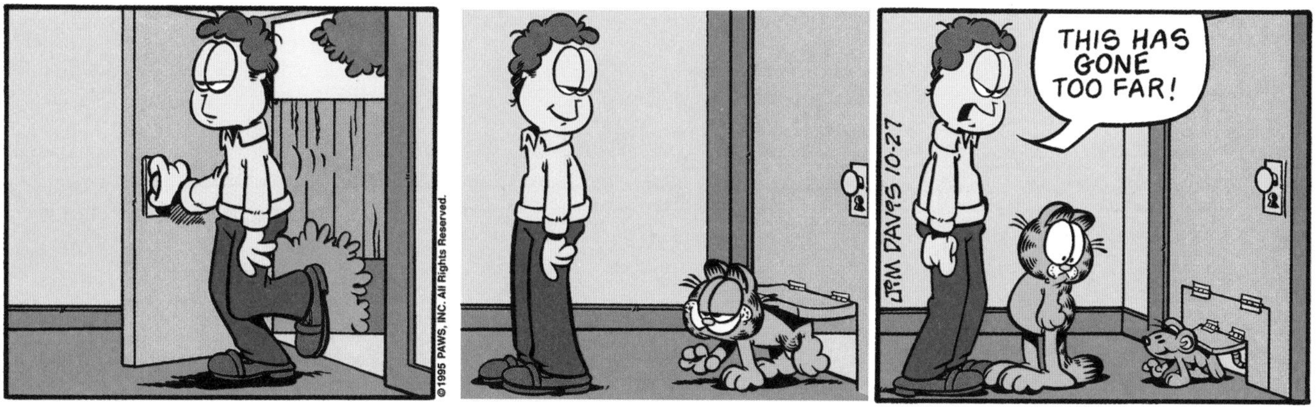

THIS HAS GONE TOO FAR!
JIM DAVIS 10-27
© 1995 PAWS, INC. All Rights Reserved.

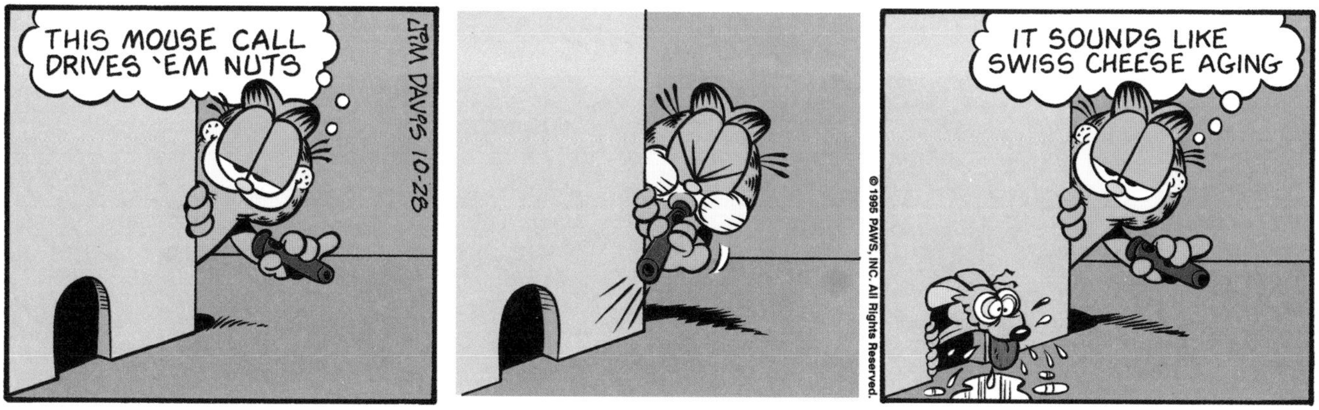

THIS MOUSE CALL DRIVES 'EM NUTS
IT SOUNDS LIKE SWISS CHEESE AGING
JIM DAVIS 10-28
© 1995 PAWS, INC. All Rights Reserved.

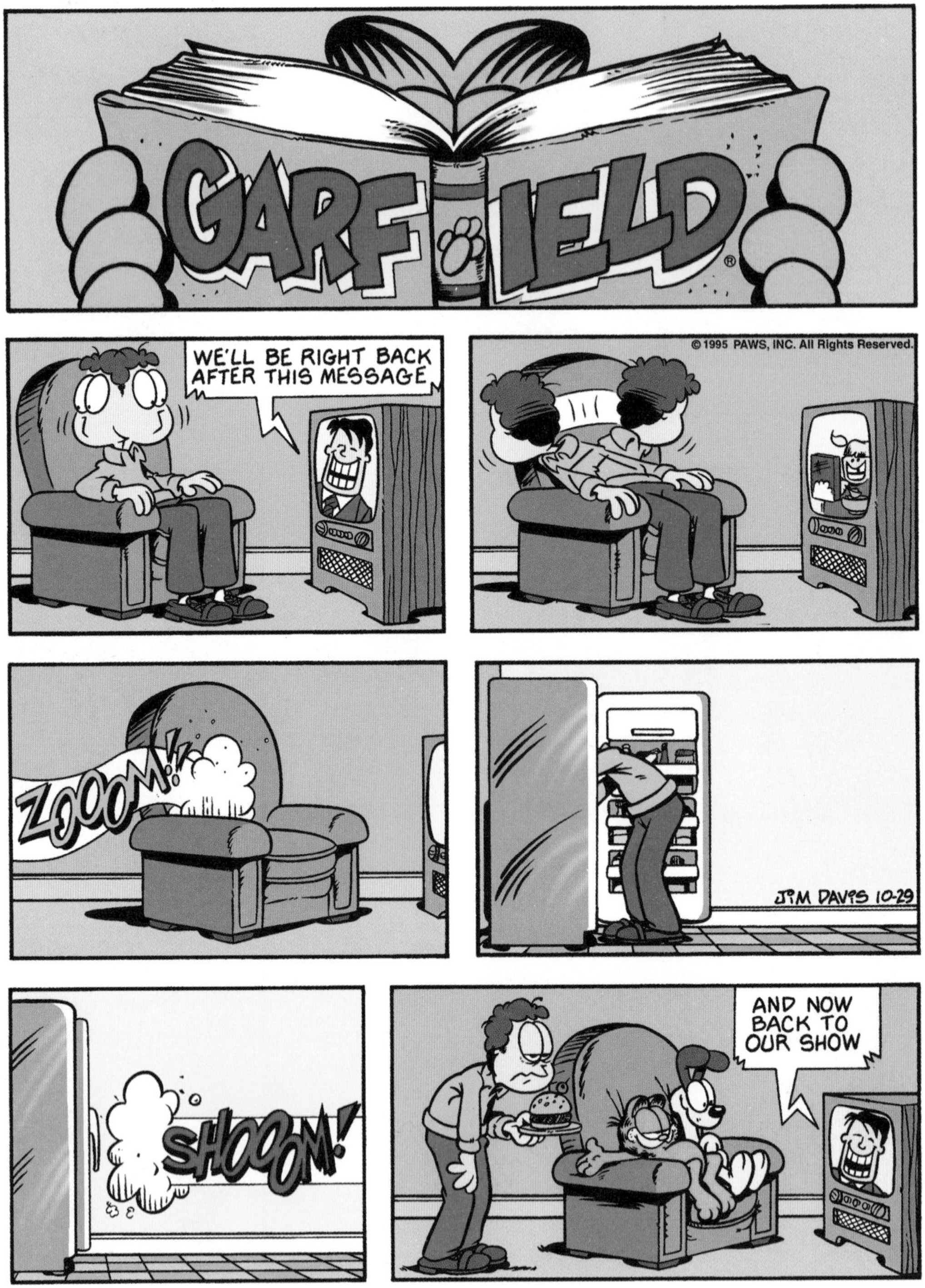
GARFIELD
© 1995 PAWS, INC. All Rights Reserved.
WE'LL BE RIGHT BACK AFTER THIS MESSAGE
ZOOOM!!
JIM DAVIS 10-29
SHOOOM!
AND NOW BACK TO OUR SHOW

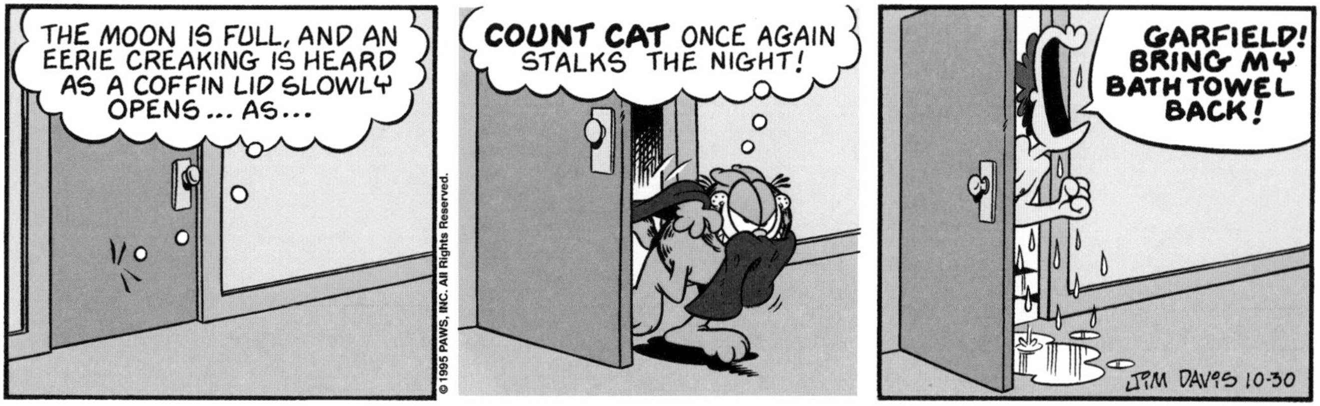
THE MOON IS FULL, AND AN EERIE CREAKING IS HEARD AS A COFFIN LID SLOWLY OPENS... AS...
© 1995 PAWS, INC. All Rights Reserved.
COUNT CAT ONCE AGAIN STALKS THE NIGHT!
GARFIELD! BRING MY BATH TOWEL BACK!
JIM DAVIS 10-30

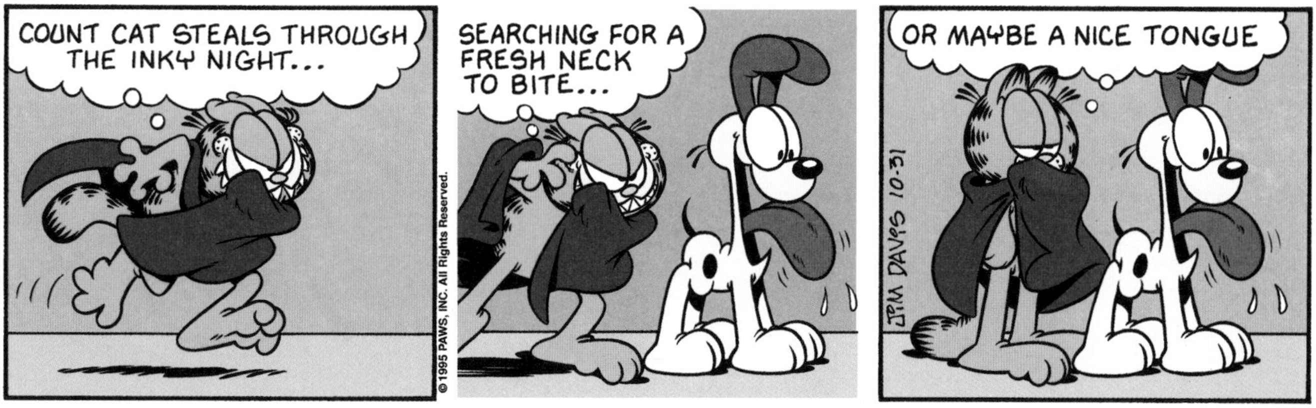
COUNT CAT STEALS THROUGH THE INKY NIGHT...
© 1995 PAWS, INC. All Rights Reserved.
SEARCHING FOR A FRESH NECK TO BITE...
JIM DAVIS 10-31
OR MAYBE A NICE TONGUE

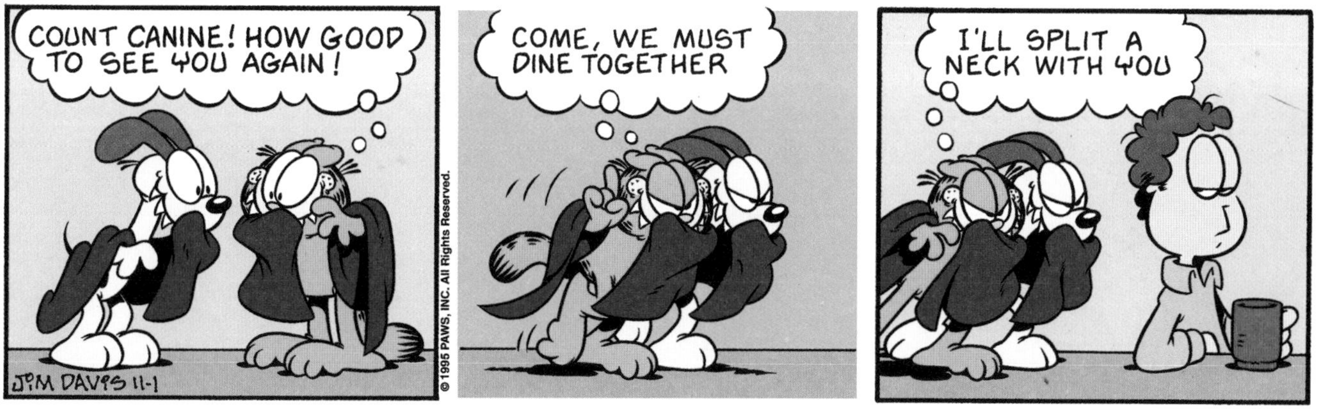
COUNT CANINE! HOW GOOD TO SEE YOU AGAIN!
JIM DAVIS 11-1
© 1995 PAWS, INC. All Rights Reserved.
COME, WE MUST DINE TOGETHER
I'LL SPLIT A NECK WITH YOU

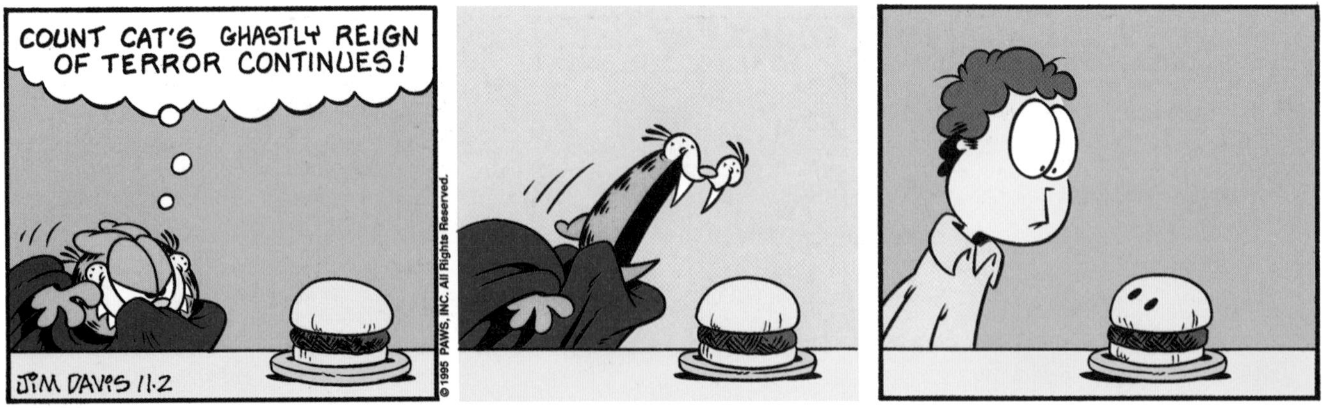
COUNT CAT'S GHASTLY REIGN OF TERROR CONTINUES!
JIM DAVIS 11·2
© 1995 PAWS, INC. All Rights Reserved.

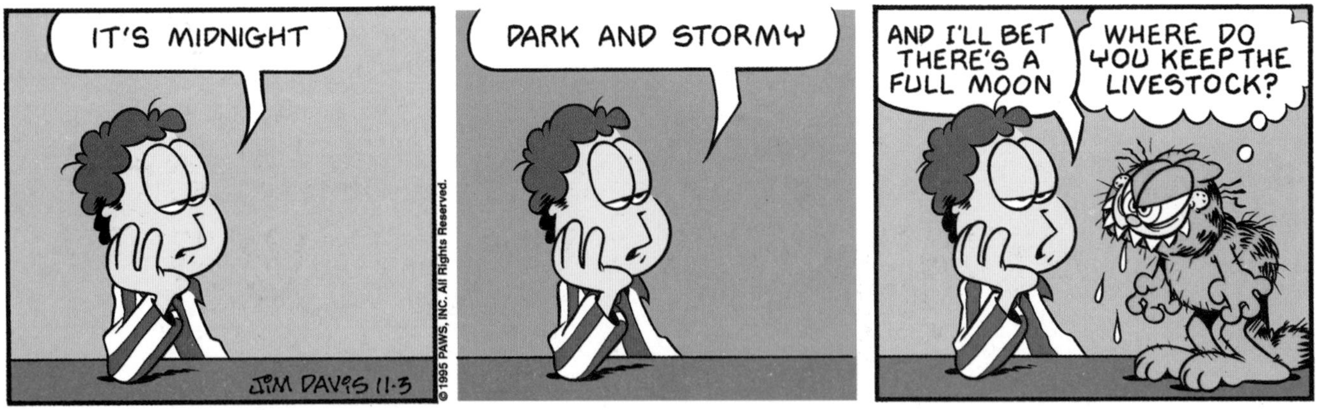
IT'S MIDNIGHT
JIM DAVIS 11·3
© 1995 PAWS, INC. All Rights Reserved.
DARK AND STORMY
AND I'LL BET THERE'S A FULL MOON
WHERE DO YOU KEEP THE LIVESTOCK?

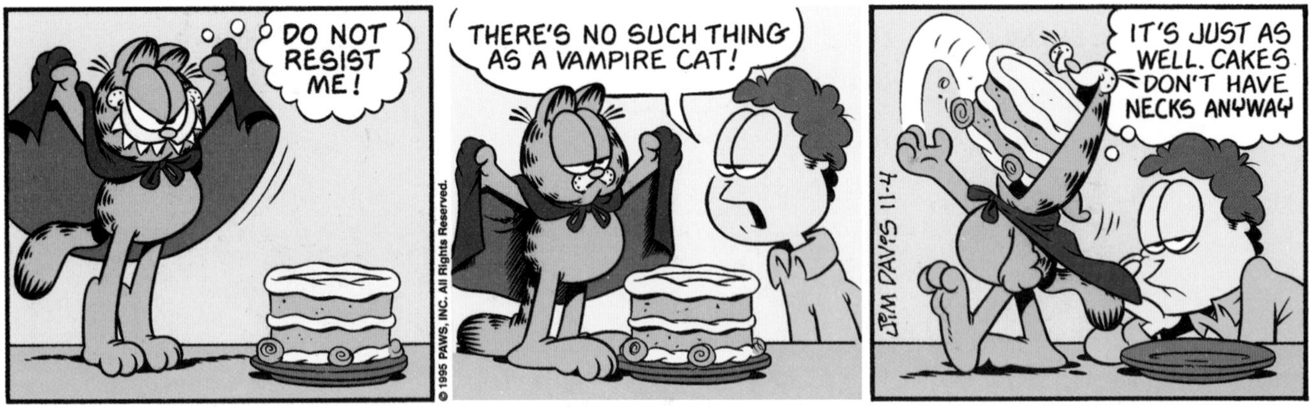
DO NOT RESIST ME!
© 1995 PAWS, INC. All Rights Reserved.
THERE'S NO SUCH THING AS A VAMPIRE CAT!
JIM DAVIS 11·4
IT'S JUST AS WELL. CAKES DON'T HAVE NECKS ANYWAY

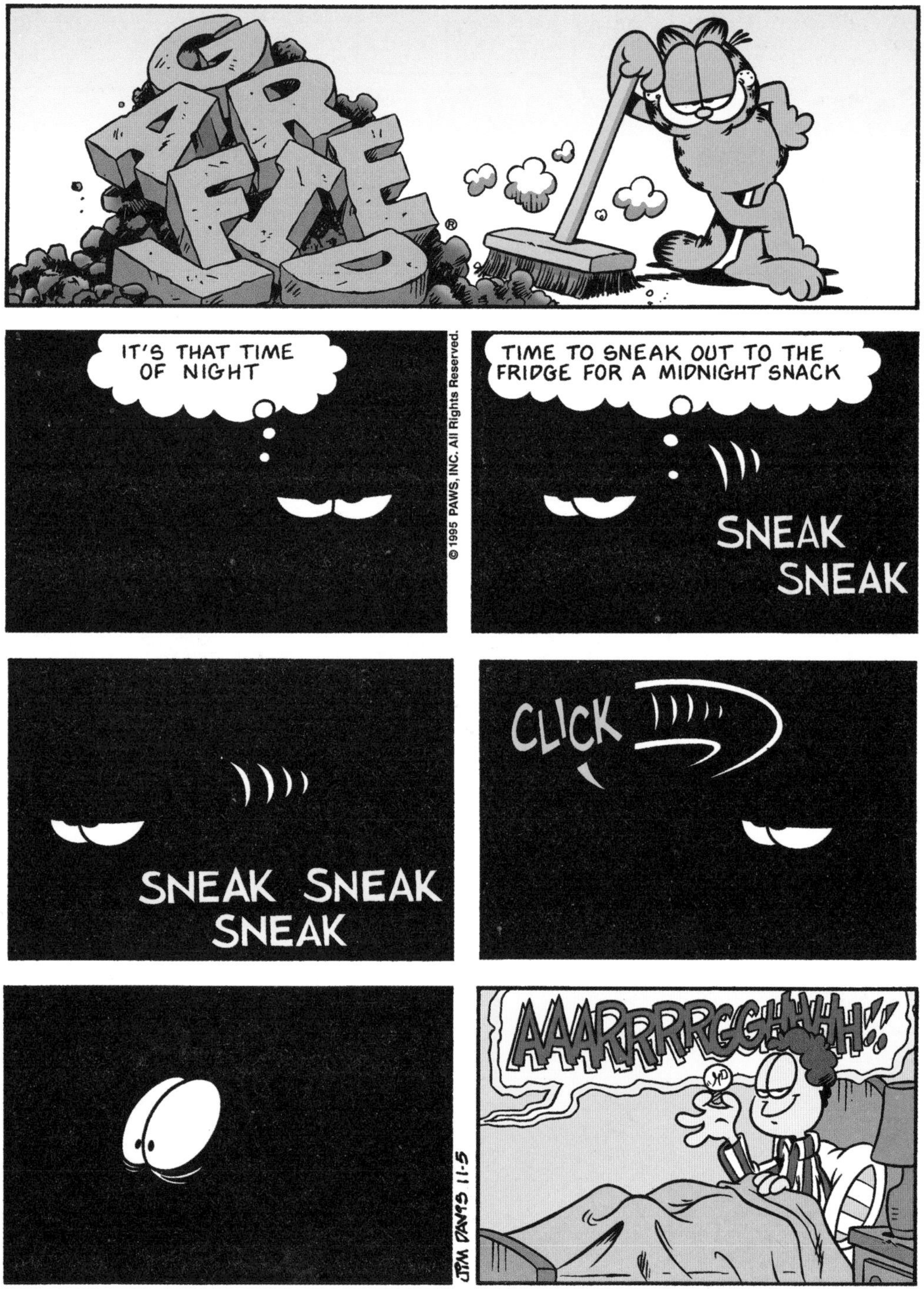
IT'S THAT TIME OF NIGHT
© 1995 PAWS, INC. All Rights Reserved.
TIME TO SNEAK OUT TO THE FRIDGE FOR A MIDNIGHT SNACK
SNEAK SNEAK
SNEAK SNEAK SNEAK
CLICK
JIM DAVIS 11-5
AAARRRRRGGHHHH!!

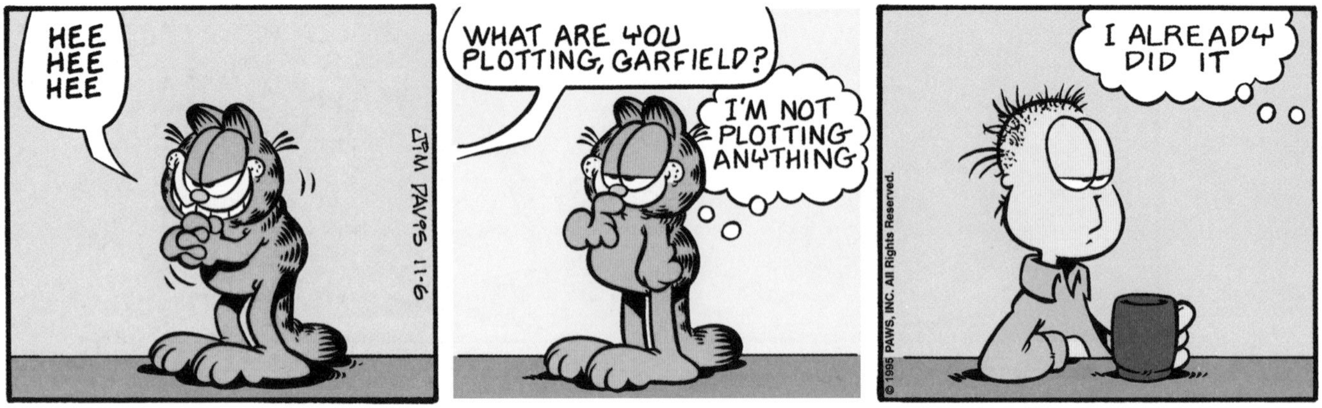
HEE HEE HEE
JIM DAVIS 11-6
WHAT ARE YOU PLOTTING, GARFIELD?
I'M NOT PLOTTING ANYTHING
© 1995 PAWS, INC. All Rights Reserved.
I ALREADY DID IT

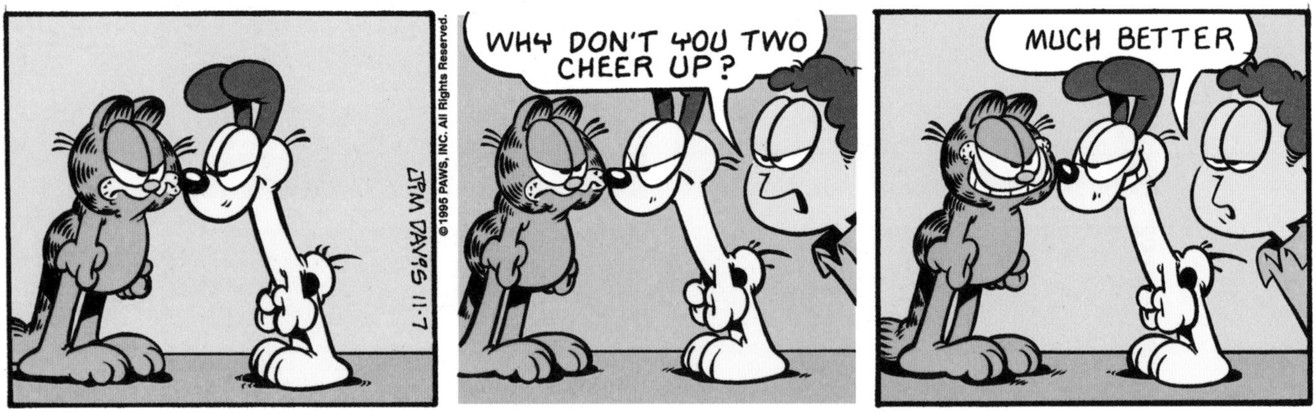
JIM DAVIS 11-7
© 1995 PAWS, INC. All Rights Reserved.
WHY DON'T YOU TWO CHEER UP?
MUCH BETTER

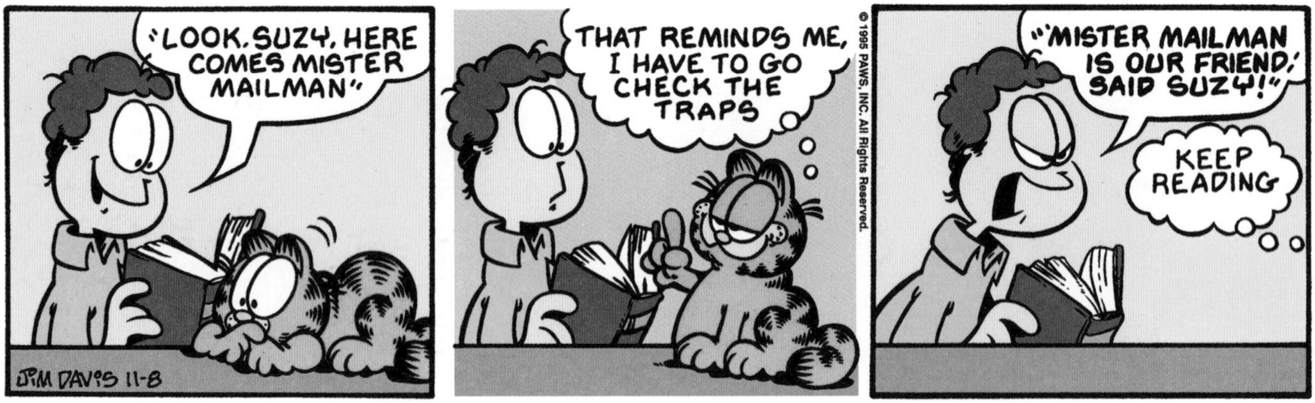
"LOOK, SUZY, HERE COMES MISTER MAILMAN"
JIM DAVIS 11-8
THAT REMINDS ME, I HAVE TO GO CHECK THE TRAPS
© 1995 PAWS, INC. All Rights Reserved.
"'MISTER MAILMAN IS OUR FRIEND,' SAID SUZY!"
KEEP READING

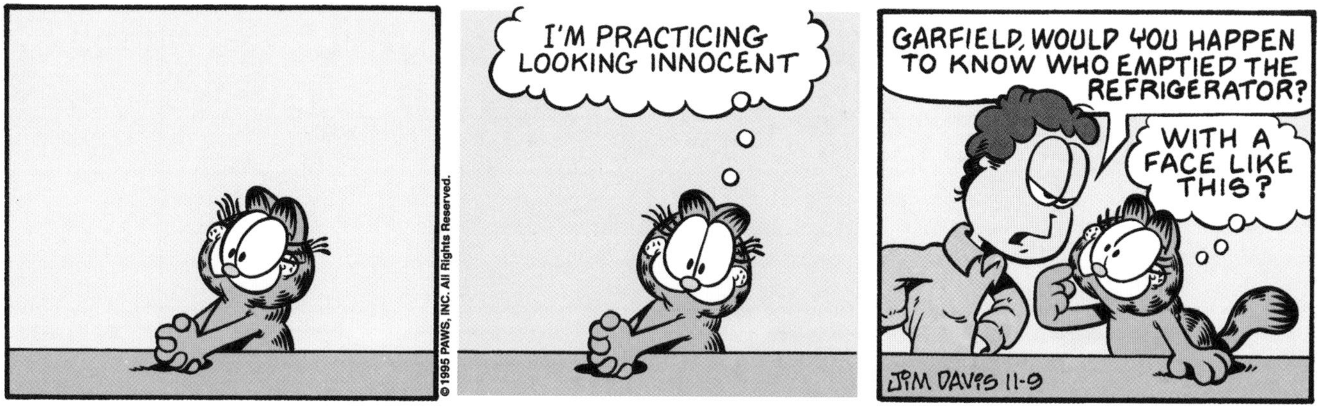
I'M PRACTICING LOOKING INNOCENT
GARFIELD, WOULD YOU HAPPEN TO KNOW WHO EMPTIED THE REFRIGERATOR?
WITH A FACE LIKE THIS?
© 1995 PAWS, INC. All Rights Reserved.
JIM DAVIS 11-9

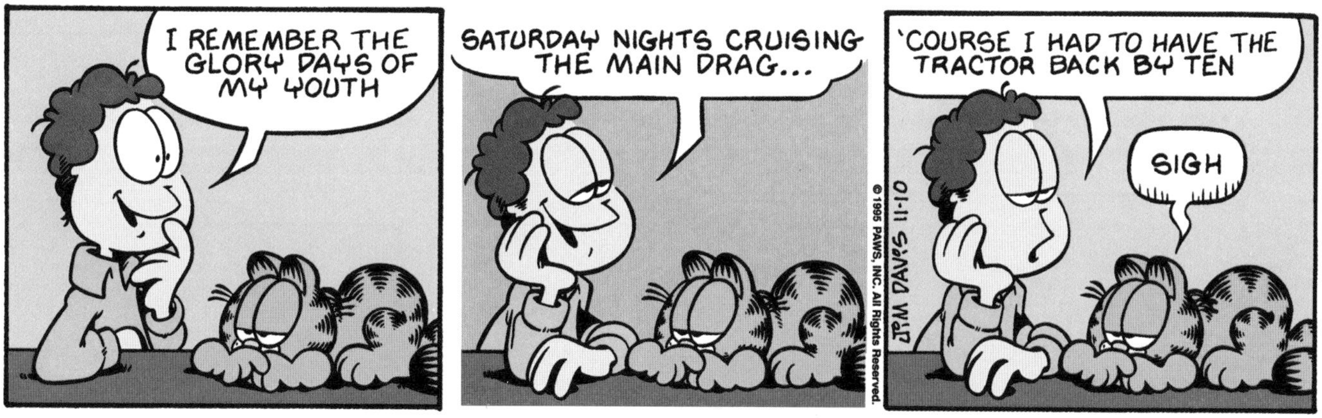
I REMEMBER THE GLORY DAYS OF MY YOUTH
SATURDAY NIGHTS CRUISING THE MAIN DRAG...
'COURSE I HAD TO HAVE THE TRACTOR BACK BY TEN
SIGH
© 1995 PAWS, INC. All Rights Reserved.
JIM DAVIS 11-10

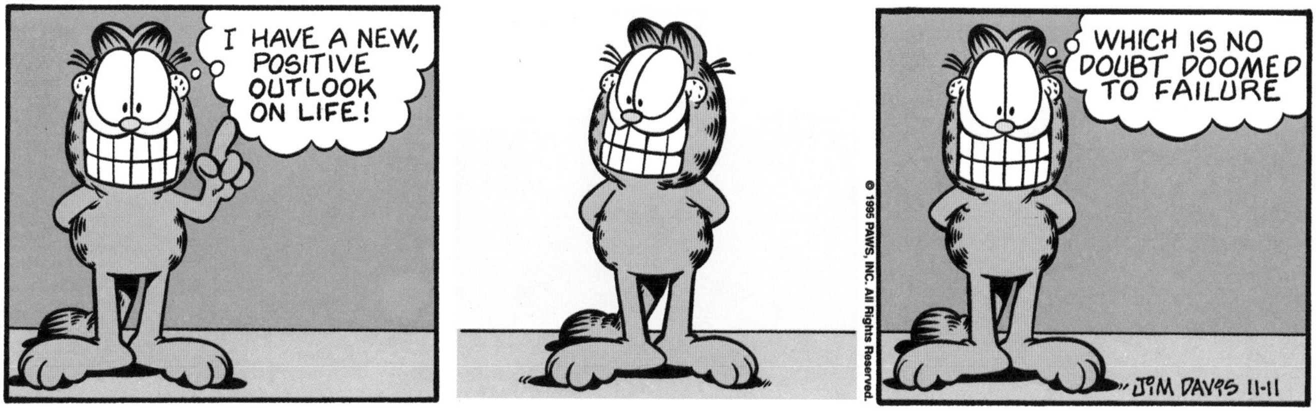
I HAVE A NEW, POSITIVE OUTLOOK ON LIFE!
WHICH IS NO DOUBT DOOMED TO FAILURE
© 1995 PAWS, INC. All Rights Reserved.
JIM DAVIS 11-11

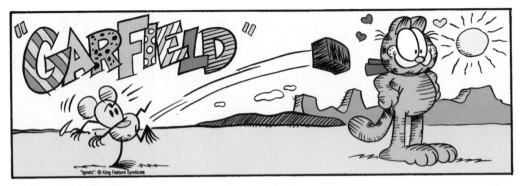

"GARFIELD"
"Ignatz": © King Feature Syndicate
GARFIELD
S P
JPM DAVIS 11-12
GARFIELD
© 1995 PAWS, INC. All Rights Reserved.

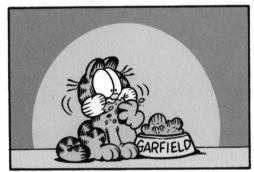

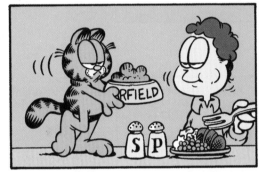

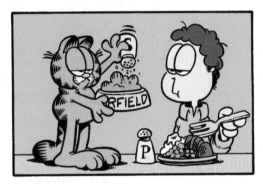

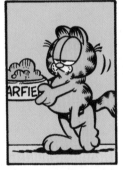

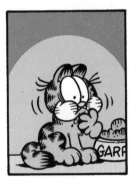

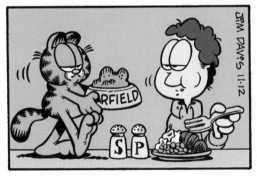

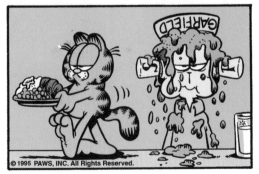

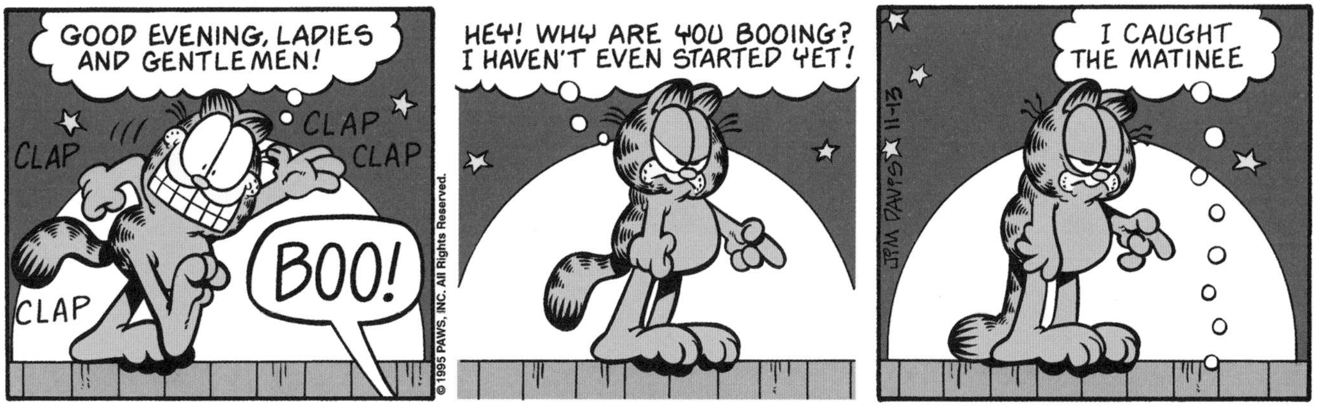
GOOD EVENING, LADIES AND GENTLEMEN!
CLAP
CLAP
CLAP
CLAP
BOO!
HEY! WHY ARE YOU BOOING? I HAVEN'T EVEN STARTED YET!
JIM DAVIS 11-13
I CAUGHT THE MATINEE

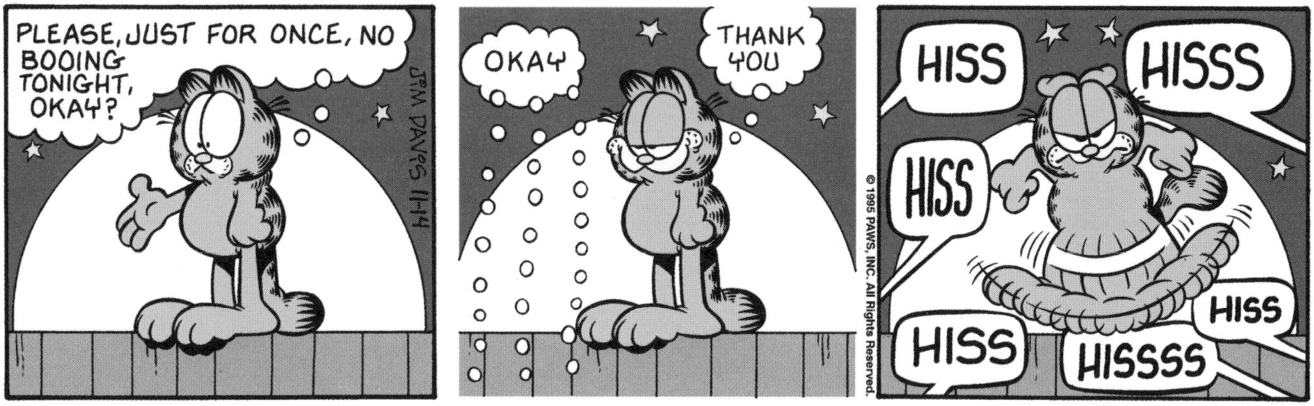
PLEASE, JUST FOR ONCE, NO BOOING TONIGHT, OKAY?
JIM DAVIS 11-14
OKAY
THANK YOU
HISS
HISSS
HISS
HISS
HISSSS
HISS

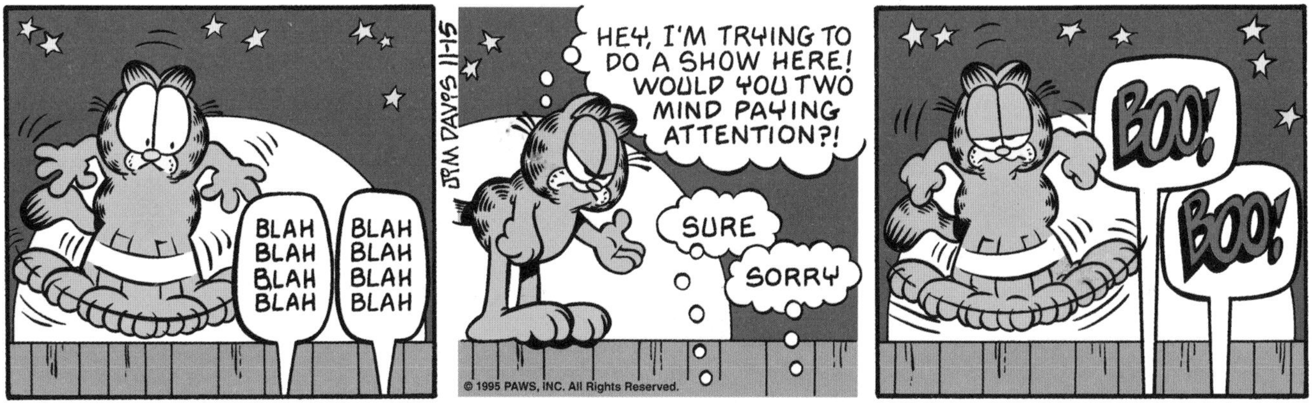
BLAH BLAH BLAH BLAH
BLAH BLAH BLAH BLAH
JIM DAVIS 11-15
HEY, I'M TRYING TO DO A SHOW HERE! WOULD YOU TWO MIND PAYING ATTENTION?!
SURE
SORRY
BOO!
BOO!

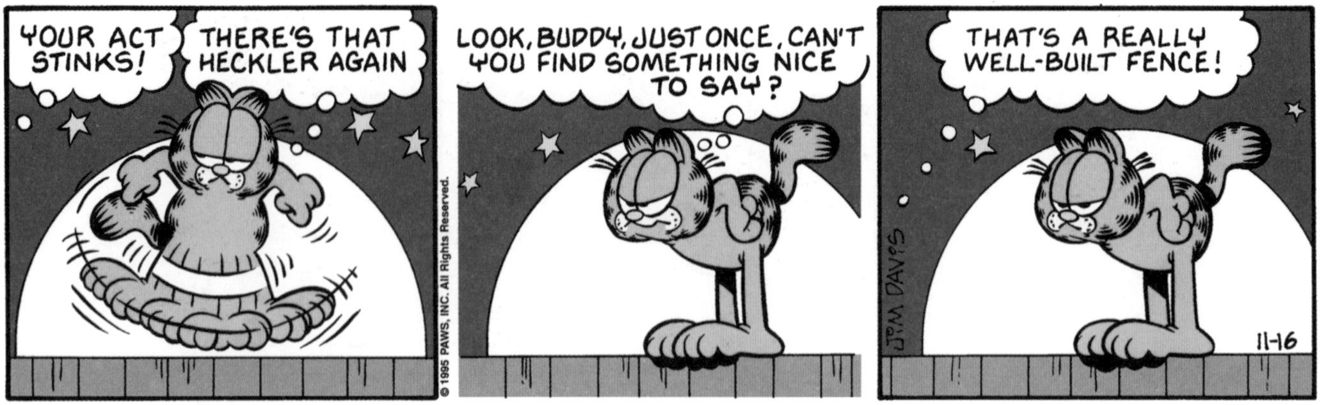
YOUR ACT STINKS!
THERE'S THAT HECKLER AGAIN
© 1995 PAWS, INC. All Rights Reserved.
LOOK, BUDDY, JUST ONCE, CAN'T YOU FIND SOMETHING NICE TO SAY?
THAT'S A REALLY WELL-BUILT FENCE!
JIM DAVIS
11-16

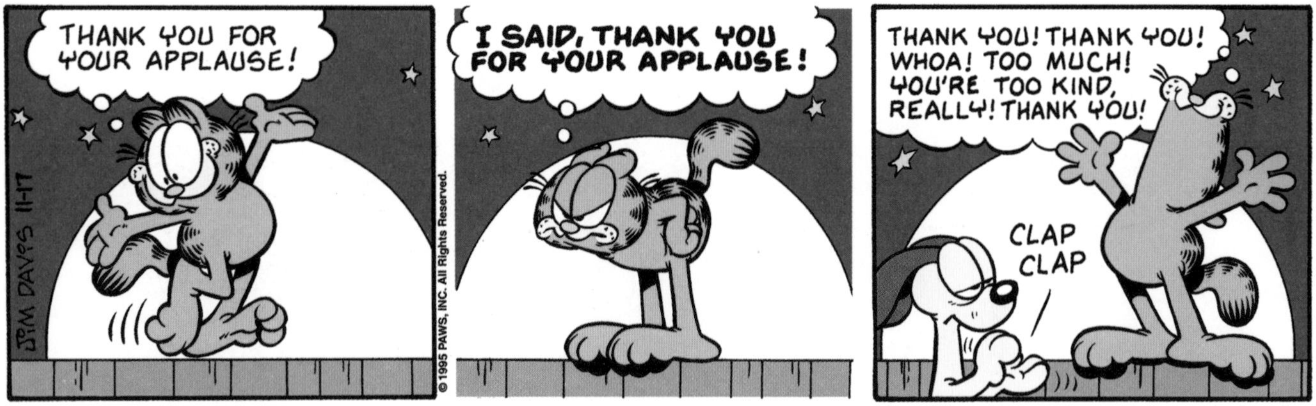
THANK YOU FOR YOUR APPLAUSE!
JIM DAVIS 11-17
© 1995 PAWS, INC. All Rights Reserved.
I SAID, THANK YOU FOR YOUR APPLAUSE!
THANK YOU! THANK YOU! WHOA! TOO MUCH! YOU'RE TOO KIND, REALLY! THANK YOU!
CLAP CLAP

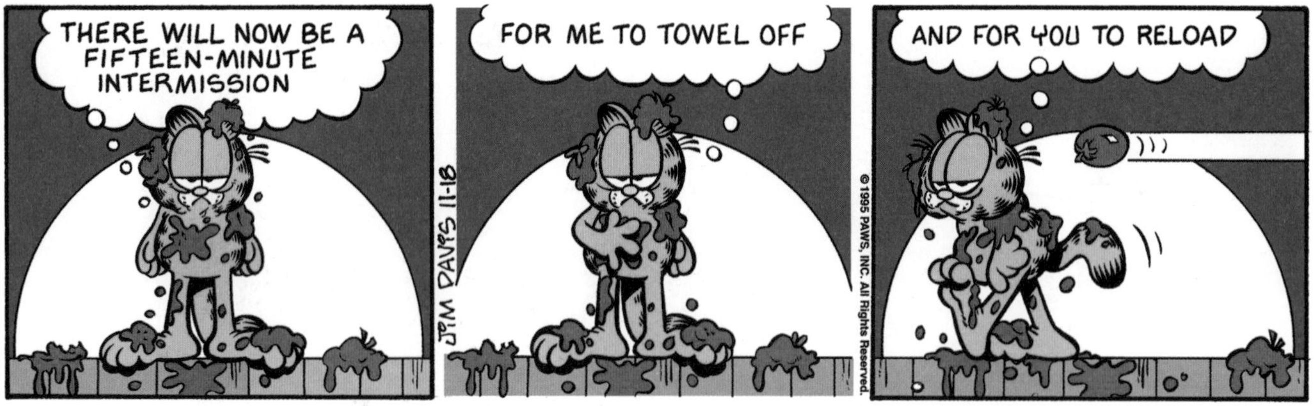
THERE WILL NOW BE A FIFTEEN-MINUTE INTERMISSION
JIM DAVIS 11-18
FOR ME TO TOWEL OFF
© 1995 PAWS, INC. All Rights Reserved.
AND FOR YOU TO RELOAD

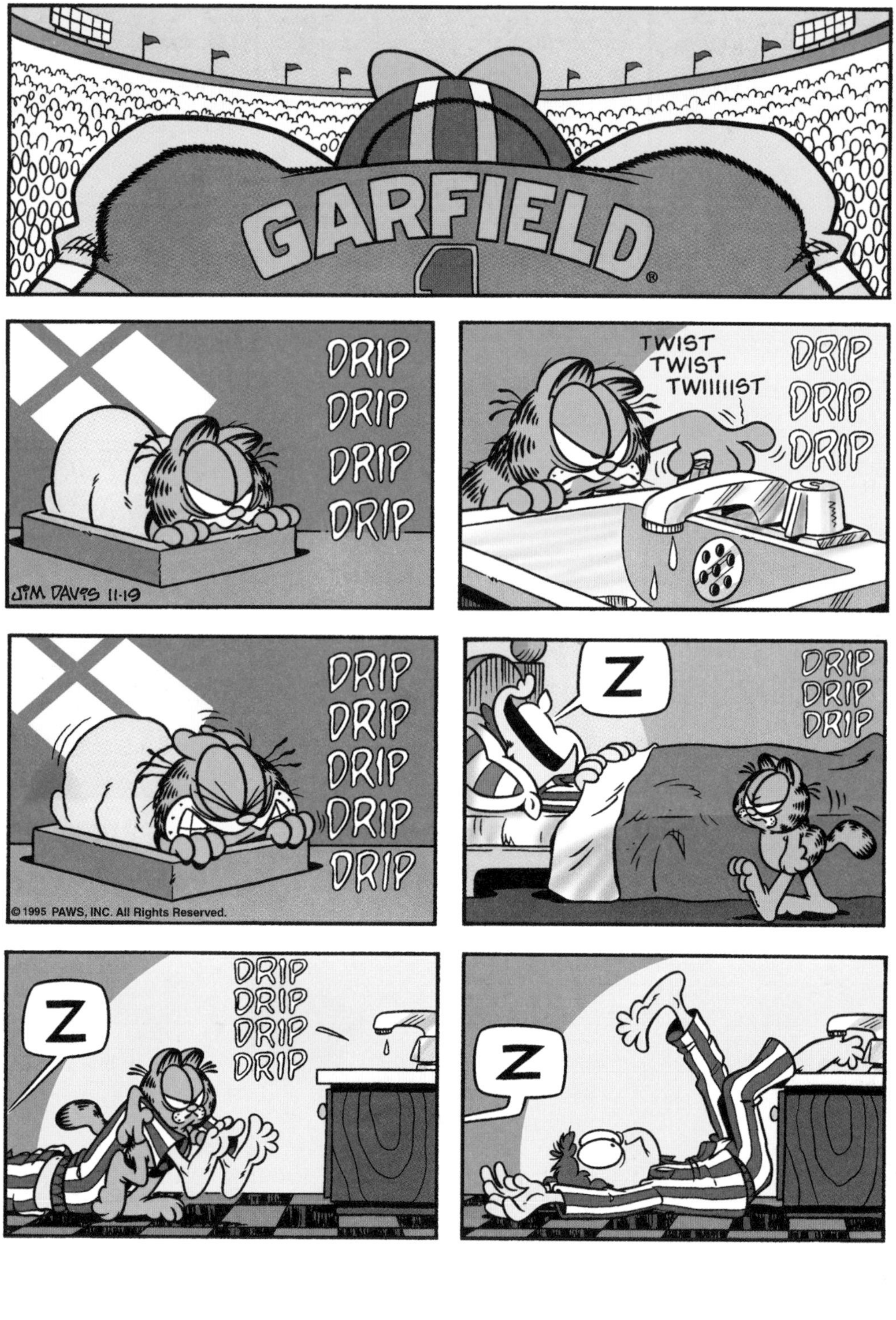
GARFIELD
DRIP DRIP DRIP DRIP
JIM DAVIS 11-19
TWIST TWIST TWIIIIIST
DRIP DRIP DRIP
DRIP DRIP DRIP DRIP DRIP
© 1995 PAWS, INC. All Rights Reserved.
Z
DRIP DRIP DRIP
Z
DRIP DRIP DRIP DRIP
Z

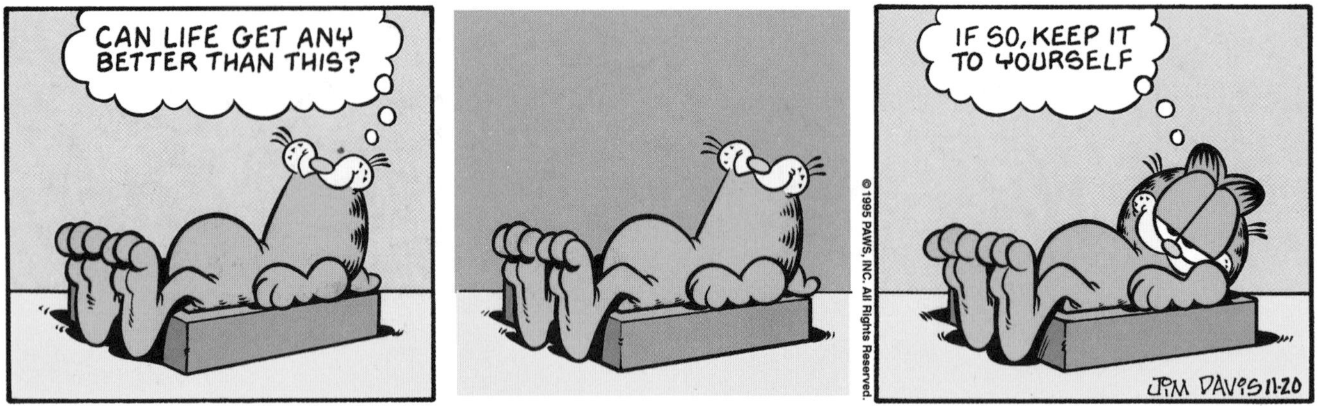
CAN LIFE GET ANY BETTER THAN THIS?
IF SO, KEEP IT TO YOURSELF
© 1995 PAWS, INC. All Rights Reserved.
JIM DAVIS 11-20

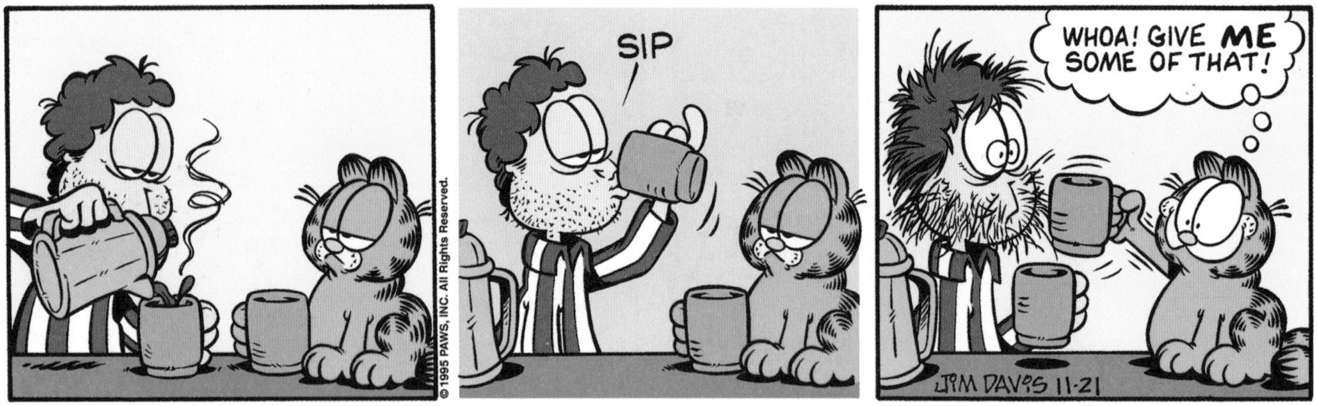
SIP
WHOA! GIVE **ME** SOME OF THAT!
© 1995 PAWS, INC. All Rights Reserved.
JIM DAVIS 11-21

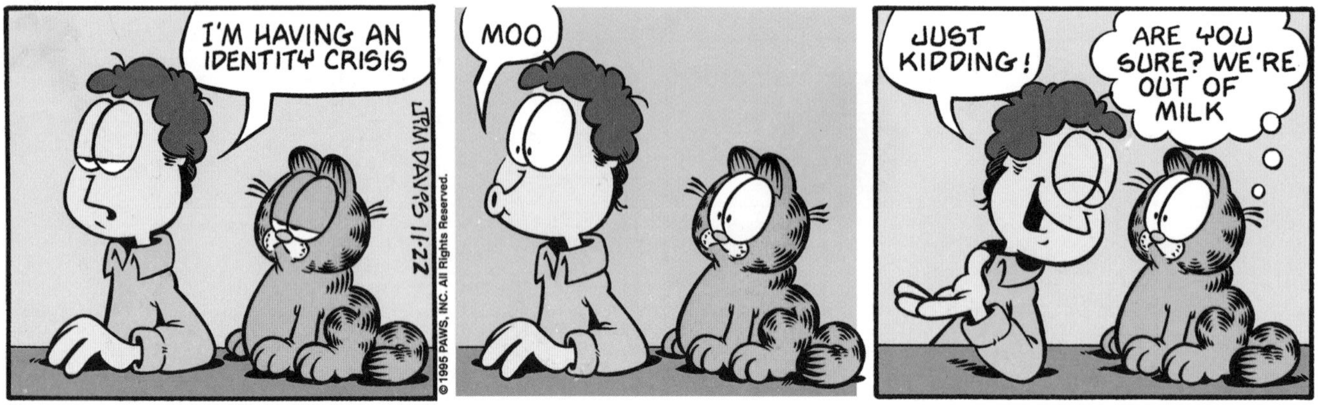
I'M HAVING AN IDENTITY CRISIS
MOO
JUST KIDDING!
ARE YOU SURE? WE'RE OUT OF MILK
© 1995 PAWS, INC. All Rights Reserved.
JIM DAVIS 11-22

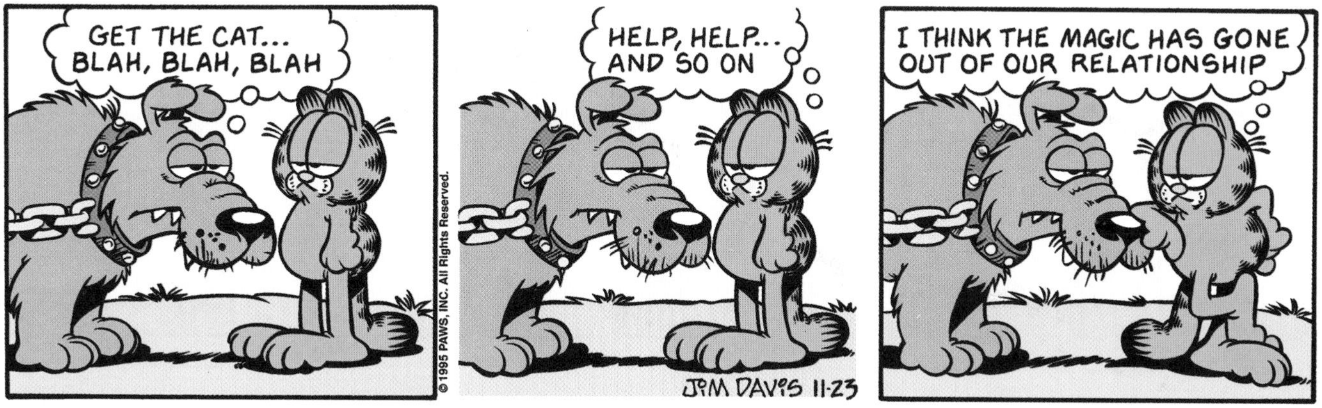
GET THE CAT... BLAH, BLAH, BLAH
© 1995 PAWS, INC. All Rights Reserved.
HELP, HELP... AND SO ON
I THINK THE MAGIC HAS GONE OUT OF OUR RELATIONSHIP
JIM DAVIS 11-23

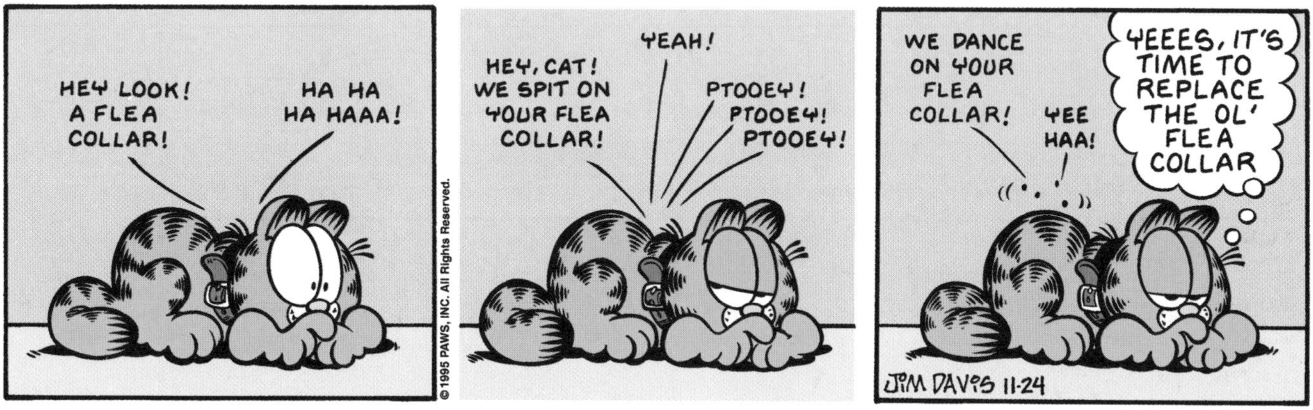
HEY LOOK! A FLEA COLLAR!
HA HA HA HAAA!
© 1995 PAWS, INC. All Rights Reserved.
HEY, CAT! WE SPIT ON YOUR FLEA COLLAR!
YEAH!
PTOOEY! PTOOEY! PTOOEY!
WE DANCE ON YOUR FLEA COLLAR!
YEE HAA!
YEEES, IT'S TIME TO REPLACE THE OL' FLEA COLLAR
JIM DAVIS 11-24

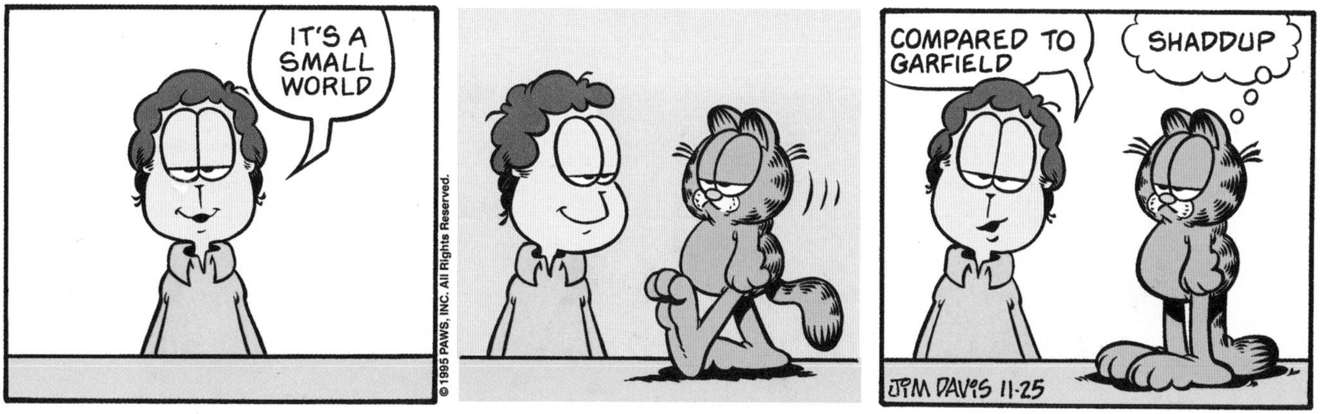
IT'S A SMALL WORLD
© 1995 PAWS, INC. All Rights Reserved.
COMPARED TO GARFIELD
SHADDUP
JIM DAVIS 11-25

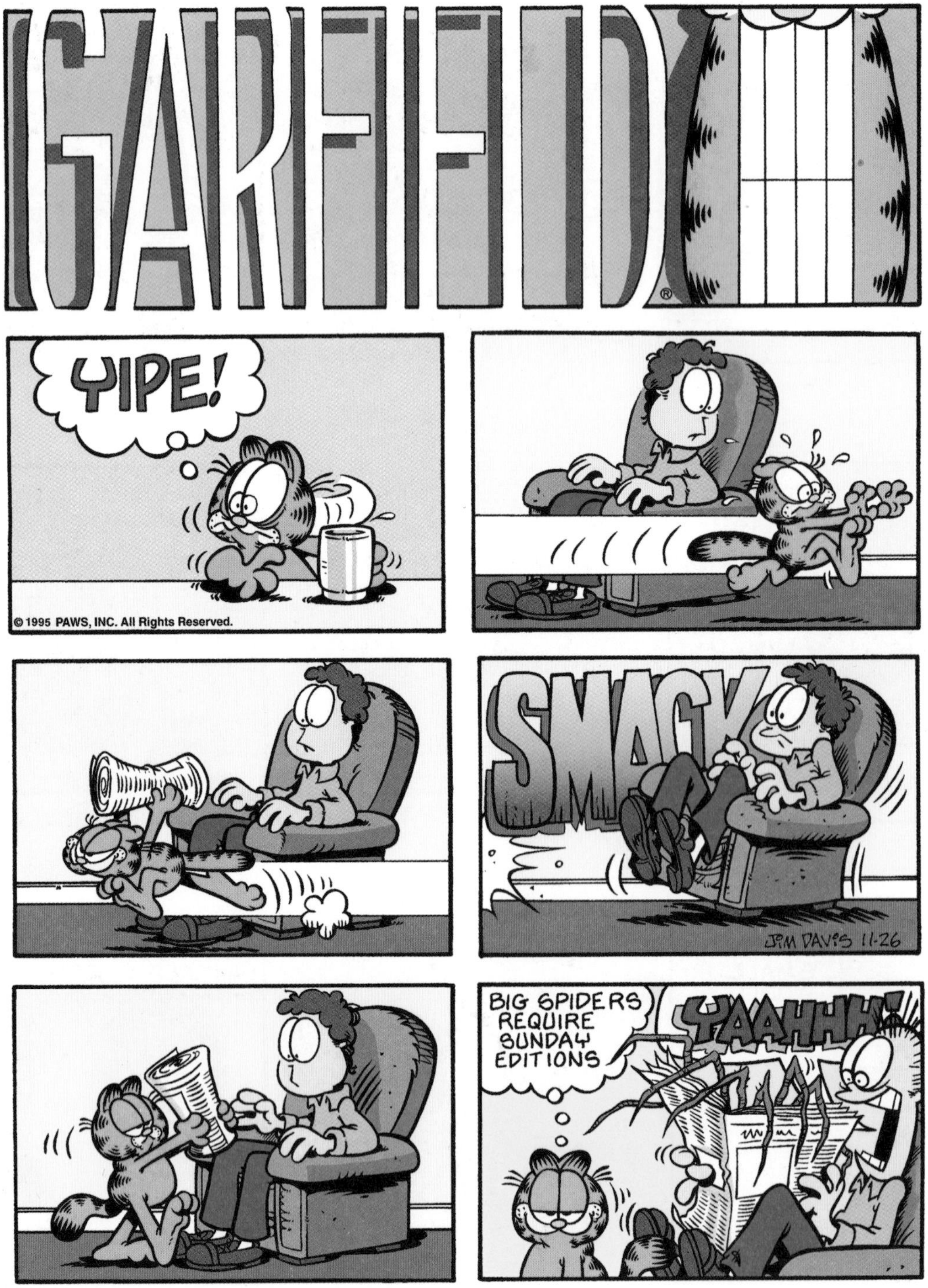
GARFIELD®
YIPE!
© 1995 PAWS, INC. All Rights Reserved.
SMACK
JIM DAVIS 11-26
BIG SPIDERS REQUIRE SUNDAY EDITIONS
YAAHHH!

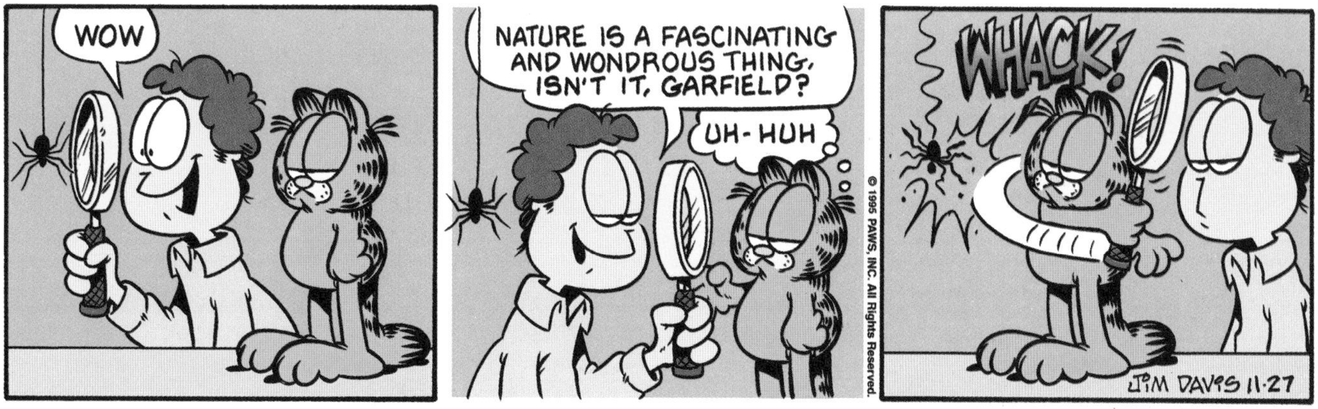
WOW
NATURE IS A FASCINATING AND WONDROUS THING, ISN'T IT, GARFIELD?
UH-HUH
© 1995 PAWS, INC. All Rights Reserved.
WHACK!
JIM DAVIS 11-27

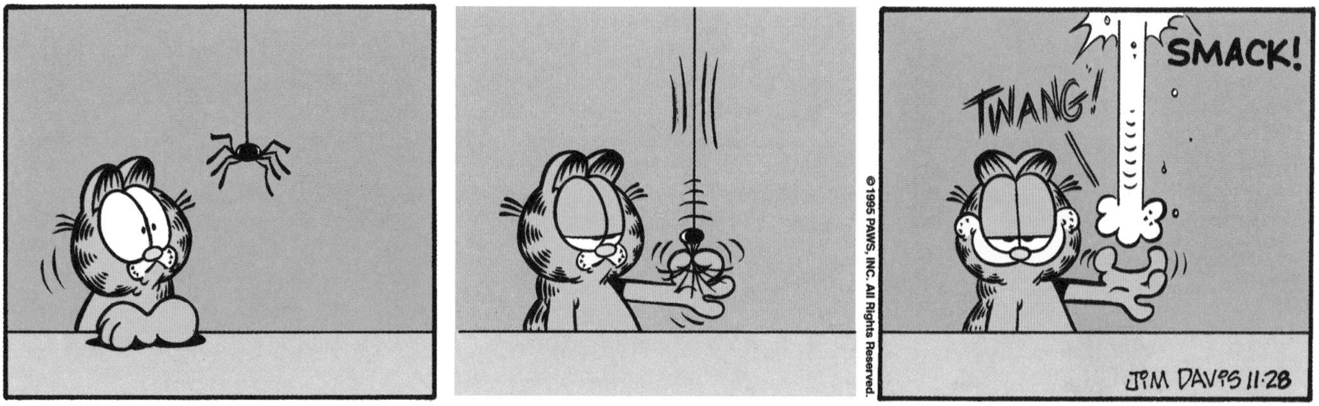
© 1995 PAWS, INC. All Rights Reserved.
TWANG!
SMACK!
JIM DAVIS 11-28

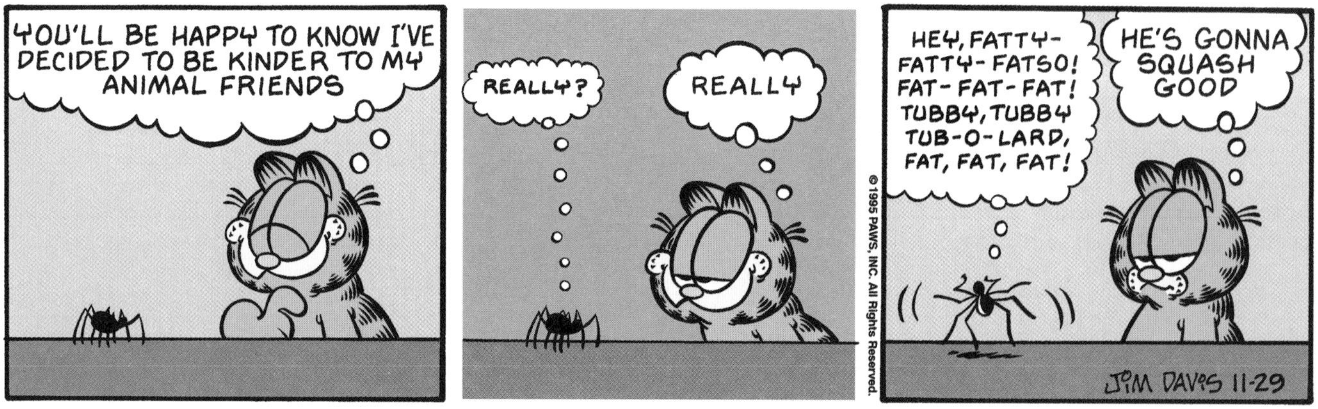
YOU'LL BE HAPPY TO KNOW I'VE DECIDED TO BE KINDER TO MY ANIMAL FRIENDS
REALLY?
REALLY
© 1995 PAWS, INC. All Rights Reserved.
HEY, FATTY-FATTY-FATSO! FAT-FAT-FAT! TUBBY, TUBBY TUB-O-LARD, FAT, FAT, FAT!
HE'S GONNA SQUASH GOOD
JIM DAVIS 11-29

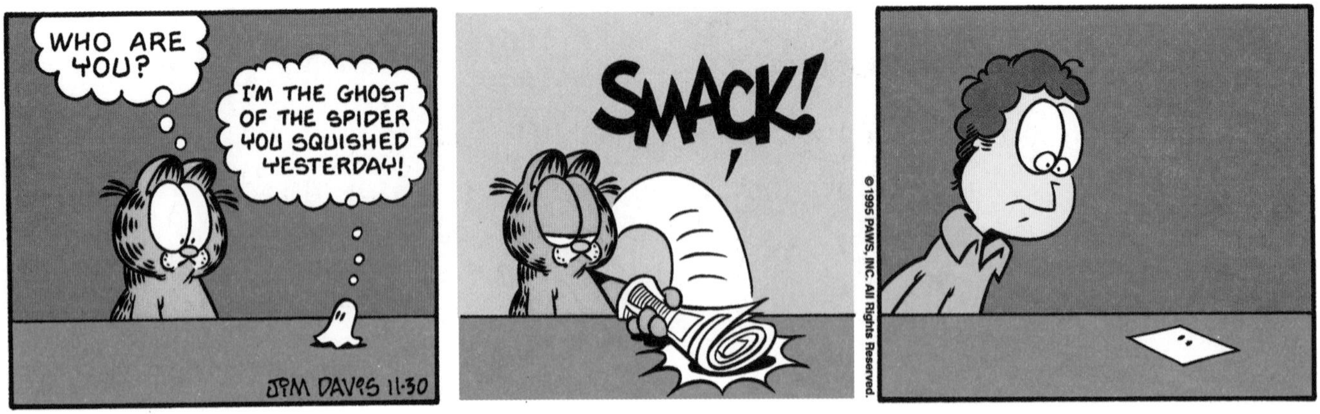
WHO ARE YOU?
I'M THE GHOST OF THE SPIDER YOU SQUISHED YESTERDAY!
JIM DAVIS 11-30
SMACK!
© 1995 PAWS, INC. All Rights Reserved.

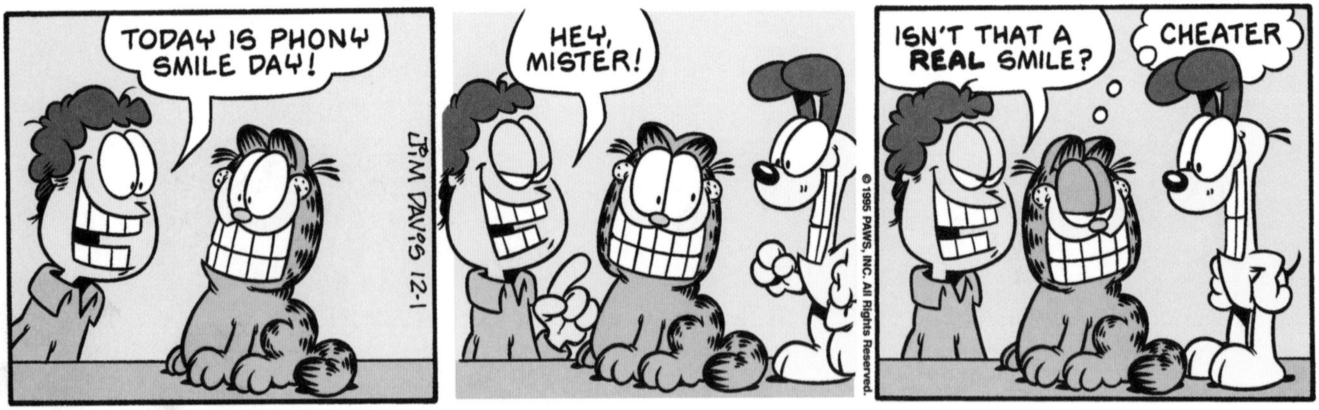
TODAY IS PHONY SMILE DAY!
JIM DAVIS 12-1
HEY, MISTER!
© 1995 PAWS, INC. All Rights Reserved.
ISN'T THAT A **REAL** SMILE?
CHEATER

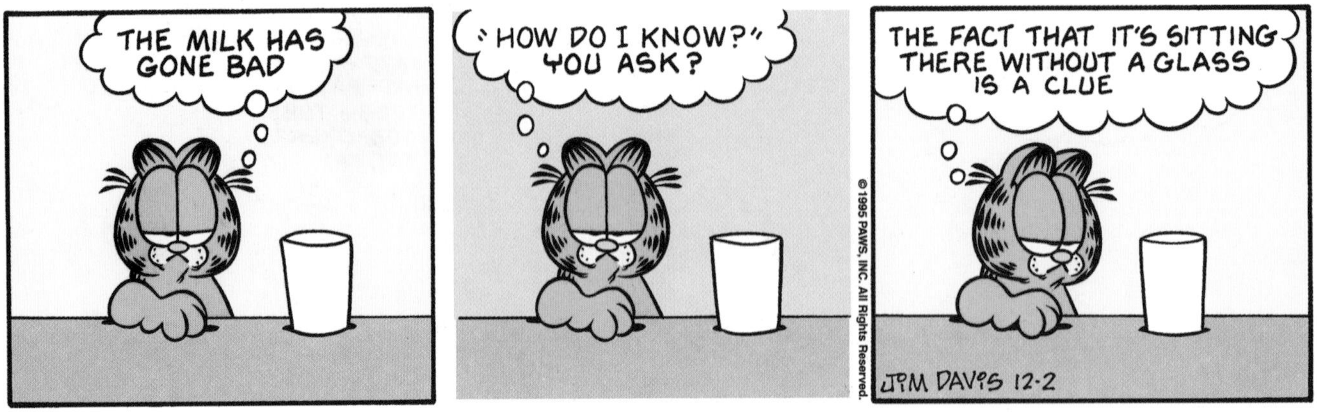
THE MILK HAS GONE BAD
"HOW DO I KNOW?" YOU ASK?
© 1995 PAWS, INC. All Rights Reserved.
THE FACT THAT IT'S SITTING THERE WITHOUT A GLASS IS A CLUE
JIM DAVIS 12-2

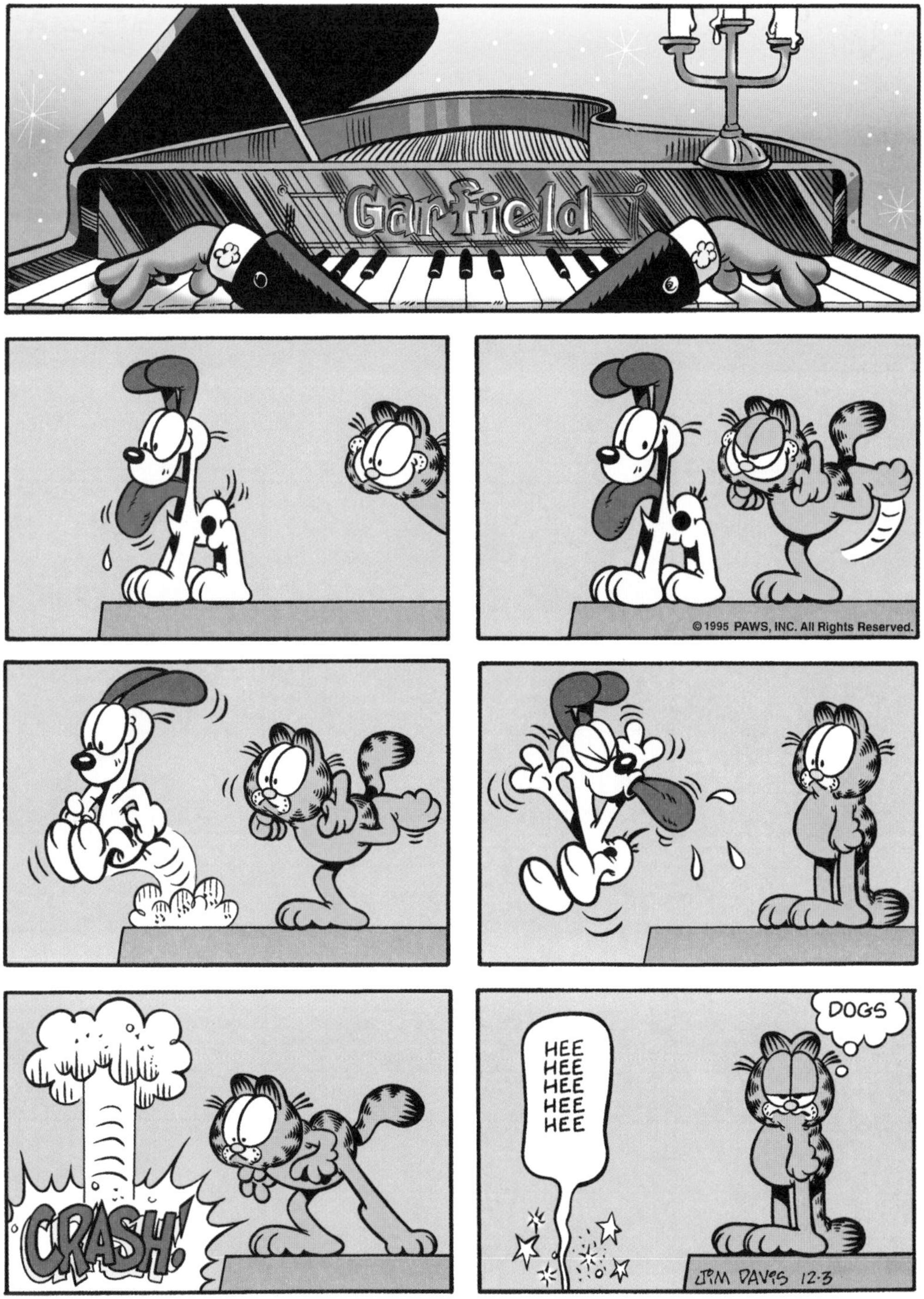
Garfield
© 1995 PAWS, INC. All Rights Reserved.
CRASH!
HEE HEE HEE HEE HEE
DOGS
JIM DAVIS 12-3

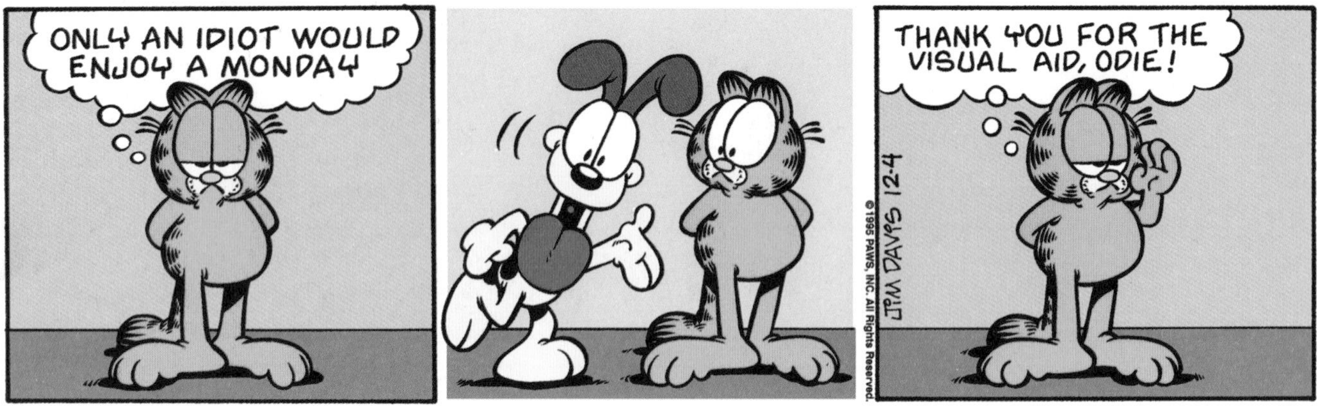
ONLY AN IDIOT WOULD ENJOY A MONDAY
© 1995 PAWS, INC. All Rights Reserved.
JIM DAVIS 12-4
THANK YOU FOR THE VISUAL AID, ODIE!

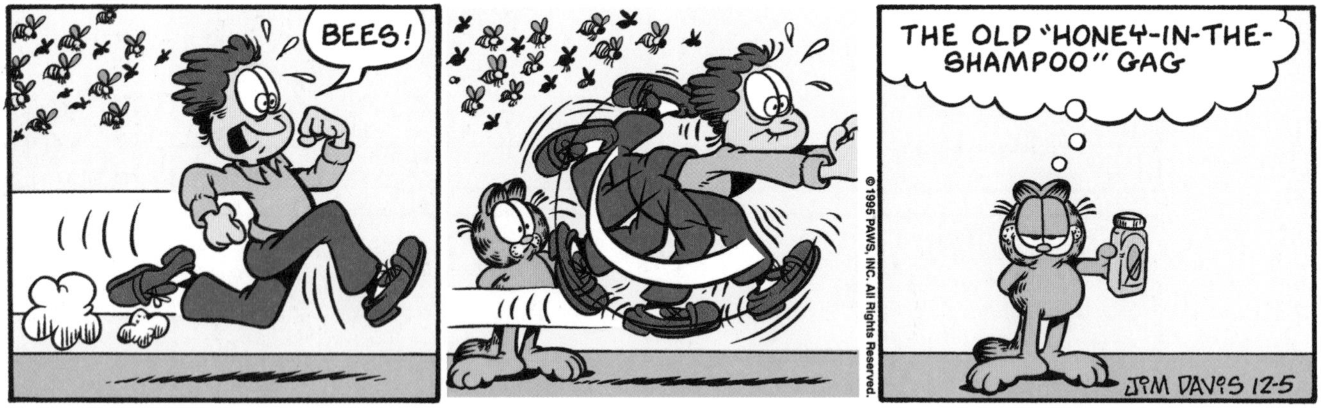
BEES!
© 1995 PAWS, INC. All Rights Reserved.
THE OLD "HONEY-IN-THE-SHAMPOO" GAG
JIM DAVIS 12-5

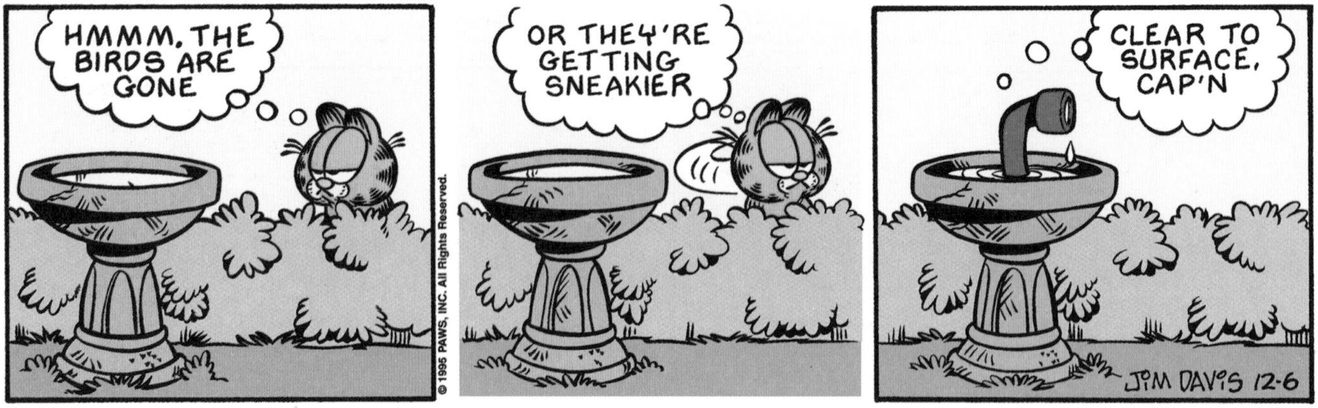
HMMM, THE BIRDS ARE GONE
© 1995 PAWS, INC. All Rights Reserved.
OR THEY'RE GETTING SNEAKIER
CLEAR TO SURFACE, CAP'N
JIM DAVIS 12-6

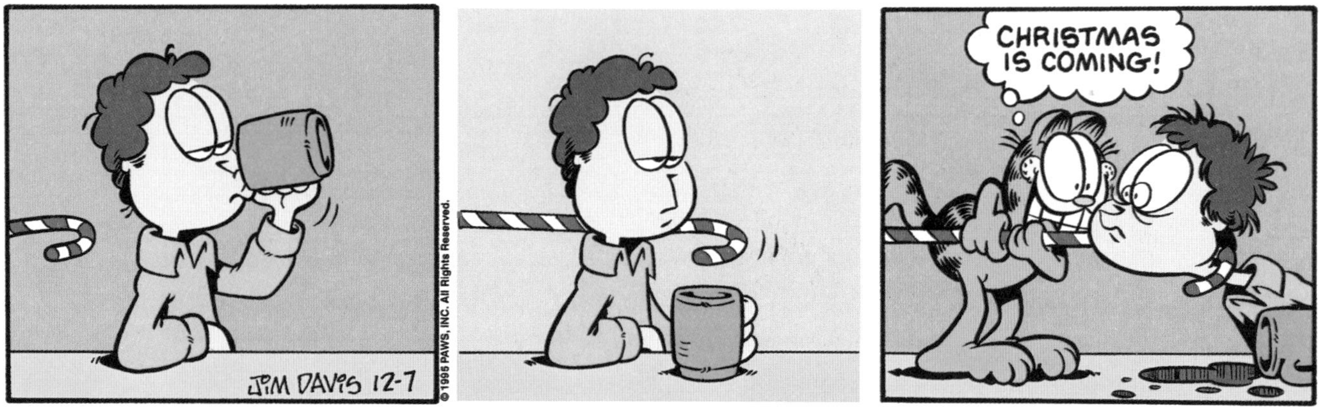
JIM DAVIS 12-7
© 1995 PAWS, INC. All Rights Reserved.
CHRISTMAS IS COMING!

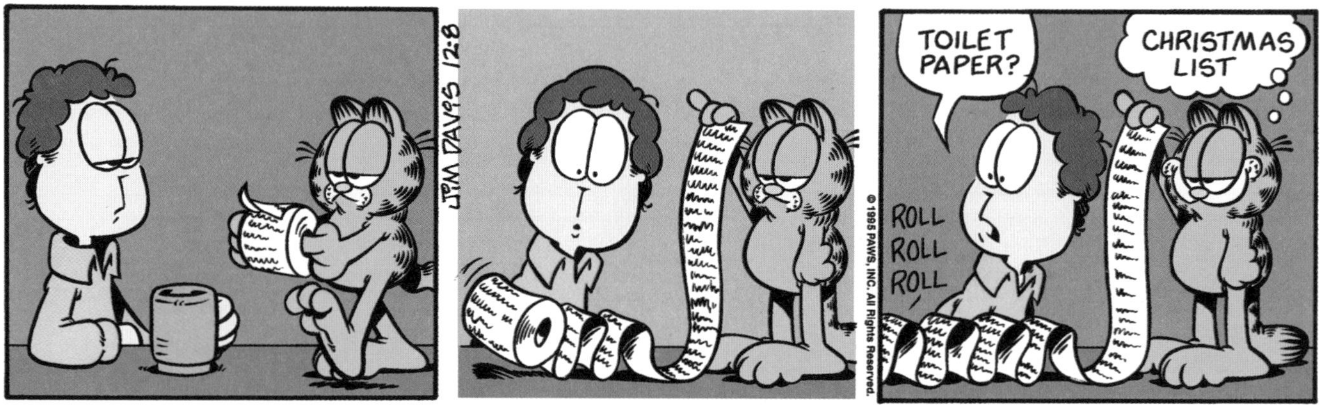
JIM DAVIS 12-8
© 1995 PAWS, INC. All Rights Reserved.
ROLL ROLL ROLL
TOILET PAPER?
CHRISTMAS LIST

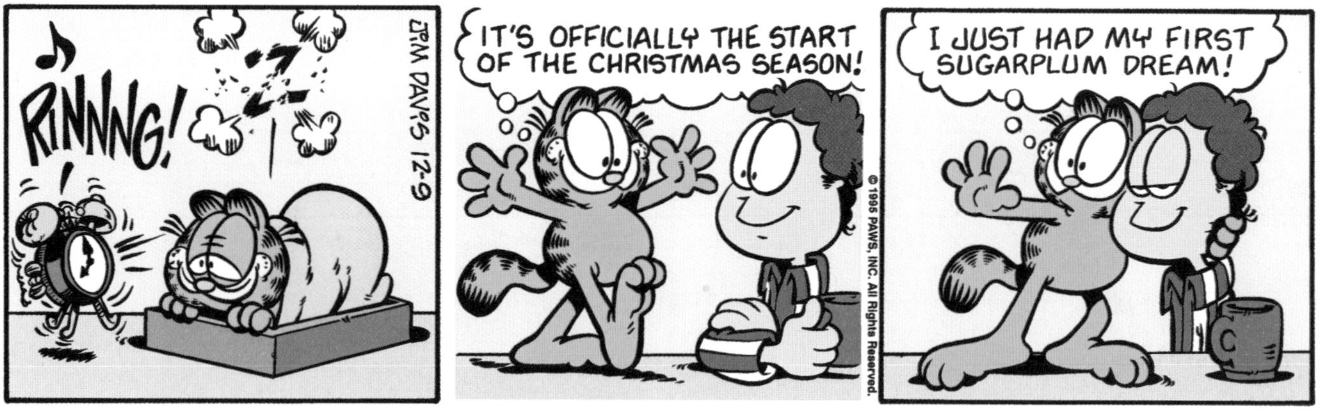
RINNNG!
JIM DAVIS 12-9
IT'S OFFICIALLY THE START OF THE CHRISTMAS SEASON!
© 1995 PAWS, INC. All Rights Reserved.
I JUST HAD MY FIRST SUGARPLUM DREAM!

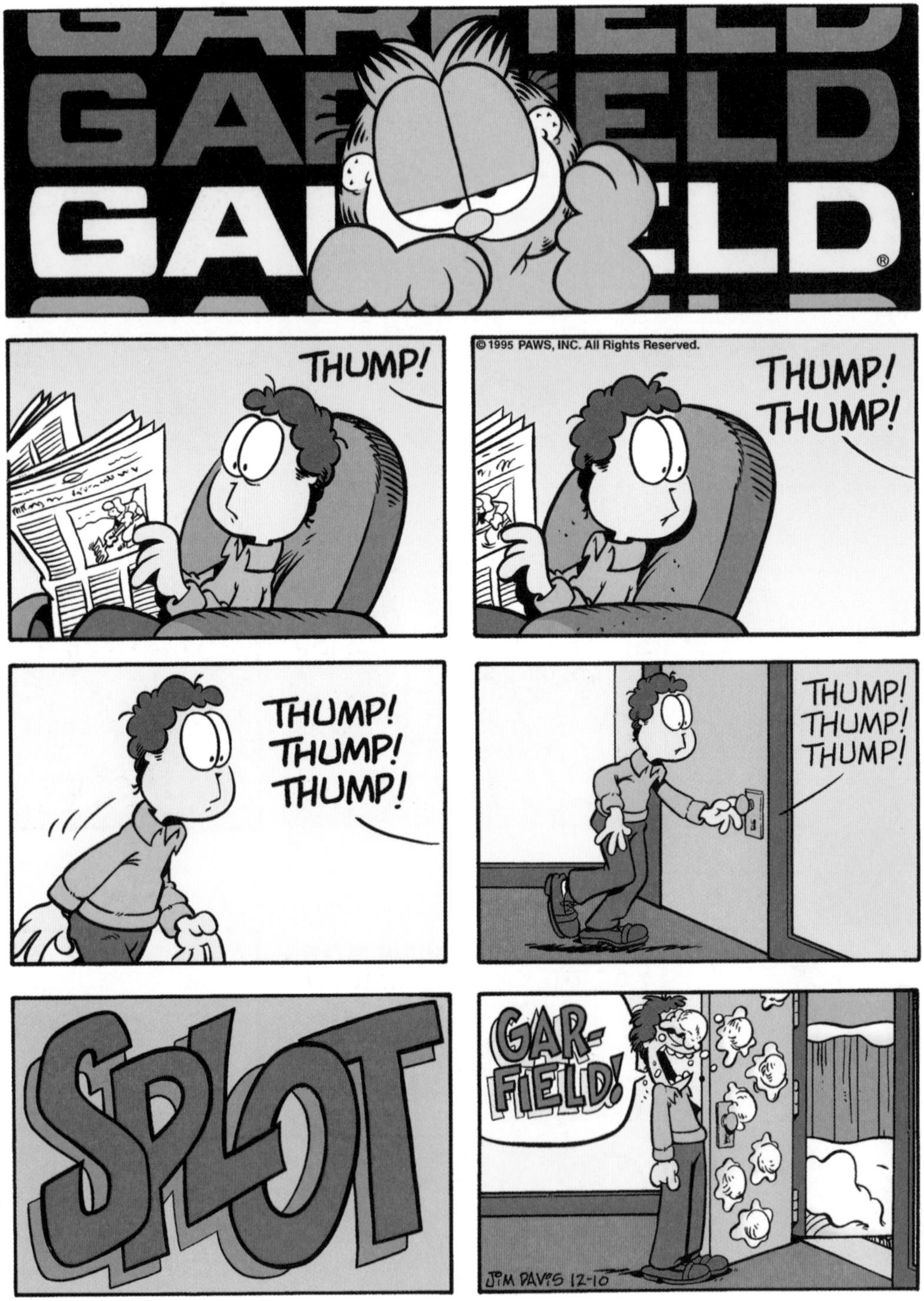
GARFIELD
© 1995 PAWS, INC. All Rights Reserved.
THUMP!
THUMP! THUMP!
THUMP! THUMP! THUMP!
THUMP! THUMP! THUMP!
SPLOT
GAR-FIELD!
JIM DAVIS 12-10

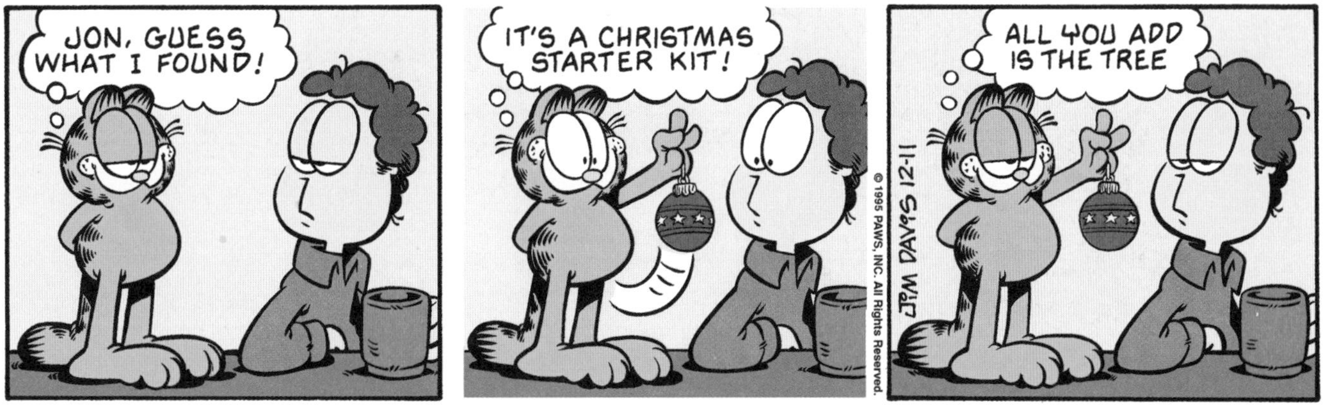
JON, GUESS WHAT I FOUND!
IT'S A CHRISTMAS STARTER KIT!
ALL YOU ADD IS THE TREE
JIM DAVIS 12-11
© 1995 PAWS, INC. All Rights Reserved.

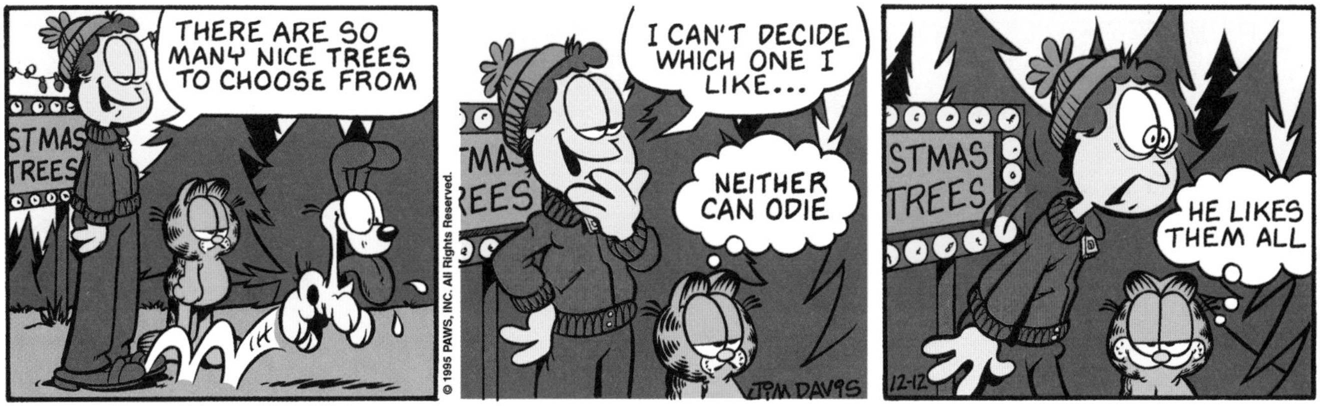
THERE ARE SO MANY NICE TREES TO CHOOSE FROM
STMAS TREES
© 1995 PAWS, INC. All Rights Reserved.
I CAN'T DECIDE WHICH ONE I LIKE...
NEITHER CAN ODIE
JIM DAVIS
HE LIKES THEM ALL
12-12

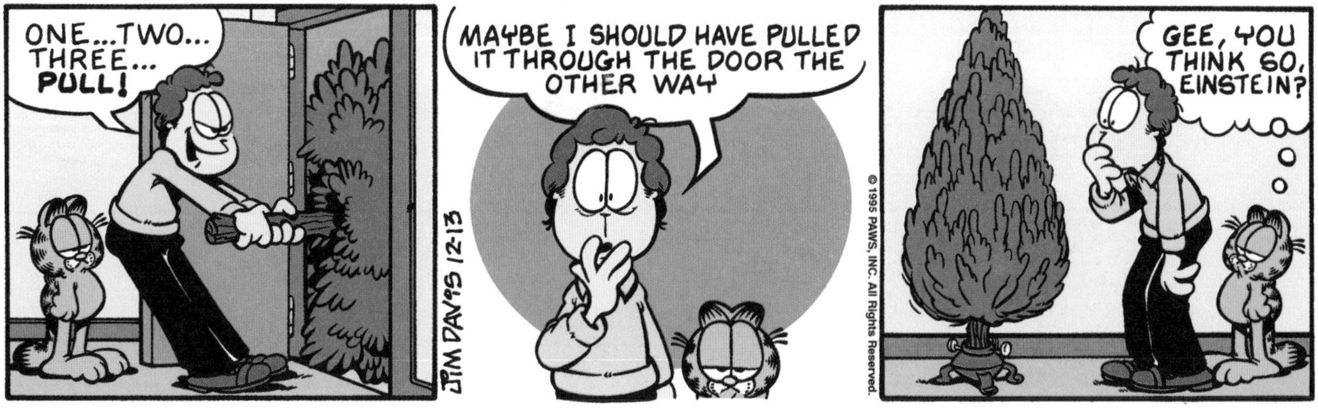
ONE...TWO... THREE... **PULL!**
JIM DAVIS 12-13
MAYBE I SHOULD HAVE PULLED IT THROUGH THE DOOR THE OTHER WAY
© 1995 PAWS, INC. All Rights Reserved.
GEE, YOU THINK SO, EINSTEIN?

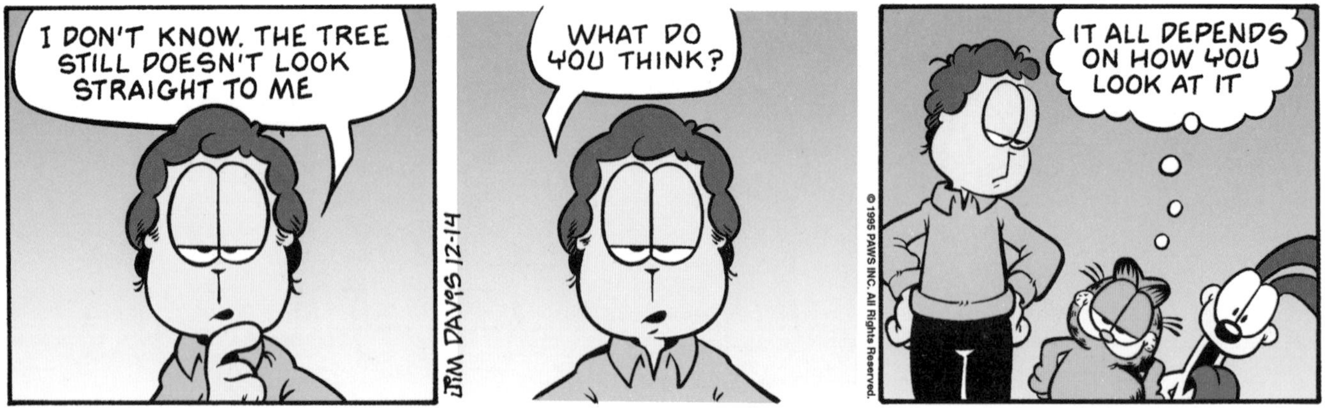
I DON'T KNOW. THE TREE STILL DOESN'T LOOK STRAIGHT TO ME
JIM DAVIS 12-14
WHAT DO YOU THINK?
© 1995 PAWS INC. All Rights Reserved.
IT ALL DEPENDS ON HOW YOU LOOK AT IT

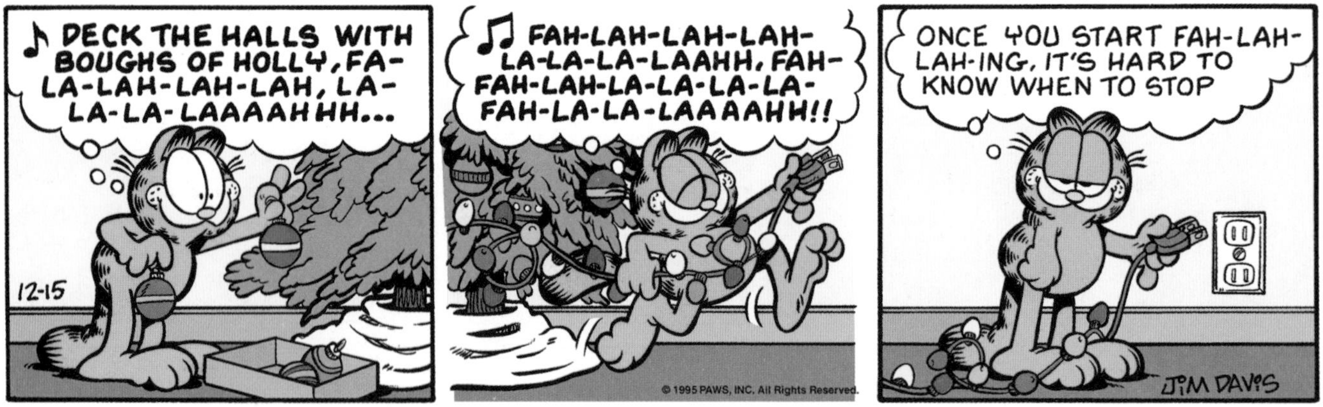
♪ DECK THE HALLS WITH BOUGHS OF HOLLY, FA-LA-LAH-LAH-LAH, LA-LA-LA-LAAAAHHH...
12-15
♫ FAH-LAH-LAH-LAH-LA-LA-LA-LAAHH, FAH-FAH-LAH-LA-LA-LA-LA-FAH-LA-LA-LAAAAHH!!
© 1995 PAWS, INC. All Rights Reserved.
ONCE YOU START FAH-LAH-LAH-ING, IT'S HARD TO KNOW WHEN TO STOP
JIM DAVIS

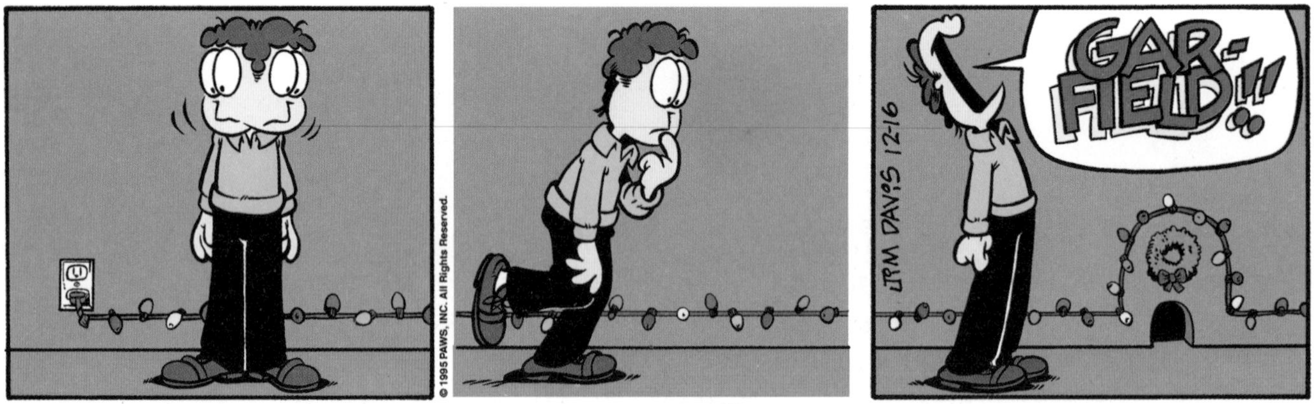
© 1995 PAWS, INC. All Rights Reserved.
JIM DAVIS 12-16
GAR-FIELD!!!

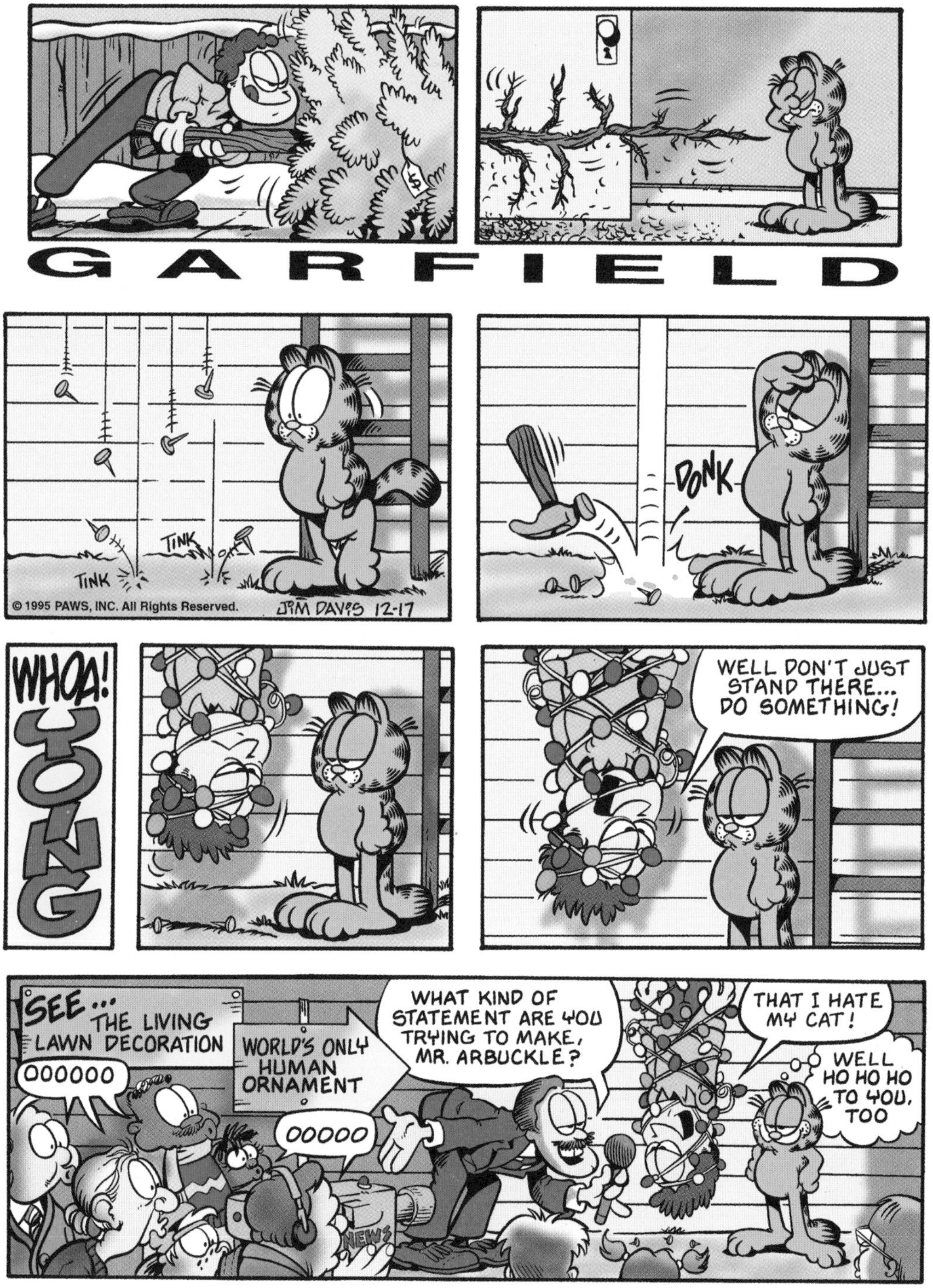
GARFIELD
TINK
TINK
© 1995 PAWS, INC. All Rights Reserved.
JIM DAVIS 12-17
DONK
WHOA!
YOING
WELL DON'T JUST STAND THERE... DO SOMETHING!
SEE... THE LIVING LAWN DECORATION
WORLD'S ONLY HUMAN ORNAMENT
OOOOOO
OOOOO
NEWS
WHAT KIND OF STATEMENT ARE YOU TRYING TO MAKE, MR. ARBUCKLE?
THAT I HATE MY CAT!
WELL HO HO HO TO YOU, TOO

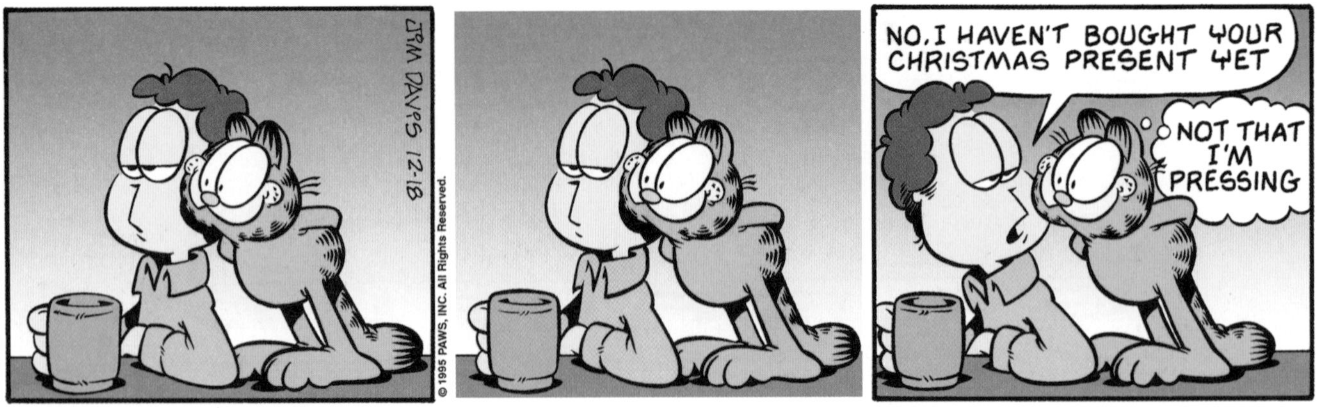
JIM DAVIS 12-18
© 1995 PAWS, INC. All Rights Reserved.
NO, I HAVEN'T BOUGHT YOUR CHRISTMAS PRESENT YET
NOT THAT I'M PRESSING

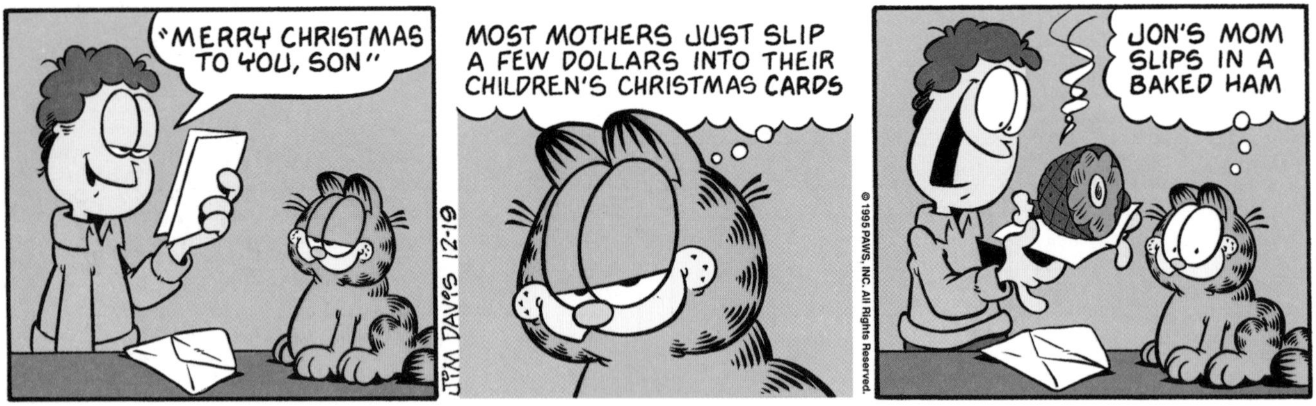
"MERRY CHRISTMAS TO YOU, SON"
JIM DAVIS 12-19
MOST MOTHERS JUST SLIP A FEW DOLLARS INTO THEIR CHILDREN'S CHRISTMAS CARDS
© 1995 PAWS, INC. All Rights Reserved.
JON'S MOM SLIPS IN A BAKED HAM

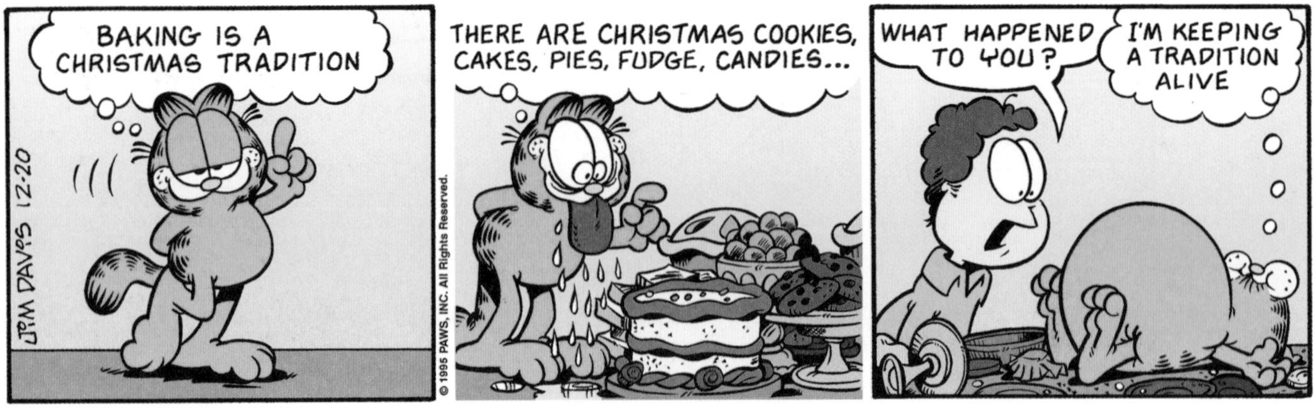
BAKING IS A CHRISTMAS TRADITION
JIM DAVIS 12-20
© 1995 PAWS, INC. All Rights Reserved.
THERE ARE CHRISTMAS COOKIES, CAKES, PIES, FUDGE, CANDIES...
WHAT HAPPENED TO YOU?
I'M KEEPING A TRADITION ALIVE

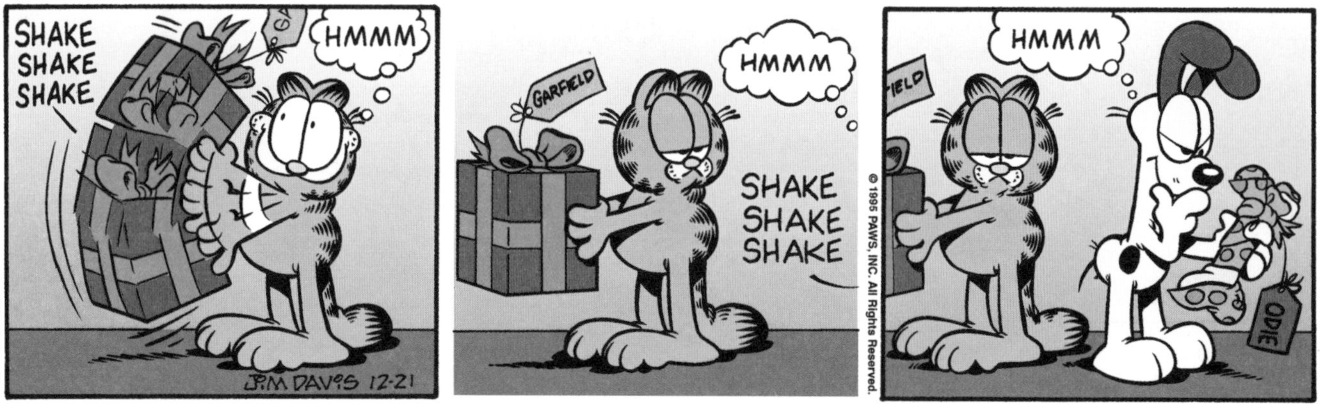
SHAKE
SHAKE
SHAKE
HMMM
HMMM
GARFIELD
SHAKE
SHAKE
SHAKE
HMMM
ODIE
JIM DAVIS 12-21

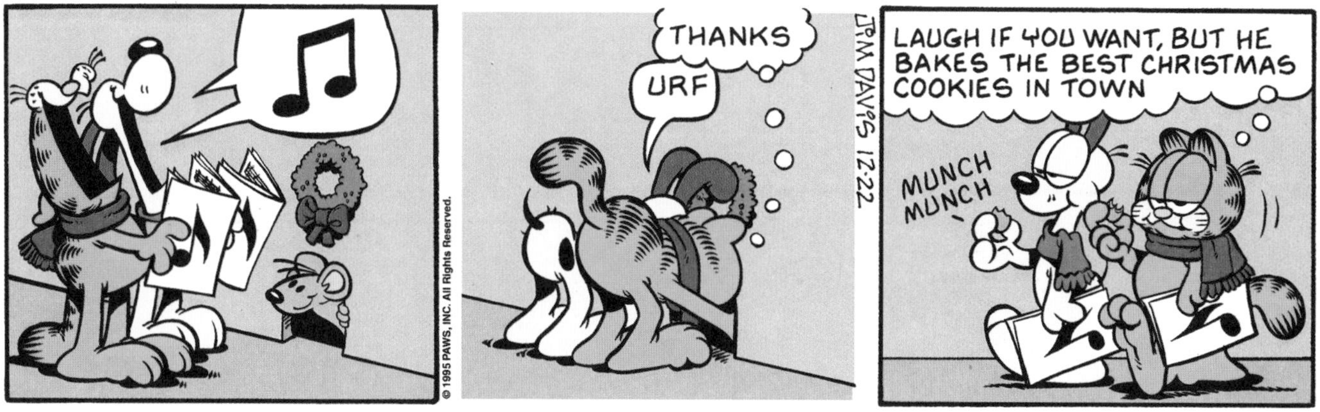
URF
THANKS
LAUGH IF YOU WANT, BUT HE BAKES THE BEST CHRISTMAS COOKIES IN TOWN
MUNCH
MUNCH
JIM DAVIS 12-22

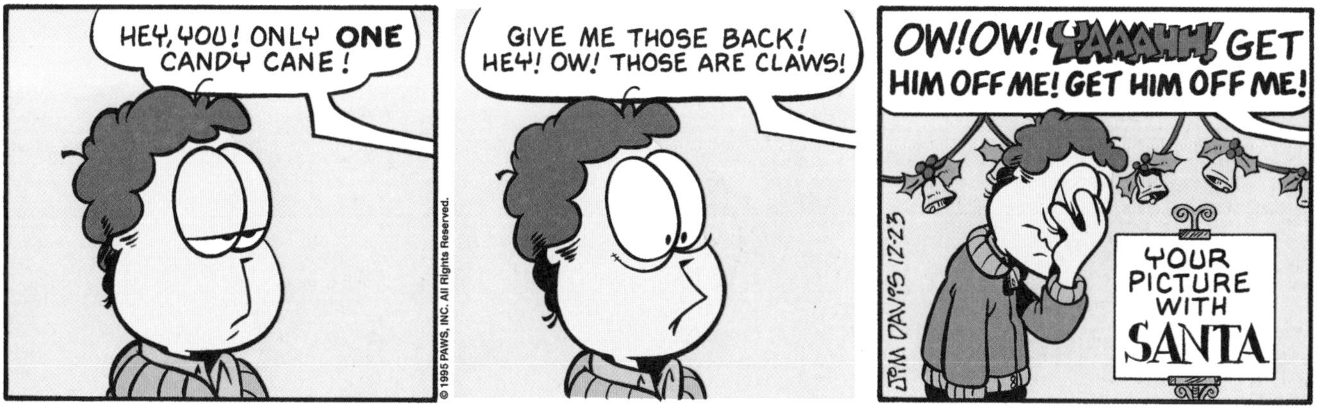
HEY, YOU! ONLY ONE CANDY CANE!
GIVE ME THOSE BACK! HEY! OW! THOSE ARE CLAWS!
OW! OW! YAAAHH! GET HIM OFF ME! GET HIM OFF ME!
YOUR PICTURE WITH SANTA
JIM DAVIS 12-23

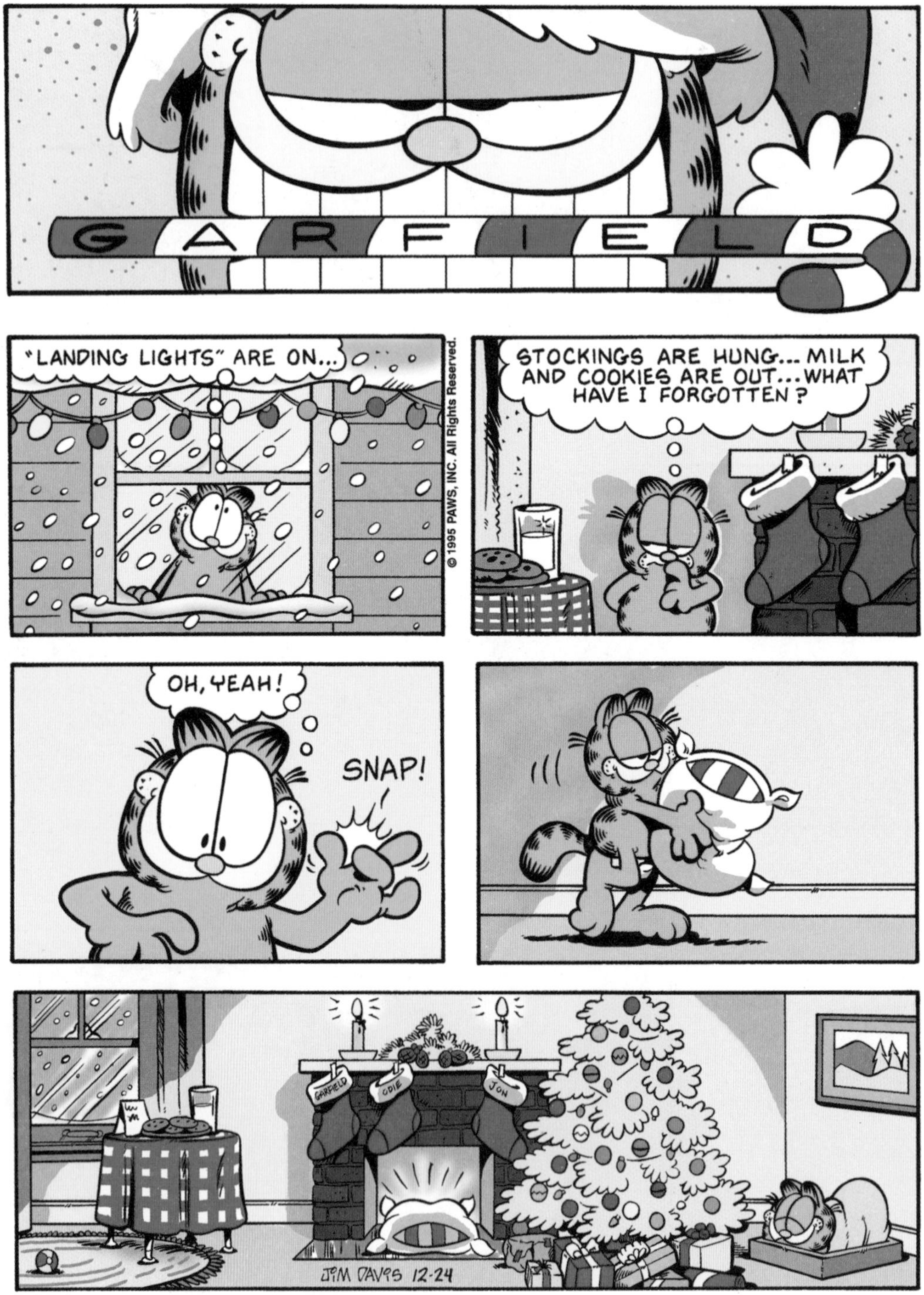
GARFIELD
"LANDING LIGHTS" ARE ON...
© 1995 PAWS, INC. All Rights Reserved.
STOCKINGS ARE HUNG... MILK AND COOKIES ARE OUT... WHAT HAVE I FORGOTTEN?
OH, YEAH!
SNAP!
GARFIELD
ODIE
JON
JIM DAVIS 12-24

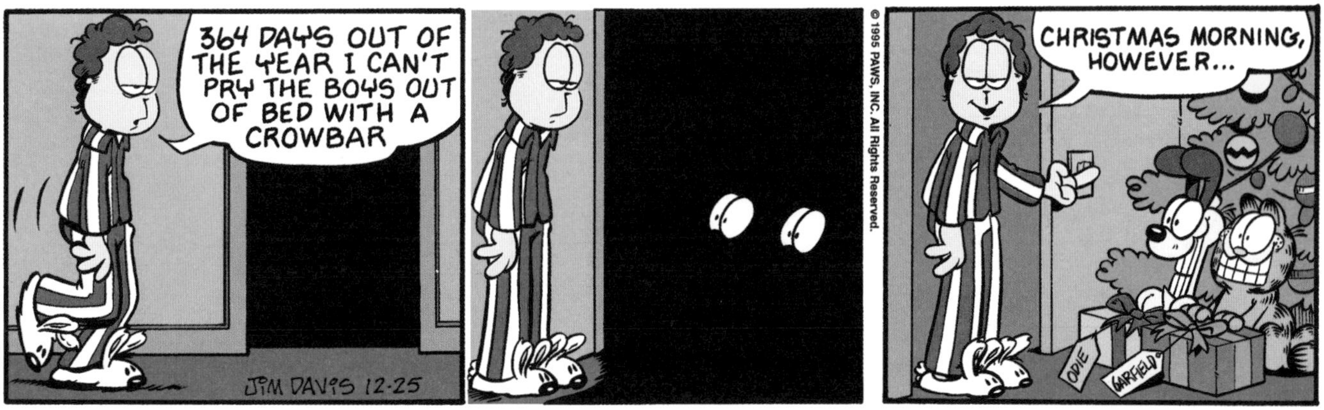
364 DAYS OUT OF THE YEAR I CAN'T PRY THE BOYS OUT OF BED WITH A CROWBAR
JIM DAVIS 12-25
CHRISTMAS MORNING, HOWEVER...
ODIE
GARFIELD
© 1995 PAWS, INC. All Rights Reserved.

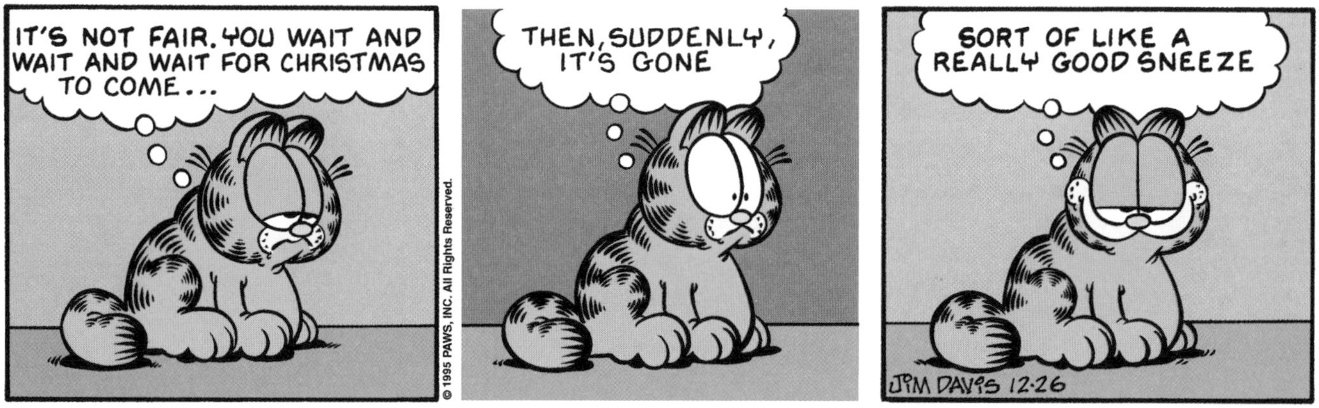
IT'S NOT FAIR. YOU WAIT AND WAIT AND WAIT FOR CHRISTMAS TO COME...
THEN, SUDDENLY, IT'S GONE
SORT OF LIKE A REALLY GOOD SNEEZE
JIM DAVIS 12-26
© 1995 PAWS, INC. All Rights Reserved.

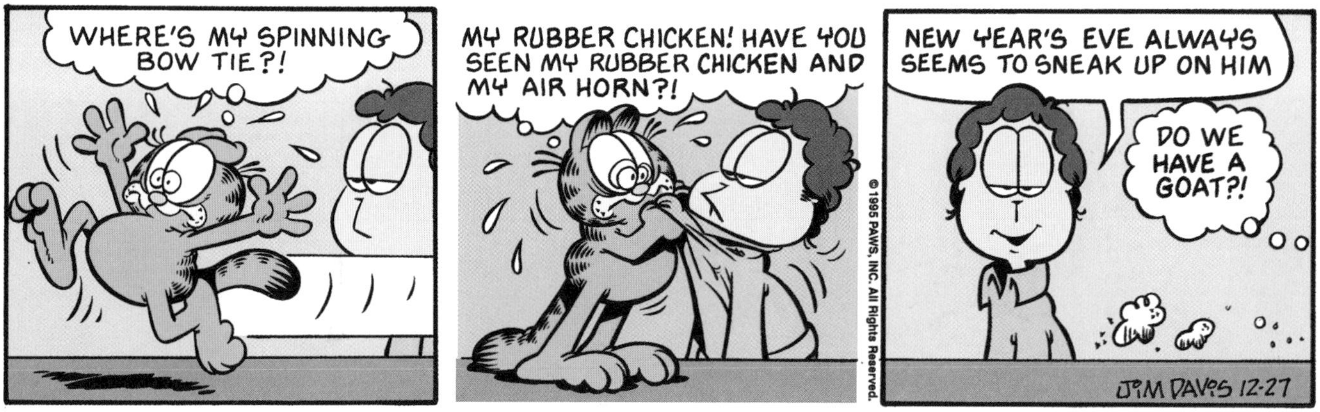
WHERE'S MY SPINNING BOW TIE?!
MY RUBBER CHICKEN! HAVE YOU SEEN MY RUBBER CHICKEN AND MY AIR HORN?!
NEW YEAR'S EVE ALWAYS SEEMS TO SNEAK UP ON HIM
DO WE HAVE A GOAT?!
JIM DAVIS 12-27
© 1995 PAWS, INC. All Rights Reserved.

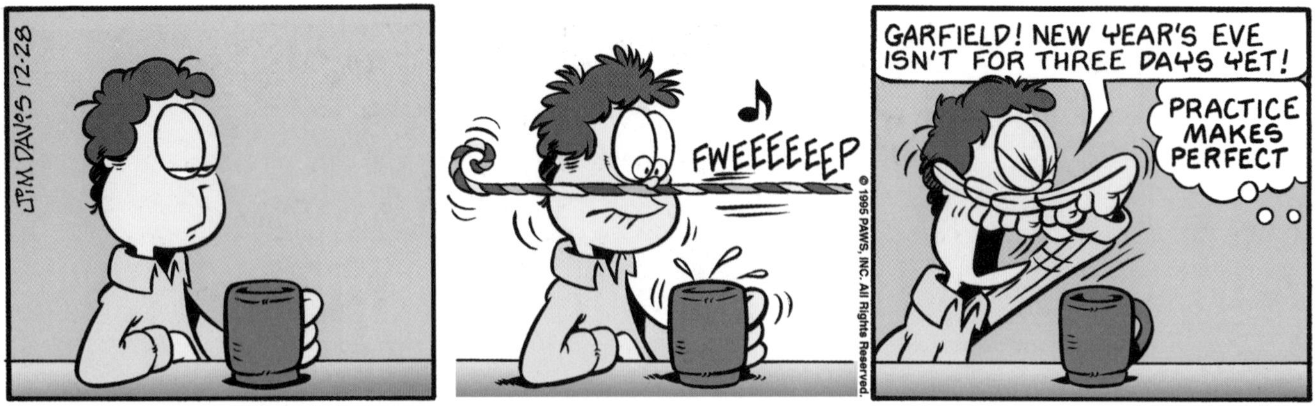
JIM DAVIS 12-28
FWEEEEEEEP
GARFIELD! NEW YEAR'S EVE ISN'T FOR THREE DAYS YET!
PRACTICE MAKES PERFECT
© 1995 PAWS, INC. All Rights Reserved.

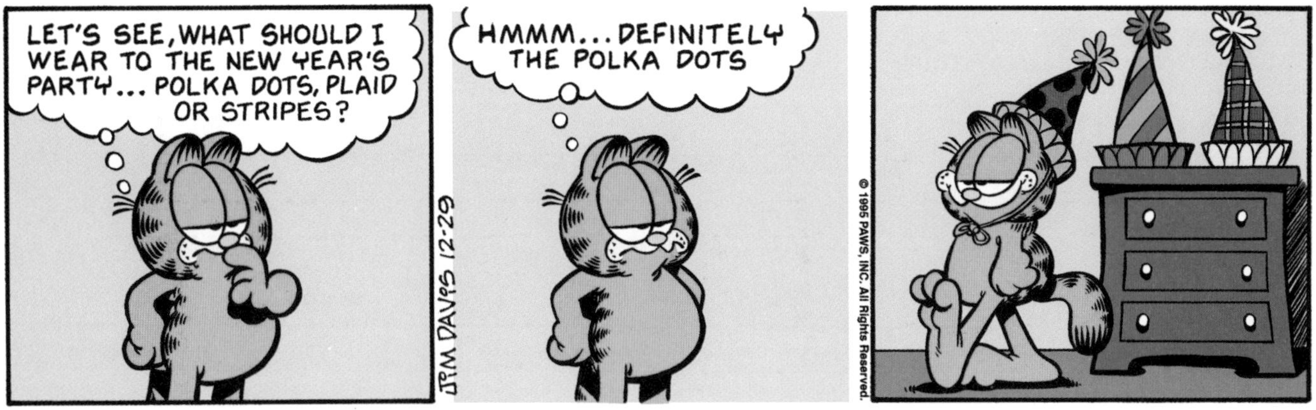
LET'S SEE, WHAT SHOULD I WEAR TO THE NEW YEAR'S PARTY... POLKA DOTS, PLAID OR STRIPES?
JIM DAVIS 12-29
HMMM... DEFINITELY THE POLKA DOTS
© 1995 PAWS, INC. All Rights Reserved.

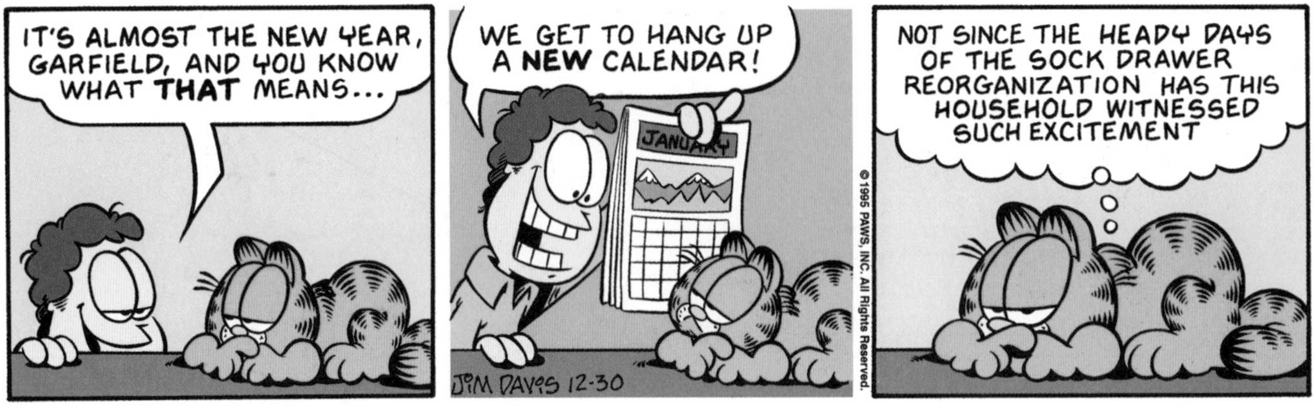
IT'S ALMOST THE NEW YEAR, GARFIELD, AND YOU KNOW WHAT THAT MEANS...
WE GET TO HANG UP A NEW CALENDAR!
JIM DAVIS 12-30
NOT SINCE THE HEADY DAYS OF THE SOCK DRAWER REORGANIZATION HAS THIS HOUSEHOLD WITNESSED SUCH EXCITEMENT
© 1995 PAWS, INC. All Rights Reserved.

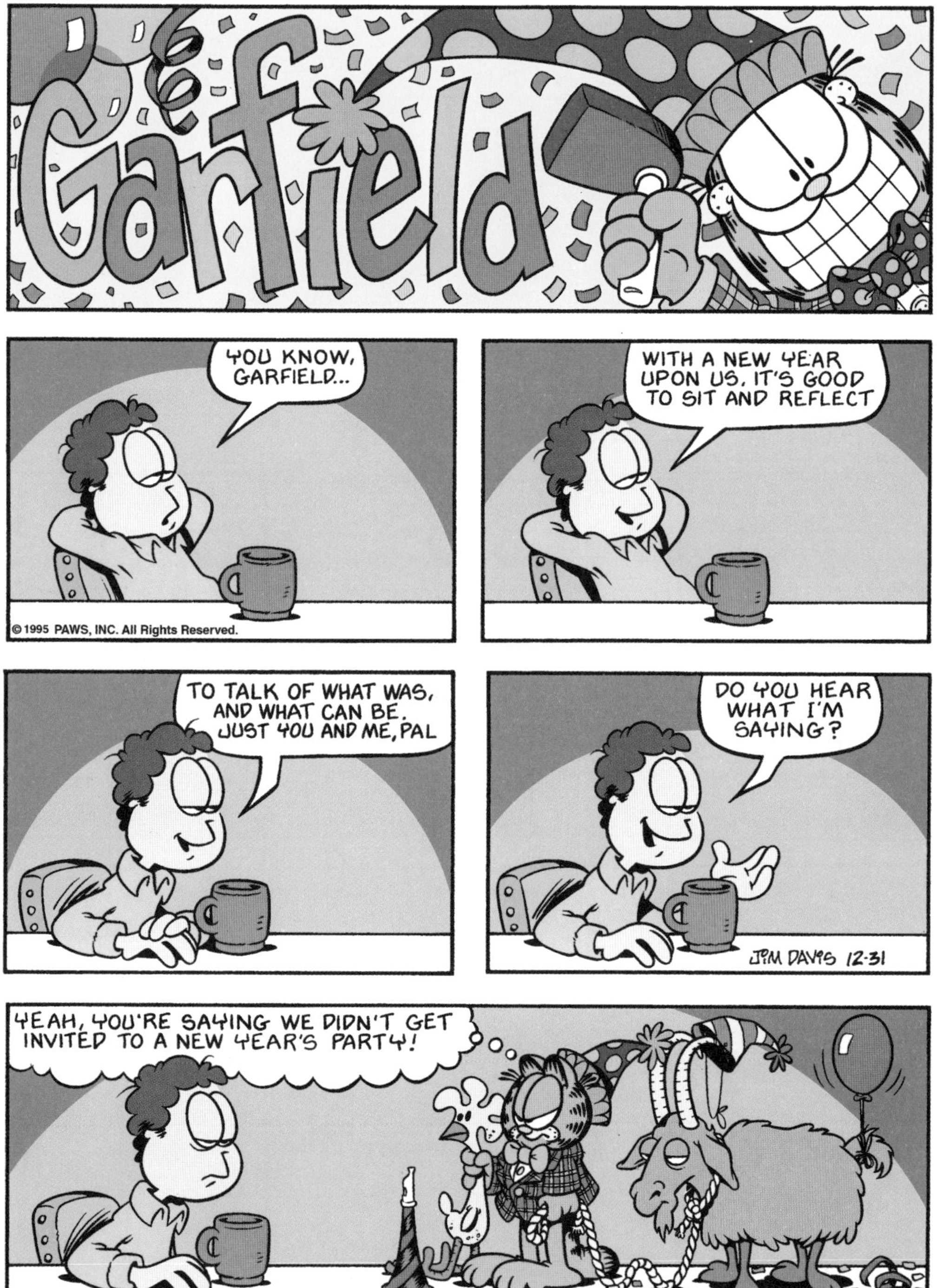
Garfield
YOU KNOW, GARFIELD...
WITH A NEW YEAR UPON US, IT'S GOOD TO SIT AND REFLECT
TO TALK OF WHAT WAS, AND WHAT CAN BE. JUST YOU AND ME, PAL
DO YOU HEAR WHAT I'M SAYING?
JIM DAVIS 12-31
YEAH, YOU'RE SAYING WE DIDN'T GET INVITED TO A NEW YEAR'S PARTY!

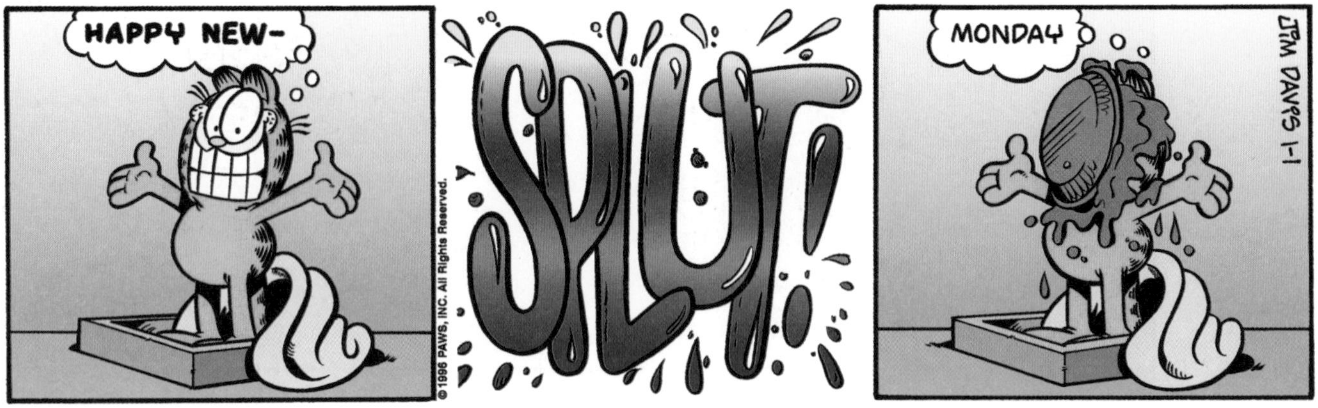
HAPPY NEW-
SPLUT!
MONDAY
JIM DAVIS 1-1
© 1996 PAWS, INC. All Rights Reserved.

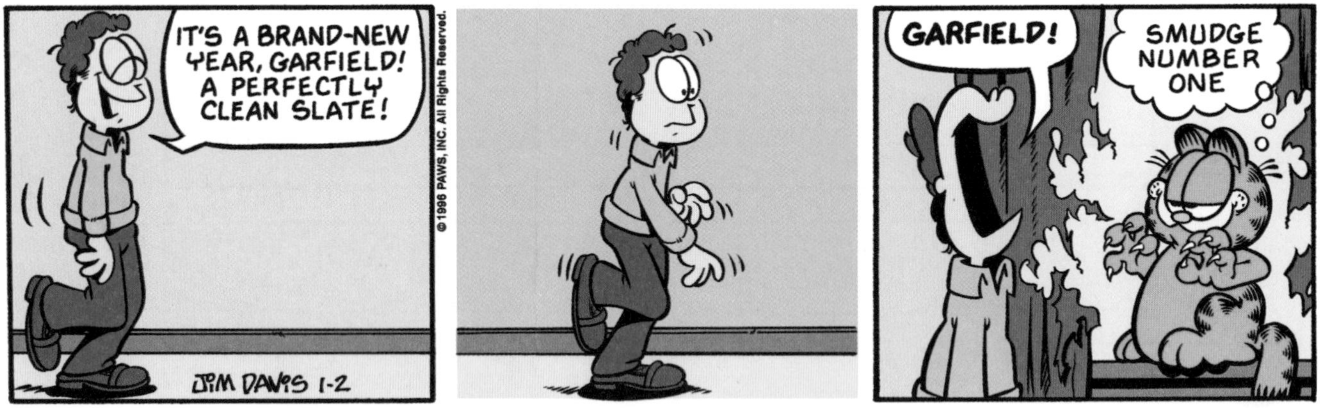
IT'S A BRAND-NEW YEAR, GARFIELD! A PERFECTLY CLEAN SLATE!
JIM DAVIS 1-2
© 1996 PAWS, INC. All Rights Reserved.
GARFIELD!
SMUDGE NUMBER ONE

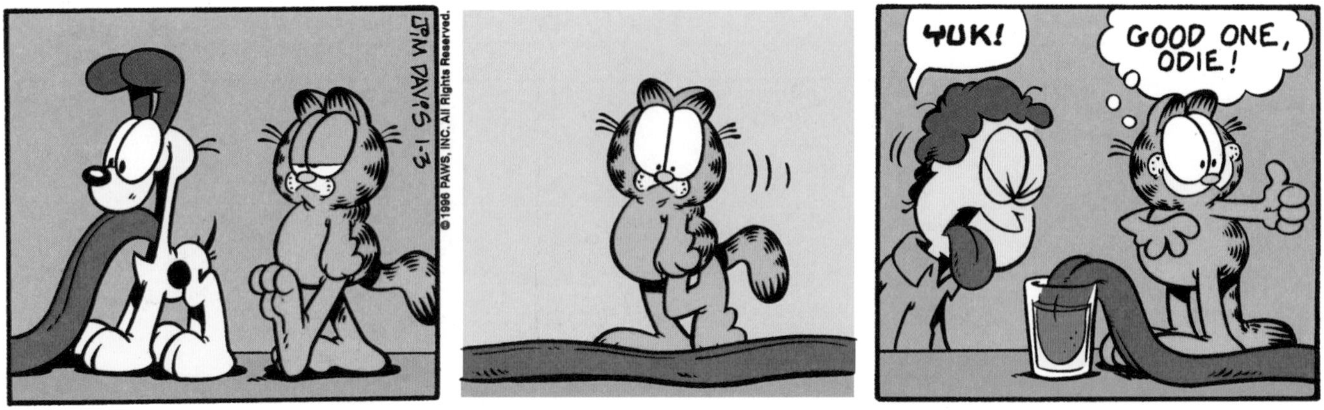
JIM DAVIS 1-3
© 1996 PAWS, INC. All Rights Reserved.
YUK!
GOOD ONE, ODIE!

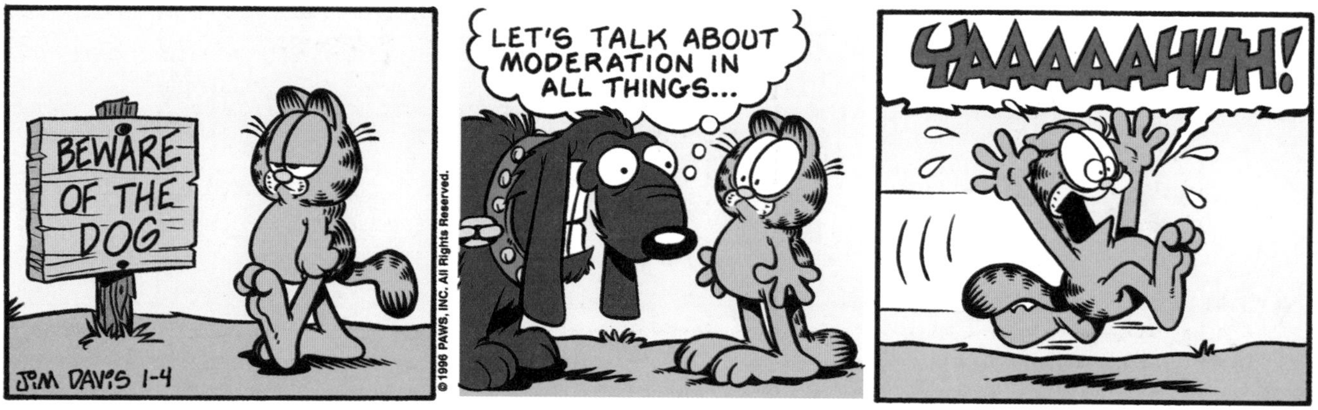
BEWARE OF THE DOG
JIM DAVIS 1-4
©1996 PAWS, INC. All Rights Reserved.
LET'S TALK ABOUT MODERATION IN ALL THINGS...
YAAAAAHHH!

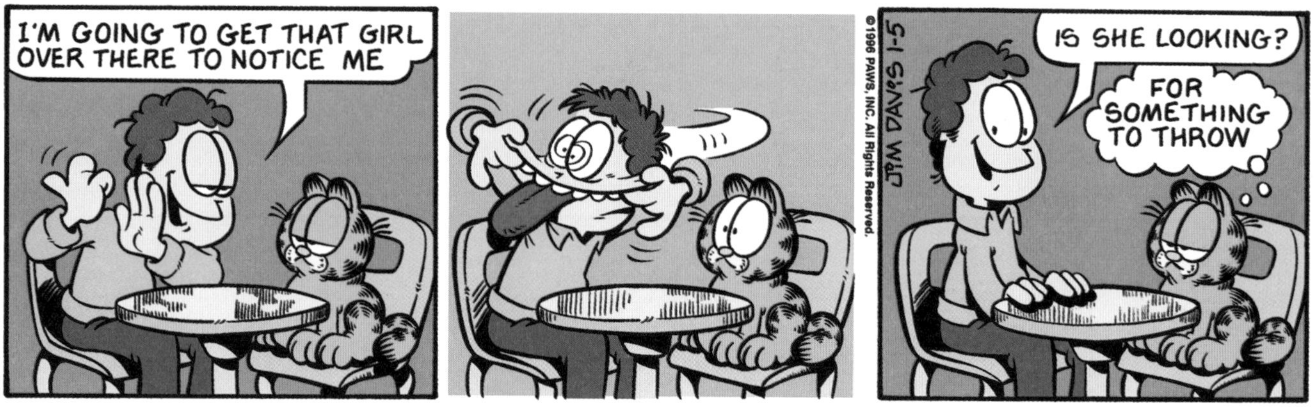
I'M GOING TO GET THAT GIRL OVER THERE TO NOTICE ME
©1996 PAWS, INC. All Rights Reserved.
JIM DAVIS 1-5
IS SHE LOOKING?
FOR SOMETHING TO THROW

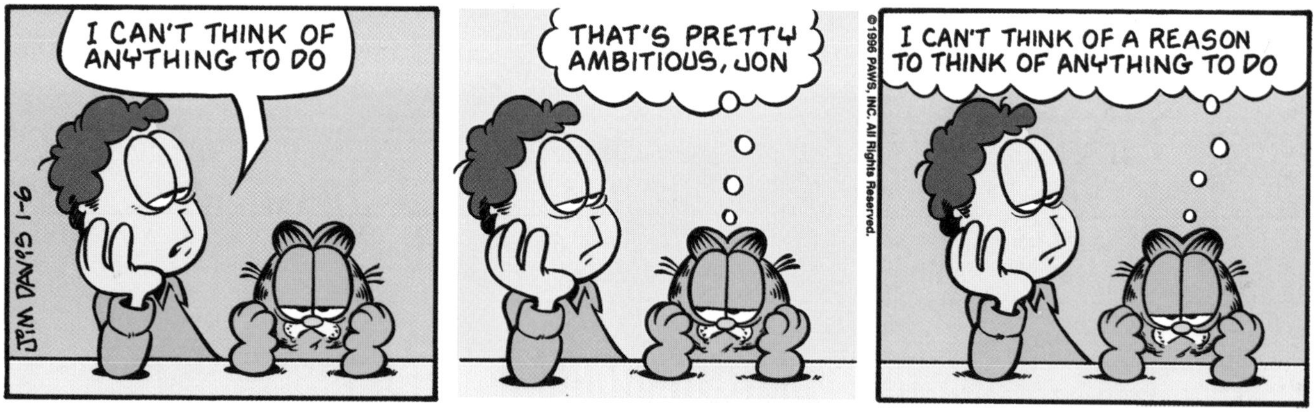
I CAN'T THINK OF ANYTHING TO DO
JIM DAVIS 1-6
THAT'S PRETTY AMBITIOUS, JON
©1996 PAWS, INC. All Rights Reserved.
I CAN'T THINK OF A REASON TO THINK OF ANYTHING TO DO

GARFIELD®
THE FIRST SNOWFLAKE OF WINTER!
© 1996 PAWS, INC. All Rights Reserved.
JIM DAVIS 1-7

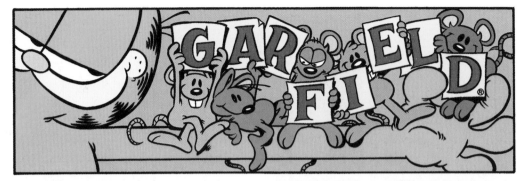

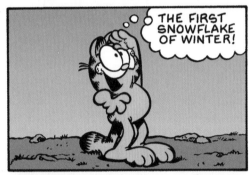

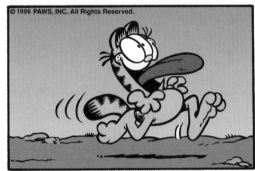

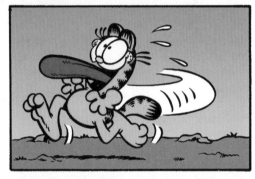

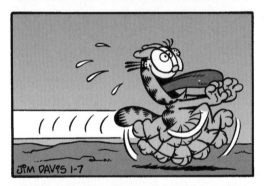

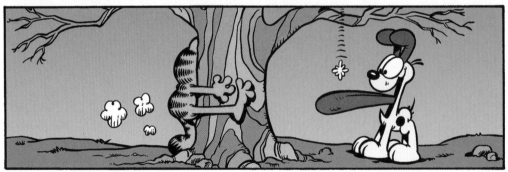

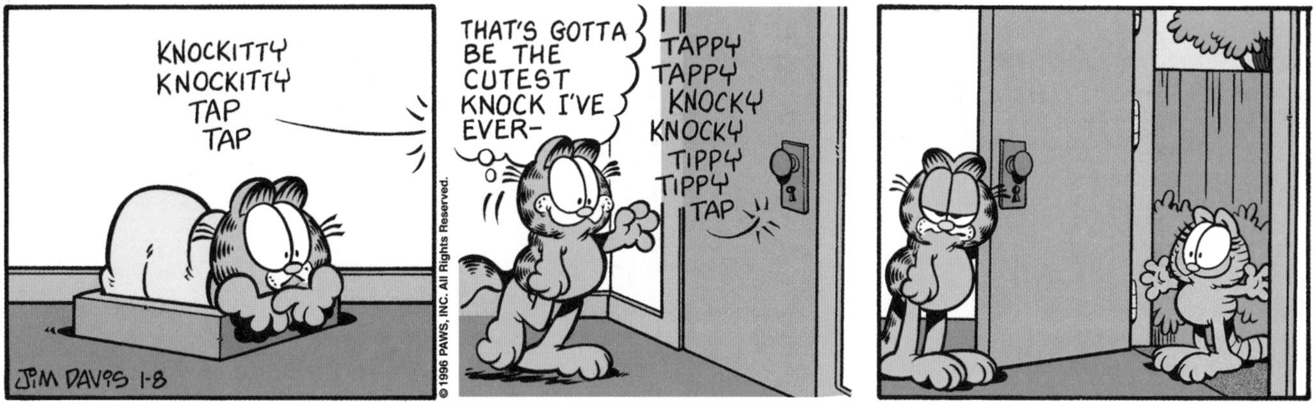
KNOCKITTY KNOCKITTY TAP TAP
JIM DAVIS 1-8
© 1996 PAWS, INC. All Rights Reserved.
THAT'S GOTTA BE THE CUTEST KNOCK I'VE EVER-
TAPPY TAPPY KNOCKY KNOCKY TIPPY TIPPY TAP

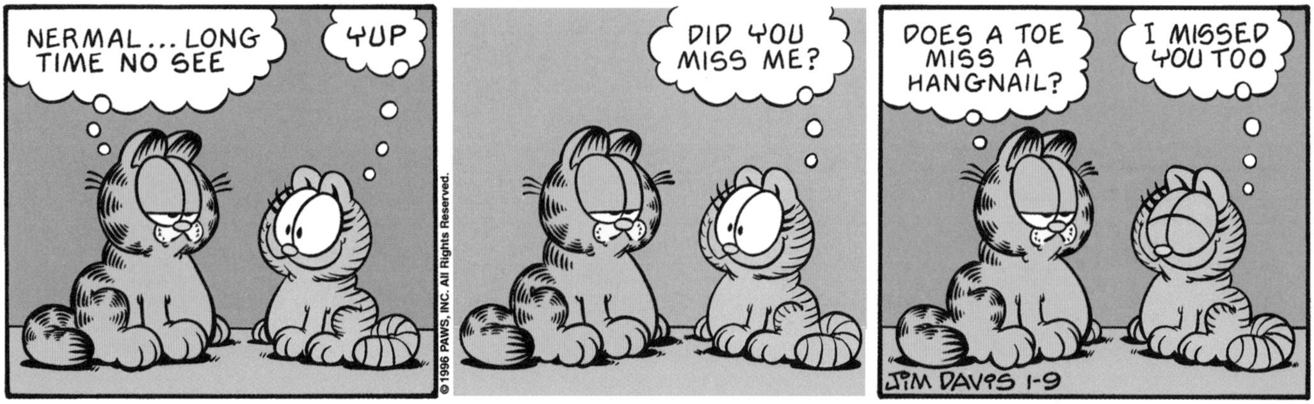
NERMAL... LONG TIME NO SEE
YUP
© 1996 PAWS, INC. All Rights Reserved.
DID YOU MISS ME?
DOES A TOE MISS A HANGNAIL?
I MISSED YOU TOO
JIM DAVIS 1-9

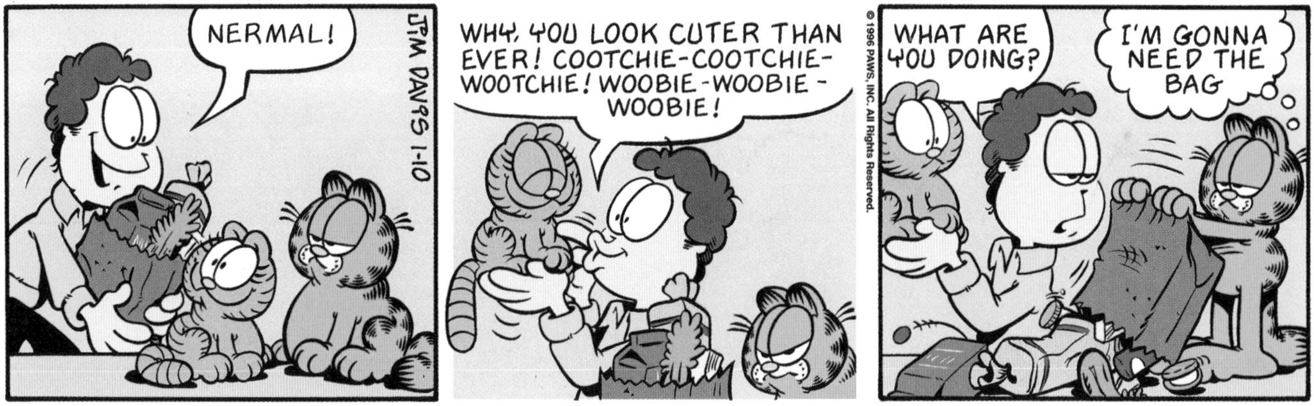
NERMAL!
JIM DAVIS 1-10
WHY, YOU LOOK CUTER THAN EVER! COOTCHIE-COOTCHIE-WOOTCHIE! WOOBIE-WOOBIE-WOOBIE!
© 1996 PAWS, INC. All Rights Reserved.
WHAT ARE YOU DOING?
I'M GONNA NEED THE BAG

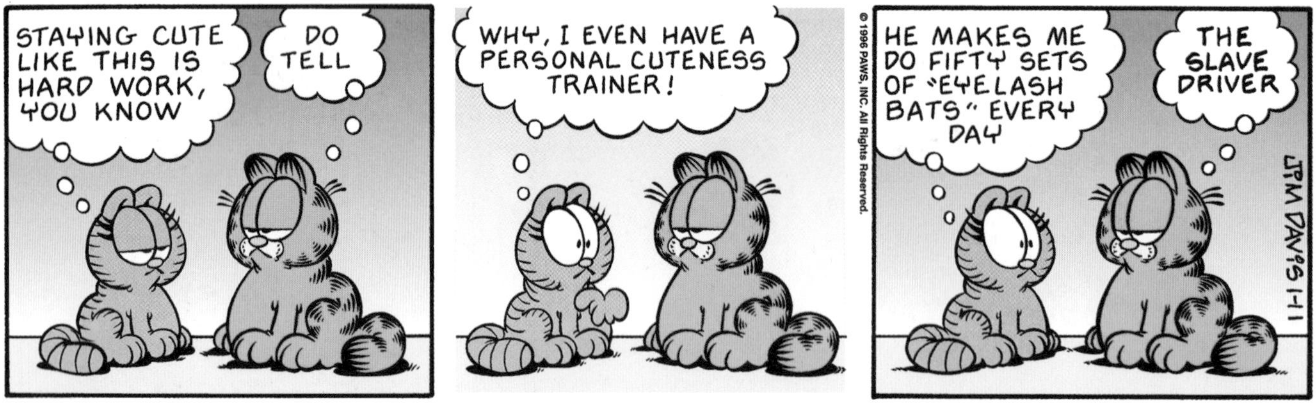
STAYING CUTE LIKE THIS IS HARD WORK, YOU KNOW
DO TELL
WHY, I EVEN HAVE A PERSONAL CUTENESS TRAINER!
© 1996 PAWS, INC. All Rights Reserved.
HE MAKES ME DO FIFTY SETS OF "EYELASH BATS" EVERY DAY
THE SLAVE DRIVER
JIM DAVIS 1-11

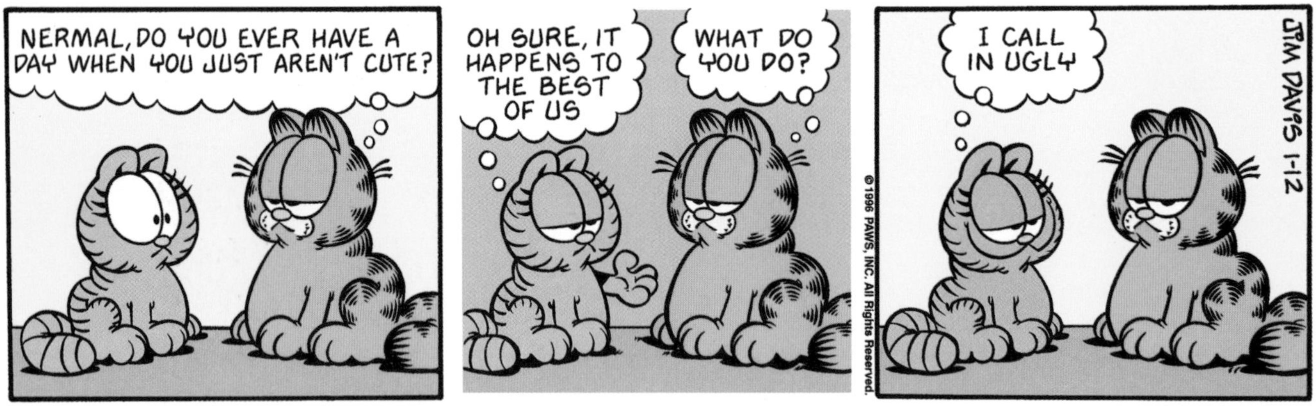
NERMAL, DO YOU EVER HAVE A DAY WHEN YOU JUST AREN'T CUTE?
OH SURE, IT HAPPENS TO THE BEST OF US
WHAT DO YOU DO?
© 1996 PAWS, INC. All Rights Reserved.
I CALL IN UGLY
JIM DAVIS 1-12

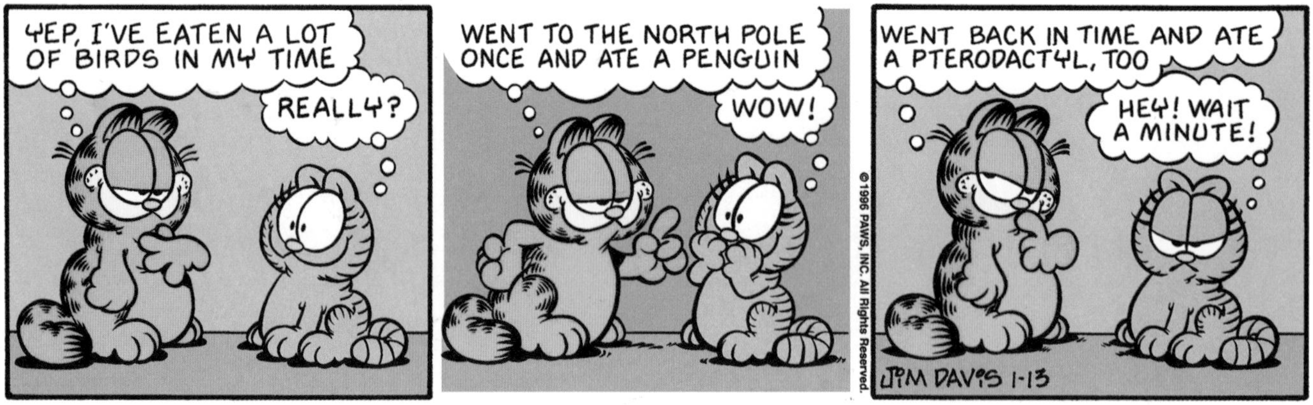
YEP, I'VE EATEN A LOT OF BIRDS IN MY TIME
REALLY?
WENT TO THE NORTH POLE ONCE AND ATE A PENGUIN
WOW!
© 1996 PAWS, INC. All Rights Reserved.
WENT BACK IN TIME AND ATE A PTERODACTYL, TOO
HEY! WAIT A MINUTE!
JIM DAVIS 1-13

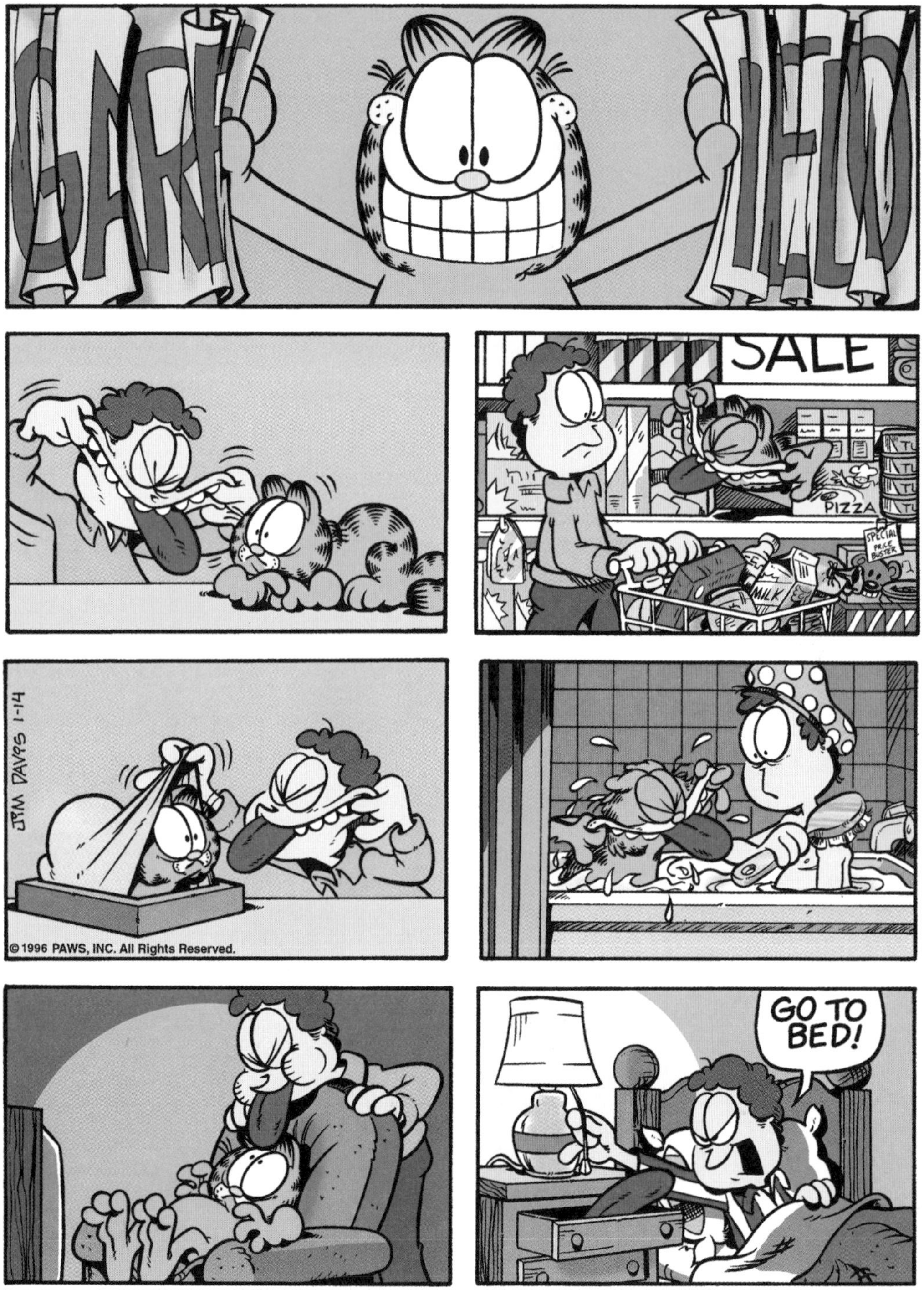
SALE
PIZZA
SPECIAL PRICE BUSTER
MILK
JIM DAVIS 1-14
© 1996 PAWS, INC. All Rights Reserved.
GO TO BED!

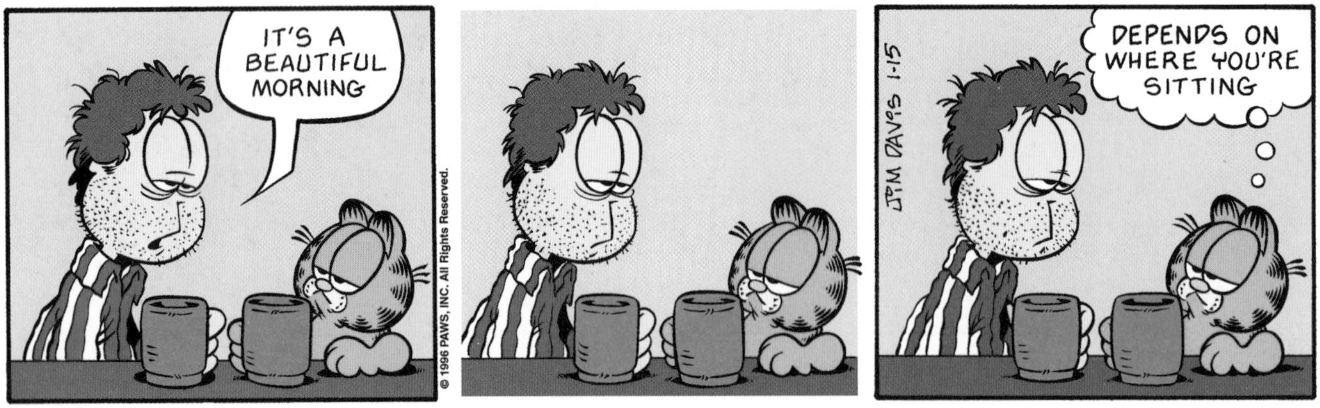
IT'S A BEAUTIFUL MORNING
© 1996 PAWS, INC. All Rights Reserved.
JIM DAVIS 1-15
DEPENDS ON WHERE YOU'RE SITTING

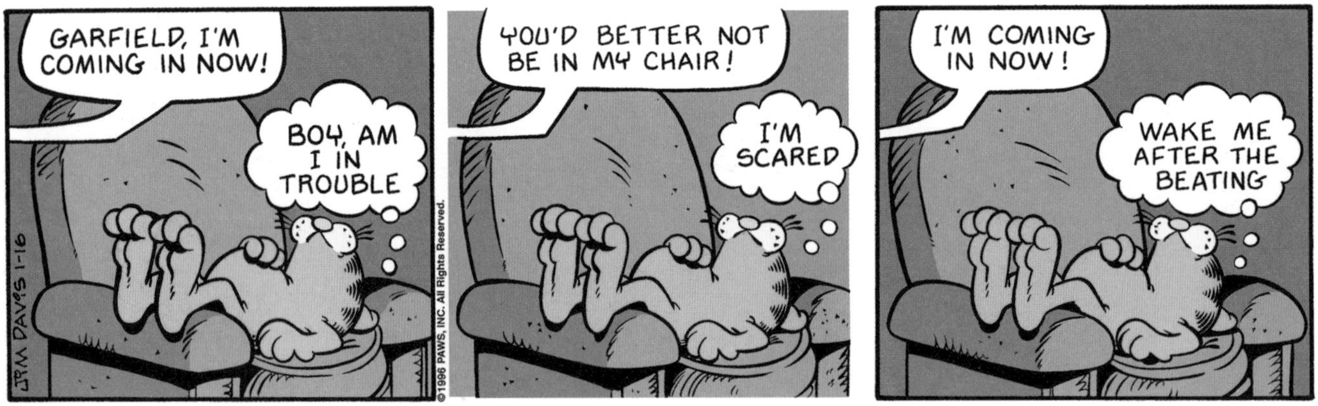
GARFIELD, I'M COMING IN NOW!
BOY, AM I IN TROUBLE
JIM DAVIS 1-16
©1996 PAWS, INC. All Rights Reserved.
YOU'D BETTER NOT BE IN MY CHAIR!
I'M SCARED
I'M COMING IN NOW!
WAKE ME AFTER THE BEATING

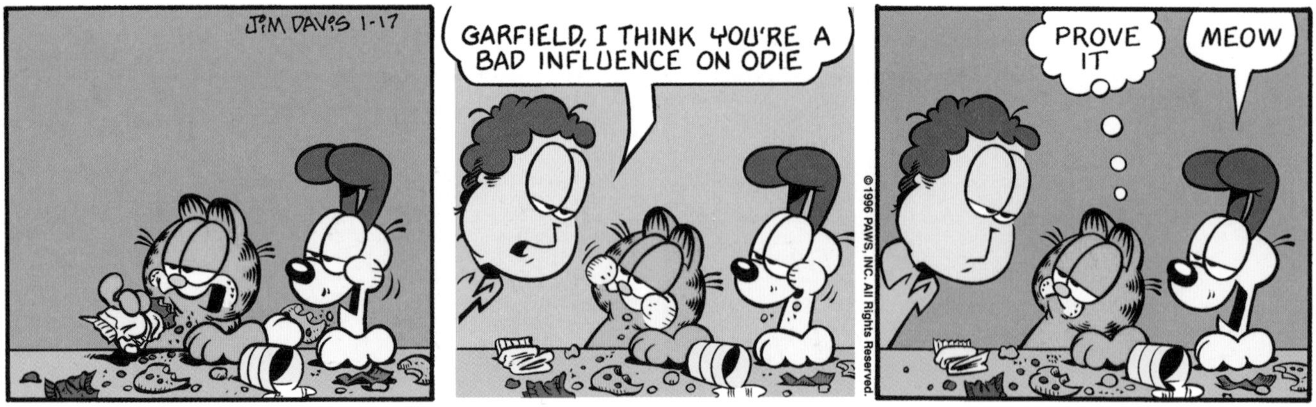
JIM DAVIS 1-17
GARFIELD, I THINK YOU'RE A BAD INFLUENCE ON ODIE
©1996 PAWS, INC. All Rights Reserved.
PROVE IT
MEOW

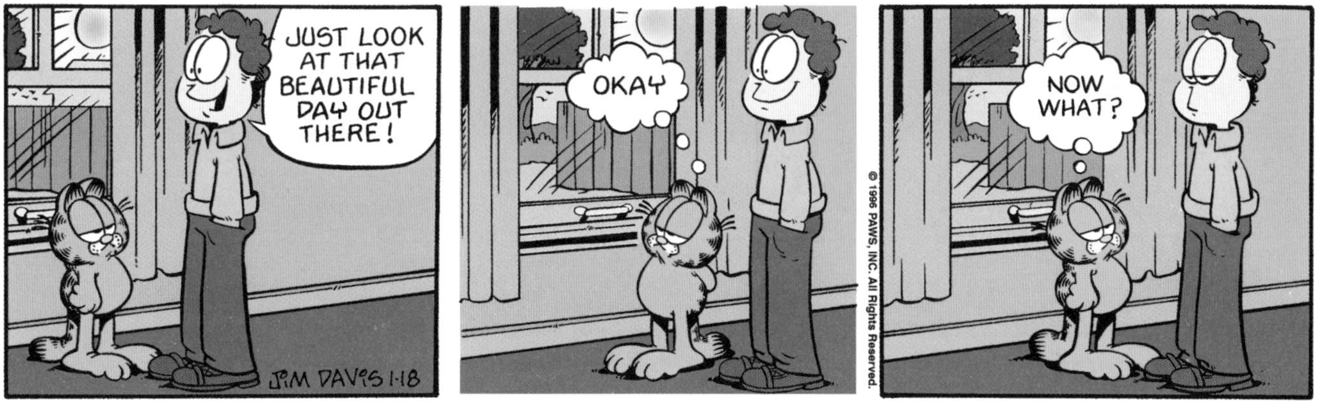
JUST LOOK AT THAT BEAUTIFUL DAY OUT THERE!
OKAY
NOW WHAT?
JIM DAVIS 1-18
© 1996 PAWS, INC. All Rights Reserved.

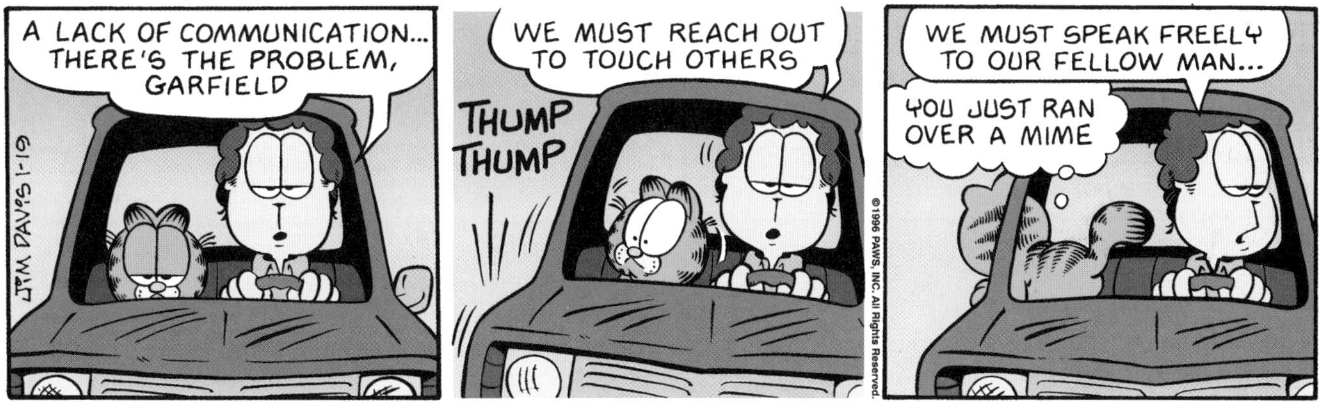
A LACK OF COMMUNICATION... THERE'S THE PROBLEM, GARFIELD
JIM DAVIS 1-19
WE MUST REACH OUT TO TOUCH OTHERS
THUMP THUMP
WE MUST SPEAK FREELY TO OUR FELLOW MAN...
YOU JUST RAN OVER A MIME
© 1996 PAWS, INC. All Rights Reserved.

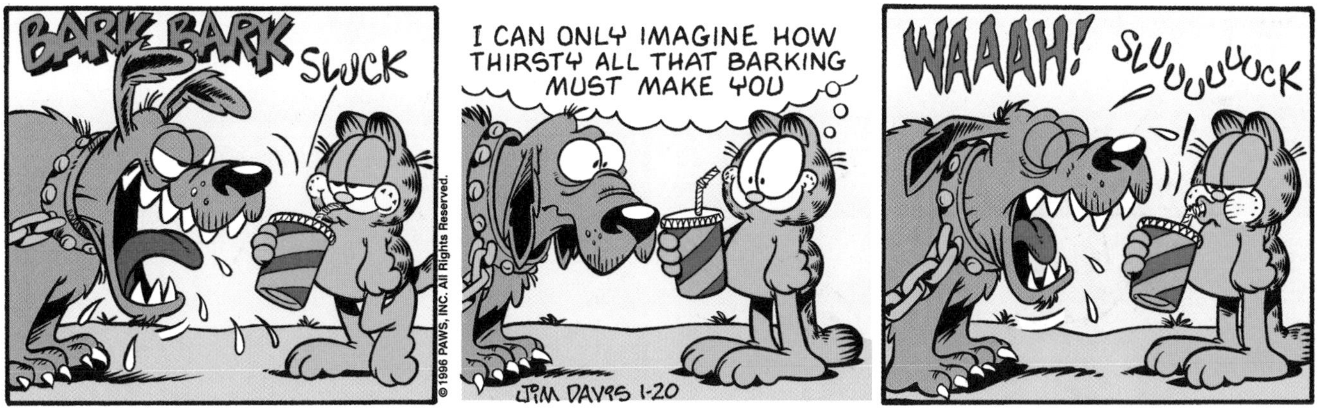
BARK BARK
SLUCK
© 1996 PAWS, INC. All Rights Reserved.
I CAN ONLY IMAGINE HOW THIRSTY ALL THAT BARKING MUST MAKE YOU
JIM DAVIS 1-20
WAAAH!
SLUUUUUUCK

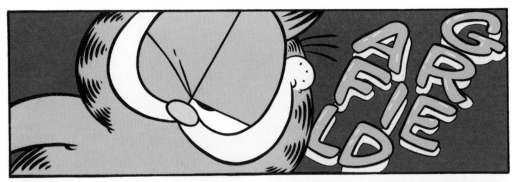

NOW YOU KNOW WHAT IT FEELS LIKE TO BE THE LAST DOUGHNUT

JIM DAVIS 1-21

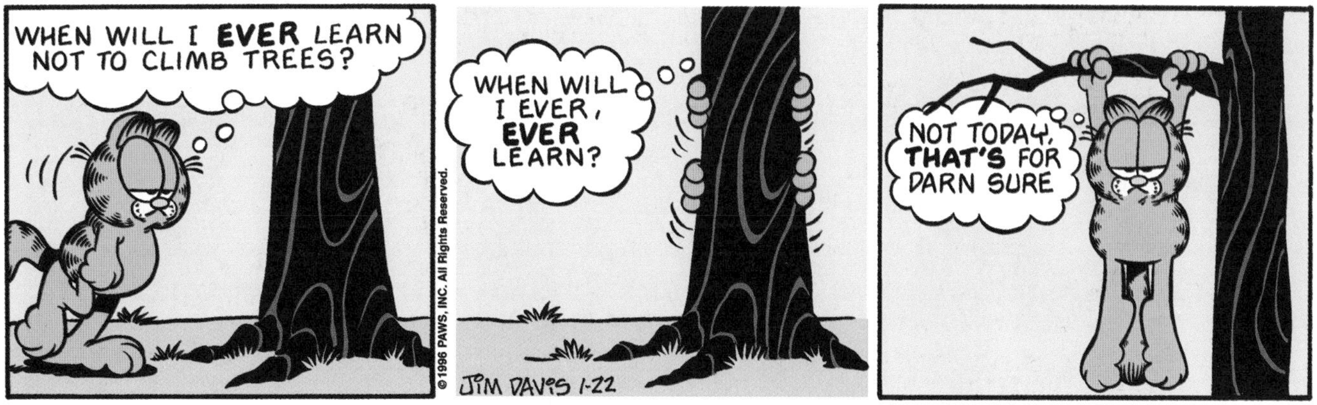
WHEN WILL I **EVER** LEARN NOT TO CLIMB TREES?
WHEN WILL I EVER, **EVER** LEARN?
© 1996 PAWS, INC. All Rights Reserved.
JIM DAVIS 1-22
NOT TODAY, **THAT'S** FOR DARN SURE

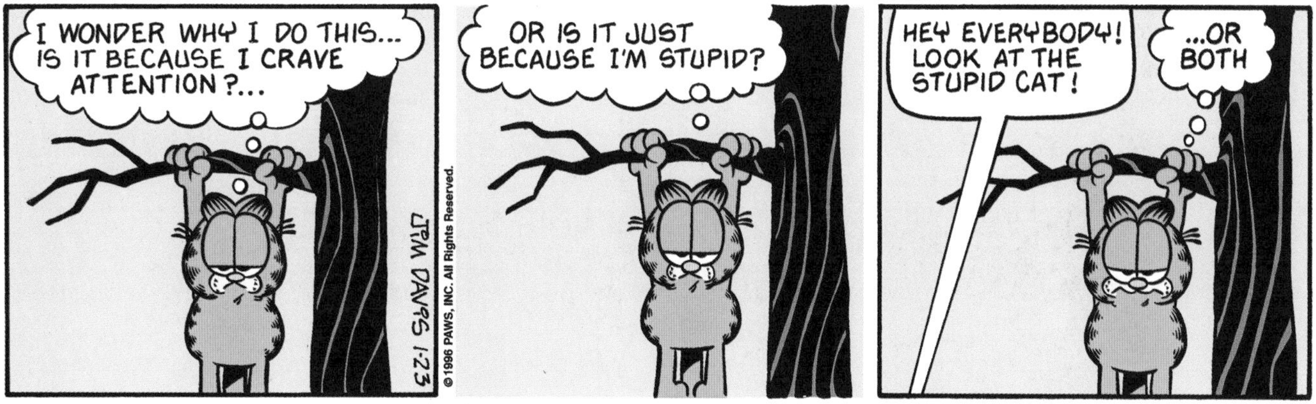
I WONDER WHY I DO THIS... IS IT BECAUSE I CRAVE ATTENTION?...
JIM DAVIS 1-23
© 1996 PAWS, INC. All Rights Reserved.
OR IS IT JUST BECAUSE I'M STUPID?
HEY EVERYBODY! LOOK AT THE STUPID CAT!
...OR BOTH

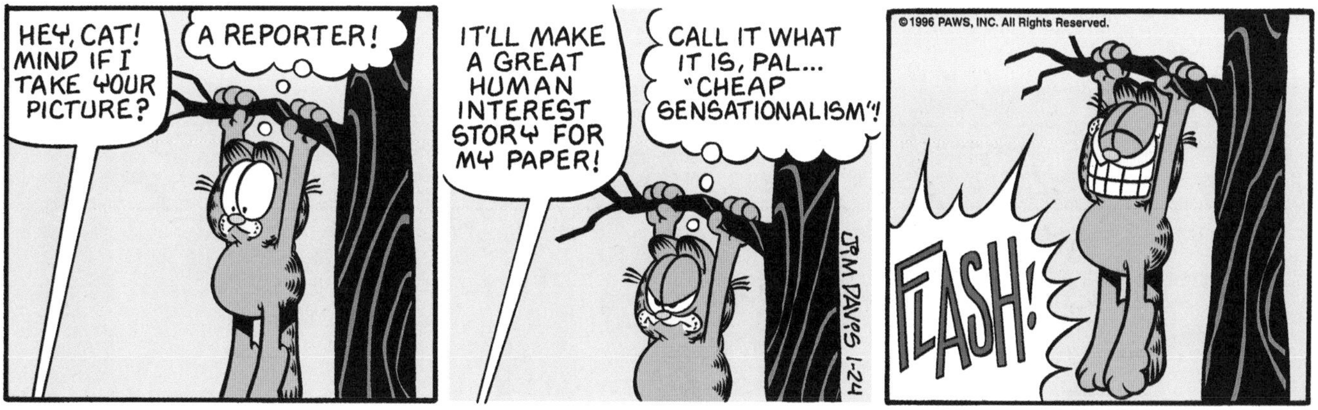
HEY, CAT! MIND IF I TAKE YOUR PICTURE?
A REPORTER!
IT'LL MAKE A GREAT HUMAN INTEREST STORY FOR MY PAPER!
CALL IT WHAT IT IS, PAL... "CHEAP SENSATIONALISM"!
JIM DAVIS 1-24
© 1996 PAWS, INC. All Rights Reserved.
FLASH!

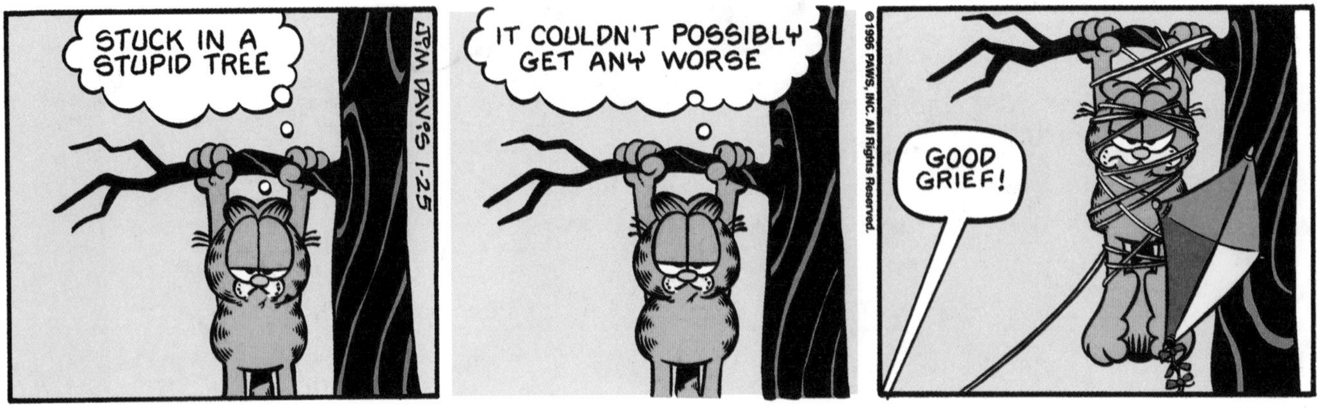
STUCK IN A STUPID TREE
JIM DAVIS 1-25
IT COULDN'T POSSIBLY GET ANY WORSE
© 1996 PAWS, INC. All Rights Reserved.
GOOD GRIEF!

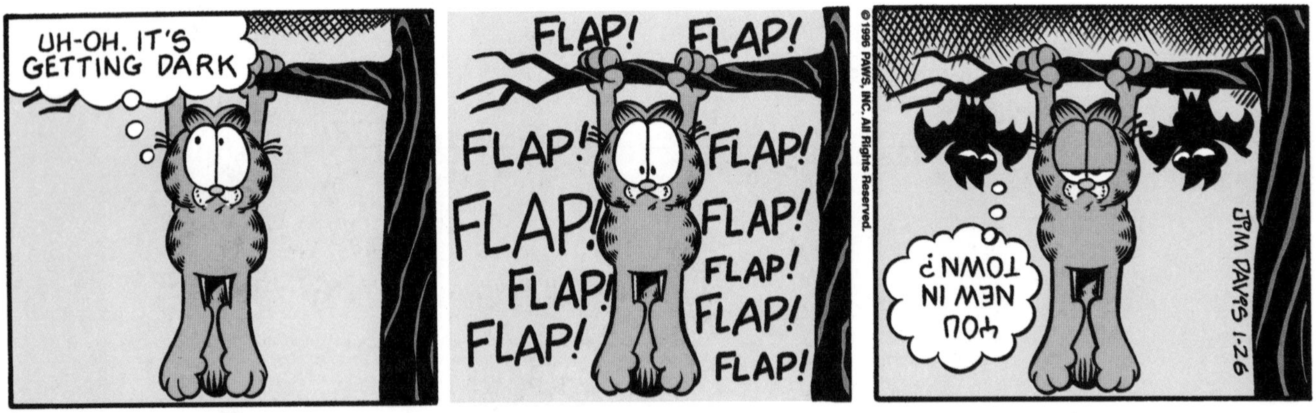
UH-OH. IT'S GETTING DARK
FLAP! FLAP! FLAP! FLAP! FLAP! FLAP! FLAP! FLAP! FLAP! FLAP! FLAP!
© 1996 PAWS, INC. All Rights Reserved.
YOU NEW IN TOWN?
JIM DAVIS 1-26

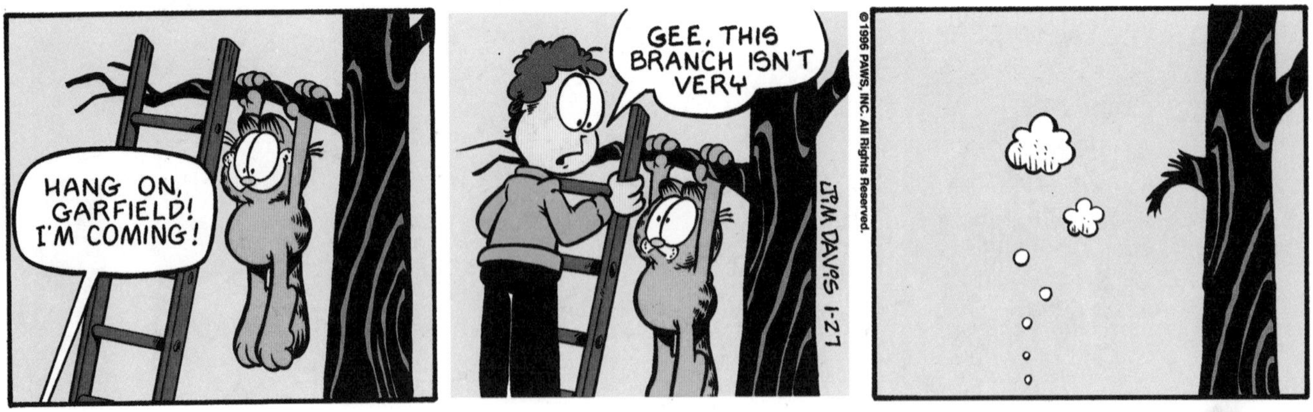
HANG ON, GARFIELD! I'M COMING!
GEE, THIS BRANCH ISN'T VERY
JIM DAVIS 1-27
© 1996 PAWS, INC. All Rights Reserved.

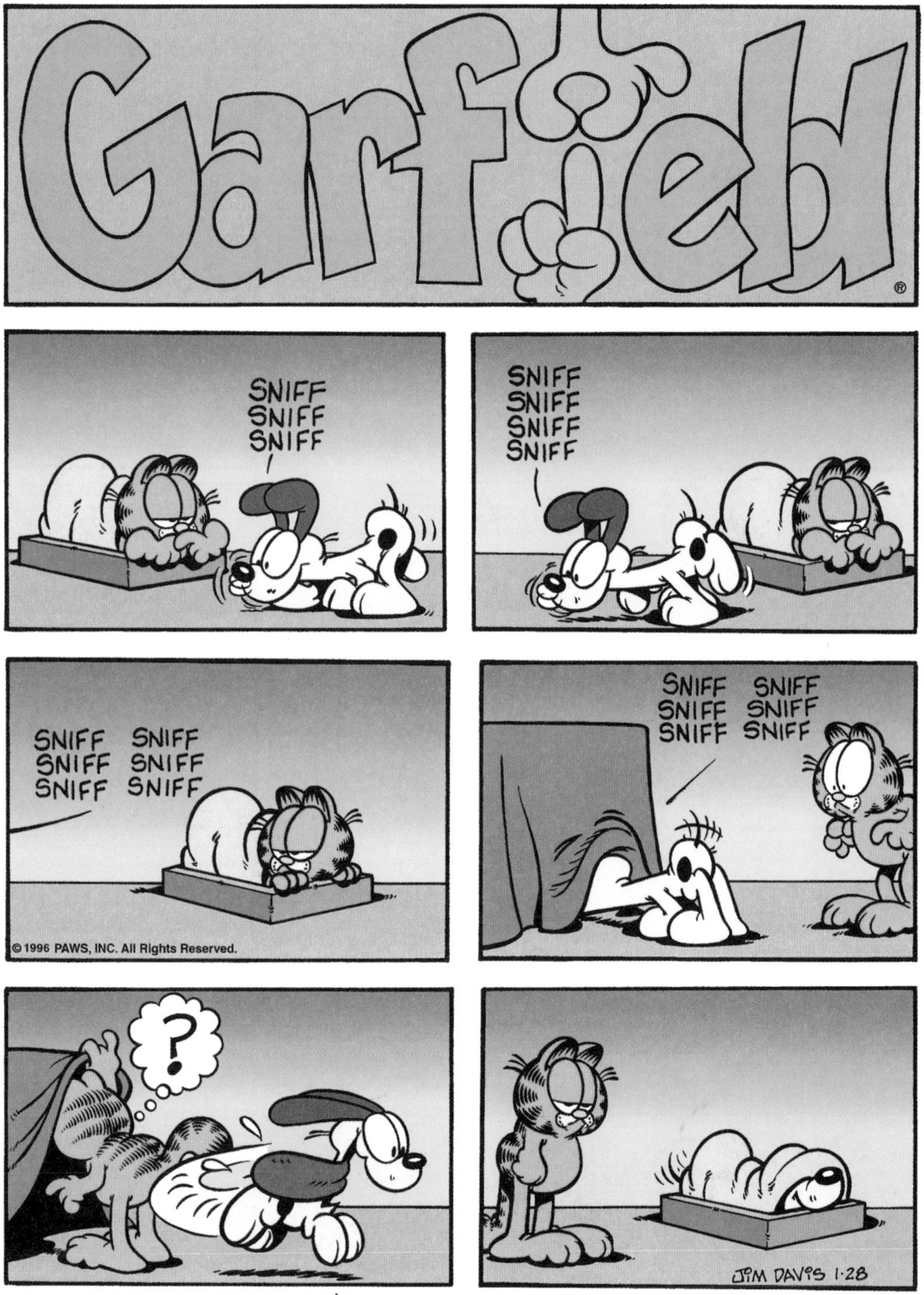
Garfield®
SNIFF SNIFF SNIFF
SNIFF SNIFF SNIFF SNIFF
SNIFF SNIFF SNIFF SNIFF SNIFF SNIFF
© 1996 PAWS, INC. All Rights Reserved.
SNIFF SNIFF SNIFF SNIFF SNIFF SNIFF
?
JIM DAVIS 1·28

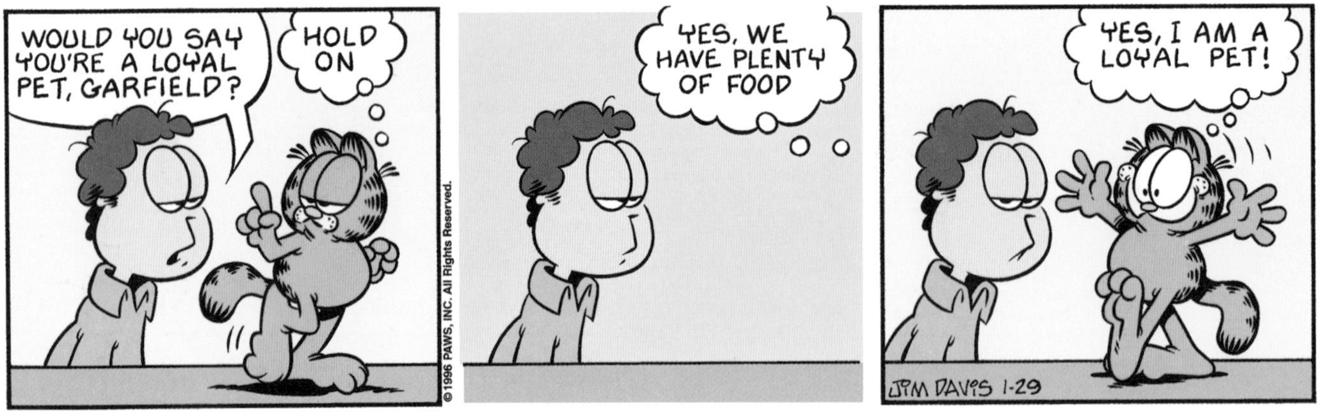
WOULD YOU SAY YOU'RE A LOYAL PET, GARFIELD?
HOLD ON
YES, WE HAVE PLENTY OF FOOD
YES, I AM A LOYAL PET!
JIM DAVIS 1-29
© 1996 PAWS, INC. All Rights Reserved.

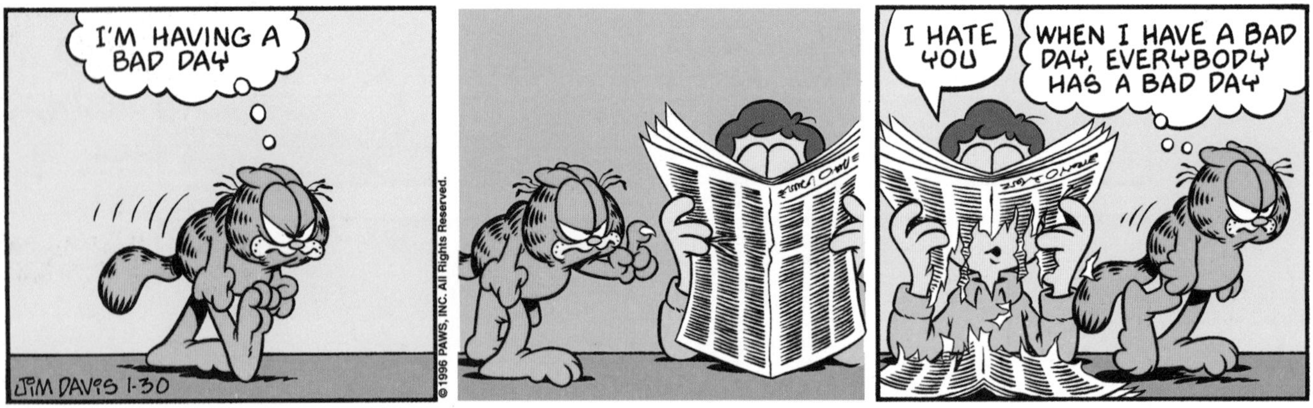
I'M HAVING A BAD DAY
JIM DAVIS 1-30
I HATE YOU
WHEN I HAVE A BAD DAY, EVERYBODY HAS A BAD DAY
© 1996 PAWS, INC. All Rights Reserved.

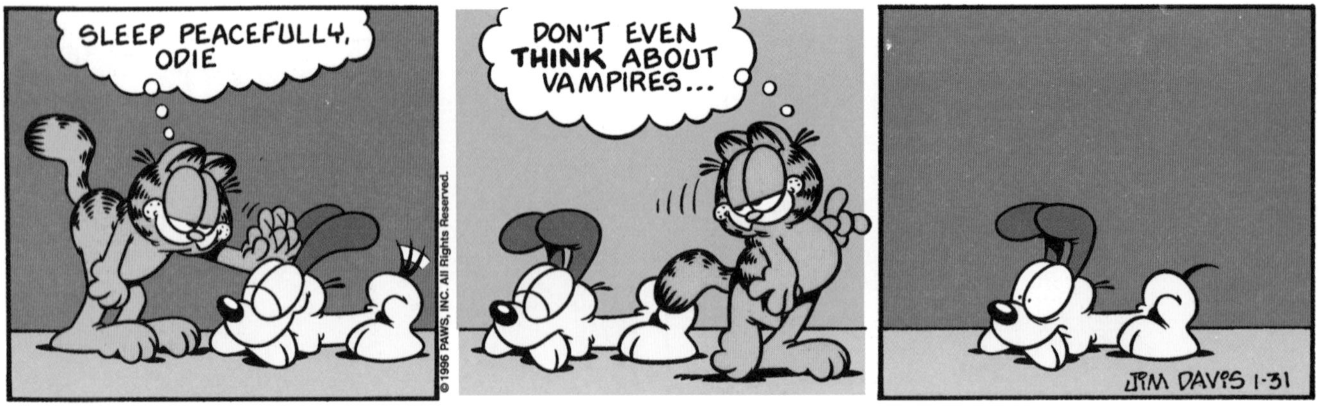
SLEEP PEACEFULLY, ODIE
DON'T EVEN **THINK** ABOUT VAMPIRES...
JIM DAVIS 1-31
© 1996 PAWS, INC. All Rights Reserved.

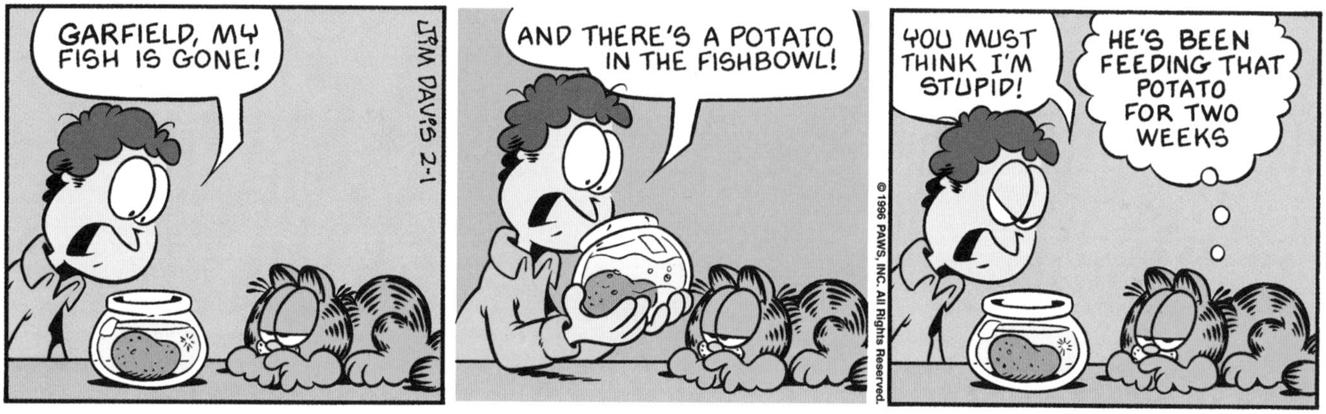
JIM DAVIS 2-1
GARFIELD, MY FISH IS GONE!
AND THERE'S A POTATO IN THE FISHBOWL!
© 1996 PAWS, INC. All Rights Reserved.
YOU MUST THINK I'M STUPID!
HE'S BEEN FEEDING THAT POTATO FOR TWO WEEKS

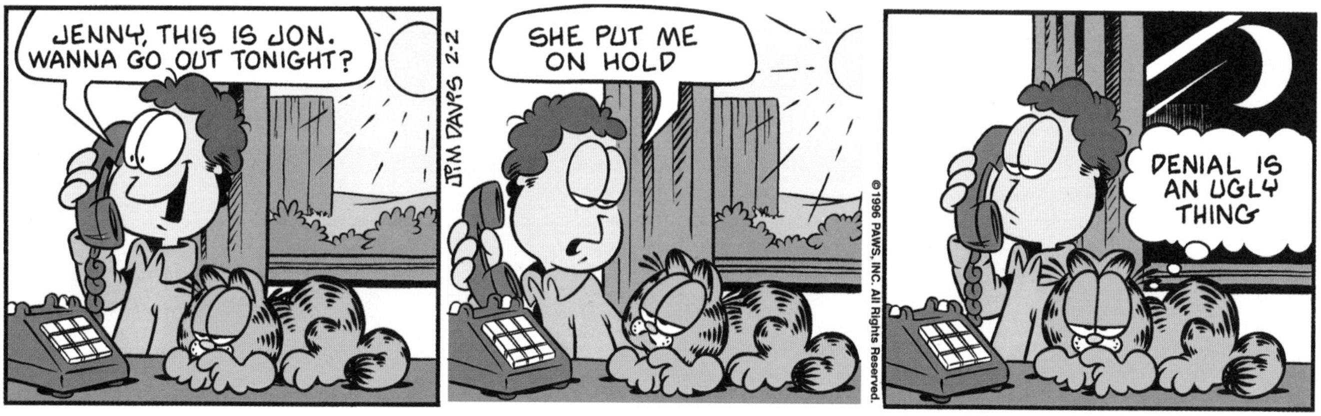
JENNY, THIS IS JON. WANNA GO OUT TONIGHT?
JIM DAVIS 2-2
SHE PUT ME ON HOLD
© 1996 PAWS, INC. All Rights Reserved.
DENIAL IS AN UGLY THING

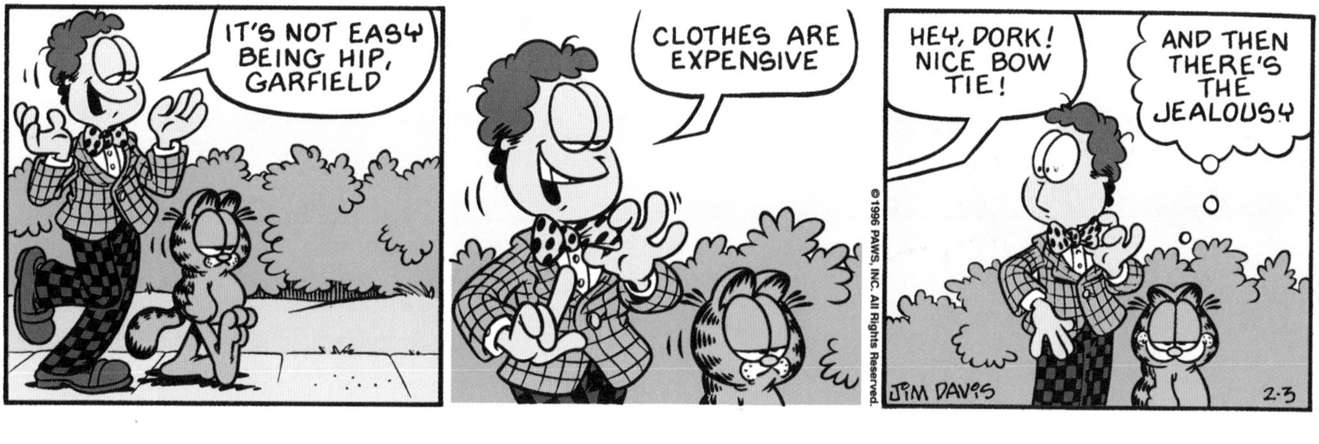
IT'S NOT EASY BEING HIP, GARFIELD
CLOTHES ARE EXPENSIVE
© 1996 PAWS, INC. All Rights Reserved.
HEY, DORK! NICE BOW TIE!
AND THEN THERE'S THE JEALOUSY
JIM DAVIS
2-3

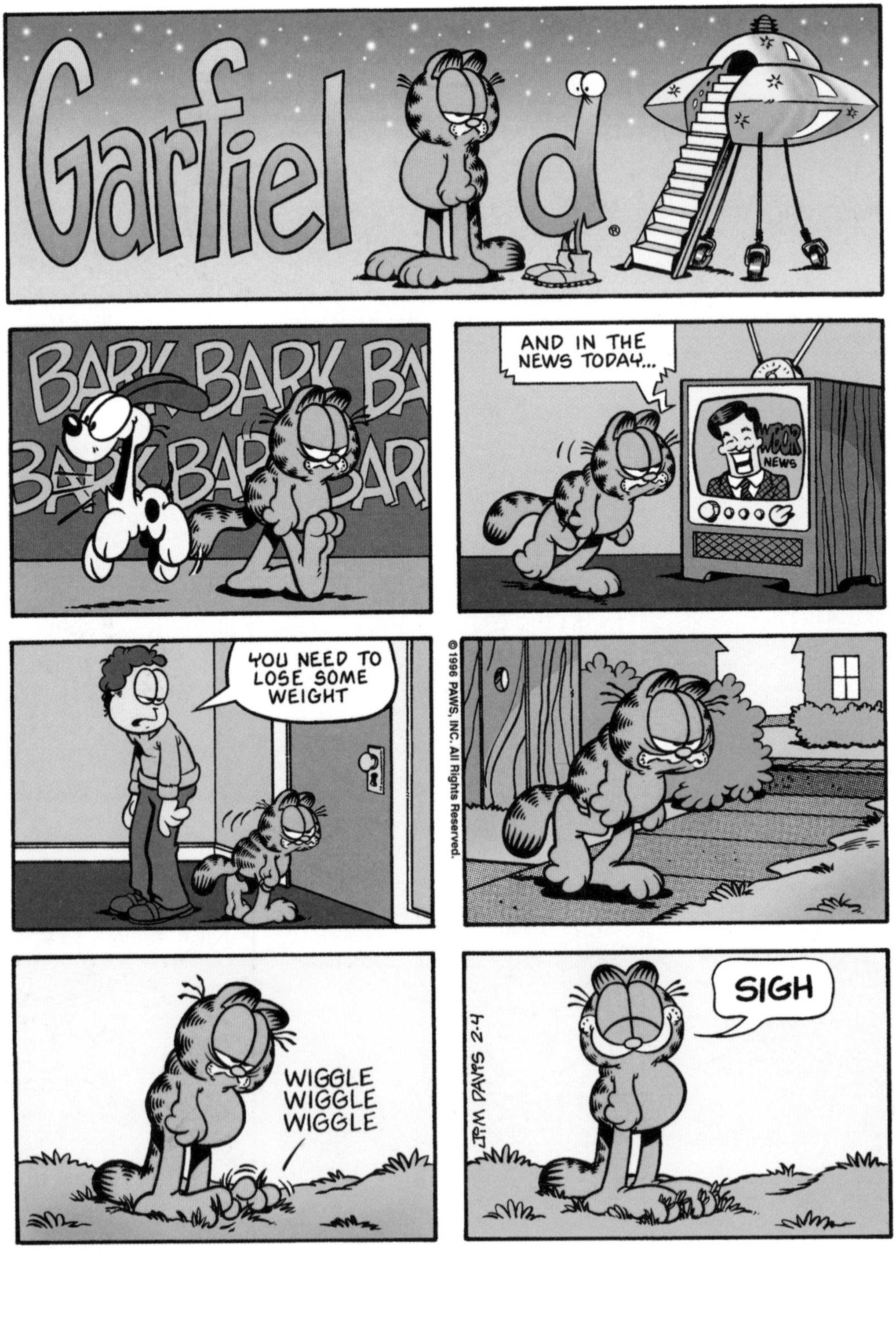
Garfield
BARK BARK
AND IN THE NEWS TODAY...
WDOR NEWS
YOU NEED TO LOSE SOME WEIGHT
© 1996 PAWS, INC. All Rights Reserved.
WIGGLE WIGGLE WIGGLE
JIM DAVIS 2-4
SIGH

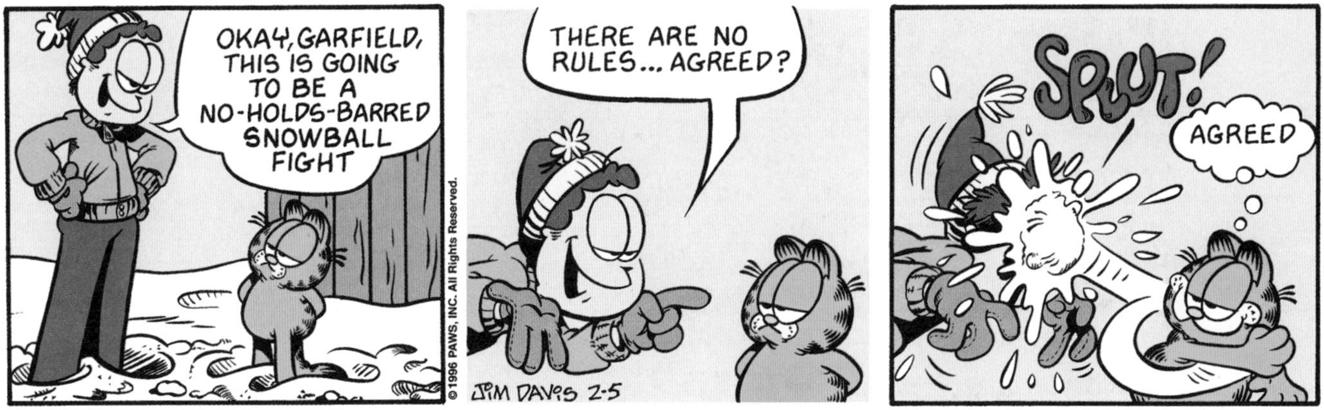
OKAY, GARFIELD, THIS IS GOING TO BE A NO-HOLDS-BARRED SNOWBALL FIGHT
© 1996 PAWS, INC. All Rights Reserved.
THERE ARE NO RULES... AGREED?
JIM DAVIS 2-5
SPLUT!
AGREED

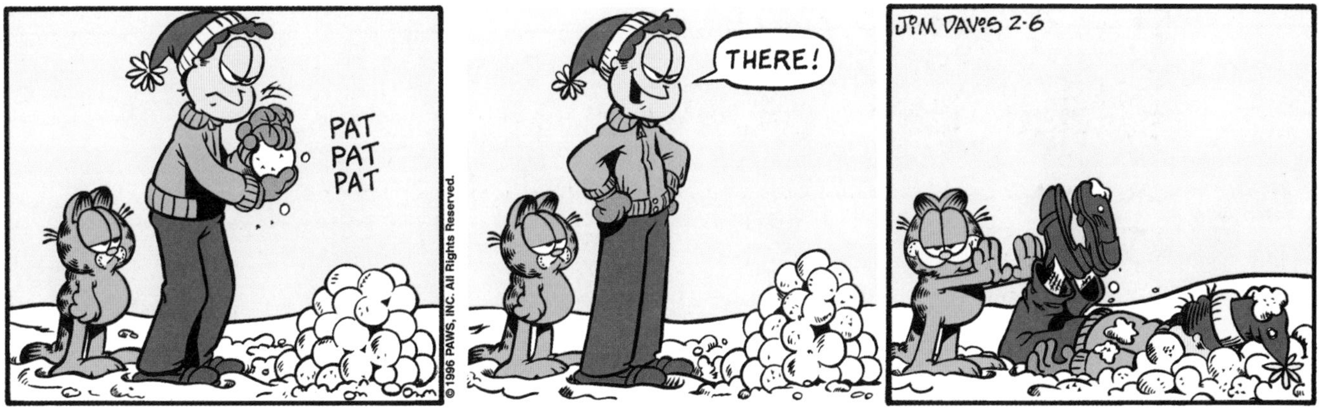
PAT PAT PAT
© 1996 PAWS, INC. All Rights Reserved.
THERE!
JIM DAVIS 2-6

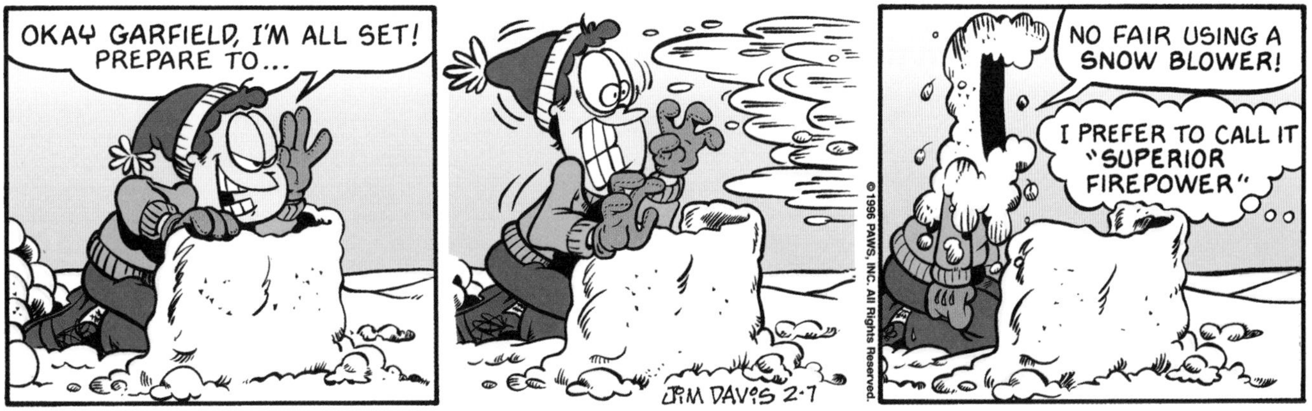
OKAY GARFIELD, I'M ALL SET! PREPARE TO...
JIM DAVIS 2-7
© 1996 PAWS, INC. All Rights Reserved.
NO FAIR USING A SNOW BLOWER!
I PREFER TO CALL IT "SUPERIOR FIREPOWER"

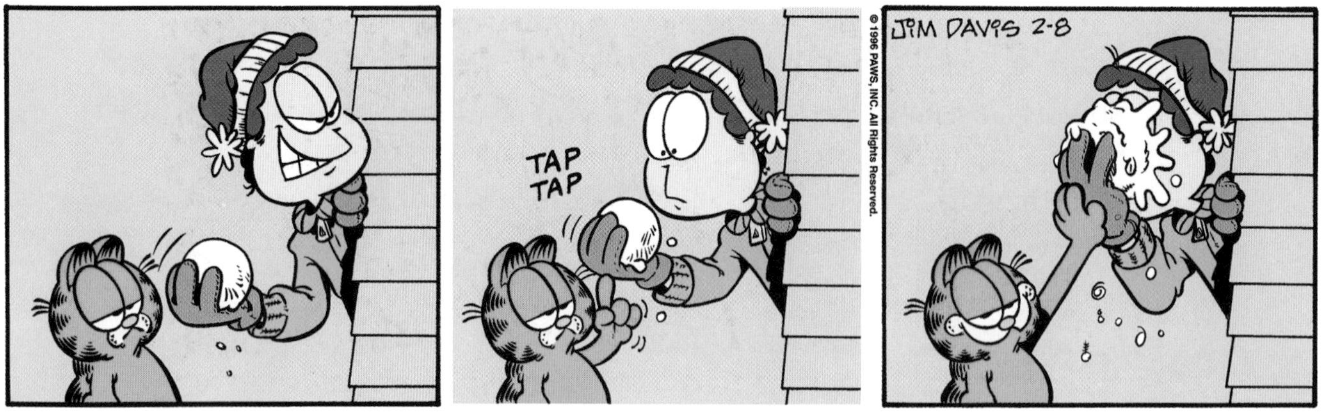
TAP
TAP
JIM DAVIS 2-8
© 1996 PAWS, INC. All Rights Reserved.

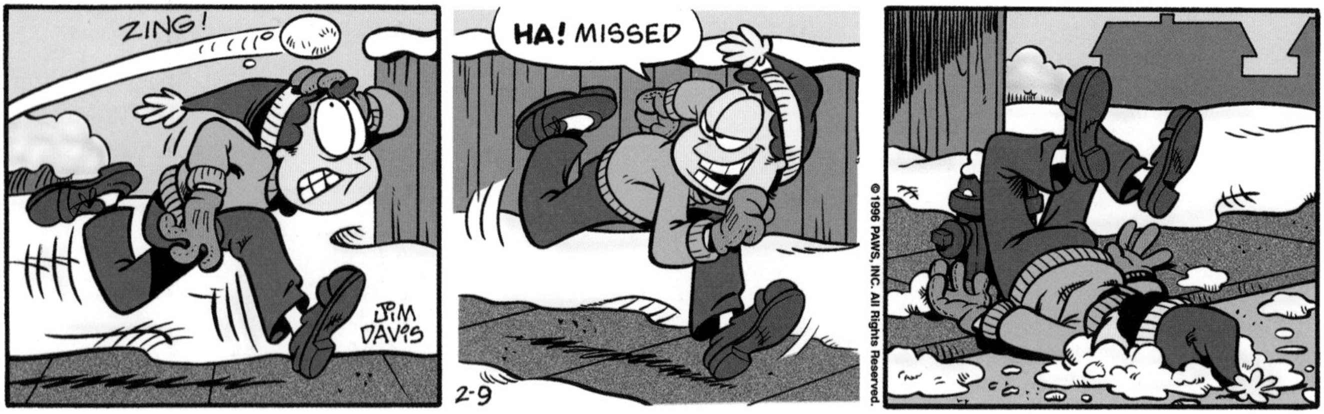
ZING!
JIM DAVIS
HA! MISSED
2-9
© 1996 PAWS, INC. All Rights Reserved.

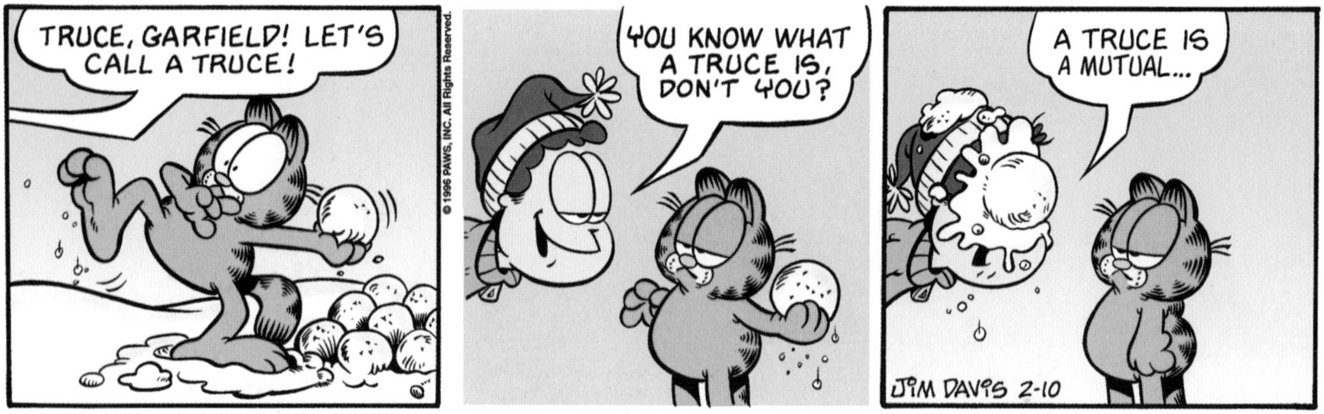
TRUCE, GARFIELD! LET'S CALL A TRUCE!
© 1996 PAWS, INC. All Rights Reserved.
YOU KNOW WHAT A TRUCE IS, DON'T YOU?
A TRUCE IS A MUTUAL...
JIM DAVIS 2-10

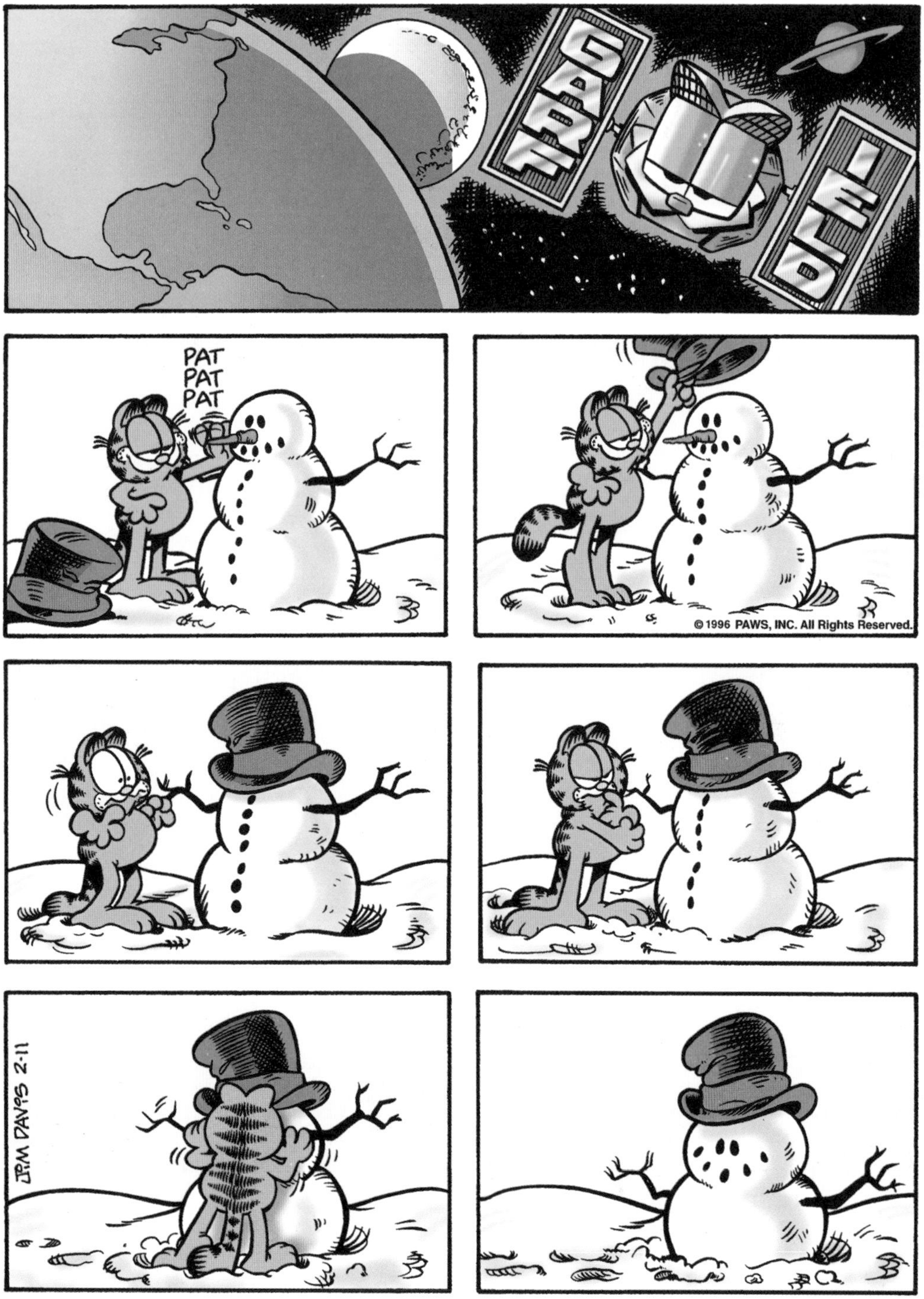
GARFIELD
PAT
PAT
PAT
© 1996 PAWS, INC. All Rights Reserved.
JIM DAVIS 2-11

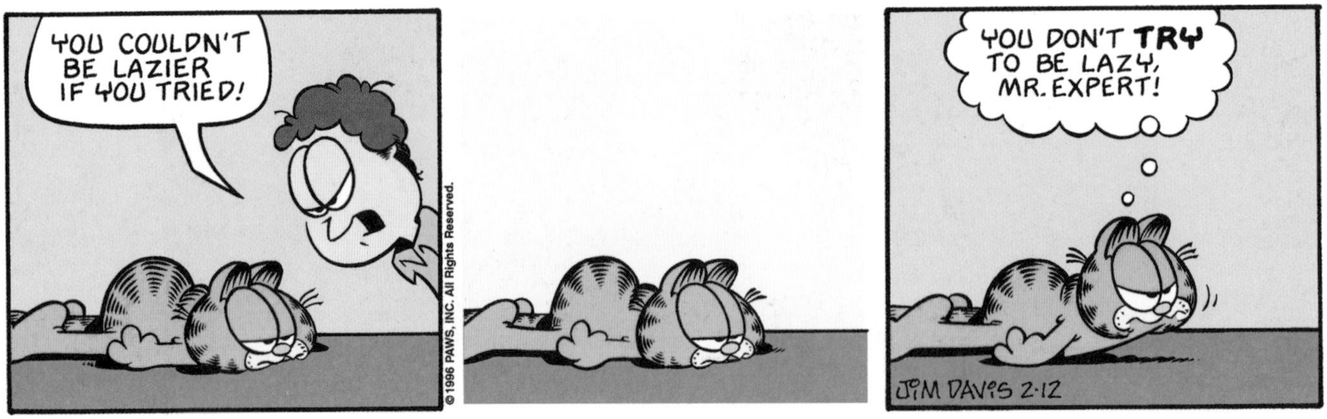
YOU COULDN'T BE LAZIER IF YOU TRIED!
© 1996 PAWS, INC. All Rights Reserved.
YOU DON'T TRY TO BE LAZY, MR. EXPERT!
JIM DAVIS 2-12

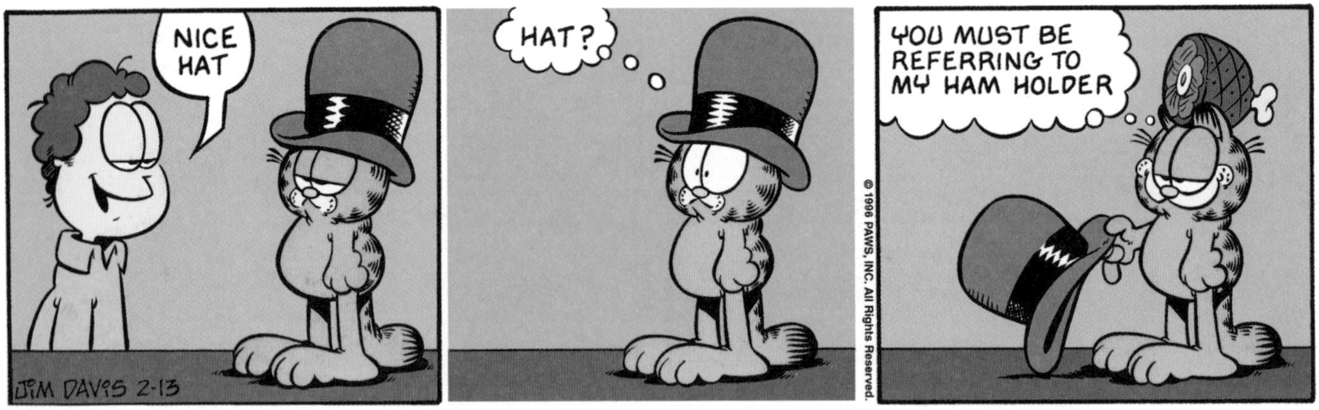
NICE HAT
JIM DAVIS 2-13
HAT?
© 1996 PAWS, INC. All Rights Reserved.
YOU MUST BE REFERRING TO MY HAM HOLDER

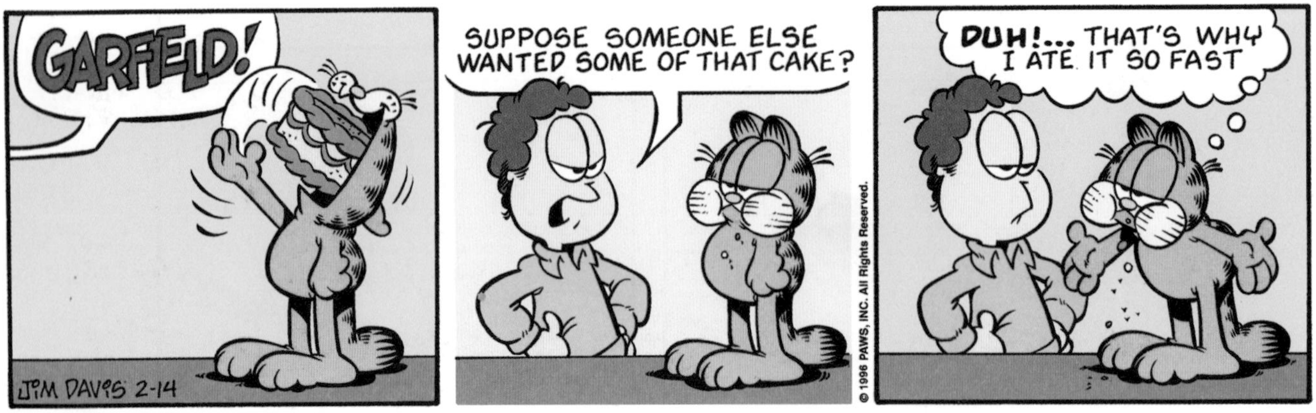
GARFIELD!
JIM DAVIS 2-14
SUPPOSE SOMEONE ELSE WANTED SOME OF THAT CAKE?
© 1996 PAWS, INC. All Rights Reserved.
DUH!... THAT'S WHY I ATE IT SO FAST

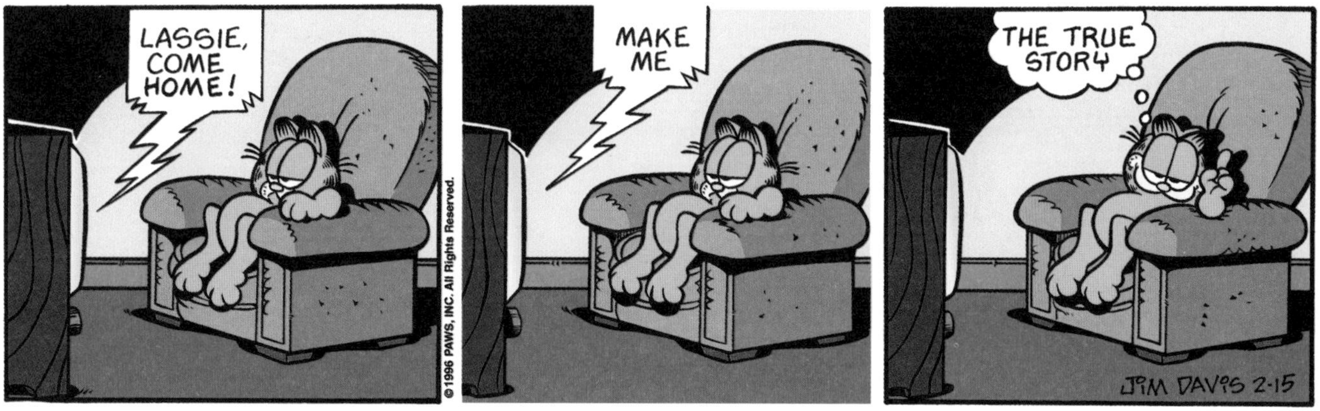
LASSIE, COME HOME!
MAKE ME
THE TRUE STORY
JIM DAVIS 2-15
©1996 PAWS, INC. All Rights Reserved.

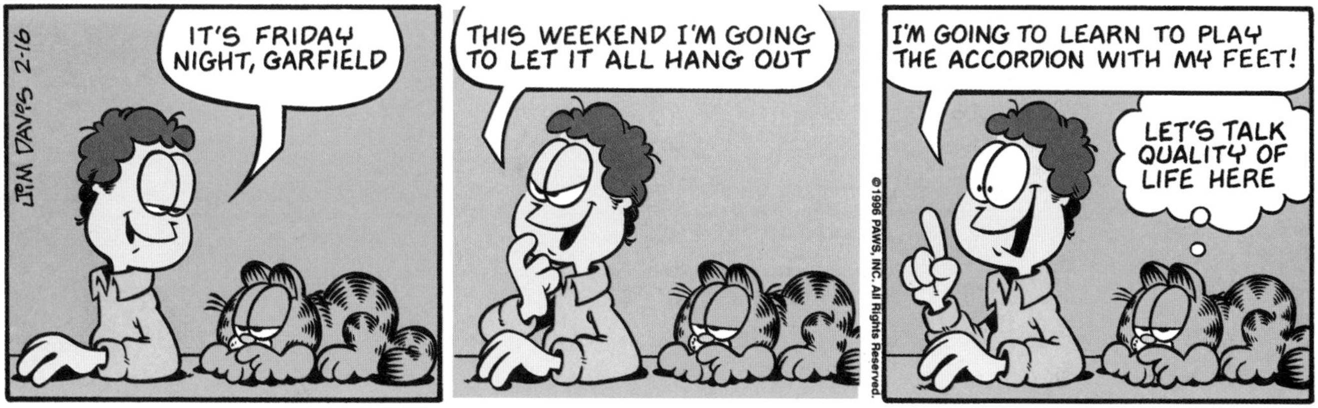
JIM DAVIS 2-16
IT'S FRIDAY NIGHT, GARFIELD
THIS WEEKEND I'M GOING TO LET IT ALL HANG OUT
I'M GOING TO LEARN TO PLAY THE ACCORDION WITH MY FEET!
LET'S TALK QUALITY OF LIFE HERE
©1996 PAWS, INC. All Rights Reserved.

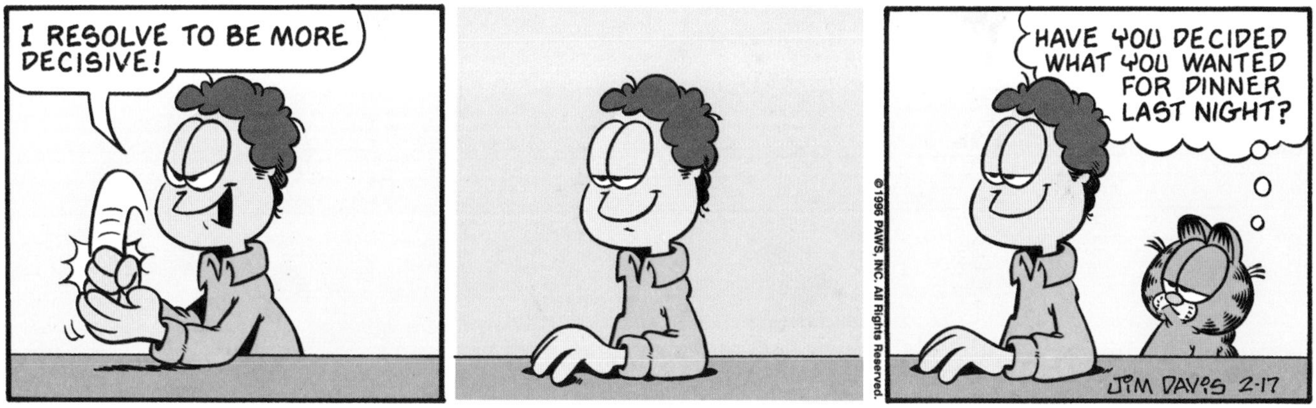
I RESOLVE TO BE MORE DECISIVE!
HAVE YOU DECIDED WHAT YOU WANTED FOR DINNER LAST NIGHT?
JIM DAVIS 2-17
©1996 PAWS, INC. All Rights Reserved.

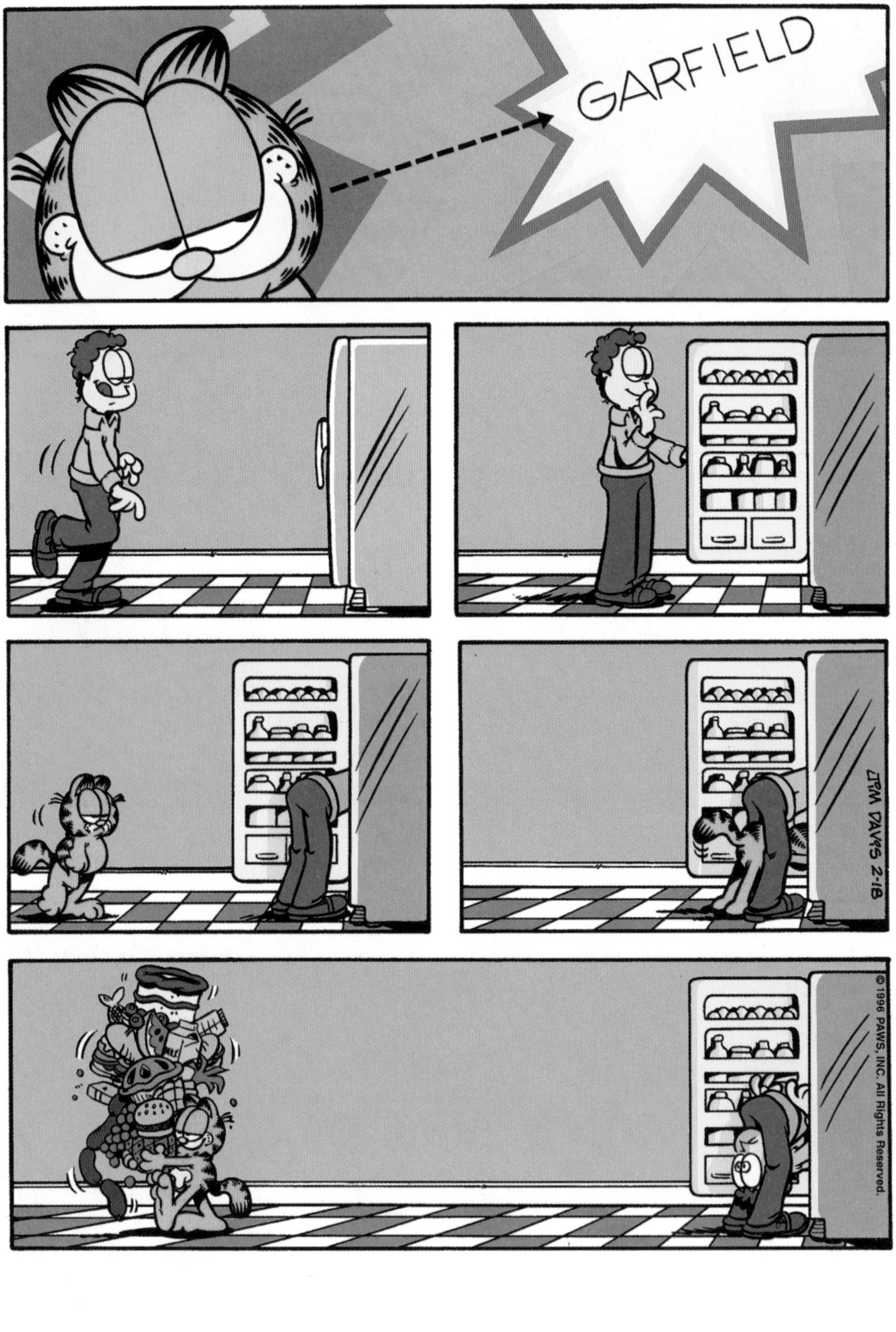
GARFIELD
JIM DAVIS 2-18
© 1996 PAWS, INC. All Rights Reserved.

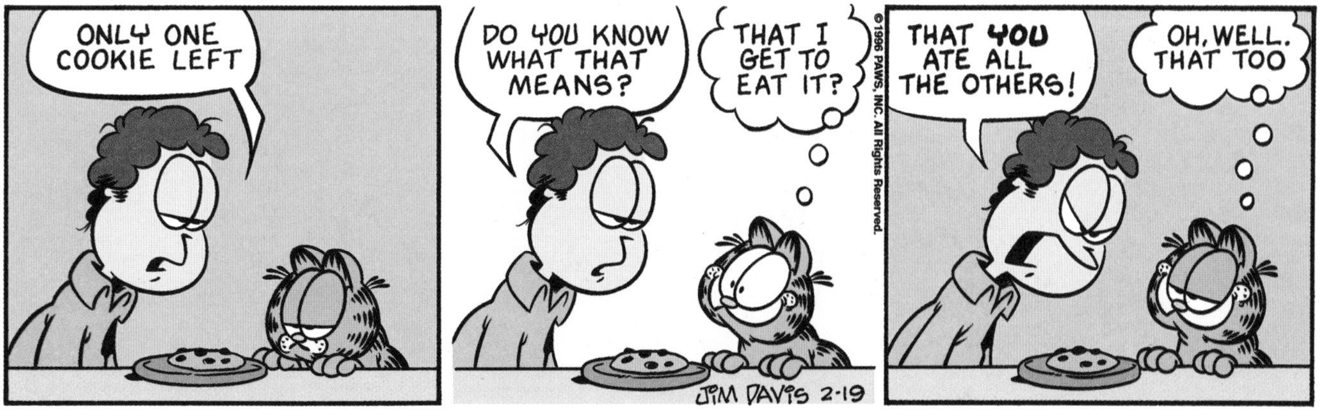
ONLY ONE COOKIE LEFT
DO YOU KNOW WHAT THAT MEANS?
THAT I GET TO EAT IT?
THAT YOU ATE ALL THE OTHERS!
OH, WELL. THAT TOO
JIM DAVIS 2-19
© 1996 PAWS, INC. All Rights Reserved.

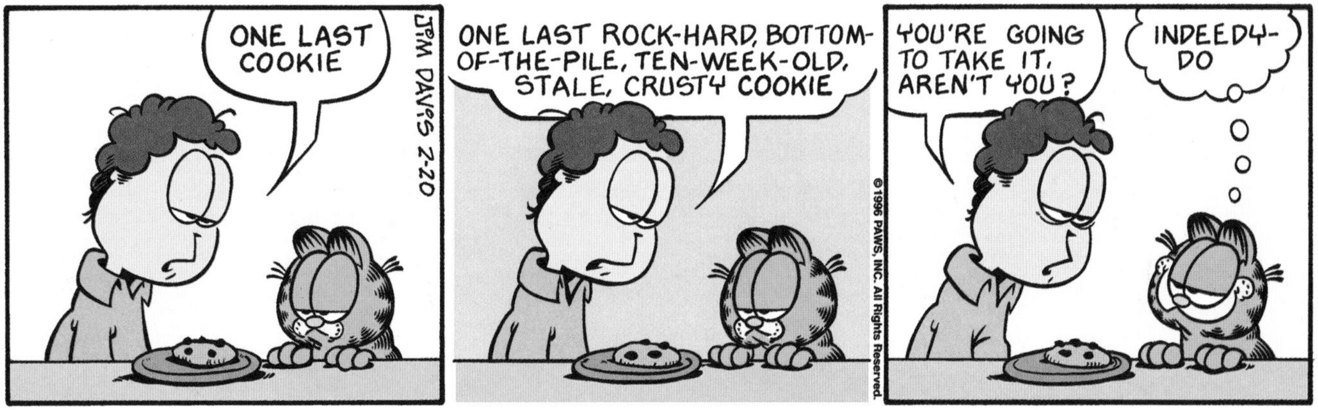
ONE LAST COOKIE
ONE LAST ROCK-HARD, BOTTOM-OF-THE-PILE, TEN-WEEK-OLD, STALE, CRUSTY COOKIE
YOU'RE GOING TO TAKE IT, AREN'T YOU?
INDEEDY-DO
JIM DAVIS 2-20
© 1996 PAWS, INC. All Rights Reserved.

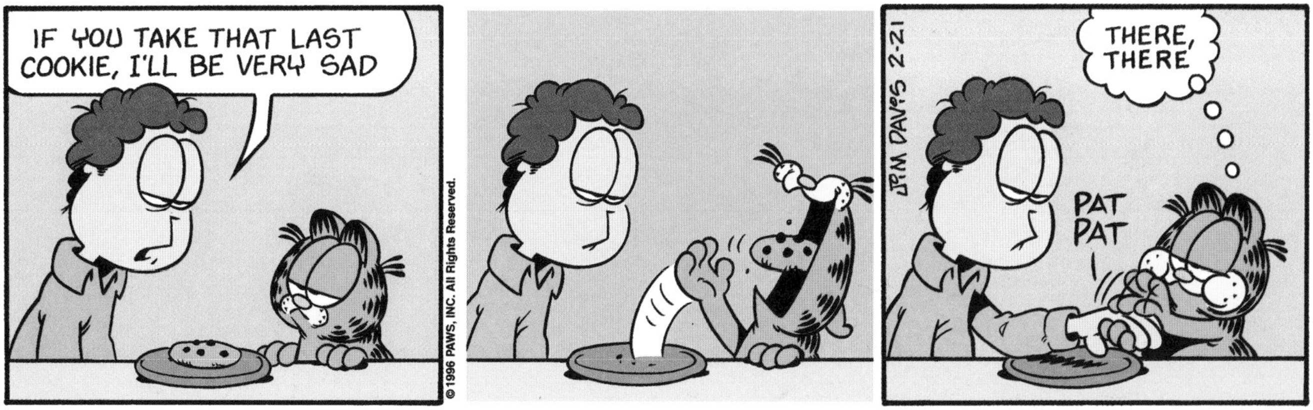
IF YOU TAKE THAT LAST COOKIE, I'LL BE VERY SAD
THERE, THERE
PAT PAT
JIM DAVIS 2-21
© 1996 PAWS, INC. All Rights Reserved.

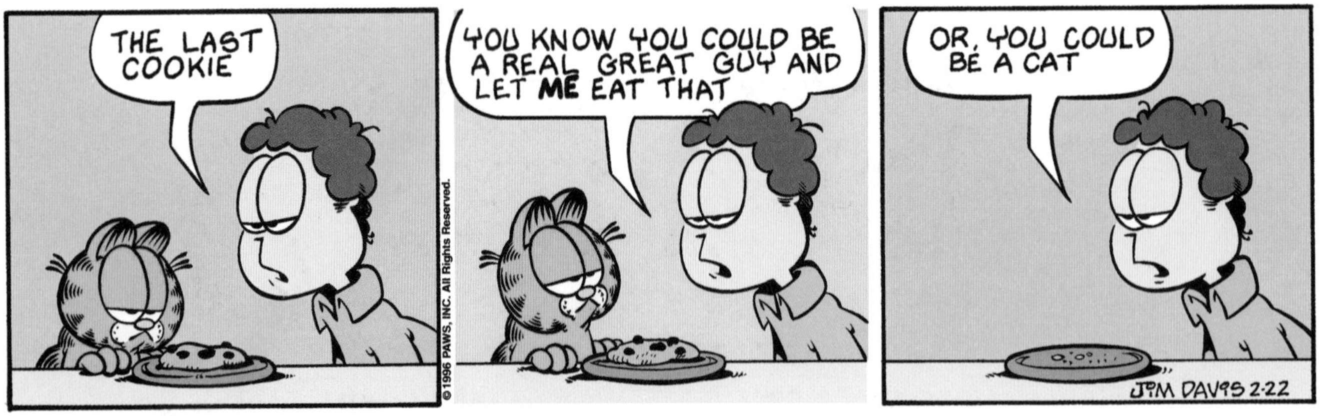
THE LAST COOKIE
YOU KNOW YOU COULD BE A REAL GREAT GUY AND LET **ME** EAT THAT
OR, YOU COULD BE A CAT
© 1996 PAWS, INC. All Rights Reserved.
JIM DAVIS 2-22

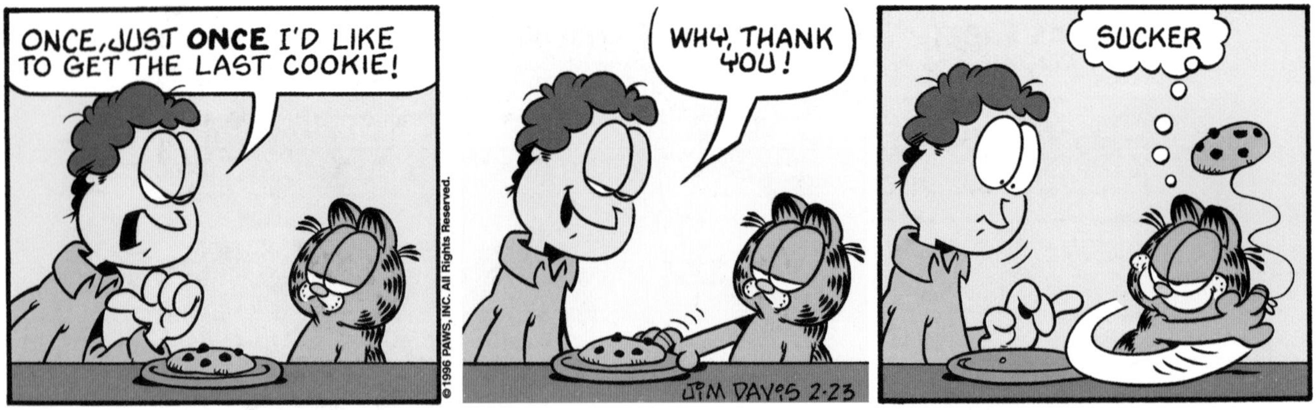
ONCE, JUST **ONCE** I'D LIKE TO GET THE LAST COOKIE!
WHY, THANK YOU!
SUCKER
© 1996 PAWS, INC. All Rights Reserved.
JIM DAVIS 2-23

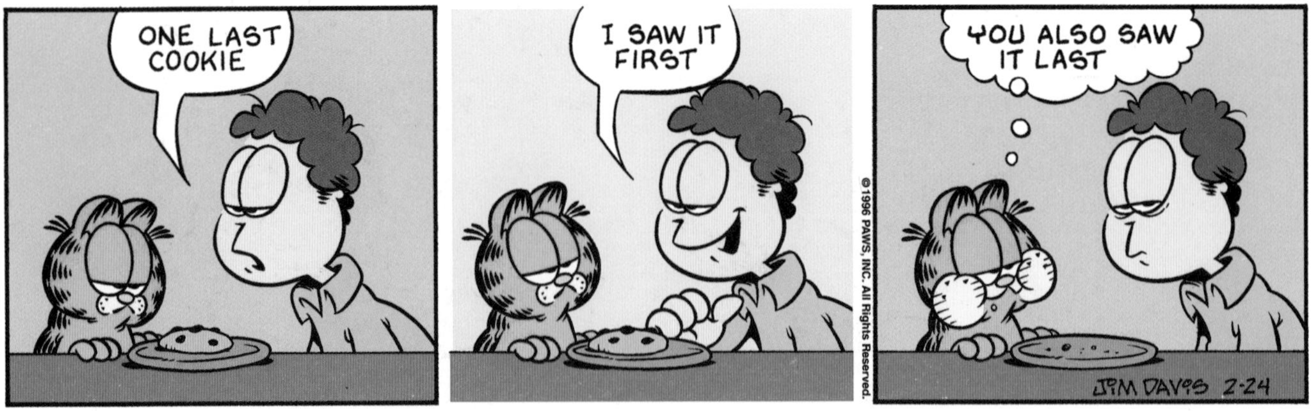
ONE LAST COOKIE
I SAW IT FIRST
YOU ALSO SAW IT LAST
© 1996 PAWS, INC. All Rights Reserved.
JIM DAVIS 2-24

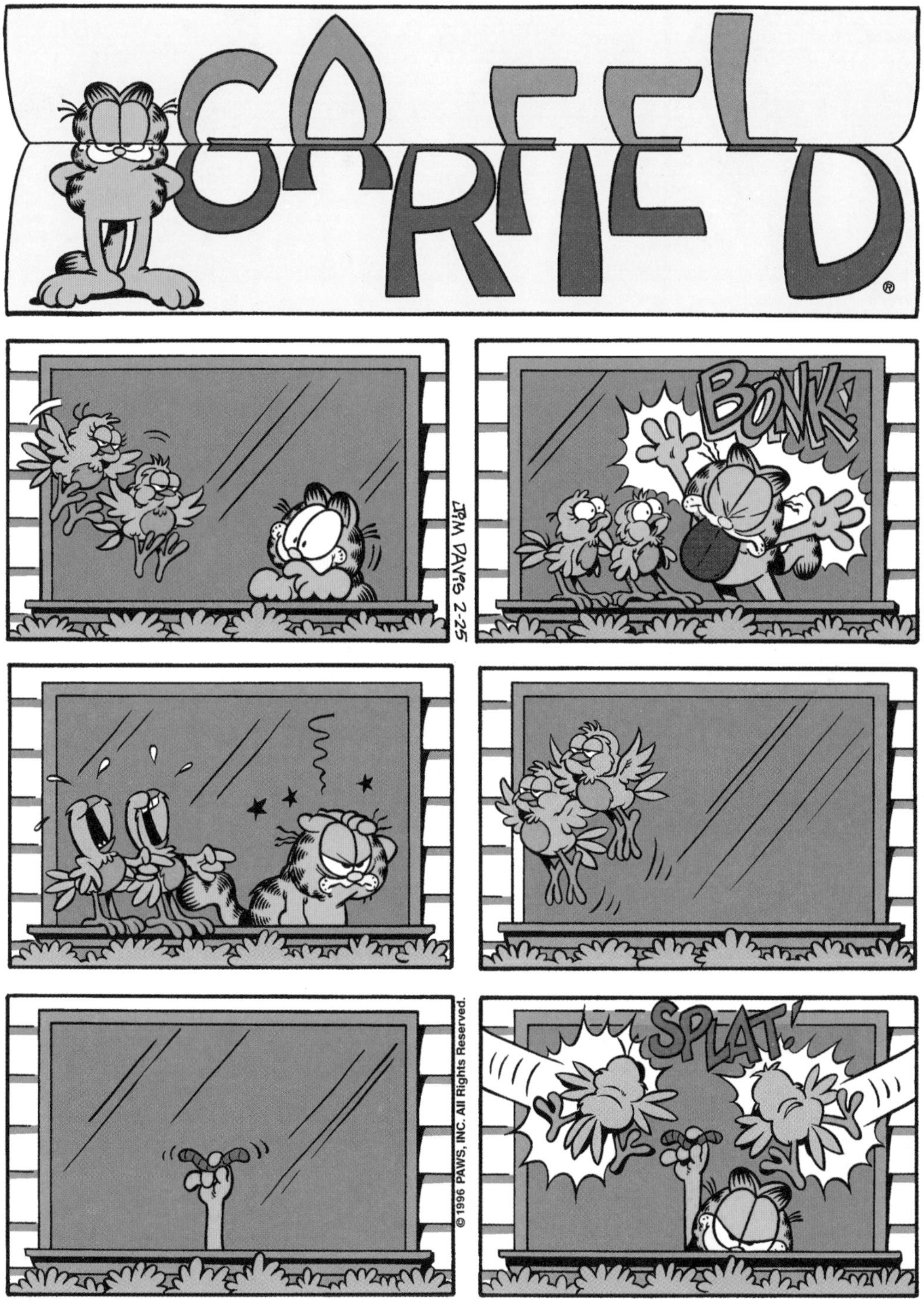
GARFIELD
JPM DAVIS 2-25
BONK!
SPLAT!
© 1996 PAWS, INC. All Rights Reserved.

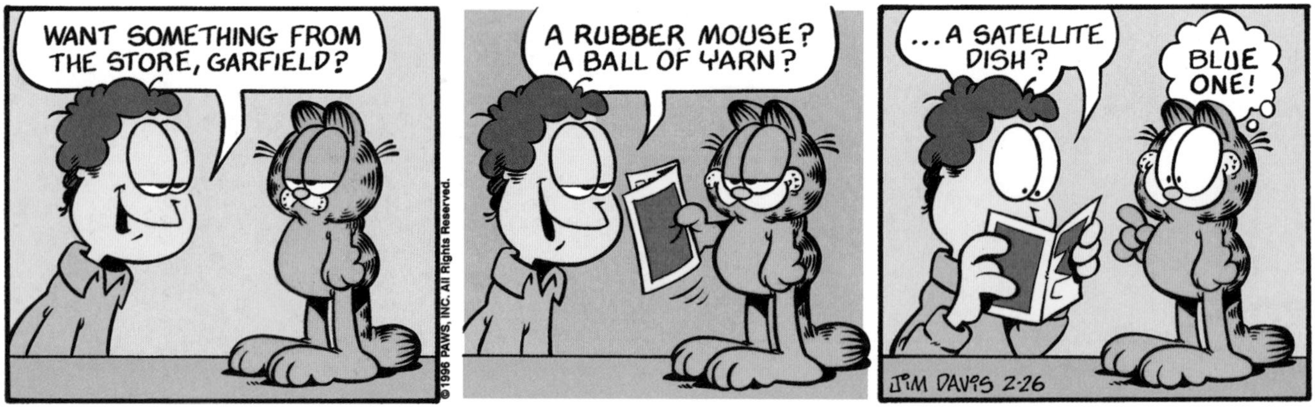
WANT SOMETHING FROM THE STORE, GARFIELD?
© 1996 PAWS, INC. All Rights Reserved.
A RUBBER MOUSE? A BALL OF YARN?
...A SATELLITE DISH?
A BLUE ONE!
JIM DAVIS 2-26

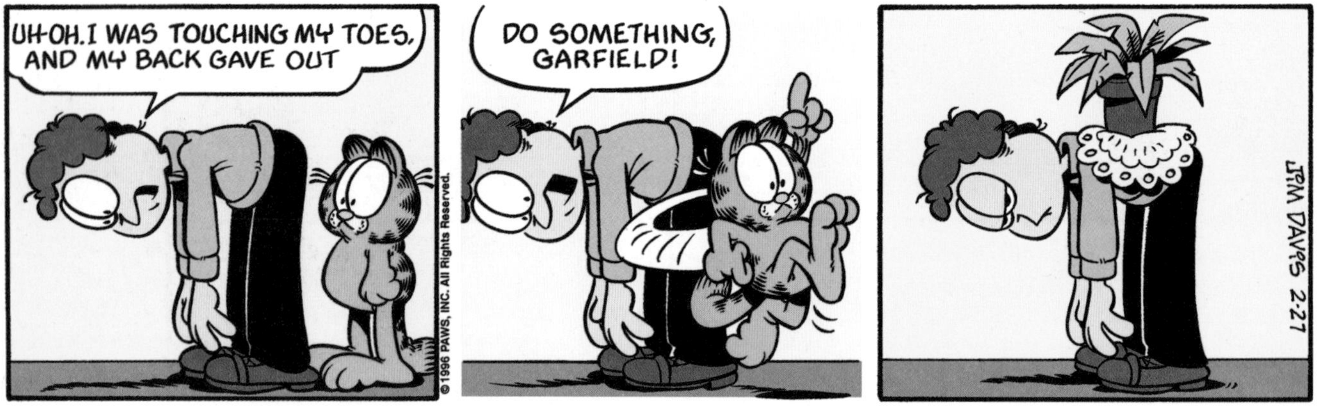
UH-OH. I WAS TOUCHING MY TOES, AND MY BACK GAVE OUT
© 1996 PAWS, INC. All Rights Reserved.
DO SOMETHING, GARFIELD!
JIM DAVIS 2-27

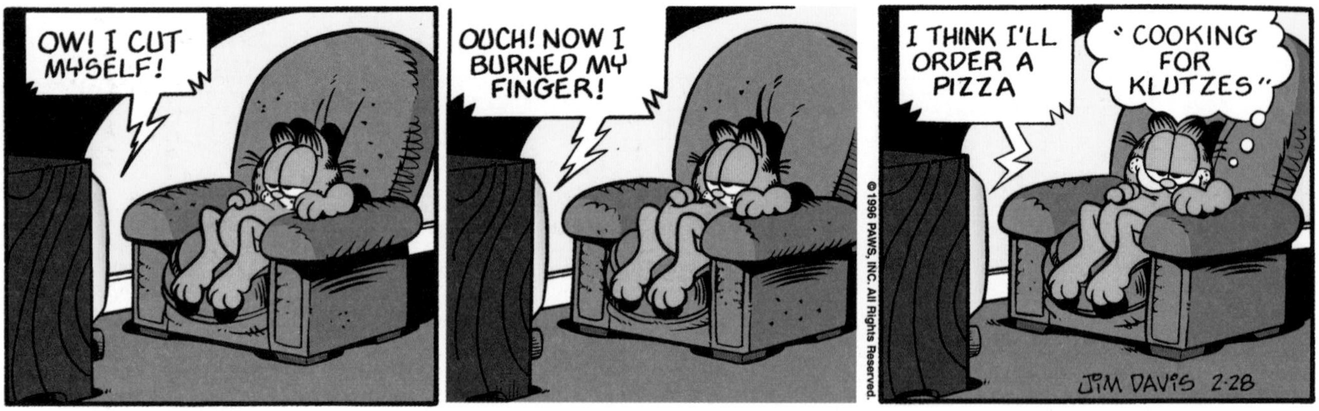
OW! I CUT MYSELF!
OUCH! NOW I BURNED MY FINGER!
© 1996 PAWS, INC. All Rights Reserved.
I THINK I'LL ORDER A PIZZA
"COOKING FOR KLUTZES"
JIM DAVIS 2-28

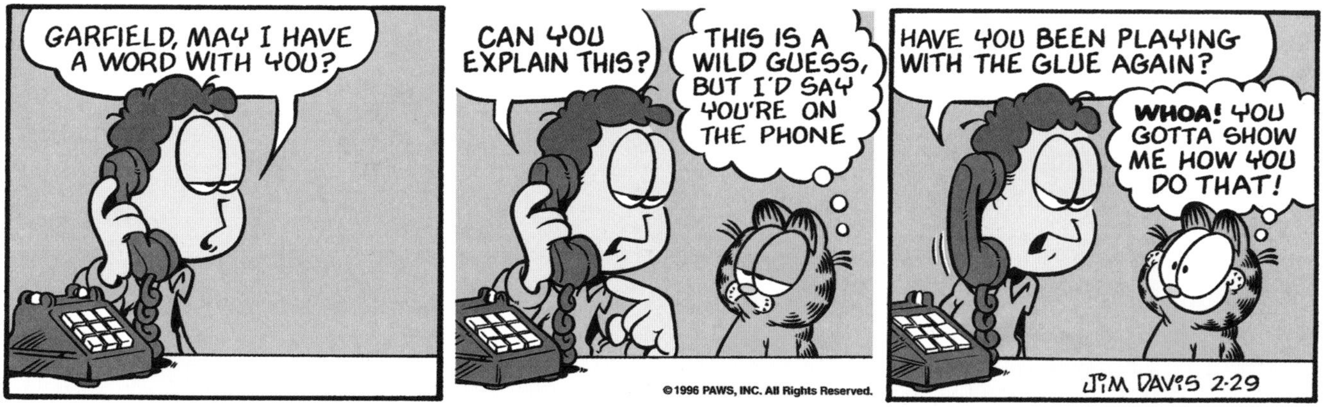
GARFIELD, MAY I HAVE A WORD WITH YOU?
CAN YOU EXPLAIN THIS?
THIS IS A WILD GUESS, BUT I'D SAY YOU'RE ON THE PHONE
HAVE YOU BEEN PLAYING WITH THE GLUE AGAIN?
WHOA! YOU GOTTA SHOW ME HOW YOU DO THAT!
©1996 PAWS, INC. All Rights Reserved.
JIM DAVIS 2-29

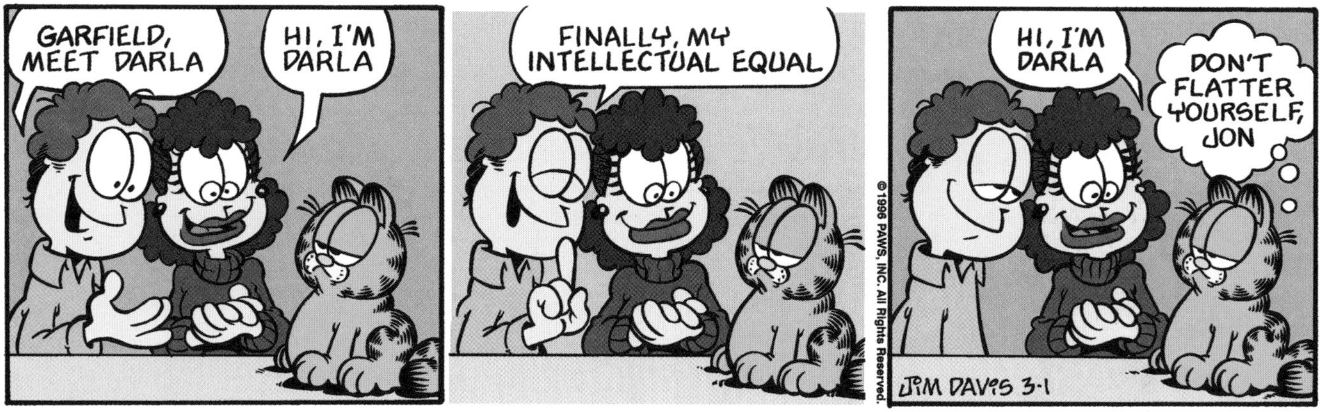
GARFIELD, MEET DARLA
HI, I'M DARLA
FINALLY, MY INTELLECTUAL EQUAL
HI, I'M DARLA
DON'T FLATTER YOURSELF, JON
©1996 PAWS, INC. All Rights Reserved.
JIM DAVIS 3-1

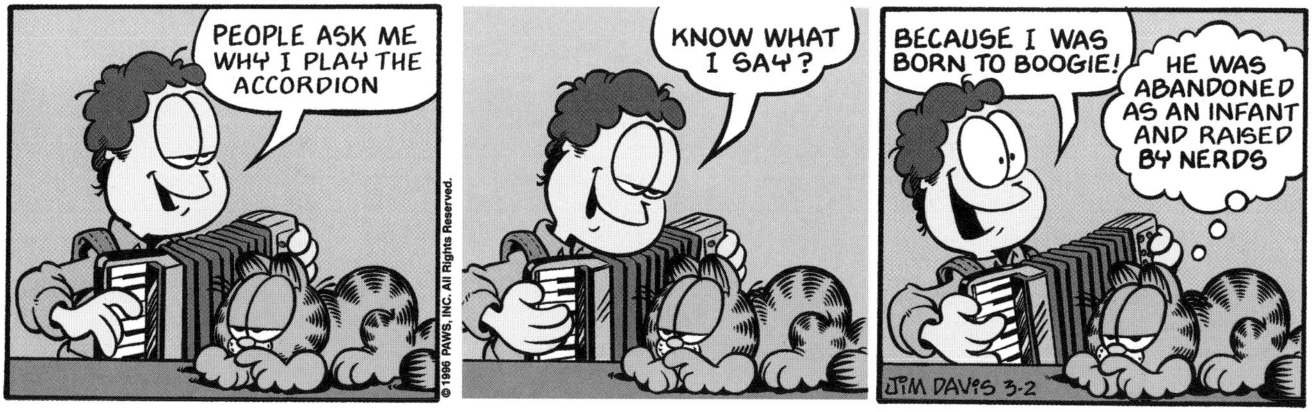
PEOPLE ASK ME WHY I PLAY THE ACCORDION
KNOW WHAT I SAY?
BECAUSE I WAS BORN TO BOOGIE!
HE WAS ABANDONED AS AN INFANT AND RAISED BY NERDS
©1996 PAWS, INC. All Rights Reserved.
JIM DAVIS 3-2

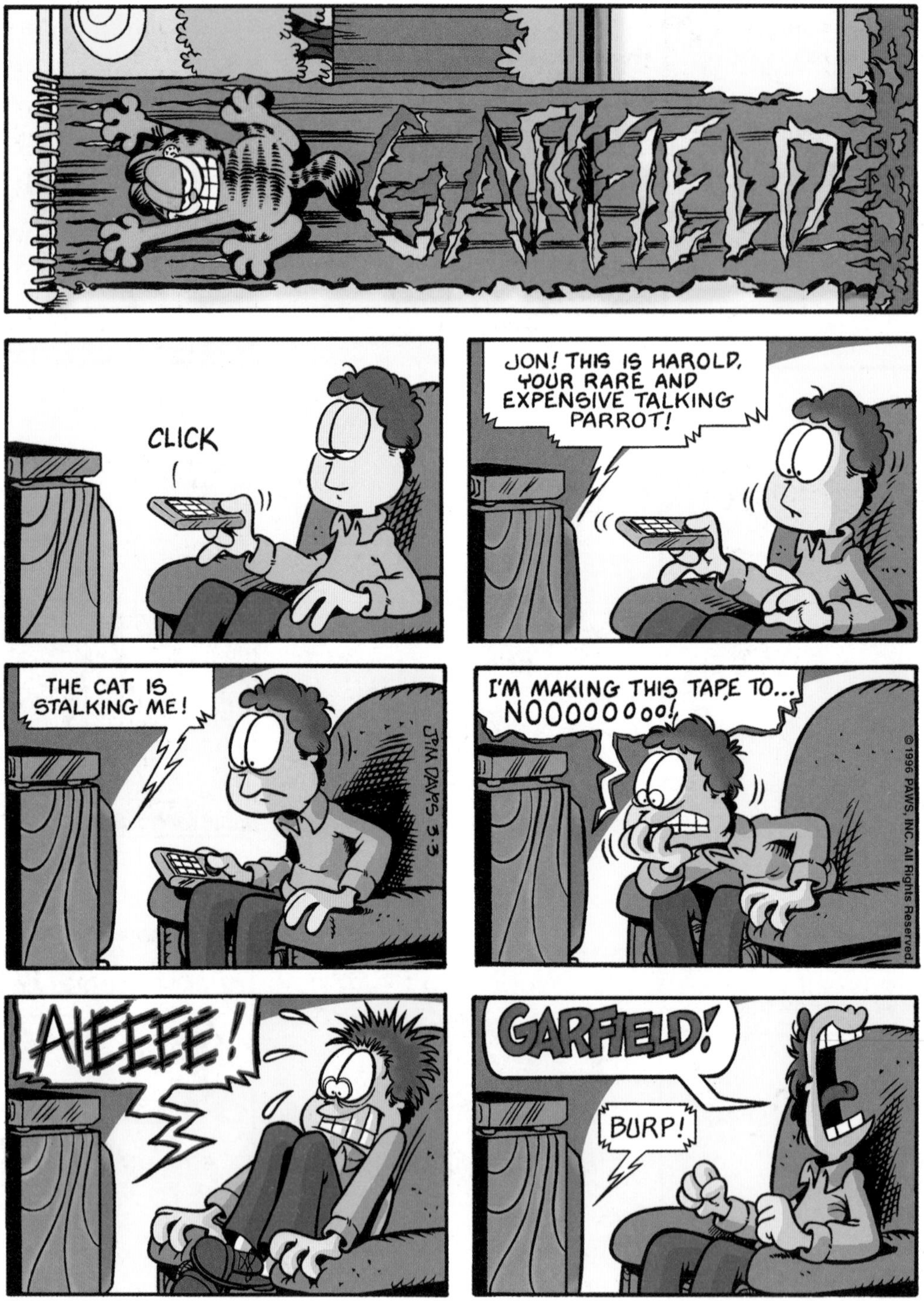
GARFIELD
CLICK
JON! THIS IS HAROLD, YOUR RARE AND EXPENSIVE TALKING PARROT!
THE CAT IS STALKING ME!
JPM DAVIS 3-3
I'M MAKING THIS TAPE TO... NOOOOOOoo!
© 1996 PAWS, INC. All Rights Reserved.
AIEEEE!
GARFIELD!
BURP!

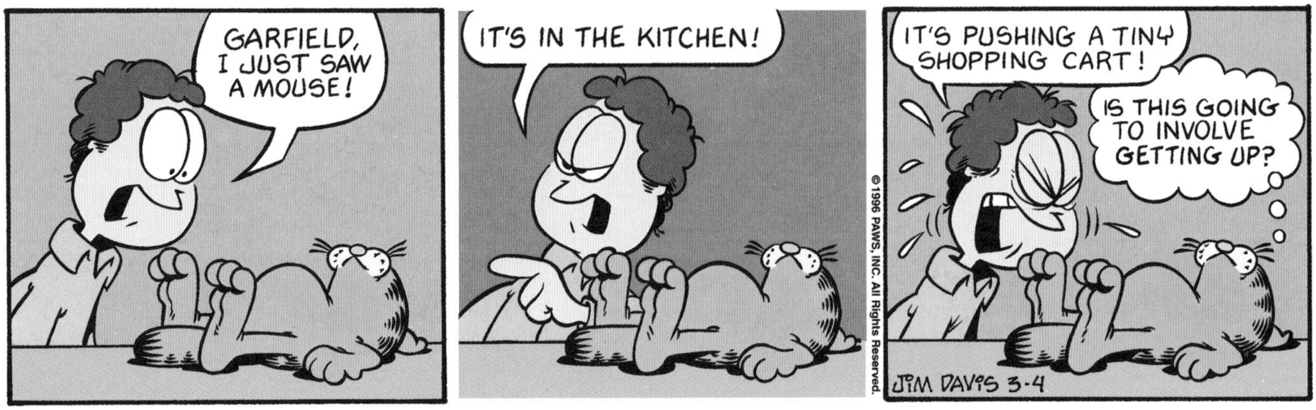
GARFIELD, I JUST SAW A MOUSE!
IT'S IN THE KITCHEN!
©1996 PAWS, INC. All Rights Reserved.
IT'S PUSHING A TINY SHOPPING CART!
IS THIS GOING TO INVOLVE GETTING UP?
JIM DAVIS 3-4

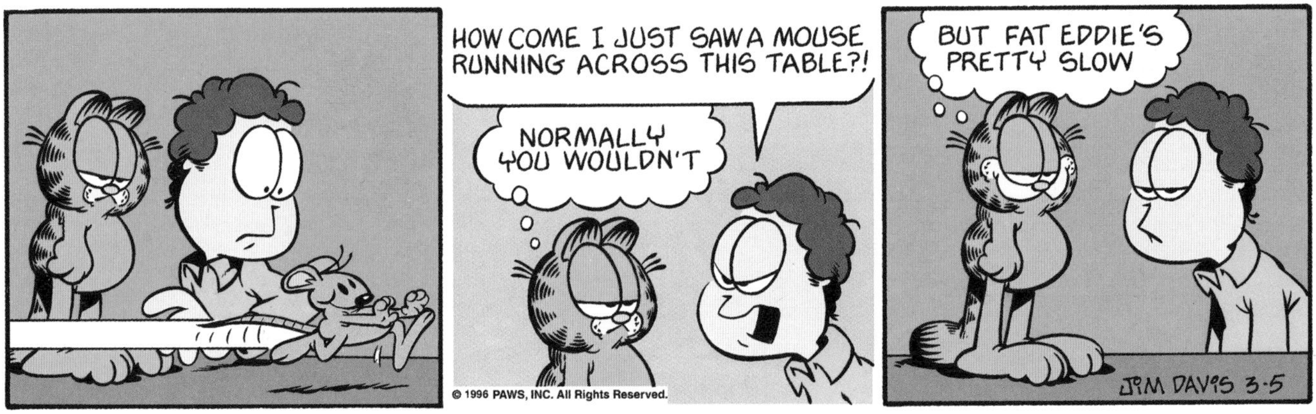
HOW COME I JUST SAW A MOUSE RUNNING ACROSS THIS TABLE?!
NORMALLY YOU WOULDN'T
© 1996 PAWS, INC. All Rights Reserved.
BUT FAT EDDIE'S PRETTY SLOW
JIM DAVIS 3-5

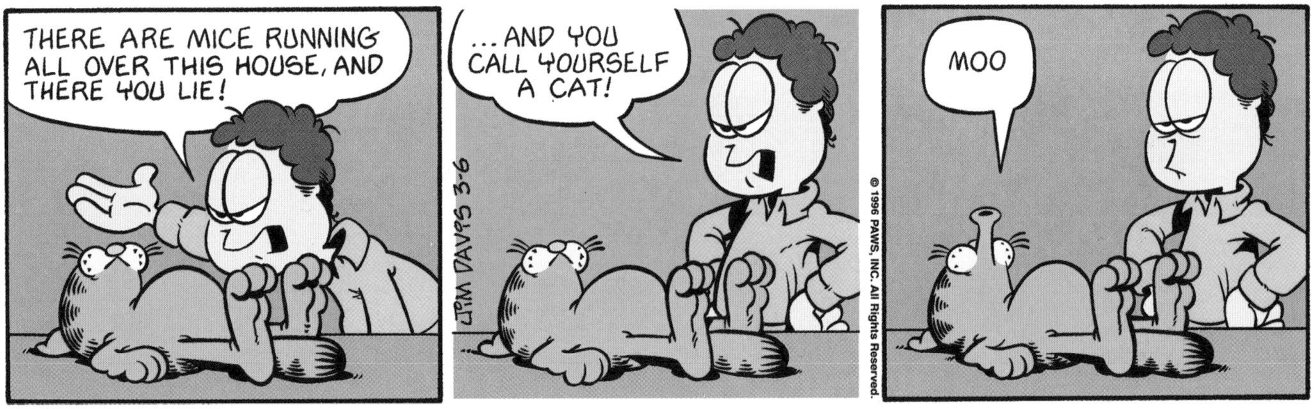
THERE ARE MICE RUNNING ALL OVER THIS HOUSE, AND THERE YOU LIE!
JIM DAVIS 3-6
...AND YOU CALL YOURSELF A CAT!
© 1996 PAWS, INC. All Rights Reserved.
MOO

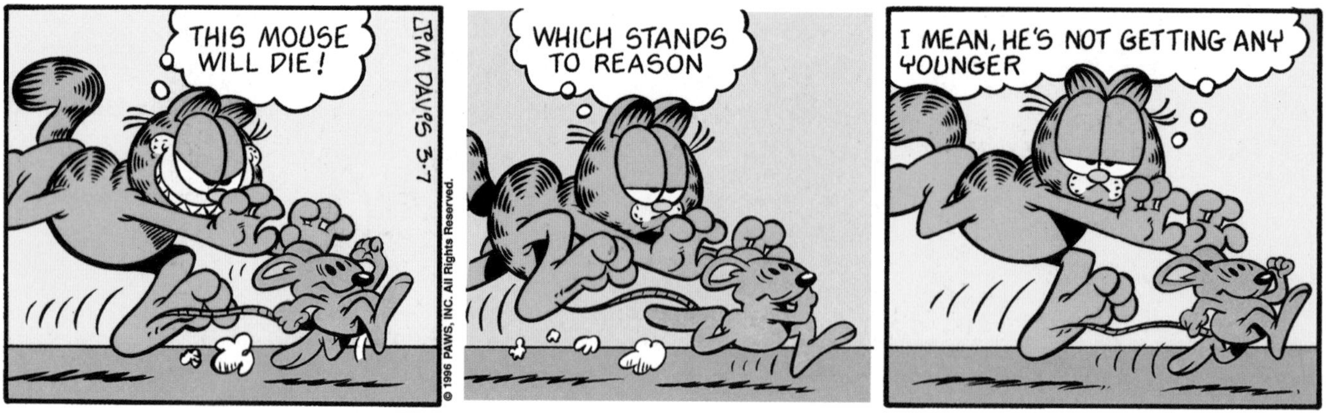
THIS MOUSE WILL DIE!
JIM DAVIS 3-7
© 1996 PAWS, INC. All Rights Reserved.
WHICH STANDS TO REASON
I MEAN, HE'S NOT GETTING ANY YOUNGER

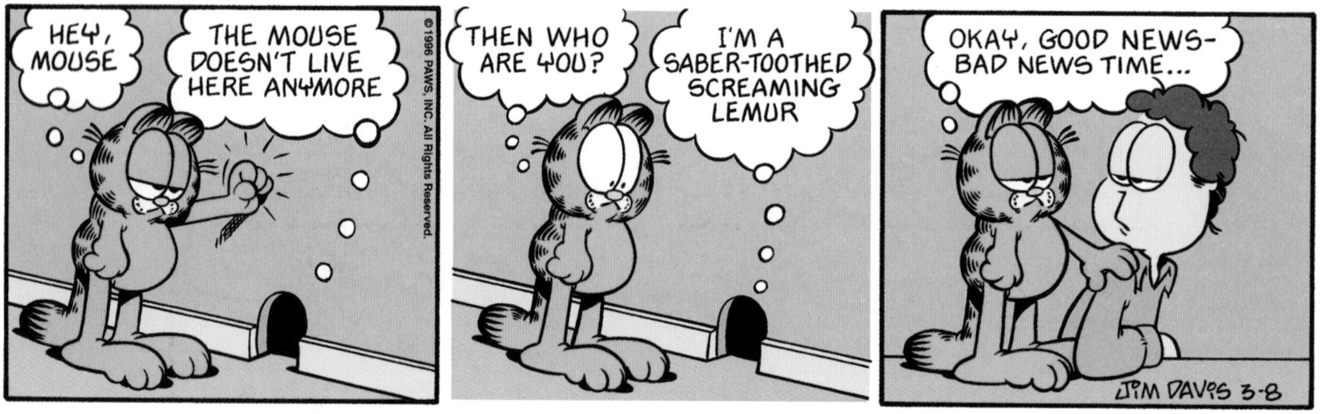
HEY, MOUSE
THE MOUSE DOESN'T LIVE HERE ANYMORE
© 1996 PAWS, INC. All Rights Reserved.
THEN WHO ARE YOU?
I'M A SABER-TOOTHED SCREAMING LEMUR
OKAY, GOOD NEWS-BAD NEWS TIME...
JIM DAVIS 3-8

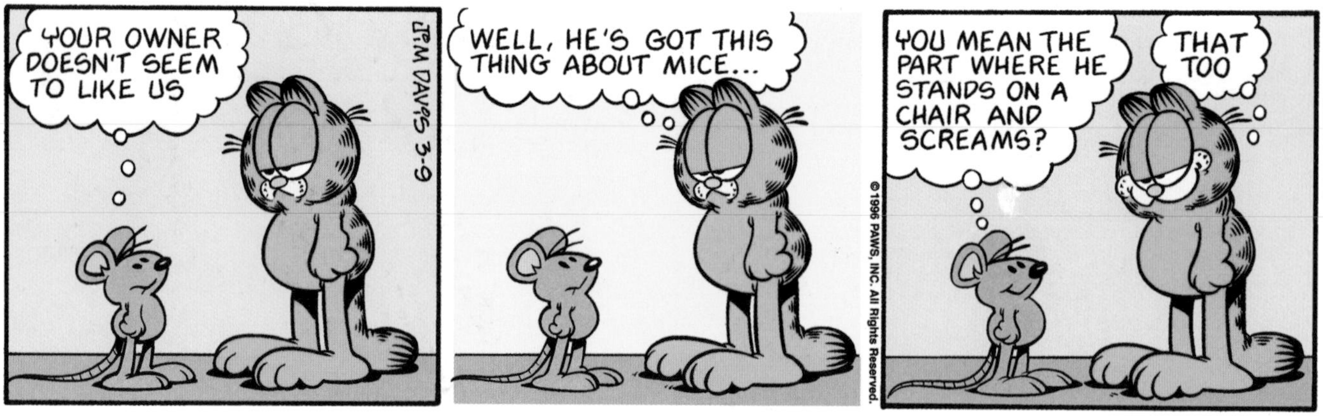
YOUR OWNER DOESN'T SEEM TO LIKE US
JIM DAVIS 3-9
WELL, HE'S GOT THIS THING ABOUT MICE...
© 1996 PAWS, INC. All Rights Reserved.
YOU MEAN THE PART WHERE HE STANDS ON A CHAIR AND SCREAMS?
THAT TOO

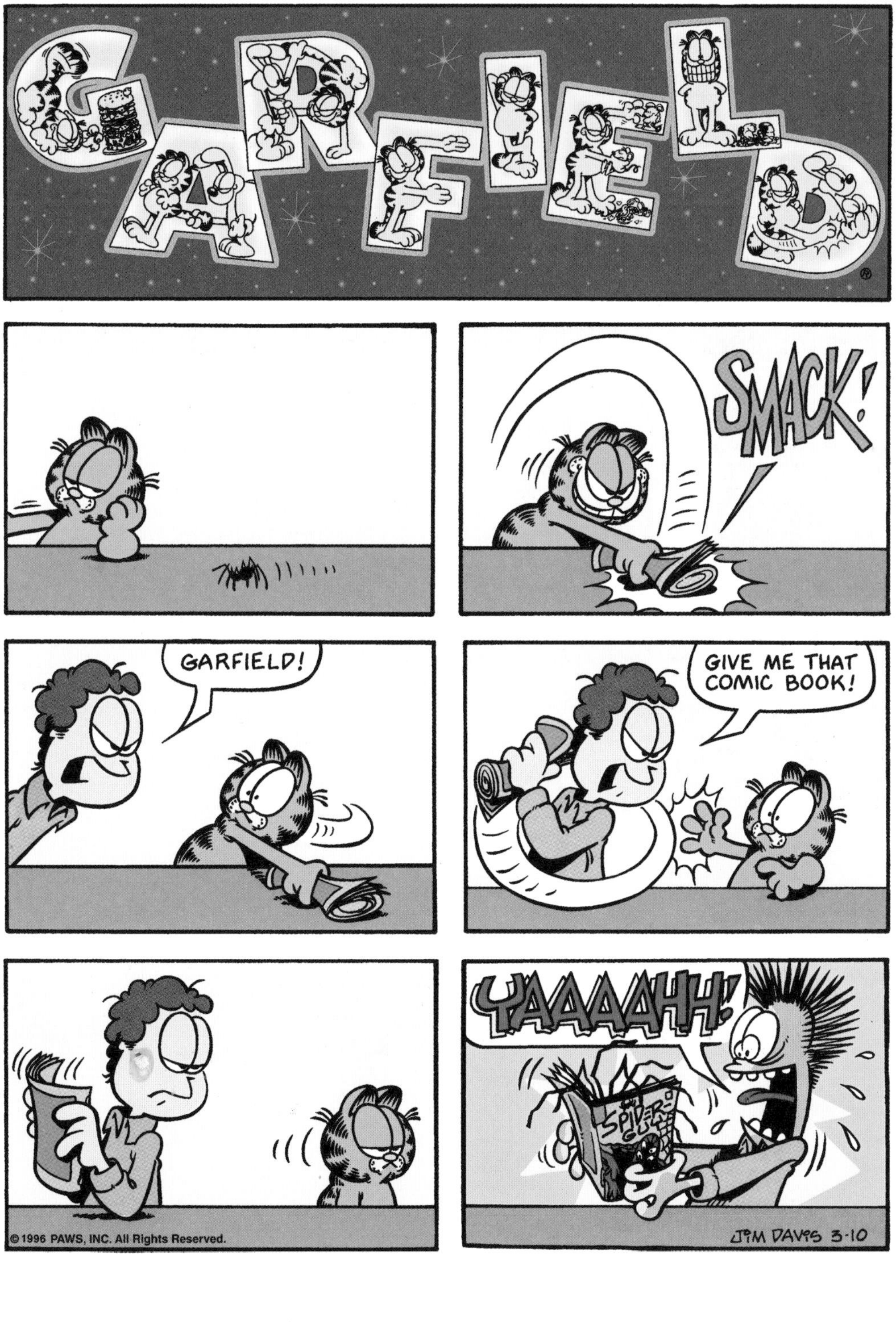
GARFIELD
SMACK!
GARFIELD!
GIVE ME THAT COMIC BOOK!
YAAAAHH!
SPIDER-GUTS
© 1996 PAWS, INC. All Rights Reserved.
JIM DAVIS 3-10

HERE'S MY SIXTH-GRADE REPORT CARD!
MY PARENTS WERE SO PROUD
"JON HAS NOT SHOVED ANY CRAYONS UP HIS NOSE THIS TERM"
©1996 PAWS, INC. All Rights Reserved.
JIM DAVIS 3-11

JIM DAVIS 3-12
GARFIELD, MY HAIRLINE IS RECEDING
BUT IT REALLY ISN'T NOTICEABLE
HEY FOREHEAD BOY!
JUST A LUCKY GUESS
©1996 PAWS, INC. All Rights Reserved.

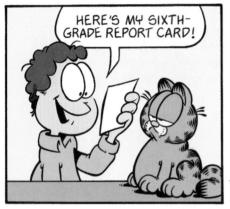

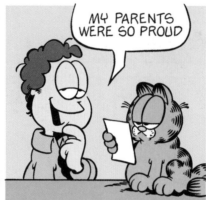

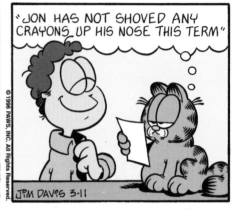

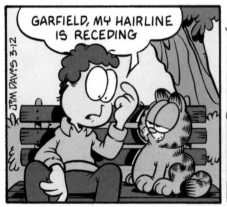

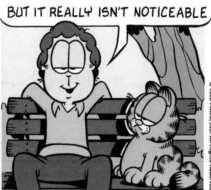

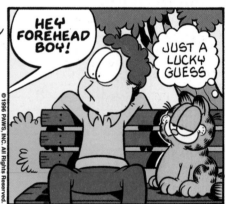

[redacted]

"Don't make me beg!"

IF ODIE WERE PRESIDENT, HE WOULD...

- Replace Washington Monument with giant fire hydrant
- Start every press conference with an Underdog cartoon
- Repeal oppressive leash laws
- Have all cats de-clawed
- Require mailmen to wear short pants
- Be the first chief executive to lick himself in public!

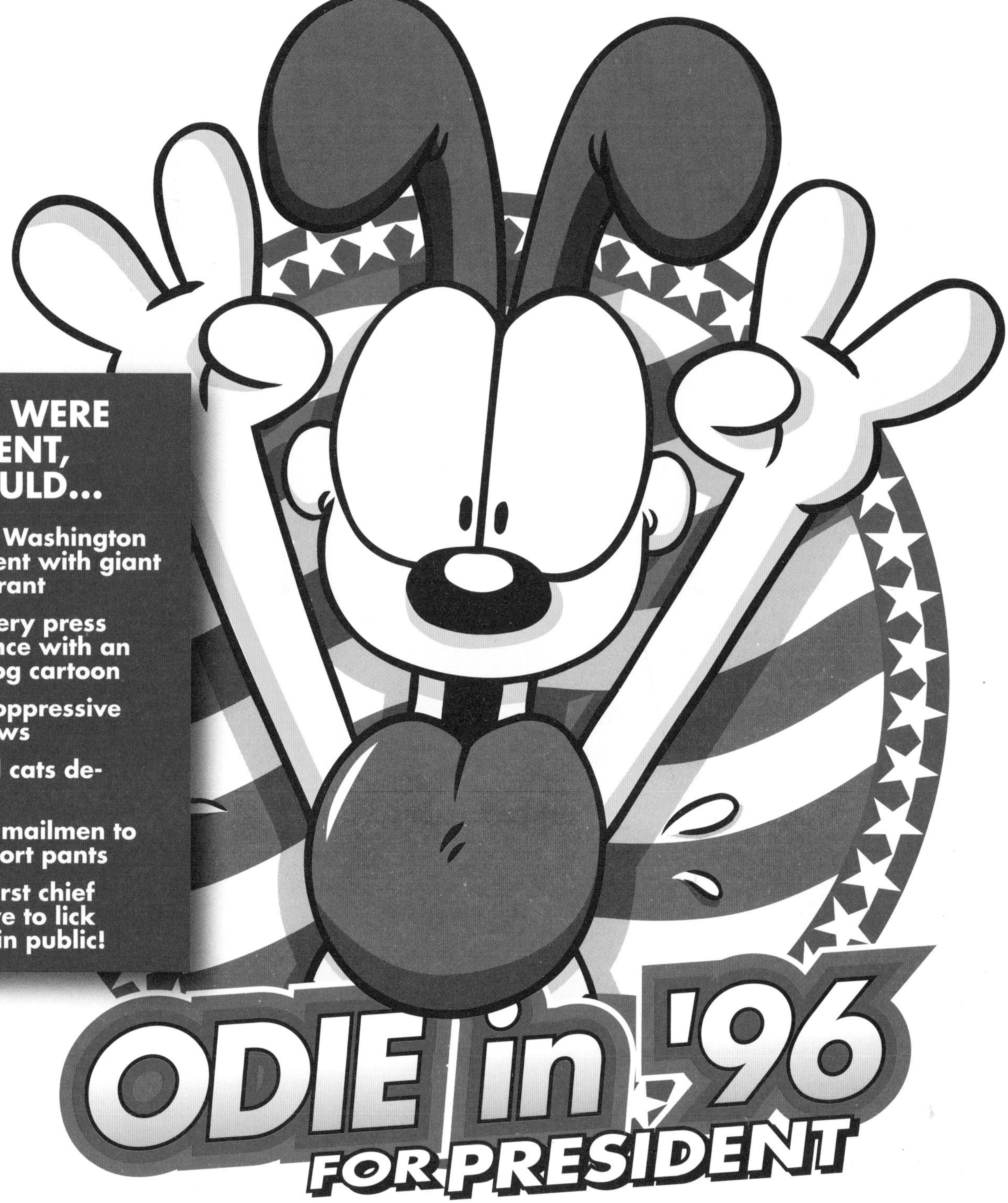

ODIE in '96
FOR PRESIDENT